THE LIMITS OF FOREIGN POLICY

CHRISTOPHER THORNE

THE LIMITS
OF FOREIGN POLICY

The West, the League
and the Far Eastern Crisis of
1931–1933

G. P. PUTNAM'S SONS, NEW YORK

FIRST AMERICAN EDITION 1973

© CHRISTOPHER THORNE 1972

SBN: 399-11124-7

Library of Congress Catalog

Card Number: 72-95740

PRINTED IN THE UNITED STATES OF AMERICA

To Pierre Renouvin and Stephen Roskill

CONTENTS

MAPS
(by Patrick Leeson)

PREFACE

MY CURIOSITY concerning the Far Eastern crisis of 1931 to 1933 was first aroused by the frequent assertion that here lay the true starting point of the Second World War and the moment when the structure of international peace which had been erected after 1918 was overthrown, or betrayed, or both. In addition, I observed that since Reginald Bassett's *Democracy and Foreign Policy*, published twenty years ago, no close study had been made of the British involvement in this crisis, for which there were now available not only the mass of official documents in the Public Record Office but also numerous collections of private papers, including those of men like Gilbert Murray and Viscount Cecil who stood outside the ranks of regular officials, and who had been one of Bassett's principal objects of attention. No sooner had I begun to delve into this unpublished material on British Far Eastern policy, however, than it became clear that the subject was so closely interwoven with its American counterpart that any attempt to isolate the former would be unsatisfactory in many ways; at the same time I began to feel that, despite the work which had already been produced on the United States side of things, there might be something I could contribute in that sphere as well in terms of both broad perspective and detailed analysis. Rashly, therefore, I plunged deeper into the subject, to be met with great kindness and assistance from American scholars already established there. In particular I wish to thank Dr. Dorothy Borg of Columbia's East Asia Institute, to whose fine work on United States policy from 1933 onwards all students are lastingly indebted, and with whom I was able to spend several days of invaluable discussion in New York.

Besides developing a comparison of British and American policies and policy-making in this way, I was also able to broaden the study in directions that were suggested by three other considerations: the role of the League of Nations and of Britain within that organisation; the complex connections, not yet adequately explored, I felt, between Far Eastern affairs and the shifting, triangular relationship between the United States, Britain and France; and above all the entire Western presence in the Far East, with its attendant images of and approaches to that part of the world. Again, I was fortunate to be able to get at newly-available or unused archive material, even if the means had sometimes to be circuitous and the result on occasions was disappointing. In the case of the League collection at Geneva (for which a 40-year rule operates), there proved to be more quantity than quality. In Paris (where a 30-year rule now obtains, but only in theory) my search was made possible only by the great kindness of Professor Pierre Renouvin, chairman of the commission which is engaged in publishing the series of *Documents Diplomatiques Français*, who worked on my questions in areas of the Quai d'Orsay archives which are at present forbidden to outsiders. Our correspondence and discussions on the spot have provided a pleasure which is inadequately repaid in the dedication of this book.

Meanwhile on German policy concerning the crisis there was the substantial amount of photostat material from the Foreign Ministry in Berlin which is preserved by the Foreign Office in London. In general, however, the German line in 1931–3 was to keep out of the affair as far as possible, and since this was obviously even more the case with the Italians—except where matters of show were concerned, as touching on their usual pretence to Great Power status—I forebore to pursue my enquiries in Rome. For the Dutch, on the other hand, Far Eastern events clearly held great significance, and for enabling me to overcome the language problem involved I am most grateful to Dr. M. J. Meijer, until recently Counsellor of the Netherlands Embassy in Tokyo and a specialist in Chinese law, who both alone and with me impatiently at his elbow toured the archives of The Hague in search of relevant material. Alas, the number of available documents which contain comment, and not simply factual report, is slender in the extreme, even where communications between the home government and Batavia were concerned. To a large extent this is a result of burnings carried out in May 1940; enough material has survived, however, to make it plain that Dutch policy at the time amounted to little more than resolute, cryptic and anxious passivity—disappointing for the historian, but no doubt sensible in the circumstances, and in itself something of a saving in bureaucratic stationery.

The focus of my work has thus been on the West, and I can make no claim to have contributed in pioneering fashion to the actual Far Eastern aspects of the crisis. Even so, I was anxious to measure the various Western estimates of what was occurring against the situation as it is now known to have existed in Japan, Manchuria and the remainder of China. In this respect the massive and unpublished documentation and proceedings of the International Military Tribunal that sat in Tokyo after the war provided one important source—though suspect in various respects. In addition, however, I must acknowledge my general debt to those Far Eastern specialists whose studies, of Japanese policy in particular, are cited throughout the book. My own access to Japanese-language sources has also been made possible through the tenacity and cheerfulness of my student, Haruko Kinase, who translated for me key sections of the multi-volumed *Taiheiyo senso e no michi: kaisen gaiko-shi*, and through the kindness of James Morley, Director of Columbia's East Asia Institute, who allowed me to read in typescript such portions of the same work as have been translated for eventual publication in edited form. Dr. Shumpei Okamoto, who is one of those engaged in this Columbia project, also encouraged me to invade his home in order to read and discuss these matters far into a Philadelphia evening.

Having thus broadened the enquiry to take in Western policies as a whole and set them against Japanese developments, I found myself required to go back into at least the preceding thirty years or so in order to establish an adequate framework within which to examine the commitments, resources and attitudes of these Western states during the comparatively brief period of the crisis itself. The Manchurian episode was to raise such broad questions concerning both collective security and international politics in the Far East that I felt bound to offer more than a brief, preliminary nod in that direction, however much this meant incurring further debts to existing works. Too often, it seemed to me, the events of 1931–3 had been looked at simply in the light of the crises that followed, culminating in the Pacific war of 1941. Such a perspective appeared to have given rise to various facile claims and criticisms which began to lose much of their substance if one did not start with the notion of 1931 as a sudden 'turning point'; in addition, it was a perspective which I felt had sometimes led to certain underlying issues being played down or neglected entirely. Hence, the first quarter of this book searches back in a way which is, of course, instinctive and proper for any self-respecting historian. At the same time, however, both this section and the remainder of the work also represent an attempt to bring together a number of closely related studies in foreign policy analysis, a subject which, in Britain at least, remains sufficiently unfamiliar to require a brief word on the approach I have adopted in that connection.

In common with many who have been trained as historians, I have to admit to a deep scepticism regarding the search which is being conducted by some political scientists for general theories and predictive formulae that can be applied to international relations. If historians themselves can often become lost in minutiae, then equally, the designing of theoretical patterns at a quasi-theological level can degenerate into a self-indulgent and fruitless pastime, however attractive the notion of discovering all-embracing explanations and solutions for international conflict, say, in an age when such a phenomenon threatens to destroy mankind itself. And while so-called 'laws' of international relations as a whole are unlikely to rise above trivial generalisations, the theoretical structures which have been erected around a particular subject such as foreign-policy decision-making are often open to serious objections: they tend to be unduly static, for example, to allow insufficiently for the on-going nature of foreign policy, where the conscious, major decision is the exception rather than the rule, and to have nothing to offer when it comes to weighing the relative significance of any one factor on a specific occasion. Or to take another field of enquiry which is rapidly being extended, not all students of game theory are modest enough to admit as Anatol Rapoport has done that the practical application of such principles in international relations 'is beset with well-nigh insuperable difficulties',[1] while their application in the study of past decisions would scarcely seem to be any more fruitful.

Yet despite the various objections which are rightly raised against some of the claims that have been made for theoretical approaches to international relations, the more traditional discipline of narrative diplomatic history, even when practised by a master of that craft, is surely also open to question in a number of respects. For example, many such studies—and I do not except my own—have often adopted a brusque approach (apparently supported by a number of unstated and perhaps unrecognised assumptions)

[1] A. Rapoport, 'International Relations and Game Theory', in B.B.C., *Decision Making* (London, 1967).

where causality is concerned, and in this context have failed to make use of work being done in neighbouring areas of study such as social psychology. Or again, that approach to international history which treats states as so many billiards balls, each one a discrete unit with its own neat and ready-made set of aims and interests, bears little relation to the world of international politics as it now exists—or perhaps ever existed. And if this last kind of exercise is now dying away, the immensely complex nature of foreign policy formulation (whether or not perceived as such by those concerned) is still frequently simplified to the point of falsification, either by isolating a single aspect of that policy from all other issues that were having to be faced by officials at the time, or by ignoring the interplay between international factors and those arising within domestic politics. Theoretical models of such a subject have their dangers, but provided they are flexible enough always to respond to and be refined by the material to which they are applied, an initial scheme of analysis of this kind can at least assist the student in recognising and finding his way through the plethora of considerations to which foreign policy gives rise.

In addition to being a historical study of the crisis of 1931–3, therefore, the present work attempts to show some awareness of what Stanley Hoffmann has called 'the long road to theory' in international relations,[1] and I have acknowledged my broad debt to a number of relevant works in a separate bibliography. Nevertheless I have tried not to let the scaffolding of foreign policy analysis obtrude on the reader's attention in the finished product. It is enough to mention here that an attempt to reveal the various layers that can be present in an international exchange will sometimes involve returning to a single episode from several different directions, and that a basic pattern has been followed in this respect in Part Two of the book, which deals with the crisis itself. Within each chronological section, events in the Far East are first outlined in the form in which they were publicly known in the West at the time, and are followed by an account of the manoeuvrings—between the Japanese army in the field and the government in Tokyo, say—that were taking place behind the scenes. By moving on from there to an account of how individual Western governments and the League of Nations reacted publicly to these events, I hope to enable the newcomer to the period to orientate himself at the outset; he will also then have the knowledge with which to embark upon an examination of how non-official pressure-groups, individuals and newspapers in various countries themselves reacted to what they saw as happening in both East and West. Finally, one turns to the way in which the policy of each government was arrived at, the views that were held in official circles of the foregoing domestic opinion, the information and advice that was being received in private from abroad, the options that were seen as being open and the reasons for whatever choice—or the refusal to choose—that was then made. At times, of course, the pattern of events requires a change in that of presentation, so that during the Shanghai crisis in 1932 it is the comparison of British and American policies and the

---

[1] S. Hoffmann, 'International Relations: The Long Road to Theory', in J. N. Rosenau (ed.), *International Politics and Foreign Policy* (New York, 1961). Cf. K. Knorr and J. N. Rosenau (eds.), *Contending Approaches to International Politics* (Princeton, 1969), esp. the essay by D. Vital.

exchanges between those two countries which are brought to the fore. In brief, the book does not have a purely narrative framework, nor does it fashionably attempt to measure the factors involved to four places of decimals, however disappointing the result may be to unyielding champions of each of these extreme approaches to international relations. If it contributes in some small way to bridging the gap between historians and others in this area of study, then I shall be pleased enough.

Explanations completed, I can turn to the more straightforward and rewarding task of acknowledging my debt to those who were themselves involved in some way in the Far Eastern crisis and who, between them, have given up many hours to answering my questions, either by letter or in interview or often both. Occasionally it transpired that the passage of forty years had considerably narrowed the memory, although it was a help in itself when this was readily admitted; in some instances, and notably where Mr. Noel-Baker is concerned, my own interpretation has come to diverge sharply from the one offered to me by a participant in the event; at no time have I relied upon oral testimony for a major point without extensive documentary support. Nevertheless, my 'feel' of the subject has been greatly enhanced by those concerned, and my warm thanks are due to Ambassador Thanassis Aghnides, then Head of the Disarmament Section of the League Secretariat; to Dr. Salvador de Madariaga, who was a major contributor to the debate at Geneva in his capacity as a member of the Spanish delegation there; to Ambassador René Massigli, who performed a similar service for France and was Head of the League of Nations Department in the Quai d'Orsay; to F. P. Walters, later Deputy Secretary-General and historian of the League, who was then Chef de Cabinet to the Secretary-General, Sir Eric Drummond; to Adrianus Pelt, one of those officials of the League Secretariat who accompanied the Lytton Commission to Manchuria, and to Major-General William Biddle of the U.S. Army, who also accompanied that Commission as a Lieutenant and aide to the American member, General McCoy; to E. H. Carr, who in 1931–3 was Assistant Adviser on League of Nations Affairs in the British Foreign Office, and to Sir Frank Roberts, who was then a junior official in the Far Eastern Department of that same organisation; to Clark Eichelberger, then a senior official of the American League of Nations Association, Philip Noel-Baker of the British League of Nations Union (who was also personal assistant to Arthur Henderson, President of the Disarmament Conference), and Walter Lippmann, whose private correspondence with the Secretary of State and others was almost as extensive as his public comments on the course of the crisis. Finally, with the leading Far Eastern officials of the State Department at the time no longer being available to be plagued with my questions, Professor George Kennan kindly allowed me to try out on him some of my tentative conclusions concerning the American Foreign Service, of which he was then a member. I hope that these and other surviving participants in the events recorded below will forgive my referring to them in the text in the style usually accorded to historical figures.

I must further express my gratitude to the following for granting me permission to quote unpublished, copyright material: Her Majesty the Queen; M. Thanassis Aghnides; Earl Baldwin of Bewdley; E. H. Carr, Esq.;

Lord Chatfield and the Dowager Lady Chatfield; Lord Hankey; the Harvard College Library; Professor Ann Lambton; the Librarian and trustees of the Austen Chamberlain Papers, Birmingham University Library; Walter Lippmann, Esq.; Mrs. Dorothy Lloyd; Malcolm MacDonald, Esq.; the Rt. Hon. Philip Noel-Baker; Mrs. Trekkie Parsons; Lord Simon; the Stimson Literary Trust, and Dr. Arnold Toynbee. I have not in every case been able to trace if and where rights over material are reserved, and should there remain those whose permission I ought to have obtained, I ask them to accept a belated apology.

My thanks also go to the staff of the numerous archives and libraries in which I have worked on this study. Without their ready assistance my task would have been difficult in the extreme, and I hope they will understand if I do not name them here individually, their institutions being set out in the list of sources at the end of the book. I would like to mention in particular, however, those who have helped me in four major centres: the Public Record Office in London, the National Archives and Library of Congress in Washington, and the library of Chatham House, where I obtained much of my secondary material. In addition, I must thank Miss Dale Anderson of the East Asia Institute of Columbia University; Hugh Collar, Esq., former Secretary of the China Association, who guided me in the workings and records of that body; Victor-Yves Ghébali of the Carnegie Foundation's Geneva centre; the Hydrographer's Department of the Royal Navy, which supplied distances for the strategic map of the Far East; Captain Kent Loomis, U.S. Navy, who advised me on the archives of that Service; Dr. Herman Kahn, former Director of the Roosevelt Memorial Library at Hyde Park, who spared me unnecessary labours there; David Marquand, M.P., who allowed me to work on the MacDonald Papers in his London home; Professor A. Temple Patterson, who made the Chatfield Papers available to me, and C. H. Rolph, Esq., in whose home I read material from the Kingsley Martin Papers. I am also most grateful to my colleague, Dr. John Chapman, and to Professor James Crowley of Yale for advice at an early stage of my enquiries.

There remain three other scholars to whom I am particularly indebted, however necessary and proper it is for me to add that the responsibility for everything that follows is mine alone. Dr. Ian Nish of the London School of Economics, having already written two outstanding studies of Anglo-Japanese relations in earlier periods on which I could lean, now offered valuable comments on the more particularly Far Eastern portions of my typescript. An even greater labour was undertaken by Professor Akira Iriye of the University of Chicago, who found time to read the entire book and to give me the benefit of his extensive knowledge of trans-Pacific relations between the wars. Finally, at all stages of the work I have received from Captain Stephen Roskill of Churchill College, Cambridge, encouragement extending far beyond those matters concerning naval policy and Sir Maurice Hankey that sent me to him in the first place. To him, as to Pierre Renouvin, I offer this book as a tribute to both scholarship and kindness.

The widespread investigations on which this book is based would not have been possible without an award from the Social Science Research Council. The University of Sussex also helped to meet the cost of some of my travels within Europe, thus conniving at a somewhat free rendering of its motto, 'Be Still and Know', as well as granting me a term's leave of absence in which to complete the final draft. These same travels from one archive to another were greatly lightened by the hospitality of three friends and their families: Professor Robert Webb in Washington, Marshall Mascott in New York and Marcel Delessert in Geneva; in London, Christopher Sinclair-Stevenson of Hamish Hamilton has been a most helpful partner in the enterprise. Meanwhile my own family have accepted my lengthy mental and physical absences with so delicate a blend of regret and encouragement that they leave no room for greater admiration and gratitude on my part.

CHRISTOPHER THORNE

January 1972

NOTES ON ABBREVIATIONS, REFERENCES, ETC.

Abbreviations used in the text.

C.E.R.	Chinese Eastern Railway.
C.I.D.	Committee of Imperial Defence.
C.I.G.S.	Chief of the Imperial General Staff.
L.N.A.	League of Nations Association (U.S.A.).
L.N.U.	League of Nations Union (G.B.).
S.M.R.	South Manchurian Railway.

Abbreviations used in references.

AA.	Photostat records of the German Foreign Ministry (Auswärtiges Amt.)
ADM.	Admiralty records, Public Record Office, London.
AQD.	Archives of the French Ministry for Foreign Affairs, Quai d'Orsay, Paris.
CAB.	Cabinet, Cabinet Office and C.I.D. records, Public Record Office, London.
DBFP.	*Documents on British Foreign Policy, 1919–1939*, Second Series.
DDF.	*Documents Diplomatiques Français, 1932–1939*, 1re Série.
DGFP.	*Documents on German Foreign Policy, 1918–1945*, Series C.
DO.	Dominions Office records, Public Record Office, London.
DS.	Department of State decimal files, National Archives, Washington, D.C.
FO.	Foreign Office files, Public Record Office, London.
FRUS.	*Foreign Relations of the United States.*
IMTFE.	International Military Tribunal for the Far East, mimeographed records, Imperial War Museum, London.
LN. Archives.	League of Nations Archives, Palais des Nations, Geneva.
LNOJ.	*League of Nations Official Journal.*
Lytton Report.	League of Nations, *Appeal by the Chinese Government: Report by the Commission of Enquiry.*
PM.	Prime Minister's files, Public Record Office, London.
RA.	Royal Archives, Windsor Castle.
T.	Treasury files, Public Record Office, London.

Further notes

Unless otherwise stated, numbers in references are to pages. In order to reduce the weight of footnotes a little I have included full details of sender, recipient and date only where such information appeared to be of immediate value to the reader; elsewhere, only the document and file or volume number is given. Where no file or box number is given for personal papers, it indicates the absence of any permanent classification scheme.

I have given Japanese names in the text in their native version, that is with the surname before the given name; on the other hand I have not included Japanese accents, which would be meaningless to the great majority of readers and which to the remainder will be obvious in their absence. In references, I have distinguished between matter obtained from the original, Japanese volumes, *Taiheiyo senso e no michi*, and that obtained from the incomplete and edited translation in the East Asia Institute, Columbia University, 'The Road to the Pacific War'. *The Times* refers to the London paper, the *New York Times* being given in full. For the sake of brevity I have generally used the term 'Far East' as spilling over to embrace also those parts of South East Asia and Australasia that were likely to be involved in any major conflict between Japan and Western powers; when dealing specifically with any one of these areas I have named it in the more usual way. Although the Soviet Union lies to the West of China, it is not included within my use of the term, 'the West'.

Unless otherwise stated, the times given are local. In order to arrive at the relative situation, the following variations from Greenwich Mean Time should be applied: Geneva, + 1 hour; Hongkong, Philippines and Shanghai, + 8 hours; Japan and Manchuria, + 9 hours; New York and Washington, – 5 hours; San Francisco, – 8 hours.

C.G.T.

'I remember in particular one long and violent argument on evolution, in the reality of which Lawrence always passionately disbelieved. "But look at the evidence, Lawrence," I insisted, "look at the evidence." His answer was characteristic. "But I don't care about evidence. Evidence doesn't mean anything to me. I don't feel it *here*." And he pressed his two hands on his solar plexus.'

ALDOUS HUXLEY, introduction to
The Letters of D. H. Lawrence

'We have of the universe only formless, fragmentary visions, which we complete by the association of arbitrary ideas, creative of dangerous suggestions.'

MARCEL PROUST, À *la Recherche du Temps Perdu*
(trans. C. K. Scott Moncrieff,
1969 edition, vol. 11, 218).

PART ONE
EXPOSITION

CHAPTER ONE

SUMMARY AND PERSPECTIVE

AT ABOUT 10.20 p.m. on the 18th of September, 1931, at the instigation of staff officers of Japan's Kwantung Army, an explosion occurred on the Japanese-run South Manchurian Railway just north of Mukden. Little damage was done to the track—a Mukden-bound express passed safely over the spot shortly afterwards—but the detonation could be denounced as the work of Chinese saboteurs; it thus provided a sufficient pretext for bringing about an immediate skirmish with Chinese troops in the vicinity, and enlarging operations thereafter. Morishima Morito, who was first assistant to the Japanese Consul General at Mukden, learned the news an hour later when he was summoned to the office of the Kwantung Army's Special Service Agency and told by Colonel Itagaki Seishiro that the Army had been mobilised to meet the emergency. When Morishima urged that diplomatic negotiations should be relied upon for settling the matter, another officer, Major Hanaya Tadashi, menacingly drew his sword and indicated that no interference in the Army's business would be tolerated.[1] Shortly before midnight, the news also reached the Commanding General of the Kwantung Army, Honjo Shigeru, at his headquarters in Port Arthur, 250 miles to the south. By the time he left for Mukden at 3 a.m., and prompted by other staff officers who were involved in the conspiracy, he had issued a series of orders which brought into action all Japanese forces in Manchuria; help was also requested from the Japanese Commander in Chief in Korea.[2] Already, many key points in Mukden had been seized from the Chinese, despite the greatly superior number of their troops. At Antung, Changchun and other towns, the same process was taking place. In the words of the League of Nations' subsequent Commission of Enquiry, the Japanese proceeded to execute their contingency plans 'with swiftness and precision', against opponents who were not only surprised and disorganised, but soon afterwards under orders not to resist.[3]

In Japanese official circles, an incident of some kind in Manchuria was not unexpected. Indications that something was being planned had been available

---

[1] IMTFE, *Exhibit* 245, Morishima affidavit.

[2] IMTFE, *Proceedings*, 18, 892–5, 19,326; ibid, *Judgment*, 558. It appears uncertain whether General Honjo was aware at the time that the explosion had been instigated by his own officers. In a note written before his suicide in 1945, he insisted that his Army had acted in self-defence. Ibid, *Exhibit* 2401.

[3] *Lytton Report, 71.*

on the spot,[1] and reports to this effect had reached the Foreign Minister, Baron Shidehara, in Tokyo.[2] The timing of the operation had, indeed, been advanced in order to forestall the delivery—by a member of the army's General Staff in Tokyo who was privy to the conspiracy—of letters from the Minister of War and the Chief of the General Staff; these letters warned against any incident and conveyed a recent admonition by the Emperor that discipline in the army must be restored.[3]

Shidehara's awareness of the nature of the problem facing the Japanese Cabinet was reinforced by a series of telegrams from his Consul General in Mukden on the morning following the explosion. In these, the latter concluded that the incident had been 'wholly planned by the Army' and would be followed by operations throughout the zone of the South Manchurian Railway.[4] Although the Cabinet decided that morning to make every effort to avoid an extension of the conflict, the situation was in fact already passing beyond their full control. The army authorities in Tokyo had earlier decided not to impede the Kwantung Army's aggressive measures in South Manchuria, and messages to this effect arrived in Mukden alongside restraining ones from the Cabinet. 'Please understand,' telegraphed the Vice Chief of the General Staff, 'that you are not restricted in taking necessary actions for accomplishing your proper duties or for self-defence of the Army, should the change of circumstances so demand'. Meanwhile all steps should be taken to eliminate 'unpatriotic acts' by those Japanese diplomats and railway officials who were sending groundless reports back to Tokyo concerning the Army's activities.[5] By invoking the Imperial 'right of supreme command' and according generous latitude to General Honjo on the spot, the central military authorities thus thrust the Cabinet on to the defensive; in turn, they were soon sustained by the surge of enthusiasm throughout Japan which accompanied the progress of the country's advancing forces.

In this fashion, the Manchurian crisis was launched upon its course. Despite earlier warnings by some observers in the area, it took the West greatly by surprise. Financial and economic chaos, not the danger of armed conflict, had been in the forefront of all minds. As recently as 10th September, Viscount Cecil had declared to the Twelfth Ordinary Session of the League Assembly:

> I do not think that there is the slightest prospect of any war. I know . . . how rash it is to prophesy as to the future of international affairs; but, nevertheless, I do not believe that there is anyone in this room who will contradict me when I say that there has scarcely ever been a period in the world's history when war seemed less likely than it does at the present.[6]

[1] E.g., IMTFE, *Proceedings*, 18,933. Broader and more recent Japanese sources will be cited in chapters 2 and 5.
[2] IMTFE, *Exhibit* 156, Shidehara affidavit, and *Proceedings*, 2,006.
[3] Takehiko Yoshihashi, *Conspiracy at Mukden* (New Haven, 1963), 154–159.
[4] IMTFE, *Exhibit* 181.
[5] Ibid, *Exhibits* 3421A, 3422B. Cf. Yoshihashi, 7–10; J. Crowley, *Japan's Quest For Autonomy* (Princeton, 1966), 122–24; S. N. Ogata, *Defiance in Manchuria* (Berkeley, 1964), 60–65. [6] LNOJ, *Special Supplement No. 93* (Geneva, 1931), 59–60.

Tension and the distant prospect of renewed conflict were thought of in terms of Europe rather than of the Far East, as Cecil indicated in the same speech when he observed that a genuine Franco–German rapprochement would remove 'seventy-five per cent of the political unrest of the world'. As news filtered through of the Mukden incident and its consequences, political figures like Cecil, as well as attentive publics[1] in the West, had to turn to a political geography that was as unfamiliar as the historical background was complex.[2]

Yet by the time the fighting came to an end twenty months later, the map of Manchuria was almost as common a feature of the world's newspapers as those of Korea and South East Asia were to become in later years. Japanese forces now controlled the whole of Manchuria, together with the neighbour-ing province of Jehol, and manipulated the new, puppet régime of Man-chukuo; in the plain south of the Great Wall they had demonstrated that Peking and Tientsin also lay within their grasp. Their overwhelming victory was reflected in the terms of the truce signed by the Chinese at Tangku in May 1933, and the thirty to forty-mile-wide demilitarised zone that was then constituted (to be policed by Chinese, but not by any armed units that might 'provoke the feelings' of the Japanese) provided a base from which further pressure could be exercised against Northern China.[3]

Four years later, the Kwantung Army moved forward again, and in 1941 the Sino–Japanese struggle became merged in the Second World War. It was therefore scarcely surprising that by the end of that war the Manchurian episode had come to be seen as an early link in a clear and carefully planned chain of events. Count one of the indictment at the Far Eastern war-crimes trial described the process as a conspiracy on the part of a number of Japanese political and military figures, reaching back to 1928,[4]

> to have Japan, either alone or with other countries, wage wars of aggression against any country or countries which might oppose her purpose of securing the military, naval, political and economic domination of East Asia and of the Pacific and Indian Oceans and their adjoining countries and neighbouring islands.[5]

Under this count, verdicts of guilty were brought in against several of the accused, and opinion in the West (as, presumably, in the Soviet Union) appears to have been content with such an explanation, in so far as there is any reflection upon the matter. It is interesting to note, however, that the Tribunal itself was not unanimous in accepting this interpretation of events as an adequate one. The member from India, Mr. Justice Pal, held that the

[1] For a discussion of the possible sub-divisions of public opinion in relation to foreign policy, see, e.g., J. N. Rosenau, *Public Opinion and Foreign Policy* (New York, 1961). I follow his definition of the attentive public as 'opinion-holders who are inclined to participate (in the opinion-making process) but lack the access or opportunity to do so'.

[2] See, e.g., H. Wilson, *Diplomat Between Wars* (New York, 1941), 261.

[3] IMTFE, *Exhibit* 193. Cf. D. Borg, *The United States and the Far Eastern Crisis of 1933–8* (Cambridge, Mass., 1964), 36–8.

[4] The year in which the Chinese ruler of Manchuria, Marshal Chang Tso-lin, was assassinated by members of the Kwantung Army.

[5] IMTFE, *Judgment*, Part A, Chapter 1; cf. Part B, Chapter V.

term 'war' should be taken as relating only to Sino–Japanese hostilities from 1937 onwards, and that there, as in the preceding period, the Tribunal 'should not avoid examining the whole of the circumstances, political and economic, that led up to these events'.[1] Also, as will be seen later, subsequent students of Japanese politics in the 1930s have again found reason to question the 'simplistic and linear' interpretation which was based upon the existence of conspiracy and the execution of a master-plan.[2] The present writer is not qualified to advance a bold opinion on the legal arguments of Mr. Justice Pal (whose historical surmises, it may be observed in passing, were not always accurate), or on the detailed formulation of Japanese policy in the years before Pearl Harbour. Nevertheless, without in any way suggesting at the outset that the Manchurian crisis did not mark a significant moment in Japanese politics, or that there was no aggressive intent among Japanese officials in the 1930s, one can at least agree that an enquiry into the origins of a war should entail more than a search for conspiracy on the part of those who struck the first blows, however abundant the evidence seeming to point in that direction. Where this study is concerned, especially, an analysis of Western policies during the 1931–3 episode gives rise to questions about the impact upon Japan of decisions taken in Western capitals in earlier years; it also entails an examination of the general conduct in international politics of those who were to set up the Far Eastern Tribunal after their victory in 1945.

During the crisis itself, when chauvinistic and militaristic features of the Japanese scene became pronounced, there were those in the West who concluded that this would prove to be no more than a temporary aberration. For others, as will be seen, the material interests of their own country did not appear to be threatened by what had occurred. Even those who were most outspoken in their condemnation of Japanese aggression could find the basic —and, presumably, remediable—cause to lie with the economic and commercial recession of the period, rather than in a conspiracy with hemispheric ambitions.[3] It is true that in both Washington and London there was much disquiet over the possibility of a clash with Japan; but only a small minority in official circles saw this as something inevitable, or as deriving from a Japanese intention to attack the West when fully prepared. Only occasionally during the events of 1931–3 does one find the thought expressed that in the long term they might prove to be a major step towards hastening the end of four centuries of Western dominance in Asia. Rare, too, was the belief that the Japanese might be facilitating that very extension of communist influence in China which it was one of their aims to prevent. In France particularly,

[1] Ibid, *Judgment*, Dissenting Opinion of Mr. Justice Pal (vols. 157–8). Justice Pal, whose opinion ran to 1,235 pages, also raised the question of how to define an 'aggressive war', and recalled, for example, that the Soviet Union, despite her neutrality pact with Japan, had declared war against the latter in 1945. Cf. R. J. Butow, *Japan's Decision to Surrender* (Stanford, 1964), 155–8. At the time of writing I have been able to see only publisher's advance summaries of R. Minear's *Victor's Justice: The Tokyo War Crimes Trial* (Princeton, 1972).

[2] Yoshihashi, 238. See below, 373ff., 417.

[3] E.g., A. J. Toynbee, *Survey of International Affairs* (hereafter *Survey*), *1931* (London, 1932), 399–403.

but also in British and American official circles, the more common thought was that Japan was the one bulwark of order and defender of Western interests in Asia against the forces of chaos and bolshevism:

Le Japon, nation civilisée, notre allié loyal de la guerre, qui seul représente et défend à l'Orient du monde l'ordre social et la paix contre une sauvage anarchie, qui, seul, pour le moment, a le pouvoir de barrer la route à la vague sanglante de bolshevisme, est pour nous Français un des invincibles ramparts de notre Indochine.[1]

Nevertheless, if a long-term threat to the West in Asia was thus unperceived in some quarters, the challenge posed by Japan's actions to the League of Nations and to the hopes reposed in collective security was readily apparent, despite those who argued that the location and particular circumstances of the conflict rendered it inappropriate as a test of that organisation and the system for which it stood.[2] The Finnish delegate to the special session of the Assembly in March 1932 posed what had by then become a common question: 'Is the League really a live force and does it constitute a real guarantee? Or, whenever a vital and universal question of security arises, when it is faced with a dispute between world Powers, is it no more than a debating body . . .?'[3] In the aftermath of the crisis, even the most fervent champions of the League were having to confess that it had 'never sunk to so low an ebb in influence and prestige'.[4] In retrospect, therefore, the episode came to be widely thought of as a decisive moment, as 'the turning point', in Lord Cecil's words, for an organisation that had until then achieved 'almost unbroken success'.[5] The historian of the League is another who has employed the description 'turning point' for an event when 'for the first time not only the action of the Council and Assembly, but the fundamental moral and political conceptions on which the Covenant was based were exposed to a powerful and determined attack'.[6]

Thus, while the crisis was soon to influence some American historians, for example, when they advocated the need for disengagement by the United States in the Far East,[7] to other sections of contemporary opinion, in Britain especially, it appeared that if aggression in Manchuria were allowed to succeed in defiance of the League, the inevitable result would be the

[1] *Le Temps*, 21 November, 1931.
[2] See Toynbee, *Survey, 1931*, 505–8, where 'an authoritative observer' developed this view, and suggested that in Europe the moral force of public opinion against aggression would still prove 'well-nigh irresistible'.
[3] LNOJ, *Special Supplement No. 101* (Geneva, 1932), 49.
[4] Noel-Baker memorandum, 5 July, 1933, Cecil Papers (British Museum), Add. 51108.
[5] Viscount Cecil, *A Great Experiment* (London, 1941), 220–1.
[6] F. P. Walters, *A History of the League of Nations* (London, 1967), 465, 499.
[7] See the essays in D. Borg (ed.), *Historians and American Far Eastern Policy* (New York, 1966). Dr. Borg's paper, 'Two Historians of the Far Eastern Policy of the United States: Tyler Dennett and A. Whitney Griswold.', prepared for the Hakone conference of Far Eastern historians in 1969, is also valuable. On July 16th, 1933, Professor Dennett wrote to a friend in the State Department: 'So far as I can see, Japan's special position is established, and . . . I didn't raise my boys to be soldiers to displace Japan.' Stanley Hornbeck Papers, box 140.

recurrence of war elsewhere. Not surprisingly, the Chinese themselves were among the most insistent in their warnings to this effect:

> The absence of any effective action from the League in this case has encouraged those who have all along been proclaiming the belief that might is right. It has, in fact, placed a premium on aggression. It has given a new impetus to those in different countries who advocate and strive for an increase in armaments in the name of national defence, since treaties guaranteeing security may be disregarded with impunity . . . All the signs in the Far East point to a major conflict within a few years . . . If we wish to enjoy the fruits of peace, we have to pay for them too. We have arrived at a cross-roads of the World's destiny . . . It means disarmament or rearmament, economic recovery or continuance of the world crisis; it means, in fact, war or peace. These are the alternative roads before us. For the sake of civilisation . . . I sincerely hope that we shall all choose wisely.[1]

Again, this interpretation was widely repeated in later years. Just as it appeared evident that a single, direct line and intention ran through Japanese policy from 1931 to 1941, so the succeeding crises of international politics in the 1930s could be seen as stemming from the triumph of militarism in Manchuria. 'Above all,' wrote Cecil in 1941, 'it encouraged aggressive Powers in Europe—first in Italy and then Germany—to set at naught the barrier so laboriously erected at Geneva against aggression and brought us step by step to the present grave position.'[2] Henry Stimson similarly found in 1947 'the road to World War II . . . now clearly visible . . . from the railway tracks near Mukden to the operations of two bombers over Hiroshima and Nagasaki'.[3] For Sumner Welles, 'the failure of the League to take action in this case was the chief cause for Mussolini's aggression against Ethiopia; for the triumph of Fascism in Spain; and for Hitler's decision to proceed with the creation by force of his "Greater Germany" '.[4] Historians, too, came to discern the same relationship between events: 'The road from Manchuria led directly through Ethiopia to Spain, to Munich and Warsaw, and back across the Pacific to Pearl Harbor.'[5] 'The precedent would not be lost upon Europe, and out of a widening series of international crises would come eventually a crisis in world order.'[6]

The corollary of this pre-Ruskian variety of 'domino theory' was that determined and relatively painless action in 1931 would have avoided the ensuing evils inflicted upon the world by the dictators. In the same way as the 1936 reoccupation of the Rhineland came to be seen as the moment when

---

[1] LNOJ, *Special Supplement No. 115* (Geneva, 1933). The drafting of this speech by Dr. Wellington Koo in September, 1933, may have been assisted by sympathetic Western delegates or members of the Secretariat, a process which was certainly taking place in 1932.

[2] Cecil, 235–6.

[3] H. L. Stimson and M. Bundy, *On Active Service in Peace and War* (New York, 1948), 221.

[4] S. Welles, *The Time for Decision* (London, 1944), 29. The writer's reference in the same paragraph to 'the Baldwin Government in England' at the time gives some indication of the book's general reliability.

[5] S. R. Smith, *The Manchurian Crisis, 1931–2* (New York, 1948), 237.

[6] R. H. Ferrell, *The American Secretaries of State and Their Diplomacy*, XI (New York, 1963), 219.

the peace-loving nations could have 'stopped' Hitler, so it was declared or implied that democracy could have put a curb on the world's militarism during the Manchurian crisis. This belief became sufficiently implanted to itself influence the course of history, and just as the Rhineland 'parallel' instructed Eden and his associates before the Suez war, so Assistant Secretary of State (as he was then) Dean Rusk believed that the United States decision to intervene in Korea 'was in the process of being made for an entire generation since Manchuria'.[1]

Such familiar conclusions as to the significance and consequences of the 1931-3 crisis will be reassessed in the final chapter of the present work; in Parts 2 and 3, so will the related criticisms levelled against those responsible for the conduct of British and American policies during the period. For the sense, outlined above, of a great opportunity lost and a lofty cause betrayed sharpened much of the comment concerning the actions—or lack of them— of those two countries. France, and even China herself were on occasions criticised for their part in the failure to repulse the Japanese;[2] the League as a whole was condemned in some quarters for the failure to achieve a settlement;[3] but the anti-Japanese hopes of the time and hence much of the subsequent blame rested above all upon Britain and the United States.

The weight and substance of contemporary criticism was by no means the same for the two of them, however. Despite some concern in the United States for the fate of China, those Americans who wished for a more active policy to be pursued against Japan were a minority with little influence in Congress. The main accusation brought at the time against the Secretary of State, Henry Stimson, was rather that he was dangerously entangling the country in the affairs of a weak and futile League of Nations, or that his tactics were exposing the United States to rebuff and diplomatic isolation. And while on several occasions there was criticism in Geneva of the uncertainty which shrouded American policy, the very existence of that increased degree of consultation which was accorded the League by Stimson was sufficient to arouse the gratitude of those who desired to see the forces of aggression repulsed. The United States did not, after all, bear the obligations of a signatory of the Covenant, and those who proclaimed the League to be the custodian of world peace could scarcely suggest publicly that the initiative for halting a conflict between member states should be transferred and supplied elsewhere.

[1] G. D. Paige, *The Korean Decision* (New York, 1968), 331, 174. Cf. the post-war anti-appeasement material in the Hornbeck Papers, boxes 16, 95, 113 and 127.

[2] As will be seen below, France was widely suspected of having a secret understanding with Japan; so, too, for a period, was Germany. The Chinese were subsequently accorded a large measure of responsibility by several critics. In 1944, for example, Walter Lippmann, amending somewhat his contemporary emphasis, wrote: 'What one might have done, what the League might have done, if China had been willing and able to fight, no one can say. The fact is that China did not resist, and this is sufficient and conclusive reason, far more significant than any other reason, why Japan was not stopped. . . . The world can only help those who help themselves.' *United States War Aims* (London, 1944), 9. Walters, too, writes: 'The failure of (Chinese) troops to resist the Japanese was in essential contradiction to the basis of the League system.' Op. cit., 497. Such assertions will be examined below. [3] E.g., L. S. Amery, *My Political Life*, *III* (London, 1955), 155.

Indeed, the assumption frequently made by observers was that 'the United States was sincerely desirous that effective international action should be taken to guard against any permanent and irrevocable alteration of the *status quo* in the Far East', and that she lacked only an 'indispensable partner' in the shape of Britain.[1] The question of exactly what 'effective action' the United States was prepared to take was seldom pursued far, and was studiously avoided in Washington itself; but even when it had eventually been made clear that the Hoover Administration would not contemplate the employment of economic sanctions against Japan, critics like Cecil (who had acknowledged that nothing effective could be achieved without American participation) still reserved their most bitter comments for the British Government.[2]

The impression of American initiative and British obstruction was reinforced in some people's eyes by the appearance in 1936 of Stimson's own version of events, particularly as regards the failure of London to join Washington in a joint démarche against the Japanese attack at Shanghai in February 1932.[3] There had already been sharp exchanges in private in 1934 and 1935 between British and American politicians and diplomats, over the accusation that the latter had been 'let down' during the crisis[4] (although one of the principal advisers on British policy was later to comment publicly that Stimson's memory 'has deceived him', and that full accord between the two countries in 1932 might have been reached but for 'symptoms of a certain impatience in American diplomacy'[5]). Herbert Hoover, for his part, while recalling in his memoirs his own opposition when Stimson had toyed with the idea of employing sanctions, managed also to convey the suggestion that the West's failure to resort to such a weapon sprang from the benighted policies of Britain and France, who had 'imperialist titles to parts of China, exactly like what [sic] Japan was trying to establish', who shared with Japan 'a trade-union sentiment among empires', and who (unlike America) had 'few moral grounds for complaint against the Japanese action'.[6]

Inevitably, the counter-charge that it was the United States which had 'let down' the League did eventually emerge, especially once the country had become involved in the World War, with criticism being directed, either against those earlier publics and administrations that had held aloof from the new organisation, or against the hesitations of American policy during the crisis itself.[7] More frequently, however, historians have come to emphasise Stimson's sins of commission rather than of omission. His efforts, it is

---

[1] Toynbee, *Survey, 1932* (London, 1933), 516–17, 527–48. Cf. G. P. Gooch in *The Problems of Peace*, 7th Series, (London, 1933), 260.

[2] E.g., Cecil, 226, 234; cf. Philip Noel-Baker in J. Raymond (ed.), *The Baldwin Age* (London, 1960), 98.

[3] H. L. Stimson, *The Far Eastern Crisis* (New York, 1936), 155, 164.

[4] See below, 247, 401.

[5] Sir John Pratt, letter in *The Times*, 10 November, 1938, and *War and Peace in China* (London, 1943), 228.

[6] *The Memoirs of Herbert Hoover, 1920–33* (London, 1952), 366–70. Hoover exaggerated the early differences between Stimson and himself over sanctions.

[7] E.g., Smith, *Manchurian Crisis*, 233, 260; D. F. Fleming, *The United States and World Organization, 1920–1933* (New York, 1938), passim.

held, were 'based on premises many of which were unfounded in fact or history';[1] his policy outran the resources at his disposal,[2] reflected the ambiguity of the American conception of the national interest in the Far East,[3] and manifested an unsound legalistic and moralistic approach to international politics in the area.[4] Thus, even with increased criticism of the American side of things, there remains a sharp contrast between the picture commonly drawn of United States policy on the one hand (in this version, idealistic to a fault, and tending to ignore some of the limits marked out by the realities of the situation), and of British policy on the other (only too ready to withdraw within those limits in an unenlightened and timid pursuit of immediate self-interest).

In this respect, there has been far greater continuity (with a few exceptions) in the charges levelled against British policies, stemming from the anger and frustration of the Government's critics during the crisis itself. As will be seen later, these contemporary opponents were not always as confident and clear-minded as they made it appear in subsequent memoirs; moreover, the evidence strongly suggests that those who were ready to face the cost of drastic action against Japan were a minority, as in America.[5] Nevertheless their concern for the maintenance of the League and its Covenant as the one hope of preventing a return to the nightmare of 1914–18 was ardent enough, was echoed (with whatever reservations in practice) by a sufficient number of their countrymen,[6] and lent itself so readily to the search for 'guilty men' after the onset of war in 1939, that it blazed a trail for the criticism that followed. The strong impression was thus formed of a Foreign Secretary, Sir John Simon, together with a group of Tories who dominated the National Government and who spoke for the business interests of 'the City', pursuing a wholly cynical and short-sighted policy. These men and their supporters, it was suggested, were hostile towards an insurgent China and timorously sympathetic towards a masterful Japan which was behaving as they would have liked to behave towards the upstart Indians;[7] they were jealous of the growing naval power of the United States and indifferent to the fate of the

[1] A. W. Griswold, *The Far Eastern Policy of the United States* (New York, 1937), 437.

[2] A. Rappaport, *Henry L. Stimson and Japan, 1931–1933* (Chicago, 1963), 201–3. Cf. W. L. Neumann, *America Encounters Japan* (Baltimore, 1963).

[3] See e.g., the essay by Neumann in A. De Conde (ed.), *Isolation and Security* (Durham, N. Carolina, 1957).

[4] E.g., G. Kennan, *American Diplomacy, 1900–1950* (New York, 1951), 44, and R. N. Current, *Secretary Stimson: A Study in Statecraft* (New Brunswick, 1954), 254 ff.

[5] This opinion is based on a study of the press, Parliament and private papers concerning the League of Nations Union in particular. Cf. R. Bassett, *Democracy and Foreign Policy* (London, 1952).

[6] It is now generally recognised that the questions asked in the 1935 Peace Ballot were tendentious, and that the inferences that could be drawn from the result were in many cases not borne out by public attitudes during an actual test of collective security. Nevertheless, nearly seven million people were ready to approve in principle the notion of military sanctions, and around ten million the idea of employing economic sanctions against an aggressor if necessary.

[7] Toynbee, *Survey, 1932*, 523–4.

League and the cause of collective security. Simon's name, in particular, became associated with deviousness. The essence of his diplomacy was seen, in Arnold Toynbee's words, as a skilfully anachronistic endeavour 'to finesse in the manner of those eighteenth-century diplomatic virtuosi who sought to save their own countries and "to preserve the Balance of Power" by deftly playing off one neighbour against another at the least possible risk to themselves'.[1] Many American historians have followed on in this vein, 'spineless temporising', for example, serving as one summary that may be thought scarcely to rest on a careful analysis of the complex problems involved.[2] Perhaps it is not surprising that on one of the comparatively rare occasions when Simon and his policy have been defended, it is in terms as fulsome as those of the majority have been sour.[3]

Thus, although the 1931–3 episode is now less well-known than the subsequent pre-war crises in Europe, it has frequently been referred to in the light of the global conflict that followed. Of course the historian will always be affected by his own experiences and environment (in the present case, for example, it will be apparent to American students that Pacific relations can sometimes look different from a European standpoint, and to all readers that the book is written in the wake of the American débâcle in Asia), and includes such hindsight as an inevitable part of his possessions: it is his job to try to be wise after the event. In similar fashion, anyone seeking to analyse foreign policy must arrogate to himself the status of an 'omniscient observer' when depicting, say, the options, whether or not perceived at the time, that were open to policy makers, and in general the 'operational milieu'[4] within which the latter were working. Such an approach is of limited value, however, unless accompanied by an appreciation of why events and possible responses to them were seen by those concerned at the time in the way they were. This is a truism, but it would seem to require restating for an event that has acquired for many the emotive label of a moment when the cause of peace was lost or even betrayed.

Furthermore, if it is impossible to ignore the context provided by later events, it is also essential to see the responses of the West in the setting of previous political, economic and strategic developments in the Far East. If historical 'roads' are well-nigh irresistible, at least their starting points can be chosen on firmer grounds than those of mere overt crises. Of equal importance in this case were the existing structure and capabilities of the League, together with the particular strains to which the post-war hopes for a new level of international security and morality were being subjected from other quarters during the period of the Far Eastern crisis. Seldom has there been a period when men have been forced to reexamine so intensively their

[1] Ibid, 540; cf. 526 ff.

[2] E. E. Morison, *Turmoil and Tradition* (Boston, 1960), 369. Cf. Ferrell, 220, 230; Rappaport, 136.

[3] Bassett, 624–5.

[4] I.e., the total setting as seen by the 'omniscient observer' and as distinct from the 'psycho-milieu' or setting as perceived by the individual concerned. See H. and M. Sprout, *The Ecological Perspective in Human Affairs* (Princeton, 1965).

basic assumptions and approaches to international politics: to face the
question of whether to make one final, major attempt to achieve a substantial measure of arms reduction and limitation, or to rearm for the
purpose of deterrence; of whether to seek safety by undertaking new commitments to other states, or by preserving the maximum freedom of manoeuvre; of whether to rely on the League and collective security, or on the
old diplomacy and 'balance of power', or on what Simon described as 'a
judicious mixture' of the two. Baldwin, Stimson and Herriot, for example,
were all burdened with this sense of the necessity for fundamental choice
within ominous and urgent circumstances. For Britain and France, these
pressing questions would have existed even had there been no movement of
Japanese troops in Manchuria; yet although in the preceding years Far
Eastern problems had tended to be treated in isolation within world politics,[1]
they now added their complications to the wider problems of peace and
security. They also became entangled with other issues around which revolved relations between Europe and the United States, notably debts and
disarmament. If the considerations facing the policy-makers are to be fully
appreciated, therefore, the 1931–3 crisis must be set partly within the whole
relationship between Washington, Paris and London. Similarly, it must be
related to the changing domestic political situation of each country, the focus
and degree of intensity of public opinion, the efforts of pressure groups and
the domestic consequences of the current international financial and
economic crisis.

In other words, it is necessary to try to place oneself alongside those
responsible for foreign policy in that complex area where the domestic and
international environments overlap,[2] where a large number of desiderata
must be weighed one against the others and against the means available,[3] and
where the dominant impression may well be (as it was for John Kennedy
after six months in office), how little one can control the international factors
with which one is confronted. At the same time, however, it is important to
recall that it is possible and even easy for those immersed in the day-to-day
formulation and practice of foreign policy to exaggerate this intractability
and unpredictability of the international environment, to shun the formulation of longer-term policies and to adopt a purely reflexive, 'in-basket'
approach[4] (or what has more grandly been termed 'the science of muddling
through'[5]). In this way the traditions, structure and functioning of the

[1] See A. Iriye, *After Imperialism* (Cambridge, Mass. 1965).
[2] See, e.g., J. N. Rosenau (ed.), *Linkage Politics* (New York, 1969).
[3] On the problems of multi-valued choices in general, see, e.g., G. Vickers, *Value Systems and Social Process* (Harmondsworth, 1970), and D. Braybrooke and C. E. Lindblom, *A Strategy of Decision* (New York, 1963), 23 ff. On the problems in relation to foreign policy in particular, see, e.g., J. Frankel, 'Towards a Decision-Making Model in Foreign Policy' in W. J. Gore and J. W. Dyson (eds), *The Making of Decisions* (New York, 1964), and G. Hugo, *Britain in Tomorrow's World: Principles of Foreign Policy* (London, 1969).
[4] See, e.g., Z. S. Steiner, *The Foreign Office and Foreign Policy, 1898–1914* (Cambridge, 1969); D. Vital, *The Making of British Foreign Policy* (London, 1968); B. M. Sapin, *The Making of United States Foreign Policy* (New York, 1966), 373.
[5] See the essay by Lindblom in Gore and Dyson, op. cit.

foreign-policy machine can themselves help condition a state's choice of policies, as can the personalities of those involved. Thus, while the various limits perceived by those responsible for foreign policy require detailed appreciation, one returns to the necessity of measuring them against the limits—whatever their degree of flexibility—that the student must arrogantly declare to have existed 'in fact'; likewise, the policy-maker's view of what was at stake in material and other terms must be set alongside a more distant judgement. After first seeking to fulfil Mr. Justice Pal's desire for a consideration of 'the circumstances, political and economic, that led up to these events', the present section of the book is devoted to the beginning of these tasks.

CHAPTER TWO

THE SETTING IN THE FAR EAST, I

To the Washington Conference of 1921

THE CRISIS of 1931–3 occurred at a time when the power and influence of the West in the Far East were in decline. Resisted by some, unrecognised by others, the process was more clearly revealed by the harsh events of those twenty months, and was hastened by the upsurge of Japanese power to which those same events testified. In both tangible and intangible ways, this decline had already set some of the major limits to what various Western states could achieve in the area. In turn, differences of recognition and response to this setting lay at the root of many ensuing conflicts of opinion and policies within and between those states.

For four centuries, the ships of Portugal, the Netherlands, England, France and, later, the United States, had perpetuated the age of Western dominance in Asia.[1] In the Far East, the final surge of conquest had taken place only recently—too recently for some to adjust to the swift changes thereafter—following the British defeat of China in the war of 1839–42. Prompted by complex and changing combinations of motives, varying in the policies which they sought to impose upon the areas under their influence or control, the Western states nevertheless appeared by the end of the nineteenth century to be at one in their triumph over the East. It seemed irrelevant that in China, for example, where concessions were now demanded almost at will, there had flourished a civilisation which for centuries had far outstripped the West in the organisation of its society and the achievements of its technology.[2] It was post-Renaissance European science and technology that was now endowed with universal significance; alien concepts of European law, religion, philosophy and politics that were confidently thrust forward for the benefit of a people 'awakening from the sleep of twenty centuries'.[3] 'Better fifty years of Europe than a cycle of Cathay.' The race was to the strong, and had duly been won.

[1] Other states were involved, though less significantly. See, e.g., K. M. Panikkar, *Asia and Western Dominance* (London, 1953), and M. Edwardes, *Asia in the European Age* (London, 1961).
[2] See, e.g., J. Needham, *Science and Civilisation in China*, vol. I (Cambridge, 1954).
[3] See J. Needham, *Within the Four Seas* (London, 1969) essays 1 and 16; O. Lattimore, *Manchuria, Cradle of Conflict* (New York, 1932), 157; C. P. Fitzgerald, *The Chinese View of Their Place in the World* (London, 1964). The quotation is from W. J. Bryan, *Memoirs*, (Philadelphia, 1925), 312.

There is, no doubt, a temptation for those living in a post-imperial Europe, influenced by a very different climate of opinion and often by a sense of guilt, to cast into one stereotyped mould the men who encouraged and carried out Western expansion into Asia. That such a view would be false may readily be shown by the contrasts to be found, for example, among those who administered British India in the eighteenth and nineteenth centuries. It is also possible, of course, to claim that, from some standpoints, considerable benefits were conveyed, as well as obtained, by the West in this age of empire,[1] an issue that will be left to those more skilled in the study of comparative values. It is relevant to the events of the 1930s, however, that, fundamentally, this Western position had been obtained by force and in the pursuit of self-interest. It is also relevant that the pursuit of profit had come to be seen as coinciding with a civilising mission, or at least as deriving from the inherent superiority of one's own civilisation.[2]

That driving power of confidence and mission manifested itself in various guises during the final phase of Western expansion into the Pacific: among them was the attempt to transplant the essence of France into Indo–China, and the decision of McKinley to annex the Philippines and thereafter 'uplift, civilise and Christianise them'. Its influence remained strong in certain quarters in 1931, and MacArthur, for example, was to carry it with him in his mental baggage when he arrived to control Japan in 1945. Apart from the disruptive effects of Western concepts—like Western technology[3]—on much of Asian society, however, the process of propaganda carried within it the seeds of its own destruction, as Asian nationalisms 'developed directly by resistance and indirectly by the recovery of historical sense and pride in cultural achievement as a result of Western contact'.[4] Even where a nation like Japan appeared to have absorbed Western principles in many ways (to the extent that, in 1931, a highly knowledgeable observer saw Manchuria as the centre of rivalry for three types of civilisation, Chinese, Russian and Western, with Japan as 'the chief protagonist of the Western (one)'[5]), one outcome was to be a blow, struck partly in the name of Asian resistance to the invader, from which the standing of the West in that area of the world never recovered.

That this might be the outcome within fifty years appeared most unlikely at the turn of the century. In Indonesia, the Dutch were presiding over islands rich in raw materials,[6] while in Indo–China a new and extensive

[1] In terms of extra-territoriality, for example, see W. R. Fishel, *The End of Extraterritoriality in China* (Berkeley, 1952), 50, 217–18; cf. D. G. Hall, *A History of South East Asia* (London, 1968), 802–3, and Panikkar, 324 ff. Panikkar's comment should also be borne in mind (ibid, 301) that 'far from rejecting the West, the, nations of Asia have been at pains to assimilate the culture of Europe in its wider aspects and to benefit by it in the reorganisation of their own societies'. Cf. G. Wint, *The British In Asia* (New York, 1964).

[2] Cf. M. Beloff, *Imperial Sunset*, vol. I (London, 1969), 32–3. Sir Ernest Satow wrote that Englishmen who arrived in China from India 'were accustomed to domineer over Asiatics'. Quoted in G. Hudson *The Far East in World Politics* (London, 1939), 15, a book that has stood the passage of time remarkably well.

[3] See, e.g., G. C. Allen and A. G. Donnithorne, *Western Enterprise in Far Eastern Economic Development* (London, 1961), 232. Cf. Wint, 124.

[4] Panikkar, 321–2; cf. Hall, cap. 41.   [5] Lattimore, vii.   [6] See Hall, 583.

French Union had been formed in 1887. From India, the supreme possession of her Empire, Britain had reached out into Burma and Malaya; North Borneo, Brunei, Sarawak, Sikkim, part of New Guinea and the Fiji islands were now hers, and the 'forward movement' from India was about to assert its influence in Tibet.[1] Even had the supreme motive of trade been removed, the existence of Australia and New Zealand would itself have assured a major British strategic interest in the Pacific, where Germany had obtained the Bismarck Archipelago, the Northern Solomons and part of New Guinea. The United States, too, having fulfilled the immediate requirements of manifest destiny, had embarked upon a Pacific expansion, with the purchase of Alaska and the Aleutians, the acquisition of Midway island, and in 1898, the annexation of Hawaii, Guam, Wake and the Philippines.[2]

In China, domination by the West was enshrined in the system of treaty ports, foreign settlements and concessions, extraterritorial legal privileges and taxation advantages which had been built up after 1842. Since the details of this system can be found elsewhere,[3] it is sufficient to note here that, as a consequence, China had surrendered her sovereignty over Macao and Hongkong, had elsewhere leased in perpetuity areas in which foreigners could reside and trade under Western law, in addition, notably at Shanghai and Tientsin, had recognised the establishment of foreign municipal administrations, and had bound herself to a low level of customs duties on imports, exports, and the transit of goods inland. During the closing years of the nineteenth century, she had also granted the Western powers and Russia naval bases, together with a controlling financial interest or concessions involving railways and industrial development. The Boxer rising had served only to increase the outward signs of this foreign control.

In this process, creative in many minds of images of China and the Chinese which were unlikely to be radically altered without some drastic reversal of events or the passage of generations,[4] Britain had played a leading part. 'First and last', in the words of one of her officials in China, 'British policy aimed at the furtherance of (her) trade',[5] and while on these grounds a peaceful and prosperous China would be welcomed, there was far less emphasis on the civilising mission which figured so prominently in policy towards India. A sense of superiority was there, and the concept of British prestige was prominent in the minds of those who transacted their country's business on the spot;[6] unlike the case of the United States, however, the national interest in China could be adequately measured in goods and cash,

---

[1] Although not without considerable differences over policy between the Government of India and the new Liberal Government, a foreshadowing of differing emphases in 1932–3.

[2] I would incline to agree with those American historians who see the 1898 development as a quantitative rather than a qualitative change.

[3] See Fishel, cap. 1.; Pratt, passim; Sir E. Teichman, *Affairs of China* (London, 1938); E. M. Gull, *British Economic Interests in the Far East* (London, 1943); Allen and Donnithorne, Appendix D.

[4] See K. Deutsch and R. Merritt, 'Effects of Events on National and International Images', in H. C. Kelman (ed), *International Behavior* (New York, 1966).   [5] Teichman, 50.

[6] Gull, 43. Cf. V.G. Kiernan, *The Lords of Human Kind* (London, 1969).

and until 1898 British trade outstripped that of other states.[1] Even when this position had been lost (by 1914, the exports of both Japan and the U.S.A. to China exceeded Britain's) and the China trade had come to be rivalled by that with other Far Eastern areas,[2] British money continued to represent by far the largest portion of foreign investment in that country.[3]

The interests of other European states in China in this period need not be examined in detail. Those of Germany were to disappear territorially and decline financially with the 1914–18 war; following developments in Indo-China, those of France became concentrated (apart from a few concessions, of which the one at Shanghai was the most important) in the southern provinces of Kwangtung, Kwangsi and Yunnan;[4] those of Italy were merely designed to minister to the pretext that she was a major power. The involvement of the United States was more complex, however. Ostensibly bound to China by a deeply embedded hostility towards imperialism,[5] she had nevertheless been quick to follow Britain in securing treaty-port and extra-territorial advantages, together with a position in the privileged foreign communities at Shanghai and Tientsin. As late as the 1894 Sino–Japanese war, moreover, the 'modern civilization' of Japan was being widely and favourably compared in America to China's 'barbarism, or a hopelessly antiquated civilization'.[6] And, as in Britain's case, there were powerful commercial motives behind American policy, with tobacco, oil and other industries pursuing a vision of an almost limitless market, akin to that dream which hovered brightly over Lancashire.[7]

Material interests alone, however, are insufficient as an explanation for the eventual degree of United States concern for the fate of China. (By 1914 her investments in that country were still less than one tenth of Britain's, and only just over one quarter of Japan's.) For a certain number of vocal Americans, China was becoming the focus for a sense of mission in a way which was scarcely ever the case in Britain. As Woodrow Wilson grew to see

[1] For the British share of expatriates, trade, investments, firms and shipping in 1899, see C. F. Remer, *Foreign Investments in China* (New York, 1933), 417. For details of British enterprises, see Gull, part III, and Allen and Donnithorne, caps. VI–IX. Cf. Pratt 85–7 and 192–3 on British involvement in China's Maritime Customs Administration.

[2] In 1913, British exports to China were valued at £19½ million, to Japan, £15 million, and to Malaya, Burma and the Dutch East Indies together, £18 million.

[3] In 1914, 37·7 per cent of foreign investments were British, 13·6 per cent Japanese. Although these foreign investments were not remarkably large, circumstances gave them 'a political importance out of all proportion to the economic consequences attributable to them'. Remer, *American Investments in China* (Inst. of Pacific Relations, Honolulu, 1929), 17.

[4] See H. S. Ellis, *French and German Investments in China* (Honolulu, 1929), and R. Levy, *French Interests and Possessions in the Far East* (New York, 1941).

[5] For an example of the pervading image of the U.S.A. as having been above all acts of acquisitive self-interest, see S. K. Hornbeck, *The United States and the Far East* (Boston, 1942), 12–15.

[6] Quoted in Neumann, 105.

[7] There were also those Chinese who suggested that America's policy of preserving China's integrity only cloaked economic aggression against her. A. Iriye, *Across the Pacific* (New York, 1967), 5, 17, 42, 86, 90.

his country's destiny as being, in the widest terms, 'to do the thinking of the world' during man's advance towards the triumph of democracy, so he and others saw China in particular as a special ward which would be guided into a future of happiness and prosperity on the American model. 'One's image of America produced an image of the world and, if indirectly, an idea of Asia.'[1] The belief owed much to the sustained efforts of American missionaries in China since around 1830, and above all to the surge of enthusiasm for their cause between 1890 and 1920.[2] At a deeper level, its attraction may be attributable in part to the reconciliation it appeared to offer between the potentially conflicting values of Christian charity and of the competitive business ethic, each deeply ingrained in American society.[3] Fostered also by a superficial interpretation of the adoption of a republican form of government in China in 1912, an image was thus established—for those who cared —of a guardian-pupil relationship that was at once good for the pocket and in the highest interests of mankind. The missionaries themselves tended to seek the remedy for China's problems in the development of a Westernised society,[4] and as John Dewey was vainly to warn in 1926,

> We have presented a certain type of culture to China as a model to be imitated. As far as we have gone at all, we have gone *in loco parentis*, with advice, with instructions, with example and precept . . . Such a part arouses expectations which are not always to be met . . . There is something of this sort in the temper of China towards us today, a feeling that we have aroused false hopes only to neglect the fulfilment of obligations . . . On the other side, parents are rarely able to free themselves from the gratitude that is due to them; failure to receive it passes readily into anger and dislike.[5]

The 'false hopes' of which Dewey spoke were linked with what has rightly been described as the ambiguity and ambivalence of American policy in the area, and from the limits which, in practice, were placed upon the exercise of a guardian's functions. Whatever the admixture of realism with idealism in the making of day-to-day policy—over Secretary of State John Hay's two 'Open Door' notes at the turn of the century, for example[6]—strong inconsistencies emerged once one took into account the powerful factors of symbols and aspirations. Hay's notes, for example, came to be thought of as establishing new and enlightened standards for less selfless states to follow

[1] Iriye, *Across the Pacific*, 5; cf. ibid. 326 ff. Cf. S. Hoffmann, *Guliver's Troubles* (New York, 1968), 123.

[2] See P. Varg, *Missionaries, Chinese and Diplomats* (Princeton, 1958); J. Lutz (ed.) *Christian Missionaries in China: Evangelists of What?* (Boston, 1965); E. Burn, *The American Idea of Mission: Concepts of National Purpose and Destiny* (New Jersey, 1957). By 1920, American missionaries in China numbered over 3,000, with a capital investment in schools, hospitals, etc. of around $12 million.

[3] See G. A. Almond, *The American People and Foreign Policy* (New York, 1960), 52 and D. M. Potter, *The People of Plenty* (Chicago, 1954), 60.

[4] Varg, *Missionaries*, 95.

[5] Quoted in H. Isaacs, *Scratches on our Minds: American Images of China and India* (New York, 1963), 196.

[6] See, e.g., Borg (ed.), *Historians and American Far Eastern Policy*; and Iriye, *Across the Pacific*, 81–8; W. I. Cohen, *America's Response to China* (New York, 1971), 48 ff.

in preserving the territorial and administrative integrity of China; it was less remarked that they allowed for the continuance of existing privileges and spheres of influence of foreign powers—including those of the United States, or that they contained no guarantee of China's integrity; it did not become a symbolic act when Hay in effect recognised that Manchuria was virtually a Russian province, or when he proposed, within six months of his 'integrity' appeal, that China should concede to America a naval base in Fukien.[1] Moreover, the two powerful currents of isolationism and the new imperialism,[2] although often to coexist in one person in a Far Eastern context,[3] were liable to impart an uncertain course to American policy when faced with the power and interests of other states in the area; and in particular, they helped perpetuate that peculiarly American dilemma concerning the use or potential role of force in international relations.[4] It also remains extremely uncertain just how many Americans in this period were seriously concerned with Chinese matters. Recent scholarship has tended to stress the gulf between the relatively few enthusiasts and the largely indifferent mass of the population,[5] while in relation to the long-term instability of American attitudes and behaviour towards China, social-psychologists would not be surprised to find this connected with an unstable focus of attention in the first place.[6]

Russia constituted one complicating factor for all Western powers in China, having resumed her eastward advance in the second half of the nineteenth century and secured the maritime provinces bordering on the Pacific by the Treaty of Peking in 1860.[7] With the aid of French money, a more direct route to Vladivostok had then been made across Chinese territory in Manchuria in the shape of the Chinese Eastern Railway; in 1897–8 there followed the seizure of Port Arthur (which, unlike Vladivostok, was not icebound for part of the year), the obtaining of a lease on the Liaotung peninsula, and permission to extend the C.E.R. southwards (by the section that was to become the South Manchurian Railway) into the newly-acquired region. Despite her ensuing defeat by Japan in 1905, which entailed the surrender of these southern interests, and despite the continuance of Chinese suzerainty over the area, Russia maintained her economic and political predominance in Northern Manchuria and along the C.E.R., by arrangement

[1] Neumann, 119; R. H. Clyde, *The Far East* (Englewood Cliffs, N.J., 1958), 348–53.

[2] Each is a portmanteau term, within which there tend to be grouped very differing phenomena. They will be examined in later chapters.

[3] Thus, Senator Albert J. Beveridge, later scourge of the League and European entanglements, in 1900: 'The power that rules the Pacific is the power that rules the world. And with the Philippines, that power is and will forever be the American people.' Quoted in S. Adler, *The Isolationist Impulse* (New York, 1960), 25. Cf. J. D. Singer (ed.), *Human Behavior and International Politics* (Chicago, 1965), 257.

[4] See, e.g., Almond, cap. III; K. W. Thompson, *Political Realism and the Crisis of World Politics* (Princeton, 1960).

[5] See, e. g., P. A. Varg, *The Making of a Myth* (East Lansing, Michigan, 1968), 117 and passim; Cohen, 165.

[6] See, e.g., Kelman, 159 ff.

[7] See P. S. Tang, *Russian and Soviet Policy in Manchuria and Outer Mongolia, 1911–1931* (Durham, N. C., 1959). 31·3 per cent of foreign investments in China were Russian in 1902.

with the Japanese. And although the Soviet Government declared in 1918 their readiness to renounce the tsarist conquests in Manchuria, they were not long in reasserting their influence along the railway to Vladivostok, and adopting a policy 'basically similar to that of Tsarist Russia'.[1]

Russia's presence in the Far East was of deep concern to Britain. For the United States, however, a greater problem was presented by the spectacular rise of Japan to the status of a major power. In the half century following the arrival of Perry's black ships in 1853, the Japanese, determined to avoid the fate of China,[2] had set out to learn from the West, reforming their already-weakened structure of internal authority by the Meiji restoration of imperial power in 1867–8, and decking it out with a written constitution in 1889. As zealously imitative, native commercial and industrial enterprises reached maturity, those of the West were relegated to a subordinate role,[3] while with American encouragement an end was brought to treaties which had conceded the foreigner extraterritorial privileges. In many Western eyes, such developments appeared both admirable in themselves and flattering to the notion of Western leadership. In this light, it was easy to overlook, for example, the intense social stresses occasioned by rapid economic change at the expense of Japan's rural areas,[4] or the independent and potentially decisive power accorded to the Supreme Command vis-à-vis the newly-democratic Cabinet.[5] It was also possible for the moment to ignore the potential consequences of Japan's absorption of the aggressive aspects of Western nationalism, epitomised in 1897 by the adoption in the Naval and Military College of Mahan's *The Influence of Sea Power Upon History*, which taught that the dynamic nation must expand, and needed strength at sea for this purpose.[6]

Already, in fact, Japan was displaying both expansionist desires and naval power. The Kurile, Bonin and Ryukyu islands had been acquired by the end of the 1870s. Far more striking was the swift defeat of China in the war of 1894–5, which brought with it Formosa, the Pescadores, and a predominant position in Korea. Initially it had also brought Port Arthur and the Liaotung peninsula, but these had been surrendered on the 'advice' of Russia, France and Germany that such a seizure would disturb the peace of the Far East. When Russia shortly afterwards took the same area for herself amid the general scramble for bases and annexations, the apparent hypocrisy of Western approaches to international politics was bitterly noted.[7]

The setback to Japanese ambitions was only brief, however, and by 1902 the country's emergence as a major Far Eastern power was being accorded

---

[1] Tang, 148. On the secret Russo–Japanese agreements of 1907, 1910 and 1912, and their alliance of 1916, see ibid, 61–5.

[2] See, e. g., Hudson, cap III.

[3] Allen and Donnithorne, 243.

[4] G. C. Allen, *A Short Economic History of Modern Japan* (London, 1962), 61.

[5] T. Takeuchi, *War and Diplomacy in the Japanese Empire* (London, 1936), 15–17; Iriye, *Across The Pacific*, 12, 50.

[6] Neumann, 58–9, 99–104; cf. Royal Institute of International Affairs, *Nationalism* (London, 1939), 186–7.

[7] Clyde, 29–41; R. Storry, *A History of Modern Japan* (Harmondsworth, 1960), 126–8.

recognition by an alliance with Britain.[1] An exhausting but triumphant war with Russia in 1904–5 led to the acquisition of the latter's Liaotung lease and the railway northwards to Changchun, together with half the island of Sakhalin and recognition of a paramount interest in Korea;[2] five years later Korea was formally annexed. Finally, the First World War brought new opportunities for expansion, and an indication that it might be sought if necessary beyond the existing framework of imperialist understandings with the Western powers. As Britain's ally, Japan seized Germany's possessions in the Chinese province of Shantung, an acquisition China was forced to recognise in the face of the Twenty-One Demands presented to her by the Tokyo Government in 1915, as she was obliged at the same time to extend Japanese rights in South Manchuria and Inner Mongolia.[3] The economic benefits of the war to Japan were also considerable in the short run, and although little was gained from an attempt to thrust away any further Russian (now Soviet) threat, by means of a military expedition to Siberia in 1918–22, the award of League of Nations mandates over three groups of former German Pacific islands, the Carolines, Marshalls and Marianas, was potentially of immense strategic significance. For Japan in 1919, there appeared good reason to believe that war paid. Britain especially among the Western powers had offered her some encouragement, and she seemed to have learned the game remarkably well—too well, indeed, for comfort in the West, where in any case the rules of that game were about to be changed.

Moreover, it is of the utmost importance for any study of the events of 1931–3 to note that when those rules were changed in 1919 with the advent of the League of Nations, Japanese politicians were, in private, extremely cool about the idea. Baron Shidehara himself—soon to be thought of as a Westerner in all but birth, so to speak, who epitomised Japan's fundamental devotion to the League—described Woodrow Wilson's scheme as 'an extremely annoying thing for Japan'. Here was one of many incidents and aspects in which men in Britain and the United States wrongly perceived the situation by projecting on to others in Asia a self-flattering image based on themselves.[4]

For the moment, however, there was alarm rather than a sense of reassurance. In the United States, where much sympathy for Japan had remained as late as her 1904–5 war with Russia,[5] there had followed a sharp increase in concern over the potential threat which the new power appeared to pose both to the destiny of China and to American interests. Tension was heightened by such specific issues as West-coast demands for a halt to Asian immigration, by the unsuccessful attempts of 'dollar diplomacy' under President

[1] See I. Nish, *The Anglo–Japanese Alliance* (London, 1966), 74–123.

[2] See Nish, caps, XII–XIV, and Clyde, 103–41.

[3] See Clyde, 231–57. Japan also increased her influence in China by means of the Nishihari loans of 1918. Cf. I. Nish, *Alliance In Decline* (London, 1972; cited hereafter as 'Nish II'), caps. VII–XIV.

[4] I owe the point about Shidehara and the League to discussions with Dr. Shumpei Okamoto, who kindly produced and translated the relevant material for me. It will be found in Gaimusho Hyakunenshi Hensen Iinkai (ed.), *Gaimusho no Hyakunen*, vol. I (Tokyo, 1969), 704–14, and Ujita Naoyoshi, *Shidehara Kijuro* (Tokyo, 1955), 136–7.   [5] Neumann, 120–1.

Taft to secure a large foothold for American finance in the railway developments of North China and Manchuria, and by the shock of the Twenty-One
Demands in 1915. In broader perspective, the question began to arise as to
whether that part of Asia which, so pleasingly, had appeared an eager pupil,
might not produce a threat to Western dominance itself.[1] What now of the
teachings of Mahan, or the belligerent confidence of Theodore Roosevelt
('No triumph of peace is quite so great as the supreme triumphs of war'[2])?
The United States Navy in particular, itself growing rapidly in this period,
was alarmed at the increase in Japanese power, and from 1904 onwards a
'Plan Orange' which envisaged war with that country lay in the files of the
newly-constituted Joint Army–Navy Board in Washington.[3]

Despite the perception of a threat to the United States and to China,
however, the underlying policy of successive American governments reflected
above all a desire to avoid becoming involved in trouble on the ground in
the Far East. Following Hay's boast that he had not incurred 'a single commitment or promise' in the area,[4] Roosevelt, too, weighed the cost of
attempting to dictate to Japan over Manchuria, and found it unacceptable,[5]
just as he began to have second thoughts about the value of having acquired
the Philippines. The United States acquiesced when Japan absorbed Korea,[6]
and in 1908 exchanged notes with Japan which could be interpreted as
according the latter a free hand in Manchuria in return for a pledge of non-
aggression against the Philippines.[7] Further ambiguity surrounded the 1915
recognition that 'territorial contiguity created special relations' between
Japan and Shantung, South Manchuria and East Mongolia, while the
Lansing–Ishii agreement of 1917 (the former was Secretary of State), although reaffirming the 'open door' principle, also recognised Japan's 'special
interests' in China resulting from her geographical propinquity. Lansing
himself had observed in 1914, in response to a Chinese appeal for protection
against Japan, that 'it would be quixotic in the extreme to allow the question
of China's territorial integrity to entangle the United States in international
difficulties', and the Joint Board's suggestion for a transfer of naval power
to the Pacific had already been turned down. Even the American protest
against the Twenty-One Demands invoked only the sanction of non-
recognition,[8] while at the 1919 peace conference, an unhappy Wilson was
unable to deny the Japanese those gains already noted. China had obtained
sympathy in this period, but little more. As Professor Iriye has put it, while

---

[1] Iriye, *Across the Pacific*, 60, 124.

[2] Quoted in R. Hofstadter, *The American Political Tradition* (London, 1962),
210; cf. R. Hofstadter, *Social Darwinism in American Thought* (Boston, 1955).

[3] Records of the Joint Army–Navy Board (hereafter Joint Board), Record
Group 225/322, National Archives, Washington; L. Morton, 'War Plan Orange.
Evolution of a Strategy', in *World Politics*, January 1959.

[4] Quoted in Adler, 27.

[5] Griswold, 131–2.

[6] Nish, 329–30. On the Taft–Katsura memorandum of 1905, see the article by
J. Chay in *Pacific Historical Review*, XXXVII, 1968.

[7] See T. A. Bailey, 'The Root–Takahira Agreement of 1908' in *Pacific Historical
Review*, IX, 1940.

[8] Clyde, 418–31; Neumann, 148.

China *as an idea* played a crucial role in U.S.–Japanese relations, 'Sino–American friendship had no solid foundation in fact'.[1] As for the Japanese, they could observe that, with the Monroe doctrine firmly lodged in the Covenant of the new League, and American sovereignty maintained in the Philippines, it was President Wilson who declared lost, through lack of unanimity, their amendment to add to the Covenant a declaration of racial equality.[2] It was not difficult to assume that any idealism emanating from Washington was merely a cloak for national self-interest; with Professor Neumann, one must add that 'sometimes this assumption was valid'.[3]

Wilson's twisting and turning in 1919 was not attributable solely to the pursuit of self-interest, however, nor simply to a lack of clarity as to where that self-interest lay in terms of the Far East. The President's difficulties over Japan arose in part from the policies which had been adopted by his two main war-time allies, Britain and France. Britain and Australia, for example, led the opposition to Japan's racial-equality amendment, which Wilson had himself helped to draft. In contrast—and yet equally embarrassing—Britain and France had secretly undertaken in 1917 to support Japan's claim to Shantung; Britain in the same year had secretly agreed to her acquisition of Germany's Pacific islands, in return for naval assistance in the Mediterranean; France had welcomed Japan's Siberian expedition as a possible help in keeping open the eastern front against Germany. For both countries, the Mediterranean and, of course, Europe were ultimately areas of greater concern. Despite the activities of her own missionaries in China,[4] France manifested none of America's emotional involvement in the fate of that country, and before the war, happy to see her ally, Russia, reconciled with Japan, had also come to her own agreement with Tokyo over spheres of influence.[5]

Like France, Britain had perceived threats from directions other than Japan, whose navy she had helped train and whose commercial and industrial progress was widely, if patronisingly, admired. Moreover, behind the jingoistic flourishes as the nineteenth century drew to a close, the 'gesture of defiance flung . . . to the nations of the world' by the Jubilee of 1897,[6] Curzon's assertion that Britain was and would remain 'the first Power in the East',[7] there had lain a sense of uneasiness, a questioning, by some, of imperial assertion in South Africa, even a consciousness of decline.[8] In 1864,

[1] Iriye, *Across the Pacific*, 112. Shortly before the end of the war, a study prepared in the U.S. Navy Department suggested that 'it was of vital interest to the United States to turn Japan towards the Continent of Asia.' S. W. Roskill, *Naval Policy Between the Wars*, I (London, 1968), 88.

[2] Neumann, 153–7; A. Zimmern, *The League of Nations and the Rule of Law* (London, 1939), 262 ff.; Nish II, 269–71.

[3] Neumann, 160.

[4] Levy, 7–10.

[5] Nish, 359–60. The agreement referred to Korea, Manchuria and Fukien for Japan, Indo–China and South China in the case of France. On the significance of various European/Far Eastern agreements of this period, see Hudson, 139–40.

[6] E. Halévy, *Imperialism and the Rise of Labour* (London, 1961), 40.

[7] Quoted in Nish, 12–13.

[8] D. Thomson, *England in the Nineteenth Century* (Harmondsworth, 1950), 203; G. M. Young, *Victorian England: Portrait of an Age* (London, 1960), 183.

the limits to British power and influence on the continent of Europe had been made more plain during the Austro-Prussian war with Denmark,[1] while since the 1870s the predominant position of British industry and even finance had been threatened and, in some respects, lost.[2] The Boer War, although apparently demonstrating imperial solidarity, had not removed the centrifugal tendencies within those territories. While in detail qualifications would have to be made to the notion of a steady decline of relative power, a situation was already emerging which was to bear heavily upon the policy-makers of the 1930s: in terms of military capability, financial resources, and mental commitment, Britain was over-extended even before 1914.[3]

In such circumstances, some of the strongest pressures upon the men conducting foreign policy are likely to be transmitted by those responsible for the country's financial affairs, whatever the other factors involved and however misguided or short-sighted financial advisers may appear on specific occasions. It is well known that this has been a feature in Britain and the United States since 1945, and its relevance to 1931-3 will be demonstrated below. In 1901, it appeared in the shape of the Chancellor of the Exchequer, Sir Michael Hicks Beach, who urged the need for economy at a time when the Admiralty were trying to find the means of meeting a growth of Franco-Russian naval power in the Far East.[4] It was a strong argument for an alliance with Japan, whose military aid Britain had already had to solicit when the Boxer disturbances in China coincided with war in South Africa and a threatening situation in Europe.[5] By 1902-3, in the words of Dr. Nish, the Japanese fleet 'was capable of dominating "naval politics" ' in the Far East,[6] and in 1905 Britain's China-seas battleships departed for home waters. By 1911, it was being recognised that the country's Far Eastern possessions were secure only so long as the alliance with Japan lasted,[7] and as Churchill admitted at the time, the First World War underlined the fact.[8] The problem had changed merely in size, not in nature, when in 1939 the Admiralty could offer only the 'hope' of sending one battleship to the Far East by 1942.[9]

The strategic and financial arguments for an alliance with Japan did not mean that the interests of the two countries were seen in London as being identical, and did not obscure the British concern not to see China dominated by Japan or any other single power. The alliance as first concluded in 1902 was intended to preserve the status quo, not to encourage Japan to alter it.[10] True, the revision of the alliance three years later did entail a recognition of each other's 'special interests . . . in the regions of Eastern Asia and of India',

[1] A. J. P. Taylor, *The Struggle for Mastery in Europe, 1848-1918* (London, 1954), 146-9.

[2] E.g., W. W. Rostow, *British Economy of the Nineteenth Century* (Oxford, 1948), and A. Briggs, 'Economic Interdependence and Planned Economies', in *New Cambridge Modern History*, XII (Cambridge, 1960).

[3] See, e.g., Beloff, op. cit.

[4] Nish, 174-7; Steiner, 52.   [5] Nish, 80-1.

[6] Ibid, 36.   [7] Beloff, 103.

[8] Nish II, 97. Cf. ibid, 84 ff., 150, 171, 228. By 1918, the U.S. Navy were also seeking Japanese assistance; Neumann, 149.

[9] See C. Thorne, *The Approach of War, 1938-1939* (London, 1967), 13.

[10] Nish, 216-36.

while London was careful not to take too strong a line thereafter over disquieting Japanese activities in South Manchuria, a region well removed from the centre of British interests in the Yangtze valley.[1] Even so, there was growing disillusionment within the Foreign Office after 1911 over the divergent aims of the two partners, and in Australia, New Zealand, Canada and India, immigration and Pan–Asian issues were helping to increase fear and hostility towards Japan.[2] By 1919, several British officials were attributing to Japan militaristic and rapacious qualities, while rejecting the more extreme Japanese claims to a special position in Manchuria and Mongolia.[3]

Moreover, the potential conflict between a policy of cooperation with Japan and that of drawing closer to the U.S.A. had already become apparent—again, foreshadowing a major feature of the 1931–3 crisis. The 1911 revision of the alliance with Japan had been planned on the British side partly in order to avoid the possible consequence of having to fight against the United States, and by 1919 there was a strong belief in the Foreign Office that it should be replaced by an entente between the three countries. Anxiety to avoid a naval race with America and not to alienate her at a time of debt negotiations pointed in a similar direction.[4] The ending of the alliance was indeed one of the measures which the U.S.A. was determined to achieve when she called the Washington Conference in 1921.

By then Japan had done more than raise the level of her military power in the Far East, for her defeat of Russia in particular had helped diminish the prestige of the West in Asia, a process further hastened by what was seen as the European civil war of 1914–8.[5] However restricted in numbers, nationalist opposition to the status quo was gathering strength from India eastwards. When the French opened the University of Hanoi in 1907, an outburst of student nationalism forced them to close it a year later; in Indonesia, the impact of the Russian Revolution fostered the organisation of opposition to Dutch rule; disillusionment with the terms of the 1919 peace settlement sparked off the May Fourth movement in China, which was later seen as a milestone on the road to internal revolution and the rejection of foreign domination.[6] Suggestions were heard that, in the face of such unrest, the imperial powers should 'draw near together in sympathy'.[7] The system under which China had been carved into spheres of influence by agreement among the powers was not to be resumed, however. The new mood in China was directly opposed to it; the appeal of the triumphant Bolsheviks in Russia

[1] Ibid, 258, 331–52; Hudson, 155–7.

[2] P. Lowe, Great Britain and Japan, 1911–1915 (London, 1969), caps. 1, 7, 8. Cf. Nish II, passim, esp. caps. II, VII, XIV.

[3] W. R. Louis, British Strategy in the Far East, 1919–1939 (Oxford, 1971), caps. 1, 2.

[4] Lowe, 309, Nish, 297, Louis, loc. cit. The anti-German and anti-Russian reasons for the alliance had also lost much of their force. Cf. Nish II, caps. II, XVI, XVIII.

[5] Panikkar, 197 ff. and C. P. Fitzgerald, The Birth of Communist China (Harmondsworth, 1964), 84.

[6] See F. Schurmann and O. Schell (eds.), China Readings, vol. 2 (Harmondsworth, 1968), 64–86.

[7] Hansard, Parliamentary Debates, House of Commons, vol. 184, col. 516. This speech by Sir H. Norman is a particularly interesting one.

both condemned it and pointed the way to its destruction; the United States herself was anxious to 'restore the equilibrium' in the Far East on the basis of an enlightened cooperation that would put an end to imperialist diplomacy.[1] Such pressures guaranteed that the Washington Conference would mark the end of the pre-war pattern. They did not guarantee an agreed or successful replacement.

Washington and after: China, the Soviet Union and Japan

The main agreements reached at the Washington Conference of 1921–2 can briefly be summarised. Partly under United States and Canadian pressure, an end was made to the Anglo–Japanese alliance,[2] the interment being tactfully veiled behind an undemanding treaty between the U.S.A., Britain, France and Japan, by which the signatories agreed to respect the status quo and to confer should any external threat or dispute between them jeopardise their insular possessions in the Pacific.[3] More importance was attached to the Nine Power Treaty,[4] in which China's sovereign independence was re-affirmed and respect pledged for her 'territorial and administrative integrity'. No obligation was undertaken to defend this integrity, however, article VII merely allowing for 'full and frank communication' should any signatory feel that the situation so warranted; and while the principle of equal opportunity for commerce and industry was reiterated and the notion of spheres of influence condemned, a clause which stated the intention of signatories not to impair one another's security was taken by Japan (not without a certain fudging of the matter in private on the American side) as being tacit recognition of her special position in Manchuria.[5] Meanwhile, outside this treaty, Japan agreed to withdraw the more extreme of her Twenty-One Demands and to modify some of the concessions made by China under the heavy-handed treatment of 1915; she also came to an understanding with China on surrendering Shantung, promised to withdraw her troops from their Siberian expedition, and later accepted the cancellation of the Lansing–Ishii agreement of 1917.

In many ways, however, the most significant agreement to emerge from the conference was the Five Power Treaty. This fixed a 5.5.3 ratio in capital ships (battleships and battlecruisers) and aircraft carriers between the

[1] See, e.g., a memorandum of March 1921 on the Anglo–Japanese alliance, Hornbeck Papers, box 12, and one of December, 1921, ibid, box 159; also A. Iriye, *After Imperialism* (Cambridge, Mass., 1965), 1–15.

[2] See Beloff, 336–43; Hudson, 184–5; Louis, cap. 3; Nish II, caps. XX–XXIII; N. Mansergh, *Survey of British Commonwealth Affairs: Problems of External Policy, 1931–1939* (London, 1952), 148 ff; J. C. Vinson 'The Imperial Conference of 1921 and the Anglo–Japanese Alliance', in *Pacific Historical Review*, XXXI, 1962.

[3] The intentionally harmless nature of the pact reduces the surprise that would otherwise attach to an American promise in advance that she would confer on an issue of security—especially one in which France was involved.

[4] Original signatories were Belgium, Britain, China, France, Italy, Japan, the Netherlands, Portugal and the U.S.A. Several other states adhered later.

[5] S. Asada, 'Japan's "Special Interests" and the Washington Conference, 1921–22', in *American Historical Review*, LXVII, October 1961.

U.S.A., Britain and Japan respectively (France and Italy each obtained 1.75), with a 35,000-ton limit on the size of battleships and a ten-year 'holiday' in the building of these vessels. At the same time it imposed a halt on the further fortifying of various potential bases in the Western Pacific: for Japan, Formosa, the Bonin, Kurile and Ryukyu islands, the Pescadores, and (in reaffirmation of the conditions of the League mandate) the Marianas, Carolines and Marshalls; for Britain, Hongkong—but not Singapore or islands adjacent to Australia, New Zealand and Canada; for the United States, Guam, the Philippines, the Aleutians, and various small islands west of Hawaii.[1]

The strategic consequences of this treaty will be examined in the next chapter. But while this and other aspects caused much tension within delegations, as well as between them, the overall intention of the conference was apparently clear to the Japanese and British Governments, as well as to the American one. An end was to be made to naval rivalry, territorial expansion and self-seeking agreements restricted to a small number of interested parties. In their place were to be multinational dealings in the common interest, with an emphasis on equal commercial opportunity, and security for Japan in her own waters in return for a position of over-all naval inferiority.[2]

An attempt was thus made to lift international relations in the Far East on to a new plane. It complemented the similar attempt enshrined in the League of Nations Covenant, nominally in global terms, but in practice directed towards Europe in particular. Like this other attempt it failed. The system it envisaged, like the League one, proved to rest on certain unwarranted hypotheses, and failed to accommodate the reactions of those— the Chinese in this case, like the Germans in the other—who rejected the inferior status which they retained under the new agreements. Both systems lacked the adherence of states—the U.S.S.R. in one case, the U.S.A. and U.S.S.R. in the other—which occupied potentially crucial positions relating to the outcome of what was being attempted; both were to encounter fundamental problems involving spheres of influence and arising from inequalities of military and economic power or potential, quite apart from any expansionist or bellicose intentions on the part of those possessing such power. In the ensuing period, the Far East was only one sphere in which dilemmas arose from the coexistence of continuing separate material interests with a proclaimed and common self-denying code; from a combination of doubts as to the adequacy of the new system with a reluctance to admit its failure or pay the price of an alternative. In the event, the intention behind the Washington agreements had been substantially undermined well before the obvious blow struck against it by the Japanese in 1931. The crisis that then occurred would have as a part of its setting a state of international relations in the Far East in which the diplomacy of imperialism had been succeeded by confusion.

The Washington treaties had attempted to regulate relations between imperial powers, but they had not put an end to the empires themselves, any

[1] In general, see H. and M. Sprout, *Toward a New Order of Sea Power* (London, 1943), caps. 9–14.   [2] Iriye, *After Imperialism*, 16–22.

more than the 1919 peace conference had promised self-determination for
all peoples ruled by the victors. Consequently, the main signatories remained
subjected to the growing strength of Asian nationalism, whatever the local
variations in the nature of the struggle. Where concessions were made, they
failed to keep pace with the rising level and intensity of nationalist demands:
thus, in India, neither the Montagu–Chelmsford reforms (which introduced
a semi-democratic system of rule at the provincial level) nor the offer of
eventual Dominion status prevented the Congress Party from celebrating
'Independence Day' in 1930, or averted widespread civil disobedience and a
boycott of Lancashire cotton goods similar to that being practised by the
Chinese against the Japanese.[1] For the Dutch, an 'ethical policy' designed to
kill discontent by kindness could not conceal the underlying refusal to contemplate granting self-government to the East Indies, and repression only
temporarily silenced revolutionary leaders like Sukarno.[2] Despite her
attempts to bring about cultural assimilation, France, too, faced 'le malaise
indochinois', fiercely suppressing violent nationalist outbreaks like the
mutiny at Yen Bay in 1930, and striving to cut off the infiltration of revolutionary men and ideas from Southern China.[3] Meanwhile succeeding
American governments were being urged to grant independence to the
Philippines, not only by Filipino nationalists, but also by those sections of
American opinion that disliked coloured immigration and the competitive
position accorded to Philippine products within the United States under
existing arrangements.[4]

It was Chinese nationalism, however, that presented the main challenge to
the imperial powers in the Far East after the 1921–22 conference. Unlike
Germany, who had given up her former rights in that country, the Washington signatories had not gone beyond a statement of their intention to provide
every opportunity for China to develop 'an effective and stable government',
and to assist that government in achieving such reforms as would warrant the
eventual relinquishing of extraterritorial rights. The recovery of full juris-
dictional and tariff powers on their own soil thus became a rallying cry which
brought intellectuals and students, as well as workers and peasants, behind
the Kuomintang's drive for control; attempts to outbid one another by rival
factions of that party further heightened the level of anti-foreign outbursts.
Anti-Kuomintang warlords in Peking and elsewhere also sought to make use
of this current of feeling, although branded by the Nationalists as tools of
the imperialist aggressors, who were in turn 'the ultimate cause of all the
difficulties and sufferings of the Chinese people'.[5] A powerful stimulus was

[1] Toynbee, *Survey, 1931*, 159–60; cf. Edwardes, 240 ff. and B. N. Pandey, *The
Break-Up of British India* (London, 1962), caps. 4 and 5.
[2] See A. Vandenbosch, 'Nationalism in Netherlands East India', in *Pacific Affairs*,
December 1931, and Hall, cap. 43.
[3] See R. Levy, 'Indo-China, 1931–1932', in *Pacific Affairs*, March 1932; Hall,
cap. 44; P. Renouvin, *La Question d'Extrême Orient, 1840–1940* (Paris, 1953),
356 ff.
[4] Clyde, cap. 33; Hall, cap. 45; G. A. Grunder and W. E. Livezey, *The Philippines
and the United States* (Norman, Oklahoma, 1951).
[5] Quoted in Iriye, *After Imperialism*, 93; cf. Fitzgerald, *The Birth of Communist
China*, 58–70.

provided by the incident of 30 May 1925, when the foreign-controlled police
in the International Settlement at Shanghai killed some of those who were
demonstrating against the arrest of strikers in a Japanese-owned mill; there
followed a widespread campaign against foreign businesses, goods and
individuals, and in 1926–7 new reverberations from the triumphant progress
of the Kuomintang's expedition northwards from Canton. Crowds overran
the British concessions at Hankow and Kiukiang; in Nanking, Nationalist
soldiers killed several foreigners and, with the capture of the Chinese portion
of Shanghai, came face to face with the forces of the West. By the end of 1928
the Nationalist unification of the country appeared almost complete, with
Peking·taken from the warlords (although the capital was then transferred to
Nanking) and Manchuria unified with the rest of China. Britain and a
number of Western states with smaller interests had already surrendered
some of their privileged areas, and an agreement on tariff autonomy was
near at hand;[1] now demands were received for the speedy return of the
remaining settlements and leased territories. An initial deadline of January
1930 was softened by negotiation, but the main reservations sought by Japan
and the Western powers were rejected. In May 1931, a new declaration by
the Nanking government raised the prospect that it would unilaterally terminate extraterritoriality on January 1, 1932. This produced further concessions on the part of Britain and the United States, but matters had not
got beyond the stage of draft agreements when the Manchurian crisis
intervened.[2]

This assault by Chinese nationalists upon both the political assumptions
and gradualist temper of the 1921–2 agreements owed much (though by no
means everything) to the encouragement of Soviet Union. Signs were not
lacking elsewhere of a communist-inspired threat to the position of the
imperial powers (there had been a communist-led revolt in Indonesia in 1926;
the French were able to drive underground, but not to crush, the Vietnamese
communists of Ho Chi Minh; communist influence in the trade-union movement in India stirred anxieties in Whitehall about the old threat from the
north of the sub-continent), but it was in China that Soviet policy gained its
most notable successes in the 1920s.[3] Disillusioned with the lethargy of the
Washington powers, Sun Yat-sen turned to Moscow for assistance, while in
Canton an alliance was concluded between the Kuomintang and the Chinese
Communist Party. At the same time (1924), China recognised the Soviet
Government and accepted the perpetuation of the latter's influence in North
Manchuria through joint Sino–Soviet management of the Chinese Eastern
Railway. By the time Moscow's efforts received their sudden setback when
Chiang Kai-shek turned on the Communists in 1927, the inadequacy of the
Washington framework had been demonstrated and the Western powers
were on the defensive. Ironically, it was the Soviet Union which, in 1929,
delivered the sharpest rebuff to date to China's attempts to recover her full
sovereignty, when mounting trouble over control of the C.E.R. was resolved

[1] Fishel, caps. VII and VIII; Iriye, *After Imperialism*, 254–88.
[2] Fishel, cap. IX.
[3] See Fitzgerald, the *Birth of Communist China*, 55 ff.; Tang, caps. IV ff.; S.
Schram, *Mao Tse-tung* (Harmondsworth, 1971), caps. 3–6; M. I. Goldman, *Soviet
Foreign Aid* (New York, 1967), 1–12; Lattimore, 244 ff.

by a brisk Soviet military victory in the area and a resumption of the status quo. It was to be Japan, not China, that successfully pushed back Soviet influence in Manchuria.[1]

Chiang Kai-shek's break with the Communists had not removed the latter from the Chinese political scene, but only complicated that scene still further, as Chu Teh, Mao Tse-tung and others, evading both the inappropriate instructions of the Comintern and the encircling attempts of the Kuomintang armies, built up rural bases in Kiangsi and elsewhere.[2] The Kuomintang itself remained split into a number of factions, and the armies of former warlords still preyed upon many parts of the country; in Manchuria, despite his proclaimed (and in some ways genuine) adherence to the central régime, its ruler after 1928, Marshal Chang Hsueh-liang, enjoyed both fiscal and political autonomy. Communist attacks on Kuomintang areas and foreign possessions in central China were becoming more pronounced. Banditry was widespread. In the spring of 1931, a separate government, hostile to Chiang Kai-shek, was proclaimed in Canton, and in July a rising of warlords in the north diverted more of Nanking's troops from their campaign against the Communists. One glance at the newspapers[3] was enough to reinforce the images of China held by those who had long seen her as congenitally chaotic and generally inferior in the political, social and economic skills of the modern world.[4] To add to the obstacles facing the Nanking régime, the world economic depression had struck China hard.[5] Then, in August 1931, the Yangtze and Yellow rivers burst their banks. Thousands of square miles were inundated and hundreds of thousands of peasants lost their lives; by early September, on the eve of the Japanese attack in Manchuria, it was estimated that eighteen million people were urgently in need of relief.[6]

Faced with the continuing fissiparity of Chinese politics, together with aggressive Nationalist demands and independent Soviet manoeuvrings, the main Washington signatories came to rely upon independent action rather than the coordinated policies which had been envisaged. A tariff conference at Peking in 1925–6 provided the final attempt of the U.S.A., Britain and Japan to develop a common approach to the area. Thereafter they converged only occasionally. 'Their different interests in China', writes Dr. Iriye, 'were stronger than their interests in cooperation to found a basis of

---

[1] On Soviet–Japanese relations in this period, see G. A. Lensen, *Japanese Recognition of the U.S.S.R.* (Tallahassee, Florida, 1970).

[2] See Schram, 106–66, and *Lytton Report*, cap. I.

[3] Headlines from a single issue of the *North China Herald* (21 July 1931) convey the confusion of the time: 'Civil War in North'; 'Harbin Police Violence'; 'Nanking's War on Reds'; 'Another Missionary Kidnapped'; 'Fire Opened on Rescue Ship'; 'Canton Orders Armaments'; 'Anxious Eyes to the Frontier'; 'Effects of Anti-Japanese Boycott and Civil War: Price of Foodstuffs'. Cf. Toynbee, *Survey, 1931*, 406–20.

[4] On the reinforcing of images and the avoidance of dissonance, see Kelman, 82–3, 159; Festinger, *A Theory of Cognitive Dissonance* (Stanford, 1962); K. E. Boulding, *The Image* (Ann Arbor, 1956); J. De Rivera, *The Psychological Dimension of Foreign Policy* (Columbus, Ohio, 1968), caps. 2–4.

[5] Iriye, *After Imperialism*, 278–80.

[6] See *North China Herald*, 4 August, 8, 15 September 1931; LNOJ, *Special Supplement No. 93*, 42.

postwar international relations. They felt their interests could better be safeguarded and promoted through bilateral agreements with China rather than through multilateral agreements. They were unwittingly putting an end to one act of the Far Eastern drama and ushering in the next.'[1] The Western powers, and not Japan alone, it should be noted, contributed to this process. And in the United States and Britain, as in Japan, there was a tendency among political leaders to assume that such actions in defence of their Far Eastern interests could be pursued without necessarily engendering conflict among the three of them, a tendency which contrasted strongly with the forebodings of those with specifically military responsibilities. In part, no doubt, the difference can be attributed to the nature of the subject that military planners are paid to think about, and it would also be difficult to deny that such plans and forebodings may themselves contribute towards bringing about the conflict in question. Nevertheless, the interlocking nature of international relations in this period was sometimes better perceived by the 'brass hats' than by the 'frocks'.

Aside from those territories she had already absorbed, such as Korea and Formosa, Japan's interests were overwhelmingly concentrated in China, and above all in Manchuria. By 1931 there were over 250,000 Japanese nationals in China,[2] forming 70 per cent of the foreign population, and in Shanghai over 38 per cent; Japan supplied around a quarter (in value) of the country's imports, and took a similar proportion of her exports. Of the foreign investments in China, Japanese money represented 35·1 per cent, slightly less than the British figure but far in advance of the American one; moreover, whereas China was the location of under 6 per cent of Britain's total overseas investments and less than 1½ per cent of those of the U.S.A., the Japanese stake there amounted to 81·9 per cent of her foreign investment. Nearly two-thirds of this Japanese money was tied up in Manchuria, above all in the wide range of commercial and industrial activities of the South Manchurian Railway.[3] Considerable proportions of Manchuria's agricultural, mining, marine, forest and manufactured products went to Japan, and while Germany, too, imported large quantities of Manchurian soya beans, the commercial and financial interests of Western states in that region were extremely small by comparison.[4]

Made up of the provinces of Liaoning, Kirin, and Heilungkiang, Manchuria covered an area equal to that of France and Germany combined,

[1] Iriye, *After Imperialism*, 87. Cf. Fishel, 69.

[2] There are slightly differing figures in *The China Year Book 1931–32* (Shanghai, 1932), and Remer, *Foreign Investments*, cap. XVII. Financial figures are taken from the latter, trade figures from the former. See also R. Akagi, 'Japan's Economic Relations With China', in *Pacific Affairs*, June 1931.

[3] Details of Japanese investments in Manchuria are given in IMTFE, *Exhibit* 2398; on Manchuria in general, see F. C. Jones, *Manchuria Since 1931* (London, 1949), and *Lytton Report*, section C, cap. 2.

[4] British exports to Manchuria amounted to around £2½ million in 1930, and investments there to around £4 million in 1932; for the U.S.A., Manchuria accounted for less than ½ of one per cent of the country's exports and of her imports in this period. Gull, 145 ff.; M. Farley, *America's Stake in the Far East* (New York, 1936), 15–16.

with timbered and mineral-bearing mountainous regions in the north-west and south-east, and a central plain running up from the Gulf of Liaotung to the region of Changchun, where the S.M.R. joined the spur of the C.E.R. Out of a population of thirty million in 1930, twenty-eight million were Chinese or Manchus who had been assimilated by Chinese culture; a large proportion of these people had arrived in the 1920s in an attempt to escape from poor conditions in Shantung and Hopei provinces especially.[1] Traditionally a 'reservoir' area for conquerors moving southwards, 'the key to the sovereignty of North China—often of all China',[2] Manchuria thus occupied a peculiar position as a land that had become racially and culturally Chinese and yet which lay beyond that ancient boundary of Chinese civilisation, the Great Wall; a territory over which China was sovereign, yet which had retained virtual independence within the new Republic. In 1931 it remained a predominantly rural area, with its few miles of road often impassable in winter; within the S.M.R. and C.E.R. zones, however, industries were helping to produce a rate of economic development well in advance of that of the rest of China.[3]

It was widely accepted that this material progress was to a large extent a tribute to the endeavours of the Japanese, whose rights in Manchuria stemmed from the victory over Russia in 1904–5, and from the 1915 agreement with China by which the lease of the Liaotung (or Kwantung) peninsula and 690 miles of S.M.R. zone was extended to ninety-nine years. Within this railway zone Japan controlled the police, taxation and public utilities, as well as stationing guards along the line itself, while her subjects in the rest of South Manchuria had the right to reside, lease land and trade there. The Lytton Commission were to conclude that probably nowhere in the world was there a country 'enjoying in the territory of a neighbouring State such extensive economic and political privileges',[4] and this situation was to provide one of the main arguments in the West for regarding the ensuing Sino–Japanese conflict as sui generis.

Great hopes were entertained in Japan of what was essentially a state enterprise in Manchuria.[5] Some of them, such as that of settling there large numbers of Japan's rapidly growing population, or that of supplying home industries with a wide range of raw materials, had yet to be realised by 1931. However, no reports on the limits to Manchuria's resources[6] were allowed to shake the accepted view that the area was vital to Japan's future, both as a source of food and materials and as a defensive barrier against the Soviet

[1] Lattimore, 201–14. [2] Ibid, 41.
[3] Jones, 12. [4] *Lytton Report*, 38.
[5] The President of the S.M.R., for example, was appointed by, and responsible to, the Prime Minister. On the other hand, the Kwantung Army was responsible, through the Minister of War, to the Emperor; the Kwantung Civil Governor was appointed by the Prime Minister; consular officials were responsible to the Foreign Office in Tokyo.
[6] See IMTFE, *Proceedings*, 2,002–3, for Major (as he was then) Tanaka's report to the General Staff on Manchuria's resources, and its reception. Cf. *Lytton Report*, 121 ff. Even one of the leading Kwantung Army plotters was ready to admit privately in 1931 that the Manchurian economy was of limited value at the time, but went on to describe the area as 'an essential base for Japan'. 'The Road to the Pacific War', vol. 1, part 2.

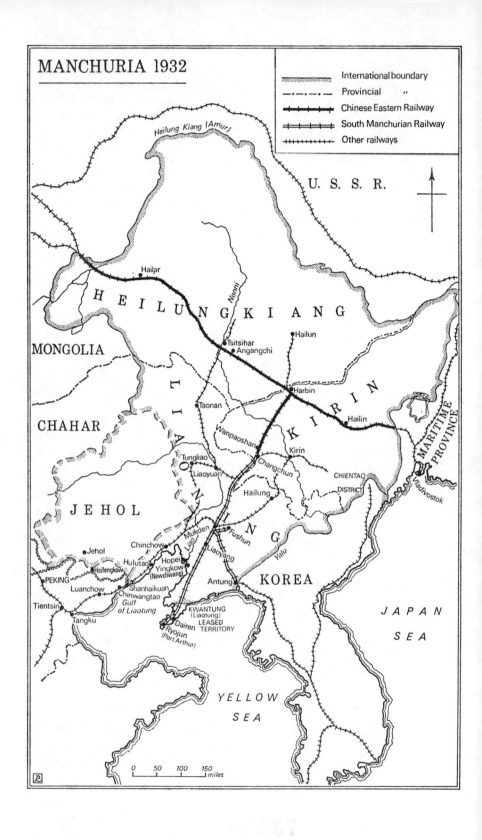

MANCHURIA 1932

International boundary
Provincial ,,
Chinese Eastern Railway
South Manchurian Railway
Other railways

U. S. S. R.

Heilung Kiang (Amur)

Hailar

HEILUNGKIANG

Nonni

MONGOLIA

Hailun

Tsitsihar
Angangchi

CHAHAR

Harbin

Taonan

Hailin

Wanpaoshan

KIRIN

Kirin

Tungliao

Liaoyuan

Changchun

CHIENTAO

DISTRICT

Vladivostok

MARITIME PROVINCE

JEHOL

Hailung

Jehol

Chinchow

Mukden

Fushun

Liaoyang

Liao

Hulutao

Hopei

Yingkow
(Newchwang)

Yalu

Hsifengkow

PEKING

Luanchow

Shanhaikuan

Antung

KOREA

Tientsin

Chinwangtao
Gulf
of Liaotung

Tangku

KWANTUNG
(Liaotung)
LEASED
TERRITORY

Dairen

JAPAN

SEA

Ryojun
(Port Arthur)

YELLOW

SEA

0   50   100   150
                    miles

Union. Nor could the memory of the sacrifices expended in that land in the war of 1904–5 be erased from the Japanese mind. 'In other words,' wrote a prominent S.M.R. official in 1931, '. . . Manchuria and Mongolia are Japan's lifeline . . . Every nation has a life-line that holds the key to its existence. As Gibraltar and Malta are to Great Britain and the Caribbean Sea to America, there definitely is an important point from which it is impossible to retreat if the nation expects to exist . . .'[1]

It is a commonplace that such notions of 'vital interest' are not measurable in purely objective terms, but rest upon subjective judgements that can change or be disproved over relatively short periods of time.[2] In 1956, the British Government was to describe the Suez Canal in Manchurian terminology as a 'lifeline' or 'windpipe' (and set about protecting it in a fashion not dissimilar to that of Japan in 1931), but the country did not collapse when the Canal was blocked in 1967. 'Vital interests' can grow, not only with the power, but with the self-esteem of the State; they reflect attitudes of mind as much as the economic or strategic 'facts' of the situation, as Macmillan revealed in 1956, for example, when he remarked that if Britain allowed Nasser to survive she would be reduced to the status of 'another Netherlands'.[3] Between 1898 and 1904 the Japanese Government had been prepared to consider abandoning to Russia their interests in Manchuria in exchange for a secure position in Korea;[4] in 1944, their Foreign Minister, Shigemitsu Mamoru, was to suggest that the Soviet Union might be offered a sphere of influence in Manchuria as part of the price for remaining neutral and exercising her good offices on Japan's behalf;[5] in 1971, Japan without Manchuria thrives exceedingly. Yet in 1931, the overwhelming majority of Japanese politicians, soldiers and public saw Manchuria as a vital interest, and the clear evidence of this was to form a powerful asset for those conducting the country's foreign relations during the Far Eastern crisis. This was to be all the more so by contrast with the uncertainty and disagreements within the United States over whether American interests in the area were 'vital' or not. It would be an example of international politics lending itself to Mill's aphorism that 'one person with a belief is a social power equal to ninety-nine who have only interests'.[6]

Japan's concern for Manchuria was strengthened as her economic difficulties increased during the great depression. Having returned to the gold standard in 1930 she suffered heavy losses to her reserves during that year and the next,[7] and widespread rural distress followed a rapid contraction in

[1] Speech of Matsuoka Yosuke, IMTFE, *Exhibit* 182; cf. ibid, 2392, 2395. In *Japan and her Destiny*, 49, Shigemitsu reiterated that 'the preservation of the rights she held in Manchuria was to Japan . . . veritably a question of life and death.'

[2] See, e.g., J. Frankel, *National Interest* (London, 1970), 73 ff.; Hugo, 36 ff., 74 ff.; J. Rosenau, 'National Interest', in *International Encyclopaedia of the Social Sciences* (New York, 1968).

[3] R. Murphy, *Diplomat Among Warriors* (London, 1964), 463.

[4] Nish, *The Anglo–Japanese Alliance*, 58.   [5] Butow, 89.

[6] J. S. Mill, *Representative Government* (Everyman edition, London, 1910), 183.

[7] By the end of 1931, the gold reserves of the Bank of Japan had fallen from 1,072 million yen to 470 million yen in two years. Allen, 106. For contemporary reports on Japan's difficulties, see FO 371, file 16241.

the American market for raw silk, a decline in Asian markets for cotton goods, and a glut of rice. A major boycott of Japanese goods in China worsened the position,[1] which was also marked by a fall in S.M.R. revenues. Economic and social dislocation, coming on top of existing tensions between rural and urban areas, strengthened in turn the appeal of those who had long been calling for drastic changes in the country's domestic structure and foreign policies.[2] Although the priorities and goals that were advocated varied considerably, the main aims of these reformers may be summarised as including an end to what was seen as a corrupt system of party politics; a fairer distribution of national wealth following the overthrow of the zaibatsu (the small number of groups like Mitsubishi which controlled much of the country's finance and industry); expansion abroad, with Manchuria and Mongolia as an essential element of the core area and a strategic base against the Soviet Union, and, after a victory over fellow-Asians in China, leadership of an awakened pan-Asian movement against the imperialism of Western intruders.[3]

These ideas have been described by Professor Maruyama as important ingredients of Japanese fascism.[4] And while some scholars would reject as misleading the actual term, 'fascism',[5] it remains important to emphasise certain features of militant Japanese nationalism which are central to a contention to be advanced later in the book, that among both governments and pressure groups in the West there was a widespread failure to grasp its nature and the extent of its hold in the 1930s: a failure to appreciate adequately the political culture[6] of Japan at the time, and one which gave rise to or facilitated major misjudgements during and after the crisis of 1931–3. The anti-liberal movement in Japan was not to overthrow the existing order by a sudden coup or electoral triumph, as it had done in Italy and was about to do in Germany, but rather took over state power by a process of consolidating support among groups already occupying the official civil and military structure. Seen from London, Paris and Washington, there was thus greater room for uncertainty as to whether a fundamental and lasting political change was taking place. It was equally significant that the movement was to

[1] By the end of December, 1931, 800,000 tons of Japanese freight lay idle in Chinese ports according to the *Japan Advertiser* of 29 December 1931. Cf. FO 371, F 520/1/10.

[2] See, e.g., Scalapino, Iriye, Takeuchi and Ogata; R. Storry, *The Double Patriots* (London, 1957), caps. 1–3.

[3] See, e.g., the extracts from the writings of Okawa Shumei in IMFTE *Exhibit* 2177A; and the ideas of the Kwantung Army's Lt. Colonel Ishihara Kanji, in 'The Road to the Pacific War', vol. 1, part 2. Cf. also the expression used by two Japanese nationalists in 1931 : 'The white race will never admit coloured peoples to full standing.'

[4] M. Maruyama, *Thought and Behaviour in Modern Japanese Politics* (London, 1963), caps. 1, 2, 3.

[5] See, e.g., Kentaro Hayashi, 'Japan and Germany in the Inter-War Period', in J. W. Morley (ed.), *Dilemmas of Growth in Prewar Japan* (Princeton, 1972). I am grateful to Dr. Morley for allowing me to see this book in proof form.

[6] For an introduction to the concept of political culture, see H. V. Wiseman, *Political Systems: Some Sociological Approaches* (London, 1967), cap. 2. Cf. G. A. Almond and S. Verba, *The Civic Culture* (Princeton, 1963), 13–14.

accentuate two existing features of Japanese politics that were alien—if not unknown—to the West: the 'rule of the higher by the lower', as Maruyama terms it—that is, the unwillingness of superiors to confront subordinates in matters wherein the latter had a direct interest—and secondly the tendency to submit to faits accomplis. In addition, while Japanese ultra-nationalists exalted the person, divinity and power of the Emperor, there was little likelihood of the latter being encouraged by his senior advisers to step down into the turmoil of the political arena to restrain actions and policies of which he disapproved. And finally, of crucial importance for Western hopes that the pressure of 'world opinion' would bring Japan back to a respect for the ideals of international behaviour presented in the Covenant, there was the conviction of Japanese nationalists that the country's actions could be judged only by the absolute values embodied in the Emperor. In Maruyama's words, 'The just cause and national conduct invariably *coexist* . . . When the nation acts, it is *ipso facto* in the just cause.'

To the reformers and a large section of the Japanese public, the 1930 London Naval Agreement in particular appeared to be a direct attack by the Western powers upon Japan's interests and safety in the Far East,[1] and economy measures forced upon the military during the 1931 financial crisis seemed to underline warnings that the nation was in danger;[2] the approaching 1932 Disarmament Conference at Geneva was also being awaited with apprehension. While Japan's civilian leaders still expected to be able to peacefully coexist and at times to cooperate with the West, others possessed an image of the situation which entailed a far greater element of conflict. 'To the military, America represented the inevitable antagonist. To the right wing, America's racial prejudice was driving Japan to seek its destiny in Asia. Above all, to the economically and socially deprived, America symbolised the existing order, both domestically and externally.'[3]

Relations with China were regarded as being particularly unsatisfactory, and although here again Japan's civilian leaders did not seek to use military force for strategic purposes, recent scholarship has emphasised the similarities between Shidehara's policies and those of the more notorious General Tanaka in the unyielding nature of their approaches to the future shape of Sino–Japanese relations.[4] The details of these relations between 1922 and 1931 can be followed elsewhere. For Japan they had not brought success. Attempts to cultivate the moderate wing of the Kuomintang had not saved Japan from the nationalist attack on extraterritoriality, and a policy of protecting the country's Manchurian interests through the local ruler, Chang Tso-lin, had not prevented the spread of nationalist unrest north of the Great Wall. Despite a carefully restrained reaction during the 1927 threat to Shanghai, there had been a clash between Japanese and Chinese troops at Tsinan in the following year. As pressures increased in Manchuria, there was a marked lack of coordination of policy in Japanese official circles, and radicals in the Kwantung Army had already murdered Chang Tso-lin in

---

[1] See, e.g., the discussions of the Privy Council's investigating committee on the ratification of the London Treaty, IMFTE, *Exhibits* 910A, 911A, and the Saionji-Harada memoirs, *Fragile Victory* (Detroit, 1968). On the Treaty itself, see below, 64.   [2] IMTFE, *Exhibits* 2393, 3414.   [3] Iriye, *Across the Pacific*, 164.
[4] E.g. Iriye, *After Imperialism*, 81, 114, 143–4, 156, 184, 191.

1928 in the hope of bringing about a major conflict.[1] Chang's successor, Chang Hsueh-liang, threw in his lot with Nanking, however, and remained loyal to the central government there. No greater success attended Japan's belated attempt to resume cooperation with Britain and the United States over various Chinese issues, despite the good-will engendered by the signing of the London Naval Agreement.[2] By the summer of 1931, with the Cabinet's policies having little to show for them, the Army Supreme Command in Tokyo had drawn up its own plan for dealing with Manchuria, with three alternatives: to obtain further concessions from a more compliant ruler of Manchuria; to replace the régime there with an 'independent', pro-Japanese one; or, if all else failed, to occupy Manchuria by force.[3]

A number of issues and incidents now combined to bring matters to a head.[4] The Chinese, maintaining that the rights acquired by Japan in 1915 and in subsequent agreements had been extorted by duress, began to develop new railway lines in Manchuria parallel to, and attracting traffic away from, the S.M.R., with Yingkow (Newchwang) and Hulutao as potential rivals to the ports worked by the Japanese. In Tokyo, this was regarded as a breach of an agreement made between the two governments in 1905. Japan also denounced Chinese acts of discrimination against Korean settlers in Manchuria, which culminated in a clash between Koreans and Chinese at Wanpaoshan in July 1931 and reprisals against Chinese living in Korea. This incident also coincided with the disappearance of Captain Nakamura, a Japanese intelligence officer who was shot by Chinese soldiers while on a secret mission in Northern Manchuria, and whose reported death aroused military and popular opinion in Japan to a new fury. Kwantung Army staff officers were now planning to put into effect the third alternative course of action envisaged by their superiors in Tokyo, the complete seizure of Manchuria, although the latter had moved only as far as contemplating action of some kind in the spring of 1932.[5] In the other camp, various Chinese delegates had met in Mukden in April to discuss means of liquidating the Japanese position in Manchuria altogether.[6] Last-minute efforts were made on both sides to negotiate a settlement of the immediate issues, and the Japanese premier, Wakatsuki, appealed for restraint.[7] On 18 September, however, Colonel Itagaki and his colleagues took matters into their own hands.

[1] Ibid, caps. V, VI.   [2] Ibid, 242–85.

[3] *Taiheiyo senso e no michi: kaisen gaiko-shi* (Tokyo, 1962–3), II, 24–5. One should, perhaps, briefly take note here of the thesis recently advanced by D. Bergamini in his *Japan's Imperial Conspiracy* (London, 1971). As part of his general contention that the Emperor Hirohito was the master-mind behind Japan's aggression throughout the period, Bergamini suggests that the former had Ishihara and others 'hand-picked' late in 1928 in order to plan the seizure of Manchuria (see, e.g., 379 ff.), and that secret links were established between the Throne and the Kwantung Army in advance of the 1931 fighting, for which the Emperor gave 'an unofficial nod'. The nature of the sources cited often makes it difficult to be convinced by this work; on Manchuria, the scholarly studies by Ogata and Yoshihashi—which Bergamini cites approvingly in his notes—have a very different tale to tell, and I see no reason to abandon them for this more lurid version.

[4] *Lytton Report*, cap. 3, remains an excellent guide.

[5] 'The Road to the Pacific War', vol. 1, parts 2 and 3, passim.   [6] *Lytton Report*, 30–1.

[7] IMTFE, *Exhibits* 246, 2395, 3536, 3537, and Shigemitsu, 63–7.

CHAPTER THREE

THE SETTING IN THE FAR EAST, II

Washington and after: the interests, policies and aspirations of the West

THE SITUATION in China; the presence of the Soviet Union in the area; the interests and experiences of Japan: all these, when filtered through the perceptions of observers on the spot and in the capitals of the West, would be among the factors affecting the formulation and conduct of policy during the crisis of 1931–3. So, too, would the perceived interests, the immediate goals and the ultimate aspirations[1] of the Western powers themselves. The present section is therefore devoted to an examination of these further elements in the setting, and the following one to the means available to the West for the defence of its interests in the Far East. In each case, it will be seen that contemporaries differed widely in their estimates of the situation, and that, in retrospect, a considerable degree of distortion appears to have been present in several instances.

In terms of territorial, and not simply trading, interests, the Western states most involved were Britain, France, the Netherlands and the United States. The position of Germany in this period also requires brief mention, however, for although she now had no possessions in the area, and a greatly diminished total of investments compared to pre-war days, her exports to both China and Japan were growing rapidly by 1931—those to China, for example, being four times more valuable than the French. The lure of the China market was a powerful one in Germany at the time, and, as already noted, the country was also the largest customer for Manchurian soya beans; the involvement of German army officers in military training for the Kuomintang helped foster these commercial ties, and in particular the growing interest of German arms manufacturers in sales to the Far East. On the other hand, a large export surplus with Japan pointed to the desirability of preserving good relations in that quarter, as did the accommodating line adopted by Japan at Geneva over such issues as Memel and reparations.[2] As with Prussia and an earlier 'eastern question', therefore, there were strong considerations making for German neutrality and passivity in any local dispute.

[1] These categories are discussed, for example, in the works on national interest cited above.

[2] On German interests, see Remer, *Foreign Investments*, cap. XX; *China Year Book, 1931–32*; K. Bloch, *Germany's Interests and Policies in the Far East* (New York, 1940). In 1932 there were about 350 German firms in China, and 60 in Japan.

The Dutch, too, had obvious grounds for caution, possessing in the East Indies one of the world's richest sources of raw materials such as oil, tin, rubber, nickel ore and bauxite. American firms like Goodyear and Standard-Vacuum Oil were established in the islands, and British interests were also involved; three-quarters of the capital invested was Dutch, however, and the need to step carefully where Japan was concerned was obvious from the immense importance that would be attached to possession of the territory's resources in any conflict involving the major powers in the Pacific.[1] Moreover, despite occasional bursts of liberal reform,[2] the Dutch still did not contemplate relinquishing the East Indies in the face of local nationalism. In this light, an orderly Japan could appear to administrators in Batavia to be more of a friend than a China that was seething with nationalist discontent,[3] and in 1931–3 there was to be something of a dichotomy in Dutch policy between the approach of an imperial power in the Far East, and that of a small European state anxious that the Covenant of the League should be upheld.

A similar ambivalence was to attach itself to the policies of France, although in Far Eastern terms this did not arise from matters of trade, in which the totals for both France herself and Indo–China were insignificant compared to those of other Western powers.[4] Paris had, indeed, invested large sums in her Asian empire,[5] and substantial amounts were also tied up in Chinese Government loans, the Yunnan Railway and Shanghai commerce.[6] Territorially, however, despite small concessions at Canton and elsewhere and a separately-administered one at Shanghai, the French stake in China was not such as to suggest the need to placate her at all costs. Indeed, rather than a potential market of 400 million, China tended to be seen by French governments as a dangerous source of unrest in Indo–China. Like the Netherlands, and unlike Britain, France would not contemplate a surrender of empire until it had been forced on the field of battle; increasingly preoccupied with her safety in Europe, she looked only for the preservation of the status quo in the Far East, and regarded the nationalist clamour there with defensive hostility. In 1932, Albert Sarraut, twice Governor General of Indo–China and now Colonial Minister, heard and warned against

[1] See Vandenbosch in *Pacific Affairs*, December 1931; Gull, 133–7, 159; Hall, 830; Farley, 25–9. The importance of the East Indies in Japanese planning in 1941, together with estimated quantities of raw materials, can be studied in N. Ike, *Japan's Decision for War* (Stanford, 1967), 217–20; cf. S. W. Kirby, *The War Against Japan*, I (London, 1957), appendix I.

[2] See A. Vandenbosch, 'Economic and Administrative Policy in the Dutch East Indies', in *Pacific Affairs*, October 1932.

[3] I owe this point to an interview with M. Adrianus Pelt who, while on extended leave from the League Secretariat in this period, worked for a time with his compatriots in Batavia, with access to official papers. Among the metropolitan Dutch in general it would seem that there was little interest in affairs of the East Indies. There was a right-wing pressure group, however, the Rijkseenheid ('Empire Unity'), who were in touch with conservative expatriates and who looked sympathetically towards Japan.

[4] See Levy, *French Interests*, 17–33; Hall, 789; *China Year Book, 1931–32*.

[5] Nearly 3 thousand million francs in Indo–China between 1924 and 1930.

[6] See Remer, cap. XIX.

the restless surf in the sea of progress, the counter-offensive of native energy stirred up by European dynamism, a peril which is all the more to be feared since the whole economic structure of Europe has been built up on what might be termed the pile-work of the colonies. Its ominous murmurings may be heard among the colonized peoples ... Now that the active forces of Europe have, as a result of the War, been scattered, now that its monetary wealth has been destroyed and industrial power overthrown by world conflict, they have grown considerably bolder and stronger.[1]

Despite sympathy for the struggles of republican China on the Left of the French political scene, therefore, and despite a pragmatic flexibility in French administration on the spot,[2] the country's policies had generally run counter to the forces that were sweeping China after the Washington Conference. It had been a French dispute with China that had helped delay the final ratification of the Washington treaties and resolutions until 1925,[3] while a Japanese emissary to Paris in 1928 had been assured by Poincaré and Briand that they fully understood his country's special position in China.[4] French trade with Japan was not of significant proportions,[5] but the interests of the two states to the north and south of China were sufficiently similar to give at least some continued sentimental meaning to the agreement they had made in that respect before 1914. General Billotte, the French C. in C. in Indo-China, was to indicate as much in 1932 to a British consular official in Yunnan, an area where the latter observed that the railway from Haiphong had given the French 'a stranglehold'.[6] In Paris, too, therefore, material and imperial interests would pull against any inclination to condemn Japan in order to preserve the League nearer home, with the added complication of those small European states who were allies of France yet more single-minded in the League cause. As in Germany's case, the temptation to avoid the difficulty by standing aside would be a strong one;[7] yet anything that threatened France's hold on Indo-China threatened also to diminish further her status as a major world power. Indifference would scarcely be possible.

Like France, Britain was essentially orientated towards a preservation of the status quo in the Far East, although where France's imperial philosophy proclaimed the extension of her indivisible self, Britain's, to adapt Lord Minto's words, suggested that she was 'a mere sojourner in the land'.[8] A partially self-imposed question mark thus hung over the British Empire in 1931, and above all over the future of India, as the second Round Table Conference wrestled with such immediate issues as budgetary control and the communal problem.[9] As seen from London, developments in the Far

[1] Quoted in R. Levy, 'Indo-China in 1931–1932', in *Pacific Affairs*, March 1932.
[2] See Teichman, 71; Toynbee, *Survey, 1931*, 427; Fishel, 205.
[3] Iriye, *After Imperialism*, 33–4.
[4] Ibid, 327, note 30. Cf. M. D. Kennedy, *The Estrangement of Great Britain and Japan, 1917–35* (Manchester, 1969), 73.
[5] Levy, *French Interests*, 41–3.   [6] DBFP, IX, No. 501.
[7] See Levy, *French Interests*, 62, where he quotes a comment of his own in 1935: 'In spite of the size of her empire in Asia and Oceania, France is fortunately outside the imbroglio of the Pacific.' Cf. Toynbee, *Survey, 1932*, 521, and Renouvin, 399–401.   [8] Quoted in Beloff, 161.   [9] See, e.g., Pandey, 135.

East could impinge upon these crucial Indian affairs in a number of ways, and in some of them Japan could be thought of as a potential source of trouble in the sub-continent. Nationalist or pan-Asian unrest, for example, over which both China[1] and the Soviet Union[2] were already regarded with suspicion, was thought of by the Aga Khan among others as a weapon to which Tokyo, too, might resort in order to embarrass the Raj.[3] Moreover the swift rise of Japanese textile exports to India was hastening the decline of the Lancashire industry in that market,[4] a menacing pattern that was also to be found affecting Britain's trade with Malaya.[5] In China, matters were more serious still, for while at the beginning of 1931 the total volume of that country's imports had increased by 23 per cent since 1913, those from Britain had declined by a third, with Germany and the U.S.A., as well as Japan, all making, in the words of a mission sent out by the Foreign Office and Board of Trade, 'substantial progress in recent years . . ., largely at Great Britain's expense'. It was seen as a crisis situation, in fact:

> Should the decline in the export trade of Britain continue much longer at its present alarming rate, the results must soon be evident in bankruptcy and disaster at home. The later consequences must be the abandonment of our great trading stations overseas, through inability to afford their maintenance any longer.[6]

Yet similar considerations could also be taken as underlining the need for continuing friendship with Japan, whatever the commercial threat she currently posed. By 1929, for example, and again in the much-reduced circumstances of 1931, Britain's trade with Japan was almost as valuable as that with China,[7] while for Australia especially among the Dominions, rapidly expanding exports to Japan (8·3 per cent of the Australian total in 1928–9; 12·1 per cent in 1931–2) and a production complementary to hers

[1] In 1931, Kuomintang agitation was being conducted for the return of 'lost' territories in North Burma, an area linked also, for the India Office, with Chinese activities in Tibet. Hall, 747–8.

[2] A Foreign Office memorandum of January 1930, for example, described Soviet intervention in China as 'on the political side a very dangerous attack on the position of the British Empire in India'. DBFP, VIII, No. 1.

[3] See Beloff, 337 and DBFP, IX, No. 520.

[4] India's own increased production, together with political unrest, had helped reduce Lancashire cotton sales there to 42 per cent of the pre-war figure by 1929. Thereafter, the U.K. percentage of all piece goods imported into British India fell from 75·2 in 1928–9 to 48·7 in 1932–3; Japan's rose from 18·4 to 47·3 in the same period. Gull, 153. Cf. Nish II, cap. XVI.

[5] 'Malaya' is used to embrace the three different constitutional areas existing at the time. Japan's share of Malaya's imports rose from 3 per cent in 1925 to 7·3 per cent in 1933; Britain's share of Malaya's manufactured imports fell from 30 to 20·1 per cent between 1924 and 1931. Gull, 137, 159.

[6] *China Year Book, 1931–32*, 189–93. In 1931, U.K. exports to China were valued at £7,858,000, to Hongkong at £4,435,000 and to Japan at £6,186,000; imports from the three were valued at £7,773,000, £406,000 and £6,952,000 respectively. Gull, 159. The declining trend in Britain's general Far Eastern trade position was to continue beyond the depression years. Ibid, 160–70.

[7] There were also loans to Japan amounting to £100 million on the London market. See FO 371, F655/1/10.

pointed in the same direction.[1] For India's raw cotton, too, the Japanese market was of great importance, and as the Secretary of State for India, Sir Samuel Hoare, was belatedly to discover and remind his Cabinet colleagues in March 1932, the trading balance lay in India's favour by a ratio of two to one.[2]

Other issues, it is true, had raised the prospect of Anglo–Japanese friction in the post-Washington period. In China, Japan's interests were seen in the Foreign Office as 'so different from those of Great Britain that her policy is bound to take a somewhat different turn from our own . . . (and) we can never count on (her) support',[3] while Britain's desire to see a united China that included Manchuria had been emphasised in public.[4] There had also been resentment in some Japanese circles at the termination of the alliance in 1921, and whilst Dominion immigration policies were a standing affront to Japanese pride,[5] Britain's construction of a major naval base at Singapore could also be construed only as a defence against the same country. Yet quite apart from the need not to clash with Japan until that continually-postponed day when the Singapore base would be completed, the dominant belief in British political circles after 1922 was that such a clash was in any case highly improbable. Both Austen Chamberlain and Arthur Henderson recognised that Japan's special interests in China stood on a somewhat different plane to those of other countries, and although clear warnings were received in London during the summer of 1931 that the Japanese Army intended to settle matters in Manchuria by force, much of the cool comment in the Foreign Office emphasised the obvious provocation being offered by the Chinese.[6] Immigration difficulties between the Commonwealth and Tokyo had been smoothed over to some extent.[7] When the Admiralty in 1925–6 pointed out the dangers that would arise should there be a confrontation with Japan, Churchill, as Chancellor of the Exchequer, poured scorn on the notion, and was upheld by the conclusions of the Committee of Imperial Defence and Cabinet that aggression against the Empire by Japan within the next ten years 'was not a contingency to be seriously apprehended'.[8] Shidehara's cooperative approach to international relations outside China encouraged the continuance of this belief, as did the moderation

[1] Japan took Australian beef, milk foods and wool. In 1934, she displaced Britain as Australia's largest supplier of textiles. Gull, 122–3, 154; Mansergh, 150–55.

[2] Far Eastern Committee of the Cabinet, minutes of 8 March 1932, CAB 27/482. On the other hand, India's trade balance with China was also highly favourable. *China Year Book, 1931–32.*   [3] DBFP, VIII, No. 1.

[4] E.g. by Austen Chamberlain in 1928. See Iriye, *After Imperialism*, 215.

[5] See Mansergh, 146–7; Beloff, 103–4, 169; Nish II, 381–2.

[6] See, e.g., Lampson to Henderson, 30 June and 18 July 1931; Lindley to Henderson, 16 July 1931, and N. Charles memorandum, 19 September 1931, DBFP, VIII, Nos. 491, 494, 493 and 505 respectively.

[7] In February 1931, for example, a 'Gentleman's Agreement' on immigration was arrived at by Japan and South Africa. DO 35/175.

[8] Roskill, 446, 450, 464. In 1924 Churchill had written to Baldwin that there was 'not the slightest chance of (a war with Japan) in our lifetime', and that Japan posed no threat to Britain's security. K. Middlemas and J. Barnes, *Baldwin* (London, 1969), 328.

of the Japanese in accepting the London Naval Agreement. 'Japan in particular . . . is unlikely to disturb the peace,' proclaimed the British Government at the Imperial Conference of 1930 when overcoming Australian and New Zealand opposition to a further postponement of the completion of the Singapore base.[1] 'Relations . . . have been excellent throughout the past year,' concluded a Foreign Office survey that summer,[2] and a year later the only two questions 'which might be said to disturb . . . cordial relations', Singapore and immigration, were happily declared to be dormant.[3] There was thus no Japanese impediment to the agreement by the C.I.D. in June 1931, that once more 'it should be assumed for the purpose of framing the Estimates of the Fighting Services that at any given date there will be no major war for 10 years'.[4] In this state of mind, the politicians, though not the military planners, entered the decade which was to end with the collapse of Britain's Far Eastern position beneath the Japanese onslaught.

In evaluating Japan's motives in the 1920s, Foreign Office officials tended to assume that the bellicosity they detected was not likely to be turned against Britain. This comforting conclusion was maintained, despite the stress that was placed upon racial issues as underlying the Far Eastern situation, and despite the uneasy recognition in some quarters that if emigration to white countries were denied to Japan, then 'it was somewhat unreasonable', in Balfour's words, 'to say that she was not to expand in a country [i.e. China] where there was a yellow race'.[5] Balfour's admission came all the easier in that the crude notion of 'yellow races' was, in fact, broken down to the extent of perceiving the Chinese to have their own special characteristics; these were generally thought of as being decidedly inferior ones which excluded their possessors, in Professor Louis' words, from 'the cardinal virtues of the English race'.[6] Time and again, one comes across images of the Chinese—'nimble-witted and unscrupulous folk';[7] 'deficient in their sense of reality'[8]—whose affective elements[9] contained a certain scorn, or at the least, despair, even where the holder appears to have

[1] Proceedings and memoranda of the Committee on the Singapore Base, CAB 32/91. The U.K. delegation argued that recent developments in the machinery for settling disputes, together with the 'deterrent effect' of the depression, had reduced the risk of war altogether. The factor before which Australia and New Zealand had to give way, however, was financial stringency, all the more so since Britain maintained that she was carrying a disproportionate share of the imperial defence burden. See, e.g., Chiefs of Staff Memorandum for the Prime Minister, October 1930, CAB 21/368.

[2] 'The Foreign Policy of the Empire', June 1930, Vansittart Papers.

[3] 'Commitments Involved in British Foreign Policy', 2 June 1931, CP 317 (31), CAB 24/225.

[4] C.I.D. minutes, 29 June 1931, CP 167(31), CAB 24/222.

[5] Quoted in Louis, 46. Cf. ibid, 175.

[6] Ibid, 139. Professor Louis usefully explores the shift of emphasis from the racial to the economic factor in the early 1930s.

[7] Lampson to Wellesley, 11 August 1929, DBFP, VIII, No. 87. Cf. Pratt, 14, 15, 66.

[8] Orde minute, 4 December 1931, FO 371, F7213/1391/10.

[9] On the structure of images, see, e.g., the works by Boulding, Kelman and De Rivera cited above.

been genuinely concerned for the welfare of China in general. And in 1938, Eden would still be describing Britain's Far Eastern need as being to maintain 'white race authority' in that part of the world.

Such images figured even more prominently among those who helped carry British trade into the Far East, and whose anachronistic outlook provided something of a parallel to the failure of many of their country's industrialists to adapt to changing world conditions or to diminish their preoccupation with unsophisticated mass markets like the Indian and Chinese ones.[1] In Shanghai, in particular, many British were to be found who neither knew nor wished to know the country in which they lived, and who resisted any concessions to Chinese nationalism, especially over extraterritoriality.[2] Scornful of the confusion of Chinese politics, indifferent to the contrasting values of Chinese civilisation, their only solution for present and future difficulties was, in the words of the Chairman of the Shanghai Settlement's Municipal Council in the spring of 1931, to 'show their teeth and teach the Chinese a lesson'.[3] Such views were echoed, though not always in such extreme form, by the China Association in Britain,[4] whose chairman, for example, referred in 1930 to 'the obsequious policy' of various governments, 'notably our own', in their dealings with China.[5] In 1931, the Association and its members were lobbying vigorously for an end to the retreat over extraterritoriality,[6] citing the conclusion of the report prepared for the

[1] E.g., C. L. Mowat, *Britain Between the Wars* (London, 1956), 270–83.

[2] See Teichman, 97; V. Sheean, *Personal History* (London, 1969), 212, 259.

[3] Johnson record of conversation with Lampson, 1 April 1931, Nelson T. Johnson Papers, box 35.

[4] The China Association had been formed in 1889 by individuals involved in the China trade. By the 1930s, company members had come to predominate over individuals. The Association had links with the Shanghai British Residents' Association, formed in November 1931, whose activities will appear below.

[5] China Association A.G.M. of 26 March 1930, General Committee Papers, 1930–1.

[6] E.g., China Association to Under Secretary of State for Foreign Affairs, 24 February 1931, and resolution of the Tientsin British Committee of Information, 15 September 1931, China Association, General Committee Papers, 1930–1 and 1931–2. Some anti-rendition communications were directed at the Foreign Office (e.g. Tientsin British Committee memorandum, 27 January, 1932, FO 800/286); some to the Prime Minister (e.g. Lionel Curtis to MacDonald, 15 August 1931, Baldwin Papers, vol. 117); some went through a variety of channels in order to be heard in Parliament (e.g., letters from G. W. Swire, chairman of the shipping and insurance firm of John Swire and Sons Ltd., which reached Baldwin and Austen Chamberlain direct, but were followed up through such men as Sir John Birchall M.P., and Sir George Bowyer, vice-chairman of the Conservative Central Office; Baldwin Papers, vol. 117). Swire, who wrote 'as a Conservative and supporter of your party', favoured the eventual surrender of extraterritoriality 'with proper safeguards'; Baldwin replied that when a suitable opportunity occurred in the Commons, 'the attitude of the Conservative Party will be made abundantly clear.' Cf. DBFP, VIII, Nos. 13, 40, 468. The Shanghai British Residents' Association, formed in order 'to mobilise and express British views on the questions vitally affecting British interests in Shanghai', paid £1,000 a year for the services of a committee, a Publicity Agent and a Political Agent in London. An active journalist member of this Committee was O. M. Green, who obtained interviews with Eden,

Shanghai Council by Mr. Justice Feetham, that the necessary preconditions for the rendition of the Settlement were far from being fulfilled, and that 'a long transition period' under the existing form of expatriate control was essential if disaster were to be avoided.[1]

This desire for a strong defence of Britain's imperial and other overseas interests was, of course, widely shared by the expatriate community in India, and by some sections of the Conservative party at home. 'Once we lose confidence in our mission in the East,' warned Churchill, 'then our presence in those countries will be stripped of every moral sanction and cannot long endure.'[2] It was also the assumption of the British Government, as well as of Justice Feetham, that satisfactory progress on the part of China was to be measured in terms of her complete absorption of certain Western principles and practices. Before the country's judicial reforms could become 'a living reality', declared a note to the Chinese Government in 1929, 'it appears necessary to His Majesty's Government that Western legal principles should be understood and be found acceptable by the people at large no less than by their rulers'.[3] In this respect, and in the development of her economy, China should follow Japan (as the *Lytton Report* was later to advise) in not resisting but learning from the West, whose past seizures of Chinese territory had naturally followed from China's own inability to maintain the standards of the civilised world.

Whatever the motives involved, such an approach entailed what can be described as cultural aggression. To stop there, however, and to depict British policy before and during the crisis of 1931–3 as having been shaped to a large degree by dynamic concepts of empire would be a crude simplication. It is worth recalling in passing that despite all the underlying notions of white superiority that remained, much emphasis had been placed at the Imperial Conference of 1921 on the Empire as a multi-racial entity that had a vital part to play in softening racial tensions in the Pacific area. More significantly, and despite the increase in empire that it had brought, the 1914–18 war had hastened the decline of self-confidence in the rightness and

for example. FO 371, F2671/65/10, F2704/65/10. On one occasion, a telegram from the China Association was read out in Cabinet. Conclusions of 24 February 1932, CAB 23/70. Other information obtained from China Association Papers, *North China Herald*, 30 November 1932, and minutes of the Shanghai Residents' Association in the possession of Hugh Collar, Esq., former Secretary of the China Association, who kindly discussed this subject with me.

[1] The Feetham Report, is summarised in the *China Year Book*, *1931–32*, 45–86. Cf. Lionel Curtis notes on the situation in China, 1931, Simon Papers (private collection). A large proportion of the Chinese Government's income was derived from Shanghai trade.   [2] Quoted in Edwardes, 229.

[3] DBFP, VIII, No. 12. Cf. ibid, No. 86. It should be noted that the Chinese Government had accepted Western legal principles and procedures as their goal (Fishel, 228), but in the light of relations between China and the West since 1842, there was unconscious irony in the assertion within the same British note that a vital Western principle of international relations which had been lacking in China was that concerning the intercourse between equal and independent states. Cf. Lattimore, 87; the comments of Mr. Justice Pal in his dissenting volumes of the IMTFE *Judgment*; Toynbee, *Survey*, *1931*, 427; Fitzgerald, *Birth of Communist China*, 38–40.

purpose of continuing dominion over others; however much feet were being dragged (or, at Amritsar, for example, callously dug in on the spot), the long-term purpose in India was linked to the surrender of power, not its extension. Regardless of the diehards, Baldwin, not Churchill, was enunciating Conservative policy by the end of the 1920s, and while the latter received little support for his campaigns among a preoccupied and largely indifferent electorate (foreshadowing their post-war reaction to the end of an Empire that had been 'created for and by "them" '[1]), the former could dimly perceive and accept that 'the unchanging East had changed', and that there was 'a wind of nationalism and freedom blowing round the world and blowing as strongly in Asia as anywhere'.[2] The basic weakness of expatriate pressure groups in the Far East lay in their inability to appeal to a highly-placed societal value (unlike, say, those groups in the United States who had helped bring about the Kellogg–Briand pact). As interest groups, for all their Conservative connections, the means they advocated were too obviously at variance with one of the goals in question, the preservation of good relations with potential Chinese customers; as attitude groups, they were non-starters beyond a restricted circle of the already-converted.[3] Their London associates, as will be seen, were to be by no means uncritically pro-Japanese during the coming crisis. With their own extreme viewpoint expressly repudiated by those responsible for the formulation and execution of British policy, they were left stranded on the shores of the China sea by the retreating tide of British imperial will, as much as by the ebb of British military power.

At a purely general level, of course, governments in London shared the aim of expatriates to preserve Britain's financial and commercial interests in the Far East. At the same, general level, however, the development of the Commonwealth (as marked by the Balfour report of 1926 and the Statute of Westminster in 1931) could not conceal the debilitating changes in power and sentiment that were taking place, and the essentially defensive outlook in official circles was not altered by the 'Nationally'-labelled Conservative electoral triumph of October 1931. Foreign policy goals remained ones of self-preservation, not of self-extension,[4] and nothing could have been further from the truth than the State Department memorandum of that time which foresaw a ruthless drive to put Britain back 'on top of the world as in the days of Queen Victoria', with 'world-wide propaganda against France and America' and 'a reversion to the Palmerstonian "damn-your-eyes" tradition in diplomacy'.[5] From the many illustrations to the contrary, a number of

[1] H. Seton-Watson in *Encounter*, July 1963.

[2] Quoted in Middlemas and Barnes, 596, 713. Cf. Beloff, cap. VII.

[3] On the distinction between interest groups and attitude groups, see, e.g., F. G. Castles, *Pressure Groups and Political Culture* (London, 1967), cap. 7. In general, see L. W. Milbrath, 'Interest Groups and Foreign Policy', in J. N. Rosenau (ed.), *Domestic Sources of Foreign Policy* (New York, 1967), a useful study, but one which does not allow sufficiently for the differences between direct and indirect forms of influence.

[4] For an elaboration of this distinction between foreign policy goals, see Wolfers, cap. 6.

[5] West European Affairs Division memorandum, 28 October 1931, DS 841.00/1220.

which will be cited during the 1931–3 episode, one might at this stage select two, since both had a Far Eastern context, and both were the products of British admirals, commonly thought of as a breed of voracious expansionists whose recipe for difficulties was gunboats. In 1931, for example, the C. in C., China Station, the fire-eating Sir Howard Kelly, warmly approved the need to negotiate a retreat over extraterritoriality, found much to admire in the Chinese, and was impressed by the state of Hankow and Wei-Hai-Wei which had been handed back to China some time before. 'Every Chinese killed,' he wrote, 'creates another slogan and another commemoration day', and could only impede friendship between the two countries.[1] At a more strategic level, the new First Sea Lord, Sir Ernle Chatfield, saw Britain in 1934 as being 'in the remarkable position of not wanting to quarrel with anybody, because we have got most of the world already, or the best parts of it, and we only want to keep what we have got and prevent others taking it away from us'.[2]

'To keep what we have got' in China after 1922 meant the preservation of trading interests and not, in the last resort, of all existing extraterritorial privileges; it also meant that one desired 'a united, well-ordered, prosperous and peaceful China' (not, let it be noted, a *powerful* China), and the preservation of that country from 'the tutelage of any single Power'.[3] That single power might be Japan; it might also be the Soviet Union, although there was a strong belief among Foreign Office officials that bolshevism, as they termed it, was fundamentally alien to the Chinese people, and was unlikely to take root among them.[4] Towards China herself, the attempt was made to combine a willingness 'to negotiate treaty revision and all other outstanding questions', as a note of December 1926 expressed it, with a readiness to resist any precipitate and damaging change in the status quo. This latter aspect was most strikingly illustrated in 1927 when, despite the reluctance of the United States and Japan to assist, Britain assembled 20,000 troops in Shanghai to meet the threat of a Nationalist assault on the Settlement there. In the words of a 1929 Foreign Office memorandum: 'Whenever real danger threatens the city, British interests, both economic and political, are so great that British troops must be sent to protect the Settlement just as though it were a British possession.'[5]

Despite this resolve, however, and the advice of Sir Miles Lampson on the spot against precipitate concessions, Britain could not conceal the under-

---

[1] Kelly to First Sea Lord, 27 June 1931, Kelly Papers, vol. 41. Cf. Personal Narrative, ibid, vol. 7, pp. 44, 50, 67–8; vol. 8, p. 10.

[2] Chatfield to Sir Warren Fisher, 4 June 1934, Chatfield Papers.

[3] DBFP, VIII, No. 1. Cf. Iriye, *After Imperialism*, passim; D. Carlton, *MacDonald Versus Henderson* (London, 1970), cap. 9; Fishel, passim; Louis, caps. 4, 5.

[4] See, e.g., DBFP, XI, No. 77.

[5] DBFP, VIII, No. 1. Cf. Austen Chamberlain's explanation to the League for the despatch of British troops in 1927, in which he maintained that conditions in China had 'modified the hypothesis upon which the Washington policy was based', and regretted that there did not appear to be any way in which the League could help settle current difficulties there. LNOJ, *March, 1927* (Geneva, 1927), 292. In 1932–3, the Japanese were quick to remind their accusers of this letter and its attendant circumstances.

lying flaw in the position of all the foreign powers in China, that 'the requirement . . . that China "put its house in order" before it could qualify for full sovereignty was not logically consistent with their insistence that, regardless of the limitations they might place upon that sovereignty, China must measure up to the criteria of responsibility of sovereign states under international law'.[1] More to the point (logical inconsistency not being unduly troublesome to framers of foreign policy), it was impossible to overlook Britain's relative lack of power in the area, and above all the danger of defeating her own ends should matters be carried to the point of a major clash with the Chinese. Hence, at times in step with the United States but more commonly alone,[2] Britain's progress became what the 1929 memorandum described as 'an enforced retreat . . . in which our main effort is directed towards preventing it from being turned into a rout'. By the spring of 1931, Britain had taken the lead among the Western powers in negotiating with the Nanking Government; in June, despite remaining differences over the length of time involved, it had been agreed in principle that Shanghai and Tientsin should be retained under extraterritorial conditions for a limited period, but that Britain's reserved areas in Canton and elsewhere would be surrendered.[3]

The considerations lying behind this retreat in China would again have to be weighed in 1931–3, this time against the one outlined earlier, of preserving friendship with Japan. For the need to win and retain the goodwill of China was seen as no light matter. Next to the existence and defence requirements of Australia, New Zealand and Malaya, it was thought of as touching on Britain's main material interest in the Far East. Despite the growing competition being experienced in the China trade, the size of that country's population helped sustain the conviction in London that there lay the great potential market of the future.[4] Moreover, even in the present, Britain's stake in China was still a large one. Hongkong's entrepot trade with the mainland, for example, rivalled that of direct American–Chinese commerce in value and dwarfed that between China and the Philippines;[5] two-fifths of foreign-going shipping from China flew the British flag,[6] and above all, British investments in China amounted to £244 million in 1931, representing 5·9 per cent of Britain's foreign total and far exceeding those of any other Western state.[7] The bulk of this money—£150 millicn of it—was located in

[1] Fishel, 219.

[2] Ibid, 69; Iriye, *After Imperialism*, 259, 273.

[3] DBFP, VIII, No. 458. Cf. ibid, No. 460. There remained much apprehension, however, over conditions in China, which were dramatised by the disappearance and subsequently revealed murder (he himself had first killed some Chinese) of an Englishman, John Thorburn. For details, see DBFP, VIII, No. 473, and FO 371, F4172/3361/10. For indignation aroused in expatriate circles, see *North China Herald*, 7 July 1931 et seq. A parallel between the Thorburn and Nakamura cases (see above, 38) was widely drawn.

[4] See, e.g., Wellesley memorandum, 1 February 1932: 'Since China is one of the great undeveloped markets of the world, it is felt . . . that our interest (there) is of greater potential value (than in Japan).' DBFP, IX, No. 239. Cf. Simon to Baldwin, 20 December 1932, Baldwin Papers, vol. 118.

[5] *China Year Book*, 1931–32.

[6] Remer, *Foreign Investments*, 373.   [7] Ibid, 74–9, 363–407.

the Shanghai area, 'the greatest port in Asia and the industrial and commercial heart of China'. Here, the 6,000 British citizens in the International
Settlement (there were another 2,000 in the French Concession) dominated
the foreign community, despite being outnumbered by the Japanese.[1] Here,
especially, no British government could be indifferent to events.

By contrast, as Griswold and other historians would be quick to point out
after the Manchurian crisis, United States material interests in the Far East
were less extensive than those of Britain, and far smaller than those of Japan.
Even in the Dutch East Indies, where the existence of American money has
already been noted (and from where, together with Malaya, the U.S.A.
derived about 90 per cent of its crude rubber and 75 per cent of its virgin tin),
the investment of the Royal Dutch Shell Company alone was greater than
that of all American firms in China and Japan combined.[2] In China, United
States investments of around $200 million at the beginning of the 1930s[3]
were not only far smaller in absolute terms than those of Britain and Japan,
but represented only 1·3 per cent of her foreign total; the British sum
remained substantially greater, even if investments in Japan and the Philippines were added to the American side of the balance. Even though the
American share of China's external trade had overtaken Britain's, it was
still well behind that of Japan,[4] while at Shanghai, where the majority of
American business interests were concentrated, the country again took third
place in terms of foreign money and citizens.[5] Possession of the Philippines,
which was still being justified in the 1920s as providing a commercial springboard into China,[6] had thus failed to produce any notable success in that
direction, and the islands themselves were accounting for as great a share of
American Far Eastern trade as was China in the early 1930s.[7] Even this
Philippine trade showed a heavy excess of imports over exports for the United
States, thus strengthening the case put forward by domestic producers (of
sugar, for example) who sought an early implementation of the 1916 promise
of eventual independence for the islands.[8] Moreover, America's Asiatic
trade as a whole showed a similar adverse balance—one that averaged $500
million annually between 1921 and 1931, in contrast to a positive balance of
$1,200 million with Europe—and the Far Eastern element amounted to only

[1] In 1931, the Municipal Council of the Settlement consisted of 5 Britons, 2
Japanese, 2 Americans and 5 Chinese. Teichman, 148–70.

[2] Farley, 29. The U.S. also derived the bulk of its tungsten and tung-oil from the
area.

[3] Remer, cap. XV. There are discrepancies, however, between Remer's figures
and those provided in a State Department paper of 2 March 1933 (Johnson
Papers, box 18). The latter gives a total of $250 million.

[4] Remer gives the 1930–1 position as 16·5 per cent for the U.S.A., 9·3 per cent
for Britain (including Hongkong), and 24·7 per cent for Japan.

[5] The State Department paper cited above gave 10,600 as the number of U.S.
citizens resident in China; Teichman, 169–70, gives the 1935 total of Americans at
Shanghai as 2,000 in the Settlement and 1,800 in the French Concession.

[6] See, e.g., G. E. Wheeler, *Prelude to Pearl Harbor* (Columbia, Missouri, 1963),
18.

[7] Farley, 14.

[8] Wheeler, 19. United States investments in the Philippines totalled around $225
to $250 million.

half the value of United States trade with Europe between 1931 and 1935.[1]

China's commercial potential, however, remained an influential picture in some American minds, while a certain popular goodwill towards that country (increased in 1931, it would seem, by the publication of Pearl Buck's *The Good Earth*[2]) was matched at the official level by Secretaries of State Kellogg and Stimson, who made clear their desire to promote close and sympathetic relations with the new Republic.[3] There was never a likelihood that the United States might seek to resist the aims of the Chinese government and people over the abolition of extraterritoriality by the extended use of military force.

Equally, however, there was no greater readiness after 1922 than there had been in the days of Hay and Lansing to contemplate the despatch of American forces in order to maintain the Open Door or to preserve China's integrity, and during his Washington Conference triumph Secretary Hughes himself had observed to his delegation that the country 'would never go to war over any aggression on the part of Japan in China'.[4] Moreover, goodwill towards China thereafter was accompanied in practice by the acknowledge-ment—forthright in some official quarters, reluctant in others—that no strong central government existed with which to negotiate, and that a state of general confusion was threatening American interests.[5] In defence of foreign lives, an American warship opened fire at Nanking in 1927, and by the beginning of the following year there were 5,000 U.S. troops and marines in Shanghai and the Peking–Tientsin region.[6] The newly-heard call of American missionaries (themselves under great pressure from Chinese nationalism) for a rapid end to the unequal treaties failed to overcome the caution of the State Department,[7] and despite earlier spurts of initiative, Washington was content to let London 'carry the ball' in the 1931 extraterritoriality nego-tiations.[8] As it was, the American intention remained to try to withhold Shanghai, Tientsin, Canton and Hankow from any surrender agreement.[9] Like Britain's policy, that of the United States was, in her own terms, essentially liberal towards China, but it, too, was conceived on an entirely occidental basis and was impelled mainly by considerations of national self-interest.[10] Likewise, in American as well as British official circles, there was to be found a disillusionment and even scorn for the Chinese that was to colour responses to the Manchurian fighting. 'If one comes here with a liking for the Chinese,' wrote the C. in C. of the U.S. Asiatic Fleet, 'and a

[1] Farley, 13–14.   [2] Isaacs, 155–8.

[3] For an appraisal of Kellogg's China policies, see D. Borg, *American Policy and the Chinese Revolution, 1925–1928* (New York, 1947). Cf. material in the Hornbeck Papers, box 76. As Professor Iriye has emphasised in a letter to me, 'The U.S. *needed* China if it was to stay an Asian power.'

[4] Asada, in *American Historical Review*, 1961. Cf. Wheeler, 11.

[5] E.g., Iriye, *After Imperialism*, passim; cf. *Annual Report of the U.S. Navy Department, 1930*, for examples of various threats to American lives and property.

[6] Iriye, 217–18; cf. Current, *Secretary Stimson*, 69.

[7] Varg, *Missionaries*, 147, 180, 194, 324.

[8] E.g., Hornbeck to Johnson, 2 March 1931, Johnson Papers, box 14. Admiral T. Craven wrote to Johnson on 29 June 1931: 'The idea hereabouts appears to be to do as little as possible and that infrequently.' Ibid, box 13.

[9] FRUS, 1931, III, 716 ff. and 918–19.   [10] Fishel, 220–1; Isaacs, 201.

sympathy for them in their many troubles, he has a hard time maintaining them. They are so lacking in anything approaching national feeling or interest, so prone to desert their post at the least threat one loses faith in them.'[1] It will be seen later that similar analyses by the Admiral during the crisis itself were accorded a sympathetic reception at the highest levels of the United States Government. Moreover, the question posed for an earlier period holds good for this one: just how many Americans were steadily and deeply concerned for the fate of China? Probably not so very many. And as Calvin Coolidge privately confessed, 'Most of us do not understand correctly what events mean in the Orient when they are correctly reported to us, which is not often.'[2]

If China had its disappointments, then commercially, at least, Japan might have seemed to offer a more promising future. By 1931, American exports to Japan were nearly $2\frac{1}{2}$ times as great as they had been before the First World War, and imports nearly $1\frac{1}{2}$ times as great, a combination which, by 1935, was accounting for 8·6 per cent of America's external trade and 42 per cent of her Far Eastern trade (compared to China's 18 per cent). On the eve of the world depression, the United States had taken 43 per cent of Japan's exports—above all, raw silk—while finding in her her third best customer after Britain and Canada, mainly for raw cotton, machinery, iron and steel, cars and other goods. $466 million of American money was invested within the Japanese Empire according to a State Department estimate in 1933.[3]

There were those in the United States, however, who were quick to raise the cry that cut-price Japanese goods were threatening domestic producers in their home market, an assertion that rested on slender foundations and ignored the favourable trade balance that existed for the U.S.A. vis-à-vis Japan from 1932 onwards, but one which found ready acceptance in the climate of crude self-regard that dominated American politics in the late '20s and early '30s. In 1930, it found expression in the shape of the Smoot–Hawley tariff act, passed by Congress and signed by Hoover over the protests of Japanese merchants, and widely seen as 'a virtual declaration of economic war on the rest of the world'.[4] As an American student of the question wrote at the time, such a policy was 'ominous for the future of countries so dependent on their foreign trade as Japan',[5] and like forthcoming British and Dutch moves in the same direction it could only strengthen the position of those in Japan who argued that their country must secure her own, wider area of commercial monopoly.[6]

[1] Taylor to Taylor, 25 September 1931, Montgomery M. Taylor Papers, box 1.
[2] Coolidge to General Frank McCoy, 7 April 1932, McCoy Papers, box 8.
[3] 'Accomplishments in Far Eastern Relations, 1929–1933', Hoover Papers; Farley, 13–14 and Griswold, 468; Allen, 156–9. The U.S.A. accounted for 35·6 per cent of Japan's imports in 1932.
[4] Hofstadter, *The American Political Tradition*, 302, note. Examples of the continuing efforts of manufacturers to obtain anti-Japanese protection will be found in the Herbert Hoover Papers, Japan Correspondence, 1929–1933.
[5] P. G. Wright, *The American Tariff and Oriental Trade* (Chicago, 1931), 82. Cf. the Hakone Conference paper by M. Wilkins, 'The Role of U.S. Business'.
[6] See Allen, 159.

Other issues, apart from naval rivalry which will be discussed later, also made for friction between the United States and Japan. Immigration was one, and long-standing West-coast antagonism to Japanese settlers succeeded in 1924 in bringing about an abrupt termination by Washington of the existing agreement on the subject, and an exclusion of further immigrants in a manner which deeply offended Japanese susceptibilities.[1] China, too, was always a potential source of American–Japanese friction, and after 1922 the United States did not conceal that there existed differences of approach and interest over Manchuria, for example, between the two countries. Nor did she respond to Shidehara's belated attempts to coordinate their respective China policies in the period preceding the 1931 crisis. As in Japanese government circles, however, the prevailing assumption in Washington was that differences over China could be kept apart from direct relations between the two powers, and when a conflict of interests did arise, as over a proposed loan for the S.M.R., evasion enabled the underlying dilemma to be avoided.[2] Shidehara's approach to international relations, the surrender of Shantung and Japan's willingness to compromise over naval limitation in 1930 all helped sustain a sanguine outlook, and while the contrast between Japanese stability and Chinese confusion was widely noted in the late 1920s,[3] Herbert Hoover was among those who saw in Japan a barrier to the spread of the bolshevik evil in the Far East.[4] 'All of the evidence,' wrote Assistant Secretary of State Nelson Johnson in 1928, 'seems to point to the friendliest feelings between us and the Japanese which should continue more or less indefinitely',[5] and as Minister to China he was repeating the same argument in the spring of 1931. 'I have no quarrel with your ideas as to our policy with Japan,' he wrote to the Under Secretary of State, William Castle:

For my part I feel that we should let Japan alone here in the East. I have always believed, however, that we should follow a policy . . . which would encourage the establishment and development of a strong government and nation in China . . . It is because I have never believed that Japan could or would attempt to take charge in China that I believe we should let Japan alone. The two countries can and will work out their destinies without the disappearance of either . . . but if Manchuria is destined to become part of Japan I do not see why it should necessarily embroil us.[6]

Given the general acceptance in official circles that military force would not be used to preserve the Open Door in China, the means envisaged for the pursuit of United States Far Eastern policies were thus limited. At the same

[1] See Neumann, 124 ff., 176–7.

[2] See Iriye, *After Imperialism*, 185 ff., 219, 238, 243, 282.

[3] For Stimson's appreciation of the Japanese at the 1930 Conference, see Stimson and Bundy, *On Active Service*, 169. For the views of Thomas Lamont of the Morgan financial organisation, see Iriye, *Across the Pacific*, 160. On Shidehara's amenable approach in 1921–2, see Nish II, 380–1.

[4] See Hofstadter, 285; R. G. O'Connor, *Perilous Equilibrium* (Lawrence, Kansas, 1962), 83; R. L. Wilbur and A. M. Hyde, *The Hoover Policies* (New York, 1937), 600–1.

[5] Quoted in Iriye, *After Imperialism*, 221–2; cf. material from 1927 in the Hornbeck Papers, box 433.

[6] Johnson to Castle, 25 March 1931, Johnson Papers, box 13.

time the immediate goals and more distant aspirations of those policies were
to some extent circumscribed by the deep-seated anti-imperialist traditions
and sentiments of the American body politic. In contemporary terms, this
meant that independence for the Philippines, for example, was seen as being
only a matter of time,[1] and while General MacArthur believed that the
public as a whole were indifferent to the issue,[2] many, like Senator William
Borah, were far from indifferent in believing that the country should divest
itself with all speed of the dangerous and war-engendering trappings of
imperialism. 'I am not sure,' Borah was to declare in 1933, 'that it is well for
the Filipinos, or well for the United States, to have an island of Western
culture in the midst of an oriental ocean, unless we are proposing in some
way to transform the nature of that oriental ocean, a task which I have no
desire to undertake myself.'[3] Hoover, too, although endeavouring with the
secret approval of some Filipino leaders to check the rush of Congress in
1932-3 to set an early date for the independence of the islands,[4] was basically
'anxious to get rid of them', while insisting to his Cabinet that he wanted no
more annexations within the Western hemisphere either.[5]

The President's views were linked with his profound dislike of the
European empires, which he shared with various members both of his own
administration and of the following one. Yet for all its strength, the anti-
imperialist tradition served to confuse, rather than to define, the aspirations
and policies of the United States in the Far East. Neither the coexistence of
isolationism towards Europe with expansionist inclinations in the Pacific,
nor the sense of a special mission regarding China, disappeared after 1922.
Within the Hoover Administration itself, and particularly in their contribution to the differences between Hoover and Stimson, they were to help
create an ambiguity of intent which was to contrast with the degree of
consensus to be found among even so heterogeneous a group as the second
British National Government that came to power in 1931. In India, as
already suggested, MacDonald, Baldwin, Simon, Hoare and the rest were
essentially engaged in conducting a retreat: a retreat, it is true, which was
envisaged as leading to the ultimate victory of voluntary association within
the Commonwealth, but a retreat none the less. The nineteenth-century
evangelicalism of Empire was no longer a driving force in that area; still less
was it present where the Far East was concerned. It is not unknown, however, for various ideas and attitudes from an earlier period of British history
to survive on the other side of the Atlantic, however modified their form.[6]
The confident assumptions and aspirations that had once helped carry
British commerce and Christianity eastwards were echoed before and during
the events of 1931-3, less in Whitehall than in certain quarters of official

[1] See e.g., Neumann, 170; Toynbee, *Survey, 1933* (London, 1934), 544 ff.
[2] Wheeler, 25.
[3] William E. Borah Papers, box 11. For Borah's similar views on the American
presence in Nicaragua, see his statement of 18 April 1931, ibid, box 328.
[4] See, e.g., G. E. Wheeler, 'Republican Philippines Policy, 1921-1933', in
Pacific Historical Review, XXVIII, 1959.
[5] Henry L. Stimson Diary, 28 August 1930, 26 January 1932; Hoover to
Stimson, 13 February 1932, Stimson Papers, box 305.
[6] E.g., Thompson, *Political Realism*, 79-80.

Washington. Resting partly on a belief in the universal significance of the American way of life, and sustained by the country's obvious power and potential, they were to form one of the major factors underlying the differences between American and British policies during the crisis.

For those who remained imbued with a belief in the Asiatic mission of the United States, the maintenance of the country's dominion over the Philippines, at least for the foreseeable future, was the main cause for which battle had to be joined with more selfish or short-sighted propagandists. 'If we can build up here,' wrote Governor General Leonard Wood in 1926, 'a strong, well-trained, well-disciplined people who are Christians, we shall have established a most powerful instrumentality for the extension of Christianity in the Orient, and on its extension and the extension of what is best in western civilization we must depend for the true advance to higher deeds and a better life on the part of the Oriental peoples.'[1] Wood's successor as Governor General, Henry Stimson, developed similar arguments, both in the Philippines and later as Secretary of State. To him, the Philippines represented 'an islet of growing Western development and thought surrounded by an ocean of Orientalism. They are the interpreters of American idealism to the Far East. They are on the way to becoming the base of our economic civilization in that hemisphere.'[2] Similar ideas existed among Stimson's entourage in Washington, where, complete with Filipino house-boy, he remained very much the ex-Governor General.[3]

Above all, the Philippines were seen as a vital link between the United States and China, where, in Stimson's words, 'the helpful idealism' of the former in what he later called 'our part of the world' had 'given us a foothold in the minds of the Chinese people which is pregnant with possibilities for good, provided we do not forfeit it'.[4] As before, the image was the flattering one of mentor and pupil, reinforced by the thought of a market of 400 million and the 'enormous possibilities', in Stimson's words, 'of a commerce with her which will supply her needs as she develops along the pathway of modern civilization'.[5] Thus the American pursuit of aggrandisement in China could be regarded as somehow of a more disinterested kind than that of European nations, and the belief retained that for all their discomforts, the upheavals caused by Chinese nationalism would ultimately work out in favour of the United States[6]—provided that one guarded in the meantime against being upstaged by, say, the League of Nations and its growing number of advisers in China.[7]

[1] Quoted in Wheeler, 20.

[2] Stimson to Patrick Hurley, Stimson Papers, box 312. Cf. Stimson, *Far Eastern Crisis*, 14. Cf. various memoranda and comments in the Hornbeck Papers, box 344, and McCoy Papers, box 28.

[3] See Pierrepont Moffat Diary, 19 September 1932; Regnier memorandum, 30 December 1932, Stimson Papers, box 313.

[4] Stimson to Major General W. Lassiter, 12 November 1931, Stimson Papers, box 303; *Far Eastern Crisis*, 235.

[5] *Far Eastern Crisis*, 90. Cf. Wheeler, 6.

[6] See Neumann in De Conde, *Isolation and Security*.

[7] For suspicions that League advisers might be trying to reduce American influence in China, see Hornbeck to Johnson, 10 June 1931, and Johnson to Peck, 17 July 1931, Johnson Papers, box 14.

It will be seen that one of the assumptions already observed in London, namely, that China's progress was to be measured by her adoption of Western civilisation, was also shared in Washington. Indeed, the closely-associated notion of racial superiority appears to have been at least more openly and readily enunciated in American official circles. In the case of both Hoover and Stimson, such pronouncements accompanied the fairly frequent recollection that their careers had given them each an insight into 'the Oriental mind'. Hoover, who was a survivor of the Boxer rising, had indeed spent many years in the East among what he called the 'lower races',[1] and despite his disagreements with Stimson over the Philippines, was ready to agree with him that 'the white man's burden' had to be shouldered.[2] Only 'the cooperation of the Anglo-Saxons', he believed, could now save civilisation from the disasters of the depression, since the others 'could not be counted on',[3] while he regretted that so few arbitrators trained in English law were available for international cases that 'we must practically come down to the lesser breed'.[4] Stimson agreed—only one Filipino politician, he believed, had 'a sufficiently Anglo-Saxon mind' to be thought of as a possible native governor general[5]—but went further in that, in contrast to Hoover, he found much to admire in the European, and especially British, empires. Like Leonard Wood, Stimson was a survivor of that group or school who have been termed the 'neo-Hamiltonians',[6] and who had followed Mahan and Theodore Roosevelt (an early political mentor of Stimson's) in welcoming the opportunity for the United States to further its interests through the exercise of its power. (This national interest was often identified with universal values and causes of a moral kind, but the military ethic was even more pronounced.) The merits of others who had succeeded in this game had thus to be acknowledged, and when Stimson, in 1932, was to see the U.S. Navy as holding the Japanese at bay on behalf of all Western powers, it was only a variation of General Wood's earlier conviction that tenure of the Philippines was vital for sustaining 'Anglo-Saxonism . . . in the Western Pacific, in the Far East (and) in India'.[7] In similar vein, a senior staff officer of the U.S. Army wrote in 1930 that if America were to grant the Philippines their independence, she would be removing her restraint 'over radical tendencies in political self-determination of the lesser-developed races', and thus placing an unfair burden on the other imperial powers:

[1] Hofstadter, 289; cf. Isaacs, 150–1.

[2] Stimson Diary, 14 February 1932.

[3] Stimson to MacDonald, 27 January 1932, Stimson Papers, box 304. Stimson's pencilled note of Hoover's phrase is also to be found in this box.

[4] Stimson Diary, 4 April 1932.

[5] Stimson Diary, 17 January 1929, referring to Manuel Quezon. Cf. Current, *Secretary Stimson*, 38–9.

[6] S. P. Huntington, *The Soldier and the State* (New York, 1957), 270 ff.

[7] Wheeler, 23–4. Wood's policies were in turn applauded in right-wing circles in Britain. Cf. a State Department memorandum (by J. F. Carter of the Far Eastern Division) of 2 April 1932, in which the writer thankfully observed: 'The United States, the Dominions and the British ruling class are alike race-conscious and color conscious, and the underlying instinct of the Anglo-Saxons is to preserve the Anglo-Saxon breed intact against the rising tide of color.' Hornbeck Papers, box 87.

The United States, Britain, France and the Netherlands, Western nations of white peoples, possess and administer the most important territory in the south-western Pacific—lands peopled by yellow or brown races of limited development, the majority of whom are constantly stirred by sentiments or propaganda to throw aside western control . . . China is a nation of teeming yellow millions . . . and . . . offers a vast market for international trade and capital.[1]

Even if Britain were seen, not as an ally, but as a rival, as was frequently the case within the higher ranks of the U.S. Navy, the task of the United States was not necessarily altered. 'We are Great Britain's logical successors,' wrote the Director of the Navy's War Plans Division in 1932. 'We cannot ignore our obligation to bear our share of the "white man's burden".'[2] Might not the responsibility even extend, as Stimson mused, to that of 'policing the world'?[3]

A description, however, of American Far Eastern policy on the eve of the Manchurian crisis as being motivated mainly by outward-looking and expansionist visions of the future would be as inaccurate as the picture of Tory imperialism aggressively dominating the policies of Britain's National Government. Hoover spoke for far more of his fellow countrymen than did Stimson in wanting no entanglements, whether in 'police' or 'mission' form, and in failing to appreciate, as Stimson saw it, 'the real nobility of the traditional . . . American doctrine towards China of the "Open Door" '.[4]

And yet the expansionist inclinations of Stimson and others did exist at the time, and helped perpetuate that ambiguity and confusion concerning the national interest in the Far East that has been observed in the pre-Washington period. Indeed, the question has dogged the United States from that day to this, and it is interesting to see it hovering still, ectoplasm-like, over the discussions of a group of her leading Far Eastern historians, and evoking responses that often give rise only to more questions still.[5] To pursue the subject at length would be a complex task, and one that might have to embrace, for example, such elusive concepts as national character or national style,[6] together with an examination of the relationship between the level of a state's potential power and of the aspirations of its people and politicians in international politics. Here, let it be said merely that if the adjective 'vital'

[1] Assistant to the Chief of Staff, G-2, memorandum, 6 May 1930, Joint Board records, 305. Such political promptings concerning the Far East were more typical of the Navy than the Army, however. See R. F. Weigley's paper for the Hakone conference, 'The Role of the War Department and the Army'.

[2] Director, War Plans Division, to General Board, 28 May 1932, U.S. Navy General Board, Studies, 438/2.

[3] Stimson Diary, 10 October 1931; the entry will be referred to more fully below.

[4] Ibid, 21 February 1932. The desire of Wood and others to identify the military virtues with the general public also failed.

[5] E.g., the assertion, quoted in Borg (ed.), *Historians and American Far Eastern Policy*, that 'America's interest in the Far East was based on the undeniable fact that it had become a Great Power, and thus it had to be interested in the region.'

[6] In the American case, see, e.g., Potter, *The People of Plenty*, caps. 1 and 2; D. W. Brogan, *The American Character* (New York, 1956); D. J. Boorstin, *The Genius of American Politics* (Chicago, 1953); Hoffmann, *Gulliver's Troubles*, 94 ff.

is taken to indicate that a state's survival as an independent, sovereign unit depends upon the preservation of the status quo in the territory, artery, or trade in question, then United States interests in the Far East came close to that description only where European-held areas were concerned—that is, those of Britain and the Netherlands which supplied the great bulk of her tin and rubber. Over rubber supplies, especially, there were soon to be growing anxieties in a few quarters in Washington—Herbert Feis, for example, the State Department's Economic Adviser, saw them as 'an index of American security'—but it is by no means certain that, had an emergency occurred, there would not have been an earlier development of a synthetic substitute (an American firm would be making part-synthetic tyres in 1940) or alternative sources of supply (in the early 1940s agreements were signed with Brazil, Peru, Nicaragua and Costa Rica, for example).[1] Severance of trade between the United States and South East Asia in 1931–3 would have created an extremely serious material situation for the former in the short run, but almost certainly not the kind of terminal condition that Eden was fancifully to depict for Britain were the Suez Canal to be closed to her in 1956.[2]

Many contemporary American officials would have agreed with this conclusion; like Hoover and Nelson Johnson, they believed that in measurable terms there was no interest worth fighting for (unless, of course, existing American territory were directly attacked). What, however, of the symbolic significance of possible developments in the Far East; of the manner of change, rather than the change itself? And if the area were seen as 'our part of the world', again one could not simply draw the conclusion that the greater interests of others must be allowed to prevail. To have less immediately at stake than Britain might make it easier, subconsciously perhaps, to risk antagonising Japan by condemning aggression on her part; to believe in one's own paramount interest in the destiny of China might make it seem imperative to do so.

For Britain, while it could be argued that, in the above sense, her own Far Eastern interests were not 'vital',[3] the loss of even a major portion of them would clearly have been seen by her and others as a downfall. The United States without the Philippines or her trans-Pacific trade and investments would remain a major power; without her commerce, without Malaya (perhaps even Burma and India), and without her share in maintaining the

[1] See H. Feis, *Seen From E.A.* (New York, 1966 edition), 6 ff.; also material in Hornbeck Papers, boxes 145 and 414.

[2] In terms of the defence of the United States, too, the Philippines were clearly more of a liability than an asset, Hawaii (and perhaps even Midway and other mid-Pacific islands) being adequate if an advanced, defensive base were required. It is an interesting speculation (no more; and the setting contains too many contrasts for any close parallel to be developed), what American feelings would have been had Japan possessed Hawaii, not so very different in range from the mainland to that separating the Philippines from Japan.

[3] At the beginning of the 1930s, two-thirds of Britain's overseas trade, for example, lay with Europe and North America, Europe alone accounting for over 39 per cent of her exports, while Asia as a whole accounted for less than 20 per cent. W. Schlote, *British Overseas Trade From 1700 to the 1930s* (Oxford, 1952), 79–81. Cf. Beloff, 32–3. Britain survived the loss of her China and South East Asia trade in 1941, of course, thanks mainly to her U.S. ally.

security of Australia and New Zealand, Britain's increasingly deceptive and self-deceiving guise as a major world power would be removed. Even for France and the Netherlands, the transition would not be so great, and it was mainly to the British base at Singapore that these other colonial powers looked for protection should the Japanese seek to tear down the existing order.[1]

Materially, then, and in terms of status, Britain had infinitely more at stake than the United States in the Far East, although this contrast was accompanied by another whereby, far from being agreed on a workaday policy of defence and even retreat, senior American politicians and officials were divided over aspirations which might entail expansion, if not conquest. In their short-term policies in the area, however, the two countries shared certain features and assumptions before the 1931 crisis. Each accepted the need for a retreat in the face of Chinese nationalism, but 'neither went to great lengths to demonstrate its friendship (with China) concretely until expediency dictated such action'.[2] Each recognised that Japan's interests and policies in the Far East were at variance with her own, but assumed that such differences were unlikely to impair good relations with Japan in a broader context. Each was, indeed, anxious to maintain those good relations on the basis of political amity and military peace; yet each had come to rely upon an individual, rather than a collective approach to the problems of the area, and neither thought it incongruous (for Britain, this lay in the near future) to wage a form of economic warfare against Japan at the behest of small sections of her own community. Each thus tolerated an element of confusion and incongruity within the tangle of ends and means which makes up foreign policy. And if economics could still be thought of as somehow a thing apart, each was faced with a further incompatibility whose relevance to foreign policy could scarcely be denied. For both the United States and Great Britain, between their commitments, perceived interests and aspirations in the Far East on the one hand and their capability on the other, there existed a considerable imbalance.

The West and the balance of power

The ambiguity surrounding the term 'power' in international politics is well known: Raymond Aron, for example, has pointed out that it embraces

---

[1] Again, without claiming to be able to measure a situation in 1931 by events ten years later, it is worth looking ahead to the way the respective interests of Britain and the U.S.A. were seen when the assault came. It was to be evident then, in the words of the official American strategic historian, that his own country's interests were 'not as vital' as those of Britain. Moreover, despite the urgings of MacArthur to the contrary, both the Allied and U.S. military planners continued to rank the defence and relief of the Philippines second to the need to hold on to Singapore and the Malay barrier as the key to the maintenance of Western military power in the Far East. Even when the time came to attack the newly-expanded Japanese dominions, recovery of the Philippines was not to be accorded the highest priority in strategic terms. L. Morton, *Strategy and Command: The First Two Years* (Washington D.C., 1962), 87, 156–9, 187, 448, 542. Japanese attack plans also accorded the Philippines a secondary position. Ibid, 181.   [2] Fishel, 220–1.

several different concepts which are usefully separated in the French language.[1] Here, investigations will rest upon the definition advanced by Arnold Wolfers, of power as 'the ability to move others by the threat or infliction of deprivations', this being one end of a spectrum which has at its other end 'pure' influence—'the ability to move others through promises or grants of benefits'.[2] Since the goals and aspirations of Western policies have already been noted, the emphasis concerning capabilities will be placed on the limits to what could be achieved, rather than on the positive influence which resources might have had on policy (a question already raised, for example, over the American interest in the Far East).[3] Before proceeding to such an analysis in terms of power, there are questions to raise at the 'influence' end of the spectrum. In both contexts, however, it is essential to bear in mind, not only the political structure and distribution of power in Japan at the time, but the more fundamental matters which have been briefly touched upon concerning that country's societal values and political culture.

Were leading Western states in a position to move Japan through the exercise of their prestige? At various times, after all, this had proved a significant factor in international relations, both on the extensive scale of Britain's control of Empire, for example, or more locally, in the compensation it provided the Royal Navy in 1914 for grave deficiencies in matériel and command.[4] In the present case, however, it is clear that Britain's prestige in Japanese eyes had long been in decline. In a sense, the very need for Britain to conclude the 1902 alliance had pointed in that direction, and both her appeals for naval help during the 1914–8 war and her readiness to terminate the alliance, seemingly at American dictation, contributed to the process. In Japanese military circles, there had been admiration for German, rather than for British achievements during the war itself.[5] Commercial and imperial difficulties, too, had helped undermine the country's standing, according to her Ambassador in Tokyo who was reporting 'our loss of prestige and influence' in the summer of 1931.[6] As for the United States, while her potential power was clearly greater than Britain's, her actions—or rather lack of them—in the Far East had scarcely

[1] R. Aron, *Peace and War: A Theory of International Relations* (London, 1966), 47 ff., 595.

[2] A. Wolfers, *Discord and Collaboration* (Baltimore, 1965), 103; cf. H. D. Lasswell and A. Kaplan, *Power and Society* (New Haven, 1950), caps 4, 5. Grant Hugo, in his *Appearance and Reality in International Relations* (London, 1970), 164, describes influence as 'the ability to persuade a foreign government to do something which they would not otherwise have done'. This lacks Wolfers' closer definition of the idea of persuasion, but both this work and the same author's *Britain In Tomorrow's World* are invaluable studies at a modest level of theory by a practising diplomat, and the present writer is much indebted to them.

[3] See, e.g., Hugo, *Britain in Tomorrow's World*, 96 ff.

[4] See A. J. Marder, *From the Dreadnought to Scapa Flow*, II (London, 1967), cap. I.

[5] See Kennedy, cap. II.

[6] Lindley to Henderson, 23 July 1931, DBFP, VIII, No. 495. This despatch will probably become celebrated for Lindley's lament over the decline of cricket in Japan, but that should not obscure the shrewdness of much of the remaining content.

been such as to enhance the likelihood of her securing a major alteration of course in Tokyo by the exercise of prestige alone. Shidehara himself, for example, told his colleagues during the discussions on the London Naval Agreement that 'he believed the United States would never fight for the sake of China'.[1]

If prestige alone was no great asset, the exercise of mere disapproval falls into the same category if one recalls the world-view of those officers in Tokyo and Manchuria who were planning to strike, together with the self-generating value process described by Professor Maruyama. Moreover, it is difficult to resist the suggestion that 'Great Powers, in particular, soon become inured to the disapproval which is almost a function of their status; they do not enquire whether others will praise or blame, but what they will do'.[2] What, then, could Western states *do* in the way of 'promises or grants of benefits' that might outweigh other attractions in Japanese eyes? Neither the United States nor Britain could offer an alliance, in the light of public attitudes towards 'entanglements' and of the whole new Versailles/Washington morality now proclaimed for international relations. France might be more attracted in that direction; but how much could she offer Japan in terms of power politics in the Far East, and how much could Japan offer her in terms of Europe that could offset the consequent antagonism of Britain and the United States? Similar objections would have arisen against any notion of some special armaments concession to Japan, quite apart from the obvious consequence that it would have been bound to weaken still further the Western position in the area in question. Financial assistance? Western capitals saw their own situation as being on the verge of disaster. New trading privileges? The American door had already been slammed, and the British one was about to be, with powerful sections of the public and legislature in each country determined to keep it so. An improvement of Japan's position in China? Even if one were prepared to go back upon the intentions of the Washington agreements in order to achieve this, there would remain the increased direct threat to one's own interests, and above all the hostility that would be aroused among the Chinese themselves. Some gesture to increase the prestige of the Japanese Government or moderates (early in 1932, for example, senior State Department officials were privately and vainly to explore the possibility of obtaining an honorary degree for Shidehara at Harvard[3])? Already, Western approval was equated in the eyes of many Japanese nationalists with betrayal of one's own country, as one of the delegates to the London Conference learned when he was handed a ceremonial suicide-knife as he stepped ashore on his return.

Whatever the objections to specific possibilities, moreover, one is also forced back, in general terms, to the close relationship that exists between prestige or any other form of influence on the one hand and power on the other.[4] What can other countries *do* in the way of threatening or inflicting

[1] IMTFE, *Exhibit* 910A. Shidehara was responding in part to the suggestion that the U.S.A. might be planning to put pressure on Japan after 1936.

[2] Hugo, *Appearance and Reality*, 123. Cf. 128, 176.

[3] Castle to Lawrence Lowell, 23 January; Lowell to Castle, 25 January 1932, William R. Castle Papers, Japan.

[4] See, e.g., Hugo, *Appearance and Reality*, 155, 158, 168.

deprivation? Here one is entering a field of enquiry which has grown rapidly
of late, and on which a veritable library of books could be compiled, part of
it comprehensible to the uninitiated.[1] Before examining this aspect of the
'operational milieu' of those conducting Western policies—that is, material
resources at their disposal, relative to Japan's, in 1931–3—it may therefore
be as well to recall at least some of the preliminary questions that arise when
considering the possibility of applying these resources, while not anticipating
answers that will be attempted in the next chapter. First, what is the situation within the other country, the value placed by its public and government
upon the matter at stake, the likelihood of its existing régime retaining
authority when complying with an external threat, and the complexion of
alternative régimes that present themselves? If one is relying upon a decline
in public morale to change that other country's political situation and inclinations, how influential is such a decline likely to be, even if it can be
effected?[2] What cost is one's own public likely to be prepared to bear for the
exercise, and how do such possible costs weigh against the gain, should one's
threat be called before success is achieved? How does the other party see
one's own material preparedness to bear costs (say, to commerce and
finance), and one's preparedness in terms of will and morale? Have there
been recent demonstrations of one's readiness to proceed, say, from diplomatic, to economic, to military sanctions? What are one's own immediate
physical resources, and one's capacity to utilise and increase them? (In one
terminology, what is the State's 'fat, slack and flexibility'?[3]) Can one present
the other party with a fait accompli, or is one likely to have to react to his?

Above all, what is the desired 'terminal situation',[4] and in what time-scale
should one view the existing problem? In retrospect, it is often held that the
major and lasting significance of a situation was overlooked at the time, and
that it was in such a light that vigorous responses should have been made to,
say, Hitler's Rhineland reoccupation. But there is also a contrary danger, of
transforming difficulties into major crises. As the Suez affair so amply
demonstrated, it is, of course, a matter of judgement; but in an age when
'turning points' are fashionable and panaceas abound, some mild reminder
may be in order of the value, as well as the temptations, of restraining one's
ambitions beyond the medium-term view. As a proponent of the 'better-to-
fight-in-1938' argument, the present writer is in no position to suggest that
current hopes should always outweigh future and possible dangers. Until
omniscient forecasting becomes available, however, it has to be acknowledged that by a similar process of reasoning one may all too easily end up
with the consequences of applying domino-theory in South East Asia, or of
the 'moment-of-destiny' school of thought that dominated Berlin in 1914.

.   .   .

[1] See, e.g., T. C. Schelling, *The Strategy of Conflict* (London, 1963).

[2] For examples of diminished morale during the Second World War that did not
have the effect intended, see B. Brodie, *Strategy in the Missile Age* (Princeton,
1965), 131–41.

[3] S. B. Jones, 'The Power Inventory and National Strategy' in J. N. Rosenau
(ed.), *International Politics and Foreign Policy* (New York, 1961).

[4] Hugo, *Appearance and Reality*, 51 ff.

In economic and financial terms, Japan exhibited several major weaknesses in the period leading up to the attack in Manchuria. The flight from the yen, her loss of gold reserves and the contraction of her markets abroad have already been referred to, and her total exports in 1931, for example, were only slightly over half the value of those for 1929.[1] With a population of over sixty-five million, which had been increasing at an average of nearly one million per annum since 1914, the country's prosperity clearly depended to a high degree on these exports, of which around 40 per cent went to the United States, 20 per cent to China and 20 per cent to the British Empire.[2] Similarly, Japan was also dependent on the import of certain vital raw materials. These did not include food,[3] but the textile industry drew its raw cotton from the U.S.A., India and Egypt, while machinery was also being imported extensively, mainly from the U.S.A. In addition, various materials of direct strategic significance had to be obtained overseas. In 1931, only 306,000 kilolitres of oil[4] were produced domestically, to meet a consumption of 1,239,000 kilolitres, with stocks at the end of the year amounting to only 83,000 kilolitres. Domestic production declined and imports increased in the next two years, while for certain associated products such as butanol (for high-octane aviation fuel), Japan was almost entirely dependent on imports, in this case from the U.S.A.[5] The United States also provided around 80 per cent of the oil imports and the Dutch East Indies around 10 per cent, and although there were possibilities of increasing supplies from nearer at hand (for example, from North Sakhalin), access to this commodity was to remain, as an official document acknowledged on the eve of war in 1941, 'the weak point of our Empire's national strength and fighting power'.[6] Iron ore was also imported to the tune of 1,550,000 metric tons in 1931, as against a domestic supply of 208,000 tons and 177,000 tons from Manchuria and Korea.[7] Crude rubber came from South East Asia and imports of tin in 1931–3 were over three times the size of domestic production; about half the zinc used was imported, with lead overwhelmingly and aluminium entirely so. Clearly the economic potential of the country for war was greatly inferior to that of the United States especially, and despite great efforts between 1931 and 1941 to achieve a higher degree of self-sufficiency, together with the prospect of additional resources coming from conquest, it was still tacitly accepted on the eve of Pearl Harbour that the hope could be only for a favourable, negotiated peace, not for total victory.[8]

[1] FO 371, F2469/39/23.

[2] See Allen, 111 ff., Gull, 154. Japan's own possessions accounted in 1929 for only 18 per cent of her exports, although here and in the structure of her trade as a whole, significant changes were to follow the economic and political crisis.

[3] Imports of rice and soya beans came largely from Manchuria, Korea and Formosa. One estimate suggested that only between 4 and 7 per cent of food consumed was imported, compared to 15 per cent for Germany in 1914. Paper by the American Council of the Institute of Pacific Relations, 9 March 1932, Newton D. Baker Papers, box 208.   [4] For the translation into tons, see below, 265,n.

[5] At the end of 1932, stocks totalled 88,000 kilolitres, as compared to 1,721,000 at the end of 1941. IMTFE, *Exhibit* 844. Cf. Kirby, appendix 3.

[6] Ike, 154. Cf. Kirby, cap. V.

[7] Iron ore, tin, lead, zinc and aluminium figures from IMTFE, *Exhibit* 844. Cf. Gull, 160 ff.   [8] See Ike, xxv and passim.

The perceptions of various Western policy-makers of the extent to which Japan was economically vulnerable will be noted in the study of the crisis itself. It must be observed here, however, that, quite apart from the problems involved in organising sanctions of this kind (of ensuring, for example, that they were not undermined by increased Soviet oil supplies to Japan) and of awaiting their full effect on the Japanese economy,[1] their application would have entailed considerable cost for both the British Empire and the United States. Indian and American cotton growers and Australian wool producers would have been particularly hard hit, and it was estimated, for example, that 300,000 workers in American silk mills and associated industries would be seriously affected.[2] Western investments in Japan would almost certainly be lost, while even if Japan did not respond with an attack on Western possessions in the Far East, a blockade of China would be sufficient to greatly increase the penalties paid by those seeking to coerce her. And although Japan's trans-Pacific trade routes could obviously be severed with ease by the United States at their eastern end, the far greater difficulty of cutting her lines to China and South East Asia, together with the possibility of blockade and retaliation, linked the matter of the West's economic power with that of the military balance in the area.

When examining the strengths of each side in mere numbers of ships or aircraft, various contextual factors have to be borne in mind. One is geography: the 2,091 nautical miles separating San Francisco from Honolulu, the 3,330 on from there to Guam (with the Marshalls, Marianas and Carolines on either hand), and the 1,497 miles from Guam to Manila. To the same destination from the Japanese naval base at Sasebo was 1,318 miles, and from Formosa only 543. For the British main fleet, there were 4,927 miles to cover between Suez and Singapore (more, if it refuelled at Trincomalee en route), 1,438 from there to Hongkong, or 2,172 from Singapore to Shanghai. It was 449 miles from Sasebo to Shanghai; 2,428 down to Singapore. The state and application of military technology was also an important factor: the restricted operating endurance of submarines, for example, together with the neglect of their strategic potential and the undeveloped possibilities of naval air power.[3] Internationally-agreed limitations were likewise of the greatest significance, those drawn up at Washington having been followed by the London pact of 1930. Under this second agreement the 1922 capital-ship 'holiday' was extended to 1936, a ratio of 10–10–7 was laid down for the U.S.A., Britain and Japan respectively for cruisers[4] and destroyers, and parity between the three countries was accepted for submarines, whose abolition Britain and the U.S.A. had unavailingly proposed.[5] How much the

[1] On these and other problems, see Royal Institute of International Affairs, *International Sanctions* (London, 1938), and M. P. Doxey, *Economic Sanctions and International Enforcement* (London, 1971).

[2] I.P.R. paper, March, 1932, cited above.

[3] See, e.g., Roskill, 536–42.

[4] In heavy cruisers, the Japanese conceded a ratio of less than 10–10–7 on paper on the understanding that the U.S. would delay its building programme in such a way as to give Japan 10–10–7 in practice.

[5] O'Connor, passim; Carlton, cap. 6; R. H. Ferrell, *American Diplomacy in the Great Depression* (New Haven, 1957), cap. 6; Crowley, cap. 1.

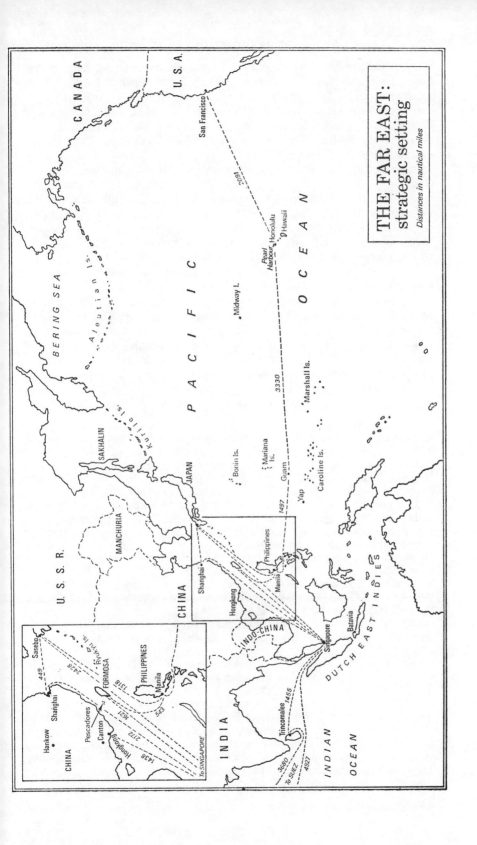

THE FAR EAST:
strategic setting

Distances in nautical miles

Western powers had surrendered in the process of these Washington and London agreements, and what alternatives had been open to them, remains a matter of debate.[1] British and American naval staffs had participated in the shaping of both sets of terms, and while Admiral William Pratt, for example, later the U.S. Navy's Chief of Naval Operations, had defended the Five Power Treaty, both the Admiralty and the U.S. Navy General Board became anxious after 1930 to see the London Agreement maintained.[2] Much naval opinion in the two countries condemned what had been done, however (extreme pacifists were also displeased),[3] and the broad context was undoubtedly one in which civilian governments and public opinion as a whole were compelling all military staffs to give ground and justify almost their very existence. This climate of opinion will be described in the next chapter, but it not only forced economies in naval construction outside treaty categories, but, in the United States especially, saw to it that building fell far short of the tonnages permitted for regulated types of vessels—it was less than a half between 1922 and 1932, in fact.[4]

Many Japanese, too, both within and outside naval circles, held that the London Agreement had jeopardised their country's safety. And yet, within a Western Pacific zone where potential enemies could not now develop major bases, Japan's forces remained a formidable proposition.[5] At sea, she had 10 battleships in commission (of which the *Nagato* and *Mutsu* carried 8 16" guns); 8 new heavy cruisers, delivered between 1926 and '29 and armed with 8" guns, with 4 more such ships being delivered in 1932; 19 light cruisers and 110 destroyers. Her 67 submarines and 3 aircraft carriers (a fourth was

[1] For example, it can be argued that Japan had achieved local superiority early in the century, and that Britain, in withdrawing her battleships, and the United States, in not building a major base in the Philippines, had then conceded as much. Britain had also not been restricted over Singapore by the new treaties, while the U.S.A. had already declined suggestions by advisers for a base on Guam. And if the current sacrifices at Washington were limited, it must also be asked how much naval expenditure the British and American governments could in any case have wrung from their legislatures thereafter. Nevertheless, it has been suggested that Britain was in effect placing the fate of her empire in American hands. Over the London Treaty, Crowley argues that it was Japan that made the sacrifices. See Neumann, 170, Griswold, 321, Crowley, cap. 1, Beloff, 343, Sprouts, *Sea Power*, caps. 7, 8.

[2] See, e.g., Disarmament Committee of the Cabinet, minutes, 7 January 1932, CAB 27/476; U.S.N. General Board to Secretary of the Navy, 6 May 1931, General Board, 438/2.

[3] Sprouts, *Sea Power*, 266–7; O'Connor, cap. 3; Roskill, cap. VIII. On the Admiralty's extraordinary arguments in 1920 for cancelling the Anglo–Japanese alliance, see Roskill, 293.

[4] Building programmes are given in Roskill, appendices C, D, E. The struggles of the two navies are best followed in this work and that of Wheeler. Cf. T. V. Tuleja, *Statesmen and Admirals* (New York, 1963), 29 ff.

[5] Unless otherwise stated, the numerical strengths of the various powers are based on figures given in League of Nations' *Armaments Year Books, 1930–33* (Geneva, 1931–3); Roskill, Appendix B; *Annual Reports of the U.S. Navy Department, 1930–32* (Washington, 1931–3). These sources do not always agree; where possible I have relied on unpublished official papers, which are cited separately. Japanese figures are taken from IMTFE, *Exhibits* 207, 706, 724, 913, 916.

delivered in 1933) were in some ways of even greater significance in terms of a possible long-range attack by Western surface fleets, naval aviation being a field in which she was rapidly gaining proficiency, thanks in part to the early assistance of a now-lagging Great Britain.[1] On land, Japan had 256,000 men (17 divisions) under arms at the beginning of 1932;[2] in the air, 1,250 military planes.[3]

As in the case of German air power in the later 1930s, there was a tendency among Western observers to over-estimate the degree of preparedness which lay behind this numerical strength. It was widely assumed in Washington, for example, that military facilities had been prepared by the Japanese in the mandated islands that lay across the route from Hawaii to the Philippines; yet although the secrecy displayed by Tokyo at the time lent colour to such a belief, one student has concluded from a search of the Japanese naval archives that the country 'made no improvement of permanent military significance in the Mandates for twenty years after she took them . . . in 1914'.[4] Similarly, it was believed in some quarters during the 1931-3 crisis itself that the Japanese had plans of attack prepared against Western possessions, whereas even as late as 1940, in the words of the official American historian, they had 'no concrete plans' for the seizure of either Guam, the Philippines, the Dutch East Indies, Burma, India or Australia, and no plans for countering American action.[5] Plans for a war against Britain, the Netherlands and the United States jointly were drawn up only in 1941.[6]

Nevertheless the capabilities and preparations of Western states themselves were so limited that Japan would be allowed ample time to improvise a successful assault were she to decide to respond in this way following, say, the imposition of economic sanctions. The Dutch, possessing only 2 cruisers and 23 destroyers in all theatres in 1931, were obviously totally dependent on British or American assistance; the French, with 9 battleships, one aircraft carrier and 19 cruisers (only one cruiser normally being in the Far East), were a stronger proposition, but could despatch a major force east of Suez only if prepared to accord a relatively strong position in European waters to a persistently upstart Italy[7] or to Germany's pocket battleships. Only Britain and the United States apparently possessed the resources to give Japan pause.

Behind the actual numerical balance in 1931-3 there lay, for all parties, the linked questions of time and armaments infrastructures, of the period taken

[1] Roskill, 58, 245, 529-31.

[2] 2 divisions were in Korea, and 2 in Manchuria. The Manchurian divisions were well above the normal strength, however, and 2 more were to be added in 1932. See *Japanese Monographs*, No. 77 (Washington, 1954).

[3] The British Air Staff estimated that 434 of the Japanese planes were first-line aircraft, with 56 more on carriers, 26 on battleships and cruisers and 16 tenderborne. CP 108 (31), CAB 24/221.

[4] T. Wild, quoted in R. D. Burns, 'Inspection of Mandates, 1919-1941', in *Pacific Historical Review*, XXXVII, 1968.

[5] Morton, *Strategy and Command*, 57-8. By 1940, however, plans existed for taking Hongkong and Singapore.

[6] Kirby, 89.

[7] France and Italy had failed to agree during the 1930 London naval talks, and had made scant progress in the matter since.

to build heavy ships or their bases, for example, or to redevelop the capacities of declining industries.[1] For Britain's Services, these factors were crystallised in the Ten Year Rule (introduced in 1919 and made onward-moving in 1928) and underlined by a defence expenditure which, alone of those of the United States and major European powers, had been reduced in absolute terms every year since the 1925 Locarno Treaty.[2] Government demands for the effecting of 'the utmost economy' had been particularly strong in the period preceding the crisis of 1931, a year in which defence took $2\frac{1}{2}$ per cent of the country's budget, compared to 4 per cent for the U.S.A. and 5 per cent for France. In that year, too, the Ten Year Rule was reaffirmed, as we have seen, despite the view advanced in a preliminary Foreign Office tour d'horizon, that in Europe, where the seeds of war remained abundant, the existing 'frozen pattern' was unlikely to last long.[3]

Senior officers of armed forces are, of course, notoriously prone to putting the worst possible interpretation on the state of their resources, and with a Disarmament Conference approaching, those of our period were not likely to prove exceptions.[4] There is also one school of thought that holds that if these men and their politicians had been more zealous in achieving a disarmament agreement in 1932, the subsequent perils would have been averted by means better and cheaper than those of arming oneself against attack. Be that as it may, hazards had already begun to form by 1931, when to meet world-wide security commitments the British Army possessed 147,764 men in Europe, 60,000 troops on the Indian regimental establishment, 3 cavalry regiments and 8 infantry regiments in Egypt and the Sudan, and 5 cavalry regiments and 45 infantry battalions in India.[5] One Indian battalion was stationed in the Federated Malay States; Singapore also had one battalion,

---

[1] In December 1932, for example, the Board of Admiralty was to estimate that it would cost around £22 million to bring the fleet to operational readiness. First Lord to Chancellor of the Exchequer, 14 December 1932, ADM 167/87. For the Admiralty's concern over the run-down of British armament firms, see ADM 167/84.

[2] From £110·6 million in 1925–6 to £92·4 million in 1931–2 and £88·9 million in 1932–3. U.S. expenditure had risen from $585 million in 1925–6 to $702 million in 1931–2, declining to $632 million in 1932–3. Japanese expenditure was fairly steady, until it rose sharply in 1932–3. Table E, vol. 1 of the Report of the Defence Requirements Sub-Committee of the C.I.D., 23 October, 1934, CAB 16/109. On Treasury pressure in general, see W. K. Hancock and M. Gowing, *British War Economy* (London, 1949).

[3] CP167(31), CAB 24/222. The conclusion of the memorandum, following so unnaturally from its content, can be explained in part by the desire to hold matters steady until the Disarmament Conference had met. Military planners were also emphasising new dangers in Europe, a War Office memorandum of January 1931, for example, raising questions over the possibility of massive German rearmament, a Franco–German clash over the Rhineland, and a Polish–German one over the Corridor. MacDonald Papers, RM 1/37.

[4] See, e.g., B. H. Liddell Hart, *Memoirs*, I (London, 1965), 185.

[5] The forces available in India were thought 'barely adequate', but possible additions had to be weighed against the likelihood of increasing discontent in that country by raising taxation. C.I.D. Sub-Committee on the Defence of India, 1931–1934, CAB 16/85.

while 2 were shuttling between Hongkong and Shanghai.[1] The aim in the Far East was to raise these numbers to 2 battalions at Singapore and 5 at Hongkong, but in 1931 this seemed as remote as did the provision of accompanying air and sea defences at the latter port (the Treasury had quickly raised objections to the expenditure involved, insisting, for example, on the deferment of work required if a squadron of flying boats were to move to Hongkong to replace the recently-withdrawn Fleet Air Arm flight).[2] The R.A.F. had a total of only 249 aircraft stationed abroad, 96 of them in India; at Singapore there were a mere 12 torpedo bombers and 4 flying boats.[3]

Imperial defence rested above all upon the Royal Navy, however, with a small amount of Dominion support potentially available, though not integrated as things stood.[4] The heart of the fleet was still held to be the 12 battleships and 3 battlecruisers (the number immediately available was reduced by repairs[5]), rather than the 6 aircraft carriers, while anxiety was persistently expressed over the number of cruisers available for commerce protection (now 50, under the London Agreement, as opposed to the 70 believed to be necessary[6]) and over the general requirement of meeting commitments on a world-wide scale.[7] In the Far East, the C. in C. China had on station in the autumn of 1931 (again, not all ships were immediately available) 5 cruisers and the aircraft carrier *Hermes*, 9 destroyers, 6 sloops, 11 submarines and a number of smaller vessels. What he lacked, however, and what the main fleet would lack if it attempted to move to the Far East, was a base possessing anything more than token defences. Hongkong, for example, possessed limited aerodrome facilities, no shore-based aircraft, and no boom, mine or anti-submarine defences, while its guns were antiquated, few in number, and lacking in the range to repel an attack even by cruisers.[8]

[1] 'Strength, Distribution and Organisation of the Military Forces in Relation to their Commitments and Duties', 22 April 1931, DC(P)15, CAB 16/102. It was estimated that Japan could put 34 divisions in the field within 3 months of mobilisation. C.I.G.S. memorandum of 31 March 1931, CAB 27/476.

[2] FO 371, F1070 and 2032/1070/10.

[3] Chief of Air Staff memorandum, 27 April 1931, CP 108(31), CAB 24/221. Cf. CP 104(32), CAB 24/229. At the time, the vulnerability of London in terms of a possible clash with France (990 first-line planes) was the main preoccupation.

[4] Australia possessed 4 cruisers, 6 destroyers, 2 submarines; New Zealand, 2 cruisers; Canada, 2 destroyers. On Canadian resentment, for example, against any suggestion of being bound by British decisions, see L. Eayres, *In Defence of Canada*, I (Toronto, 1964), 13 ff.

[5] During 1931, *Iron Duke* and *Marlborough* were withdrawn from service; *Barham* was rebuilding (completion, 1933) and *Ramillies* and *Repulse* were to pay off in 1932 for major repairs. ADM 167/84.

[6] See First Sea Lord memorandum, 14 April 1931, CP 100(31), CAB 24/220.

[7] See Board minutes, 10 December 1931, ADM 167/83.

[8] Hongkong's 9·2″ guns had ranges of 19,700 or 12,600 yards. Modern 8″ naval guns had a range of 29,200 yards, and 16″ guns of 38,400 yards. All details on bases are taken from a report of the Chiefs of Staff Sub-Committee on the Far East, 22 February 1932, and Chiefs of Staff Annual Review, 1932, CP 104(32), CAB 24/229. On earlier plans and preparations, see Roskill, 354, 404–11, 459–63, 537.

Singapore was the key, however, and, like the fleet's oil reserves,[1] it bore the marks of repeated government economies. Work on the base, first authorised in 1921, had been abandoned and restarted in 1924, slowed down in 1928, slowed down and suspended where possible in 1929, and, as already noted, deferred again in 1930.[2] Now, its floating dock and oil-fuel reserves lay open to attack, even from seaward (the possibility of a large-scale assault from the landward side having been ruled out[3]). No 15" guns had been installed as the Admiralty desired; the 5 9·2" guns were old and unsuitably mounted, and were supplemented by only 6 6" and 8 anti-aircraft guns, together with a few howitzers. Even so there were enough regular soldiers to man only a portion of these weapons, many of which were not even sited to defend the incomplete naval base, and it was thought that it would take about six weeks for an additional division to arrive from India or the U.K. Anti-submarine and other seaward defences were virtually non-existent, and the comparable air defences have already been listed; at Trincomalee, where the fleet would need to refuel on its voyage out, the oil supplies were without even this token protection.

Yet unless Singapore could be held intact during the thirty-eight days that it was now estimated it would take the main fleet to arrive (with ten more days to reach Hongkong), then the heavy units could not advance beyond India. This was recognised in the Admiralty, where it was also calculated that the Japanese fleet could be off Singapore in ten days and then destroy the base facilities and oil supplies at its leisure. The gap could be filled, it seemed, merely by hoping for the best, and when Vice-Admiral Sir Frederick Dreyer took over as Deputy Chief of Naval Staff in 1930, he found that the trek to the Far East remained the only war plan in existence; similarly, when he became C. in C. China in January 1933, he found no war plan prepared for that station.[4] Even in the Admiralty, plans on the file in 1933 were still

[1] Oil reserves were intended to be at the level estimated for 1 year's supply in a major war: 7½ million tons. After repeated cutting at the estimate stage, they totalled 4 million tons at the end of 1931. See ADM 167/83, 87, and Admiralty memorandum on Commonwealth Naval Policy, 19 June 1930, CAB 32/77.

[2] See CAB 32/77, 91. Cf. Roskill, 289–90, 339, 420; Kirby, 6–9.

[3] A landward assault was discounted on the grounds of the nature of the terrain. In view of the consideration raised by Mr. Geoffrey Hudson in Louis, 236–7, it should perhaps be emphasised that in constructing the seaward-facing defences of Singapore, little or no account was taken of having France as a possible ally. In their report of March 1932, cited above, the Chiefs of Staff declared that 'an alliance with France in a war with Japan would not be likely to prove of material assistance on the outbreak of war.' In a letter to the C. in C., China, of 2 February 1934, Chatfield, for example, merely argued that the Japanese would be unlikely to attack Singapore once its defences were completed because they might lose some of their precious capital ships in doing so. Chatfield Papers. In 1938, there was again no expectation of French help.

[4] Dreyer to Chatfield, 12 December 1933, Chatfield Papers. Captain Roskill, who is proceeding with his study of naval policy in this period, has kindly confirmed that he has discovered no new strategic plans in the Admiralty records for the early 1930s. On the inadequacy of inter-service cooperation in the area, see Kirby, 4, 54–5. Dreyer found much comforting talk among military and naval officers to the effect that Japan would not risk sending her heavy ships south of Hongkong. Dreyer to Chatfield, 19 August 1933, Chatfield Papers.

based on the assumption that Singapore was adequately defended, giving the China forces the task of defending Hongkong instead.[1] As First Sea Lord Chatfield could, and did, change this sort of thing. But at the political level, there had been little alteration when the crisis broke since the warnings of Beatty and others had gone unheeded in the 1920s.[2] In April 1931, Chatfield's predecessor could only repeat that Japan 'would seem . . . secure against serious naval interference by any other Power . . . The number of (our) capital ships is now so reduced that should the protection of our interests render it necessary to move our Fleet to the East, insufficient vessels of this type could be left in Home Waters to insure the security of our trade and territory in the event of any dispute arising with a European Power'.[3] Such a dispute was not an immediate likelihood, of course, but the First Lord of the Admiralty, Austen Chamberlain, was correct in pointing out to his Cabinet colleagues in August of the same year that, on a logical interpretation of the Foreign Office memorandum on the subject, the Ten Year assumption was invalid. He asked it to be placed on record that, even apart from the fresh economies it was now being called upon to make, the Navy 'was not capable of carrying out its tasks if a major war should break out'.[4]

At least those tasks themselves were clear enough as regards the preservation of Britain's trade, possessions and Dominions in the Far East.[5] For the United States Navy, however, not only was there the problem of inadequate resources, but also of much obscurity as to what those resources were ultimately for. In part, the Navy and Joint Board themselves had helped to create this confusion, with their own hotch-potch of racialism and the democratic mission, of self-interest and self-sacrifice; with their waverings between supporting the British or striving against them for the riches of the Orient, between viewing the Philippines as the likely cause of a well-nigh inevitable war with Japan, or as an asset with which to fight such a war.[6] The Navy *had* to believe that the Far East was vital to the United States in order to bolster its own existence, just as it had to maintain its dubious Pacific war plans as a basis for demanding more appropriations for its building programme. Senior officers and planning staff could—and sometimes did—rightly complain, however, that the problem in essence derived from that political failure which has already been noted, to define clearly the national interest in the Far East and to adopt one's policies accordingly. As the State Department's senior disarmament official observed when the 1932

[1] Chatfield to Dreyer, 1 June 1933, Chatfield Papers.

[2] For Beatty's 1924 warning, for example, see Roskill, 420.

[3] CP 100(31), CAB 24/220.

[4] Cabinet conclusions, 31 August 1931, CAB 23/68. Cf. Board of Admiralty minutes for 1930 and 1931, ADM 167/81, 83.

[5] The ambiguities created by obligations under the League Covenant will be mentioned below.

[6] See, e.g., Joint Board to Secretaries of the Navy and War, 23 October 1931, and the Joint Planning Committee's report of 28 February 1934, both in Joint Board, RG 225/305. For an example of a pertinent Congressional question, see Wheeler, 128. On these issues, the Hakone conference paper by W. H. Heinrichs, 'The Role of the U.S. Navy', is useful. On the unrealistic thinking of the Navy in the preceding period, see W. R. Braisted, *The United States Navy in the Pacific, 1909–1922* (Austin, Texas, 1971), 577.

Geneva conference was drawing near, the need was to arrive at some agreement on the function of the Navy, 'the purpose for which we hold our fleet
in being'.[1]

Like the U.S. Army, Marine Corps, and, to a lesser extent, Air Corps,[2]
the Navy had long been feeling the effects of a political climate which led to
drastic economies.[3] In his Annual Report for 1931, the Secretary of the
Navy, Charles Francis Adams, went so far as to question publicly, at least
by implication, his own Government's allocation, which 'many of the most
experienced and far-seeing officers' felt was inadequate for 'minimum
requirements within treaty limits'.[4] One senior officer was to describe the
situation in the autumn of 1932 as being so bad that the once-decried London
Agreement was now thought of as vital protection,[5] while Admiral Pratt,
though set apart from most of his colleagues by his intelligent acceptance of
disarmament measures and financial limitations, regarded the position vis-
à-vis Japan as 'simply appalling'.[6]

Despite major developments in naval aviation, the Navy possessed only 4
aircraft carriers at this time, devoting its main efforts to modernising the 15
capital ships now permitted by treaty. In 1932, however, only 11 of these
battleships were in full commission, while in modern heavy cruisers Japan
possessed a superiority in the ratio of 10 to 7.[7] In the Far East, the Asiatic
Fleet was little more than a token force, consisting, in the summer of 1932, of

[1] Moffat Diary, 11 August 1931, 31 May 1932. Cf. Wilson, 247–8, and material
in the Hornbeck Papers, box 423.

[2] In the air, the basis had been laid for rapid expansion in an emergency (Roskill,
468–9), with over 1,000 land-based planes, 171 on carriers, 84 on battleships and
cruisers and 51 on tenders [CP 108 (31), cited above]. The major step forward made
possible by the B–17 was still some way off, however. The U.S. Army had been
reduced to negligible proportions. The Marine Corps was being reduced, and no
permanent increase could be made in its Shanghai contingent, despite appeals from
the local commander. C. in C. Asiatic Fleet to Commandant, Marine Corps, 5
April 1932; Commandant, Marine Corps, to Chief of Naval Operations, 9 May
1932, U.S. Navy, Office of the Secretary, General Correspondence, EF16/P9–2,
320128.

[3] $82 million a year was being saved by taking ships out of commission and
undermanning; $96 million a year by not taking up permitted treaty replacements.
See *Annual Report of U.S. Navy Department, 1932*, and Admiral W. V. Pratt, 'Our
Naval Policy', in *U.S. Naval Institute Proceedings*, vol. 58, 1932.

[4] *Annual Report of U.S. Navy Department, 1931*; cf. Adams to Taylor, 13
December 1932, Taylor Papers, box 1. For Navy League propaganda at this time,
see U.S.N. General Board, Disarmament Papers, series X, XI, XII, and A.
Rappaport, *The Navy League of the United States* (Detroit, 1962).

[5] Moffat Diary, 10 September 1932.

[6] U.S.N. General Board, Hearings, 14 January 1932, 1–68; 'Gambling In
National Defence Securities', 9 January 1933, William V. Pratt Papers,
Correspondence.

[7] 'State of U.S. Fleet', July 1932, U.S.N. General Board, Studies, 420/1, 420/6;
Wheeler, caps. 5–7; Tuleja, 87–8. The battleships *Mississippi* and *New Mexico*
were due to complete modernisation in January 1933; *Idaho*'s completion date was
indefinite. In 1932, the carriers *Saratoga* and *Langley* were attached to the main
fleet; the scouting force, which usually operated separately, consisted of 11 cruisers
and the carriers *Lexington* and *Wright*.

one cruiser, the *Pittsburgh* (whose 6" guns were in such disrepair they were excluded from target practice), 18 destroyers (all with hull deterioration from over eleven years' continuous commissioned service and with no vessel properly equipped as leader), and 7 submarines. There were no fleet tugs, while the cruiser *Rochester*, sent as a reinforcement during the Shanghai crisis, was a thirty-nine-year-old, nine-knot coal burner, of 'no military value'; radio codes were not such as to provide for operational secrecy. In the words of the Fleet's commander, it was 'inadequate to carry out the assigned mission in the Manila Bay area under other than peacetime conditions'.[1] Base facilities were likewise deficient, and indeed, with the partial exception of Pearl Harbour, little had been done even to provide the facilities required by the main fleet nearer home since its transfer to Pacific waters in 1921.[2] Even so, War Plan 'Orange' remained in force, its basis, in naval eyes, lying in political assumptions that were in several respects far removed from those of the State Department and succeeding governments: that Japan aimed at commercial and political hegemony in the Far East; that a continuing clash between her interests and those of the United States was inevitable, and that 'the . . . adjustment of controversial problems with governmental planes so wide apart . . . could not be permanent and could be maintained only by force'.[3]

As revised in 1928 and in force during the 1931–3 crisis, plan 'Orange' laid down the intention 'to establish at the earliest date United States naval power in the Western Pacific in strength superior to that of Orange'. Whilst the main fleet was dashing across from San Francisco or Hawaii, therefore, the primary task of military and naval forces in the Philippines was 'to hold the entrances to Manila Bay'. The fleet would then arrive, and from the Manila base proceed to conduct an offensive against Japan's vital sea lanes.[4] At the time, however, such an operation would have been every bit as hazardous as the Royal Navy's hopeful slog towards a scarcely-defended Singapore. To those responsible for its execution (believing as they did that the mandated islands were being fortified) it appeared virtually impossible. The 2–1 ratio which the Navy's General Board had believed 'the only safe one to maintain towards Japan until such time as she adopts a government similar to ours and is actuated by ideals in harmony with our own'[5] was far from being achieved. Despite work on the beginning of a 'fleet train', vital elements making for flexibility of movement were still missing.[6] Although there had been some recognition of the importance of air power for the defence of the Philippines,[7] those islands remained extremely vulnerable, and their stocks

[1] Annual Reports of C. in C., Asiatic Fleet, 1929–1933, U.S. Navy Department, Office of the Secretary, General Correspondence, EF16A9/1, 300630, 300633, 320711, 330710.

[2] Wheeler, 73–9.

[3] Ibid, 46, 55, 60, 81.

[4] Joint Board, RG 225/303. In the event of an Anglo–Japanese ('Red-Orange') war with the U.S.A., priority was to be given to the Atlantic, a choice which was to be repeated in the 1940 'Plan Dog' relating to an Anglo–American coalition fighting a two-ocean war. Morton, *Strategy and Command*, cap. 1, and 81–3.

[5] Wheeler, 55.

[6] Ibid, 84–6; Roskill, 541–2.   [7] Wheeler, 97.

of oil were inadequate for full fleet operations.[1] As in Whitehall, much detailed preparation also appears to have gone by default, the main fleet, for example, not having a complete operating plan for use under 'Orange', even by July 1933.[2]

The consequences of this situation had long been perceived in some quarters, the Navy's planners, for example, having concluded in 1922 that the Japanese could not be prevented from taking the Philippines. During the Far Eastern crisis itself, and again in 1934, the local commanders were to point out that, although the fortress of Corregidor at the entrance to Manila Bay might be held for even a year, the Japanese could still outflank it and deny the use of the Bay to the U.S. fleet.[3] Changes in relative strengths and in the techniques of war, they wrote, had nullified the supposed value of the base, the defence of which was 'futile with the forces available'.[4] When the C. in C. of the main fleet also wrote to Washington to say that 'Orange' was impracticable, the Chief of Naval Operations admitted in reply that the dash across the Pacific would have to be abandoned; instead, after overcoming enemy resistance, a preliminary base would be established in the mandated islands before moving on.[5] 'We are unable to defend the Philippines,' wrote the Navy's Director of Plans in 1932—adding, so ignorant were the two countries of each other's position, that Britain was securely placed because of Singapore and probably had a secret agreement with Japan in any case.[6] The large element of fantasy in plan 'Orange' was not then removed, for that would have challenged too many cherished claims and assumptions; but before long the Secretaries of the Navy and of War were also admitting that an immediate conflict with Japan in the Far East 'would have to be fought under conditions that might preclude its successful prosecution'. [7]

For both the United States and British navies, their difficulties concerning the Western Pacific were compounded by two other considerations. One was the existence of other obligations or areas of concern. The Royal Navy, for example, had not only to watch the Mediterranean and other seas in the

[1] Report of Local Joint Planning Committee, Hawaii, 4 May 1930, Joint Board, RG 225/303; Report on Philippines Air Forces, ibid, RG225/350(458); Philippines Joint Planning Report on Oil Facilities, 18 August 1930, ibid, RG 225/305. Immediate war-time oil needs for the Philippines were estimated at 2½ million barrels; current storage facilities amounted to around 270,000 barrels. In 1928, Army planners had estimated that, to meet a likely Japanese attack of 300,000 troops within thirty days, the defence could muster 11,000 troops (7,000 of them Filipinos), 9 bombers and 11 pursuit planes. Morton, 'War Plan Orange', loc. cit.; Wheeler, 90.

[2] C.N. Ops. to C. in C., U.S. Fleet, 13 July 1933, enclosed in U.S.N. General Board copy of War Plan Orange, 1938, W.PL 13–14, vol. 2.

[3] Local plans provided for a withdrawal to Corregidor after fifteen days of fighting, leaving the air bases, dry dock and oil storage facilities at the Navy's Cavite yard undefended.

[4] Taylor to Pratt, 31 January 1933; Parker and Upham to Joint Board, 1 March 1934, Joint Board, RG 225/325(533).

[5] C. in C., U.S. Fleet to C.N. Ops., 24 August 1934; C.N. Ops. to C. in C., 10 December 1934, enclosed in War Plan Orange, 1938 copy, cited above.

[6] Memorandum of 28 May 1932, U.S.N. General Board, 438/2.

[7] Letter to Secretary of State, 26 November 1935, Joint Board, RG225/305(573).

national interest, but to be prepared to carry out what could be extensive tasks under the Covenant of the League of Nations, 'the British sailor's nightmare' as Chatfield was later to describe it.[1] This commitment did not exist for the U.S. Navy, although some were looking to its power to enable the country to play a decisive, 'balancing' role in world politics.[2] Even so, the Atlantic, as well as the Pacific, was there to be guarded, and the problems of a two-ocean strategy and of the rapid transit of units through the Panama Canal were lasting preoccupations.[3] The scenario of the 1932 war game illustrates the point (the game coincided with the Shanghai crisis, but had been planned a year before), for it envisaged the United States facing a coalition, 'Black',[4] which, while not stated as such, clearly comprised Japan and Britain.[5] In retrospect, the notion of a British attack appears a little far-fetched (a well-matured revenge for Yorktown? an over-exuberant attempt to cut through the debt problem?), and while such a possibility had been ruled out on the British side before 1914[6] even the American planners were now coming to think of an Anglo–Japanese assault as somewhat unlikely. The episode points to the second remaining consideration, however: the existence of a continuing sense of rivalry, together with the absence of any cooperation against Japan or any other potential enemy.

This point needs little development here. Fundamentally, the lack of military cooperation was a political matter, and will therefore be touched upon in the next chapter; images of the other nation held by military officials will also emerge throughout, together with those of diplomats and politicians. In British naval circles, despite the acceptance of parity for the United States, the latter was still frequently thought of as jealous, unreliable, and indifferent to Britain's security. In Washington, despite the London Naval Agreement, the conflicting desiderata of the two navies over further limitations, especially those concerning cruisers and battleships,[7] was often seen as reflecting an underhand attempt on Britain's part to deny the new power

---

[1] Lord Chatfield, *It Might Happen Again* (London, 1947), 90. A major preoccupation in this connection, of course, was the reaction the U.S.A. might display over freedom of the seas and neutral rights.

[2] In his 1932 'Naval Policy' article, for example, Pratt wrote: 'With parity [with Britain] in our hands, we become practically the balancer of power in any war threatening to become a world war, and as we decide, the war is apt to go. . . .'

[3] See, e.g., Pratt to the Secretary of the Navy, 12 April 1933, Pratt Papers; Joint Board, RG 225/304, 325(598), 326–1(562). Cf. Roskill, 541 ff.

[4] Not to be confused with the colour scheme of the war-plans catalogue, in which 'Black' referred to Germany.

[5] Joint Board, RG 225/350(491). Perhaps the planners had read that early will of Cecil Rhodes, in which he had left money for the founding of a secret society for the recovery of the U.S.A. within a federated Empire.

[6] Beloff, 168; Roskill, 25, 73, 214 ff.

[7] Broadly speaking, the U.S. Navy, with Pacific distances in mind, wanted large battleships (35,000 tons) and cruisers (10,000 tons), with corresponding gun calibres (16" and 8" respectively). With their greater number of bases, the Royal Navy were prepared to see sizes reduced in order to obtain a greater number of vessels. There were, of course, differences of opinion within each side; Pratt, for example, was ready to see the battleship displacement ceiling reduced, to the horror of his colleagues.

its place on the world's oceans. At times it was recognised that the interests of the two countries 'marched together' in the Far East.[1] But to suggest, as it has been done, that Anglo–American cooperation, as 'the logical answer', helped 'isolate' Japan between 1927 and 1936 is highly questionable.[2] Nothing in the nature of joint planning took place, while in 1931 and 1932 some American officers were still writing feverishly of the need for protection against Britain.[3] 'The British policy of domination of world markets,' ran a General Board study in 1934, 'is in serious economic competition with the United States. The British policy of naval supremacy is a potential danger to American territory and commerce.'[4] In the words of Captain Roskill, the two navies 'were studying their problems not only in total isolation from each other, but with a degree of suspicion towards each other that often amounted to overt hostility'.[5] Their lack of cooperation extended also to the forces of France and the Netherlands.[6] Even in 1941, as Cordell Hull acknowledged at the time, it was to remain a possibility that the United States would not go to war alongside the European imperialists unless her own territory was attacked, together with theirs, by the Japanese.[7]

In 1931–3, neither Britain nor the United States possessed so great an influence with Japan that her government could be prompted to defy powerful domestic groups or public sentiment by some positive inducement. Nor was either in a position to coerce Japan by economic sanctions without considerable social and economic cost to itself. If such sanctions were attempted, and if the Japanese in some way defied them by the exercise of their local military superiority (at the least, say, by blockading all China's trade), then the Western powers would find themselves initially at a serious disadvantage. A situation long foreseen by naval planners on both sides of the Atlantic would then obtain. A total war could doubtless be won, especially if conducted by the two powers in close cooperation. To do so, however, would take time—Hoover was told four to six years for the United States alone, two years 'if the British would put their entire fleet under joint command'[8]—and was likely to be preceded by the loss of territory and shipping on an extensive scale. There was little possibility of seizing a local bargaining counter, but rather, the strong probability of being faced with some particularly uncomfortable fait accompli. As for the United States over Hungary in 1956, say, the situation did not readily allow for the application of effective military pressure by carefully limited stages. As in that case, too,

[1] E.g., Wheeler, 62.

[2] G. E. Wheeler, 'Isolated Japan', in *Pacific Historical Review*, XXX, 1961.

[3] E.g., Naval War College memorandum, 23 October 1931, and Director of War Plans memorandum of 28 May 1932, U.S.N. General Board, 438/2.

[4] 'Study Regarding the U.S. Position at the London Naval Conference of 1935', 10 October 1934, U.S.N. General Board, Disarmament Papers, series XIII, 1.

[5] Roskill, 112.

[6] See Mansergh, 158; Kirby, 14; Morton, *Strategy and Command*, 101.

[7] Morton, *Strategy and Command*, 125–6.

[8] Hoover, *Memoirs, 1920–1933*, 367–8. No such estimates have been found by the writer in British archives.

the possible price of compelling the other party to back down could readily be seen to be so high that one might wish to avoid acknowledging that the affair had ever been a test of nerve and resolution in the first place.[1] If Japan decided to act on the basis that the issue was, literally, a vital one, the choice for the West could only be that between acquiescence and the acceptance of a large step up on to the plane of a possible major war.

In both London and Washington, as in Tokyo, the possibility of conflict existed in the minds of many, probably most, senior military officials before the crisis of 1931–3 broke out. The images of the situation were by no means the same in each case, however. The highest degree of similarity was to be found between the Americans and Japanese, where there existed something of a mirror-like perception of threat and the ultimate likelihood of battle.[2] In British military (and especially naval) circles, on the other hand, war with Japan was seen as a possibility for which the country was dangerously unprepared, but not one that either Japanese intentions or 'historical destiny' made likely. There were to be further contrasts, as will be seen, between the extent to which various politicians in the West perceived the existing balance of power, as it has been set out above. For all these men, however, both the question of coercion and the issues raised by the Sino–Japanese conflict had to be seen and responded to in the context of domestic situations, domestic attitudes towards international relations and the state of those relations between one another in the West. As the final aspects of the setting, therefore, these will be examined in the next chapter.

[1] There were, of course, important differences—not least the existence of nuclear weapons—between the 1931 and 1956 situations, but the comparison remains instructive. To use the terminology of Roberta Wohlstetter ('Cuba and Pearl Harbor', *Foreign Affairs*, vol. 43, No. 4, 1965), one could say that apart from a preliminary withdrawal of ambassadors, the alternatives open to the West to coerce Japan were such as to quickly render the slices of action very thick.

[2] On mirror images, see, e.g., Kelman, 255 ff., and on threat perception generally, ibid, 295 ff., 395 ff. See also De Rivera, 363 ff., 425, on this and the tendency 'to oversimplify the other's motivation, overrationalize his decisions, and neglect his completely different frame of reference'.

CHAPTER FOUR

THE SETTING IN THE WEST

Domestic politics and diplomatic resources

THE THREE most powerful Western states involved in the Far Eastern crisis were led by men who, in terms of domestic politics, were insecure and on the defensive. In the French Third Republic, of course, this could almost be assumed as one element of the situation. Since January 1931, Pierre Laval[1] had headed one of the conservatively-oriented governments whose tenure of power since 1930 had been facilitated by the refusals of Blum and the Socialists to help the Radicals form an administration.[2] Elections due for the summer of 1932, however, might provide a further opportunity for a revival of a Cartel des Gauches. Meanwhile, there was no great harmony between Laval and his Minister for Foreign Affairs, Aristide Briand. For all his basic pragmatism and awareness of the problems of French security in terms of power politics, Briand's faith in the League aroused scepticism and derision in many French nationalists; a vain and unhappy candidature for the Presidency of the Republic had further weakened his political position in the summer of 1931, and age and ill-health were taking their toll. By the time Laval seized the opportunity of the death of his Minister for War to reform his government in January 1932, to the exclusion of Briand, the latter was already in eclipse and had only a few months to live. In Herriot's words, 'Aristide Briand, le pacificateur, est mort comme un exilé dans son propre pays'; he died, writes Professor Duroselle, 'dans la tristesse et dans l'échec'.[3] Even within the Quai d'Orsay, it seems that Briand did not always receive the full sympathy and support of his officials during this last period of his life. Among the fonctionnaires of that formidable but creaking apparatus, guided by Philippe Berthelot as Secretary General, René Massigli was one of the few with a firm belief in the League of Nations, and senior officials appear to have guided French diplomacy during the opening stages of the Far Eastern crisis with only passing reference to Briand.[4]

[1] For a recent reassessment, see G. Warner, *Pierre Laval and the Eclipse of France* (London, 1968).   [2] See, e.g., J. Colton, *Léon Blum* (New York, 1966), 77.

[3] M. Soulié, *La Vie Politique d'Edouard Herriot* (Paris, 1962), 335 ff.; G. Suarez, *Briand*, VI (Paris, 1952), 361–70; J-B Duroselle, *La Politique Extérieure de la France, de 1914 à 1945* (Paris, 1965), 205–10.

[4] See the study by R. Challener in G. Craig and F. Gilbert (eds.), *The Diplomats* (Princeton, 1953). Historians are handicapped in trying to reconstruct the dialectic lying behind French policy, since there was no circulation and minuting process in

During 1931, the general decline in economic activity was beginning to affect France, with the Government in turn raising some tariffs, cutting back its budget, and accepting the Hoover moratorium on debts and reparations only with much grumbling over the loss of income involved. Compared to Britain, however, and even more to the U.S.A., France was only mildly affected by the depression until the summer of 1932.[1] It was European political and security issues which preoccupied France in the autumn of 1931: unresolved naval differences with Italy; the growing German clamour for an end to the Versailles restrictions, and the approaching dilemma over disarmament. Forthcoming skirmishes in Manchuria might seem of little importance by the side of even a single event nearer home, like the launching of the pocket-battleship *Deutschland* in May.

In the United States, there existed a sense of political insecurity despite the year or more that remained to Herbert Hoover before he had to seek a further term of office at the polls.[2] Certainly, it was a situation scarcely to have been imagined when Hoover had entered the White House in 1929, the man who had made good in business, in relief work far beyond America, and as Secretary of Commerce under Harding and Coolidge. A much-travelled mining specialist and a person whose name had become known to millions in Europe during the Great War, he had taken up office to the accompaniment of widespread acclaim and expectation. In the words of one journalist, the country had summoned the great engineer to solve its problems and sat back to watch the performance.[3]

Despite his abilities, however, Hoover was not well-equipped as a political animal, and remained far removed from the Republican bosses who had been less than overjoyed at his nomination in 1928. He tended to be shy, labouring immensely hard—excessively so, some observers thought,[4] but disliking the inescapable trivia of politics and seldom relaxing among other than close friends. His written and spoken style tended to clumsiness, while an abruptness of manner was to make itself felt in international as well as domestic politics in the months ahead.[5] At the same time he was highly sensitive to

the Quai d'Orsay similar to that in the Foreign Office, nor were records kept of the kind preserved in the British Cabinet Conclusions. In the first ten months of the Far Eastern crisis, it appears that little was attempted in the Quai in the nature of a long-term analysis of the Far Eastern scene.

[1] A. Sauvy, 'The Economic Crisis of the 1930s in France', in *Journal of Contemporary History*, vol. 4, No. 4, 1969; Toynbee, *Survey, 1931*, 35, 130, 152.

[2] There is no adequate biography of Hoover. See the effusive E. Lyons, *Herbert Hoover: A Biography* (New York, 1964); R. Hofstadter, *The American Political Tradition*; Wilbur and Hyde, *The Hoover Policies*; W. S. Myers, *The State Papers and other Public Writings of Herbert Hoover* (New York 1934, 2 vols.); W. S. Myers and W. H. Newton, *The Hoover Administration* (New York, 1936). Hoover's own *Memoirs* (London, 1952-3) are essential, though not always accurate, and his social and economic philosophy is set out in his *American Individualism* (New York, 1922). His private papers for 1931-3 are thin on matters of foreign policy.

[3] *New York Times*, 2 March 1930, quoted in A. U. Romasco, *The Poverty of Abundance* (London, 1968), 203.

[4] See, e.g., W. Lippmann, *Interpretations, 1931-3* (London, 1934), 68; Stimson Diary, 11 October 1931.

[5] For a contemporary comment, see, e.g., Moffat Diary, 10 January 1933.

criticism, a characteristic that had become marked by the autumn of 1931. When accused by the President of the Navy League, for example, of 'abysmal ignorance' and folly concerning that Service, Hoover quickly lashed back in a manner which appeared to many to impair the dignity of his office, as well as to bring adverse political consequences. 'For the next eighteen months,' he told Stimson, 'he intended to fight everything.'[1]

Above all, he would fight to bring the country out of the darkness of economic recession by means which would not impair the essential glories of its society: individual freedom to face up to 'the emery wheel of competition' and to strive for life's prizes in a race for which the government ensured only an equal start and 'fairness' thereafter. True, this did not mean a fatalistic response to the depression (as Andrew Mellon, Hoover's Secretary of the Treasury, would have liked), and the President's attempts to halt the downturn in the cycle have even been described as being of pioneering significance.[2] Government compulsion or direct, government relief remained anathema to the President, however. The great task in Washington, apart from encouraging self-help, was to slash government spending in order to obtain a balanced budget and a restoration of business confidence. Thus, urged on by men like Thomas Lamont of the J. P. Morgan company, Hoover became locked in conflict with Congress over this issue as the financial crisis deepened in 1931–2. He saw himself as facing difficulties greater than those which had challenged any President since Lincoln;[3] he and the nation were 'at war with destructive forces in a hundred battles on a hundred fronts';[4] this crisis came before all others.

By the time the Manchurian affair came to a head, Hoover was desperately in need of success. Gross national product was well into the slide that was to take it to a third of its 1929 figure by 1933.[5] Construction activity was plummeting, too;[6] businesses and banks were failing in hordes (2,298 banks in 1931 alone);[7] farm surpluses mocked the poverty of those who had laboured to produce them. In the cities, the growing mass of the unemployed passed far beyond the limits of local welfare resources: 40 per cent of the work force in Chicago by October 1931, and 800,000 in New York by the end of the year; over eight million across the country as a whole by then,

[1] Stimson Diary, 29 October 1931; Moffat Diary, 29 October, 1 December 1931; *Washington Post*, 30 October 1931; *New York Herald Tribune*, 30 October, 5 November 1931; Rappaport, *The Navy League*, cap. VII.

[2] Romasco, 231.

[3] Hoover to Charles Adams, 11 August 1931, Hoover Papers, Presidential personal file.

[4] See Romasco, 175 ff. Nevertheless, Hoover had had a burst of hope in the spring of 1931, writing on 11 March to ask General Dawes to come back from Europe 'with a strong statement as to the infinitely better leadership we have had in this depression than that which has been shown abroad . . . We have had no doles and no action which permanently undermines our social system. We begin to emerge from the depression . . . without disorganization and bankruptcy . . . We have no human suffering . . . and we have maintained our standards of living'. Dawes Papers, Hoover file. When the President wrote this, there were around seven million unemployed in his country.

[5] J. K. Galbraith, *The Great Crash* (Harmondsworth, 1961), 186.

[6] Romasco, 57.   [7] Ibid, 86.

eleven million by October, 1932, and nearly thirteen million in 1933—about one in four of the work force.[1] With revenues declining, the Federal budget for the year ending 30 June 1931 showed a deficit of $903 million, and its successor, one of $2,885 million. Fears that the country might follow Britain off gold brought a swift drop in the reserves between September and November 1931, and a total loss of $1,100 million in gold over only nine months.[2] Before this avalanche, Hoover's exhortations for wages and employment to be maintained had been swept aside. His special committees could offer only platitudes, the Federal Farm Board had failed to lift prices by its purchases, and his brand-new National Credit Corporation was defunct within two months. In the press, with which his relations were strained to the limit, the President was now bitterly attacked. 'Hoover breadlines' and 'Hoovervilles' had become common terms of implied abuse. On Capitol Hill, where Republicans had controlled both houses in 1929, the Administration would have to face a Seventy-Second Congress in December that had a Democratic majority in the House of Representatives, and in the Senate a notional Republican majority which was at the mercy of those 'Progressive' Republicans who had their own ideas for meeting the economic crisis. Where Hoover was determined to retrench, many Congressmen were set upon spending, and the result was anger and obstruction on each side, all the more so since everyone had his eyes on the Presidential election that was to follow in 1932. To Hoover, not only his own position but the destiny of America would depend on the result. 'This campaign,' he was soon to declare, 'is between two philosophies of government.' It was the crucial stand of conservative liberalism against the evil of collectivism. Stimson wrote privately of his leader: 'He has wrapped himself in the belief that the state of the country really does depend upon his reelection. It constantly entered into his policy.'[3]

This preoccupation, coupled with the fight against economic catastrophe, greatly reduced the amount of attention Hoover gave to foreign affairs.[4] Before this, he had taken much interest in a field with which, in Stimson's words, he was 'very thoroughly acquainted',[5] and where his general views were fairly set by the time he reached the White House. Deeply concerned with the bolshevik menace to Western capitalist civilisation (and hence opposed to recognition of the Soviet régime[6]), he was also strongly anti-pathetic to what he saw as the linked evils of Western imperialism and a wasteful and dangerous level of national armaments. In 1920, he had called for America's entry into a League of Nations 'that was created at our insti-gation and upon which . . . our real hope of a better world revolves';[7] later,

[1] Ibid, 166 ff.

[2] *Annual Report of the Secretary of the Treasury, 1931* (Washington, 1932), and ibid, *1932* (Washington 1932); cf. Ogden Mills Papers, boxes 109–11.

[3] Stimson Diary, 14 November 1932.

[4] E.g., ibid, 22, 30 September 1931.

[5] Ibid, 28 August 1930.

[6] For a contemporary discussion, see Castle to Hoover, 14 November 1931, and 17 August 1932, Castle Papers. Hoover continued to oppose recognition, and U.S. aid to the Soviet Union after the German invasion of 1941.

[7] *Washington Star*, March 1920, in Hoover Papers, 'Bible', 13.

despite his country's failure to join the new organisation, he had proposed that the 1928 Pact of Paris should be reinforced with some arrangement for international consultation, and had approved American cooperation with the League on humanitarian and technical matters.[1] His early support for entry had been hedged with various reservations, however, and thereafter his determination that all political or military entanglements should be avoided had grown, pari passu, with the conviction that a corrupt and over-armed Europe had retained within itself the seeds of further conflict. This in turn became allied to his belief that the economic and financial depression had also sprung from this same unhealthy soil, and not from the fair land of the United States. His country still had an obligation to give a moral lead to the world, but she must seek her salvation within her own resources and her own genius.[2] Meanwhile, countries like France—which he found particularly obnoxious[3]—must be told from behind the shelter of the Smoot-Hawley tariff wall that concessions by the United States, over debts for example, would depend upon a reduction of hostilities and of armaments within Europe itself.

Hoover's domestic preoccupations did thus spill over into international politics, and came to shape his reactions in that sphere to a high degree. This is not to suggest, for example, that without the depression he might have been ready to defy opposition at home and risk the consequences of taking a strong line over the Far Eastern crisis. It is to argue, rather, that his own inclinations were reinforced by an unwillingness to do battle with powerful sections of American opinion over what he, in common with them, saw as a secondary, although dangerous, matter. Thus, Hoover's sensitivity to domestic criticism was to help modify the overt cooperation between the United States and the League during the coming crisis, just as his desire to placate the Hearst press was to help widen the gap between him and Stimson in the summer of 1932.[4] Likewise, when major industrial contributors to Republican party funds made known their wishes over such matters as arms-embargo legislation or a threat to their interests in a country like Liberia, the President was to hasten to placate them. Within the State Department, comment upon Hoover's responses, or upon initiatives like his disarmament plan of 1932, tended to pass from the disillusioned to the cynical. Many European observers would have found their own views echoed had they been able to see inside the diary of Pierrepont Moffat, for example, a senior disarmament official and then Chief of the West European Division. Hoover was 'viewing the entire (disarmament) problem from an exclusively American angle', Moffat wrote in the autumn of 1931, and in the following summer he saw the President's responses concerning

[1] See Adler, 208.

[2] See, e.g., *Washington Post*, 9 and 10 December 1931, and Lippmann's comment in *Interpretations*, 71–4; Romasco, 182–6; S. O. Levinson to Hoover, 16 September, 1931 and Hoover to Levinson, 18 September 1931, Hoover Papers; Hoover, *Memoirs, 1920–1933*, 331.

[3] See, e.g., Stimson Diary, 13 September 1931; D. Pearson and C. Brown, *The Diplomatic Game* (New York, 1935), 234–41.

[4] References to material used more specifically in later chapters will be given there.

the same matter as being shaped 'from the point of political expediency rather than success in negotiations'.[1] Whether it was his pre-election desire to win votes or his post-election anxiety to preserve his record, his views, wrote Stimson in his diary, were 'coloured solely by his domestic problems'.[2]

As a body, Hoover's Cabinet was not nearly of the same decision-making importance as Britain's, its meetings usually being fairly brief, its proceedings unrecorded and its powers quite eclipsed by those of the President himself.[3] Moreover nearly all its members, like Hoover, were immersed in the domestic consequences of the depression (in the case of Ogden Mills, who became Secretary of the Treasury, the strain was too much for his health), and few appear to have contributed to the discussions when matters of foreign policy did arise. Hoover's close friend and Secretary of the Interior, Ray Lyman Wilbur, occasionally corresponded with him on the subject, and had had some experience in the field through the Institute of Pacific Relations. (At the time, for example, Wilbur had condemned the 1924 Immigration Act as 'offensive to Japan and Asia', while in 1927 he had urged Coolidge to relinquish U.S. privileges in China as a means of helping 'the American idea' to prevail there over that of 'Soviet, minority tyranny'.[4]) The Secretary of War, Patrick Hurley, a forceful individual and champion of the retention of the Philippines, was occasionally to proffer blunt comments on the un-wisdom of provoking Japan; bitterly opposed like Hoover to European imperialism in Asia, his desire for extensive American aid to China was only to blossom during and after the Second World War, when he fought to prevent 'the loss' to his own country of Chiang Kai-shek's China, at the hands of the treacherous communists who infested the State Department.[5] Hurley's opposite number in the Navy Department, Charles Francis Adams, does not appear to have aligned at all closely his concern for the state of the Navy with an analysis of foreign policy, although his sympathy for Japan's case in Manchuria will be noted in due course. Perhaps his very lack of ambition and endeavour in this related sphere was one reason why Hoover came to wish he had appointed him Secretary of State in preference to Stimson.[6]

Henry Stimson had in any case been Hoover's fourth choice for the job when he was appointed in 1929 at the age of sixty-one. With him now lay the main responsibility for foreign policy, with Hoover occasionally prompt-ing some new move, sometimes encouraging, but above all exercising a decisive veto on policies which he believed might entail a risk of war, a prospect of lasting foreign entanglements, or an outcry within the United States. In this last year and a half of the Administration's life, 'deep

[1] Moffat Diary, 20 October 1931, 22 April, 18 and 29 June 1932.

[2] Stimson Diary, 7 June 1932. Further references to this subject will be supplied as they arise.

[3] Stimson, for example, recorded in his diary for 6 November 1931 that the two-hour meeting that day had been the longest so far.

[4] R. L. Wilbur, *Memoirs* (Stanford, 1960), 351–2.

[5] D. Lohbeck, *Patrick J. Hurley* (Chicago, 1956), 171 ff., 209 ff., 413–14.

[6] Ferrell, *American Diplomacy*, 35; cf. Moffatt Diary, 4 January 1932.

divisions of both principle and attitude'[1] between the two men were to impart a confused and disjointed look to American policies. In part, the cause lay in their contrasting personalities: where Hoover was cerebral and cautious, Stimson was emotional and impulsive; while Hoover submerged himself in his work, Stimson rapidly became listless and jaded unless he set aside considerable time for recreation. Stimson's distaste for inter-party polemics did not help matters when his President was laying about him in a desperate attempt to slay those who would lead America to ruin. Perhaps their early geographical and social environments within America—Stimson mainly East coast, Hoover mid-West and West—had something to do with it as well, although there are too many exceptions to any such categories to make them of ready explanatory value. At another level, however, the difficulty arose from a fundamental contrast of perception: as with Truman and MacArthur later, their cognitive maps of the world were radically different.[2] Somewhat loosely, one might say that between them they expressed much of the ambivalence towards international politics of their country as a whole in the late nineteenth and twentieth centuries, a subject that will be explored further in the second part of this chapter.

Stimson's political mentors had been Theodore Roosevelt and Elihu Root (a former Secretary of State), his intellectual training that of law. Having zealously pursued offenders against the community as a Federal Attorney in New York,[3] he had become Secretary of War in 1911, a post well suited to his belief in the military virtues, and one which was followed by a brief but enjoyable spell as an artillery officer on the Western Front during the Great War. Where Hoover had opposed American involvement, Stimson had felt shame at his country's initial silence over the moral question at issue, and the eventual alliance with Britain and France became for him a natural alignment in defence of democracy. In 1920, while expressing reservations over article 10 of the Covenant, he had been among those Republicans who advocated that the United States should join the League. He was not, however, a close student of European politics, his brief spells of public service after the war taking him in other directions: to Nicaragua in 1927, as a forceful mediator in a civil war there, ready to employ the threat of United States military action if necessary; to the Philippines as Governor General from 1928 to 1929, from whence he returned to Washington, as we have seen, convinced of the American mission there and on the mainland of Asia. In each tour of duty, his essentially conservative philosophy had been reinforced. Thus, his approval went out to a politician such as Trujillo of the Dominican Republic, as a preserver of stability,[4] and was to be instinctively withheld from what he described as 'a rather nasty proletarian revolution' in Salvador.[5] In 1933, as will be seen, while disapproving of what the corrupt

---

[1] Stimson and Bundy, 195–200; Hoover, *Memoirs, 1920–1933*, 366. On Stimson, see Morison's *Turmoil and Tradition*, which is benevolent, and Current's *Secretary Stimson*, which is hostile. Ferrell offers a useful portrait in his *American Secretaries of State*. Pearson and Brown provide tart comments.

[2] See De Rivera, 247 ff.

[3] Ferrell points out that, in this post, Stimson had used exposure and public opinion as weapons with which to threaten wrongdoers. *American Secretaries*, 164.

[4] Stimson Diary, 13 October 1930.   [5] Ibid, 25 January 1932.

dictator, Machado, was doing in Cuba, he regarded him as at least possessing the merit of suppressing revolt and thus holding that country safe for business.

For all his Asian hopes, Stimson came to the State Department accepting what was already the predominant assumption there, that a modus vivendi with Japan was both possible and likely. Thereafter, he was impressed by Shidehara's approach to international relations, and by the concessions made by the Japanese at the London Naval Conference in 1930. That meeting had also marked a major step towards the main goal he had set himself in his new office: the improvement of Anglo-American relations. At the same time, however, it had revealed a lack of patience on the Secretary's part over diplomatic manoeuvrings, a characteristic to which those who observed him invoking the Pact of Paris in 1929 (in relation to the Sino-Soviet clash in Manchuria) could add that of an insensitivity to the opposing views of other countries, together with an a priori, legalistic approach to international politics, and an ability to deceive himself as to the efficacy of his own policies. Not all these features were to be of fixed strength: by the end of 1932 Stimson would be much more appreciative than Hoover of the difficulties of various European states, taking a longer and broader view altogether of the international scene. In that European context, especially, he was to end as a far more mature Secretary than the one who had blithely charged into the Sino-Soviet dispute. His basic make-up did not change, however. He remained a rigid personality, with little sense of humour and a strong sense of his own importance; a man who at times had acute doubts as to the policy he should pursue, but who in public laid down all the more dogmatically his chosen formula for success. Happier giving orders than seeking opinions ('I suggest,' wrote his Under Secretary to a somewhat insecure and effusive diplomat in the field, 'that you be very careful to let him talk when he wants to talk'[1]), he tended to treat subordinates in an insensitive manner, and to subject them to his varying moods when he descended upon the State Department from his country gentleman's home above the Potomac.[2] His relations with the press, too, were often strained, although here there were clearly faults on both sides, and he was on good terms with individuals such as Walter Lippmann, whose advice and approval he valued.[3]

Stimson was a man of considerable ability, being able, for example, to master the complex background to a new question with speed and thoroughness.[4] On the other hand, routine business—what he called 'Department chicken-feed'[5]—bored him; crises exhausted him, but in a sense his own

---

[1] Castle to Prentiss Gilbert, 28 November 1931, Castle Papers, Switzerland.

[2] See, e.g., Moffat Diary, 29 September 1931; 20 July 1932.

[3] See, e.g., Stimson's 'great relief' at Lippmann's approval of his Manchurian policy, Diary, 24 September 1931. Stimson took to meeting a select group of newsmen at his home, Woodley, with bêtes-noires like Drew Pearson (see Diary, 13 January 1932) excluded. The Far Eastern crisis offers several examples, in Washington and London (and almost certainly, Paris) of the press being used by official circles as an instrument of policy, on which question see B. C. Cohen, *The Press and Foreign Policy* (Princeton, 1963), passim.

[4] E.g., Moffat Diary, 15 September 1932.   [5] Ibid, 14 March 1932.

approach helped create them, while he defied the nature of international politics in his concentration on a single issue to the exclusion of others.[1] His relations with permanent State Department officials were in consequence distant and intermittent. A childless and, one feels, a somewhat lonely man, he preferred to surround himself with a small, faithful staff, to take his exercise and often to breakfast with them at his home, and to hammer out policies in this *cercle intime* of a Governor General. From the Philippines he had brought Captain Regnier as his military aide; in the new office of special assistant to the Secretary, he installed Allen T. Klots, the son of an old friend. The death, in March 1931, of his Under Secretary, Joseph Cotton, having grieved Stimson greatly, the former's role as 'counsellor, guide, and friend' was thereafter increasingly taken over by James Rogers, former Dean of the University of Colorado Law School, who had come into the Department as an Assistant Secretary.[2] This intimacy did not extend, however, to Cotton's replacement as Under Secretary, William R. Castle, whose appointment Stimson later publicly regretted. Coming from a wealthy Hawaiian–American background, a career officer who had been an Assistant Secretary and, briefly, Ambassador to Japan in 1930, Castle was an ardent Republican,[3] and closer to Hoover than to Stimson. In addition, his approach to international politics was calmer and more pragmatic than the Secretary's, and his stay in Japan had reinforced the belief that that country's predominance in eastern Asia was not only inevitable but, as a stabilising factor, in the interest of the United States. At times, Castle's influence was to help push American policy during the crisis closer to that of Britain, although ironically, and despite being a friend of Sir Robert Vansittart, he was less intense than Stimson in the pursuit of Anglo-American harmony.[4] The remaining official in Washington most concerned with Far Eastern policy, Stanley K. Hornbeck, was Chief of that Division in the State Department. A tense and humourless man, who at times in private showed a prickly awareness of being outside the East-coast élite circle of Groton, Harvard, Yale, etc. that constituted an important part of the American Foreign Service,[5] Hornbeck had had a fairly brief experience of the Far East as a teacher in China. As one of the 'bureaucratic chieftains' in the State Department in the 1930s,[6] he was to play a significant role in the shaping of American policy. To this end, while reacting in insecure fashion to any hint of criticism,[7] he churned out a flood of memoranda with a pedantic thoroughness that wearied Stimson;[8] a greater disadvantage was the rapidity

[1] E.g., ibid, 13 October, 1931; 12 January 1933.
[2] See ibid, 21 March 1932.　　　　　　　[3] E.g., ibid, 8 November 1932.
[4] See Stimson and Bundy, 192; Rappaport, *Henry L. Stimson*, 37–8; Lord Vansittart, *The Mist Procession* (London, 1958), 386.
[5] The resentment appears, for example, in Hornbeck's draft autobiography, Hornbeck Papers, box 496. Cf. W. H. Heinrichs, *American Ambassador* (Boston, 1966), cap. 7.
[6] See the paper prepared by W. H. Heinrichs for the 1970 Cuernavaca conference of Far Eastern historians, 'American–East Asian Relations'.
[7] E.g., Castle to Johnson, 10 March 1931, Johnson Papers, box 13; Hornbeck to Johnson, 14 November 1932, ibid, box 15.
[8] Stimson Diary, 23 November, 1931.

with which he tended to shift his tactical emphasis (when reading a document, he frequently underlined and side-lined so much of it as to lose all clarity); a greater one still, especially in the period immediately before the Pacific war, was that on major issues he was quite often wrong.

Traditionally, the State Department and professional diplomats played a less prominent role in the formulation of American policy than was sometimes the case in Europe.[1] In 1931–33, it is true, other departments, such as the Treasury, did not intervene in foreign policy to the extent that occurred in the following period.[2] Since the 1914–18 war, however, the outer limits set by mass opinion had appeared to be strongly defined,[3] and should they tend to blur a little at times there was always the vociferous and formidable William E. Borah to re-score them in an isolationist direction from his seat as Chairman of the Senate Foreign Relations Committee.[4] Even within the area of manoeuvre that remained, however, it would seem that the American diplomatic machine did not at this time make the best use of the high level of ability of many of the men who staffed it. Stimson's own methods contributed to, but were not primarily responsible for, this state of affairs. If one commonly-observed danger of having a tightly-knit group of professional diplomats is the development of an isolated and inflexible set of norms which will preclude adaptability and originality, an institution that carries among its higher levels large numbers of passing, political appointees of questionable competence is likely to suffer from the equally grave defects of impaired efficiency, and the lack of a common language that makes for clarity and conciseness. Only below the grade of Minister had the American Foreign Service been placed on a merit basis in 1924, and it remained poorly paid. Moreover, a sizeable proportion of the higher posts went to non-professional members of 'a caste of wealth',[5] and in that case much of the valuable reporting would have to come from a career man in a lower position, as was done by the Counsellor in London, Ray Atherton, under both General Charles Dawes and Andrew Mellon. In Paris, Ambassador Walter Edge was himself a fairly shrewd reporter, but his grasp of French was limited.[6] In Tokyo, the Ambassador at the outbreak of the 1931–33 crisis, W. Cameron Forbes, was a wealthy ex-Governor General of the Philippines whose political intelligence and reporting were lamentable, and whose private journal reflected an overriding interest in polo and the social

[1] See the study by D. Perkins, in Craig and Gilbert.

[2] See the Hakone Conference paper by L. Gardner, 'The Role of the Commerce and Treasury Departments'.

[3] See in general, Rosenau, *Public Opinion*, 35–9; Almond, 66; K. Waltz, *Foreign Policy and Democratic Politics* (London, 1968), 8–18.

[4] For an admiring biography see C. O. Johnson, *Borah of Idaho* (New York, 1936), and for a more critical sketch, Adler, 160–2. On the generally negative role of Congress, see the paper prepared for the Hakone Conference by W. S. Cole, 'The Role of the United States Congress and Political Parties'.

[5] B. D. Hulen, *Inside the State Department* (New York, 1939), 99; Joseph Grew, Diary, 30 November 1932. British embassies, too, are of course sometimes given to political figures, but less frequently.

[6] Edge to Castle, 14 July 1931, Castle Papers, France.

round.[1] His successor, Joseph Grew, was to find the Embassy in poor shape in 1932; by contrast, Grew was an able 'career diplomat' (Johnson in China was also a professional), although he himself described the term as being one of disapprobation in the United States.[2]

Financial stringency pressed hard on the State Department in this period and helped weaken morale further;[3] some sections were seriously short of personnel,[4] and the Far Eastern crisis produced a distinct creaking from within the building that lay like some antiquated liner, moored alongside Pennsylvania Avenue.[5] If surviving records are any guide, current exasperation with inefficient filing systems and bureaucratic procedures was well founded.[6] Compared to the Foreign Office, the dialectical process was extremely haphazard,[7] while, as in London, there was little or no time and encouragement for officials to sit back from day-to-day business and achieve anything like a broad perspective or a basis for contingency plans.[8] Communication between the centre and diplomats abroad was also seriously deficient. Grew, for example, was to receive only the barest of instructions before leaving for Tokyo in the middle of the crisis (after talking to Hoover, Stimson, Castle, Rogers, Hornbeck and Hurley, he found that no two of their minds tallied on the subject of Japan), and four months after his arrival 'had not the slightest idea whether (his) despatches were considered useful'. Relevant communications between Washington and other capitals were often not repeated to him ('it's like playing baseball without being able to see the pitcher'), and he was obliged to keep up to date through his British colleague; had it not been for a private exchange of diaries with Castle and

[1] W. Cameron Forbes, Journal, Second Series, IV, 176–305. 'Deeply humiliated' at his failure to observe and report signs of impending trouble in Manchuria, Forbes by implication blamed his staff when apologising to Stimson. He later informed his successor, however, that the staff were excellent, apart from the person in charge of his social arrangements. Apparently Forbes was not the least competent of such American ambassadors. As has been written of that recruit squad of the French Army in which Marcel Proust passed out 63rd out of 64, one cannot help speculating about the candidate at the bottom of the list.

[2] Grew to S. N. Nye, 13 December 1932, Grew Papers.

[3] E.g., Castle to Hugh Wilson, 15 August 1932, Castle Papers, Switzerland; Davis to Castle, 27 September 1932, ibid.

[4] E.g., Moffat to Carr, 1 December 1932, Moffat Papers, vol. 22; Hornbeck Papers, material in boxes 143, 147, 170, 184.

[5] E.g., Hornbeck to Johnson, 26 September 1931, Johnson Papers, box 14: 'If we have seemed "unresponsive", please invoke your memory of the machinery and methods of the department, and take into account that we have been flooded with telegrams.'

[6] E.g., Moffat Diary, 9, 10 February 1932.

[7] Written comment, such as there was, was frequently separated from the material being commented upon, for example.

[8] In 1930, there had been a flurry of suggestions for greater research facilities within the State Department. Urgent memoranda on the subject by MacMurray and Hornbeck are particularly interesting, and offer something of a parallel to the efforts of Wellesley within the Foreign Office which are noted below. They will be found in the Hornbeck Papers, box 146. There is a memorandum (of 1931?) by E. H. Dooman, concerning the Far Eastern Division being 'entirely preoccupied with affairs of the moment', in the McCoy Papers, box 78.

with his son-in-law, Moffat, he would have been left in greater ignorance still. Moffat himself took over as Chief of the West European Division in circumstances of 'utter disorganization', learning only indirectly that he was to have the post, and with no word from Stimson on the subject. In Grew's mind, one could only hope that the Department might one day 'be shattered to bits and remoulded'.[1] Any successes for American diplomacy during the crisis would have to be achieved despite its own system, not because of it.

For Britain, insecurity existed at the highest political level despite an apparently overwhelming public support for the government of the day. In August, MacDonald's second Labour ministry, pre-Keynesian and crypto-socialist, unable either to protect the welfare of its supporters or to prop up a system in which it did not believe, had been terminated amidst much drama and bitterness.[2] The formation of a National Government in its place brought no radical solution to the economic and financial problems of the day, but to King and country alike it seemed not only necessary for obtaining loans, but a comforting thing to do, a gesture of defiance and solidarity in the face of danger, rather like putting the kettle on for tea during the blitz ten years later. Supported by the Conservative and Liberal parties, and given the appearance of breadth by MacDonald and a few remaining colleagues, the new régime was declared to be a temporary measure 'for dealing with the national emergency as it now exists'; once that was passed, the parties would then resume their former positions.[3] At the polls on October 27, this Government proceeded to secure overwhelming endorsement, 472 Conservative, 33 Liberal, 35 National Liberal and 13 National Labour M.P.s being returned under its banner, against an opposition of only 46 Labour, 5 Independent Labour and 4 Lloyd George Liberals. MacDonald thereupon formed his second National Ministry, and the country awaited the return of business as usual.

In retrospect, the panic and political upheavals of the time appear out of all proportion to the nature and extent of the depression itself, which was far less acute than in the United States. Although the volume and value of her exports fell swiftly between 1929 and 1931, the terms of trade were moving significantly in Britain's favour. Real national income fell below the 1929 level only in 1932, and then marginally; real wages rose every year from 1929

[1] Grew Diary, 27 June, 16 July, 20 December, 1932; Grew to H. Shaw, 18 April 1932, Grew Papers; Moffat Diary, 13, 14 July 1932. In the post-war period, Ambassador George Kennan's experience in Washington before leaving for Moscow was to be not unlike Grew's.

[2] See A. J. P. Taylor, *English History, 1914–1945* (Oxford, 1965), 284–97; Mowat, 386–412; R. Skidelsky, *Politicians and the Slump* (London, 1967), caps. 13 and 14; H. Nicolson, *King George the Fifth* (London, 1952); R. Bassett, *Nineteen Thirty One; Political Crisis* (London, 1958). When reading this book of Bassett's, and his *Democracy and Foreign Policy*, it is worth recalling that he was an active National Labour supporter at the time. See e.g. a letter of his in M. Gilbert, *Plough My Own Furrow* (London, 1965), 225–6.

[3] MacDonald was Prime Minister, Baldwin Lord President of the Council, Snowden Chancellor of the Exchequer, Samuel Home Secretary, Reading Foreign Secretary and Chamberlain Minister of Health.

to 1933. There was no collapse of financial institutions, as in America and parts of Europe, and when, despite the existence of the newly-minted National Government, the cherished gold standard had to be abandoned on September 21, 1931, the consequences were remarkable only for being unremarkable.[1] An upswing in the economy was to be under way by the autumn of 1932 and to become strong in 1933.[2]

To most people in Britain, however, things seemed very different. For an Arnold Toynbee, the apparently imminent collapse of Western civilisation conjured up the parallel of the disintegration of the Roman Empire.[3] For the mounting number of unemployed—$2\frac{1}{2}$ million by the end of 1930; 2,700,000 by the middle of 1931, and a peak of just under 3 million early in 1933—it meant present wretchedness. For members of the Government, it could be measured in a continuing flight from the pound (speeded up by the news of disturbances in the Home Fleet at Invergordon on September 15[4]) which led to the seemingly momentous decision to abandon gold. The Dominions were also in serious economic difficulties; the finances of India appeared to be poised on the verge of collapse.[5] 'In the inner circle it has been a time of the gravest anxiety,' wrote Neville Chamberlain in his diary on the 19th. 'The world is completely out of joint.' 'This has been a terrible week,' he wrote to a sister on the same day, and to his other sister on the 26th he described 'crisis after crisis coming upon us'. On October 4, he was still reporting 'a most anxious and harrowing week'.[6] 'We are in an awful state just now,' MacDonald wrote to the American Ambassador, 'and I can think of nothing but that.'[7] To Baldwin, he observed later: 'We have all been so distracted by day to day troubles that we have never had a chance of surveying the whole situation and hammering out a policy regarding it, but have had to live from agitation to agitation.'[8]

This sense of imminent disaster soon receded, but the experience had left a lasting mark on the political mood of the country and its governments, not least as regards foreign policy. A lack of confidence remained, a desire to avoid trouble and a readiness to take the short-term view if it offered more comfort than the longer one. The very pretence of a National Government was to be maintained rather than return to clear-cut divisions on party lines, and with the Labour Party broken-backed and the Liberals in decline, political debate, while often bitter, was not unduly troublesome. The same mood was reflected in the 'agreement to differ' among members of the

---

[1] The pound fell from $4·86 to $3·80, then to around $3·40.

[2] See H. W. Richardson, 'The Economic Significance of the Depression in Britain', in *Journal of Contemporary History*, vol. 4, No. 4, 1969, and L. J. Williams, *Britain and the World Economy* (London, 1971), caps. 3, 4.

[3] *Survey, 1931*, 1–8.

[4] The repercussions of the 'mutiny' were felt, not only abroad, but in the Navy for a long time to come. An exchange of correspondence in the summer of 1932 between the First Lord of the Admiralty and Admiral Chatfield, to be found in the latter's papers, is important.

[5] See Toynbee, *Survey, 1931*, 47 ff.

[6] Neville to Ida and Hilda Chamberlain, Neville Chamberlain Papers.

[7] MacDonald to Dawes, 20 September 1931, MacDonald Papers, RM 6/12.

[8] MacDonald to Baldwin, 3 December 1931, Baldwin Papers, vol. 46.

Government regarding the one policy measure, increased protection, that was produced as a positive response to the economic crisis. It was an agreement that was reached only after much tension within the Cabinet, however, with Samuel's Liberals (as distinct from the Simonite National Liberals) pledged to free trade as an article of faith, and the Conservatives, with Neville Chamberlain in the van, set upon a tariff.[1] In terms of domestic politics and personalities, in fact, it was not a particularly harmonious set of men who governed the country, a feature which is amply recorded in the private papers of those concerned, despite the nervous decision of the Cabinet itself that its own minutes should not cover points of dissent or reservation since this would be contrary to the principle of Cabinet unity.[2] Samuel, for example, was greatly disliked and distrusted by some of his colleagues,[3] while Lord Hailsham, Secretary of State for War in the second National Government, had been ruled out of the first by MacDonald on the grounds that he was 'particularly obnoxious to the Labour Party'.[4] On taking office, Hailsham observed to Austen Chamberlain that he would 'find it very difficult to be loyal to some of (his) colleagues',[5] while Chamberlain himself, First Lord of the Admiralty and privately downcast at not being recalled to the Foreign Office, found it 'a beastly atmosphere to dwell in'.[6]

For MacDonald, the growing likelihood of a tariff measure being pushed through only increased his mood of personal insecurity. He was widely praised—in the United States as well as Britain[7]—as a man who had put country before party; Baldwin, despite later murmurings in his own party, never deviated from the pre-election Conservative pledge to support him as Premier.[8] But the scorn of his former Labour colleagues, though reciprocated,[9] could not be ignored, and suggestions that he was the dupe of the Tories continued to sting him to bitter retort, as will be seen in connection with Far Eastern policy. To the King and to Baldwin he was soon writing unhappily of his anomalous position and the inescapable strains within his

[1] As early as September 12, Chamberlain, in a letter to a sister, saw things as 'moving rapidly in the direction of a tariff'. The issue caused little excitement in the country, however.

[2] Cabinet conclusions, 25 November 1931, CAB 23/69.

[3] E.g., Austen to Lady Chamberlain, 2, 14 October 1931, Austen Chamberlain Papers, AC/6/1.

[4] Neville Chamberlain Diary, 24 August 1931.

[5] Hailsham to Chamberlain, 7 November 1931, Austen Chamberlain Papers, AC/39/1-6.

[6] Chamberlain to Lady Chamberlain, 1 October 1931, ibid, AC/6/1. Ironically Simon, of whose handling of foreign policy Chamberlain was to be critical, had been encouraged by the latter to be 'not merely an outstanding Personality but a Force' in politics. Letter of 16 January 1931, Simon Papers (private collection).

[7] E.g., messages to MacDonald from Stimson, 30 October, and Thomas Lamont, 10 September 1931, MacDonald Papers, RM 6/12; Lippmann, in *New York Herald Tribune*, 10 September 1931.

[8] Neville Chamberlain Diary, 24 September, 1931; Baldwin to MacDonald, 9 August 1933, MacDonald Papers, RM 6/14; Neville Chamberlain to MacDonald, 13 October 1933, ibid, RM 5/8; T. Jones, *A Diary with Letters* (London, 1954), 56; R. R. James, *Memoirs of a Conservative*, (London, 1969), 379.

[9] E.g., MacDonald to C. Allen, 26 December 1932, MacDonald Papers, RM 3/5.

Government, suggesting that the Tories might throw him over in their rush towards protection and reacting quickly to reports of confident predictions by members of that party.[1] His eyes were beginning to give him serious trouble, and personal problems added to his worries. Although he continued to work hard and to interest himself—too much so for the liking of some Ministers[2]—in many developments, above all those concerning foreign policy, where his knowledge and skills were considerable,[3] there is ample evidence that during the autumn of 1931 he was close to a nervous break-down. At one point he told Austen Chamberlain simply that 'his mind would not work'.[4] Not surprisingly, this final period of his political career was to show up, besides the courage of the man in the face of a painful illness, his vanity and extreme sensitivity to criticism, his substitution of eloquence for analysis, and his tendency to dissemble rather than argue out a point with those—the King, for example, or Henry Stimson—whose good opinion he valued. His skills as an international negotiator were not entirely gone, as will be seen later, and in Cabinet, too, he could still push through business with expedition and shrewdness. But his general decline was unmistakable.

In foreign affairs, as well as matters of trade, there were to be further disagreements between members of MacDonald's Government. Yet there also existed a large area of common ground between leading members of the Cabinet, and, given the disagreements and insecurity that were attached to other subjects, it is not surprising (particularly in the light of subsequent studies of small-group behaviour[5]) to find that there was an eagerness to occupy that ground together whenever possible. Over immediate Far Eastern policies there was thus to be little dispute, and the suggestion, so frequently made, that they were dictated by the Tories and their friends in the City is not supported by the evidence now available. Neither the Labour nor the Liberal members of the Government were to display any strong predilection for China's cause as opposed to that of Japan; few of the Tories were to be uncritically pro-Japanese; over the decisive matter of Britain's interests and resources in the area, there was to be unanimity.

Of Stanley Baldwin, MacDonald had correctly written some years before

[1] E.g., MacDonald to Baldwin, 5 September, 2 October, 3 December 1931, Baldwin Papers, vols. 44, 45, 46; MacDonald to King George V, 14 September, 1931, MacDonald Papers, RM 5/43; this file, together with 5/44, 45, 46, is essential for an appreciation of the strains of the time.

[2] E.g., Neville to Hilda Chamberlain, 17 January, 1932, Neville Chamberlain Papers.

[3] On MacDonald's opposition to the 1914 war, see A. Marwick, *The Deluge* (London, 1965); on his abilities as an international conciliator, see Mowat, 148–9, 178 ff., 372 ff., and Taylor, 214 ff.; on his extensive foreign travel, see Lord Elton, *Ramsay MacDonald* (London, 1939), passim. I have also been helped by discussing MacDonald with his forthcoming biographer, David Marquand.

[4] E.g., MacDonald to Sir Thomas Horder, 30 August 1931, MacDonald Papers, RM 5/43; Austen to Lady Chamberlain, 2, 5 October, 2 November 1931, Austen Chamberlain Papers, AC/6/1; Simon note, 27 September 1931, Simon Papers (private collection), Personal, 1931. But cf. S. W. Roskill, *Hankey*, vol. 2 (London, 1972), 569.

[5] See, e.g. De Rivera, cap. 8; J. Klein, *Working with Groups* (London, 1963), 70, 96, 121; W. J. H. Sprott, *Human Groups* (Harmondsworth, 1958), 13, 109.

that 'on foreign politics, his personal views are, as near as no matter, the same as mine'.[1] Like MacDonald, too, Baldwin was to have his abilities widely disregarded in later years of disillusionment, but at the time his recent triumph over Beaverbrook and Rothermere—albeit a last-minute one—was a reminder of his shrewdness and tenacity in terms of domestic politics. Over the long-term, European threat to Britain's security he was also far more concerned and active within Government circles than many writers, the present one included, have given him credit for. It remains the case, however, that he was excessively withdrawn in Cabinet discussions, and that his willingness to lead and take risks in the national arena did not match the prescience he displayed in private. It is also worth repeating that the Conservatives in the Cabinet, at whose head he stood, were not now representatives of the landed aristocracy, and as a whole were more concerned to restore and expand the country's business than to pursue any Milneresque vision of Anglo-American world domination. Their determination was less to uphold the glories of empire than to preserve whatever opportunities were possible within an inescapable devolution of power.[2] Sir Bolton Eyres-Monsell, who was a close friend of Baldwin's and succeeded Austen Chamberlain at the Admiralty after the election, perhaps came nearest to the stereotype of one resistant to change. Lord Londonderry at the Air Ministry, linked by his wife's effusive social tittle-tattle to MacDonald rather than to Baldwin, was to become notorious for his opposition to the abolition of bombing, but, like Hailsham, was to respond to the Far Eastern crisis in a less one-sided and pro-Japanese way than American diplomats commonly supposed. Sir Samuel Hoare, on the other hand, was to be inclined (or perhaps further inclined) in at least an anti-Chinese direction by his work at the India Office. Departmental concern was also to colour the reactions of a colleague with a very different social background (the Great Western Railway and National Union of Railwaymen, as opposed to Harrow, Oxford and a baronetcy), J. H. Thomas, a colourful and heavy-handed character, beloved by his heavy-handed Monarch and now installed in the Dominions Office as a loyal follower of MacDonald and a token of working-class support for the new Government.[3]

None of these men, however, possessed the potential influence of Neville Chamberlain, who went to the Treasury after the election.[4] His was the key position, it seemed, in the battle to save the country from ruin, and as the recovery proceeded and tariffs came to the fore, so, too, did he. His early

[1] Quoted in Carlton, 26. On Baldwin, see the biography by Middlemas and Barnes, a useful corrective, although perhaps uncritical in places, and containing many inaccuracies on the Far Eastern crisis.

[2] See essay No. 2 in D. C. Watt, *Personalities and Policies* (London, 1965).

[3] See G. Blaxland, *J. H. Thomas: A Life for Unity* (London, 1964), cap. 26. Thomas' bluntness had already brought clashes with various Dominion leaders, especially Canadians. See A. C. Temperley, *The Whispering Gallery of Europe* (London, 1939), 180.

[4] There is no adequate biography of Chamberlain, although a new one is now in progress. That of K. Feiling (London, 1946) contains useful (but by no means always the most significant available) material from his letters and diary, as well as details of his considerable work in the field of health and social services.

succession to Baldwin as leader of the Conservatives, though recently fore-stalled by the latter, appeared to be assured, and indeed, not without reason, he already saw himself as something of a leader by default. MacDonald, he wrote on September 19, was 'worn out' and Baldwin 'useless'; hence, 'everything seems to fall on me'.[1] Having played a leading role in bringing about the formation of a National Government in the first place, he was conscious of his power, and privately boasted of his ability to put Mac-Donald in his place if ever he chose to rap the Premier over the knuckles.[2] Often cold and sometimes harsh in his dealings with others, an industrious and able administrator, the very limits of his vision reinforced his self-confident assertiveness. On foreign policy, his influence during the period of the Far Eastern crisis was to be largely a negative one, through the exercising of a powerful financial veto. Thereafter, however, he was to play an increasingly assertive role in discussions of major policy issues concerning Japan, the United States and Europe. To a significant extent, the limited nature of the foreign policy resources which he was to inherit as Prime Minister in 1937 would be of his own making.

Chamberlain's manner in Cabinet was in marked contrast to that of Sir John Simon, who succeeded Lord Reading[3] as Foreign Secretary in November, a choice not made by MacDonald out of personal liking, and one that did not prevent strained relations between the two men before a year was out.[4] A former Attorney General and Home Secretary, Simon had already signalled his loyalty to the Prime Minister, however, by offering to resign his own seat at the election if that would help the latter avoid an unpleasant contest among his former Labour supporters at Seaham;[5] his own group within the Liberal Party had also begun to move away from a rigid adherence to free trade,[6] and declared its separate existence in October. Stipulating only that he 'could not accept a place inferior to Samuel', Simon's personal preference was for the Treasury; second came the Foreign Office, where, mirroring Stimson, he could pursue 'the ambition of helping about America and debts'.[7]

Simon was to be the object of much contemporary and retrospective

---

[1] Neville to Ida Chamberlain, 19 September 1931, Neville Chamberlain Papers.

[2] E.g., letter to Ida Chamberlain 15 November 1931: 'If (MacDonald) continues to act as though he were Dictator and not P.M. I shall watch for a suitable opportunity and then show my teeth. I think he realises that at any time I choose he will have to deal with me and not S.B. and I don't at present observe any desire to get "across" me.' Ibid, 12 December 1931: 'The P.M. shows much deference to what I say and as S.B. mostly remains silent our people look to me for a lead and I see that they get it.' Neville Chamberlain Papers.

[3] Reading, a Samuelite Liberal, was a former Attorney General, Ambassador to the U.S.A., and Viceroy of India.

[4] MacDonald to Baldwin, 3 November; Reading to MacDonald, 3 November; MacDonald to Reading, 5 November 1931; MacDonald Papers, RM 5/6; Austen to Lady Chamberlain, 16 July, 10 October 1932, Austen Chamberlain Papers, AC/6/1; Hankey Diary, 3 October 1932.

[5] Simon to MacDonald, 1 September 1931; MacDonald to Simon, 3 September 1931, MacDonald Papers, RM 5/43.

[6] See Garvin to Simon, 26 June 1931, Simon Papers (private collection).

[7] Simon to Baldwin, 2 November 1931, Baldwin Papers, vol. 45.

criticism and downright dislike; even by the end of 1934, the Chief Whip was to describe him as the Government's biggest liability.[1] His manner, cool and excessively correct, 'as if he had just got out of a cold bath', in Vansittart's words,[2] did not win him friends in private, and in public his obvious cleverness often appeared linked to some slyness of purpose.[3] Men did not trust him, although some might add, as did Neville Chamberlain when recording as much in his diary, that 'this (was) doing him an injustice'.[4] Unpublished letters of the time reinforce Vansittart's assertion that behind that cold exterior was a man who longed to be liked but lacked the natural warmth or imagination to bring this about;[5] a man not indifferent to matters of principle,[6] and far from insensitive to public criticism, but one who did not possess the politician's essential knack of knowing how to give that public its required dollop of verbiage. Unlike Jimmy Thomas, there was not enough of the ham about him.[7]

As a Foreign Secretary, however, Simon possessed more serious defects, which arose in part from the nature of his own abilities. His acute mind enabled him to grasp the various facets of a problem to an extent that Chamberlain, for example, could not match. In a case such as that of France and Germany, he could put himself in their respective positions in a way that was admirable,[8] and in the weighing of many finely-balanced considerations, as over the Far Eastern dispute, his sensitivity could scarcely be improved upon. The inescapable moment of choice, however, was not for him. In Cabinet he saw his role, not as an initiator of policy, but as an agent to be given instructions, and however justifiable this might have been in theory, in practice his overburdened colleagues (especially the forceful Chamberlain) were soon to grow exasperated at receiving fine summaries of pros and cons with little accompanying advice or leadership.[9] Moreover,

---

[1] Middlemas and Barnes, 807.

[2] Vansittart, 437.　　　　　　　　[3] See, e.g., Liddell Hart, 205.

[4] Chamberlain Diary, January 1934; cf. James, 380.

[5] For a not wholly unkind portrait, see the New Statesman, 16 December 1933; for an attempted light touch, see his letter to The Times of 22 May 1931. Simon had the habit of taking officials and others by the arm, but tended then to use the wrong Christian name.

[6] In 1931, for example, as during the 1914–18 war (when he had resigned on a matter of principle), Simon ceased to draw his salary without revealing the fact.

[7] See the comment of L. S. Amery, My Political Life, III (London, 1955), 154, on Simon's realistic approach, compared to that of Eden, 'who cheerfully voiced all the popular catchwords'. In this period, Eden was Simon's Parliamentary Under Secretary. From a study of his minutes within the Foreign Office, where the 'catchwords' were somewhat different, there seems no reason to dispute Amery's comment as regards 1931–2; by 1933 (when ironically, Neville Chamberlain found him impressive: letter to Ida Chamberlain, 25 March 1933, Neville Chamberlain Papers), Eden was beginning to express some views of his own.

[8] See, e.g., his undated summary of the 1932 French and German positions, in Simon Papers (private collection), Foreign Affairs, 1932.

[9] E.g., Neville Chamberlain Diary, January 1934, on the Cabinet's disarmament discussions: 'Simon played a rather pitiable part, being apparently unable to give us a lead and always asking the Cabinet to give him instructions . . . (His) weakness has given rise to much criticism both in the Press and in the Cabinet . . . The fact

while in public he could argue a case brilliantly, in private Simon displayed a certain pillow-like quality, unduly quick to give ground, or to appear to qualify a decision, or to shelter behind his colleagues in the face of vigorous opposition. His pairing with Stimson, dogmatic and prone to over-personalise his policies, was not to be a happy one. In appreciating the complexities of international politics, Simon was the abler of the two; as a public hero, the advantage lay with Stimson; as decision-makers and negotiators, both had serious limitations.

Policy decisions in London were ultimately a Cabinet responsibility, although often formulated in advance by its various ad hoc committees, with military matters usually being examined in advance by the Committee of Imperial Defence, where leading members of the Government could receive advice from the Chiefs of Staff.[1] Within this structure (more complex than it has been sketched, of course, with the Dominions and India Offices being only two of the other elements impinging upon foreign policy), a vital linking role was played by Sir Maurice Hankey, Secretary to both Cabinet and C.I.D., and guiding spirit of many of the major sub-committees that were set up as the need arose. His influence will be observed from time to time during the crisis, but from the outset he was greatly preoccupied with the gap between Britain's commitments and resources. For all his abilities, he possessed only a restricted understanding and sympathy for some of the main social and political developments of the time, bemoaning in his diary, for example, the 'orgy of extravagance on social reform' that had helped diminish the country's fighting Services. 'Our policy in India, Egypt and China has been weak,' he added, 'and reacts on our prestige in all Eastern countries. The result has been a great fall in our prestige throughout the world.'[2]

For the Foreign Office, the whole inter-war period is usually seen as having been an unhappy one in a number of ways. Memoirs with such titles as *Diplomatic Twilight*[3] and *Diplomacy In Fetters*[4] describe the damaging restrictions encountered within and without Whitehall; historians also emphasise defects in matters of recruitment, structure and general approach.[5] Despite reforms in 1919, serious anachronisms still existed, and while overseas trade had become the responsibility of a separate department, the Treasury (whose Permanent Under Secretary, as Head of the Civil Service,

is that . . . he seems temperamentally unable to make up his mind to action when a difficult situation arises.' Chamberlain made it clear, when Thomas and others raised the possibility, that he was not himself a candidate for Simon's job; it is tempting to speculate on the outcome for the country and Chamberlain had he decided otherwise. On Simon, cf. Lord Avon, *Facing the Dictators* (London, 1962), 28.

[1] See F. A. Johnson, *Defence by Committee* (London, 1960); S. W. Roskill, *Hankey, Man of Secrets*, I, II (London, 1969, '72); Watt, essay No. 7.

[2] Hankey Diary, 6 September 1931. For some of Hankey's earlier views on Far Eastern developments, see Roskill, *Hankey*, vol. 2, 367, 408–9, 435.

[3] By Sir W. Selby (London, 1953).

[4] By Sir V. Wellesley (London, 1944). Cf. Vansittart, *Mist Procession*, and Lord Strang, *Home and Abroad* (London, 1956).

[5] See the essay by G. Craig in *The Diplomats*; D. G. Bishop, *The Administration of British Foreign Relations* (Syracuse, 1961); Steiner, and Vital, op. cit.

had a right to be consulted on such matters) had prompted MacDonald to reject a cogently-argued Foreign Office submission that they should be allowed to set up their own 'politico-economic intelligence department'.[1] The Treasury itself, inevitably concerned with such matters as reparations, debts and armaments-expenditure, exercised considerable, and some felt, mischievous, influence under Sir Warren Fisher,[2] who, with his political master, Chamberlain, made up a more formidable combination than that of Simon and Vansittart. In fact, Fisher's direct influence on Far Eastern policy was to be small in 1931–33, but his fierce anti-American views were to make themselves strongly felt thereafter. Meanwhile, from 1914 onwards, pressure groups such as E. D. Morel's Union of Democratic Control had fostered a widespread distrust of professional diplomats, whose secret manoeuvrings were accepted as having been a major cause of the war. It requires only the memory of Lloyd George riding roughshod over Curzon and of Chamberlain's one-man mission in the later '30s to complete a picture of the Foreign Office in these years that must wring pity from all but the flinty-hearted.

But while many of the above limitations did hold good for much of the inter-war period, there were also considerable variations of circumstances and in the degree of influence which the Foreign Office could and did exert. The contrast with the pre-1914 years,[3] in other words, was probably less simple or clear-cut than many have believed. Variables in the later period included the policy issue involved, the domestic political situation and its leading personalities, the focus of public opinion and the relative involvement of other Whitehall departments. Public opinion, for example, was less a fixed and objective factor than a varying image in the minds of policy makers, and while Baldwin for one was later to lend strength to the suggestion that there is a common tendency to over-emphasise the restrictions involved,[4] there were other occasions when one may discern the image of

---

[1] The submission had been set out by Sir Victor Wellesley in a memorandum of 1 December 1930. His analysis of Britain's problems of industrial structure was acute, and he had interesting comments to make on the likelihood of growing clashes between Britain's interests and those of American 'economic imperialism'. Given 'the intimate connection between modern industrial developments and foreign affairs', he argued that 'our methods . . . are already ten years behind the times', with a 'complete divorce' between the economic and political work being done in Whitehall. The proposal having been rejected by MacDonald, one man in the Foreign Office was set free of other duties in 1932 to work on politico-economic affairs. MacDonald Papers, RM 1/39.

[2] Vansittart later defended Fisher from the accusations brought by Selby and others; Chatfield did the same. It should be remembered that Vansittart partly owed his own appointment to Fisher. See Watt, essays 1 and 5. Hankey's comments on Fisher will be set out in a later chapter. The latter's low opinion of the professional leadership of the armed forces was a major factor with him; the historian of the Treasury is also of no doubt as to his considerable influence on Chamberlain. H. Roseveare, The Treasury (London, 1969), 252 ff.   [3] See Steiner, passim.

[4] See, e.g., Kelman, 455; Hugo, Britain In Tomorrow's World, 166; Almond, cap. 5; M. J. Rosenberg, 'Attitude Change and Foreign Policy In the Cold War Era', in Rosenau, Domestic Sources; S. Huntington, The Common Defense (New York, 1961), 250–1.

public opinion being made to coincide happily with the view of the beholder
as to what policy the situation in question requires. A recent study of the
1929–31 Government has concluded that, in matters of foreign policy,
public opinion exercised little influence; over the Far Eastern crisis, it will
be seen that the same factor was generally of less account in London than
that of publics other than one's own (as recalled for a post-1945 period, also,
by one of the Ministers involved).[1] The public's attention in the autumn of
1931 was fixed on domestic issues, and the same was true of a new and
heterogeneous Cabinet. The initial definition of the situation by the Foreign
Office was thus of considerable importance, and since this was then fully
accepted by the Government itself, further responses as matters developed
could also be shaped in that quarter. Only at moments of acute crisis was
this pattern likely to change—or, as we shall see, if a senior official sought
to move outside those policy limits that he himself had helped to construct.

As Permanent Under Secretary, Vansittart owed his position to Mac-
Donald, whose Personal Private Secretary he had been, and who had sought,
through him, to retain a strong influence on policy despite Arthur Henderson's presence as Foreign Secretary.[2] Europe, and above all the possibility
of a belligerent Germany, were the main objects of Vansittart's attention and
subjects of his mannered prose; his private life and diplomatic career had
also helped incline him towards the patient cultivation of good relations
with the United States. The Far East, together with the economic aspects of
international relations, was more the concern of one of Vansittart's Deputy
Under Secretaries, Sir Victor Wellesley—although as a recruit of the
Foreign Office and not of the Diplomatic Service in the days when they were
separate, he had won his promotion in Whitehall rather than in Tokyo or
Peking. To several leading supporters of the League of Nations, Wellesley
was and remains one of the villains of the Far Eastern drama: '(his) dead
hand,' wrote Cecil to Simon in November 1931, 'has . . . for the last three
or four years . . . resolutely opposed anything that may make the action of
the League effective in China.'[3] It needs to be recalled, therefore, that
Wellesley, while believing that Japanese expansion of some kind in Asia
could not be prevented by Britain, had been among the leading members of
that group of Foreign Office officials in 1919–21 who had emphasised the
divergence of interests between the two countries; he had advocated an
Anglo-American-Japanese entente in place of the dual alliance, and, in later
years, a policy of friendship with China and the gradual surrender of extraterritoriality.[4] In addition, while highly sceptical of the confident claims
made for the League by its supporters, he was arguing privately at the time,
as he did publicly afterwards, that 'in spite of all present appearances to the
contrary, the forces of internationalism are in the long run likely to triumph
over those of nationalism', a prospect he welcomed as being in keeping with
'economic realities'.[5]

[1] Carlton, 29; K. Younger, 'Public Opinion and Foreign Policy', in *British
Journal of Sociology*, 1955.
[2] Vansittart, 394.
[3] Cecil to Simon, 28 November 1931, Cecil of Chelwood Papers, Add. 51082.
[4] See Louis, 4, 27–8, 39, 95, 108, 144, 153.
[5] Memorandum of December 1930, cited above.

On Far Eastern matters, Wellesley paid much attention to the views of Sir John Pratt, an Anglo-Indian with long experience of China as a member of the Consular Service and now attached to the Far Eastern Department as an adviser.[1] In Washington, Sir Ronald Lindsay was an Ambassador who had been Vansittart's predecessor as Under Secretary, and whose marital ties, as well as present location, may have helped incline him towards placing a high value on the retention of close Anglo-American understanding during the coming crisis.[2] Local colour was also to enter strongly into the preferences of Sir Francis Lindley in Tokyo, a 'good, stolid Englishman' in the eyes of his American colleague,[3] but one whose despatches in the months ahead were to take on so shrill a tone that at one point he earned a strong rebuke from Wellesley. Privately, Lindley was 'not at all pro-Japanese' according to Joseph Grew,[4] but his fears during the crisis were to lend his reporting a heavy bias in that direction. Personally, too, he was now somewhat sour as he approached the end of his career, writing to the King's Private Secretary of his fading hopes of obtaining 'a good European Embassy' in querulous terms that might have been modelled on those of M. de Norpois in his Venetian backwater.[5] Lindley's colleague in China, Sir Miles Lampson, displayed greater sang-froid, a quality that had already stood him in good stead during the complex negotiations over extra-territoriality in which he had been involved at various periods since his arrival as Minister in 1926. Lampson would have claimed that he had no illusions about the chaotic nature of Chinese politics, and at times had disagreed with what he saw as unduly precipitate concessions by British governments; nevertheless he believed that major forces were in the process of remaking the country around him, and his essentially constructive attitude to the nationalist ferment set him far apart from the Western club-bar politicians in Shanghai. Meanwhile the diplomat who was later to succeed Lampson, Alexander Cadogan, was at this time Adviser on League of Nations Affairs, and of all senior Foreign Office officials was probably the one most in sympathy with the general approach—but not always the particular views—of Viscount Cecil. Cecil's own beliefs will be examined in the following section, as someone who was outside official circles at this time, even though he will appear on their fringes as leader of the British Empire's delegation to the League when the crisis occurred.

How efficient was this Foreign Office machine in 1931–33, remembering that, even then, it was only one of a number of departments involved in the policy process?[6] A separate volume would be required to do justice to this

[1] Such was the status of the Consular Service that, in theory, Pratt was junior to the rawest Foreign Office member of the Department. The Head of that Department, C. W. Orde, wrote carefully and unremarkably; in 1931, one of his team, D. MacKillop, was by contrast extremely blunt and pugnacious.

[2] As Assistant Under Secretary in 1922, Lindsay had been in favour of taking a strong line against Italy over Corfu. J. Barros, *The Corfu Incident* (Princeton, 1965), 109.

[3] Grew Diary, 22, 28 June, 13 July 1932.   [4] Ibid, 25 January 1933.

[5] Lindley to Wigram, 26 October 1932, RA G.V, P 510/55; ibid, 7 January 1933, P 510/53. The King spoke to Simon about the matter, but Lindley failed to obtai n his new post.   [6] See Kelman, 451 ff., and Vital, cap. III.

subject, and only a few, brief suggestions must suffice here, with references to neighbouring studies. In its recruitment and training, there is no doubt that the Foreign Office was to some extent handicapped in ways which have been described for both earlier and subsequent periods, and that the social and political assumptions of a man like Lindley, say, divorced him from an understanding of some of the major changes taking place in the inter-war world. Even when one has qualified that comment by reference to individuals whose perceptions, while rooted in the same system, were very different, there remains the structural deficiency which, as before 1914, 'discouraged long-term analysis'.[1] The pragmatic, day-to-day approach which has often been criticised since 1945[2] was no less predominant in 1931, while within it, the minuting and circulation procedure teetered between the creation of an impossible overload for senior officials on the one hand, and on the other, the establishment of a filtering process that tended also to reinforce a single, dominant image of a situation.[3] In brief, and in terms of communication theory, the learning capacity of the system (or rather, sub-system) as it stood was seriously limited.[4]

It would be easy to over-state such criticisms, however, and the defects that existed in the formulating of British foreign policy can in many instances be traced to conditions outside the Foreign Office itself. As one detail already mentioned suggests,[5] that organisation *had* tried to increase its learning capacity, and had been prevented from doing so. However inconclusive the results, senior officials did attempt to analyse the underlying, long-term factors in the Far Eastern scene, and, despite a tendency to revert to more comfortable assumptions, did seek to peer into a gloomy future on a number of occasions. For all its disadvantages, the minuting system permitted and even encouraged a far more extensive and coherent dialectic than was taking place within the State Department, and divergence of opinion did manage on occasions to thrust its way up through the settling mist of a corporate view. Faced with a serious and growing gap—at least half a century in the making—between the country's international commitments and resources, it was not simply the Foreign Office but governments and, ultimately, publics that failed to grapple with the situation. If this essentially dependent and even impotent role of the Foreign Office was to be dramatically demonstrated in 1938 and 1956, it was also to be significant during the crisis of 1931–33 that, despite the provision of suitable papers by officials, their political masters in the Cabinet undertook no sustained, long-term analysis of the problems which events were showing up.[6] Beset by difficulties, Government and nation alike embarked upon a period of change and danger in a mood that was predominantly weary and defensive, and with the hope that somehow matters would turn out for the best.

[1] Steiner, 210.

[2] E.g., Vital, cap. V.

[3] For an earlier illustration, see P. G. Edwards, 'The Foreign Office and Fascism', in *Journal of Contemporary History*, vol. 5, No. 2, 1970.

[4] See K. Deutsch, *The Nerves of Government* (New York, 1966), 96–7.

[5] See the 'Politico-Economic' submission, referred to above.

[6] Cf. Deutsch, 182 ff.

The search for peace

In the autumn of 1931, the international problems facing Western states were of a size and complexity unequalled since the peace settlement of 1919. Each country could offer its own analysis and proffer its own solutions, but the apparent complexity of the situation can be illustrated by a Foreign Office summary which was circulated to the Cabinet in November, and which saw the issues as being locked together 'more or less in the following order':

> The *monetary crisis* leads inevitably back to the *economic chaos* in Europe. The economic chaos, and all attempts to deal with it, involve in their turn the political questions of *reparations and debts*. These are linked by the United States with the question of *disarmament*, and the latter, in the eyes of the French Government, depends upon the problem of *security*. The problem of security in its turn raises the question of the *territorial status quo* in Europe . . ., which brings us to the conflict between *the maintenance or revision of the Peace Settlements*. . . . No matter at what link we touch the chain, we cannot find any satisfactory halting place until we have reviewed this whole series of problems.[1]

At Geneva, too, most delegates to the new session of the League's Assembly, which opened on September 7, were keenly aware of the network of dangers surrounding them. 'The world is passing through a terrible crisis,' declared their President, Nocolas Titulesco, '—a lack of confidence which began in the sphere of finance and threatens to invade every domain.'[2] The threat was soon to become a reality. In consequence, the approaching Far Eastern crisis was only one development during the next year and a half that pushed individuals and governments into reappraisals (no less painful for being unclear and inconclusive) of the hopes and means of peace and security which they had proclaimed at the end of the Great War.

This search for peace after 1918 had not, of course, been confined to the West. Japan herself had appeared to be a staunch supporter of the League, and during the coming debates on her clash with China delegates from Central and South America as well as other parts of Asia were to join in testifying to the hopes placed in the Covenant. 'The whole East,' declared the Persian delegate with pardonable exaggeration, 'saw in the League's creation the advent of a new era in which nations would cooperate on a basis of justice and equality. The era was to end rivalry between the great States and to protect the weak against unjust attack, humiliation, or mutilation by the strong.'[3]

It had been from the West, however, that the initiative had come for this attempt to raise international relations on to a new plane. While its antecedents went back into the previous century, the intensity with which it had been pursued in recent years sprang mainly from the horrors of 1914–18 as experienced in Europe, and was expressed from within a Western generation

[1] 'Changing Conditions in British Foreign Policy', 26 November 1931, CAB 27/476.

[2] LNOJ, *Special Supplement No. 93*, 30.

[3] LNOJ, *Special Supplement No. 101*, 56.

that now saw itself as being 'in a race with international anarchy'.[1] The
League of Nations, which was the main achievement of this initiative, was
essentially a Western product, its Covenant 'a British-American document,
with here and there an addition or amendment to meet the wishes of others',[2]
and its legal concepts alien to a large portion of mankind.[3] Its underlying
philosophy was rooted in Western liberalism of the nineteenth century and
earlier: in the belief that democratic states are inherently peaceful, and that
unfettered, open discussion will reveal the natural harmony between individuals and nations; that free men, seeking pleasure in preference to pain,
will cherish peace above war, and will seek the good opinion of their fellows
in this respect; that something identifiable as 'world opinion' not only
exists but will exert a powerful influence for good.

The League also did more than enshrine Western values. However much
some might have wished it otherwise, it could not be dissociated from the
political circumstances in which it was set up. Immediately, they included
the victory in war of a powerful group of Western states. In wider perspective,
they reflected the culmination of an era of Western dominance which had
been established with the help of force and maintained over large areas of
the world. Some held that the benefits were fully shared with others; many
Asians—Mr. Justice Pal in 1948, for example[4]—thought otherwise. Moreover, there was a strong element of conservatism among those who championed the League in the West. In the United States, many had been
encouraged to see it as a barrier against the spread of bolshevism[5]—a view
shared, as will be seen, by its first Secretary General. As an instrument for
improving relations between existing political entities, the new organisation,
as E. H. Carr pointed out long ago, in many ways stood to help protect,
rather than to undermine, the interests of the haves against those of the have-
nots. 'The League ought to find its most ardent defenders among Conservatives,' remarked General Smuts privately. 'But it won't. They will, of course,
try to destroy the very instrument which alone, as things are, might save
their kind of world.'[6] For all their sincere zeal, Lord Cecil, Gilbert Murray
and other British enthusiasts were observed by a close friend to arrive at
Geneva with 'the assumption, the subconscious attitude, that Britain would
rule the waves of international assemblies as she ruled the waves of the sea';
it was easier to get over 'the awkward discovery (that) the world was full of
foreigners' than it was to accept that they wished to guide their own destinies,

---

[1] Raymond Fosdick, letter of 31 July 1919, in R. B. Fosdick, *Letters on the
League of Nations* (Princeton, 1966). Despite his strong criticisms of the peace
settlement, Fosdick, like many in Britain, saw the League as 'the only thing that
stands between us and another war'.
[2] A. Zimmern, *The League of Nations and the Rule of Law* (London, 1939), 243.
On the founding of the League, see also Walters, op. cit.; D. Hunter Miller, *The
Drafting of the Covenant* (2 vols., New York, 1928); F. H. Hinsley, *Power and the
Pursuit of Peace* (Cambridge, 1967); E. H. Carr, *The 20 Years' Crisis* (London,
1962); I. Claude, *Swords Into Ploughshares* (London, 1964).
[3] See Needham, *Within The Four Seas*, 23.
[4] IMTFE, *Judgment*, dissenting opinion of Mr. Justice Pal, 732–4.
[5] W. F. Kuehl, *Seeking World Order* (Nashville, Tenn., 1969), 326.
[6] N. Angell, *After All* (London, 1951), 230.

or that 'renunciation of force as a means of national policy pointed towards renunciation of fruits of past wars which were kept by force or the threat of it'.[1] Few embraced the League in the belief that the British Empire—still less the French—ought thereby to be speedily diminished. Supporters of the League and of international enlightenment in the United States, for example, were often at one with those who dreamed of national destiny in seeing the dutiful imbibing of Western ideas as being the chief merit of the Chinese, 'the one great people of the Orient', as James Shotwell termed them, 'who are schooling themselves in democracy'.[2]

The Covenant could not change the rules of the international game in a way that would prevent cultural aggression; nor did it place restrictions on economic exploitation or warfare. To desire a return to peace after 1919 could and usually did coexist with an underlying belief in the survival of the fittest through the unregulated workings of the business cycle: 'being a good internationalist was . . . readily equated with being a devotee of the non-intervention of Governments.'[3] Domestically, this could mean passivity in the face of hardship; internationally, however, it was not strong enough to prevent the erection later of nationalist tariff barriers or the waging of a campaign against a country like Japan that appeared to be succeeding only too well at the trade game. Again, the Covenant laid no political obligations on the victorious powers in respect of their existing colonial possessions, and only very general ones on those who received further territories as Mandates; on racial equality, as we have seen, it remained deliberately silent.

These observations are made, not with the intention of decrying the League from the standpoint of very different times, or of denying that, in 1919, it marked a great and sincere attempt to remove the shadow of war from mankind. But despite its endeavours in other parts of the world—its technical, medical and economic advice to China, for example—the League's essence was a Western one, and so, too, was the emphasis of most of its proceedings. Brazil and other states had warned against this; in 1931, Briand's scheme for European Union was arousing particular suspicion among Asiatic delegations, and only shortly before the Manchurian crisis, a member from India was addressing the Assembly on the dangers of Euro-centrism.[4] Cecil's remarks, quoted earlier, on the proportion of the world's troubles that could be traced to Franco-German tension, could only have confirmed this disquiet.

The League was also conservative in another sense. For such a major attempt to be made to place international relations on a new footing, a serious shock to the existing order is required. At the same time, the perceived nature of that shock will greatly influence the design of any organisation set up in its wake, which, in large measure at least, will be intended to prevent its recurrence. This had been the case in 1815 and was to be so again in

[1] S. de Madariaga, 'Gilbert Murray and the League', in G. Murray, *An Unfinished Autobiography* (London, 1960); cf. Toynbee, in ibid, 216.

[2] J. T. Shotwell, *On the Rim of the Abyss* (New York, 1937), 276; cf. Iriye, *Across the Pacific*, 248.

[3] A. Shonfield, 'The Economic Factor in International Relations', in *International Affairs*, November 1970.

[4] LNOJ, *Special Supplement, No. 93*, 49–50; Walters, 433.

1944–45. It was true of the League, whose Covenant represented an endeavour to prevent the onset of war 'by default'; it reflected the belief that somehow Europe had stumbled into the conflict of August 1914 through shortcomings all round and a lack of time and machinery that would have enabled tempers to cool and public opinion to push diplomats and politicians into a settlement of the dispute. That one state at least had deliberately worked for war in 1914 or that publics had in some cases been joyfully belligerent, while not explicitly denied, did not lie within the League's scheme of things. At the same time the Covenant conservatively, but realistically in this case, did not seek to impose a supranational authority upon its sovereign members. Acknowledging the special position of larger powers through their permanent membership of the Council, it required unanimity for nearly all decisions apart from procedural ones, accepted that a large degree of independent judgement must be retained by individual governments, and, while seeking to avoid 'resort to war', did not prohibit the use of force.[1]

From a French viewpoint, however, such an organisation was inadequate for the task of ensuring the security of its members, above all that of France against a revived Germany. Failing to obtain a separate Anglo-American guarantee and achieving little success through the ultra-nationalist policies of its governments between 1919 and 1924,[2] Paris returned to the attempt, already made during the designing of the League, to obtain greater strength for that body at its centre. Through the abortive Treaty of Mutual Assistance in 1923 and the milder but also vain Geneva Protocol of 1924, to the 1931 preparations for the Disarmament Conference, the search was for some kind of military force to be placed at the League's disposal, powers for the Council to designate the aggressor, and compulsory arbitration together with economic or if necessary military sanctions. When this, too, failed, there were all the more Frenchmen who, like Barthou, poured scorn on the new order: 'All these League of Nations fancies—I'd soon put an end to them if I were in power . . . It's alliances that count.'[3] Quite apart from the tension that was to exist in 1931–33 between France's desire to see the League

---

[1] Action under article 11 required unanimity, but under article 15 a majority of the Council could report on the facts of a dispute, and a single party to that dispute could have the case transferred to the Assembly. Even under 15, however, the Council could make only 'recommendations'; similarly, under article 10 (respect for the 'territorial integrity and existing political independence' of members), it could only 'advise' on the means by which obligations were to be fulfilled. Under the main sanctions article, 16, the Council could again only 'recommend' what military forces members should contribute. On the matter of the resort to force, an opinion of the Commission of Jurists, accepted by the Council in 1924, merely stated: 'Coercive measures which are not intended to constitute acts of war may or may not be consistent with the provisions of Articles 12 to 15 of the Covenant'; it was for the Council to decide in each case 'whether it should recommend the maintenance or the withdrawal of such measures'.

[2] See Duroselle, 181 ff.; Colton, 64 ff.

[3] Quoted in R. J. Young, 'Strategy and Diplomacy in France, 1934–1939', unpublished University of London Ph.D thesis, 1969. French bitterness had recently been heightened by the publication of letters by Stresemann, which seemed to indicate that he had been cynical in his conciliatory work with Briand.

strengthened in a European context and her inclinations as an imperial power in the Far East (and hence, as noted earlier, tension between France and her allies in central Europe who were more single-minded that the Covenant should be applied 'as completely and firmly against a powerful aggressor as against any small country...'[1]), there was also bound to be a certain schadenfreude in Paris if it were demonstrated that, as it stood, the League could not preserve its members from aggression.

French fears arose from the conviction that, if war returned to Europe, they could not escape involvement. In Britain, on the other hand, the strong desire to ensure that war should not return was accompanied by the equally powerful and traditional wish to avoid any commitments which might needlessly drag the country back into the trenches. Thus, when internationalist ideals and isolationist instincts were felt to be reconciled within the League, it was a League perceived very differently from the one desired across the Channel.

As championed during the war by a variety of individuals and groups,[2] the League idea in Britain came to command widespread support and 'all the characteristics of a creed'.[3] Here was a means of putting to an end that 'foul idol', as John Bright had called it, the balance of power—a term whose many possible meanings[4] were now restricted in most men's minds to those with pejorative connotations and associated with the causes of the recent war. Alliances were seen, like armaments and 'secret diplomacy', as leading inexorably to conflict. In the League, however, there could be established, in Woodrow Wilson's words, 'not a balance of power but a community of power'. Through the League, armaments could then be reduced 'to the lowest point consistent with national safety'; scrutinised by the League, diplomacy could proceed 'always frankly and in the public view'; on the basis of the League, one could achieve 'peace without victory'.[5] Later, when general hostility towards Germany had subsided and been succeeded by that guilt concerning the Versailles Treaty which was fostered by Keynes' *Economic Consequences of the Peace*[6] and other works, the League could also be thought of as a vehicle for reconciliation and the redress of just grievances. By the mid 1930s, collective security—'one for all and all for

[1] Sean Lester, 'The Far Eastern Dispute From the Point of View of the Small Powers', in *Problems of Peace, 8th Series* (London, 1934).

[2] See H. R. Winkler, *The League of Nations Movement in Great Britain, 1914–1919* (Metuchen, N.J., 1967), and Zimmern, passim.

[3] F. S. Northedge, 'British Opinion, the League and the U.N.', unpublished paper for a Chatham House study group, 1953. I am most grateful to Professor Northedge for lending me what appears to be the only surviving copy of his paper.

[4] See M. Wight, 'The Balance of Power', in Butterfield and Wight (eds.), *Diplomatic Investigations* (London, 1966).

[5] See L. W. Martin, *Peace Without Victory* (New Haven, 1958). For those like MacDonald who had opposed the war from the outset, the fight had been a long one. For some others, who, like Gilbert Murray, had found in the prosecution of war a harmonising of national self-interest and honour, 'a strange deep gladness' as well as tragedy, there may have been an element of atonement in the subsequent struggle for the League. See Marwick, *The Deluge*, 46–8.

[6] On the influence of this work in undergraduate circles, see, e.g., Kingsley Martin, *Father Figures* (Harmondsworth, 1969), 102.

one'[1]—commanded at least the verbal support of over ten million people, roughly half the number of those voting in the general elections of the period.

From the war onwards, the body most concerned with promoting this cause was the League of Nations Union, which had three thousand branches and nearly a million members by 1933.[2] Earl Grey and Cecil were then joint Presidents, with Baldwin, Lloyd George and Clynes as honorary Presidents, and Gilbert Murray as Chairman of an Executive Committee which included Norman Angell, the Earl of Lytton, Philip Noel-Baker and Professor Zimmern;[3] while the Union drew its strength mainly from the Left of British politics, it did also include some Conservatives among those of its members who sat in the Commons. It was Murray who played the major role in holding together a leadership which often displayed that brittle quality to be expected within attitude groups,[4] and whose fissiparous tendencies were further increased by the Union's avowed task and situation: linking and seeking to influence a state's external environment and its internal policy, each resistant to change, at a time of high international tension.[5]

The man most associated with the League in the public eye, however, was Cecil, one of the architects of the Covenant who had subsequently given what had been described in a 1930 tribute as 'unique service to the cause of international cooperation and goodwill'. Nominally a Conservative and in his own words 'a reluctant supporter' of the National Government, this 'bent figure of deep conviction and angular good-will'[6] was out of place among his party, many of whose members thought him a crank, and in 1932 was toying with the idea of joining the Liberals.[7] Despite Cecil's implied belief in the fundamental wisdom of mankind, however, there was substance in the comment of a contemporary that he was 'an aristocrat at heart';[8] at the same time his dedicated pursuit of the cause of peace was conducted in

---

[1] For a discussion and clarification of the term, see Claude, 223 ff.

[2] *The League Year Book, 1933* (London, 1933). This also gives details of other national societies. The L.N.U.'s journal, *Headway*, enjoyed a large circulation. Unfortunately the Union's records were destroyed by bombing in the war.

[3] A list of the Committee in December 1931, can be found in the Austen Chamberlain Papers, AC 39/1–6. On Murray and Cecil, 'monks of the civic religion' of international peace, see the brilliant essay by Madariaga, cited above.

[4] See Castles, 91. Clashes among the Union's leadership, which were to increase when Austen Chamberlain joined, already existed, with Cecil, for example, sometimes sharply criticising the Union's Secretary, Dr. Maxwell Garnett, for what he took to be the latter's tendency to try to initiate policy on his own. On 30 March 1931, Cecil wrote to Murray, however: 'I cannot feel that at present the people at L.O.N.U. have got their backs into this disarmament thing at all. They are much more absorbed by making their wretched machine work—a matter of infinitely small importance.' Gilbert Murray Papers.

[5] The Union bears out most, though not all, of the hypotheses on linkage groups advanced by Deutsch, 'External Influences on the Internal Behaviour of States', in R. B. Farrell (ed.), *Approaches to Comparative and International Politics* (Chicago, 1966).

[6] Vansittart, 158.

[7] Cecil to Noel-Baker, 7 October 1932, Cecil Papers, Add. 51107.

[8] Temperley, 56.

a manner which occasionally appeared devious to some observers, but which was attributable largely to that wishful thinking and frustration that was to distort the accuracy of his memoirs.[1]

Cecil had played a large part in disseminating a belief that was central to that reconciliation of internationalist and isolationist inclinations which has been referred to above: the belief that aggression could be halted by the force of world opinion:

> For the most part there is no attempt to rely on anything like a superstate; no attempt to rely upon force to carry out a decision of the Council or the Assembly of the League. What we rely upon is public opinion . . . and if we are wrong about it, then the whole thing is wrong.[2]

If a further deterrent were needed, it lay in the Covenant's provision for economic sanctions. With recent memories of the blockade of Germany and plentiful post-war examples of the debilitating effect of economic hardship, it seemed unlikely that one would have to resort to those military measures that were also allowed for. Disarmament and collective security could be seen as two sides of the same coin—as indeed they are, in a sense.[3] Adjustments to the peace settlement might have to be made, but they would not be at Britain's expense, and with the German navy at the bottom of Scapa Flow, no direct threat disturbed most people's initial optimism. (Hankey himself, it is worth recalling, had helped bring in the Ten Year Rule.) The dilemma of the 1930s,[4] between desiring peace and having to fight for it, had scarcely been noticed. On the Left there were many, within the Union of Democratic Control, for example, who at least were open in their distaste for all the coercive aspects of the Covenant.[5] Gilbert Murray himself was describing article 16 in the summer of 1931 as 'unfortunate', and was opposed to the creation of a separate League force;[6] Cecil, while moving closer to the French position on this last proposal, privately declared that he had 'for a long time believed that economic blockade is impracticable except as a part of belligerent action'.[7] At the same time, many thousands of sincere people had been encouraged to believe that their League ticket to the millennium was a free one.

Cecil, Murray and their followers can be seen as lying at one end of a spectrum of attitudes and opinions concerning peace and collective security. There were, of course, those at the opposite pole who saw in the organisation only a dangerous delusion that would place the country in jeopardy: several —not all—senior officers in the Services came into this category (the

[1] See Wilson, 218; Martin, *Father Figures*, 96 and *Editor*, 235–6; Thorne, 'Viscount Cecil, The Government and the Far Eastern Crisis of 1931', in *Historical Journal*, vol. 14, No. 4, 1971.

[2] *Hansard, House of Commons*, vol. 118, cols. 990–2, 21 July, 1919.

[3] On the need for a low level of armaments to enable collective security to function, together with the problem of circularity involved, see Claude, 236 ff.

[4] The dilemma is excellently brought out in Martin, *Editor*.

[5] See Taylor, 216.

[6] Murray to Carruthers, 7 June 1931; Murray to Lee, 29 August 1932, Murray Papers.

[7] Cecil to Austen Chamberlain, 13 January, 1932, Cecil Papers, Add. 51079.

Admiralty's fears have already been mentioned); with only the slightest concessions on his part, so too did a politician like Leopold Amery.[1] The
Conservative Party as a whole had displayed only modified rapture towards
the League idea during the war,[2] and it was on the grounds of its 'increasing
estrangement' from the L.N.U. that Austen Chamberlain reluctantly agreed,
early in 1932, to join that body's Executive Committee, despite 'more
frequently than not (having) differed from its expressions of opinion'.[3] The
ensuing clashes between Chamberlain and Cecil will be traced in later
chapters; meanwhile, Baldwin, too, continued to dislike much of the Union's
propaganda, and sought to avoid its public meetings '(where) I should have
to steer between the Scylla of cursing them and the Charybdis of mush and
poppycock'.[4]

To suggest, however, as some fervent League supporters were later to do,
that Baldwin, the National Government, senior Foreign Office officials and
others were at best indifferent and often hostile to the idea and fate of the
League would be to miss the dilemma which confronted all those who stood
somewhere between the extremes of immovable (sometimes belligerent)
chauvinism and confident (sometimes pacifist) internationalism. Much of the
hesitation and ambivalence of British defence and foreign policies between
the wars can be traced to this source. These men, too, were scarred by the
memory of 1914–18. They, too, believed that the letter and spirit of the 1919
settlement with Germany could not provide the basis for a lasting peace.[5]
They, too, accepted that a return to the pre-1914 international system would
entail renewed disaster, and hoped for some eventual change in which the
League might play a leading part. Where they doubted, they did so with an
earnest disquiet, not indifference; mid-nineteenth-century agnostics rather
than mid-twentieth-century Church of England-for-convenience. Baldwin,
for example, believed that 'great armaments lead to war', that Cecil had been
right to press for Britain to reduce her forces, and that, as a friend put it, 'the
old diplomacy brought us to the Great War'.[6] Neville Chamberlain's policies
in the later 1930s were, in part, to be a reflection of the same belief that
although alliances might be the best way 'to mobilise force and determination', they only made war the more likely.[7] It was not inconsistent when
Wellesley wrote later that 'balance of power as a policy has failed' and that
'some reliable system of "collective security" must ... always remain
(Britain's) most cherished hope'.[8] And if further illustration were needed of
the shift of outlook since the days when Eyre Crowe was reaching the top of

[1] See Amery, 141.   [2] Winkler, cap. V.
[3] Talks had been held in the summer of 1931 between L.N.U. and Conservative
officials to try to overcome what the former described as 'the apathy of Conservatives up and down the country'. With Baldwin's blessing, a scheme of county
federal councils was organised, and Chamberlain persuaded to join the Executive
Committee. Gower to Lloyd, 10 July 1931; Hills to Baldwin, 14 September 1931;
Baldwin to Fisher, 16 September 1931, Baldwin Papers, vol. 133; Austen to Ida
Chamberlain, 28 February 1932, Austen Chamberlain Papers, AC 5/1/569–682.
[4] Baldwin to Austen Chamberlain, 17 February 1933, ibid, AC 40/5–9.
[5] Appreciation of this point is lacking, for example, in Ferrell, *Secretaries of
State*, 219–20.
[6] Jones, 30, 93; Middlemas and Barnes, 361–2, 722.
[7] Thorne, *The Approach of War*, 14.   [8] Wellesley, 128–9, 136.

the Foreign Office,[1] it is supplied by Vansittart, that daily balancer of power vis-à-vis Germany in particular, who wrote privately in May 1931: 'There is much thinking and struggling ahead of us if the old pernicious doctrine of the balance of power is not to creep back. . . . The keystone of (Britain's) foreign policy is the League and the principles and undertakings for which it stands . . . We have been constantly opposed . . . to the old group system . . . (while) the League would be worth nothing if it did not sometimes attempt the impossible'.[2] 'It is of the highest importance,' wrote Lord Londonderry, one of the main disarmament 'villains' of 1932, 'that we should maintain the League of Nations, and it depends on Great Britain whether the League will develop or . . . languish.'[3]

It was not, therefore, a mere cynical gesture when the Covenant was formally and regularly placed at the head of Britain's international commitments.[4] From the outset, however, British governments, unlike the French, had seen the League as essentially conciliatory in function. The official commentary on the Covenant in 1919 had made that clear, and the 'limited League' that it envisaged corresponded with the bulk of private propaganda which had been conducted in the country before then.[5] America's subsequent refusal to participate reinforced the same attitude, while the League's Secretary General, Sir Eric Drummond, was among those who had privately argued (for obvious reasons) that Britain's obligations under the Covenant were 'extremely light'.[6] Thereafter, MacDonald's first Labour Government had rejected the Treaty of Mutual Assistance as being 'essentially a war-preparation document', and Baldwin's second Government, in the person of Austen Chamberlain and the words of Arthur Balfour, had done the same for the Geneva Protocol.[7] In the same spirit, Britain informed the League in 1928 that she regarded article 10 of the Covenant 'as the enunciation of a general principle', although one 'of great sanctity',[8] while both in general terms and over specific issues (a possible clash with Turkey over Mosul in 1925; the Bolivia–Paraguay dispute in 1928) the strong inclination was to regard economic sanctions as impracticable and unhelpful.[9] As Prime Minister in 1931, MacDonald had behind him a long

[1] For Eyre Crowe's criticism of the League idea, see Winkler, 231–2.

[2] 'An Aspect of International Relations', CP 317(31), CAB 24/225.

[3] Londonderry to Baldwin, 22 February 1932, Baldwin Papers, vol. 118.

[4] A list of such commitments, 'in order of importance', appears in a memorandum appended to Vansittart's paper, cited above.

[5] Winkler, 256–7; Cmd. 151, June, 1919.

[6] Drummond to Balfour, 29 June 1921, LN Archives, P 33. Drummond's letter was written with the Imperial Conference in mind. He asserted that Britain's obligations 'are really reduced to one thing, viz. that if a Power breaks the . . . Covenant, Great Britain will have to break off financial and economic relations with that Power. But even here there is a safeguard, since it is the British Government who will judge whether the Power has or has not broken these engagements'. In 1929, Drummond was to ponder on the possibility of helping to obtain American membership of the League by abandoning articles 'like 16'. Salter to Drummond, 20 December 1929, ibid.

[7] Zimmern, 307 ff.; Walters, cap. 24.   [8] Zimmern, 279–80. Cf. ibid, 442, note.

[9] P. J. Beck, 'Britain and the Peace-Keeping Role of the League of Nations'; unpublished Ph.D. thesis, University of London, 1971.

dislike of the inter-governmental and coercive aspects of the League, and although his belief in the value of popular participation had become soured,[1] his aversion to sanctions and binding commitments remained as strong as ever. 'Hesitating and confused minds', he believed, had concocted the sanctions provisions of the Covenant, whose only value was as 'a harmless drug to soothe the nerves'. By 1930, indeed, he had come to see them as a menace, and with Hankey's help he drafted a memorandum which laid down the Government's need to retain freedom of decision 'as to what is the best policy for the League to adopt in order . . . to carry out . . . the preservation of peace'. 'Recent publications like the "Life of Lord Carnock" and official documents,' he emphasised, 'warn us to take care that we do not repeat the errors of 1906–12.'[2] When the Far Eastern crisis occurred, in other words, it had long been accepted in Whitehall that additional resources were necessary 'to ease and complement our policy of the League', in Vansittart's phrase. As Simon was to put it concerning disarmament efforts in the summer of 1932, 'a judicious mixture of the new League methods and "old diplomacy" . . . can, I feel convinced, alone achieve the practical results for which we are striving and which the League exists to help us to realise'.[3]

In its desire to play down sanctions and binding commitments, Britain had been in accord with most Dominion governments. There, too, there had been a reaction against the 1919 settlement, while Canada in particular regarded the League with indifference or even distaste.[4] It was Canada, for example, that had helped secure a League resolution of 1924 (although technically rejected by a single vote, it became an accepted interpretation thereafter) which spelled out the need for the Council to take the geographical situation and 'special conditions' of each state into account when recommending some form of action, and emphasised that individual governments were free to decide in what degree those recommendations should be followed.[5] In the light of later recriminations over the Far Eastern episode, however, it is also important to recall that Britain and the Dominions had not been alone in applying the rule of self-interest when deciding priorities and interpretations concerning the League. The smaller states, too, who were by no means united in their approach and emphasis,[6] provided members, from Scandinavia, for example, who were anxious to avoid becoming involved in

[1] See, e.g., MacDonald to Cecil, 6 July 1931, and to Gilbert Murray, 4 January 1932, MacDonald Papers, RM 2/20 and 6/13 respectively. Cf. Carlton, caps. 1, 4. MacDonald had bitterly rejected an invitation to become an honorary president of the L.N.U. in 1923, recalling the attacks made by various people, now members of the Union, on him and his friends during the war. MacDonald letter of 12 July 1923, Murray Papers.

[2] Drafts of April 1930, MacDonald Papers, RM1/113. For Hankey's views on the League, see Roskill, *Hankey*, vol. 2, 60–1, 263, 394, 500.

[3] Simon to Cecil, 28 June 1932, FO 800/287.

[4] Mansergh, cap. IV; Eayres, 3–25.

[5] Walters, 227, 283. It was the Canadian delegate who used the well-known simile of a mutual fire-prevention society, with unequal risks, and his country's 'fire-proof house, far from inflammable materials'. Reservations concerning League members' 'geographical position . . . and situation as regards armaments' were also written into the Locarno Treaties.

[6] See Zimmern, 331 ff.

military enforcement or the damaging effect of economic sanctions. They, too, had derived satisfaction from the interpretive resolution of 1921 which envisaged that sanctions under article 16 might be partially or completely postponed by some states in order to 'reduce to a minimum the losses and embarrassments which may be entailed'. The later version of the League story as having been one in which the resolute selfishness of the larger powers triumphed over the unadulterated idealism of the smaller is one of the many myths surrounding the history of the time.[1]

By 1931, the League and its much-interpreted Covenant did have certain peace-keeping successes to their name, notably over the Greco–Bulgarian dispute of 1925 when the Council had acted swiftly under article 11.[2] On that occasion, however, the disputants had been small powers, while the major ones, fresh from signing the Locarno treaties, were in accord on the need for intervention. Two years earlier, moreover, the Corfu incident, when France had found it expedient to work in a mainly pro-Italian direction, had suggested that in conditions other than those of 1925 the League could help focus public idealism and indignation, but not ensure that the Covenant would be upheld. The episode had also underlined the problem of handling a resort to force which did not involve a declaration of war, and in all, as Drummond privately acknowledged, 'brought in question the fundamental principles which lie at the root of the public law of the new world order established by the League'.[3] Nor were the limits on what the organisation could achieve seen to be removed by subsequent studies and proposals that were intended to reveal and expand the full possibilities of the Covenant, involving, for example, article 11 and draft Model Treaties on arbitration and the halting of hostilities.[4]

These limits obviously affected the role of the League's Secretariat. In theory, this was already fairly restricted by the Covenant, which failed to accord the Secretary General, for example, some of those powers of initiative that were to belong to the office under the United Nations. Drummond himself, above all an efficient administrator, had apparently been content self-effacingly to build up at Geneva an international civil service.[5] Without a single political head in situ to whom he was responsible, however, no Secretary General could avoid playing a political role, even if only the vital one of negotiating the consensus which was essential if the Council were ever to function effectively. Some contemporaries, indeed, saw danger in the possession of such potential influence,[6] while Drummond himself recognised the sway that members of the Secretariat might exercise in various ways.[7] His own role in the League's major crises to date had been an important one,[8] and his inclination to keep such negotiations in his own hands within the Secretariat had been strengthened by the arrival at Geneva in the later

[1] See the essay by Erik Lönnroth, in Craig and Gilbert.
[2] J. Barros, *The League of Nations and the Great Powers* (Oxford, 1970).
[3] Barros, *The Corfu Incident*, appendix C.
[4] See Walters, cap. 20; Toynbee, *Survey, 1931*, 254 ff.
[5] See Walters, cap. 7.   [6] E.g., Zimmern, 481–6.
[7] See A. W. Rovine, *The First Fifty Years* (Leyden, 1970), 48–51; A. Salter, *Slave of the Lamp* (London, 1967), 262.
[8] See, e.g., Barros, *The League and the Great Powers*, 44, 120–1.

1920s of senior members of staff (from Italy and Germany especially) whose appointments and loyalties had to be seen in essentially national terms. A naturally discreet man, a person of principle as his successor, Joseph Avenol was not,[1] Drummond remained widely trusted and respected up to his departure in 1933.[2] Yet there were also murmurs against him, as will be seen, and there was a lack of steel in his personality—he was too weak a man, for example, to make a success of his later career as British Ambassador in Rome. Deeply regretting the absence from the League of the United States (it was felt by many of his staff that in his restricted social life he showed undue favours to Americans, and it was known that he hankered after the British Embassy in Washington), he embodied the organisation's Western, conservative principles and saw it as standing face to face with bolshevism, 'the two great antagonistic forces in the world today'.[3]

Drummond was among those who perceived severe limits to what the League could achieve after a decade of existence. It must work by persuasion, he wrote in 1928, and 'cannot immediately impose its will on a recalcitrant party'.[4] And besides those who, in Briand's words, 'not daring to attack it openly, allow no occasion to pass for disseminating rumours to its detriment',[5] supporters of the League also had doubts in their minds before the crisis in 1931. What could be done, asked Professor Zimmern in 1928, if that public opinion on which the organisation relied was, as he saw it, 'inert, acquiescent and largely indifferent' to foreign affairs?[6] 'What if some Nation . . . *resorts to hostilities*?' queried an L.N.U. essay in the summer of 1931. 'Is it or is it not fundamental to Peace that such a war-monger be restrained by force—that is to say by sanctions? The nations have not yet worked out any final answer . . .'[7] Well-wishers of the League in the United States wrestled with the same issue.[8] In the words of the Geneva Research Information Committee, the news from Mukden on 19 September was to raise 'the dreaded question, feared by friends . . . of the League. What would or could (it) do if a Great Power took action on its own?'[9]

When he had learned that the United States might not join the League, Drummond's reaction had been to doubt whether the organisation 'would

[1] On Avenol, see Barros, *Betrayal From Within* (New Haven, 1969). Thanassis Aghnides, then Head of the League's Disarmament Section, has written to me: 'Drummond was essentially loyal to the spirit of the Covenant. Avenol was not guided by any principle, nor did he have any strong convictions. He was essentially an opportunist and a cynic.'

[2] See, e.g. William Martin's article in the *Journal de Genève*, 30 January 1932.

[3] Quoted in Rovine, 45.   [4] Ibid, 50.

[5] LNOJ, *Special Supplement No. 93*, 69. Cf. Walters, cap. 39.

[6] *The Problems of Peace*, 3rd Series (London, 1929), 299 ff.

[7] A. Wilson, *World Security: An Essay on Sanctions* (L.N.U., London, 1931).

[8] See, e.g., the Committee for the Study of Economic Sanctions, note in Norman Davis Papers, box 8.

[9] *The League and Manchuria: Geneva Special Studies, vol. II, No. 10* (Geneva, 1931), 4. Cf. Foreign Office memorandum of June 1931, CP 167 (31) in CAB 24/222. For a contrasting, greatly optimistic contemporary assessment of the situation, see Toynbee's essay in *Pacific Affairs*, September 1931.

ever be an international instrument of really first-class importance'.[1] The ideas on which the League rested had been fostered by a sizeable number of Americans before and during the war;[2] the League's existence owed more to President Wilson than to any other man; now, it was rejected by a strange combination of disillusioned internationalists (who, like Lippmann, saw the 1919 settlement as 'immoral' and the League as a reactionary 'bureau of the French Foreign Office'[3]) and an assortment of isolationists whose domestic economic preferences spanned communism, progressivism, and bone-hard reaction.[4] The League was a trick to get American blood and money spilt again in the grimy quarrels of Europe; it would commit the United States to policies decided largely elsewhere; it would bind the country up with the devious British and the corrupt French.[5] Although the issue was not put clearly before the American public—several prominent Republicans, as we have seen, arguing that a vote for their party would still be a vote for the League—Harding's victory at the polls in 1920 was interpreted by him and others as a decisive and final rejection of the Geneva organisation.[6] The matter, remarked the new President, was now 'as dead as slavery', and others followed suit. 'This Government had definitely refused membership in the League,' ran Hoover's 1928 campaign statement. 'On this we stand.' The Democratic Party, too—not without the blessing of disciples of Wilson, like Norman Davis—sought to escape from their former leader's burdensome legacy, and their 1928 platform, while not mentioning the League, talked of 'freedom from entangling political alliances with foreign nations'. It will be seen later that in 1932 as well, the party's new Presidential candidate, Franklin Roosevelt, was to be another who reversed his views on the subject in this way.

For a time after 1920, American non-recognition of the League found expression in official policies that were as inane as they were pompous.[7] In addition, the Treaty of Mutual Assistance was abruptly rejected, and an aggressively uncooperative response returned to British enquiries concerning the Geneva Protocol.[8] Yet 'isolation' was, of course, impossible. Quite apart from the country's trading and other overseas interests, issues such as disarmament and international debts were bound to link the United States to the rest of the world, and the Washington Conference acknowledged as much. At the same time, cooperation with the League over the non-political aspects of its work grew to the point where, under an encouraging Hoover, it

[1] Drummond to Fosdick, 15 December 1919, in Fosdick, op. cit.

[2] Kuehl, passim; Martin, *Peace Without Victory*; Current, 'The United States and Collective Security', in De Conde.

[3] Lippmann to Fosdick, 15 August 1919, in Fosdick.

[4] See, e.g., Adler, and R. Osgood, *Ideals and Self-Interest in America's Foreign Policy* (Chicago, 1953); De Conde, 'On Twentieth Century Isolationism', in De Conde.

[5] For specific illustrations, see Fosdick, passim, and William E. Borah Papers, e.g. boxes 328, 341, 345. On anti-British feeling, see Sprout, *Towards A New Order* caps. 4, 5.

[6] See Adler, 105 ff.; Fleming, 17–47.

[7] See Fleming, cap. IV.

[8] See Perkins, 'The Department of State', in Craig and Gilbert.

was both cordial and extensive. The blessing of successive administrations was also forthcoming for the vain attempts of Elihu Root and others to secure, with the approval of Congress, American adherence to the Protocols of the World Court.[1] Various bodies within the United States also sought to create an informed and sympathetic international outlook among the public at large.[2] Some, like the Foreign Policy Association and Council on Foreign Relations, maintained a neutral position over the question of the League itself; others advocated American membership, but even the League of Nations Association still spoke of 'reservations, should they be deemed necessary', and it never became a mass movement as in Britain. In 1931, in fact, financial difficulties were threatening its very existence.[3]

Disarmament was a more common cause than the League, and a host of small and often radical pressure groups like the Women's International League for Peace and Freedom existed to work for it. The number and variety of such bodies did not increase the clarity or realism of the general debate on international relations, however. In particular, the subject of force attracted more emotion than careful reasoning. With Wilsonian internationalists and many isolationists both rejecting 'power politics',[4] and with the common assumption that the country's principles rose far above the selfish particulars of national interest,[5] dealers in moral platitudes had a field-day. By brandishing such platitudes, certain groups did achieve one apparent triumph—the Kellogg–Briand Pact (or Pact of Paris) in 1928, but only when it had been made clear that no cost was involved.[6] Signatories' renunciation of war 'as an instrument of national policy' was backed only by the sanction of public disapproval and 'the denial of benefits furnished by this Treaty'. 'Suppose some other nation does break (it),' Kellogg was asked, 'why should we interest ourselves in it?' 'There is not a bit of reason,' answered the Secretary. When the Japanese attacked in Manchuria in 1931, William Borah, who had been a leading advocate of the 1928 agreement,

[1] Fleming, 219–313; Adler, caps. 7–9; A. Zimmern, *The American Road to World Peace* (New York, 1953), 92 ff.; *Geneva Special Studies*, vol. III, No. 1 (Geneva, 1932); *The Problems of Peace, Sixth Series* (London 1932).

[2] See Adler, 121 ff.; R. Divine, *The Illusion of Neutrality* (Chicago, 1962); Ferrell, 'The Peace Movement', in De Conde; D. Detzer, *Appointment on the Hill* (New York, 1948); W. Cohen's Hakone Conference paper, 'The Role of Private Groups'; material in Norman Davis Papers, boxes 17 and 18.

[3] In 1923 the L.N.A. had under 50,000 members, although in 1931 it still had branches in 32 states. Its President was George W. Wickersham, with Philip Nash as Director. Nicholas Murray Butler, Raymond Fosdick, Congressman Morton D. Hull and James Shotwell were among other prominent members. On its financial problems, see Nash to Root, 19 August 1931, Elihu Root Papers, box 147; Wickersham to Davis, 8 January 1932, Davis Papers, box 35. In 1932, the Association joined other peace organisations in submitting a plank for the Democratic platform, calling for increased co-operation with—but not membership of—the League. Newton D. Baker Papers, box 145. For Lippmann's ideas in the same context, see Lippmann to Baker, 9 May 1932, ibid, box 149.

[4] See H. Morgenthau, *In Defense of the National Interest* (New York, 1951), 28–30.

[5] Hoffmann, *Gulliver's Troubles*, 114 ff.

[6] See R. H. Ferrell, *Peace In Their Time*, (New Haven, 1952).

merely concluded that it began to seem 'that leagues and peace treaties and peace pacts are not made for large nations'.[1] Meanwhile, as the French found during the 1930 naval negotiations in London, commitments were ruled out in Washington. Adherence to the World Court was still blocked in the Senate,[2] and while Stimson felt able to assure MacDonald privately that the United States would not enforce its neutral rights if the Royal Navy were blockading an aggressor condemned by the League,[3] official policy still left the matter uncertain. With the onset of depression, isolationism in its various forms began to take an even stronger hold.[4]

Even among those closely concerned with the practical aspects of relations with other states, there remained a disposition to believe in the efficacy of moral force and public opinion in world affairs, and, as in British circles, to accord a pejorative meaning to the term 'balance of power'.[5] Far more so than in the British case,[6] it also seemed easy to shrug off the common drudgery of international relations. If the 'world opinion' approach was disregarded by others, as it was when Stimson invoked the Kellogg Pact over the 1929 Sino–Soviet clash in Manchuria, there was no great pressure to acknowledge the fact or think through the implications of failure.[7] Moreover, even where there was a readiness to see the United States involved internationally to a greater degree, it tended to point in directions other than that of ordinary League membership among the herd. Within the Navy Department and Stimson's office, as we have seen, the notion, rather, of a Pax Americana, successor to the Pax Britannica, peeped through from time to time, ignoring the special conditions which had helped bring about that earlier case.[8] Less grandiose, but related nevertheless, was another idea which could claim a British precedent: that of America standing apart as the decisive 'balancer' of the international system.[9] 'In the long run,' wrote a friend to the country's former Under Secretary-General of the League, 'we shall be able to help most if we keep out, throwing our weight into the scale from time to time wherever a specific good can be accomplished thereby.'[10] The opinion of General Dawes was similar,[11] and that of Admiral Pratt has already been quoted.[12] 'The best possible thing for the United States was outside of the League,' argued Stimson in the summer of 1931. 'We would lose our influence and moral power if we were put in a position where we had to discuss on equal terms with the other nations the routine problems and squabbles of Europe ... Our real role was to throw our influence to help

---

[1] Borah to Roan, 12 October 1931, Borah Papers, box 321.
[2] Adler, 186 ff.
[3] Stimson Diary, 7 August 1931; cf. Baldwin's Albert Hall speech of 11 July 1931, widely quoted in the press the following day.
[4] See Ferrell, *American Diplomacy*, cap. 1; Adler, cap. 11.
[5] For an example, see Cordell Hull, *Memoirs I*, (London, 1948), passim, and Stimson Diary, 9 July 1931.
[6] See Hoffmann, *Gulliver's Troubles*, 98 ff.
[7] See Ferrell, *American Diplomacy*, cap. 4; Tang, 210 ff.
[8] See Sprout, *Towards A New Order*, caps. 1, 2.
[9] See Wight, op. cit.
[10] Flexner to Fosdick, 26 February 1922, in Fosdick.
[11] C. G. Dawes, *Journal as Ambassador to Great Britain* (New York, 1939), 415.
[12] See above, 75,n.

in major emergencies.'[1] During the 1931–3 crisis, this self-image of a deus ex machina was to feature in American policy as much as Britain's ambivalence over collective security did in hers, or, in Paris, a preoccupation with matters of security on the Rhine.

The crisis was also, however, to help bring about in each country some agonising reappraisals which ultimately concerned the very nature of international politics. For despite their differences (and France, for example, was clearly less beset by moral dilemmas than the other two), all three had long been affected by a confusion to which Salvador de Madariaga pointed when he talked at the time of states 'coming to the Disarmament Conference with a divided mind, feeling that we do not know where to place our faith: in national egoism or . . . international idealism'.[2] Similarly, Zimmern was soon to write of 'the characteristics of a period of transition'.[3] Not only the Baldwins and the Stimsons were to experience the difficulties involved. Cecil, for example, failed to escape them when arguing the case for a draft Model Treaty at a meeting of Foreign Office and Service chiefs in 1930. What would happen, growled an unhappy gentleman from the Admiralty, if, under such a treaty, the League wished to prevent the fleet being sent to Singapore in an emergency. In that event, answered Cecil nimbly, 'we would not be bound to accept the League recommendation. We might have excellent reasons for saying this movement must be carried out for reasons of national security.'[4] It was the justification the Japanese were to offer—sincerely so— over Manchuria. Where did one draw the line? Sending a fleet, after all, *could* be construed as being as coercive an act as firing a battery of field guns. American admirals were soon asking similar questions (concerning the Panama Canal especially) of one of their own eminent academic champions of collective security; they, too, might reasonably have found the answers they were given unsatisfactory.[5]

Areas of 'special interest' still figured prominently in the thinking of the West, as they did for the Japanese over Manchuria, and although the parallel between certain Western actions after 1919 and those of Japan in 1931–3 was by no means always a true one, it was to seem close enough to make some people in élite circles feel uncomfortable. France, for example, had at one time deemed it necessary to promote a separatist movement in the Rhineland, as well as seeking to dominate Yunnan in defence of Indo–China. For her part, Britain had signed the Kellogg Pact only on the understanding that there were 'certain regions of the world the welfare and integrity of which constitute the special and vital interest of our peace and safety', and where 'interference cannot be suffered'. A large measure of control was also still retained over a nominally independent Egypt and Britain's 'lifeline', the Suez Canal.[6] Further East, the India Office was ready to resist

[1] Memorandum in Stimson Diary, 12 July 1931.

[2] LNOJ, *Special Supplement No. 93*, 80–1.

[3] Zimmern, *The League of Nations*, 495–6; cf. Toynbee, *Survey, 1932*, 182 ff.

[4] Minutes of 24 July 1930, CAB 21/348.

[5] U.S.N. General Board, Hearings, 14 January 1932, 1–68; questions to Professor George Wilson of Harvard.

[6] See, e.g., Taylor, 276. After 1922, Britain remained opposed to any discussion of Egyptian matters by the League. Beck, op. cit.

China's influence in Tibet, where she was suzerain power, in defence of Britain's.

For the United States, Hoover was endeavouring to change things in some respects by withdrawing the Marines from Nicaragua and Haiti;[1] his Administration had also abandoned the use of non-recognition as a mark of displeasure towards South American states, and, by publishing the Clark Memorandum, had revoked the claim that the Monroe Doctrine justified United States intervention in Latin America.[2] This good-neighbour policy did not mean, however, that all thought had gone of intervening in that part of the world in what was seen as self-defence. Stimson, for example, had written publicly after his Nicaraguan mission that, just as Britain controlled the sea route to India, so the United States must ensure the safety of the Panama Canal and its approaches, even if it meant enforcing order in the Caribbean area.[3] The isthmus, he wrote later, was 'the one spot external to our shores which nature has decreed to be most vital to our national safety, not to mention our prosperity',[4] and he was to be incensed when Britain, contrary to his wishes, chose to recognise a new régime in Salvador 'in our backyard, so to speak'.[5] During the Disarmament Conference, too, Stimson, like Lord Londonderry, was to insist privately on the value of aircraft as a means of preserving the national interest—only whereas Londonderry saw this in terms of existing British territory, the Secretary of State recalled the use of planes in Nicaragua and Honduras;[6] as it will also be seen, he was to acknowledge that there was much validity in the argument of friends that Japan's position in Manchuria was akin to that of the United States in Cuba or Mexico. Even Hoover, so anxious to be rid of America's imperial trappings, had been ready to buy Bermuda and Trinidad from Britain 'for defence purposes', as well as British Honduras to use as a bargaining counter with Mexico[7] (cf. Woodrow Wilson's Second Principle: 'Peoples and provinces must not be bartered about from sovereignty to sovereignty as if they were chattels or pawns in a game'). Evidently, the problem 'of reconciling national self-interest with universal ideals'[8] still admitted of no easy solution.

Not surprisingly, the differing approaches of French, British and American governments to problems of peace and security often strained relations between them. Specific issues, too, were affecting all sides of this triangle and

[1] See FRUS, 1931, II, 780 ff., and 1932, V, 766 ff.

[2] See Ferrell, *American Diplomacy*, cap. 13. It is worth recalling that in October 1931, the U.S.A. declined a League invitation to join a special committee to study a possible pact against economic aggression. FRUS, 1931, I, 605–7.

[3] Current, *Secretary Stimson*, 33.   [4] Stimson and Bundy, 183.

[5] Stimson Diary, 25 January, 9 March 1932; cf. FRUS, 1932, V, 566 ff.

[6] Moffat Diary, 3 June 1932.

[7] Hoover, *Memoirs, 1920–1933*, 345–6. William Castle was soon to revert to the idea of taking territory in the West Indies in liquidation of the British debt. Castle to Reed, 19 December 1931, Castle Papers, England. Hoover's gunboat inclinations over Liberia will be noted in a later chapter.

[8] Osgood, 1. Cf. Shotwell's sympathetic comments on Japan's 'brave but mistaken' efforts to do in China what Britain had done in Egypt and the U.S.A. in the Caribbean. *On the Rim*, 229.

the images and expectations held of each other at the time when the Far Eastern crisis came upon them. In 1932 in particular, this aspect of the situation was also to affect and be affected by relations between Western states and Japan. To complete the setting of the crisis itself, therefore, a brief survey is necessary of matters within the Western triangle, as they stood up to the end of 1931. Above all, this means a summary of the position concerning debts and disarmament.

Britain had emerged from the Great War owing the United States about £850 million. She was owed far more by other allied governments, but failed either to get all such debts wiped out or to retrieve much of what was due to her. Saddled with a high rate of interest by the United States, she was able to make incomings exceed outgoings only by insisting on her share of reparations payments from Germany, an uncomfortable position post-Keynes, and at odds with the desire to see a reconciled Europe. Resentment at having to pay America far more than the original amount borrowed was also increased by the latter's rising tariff barriers, which impeded compensatory dollar earnings through trade.[1] France, too, resented her debt payments to the United States—despite having obtained better rates of interest than Britain, experiencing few qualms over insisting on her major share of German reparations, and becoming financially the strongest European power by the autumn of 1931.[2] The United States, on the other hand, while tending to take a Keynesian view of reparations, repulsed all suggestions from her former allies that the question should be linked to that of debts, or that debts should be cancelled.[3] In the deathless prose of Calvin Coolidge, 'They hired the money, didn't they?'

The financial collapse of Germany in the spring and summer of 1931, however, did force Hoover into proposing a moratorium on debts as well as reparations until December 1932. But as Congress was to underline when approving the move, there was still no question of debts being reduced or cancelled, despite continuing pressure from Britain and France and the dissatisfaction expressed by Laval in particular when he visited Washington in October 1931, in the vain hope of securing some consultative commitment by the United States on matters of security.[4] Hoover, Castle and others were 'thoroughly tired of giving up to Europe and allowing Europe to do us in the eye as a reward for our kindness'.[5] Hoover, in particular, regarded Laval's

---

[1] On debts alone, receipts fell short of payments between 1919 and September 1931 by £19½ million; the interest on the American debt was 3 per cent for 10 years, and 3½ for 52 years; in 1931-2, Britain bought £104 million worth of goods from the U.S., and sold her £18 million worth in return. Treasury memorandum, 14 November 1931, CAB 27/466; Cabinet conclusions of 28 November 1932, CAB 23/73. See also H. Feis, *The Diplomacy of the Dollar: First Era, 1919-1932* (Baltimore, 1950).

[2] In August 1931, French gold reserves amounted to over £486 million; the British reserve, before the 1931 crisis, was £150 million.

[3] E.g., Stimson's warning to MacDonald by telephone, 13 June 1931, Stimson Papers, box 300.

[4] See FRUS, 1931, II, 237-58; Stimson Diary, 22, 24 October 1931—a record which Hoover later found '*very imperfect*'. Hoover Papers. Cf. Warner, 45-9.

[5] Castle to Reed, 19 December 1931, loc. cit.; Stimson Diary, 29 September 1931. Cf. Cordell Hull, 171.

visit with suspicion and irritation, and made little secret of his dislike of France.[1] Over money, as over the questions of disarmament and security, it was the large existing resources of that country, not her vulnerability, that were seen in Washington,[2] and it was on that side of the triangle that tension was particularly pronounced during that autumn. There were American officials who recognised that a more flexible policy was needed towards France,[3] and there were even those who were privately ready to accept what Hoover was later bitterly to deny, that in his talks with Laval he had allowed for the possibility of future debt adjustments should difficulties in Europe persist and be faced up to by the countries concerned.[4] The most Hoover would acknowledge in private, however, was that Britain, as distinct from France, had a good case for seeking a revision of the terms of her debt,[5] while even Stimson, who would have liked to see the whole, damaging issue removed for ever, recognised that if the President made further concessions with Europe in its existing state, he would 'break his hold on his own people'.[6] The main immediate concern, therefore, was to prevent Britain and France coming together to form a united front on the question against the United States.

There were those on both sides of the Atlantic who, in 1931, were thinking around the possibility of using debt concessions as a lever to obtain a substantial measure of French disarmament.[7] Whatever one's particular view, however, attention was focussed on the Disarmament Conference which, after years of preparation and delay, was due to meet at Geneva in February 1932. For those who emphasised article 8 of the Covenant and believed, with Grey, that 'great armaments lead inevitably to war', this would be the supreme test of the new standards proclaimed for international relations in 1919. As Cecil had challengingly put it when submitting the report of the Preparatory Commission: 'It rests with Governments to give proof of their oft-repeated intention to reduce the burden of armaments and therewith the risk of war.'[8] The world had to choose, wrote Stimson privately, 'whether it is going to try the new methods . . . or whether it will drift into the old cycle of competition and war'.[9] In Britain and the United States especially, hundreds of public meetings and petitions emphasised the widespread anxiety over the outcome.

As noted in connection with the general search for peace, however, the

[1] E.g., Stimson Diary, 13 September 1931; Moffat Diary, 20 October 1931.

[2] E.g., Moffat Diary, 17–18 October 1931; Lamont to Hoover, 20 October 1931, Hoover Papers; *New York Herald Tribune*, 11 September 1931.

[3] E.g., Edge to Hoover, 9 June 1931; Edge to Castle, 28 August 1931, Castle Papers, France.

[4] Stimson Diary, 10 January, 1932. The final Hoover–Laval communiqué had implied just such a possibility that Hoover later denied.

[5] Stimson Diary, 8 September 1931.

[6] Ibid, 26 December 1931.

[7] E.g., Edge to Castle, 28 August 1931, Castle Papers, France; Stimson Diary, 27 August 1931. Eden had the same idea: note of conversation, July (no date) 1931, Stimson Papers, box 301.

[8] Cmd. 3757, December 1930.

[9] Memorandum in Stimson Diary, 10 July 1931. In general, see Toynbee, *Survey*, *1931*, part II.

Western powers disagreed over the ways in which to achieve disarmament, and even the year's arms-building truce that was brought into effect on 1 November 1931 was achieved only after much internal and international dissension.[1] For the French, with the political and military threat from Germany increasing, guaranteed security had to come before disarmament, which meant maintaining their superior strength on land while awaiting such reassurances as a League force, a consultative commitment by the United States, and an increased engagement on the part of Britain.[2] But while Britain, too, was greatly concerned to avert trouble in Europe, the pre-dominant Baldwin–MacDonald approach was not only one of avoiding commitments (Locarno, by its very generality, appeared no grave exception), but of favouring neither Germany nor France.[3] Indeed, despite misgivings over a rearmed Germany that were expressed by Austen Chamberlain and others,[4] it was widely accepted, even by the Germanophobe Vansittart, that Berlin's case was 'a very good one', and that the French security thesis was 'a very bad one (leading) nowhere'.[5] MacDonald was particularly fierce in denouncing the evils of Versailles and French tardiness in releasing Germany from its more obnoxious clauses, and continued into 1933 to attribute German nationalist excesses largely 'to the French handling of affairs'.[6]

Thus, despite French loans to the Bank of England, strain was also apparent along this side of the triangle in the autumn of 1931, with tariff and trade-quota issues contributing to the situation. Again, there were those who sought to improve matters. Lord Tyrrell, Ambassador in Paris, believed that 'the root of the difficulty . . . is our apparent failure to realise (the) French point of view',[7] and under pressure from Simon, even MacDonald agreed that the position was disquieting. 'We are returning to the Curzon régime,' he wrote at the end of the year, 'and if we are not careful we shall get Anglo–French relations into a narrow corner from which one of us will have to recede without much credit, and, in present circumstances, that one is likely to be us.'[8] Without French cooperation, after all, the problems of disarmament and reparations would not be solved, and on December 10 the Cabinet agreed on the need to establish 'close contact' with Paris on these subjects.[9] At the same time, the two countries were potential allies in resisting American demands for the continued payment of debts, but here the other two sides of the triangle, Franco–American and Anglo–American,

---

[1] See, e.g., Stimson Diary, 9 July 1931; Moffat Diary, 6 August, 11, 17, 18 September 1931.

[2] See, e.g., RA G.V, K 2330(4).

[3] See, e.g., Taylor, 214–22.　　　　　　　　　　[4] See, e.g., CAB 16/102.

[5] Vansittart memorandum of 11 January 1932, loc. cit.; cf. *History of The Times*, vol. IV, part 2, 795 ff.

[6] MacDonald to Baldwin, 15 June 1931, and to Cecil, 13 September 1932, MacDonald Papers, RM 5/6 and 6/13 respectively; MacDonald to King George V, 13 March 1933, RA G.V, K2353/19. On the War Office survey of German dangers noted earlier (January 1931), MacDonald minuted: 'I too am disturbed, and am compelled to suspect that France is cheating us.' Cf. Angell, 241–2.

[7] Tyrrell to Simon, 2 December 1931, Simon Papers (private collection), Foreign Affairs, 1931.

[8] MacDonald to Simon, 17 December 1931, ibid.　　　　　　[9] CAB 23/69.

caused MacDonald, especially, to hesitate, and to draw a picture of Anglo–French rivalry for American respect:

'I see the force of your argument,' he wrote to Simon, 'that we might join with France and give that unfortunate country some moral backing for a very self-seeking policy. I do not exactly like it because its effect may be to change our general relations with America and give the American public to understand that we are mere tools in the hands of France. That would again restore France to its position in America—a very deplorable result.'[1]

There also remained the question of the French desire for an increased British commitment in Europe. This caused far greater heart-searching in London than did the problem of finding a basis for the country's own proposals to put to the 1932 Conference, it being agreed by an all-party committee that nothing was possible unless others accepted cuts comparable to those Britain had already made on her own.[2] The French appeals created a serious dilemma, however. On the one hand was the thought that 'without some further advance by (Britain) . . . there was very little prospect of a successful issue to the Disarmament Conference', and the belief that such a failure would be 'horrible' (Simon's word), and 'a catastrophe'. On the other hand, there was the fear of being drawn into a war by commitments and events beyond Britain's control. In the end, the painful memory of 1914 was decisive. There would be no guarantees over and above Locarno; nothing involving German's eastern frontiers; nothing (and here the decision took longer) in the nature of a Mediterranean Locarno.[3] The Far Eastern crisis would make it appear all the more urgent to obtain lasting reconciliation in Europe, but it would not alter—indeed, it would reinforce—the decision that sacrifices to that end would have to be made by others.

In this, the British position bore strong resemblances to the American one. In Washington, for all Hoover's fierce desire to see disarmament achieved, it was agreed that the United States, having cut her army to the bone and regulated her navy by international agreement, could herself offer little at the forthcoming Conference beyond 'sympathy and patience'. What was needed was for the Europeans to achieve a proper peace settlement; then and only then could progress be made.[4] Partly for this reason, there was insouciance and confusion in high places in preparing for the Conference. Who should lead the delegation? Hoover wanted Borah, who declined; Stimson favoured Dwight Morrow, who died; Dawes accepted the job, but then mercifully went elsewhere; in the end, Hugh Gibson, Ambassador in

[1] MacDonald to Simon, 31 December 1931, Simon Papers (private collection), Foreign Affairs, 1931.
[2] See, e.g., CP 195(31), CAB 16/102.
[3] See, especially, Cabinets of 15 December 1931, and 13, 14, 20, 26 January 1932, CAB 23/69 and 70; cf. CAB 27/476. It is worth noting that the alternatives facing Britain if the Conference failed were described in Cabinet as (1) expensive rearmament, or (2) 'accepting a position of inferiority *to a France powerfully armed and exercising hegemony in Europe.*' Italics added.
[4] E.g., Stimson Diary, 9 July, 22 October, 6 November 1931; Moffat Diary, 11 August, 30 September, 2 October 1931; records of disarmament delegation meetings, 5 and 7 January 1932, Davis Papers, box 20. In general, see FRUS, 1931, I, 471 ff.

Brussels, took over the business in Stimson's name, with Hugh Wilson (Minister to Switzerland) and the inevitable Norman Davis among the team.[1] Small sums of money for the delegation were dragged out of Congress,[2] and attempts made to obtain positive cooperation from the reluctant majority of senior army and navy officers (it was said that the admirals were alleging over their dinner tables that Hoover was a British agent, if not a Japanese one).[3] As in London, fears were expressed over the state of the country's arms industry,[4] while Stimson himself showed little interest in the specific issues involved. A few days before the delegation was due to sail, it still had no formal instructions, inadequate funds and incomplete membership. Prompted by Hoover's alarm at attacks from pacifist quarters, a speech dealing in high-sounding generalities was hastily prepared; only a last-minute and despairing telephone call from Gibson in Geneva produced the specific proposals which he was able to put to the Conference on 9 February 1932.[5]

Naval disarmament, in particular, had long brought with it the likelihood of friction between the United States and Britain, but despite the continued suspicions of the Navy Department, Hoover and Stimson saw the visit of MacDonald in 1929 and the Naval Agreement of 1930 as having ushered in a new and cordial phase in relations between the two countries.[6] Stimson, as we have seen, gave priority to this aspect of foreign policy, and when he visited London in the summer of 1931 for talks on the financial situation, happily reported to the President that he and the British were working together 'like two old shoes'. Lunching with Hailsham, Simon, Reading, Hoare, Vansittart and others, he found them 'a very fine set of men'.[7] Other members of the American East-coast, business-cum-governmental élite, like Norman Davis, also had a wide circle of acquaintances in Britain, while in the early autumn, the struggles of the National Government to save the economy were admiringly followed with the help of Jimmy Thomas's frequent confidences to General Dawes in the London Embassy. Dawes's Counsellor, Ray Atherton, built up the drama and relief of it all by describing, in October, the 'really revolutionary sentiment among the masses', and the issue of the coming election as being between 'the forces working to defend the capitalist system and those seeking to supplant it'.[8] It was thus no wonder that Stimson, Lamont and others were jubilant at the result.

[1] Borah to Hoover, 2 September 1931; Hoover to Borah, 8 September 1931, Hoover Papers; Stimson Diary, 30 September, 12 December 1931, 18 January 1932; Moffat Diary, 26 October 1931; 15 January 1932.

[2] Stimson Diary, 13 January 1932; Moffat Diary, 11 January 1932.

[3] Moffat Diary, 6 July, 4, 18, 20, 23 November, 4 December 1931. Pratt and Hepburn were two notable exceptions among American admirals resisting disarmament.

[4] Moffat memorandum, 7 October 1931, Moffat Papers, vol. 22.

[5] Moffat Diary, 12, 13 August, 3, 6, November, 18 December 1931; 16, 21, 27, 28, 29 January, 8, 11 February 1932; memorandum of 2 October 1931, Moffat Papers, vol. 22; Stimson Diary, 14 December 1931; press cutting sent by Hoover, Stimson Papers, box 304. For Gibson's speech, see FRUS, 1932, I, 25–30.

[6] See DBFP, I, No. 77 especially.

[7] Stimson Diary, 20, 28 July 1931. Cf. Watt, op. cit.

[8] DS 841·00/1156, 1159, 1167, 1170, 1190, 1194, 1211.

Debts and naval disarmament remained as potential sources of discord, however, while Hoover, unlike his Secretary of State, was no Anglophile.[1] At least Stimson's pleasure at improved relations was shared by many on the British side, especially since, in the words of a Foreign Office memorandum, such progress 'has not entailed and does not call for the sacrifice of any essential British interest'.[2] In 1931 Vansittart could write that 'relations have probably never before been on a sounder basis than they are at the present time', while in January 1932 he was still able to record 'a degree of cordiality never before attained'.[3] MacDonald rightly felt that much of the credit for this state of affairs belonged to him, and believed, less soundly, that 'his name did carry weight in America'.[4] Reading and Simon after him were also keen to work closely with Washington, while within a wider circle, some thought in terms of a special relationship that might help Britain to stay aloof from Europe.

There remained, however, a section of the British public that, in the words of its Ambassador in Washington, 'did not very much like the United States'.[5] Resentment over the latter's stand over neutral rights in the first stages of the 1914–18 war had not entirely been erased by the subsequent alliance in arms. The termination of the Anglo–Japanese alliance had aroused similar sentiments in some quarters, and, besides Treasury anger over debts, the Admiralty's resentment over parity and exasperation over the criteria of naval limitation were never far from the surface. The imperial-preference tariff policies of Neville Chamberlain and his supporters likewise suggested transatlantic rivalry rather than cooperation. Sir Warren Fisher was only one particularly vehement representative of the many in official circles who held that American governments were never to be trusted. 'The United States have often let us down,' wrote Vansittart in his survey of January 1932, and his paper of the previous May had expressed a view that was widely held in Whitehall:

We shall doubtless continue to hear much about idealism from across the Atlantic, and to be furnished with many facile but impractical recipes for expediting the arrival of the millennium; but we must recognise that there can be no active American participation in European political problems in the near future. There will be no teething of the Kellogg Pact, or, indeed, any activity which by any stretch of the imagination could be described as the assumption of an obligation or a responsibility.

Vansittart was right. Thus, before the Far Eastern crisis arrived, British expectations of the degree of cooperation that might be obtained from the United States were already severely limited. Nothing that occurred thereafter was substantially to change such views. This, too, would be right.

---

[1] Hoover's First World War experiences in Britain had not always been happy, and he was somewhat scornful of American women who married into the British aristocracy. See the comment in Vansittart, 386.

[2] 'The Foreign Policy of the Empire', Vansittart Papers.

[3] CP 317(31), CAB 24/225; CP 4/32, CAB 27/476.

[4] Neville Chamberlain Diary, 23 August 1931.

[5] FRUS, 1932, III, 196–7.

Retrospect

On 18 September 1931, certain officers of the Japanese Army were prepared to resort to force in pursuit of what they, together with large numbers of their fellow-countrymen, perceived as a vital national interest. In the immediate locality, Western states had little at stake in material terms; in the wider setting of China, the Western Pacific, Australasia and South East Asia, Britain's material interests were substantial, those of the United States modest, both absolutely and relatively. However, whereas there was widespread agreement within official British circles on the nature and extent of these interests, in Washington there was greater ambivalence, involving the presence in some minds of aspirations of a high order. In 1931, for example, the well-worn term 'the Open Door' in China meant different things to various Americans who were closely concerned with the country's Far Eastern policies. In general, however, its role was mainly symbolic, a token of one's faith in the new framework established for Far Eastern politics at the Washington Conference and of one's confidence that, within this framework, there existed a special place for the United States as the enlightened mentor of the Chinese Republic. When Stimson wrote of 'the real nobility of the traditional American doctrine towards China of the Open Door', it was primarily an expression of the sublimated imperialism of spreading the American way of life; secondly, it also testified to a vision of China as a potential and well-nigh limitless market; only incidentally did it reflect a concern for existing material interests. In this last sense, and as relating to immediate and tangible goals, the term fitted British policy far more adequately. Yet whatever their interests, neither Britain nor the United States was in a position to influence Japan to abandon a domestically popular course of action, especially given the political culture and particular political circumstances prevailing in that country at the time. Nor could Britain or the United States seek to coerce Japan by witholding trade without considerable self-injury, while neither was in a position to defend its possessions in the Far East without sustaining immediate and severe losses. This situation applied, a fortiori, to France and the Netherlands.

In all these Western states, there was a widespread assumption in official circles that Western values were universal, and that the progress of Asian states, particularly China, should be measured in these terms. Even in Washington, there was also much adverse comment upon the state of China and the qualities of its people, while the recognition that Japan's interests diverged from those of the West was frequently accompanied by the assumption that no major or irreconcilable dispute need thereby arise. As a barrier to aggression in the area, the League of Nations, itself an essentially Western organisation, had yet to prove its ability to halt a major power that was involved in a matter which it judged to be of major importance to its existence. At the same time, two of the three leading Western states saw themselves as being in extremis financially and economically, and two of the three had growing defence problems close to home. In all of them, despite some external appearances to the contrary, the political leadership was affected in varying degrees by a sense of weakness and insecurity, and their publics were not in a mood for external risks. Among the three of them, despite elements of friendship and accord, there lay serious differences of interest, approach and opinion.

Perhaps the most striking aspect of the situation in retrospect, however, is the degree of confusion concerning the nature, goals and methods of conducting international relations that existed in men's minds in the West (and, indeed, in Japan too before the Kwantung Army supplied an unambiguous answer). In seeking to appreciate the reason for this, the historian's sense of perspective is obviously indispensable. It is relevant in that context, for example, to recall the process of decline that had taken place during the nineteenth century in that system of international management known as the Concert of Europe.[1] Stepping back even further to take in as well the period on either side of the crisis of 1931–3, one can also offer a reminder of some of the many factors that were making for a process of rapid transformation in the conditions surrounding international relations: social, economic and technological change;[2] shifts in the basis and criteria of power, in the number of actors on the international scene, the scope of their purposes and their propensity to affect one another as they shuffled forward in what Stanley Hoffmann has described as 'the chain gang'.[3] One can observe, too, the tangible and intangible factors that were eroding the primacy of Europe, not merely to produce the two super-powers whose supremacy was to be unmistakable only a decade after the Far Eastern crisis had ended, but also to hasten the self-assertion of states which in 1931 were still thought of as merely a collection of backward and subject peoples.[4] Nor should one forget the forces of political and racial aspiration that were cutting across those dominant and convenient units of international politics, states themselves.

Besides the historian's view of all this, however, it may also be useful to see the confusion that existed in 1931 in terms of concepts developed in the field of political science. In doing so, caution is obviously necessary, and no neat, theoretical 'explanation' is intended. Argument by analogy is as dangerous in purely intellectual terms as it is in everyday politics, while concepts developed within a domestic setting are not to be transferred to the international one without heed being paid to the particular attributes which set the latter apart.[5] Even where attempts have been made to develop a theory of systems relating specifically to international politics, enough questions remain—quite apart from the turgid self-indulgence of some of the works themselves—to give the historian pause.[6] Yet provided that a model of an international system[7] is recognised to be an idealised and necessarily

---

[1] See, e.g., Hinsley, caps. 10, 11.   [2] E.g., ibid, cap. 12.

[3] E.g., Hoffmann, *Gulliver's Troubles*, 52; H. Kissinger, *American Foreign Policy* (London, 1969), 53.

[4] See, e.g., G. Barraclough, *An Introduction to Contemporary History* (London, 1964), a stimulating essay, although it exaggerates 'the dwarfing of Europe'.

[5] See, e.g., Hoffmann, 10.

[6] See, e.g., J. C. Charlesworth (ed.), *Contemporary Political Analysis* (New York, 1967); also, M. Kaplan, *System and Process in International Politics* (New York, 1957).

[7] Accepting Aron's definition (op. cit., 94): 'The ensemble constituted by political units that maintain regular relations with each other and that are all capable of being implicated in a generalised war.'

simplified construction, it may at least sometimes help to clarify and raise
pertinent questions concerning long-term changes that might be taking place.
Similarly, despite the lack of a single, overriding authority, one may depict
the conduct of international relations as a changing series of games, each
with its set of rules (some of which, of course, will be enshrined in international law), played within the prevailing system.

Briefly, in 1931 the international system was in the process of changing from
what has been termed a moderate, balance-of-power one to the bi-polar one
that was to obtain at the end of the Second World War.[1] In other words,
within the structure of the system itself, and not only in men's minds, there
existed a good deal of confusion. Bi-polarity did not yet exist, for there
remained a fairly wide dispersal of power, as well as wide discrepancies in its
levels. Nor had the basis of that power yet been transformed by nuclear
weapons in such a way as to provide weaker states, paradoxically, with
greater room for manoeuvre. The 1919 settlement had left, and even enhanced, two of the European empires, while much of the self-assertion that
was soon to emerge in areas beyond Europe remained only latent. In most
European eyes, that continent was still at the centre of the international
system, with isolationism within the United States and turmoil within the
Soviet Union temporarily concealing the rising power of those two countries.
Within the League itself (where, despite its title, states and not nations or
other groupings were crucial), even the old Concert apparatus lingered on in
the form of permanent seats on the Council accorded to 'the principal allied
and associated powers'.

At the same time, however, it had been thought necessary to change the
nature and rules of the international game, away from that which had lately
been characterised by alliances and ententes. The 'balance of power' was
anathema. The result was thus the attempt to institute the new League game:
to impose it from above, as it were, upon the scarcely perceived shifts already
taking place in the international system beneath. We have seen that it was
not in fact a totally new game, nor a totally inflexible one. Nevertheless, it
did place strong emphasis on a set of normative rules—as distinct from
pragmatic ones[2]—that were enshrined in the Covenant, to a degree that
rendered it brittle at a time when changes in the system were likely to demand
flexibility, even if human frailties did not already do so.

The aim of the game might appear to be clear enough: 'the achievement of
international peace and security'. Already we encounter ambiguities and
inadequacies, however. Did this cover security of a non-political and non-
military kind; and what of those who had not, under existing circumstances,
or who offered differing definitions of what constituted security? And what
of powerful units outside the game and its rules, notably the United States
and Soviet Union—especially since in the case of the latter the political creed
involved was seen by Drummond and others as the very antithesis of all that
the League stood for? Or again, what if one of those sovereign states taking
part were unable to control groups within its borders that could impinge
upon the international scene? (Both China and Japan were soon to accuse

[1] See, e.g., Hoffmann, op. cit. 13 ff.
[2] See, e.g., F. G. Bailey, *Stratagems and Spoils* (Oxford, 1969), 4–6. Cf. ibid.,
19 ff.

each other of being in such a condition; in recent times, another example, in Palestine, has again created a certain confusion among the established players.) As for the way in which relations between states were to be conducted, these were circumscribed by the Covenant, and were to be peaceful. But the use of force was not entirely ruled out, and the question remained: was a war a war if it was not declared to be such by those involved?[1] How was 'aggression' to be defined in the first place, and if the term could be agreed upon in a military sense, what of, say, economic aggression, on which the Covenant said nothing? Finally, what would happen if someone broke the rules? Articles 15 and 16 appeared to provide a clear answer: all would act to uphold the aims of the game. Yet even if these articles could be applied to great and small alike, what of the latitude of judgement and action that was still reserved for individual players?

In brief, however sincerely one might declare one's policies to be based entirely upon the League and its Covenant,[2] or even outside the League, pronounce one's rejection of 'power politics', a host of questions remained to be answered in practice. Normative rules had been established, but pragmatic rules remained indispensable. Between those targets of foreign policy which have been termed 'possession goals' on the one hand and 'milieu goals' on the other,[3] men still had to hesitate over priorities. Now, the dilemma was about to be further underlined as General Honjo Shigeru stepped out of his bath in Port Arthur shortly before midnight on Friday, 18 September, and gave his approval to the movement of his troops who were already spreading out into the attack.

[1] On the problem, 'When Does War Exist?', see Q. Wright in *American Journal of International Law*, vol. 26 (1932), 362–8. Wright concluded: 'So long as both China and Japan deny an intention to make war, war in the legal sense could only result from recognition of a state of war by other states ... The existence of legal war is probably necessary to prove violation of Article XII of the Covenant, and is almost certainly necessary to render sanctions applicable under Article XVI.' On the general problem of defining aggression, see, e.g., Aron, 121 ff.

[2] Cf. Hugo, *Britain in Tomorrow's World*, 39, 48.

[3] I.e., 'goals pertaining, respectively, to national possessions and to the shape of the environment in which the nation operates.' Wolfers, 73–4. One should add: (i) that possession and milieu goals are not, of course, necessarily mutually exclusive; and (ii) that the general problem was also a familiar one for non-League states, as illustrated, for example, by the debate within the Soviet Union concerning 'socialism in one country' and 'permanent revolution'.

PART TWO

DEVELOPMENT

CHAPTER FIVE

OUTBREAK: FROM THE MUKDEN INCIDENT TO THE LEAGUE RESOLUTION OF 24 OCTOBER 1931

Developments in the Far East

GIVEN THE enormous disparity in the number of troops on either side,[1] the Japanese advance in South Manchuria was remarkably swift. The foundations were thus laid for the later charge that China had failed to act with sufficient vigour in her own defence, and there was scorn for the Chinese army in several quarters. Within three days of the explosion at Mukden, the Kwantung Army had secured key points along the length of the S.M.R., and also, more ominously, branched out far from the railway zone to take Kirin, where the local Chinese commander (at revolver-point, in fact) proceeded to proclaim the independence of the province. At the same time, units of the Japanese Korean Army crossed the Yalu river to reinforce their comrades in Mukden and elsewhere. The lull which followed was then shattered on 8 October, when Japanese planes attacked Chinchow, well down the railway line towards Peking, while away to the north the dissident Chinese garrison commander at Taonan (he was prompted and financed by the Japanese) marched along the railway from there towards Tsitsihar with the intention of taking over the government of Heilungkiang province; this advance was halted when the retreating loyalist troops destroyed the railway bridges over the river Nonni, but a new point of tension had thus been created. Meanwhile Tokyo was warning the Chinese Government to halt their country's widespread boycotting of Japanese goods if they wished to avoid serious counter-measures being taken.

Public opinion in Japan was soon demonstrating its excited support for what its army was doing in Manchuria.[2] The Social Democrats and other

---

[1] To meet a Kwantung Army total (including railway guards) of around 11,000, Chang Hsueh-liang controlled about 110,000 regulars in the Peking and Tientsin area, and about 140,000 more in the three provinces of Manchuria, plus Jehol. This section is based partly on Chapter 4 of the *Lytton Report*, and Chapter 5, part B of IMTFE, *Judgement*. These sources have been greatly added to, however, by, e.g., Ogata, 53 ff., Yoshihashi, cap. 6, Crowley, cap. III, and above all the second volume of the massive series, *Taiheiyo senso e no michi: kaisen gaiko-shi*, together with the abridged, typescript translation, 'The Road to the Pacific War'.

[2] See, e.g., Hugh Byas, 'All Japan Unites Against the League', *New York Times*, 14 October 1931, and his *Government By Assassination* (London, 1943), 37.

proletarian parties joined in the clamour, and attacks on Shidehara for being too moderate came from within his own, Minseito party (the Home Minister, Adachi Kenzo, even boycotted Cabinet meetings on these grounds) as well as from the main opposition, Seiyukai party. Moreover, despite public assurances that Japan 'harboured no territorial designs in Manchuria', the stated conditions upon which Tokyo would withdraw its troops began to grow steeper, from the assured security of Japanese life and property to a new Sino–Japanese agreement, reached by direct negotiation, on 'certain fundamental principles' which were not to be defined until the end of this period.

So much was readily apparent. In secret, a struggle was being waged which involved the civil leaders of the Japanese Government, the military high command and the staff of the Kwantung Army. This last body had in fact set out to win control of the whole of Manchuria, as a strategic base against the Soviet Union and as the first step in breaking what was seen as the geographic and economic impasse facing Japan. Certain senior officers in Tokyo, as we have seen, had been privy to the scheme; but the date envisaged by the main group for some kind of action had been 1932, and although it was felt essential to support the Kwantung Army once operations had begun, there remained a strong disinclination to see any move into North Manchuria that might raise the spectre of Soviet intervention.[1] As for Shidehara and his Prime Minister, Wakatsuki, they sought to prevent an extension of the Mukden clash and to settle matters swiftly with the Chinese authorities. In this they also had the approval of the Emperor, who forcefully expounded his views to Wakatsuki and called upon the General Staff to maintain discipline in the army. It was not enough, however. The Emperor's senior advisers were determined that he should not risk becoming embroiled in political controversy, and the General Staff, eventually supported by the War Minister, General Minami, were left to invoke against the Government the 'right of supreme command' which the Emperor exercised through them. Under mounting pressure from public opinion[2] and the faits accomplis in Manchuria, Wakatsuki—more inclined to give way than Shidehara—sought a compromise with Minami: the Government would not challenge the prerogative of supreme command and would provide the necessary funds for the supporting action taken by the Korean Army, which they had at first sought to prohibit; in return, the General Staff would curb the activities of the Kwantung Army.[3]

This agreement was rapidly undermined, however. While the Kwantung Army gave ground only to the extent of now aiming to install a nominally independent régime under Japanese control, the General Staff in turn began to move some of the way towards this position and in their orders left sufficient loopholes to enable the gains already made to be reinforced.[4] The prohibition on any move north towards Harbin was maintained, and for the

[1] *Taiheiyo senso e no michi*, II, 41–4.
[2] See Takeuchi, 357–66.
[3] *Taiheiyo senso e no michi*, II, 12–21. The Korean Army episode is too complex to relate in detail. But in all it demonstrated the near-impotence of the authorities in Tokyo. For Bergamini's version, see op. cit., 430.
[4] *Taiheiyo senso e no michi*, II, 27–34; IMTFE, *Exhibits* 3422 C, D, H, I, J, K.

moment accepted;[1] with the support of S.M.R. officials, however, Itagaki and his colleagues made preparations for the complete expulsion of Chang Hsueh-liang, declarations of independence by tame Chinese committees in the three Manchurian provinces, and the eventual establishment of a separate, multi-racial state there, together with Jehol and Inner Mongolia, under the nominal headship of the former heir to the Chinese throne, Hsuan-Tung (now living in Tientsin as Henry Pu-yi).[2] By the end of this period, the General Staff were being bluntly told from Mukden that the idea of an autonomous régime that would remain under Chinese suzerainty was unacceptable, while no interference by the League of Nations would be tolerated. On this last point, the General Staff and Minister of War readily agreed.[3]

The Cabinet's position was further weakened by local military initiatives, above all the bombing of Chinchow, which, apart from being intended to keep Chang Hsueh-liang on the run, was specifically aimed at forcing Tokyo into unambiguous support for the army in the field—the likelihood of international disapproval being recognised and calmly accepted.[4] Confidence was further shaken when, in mid-October, an extremist plot against the Government and existing political parties was uncovered in Tokyo.[5] The conspirators received only light sentences, Mori Kaku and other zealots redoubled their verbal attacks, and fears increased that the Kwantung Army (which had not, it seems, been directly involved in the plot) might openly defy the Government. As early as 6 October, Wakatsuki was privately saying that if public opinion were solid over Manchuria, he would follow it.[6] By the end of the period, his Ministry was on the verge of collapse.[7]

Meanwhile the possibility of fighting in North Manchuria had turned the attention of many observers towards the attitude of the Soviet Union. However, despite attacks in the Moscow press on Japan's intention of transforming Manchuria into another colony as it had Korea,[8] the official position was carefully reserved, with press denunciations of the League and Western imperialist powers also being licensed.[9] Soviet policy was, in fact, to remain one of watchful determination to avoid being dragged into a fight at a time of domestic turmoil and a place of inadequate preparation.[10] China, on the other hand, no longer had such an option. In her cities there was violent pressure, especially by students, for an all-out war against Japan, and C. T. Wang, the Foreign Minister, was assaulted by a crowd which stoned the Foreign Ministry in Nanking on 28 September.[11] With a volunteer movement

[1] See IMTFE, *Exhibits* 3422 F, G.

[2] *Taiheiyo senso e no michi*, II, 39–44; IMTFE, *Exhibits* 3479B–J; *Proceedings*, 18, 892 ff.; FO 371, F 6072/1391/10.

[3] Kwantung Army memorandum of 24 October and cable of 7 November 1931, Ogata, 102 ff.   [4] *Taiheiyo senso e no michi*, II, 85–8.

[5] See Storry, *The Double Patriots*, 86 ff.   [6] *Taiheiyo senso e no michi*, II, 163–7.

[7] Cf. Wakatsuki affidavit, IMTFE, *Exhibit*, 162; Shidehara deposition, ibid, 3479; Minami affidavit, ibid, 2435, and cross-examination, *Proceedings*, 19, 855.

[8] E.g., *Izvestia*, 16 October 1931.

[9] E.g., *New York Times*, 27 October 1931.

[10] See J. Erickson, *The Soviet High Command* (London, 1962), 357 ff.

[11] *New York Times*, 29 September 1931.

being set up, Chiang Kai-shek felt it politic to make dramatic promises of 'falling with other patriots if necessary'.[1] In a search for national unity, the Government began negotiations with the rival Canton régime, while talks on Manchuria with the Japanese Minister, Shigemitsu Mamoru, were broken off.

Diplomatic relations with Japan were not severed, however, nor did either side declare war. Instead, on 21 September, China appealed to the United States as a signatory of the Kellogg Pact to concern itself with 'the upholding of the principle of peaceful settlement of international disputes',[2] and to the League of Nations to seize itself of the dispute under article 11 of the Covenant.[3] Preoccupied with economic collapse and toiling with domestic politics, the West found itself involved.

Public reactions in the West

When examining both the public and private responses of the West during this early period of the crisis, together with that of November and December, it is important to bear in mind what was soon to become a fairly common assertion among the general criticisms that have been outlined in an earlier chapter.[4] By commentators like William Martin in the *Journal de Genève*,[5] by the *Manchester Guardian*, G. P. Gooch, Alfred Zimmern and others, it was to be held that this opening phase was the one when, with a little determination, Western governments could have brought the affair to a triumphant conclusion.[6] From the middle of 1932 this was to become Cecil's argument, too,[7] while the assertion that he was to make in his memoirs, that Japan's withdrawal from the Shanghai fighting in the spring of 1932 proved what could easily have been achieved earlier,[8] was to be echoed by the historian, Sarah Smith, when attacking the failure of the United States to cooperate wholeheartedly with the League from the outset.[9]

When one turns to the responses at the time, however, such easy confidence is as lacking in unofficial as it is in official circles. Instead, uncertainty and

[1] *New York Times*, 23 September, 1 October 1931; *North China Herald*, 6 October 1931.

[2] FRUS, 1931, III, 24.

[3] Official communications between the two combatants and the League will be found in annexes to the LNOJ for the period in question. An account of China's tactics at the League (her decision, for example, not to resort to articles 10 and 15 at the outset) will be found in W. W. Willoughby, *The Sino–Japanese Controversy and the League of Nations* (Baltimore, 1935). Willoughby was technical adviser to the Chinese delegation at the time.

[4] See above, 8ff.

[5] E.g., *Journal de Genève*, 19 February 1932. See P. de Azcarté (ed.), *William Martin: Un Grand Journaliste à Genève* (Geneva, 1970).

[6] See, e.g., Temperley, 97; Zimmern, 428; *Manchester Guardian*, 21–3 January 1932; *The Problems of Peace, 7th series*, 22–3.

[7] E.g., Cecil to St. G. Saunders, 23 March, 11 April 1932, Cecil Papers, Add. 51100.

[8] Cecil, 231–3. Cecil's assertion that 'nothing that occurred later modified these conclusions' appears to have been written before Pearl Harbour.

[9] Smith, 80, 226, 233, 237, 260.

caution were more prominent features. At Geneva, where the economic crisis dominated all thoughts,[1] news of the clash at Mukden was received, according to one eye-witness, 'with stupefaction and utter disbelief', and although press and public crowded in to hear what the Council might decide at its first meeting to consider the matter, there was little clear information as to what was actually taking place in the vast remoteness of Manchuria.[2] Moreover, despite the dialectical superiority of the principal Chinese delegate, Dr. Alfred Sze, over his Japanese rival, Yoshizawa Kenkichi, many observers suspected the accuracy of what he had to say. Only a few days earlier, Cecil had had to convey to Sze Britain's doubts, arising from the Thorburn case,[3] as to 'whether the Chinese Government really had sufficient authority to make it a useful member of the (League) Council'; now, on 25 September, he wrote to a friend that, while 'all the great Powers have been equally determined on trying to reach a settlement of the crisis', there was 'no doubt that the Chinese, after their manner, have enormously exaggerated what has been happening'.[4]

Even so, there was soon much uneasiness in and around the corridors of the League. With the Assembly concluding its session on 29 September, some of the representatives of smaller states disliked leaving matters entirely in the hands of the not very high-powered Council, especially since much of the latter's work was now being conducted in private, and within its ad hoc 'committee of five'—Cecil, Massigli for France, Curtius for Germany, Grandi for Italy, and Lerroux of Spain, who was the Council's chairman at the time.[5] Rumours also centred around the attitude of the American Government, and despite the excitement that was occasioned on 24 September, when Stimson let it be known that his country was in 'wholehearted sympathy' with the League's efforts and the Council's appeal for restraint,[6]

[1] E.g., Cecil to Reading, 1 and 21 September 1931, FO 800/226.

[2] This was despite the presence in China of Dr. L. W. Rajchman, Director of the League's Health Section and an ardent Sinophile. F. P. Walters, Chief of Section in Drummond's office, was also in China at the time, but in order to help remove Japanese suspicions he was sent to Japan, where, after discussing the crisis with Shidehara and Western diplomats, he appears to have modified his views on what could be achieved immediately. Interview with Mr. Walters, 12 December 1970. See below, 182.

[3] See above, 49,n.

[4] Cecil memorandum, 8 September 1931, Cecil Papers, Add. 51100; Cecil to Noel-Baker, 25 September 1931, ibid, Add. 51107. Cecil described Yoshizawa as 'almost inarticulate' and Sze as 'intelligent, but I think untrustworthy'. China had been elected to a non-permanent seat on the Council on September 14.

[5] At the secret meeting of the Council on 22 October, Sean Lester for Ireland was to query the practice of special consultations among the committee of five, and to request confirmation that no precedent was being established. 'A committee,' he wrote, 'which includes all the permanent and excludes representatives of the non-permanent members creates a breach in the Council which is not in accord with the spirit of equality in this remarkable international organisation.' LN Archives, R 6228. Cf. Zimmern, 381; Fleming, 398; Geneva Special Studies, II, Nos. 10 and 11.

[6] FRUS, 1931, III, 48–9; Cf. FRUS, Japan, 1931–1941, I, 9; DBFP, VIII, Nos. 519, 692.

it was already widely known that American disapproval, as well as Japanese opposition, had put paid to discussions concerning a possible commission of enquiry. No trace of this idea, or that of neutral observers, remained in the Resolution that was unanimously adopted by the Council on 30 September. This noted Japan's declared intention to withdraw her troops as soon as conditions permitted, together with China's promise to take responsibility for security in the areas so evacuated; it also urged a resumption of normal relations, and adjourned the Council until 24 October. 'In the special circumstances,' suggested Lerroux, 'a certain time has to be allowed for withdrawal . . . (and) I am inclined to think that no useful purpose would be served by continuing our discussions at the present moment.'[1] No deadline was set for the Japanese withdrawal, and no public reinforcement of the Resolution was forthcoming from Washington.

Hopes that the affair was now as good as settled[2] were shattered by the bombing of Chinchow, and after Lerroux had despatched a further appeal to Nanking and Tokyo, the Council reconvened at China's request on 13 October. Lord Reading led the British delegation, Briand took the chair in the absence of Lerroux, and Madariaga replaced the latter for Spain. A new tension now surrounded proceedings, together with renewed speculation concerning American policy; this persisted, despite the release of a message from Stimson to Drummond recalling the obligations of the Nine Power Treaty and Kellogg Pact,[3] and despite the electrifying news that Washington had accepted the Council's invitation, revealed on 16 October and opposed by Yoshizawa, to be represented at its discussions. Amidst jubilation, Prentiss Gilbert, the American Consul General in Geneva, took his seat at the Council table that evening—'an epoch in the world's endeavour to secure peace', as one spectator saw it.[4] Gilbert's speech, however, made it clear that he was there only in respect of the Kellogg Pact, having nothing to do with the machinery of the League; meanwhile the State Department had been quick to smooth over Japanese allegations that Stimson had sent an aggressive message to Tokyo concerning the Chinchow affair, and while Britain and other Council members announced on the 17th that they were drawing the attention of both Japan and China to their Kellogg undertakings, the United States followed suit only three days later.[5] Finally, no immediate and wholehearted American support was declared for the Resolution which the Council adopted against the single dissenting vote of Japan on 24 October. In this document, the Japanese were now invited to complete their withdrawal of troops to the railway zone within three weeks; the moment that was done, direct negotiations should begin between the two parties in dispute on all outstanding issues.[6] Under the unanimity requirement of article 11, Japan's vote deprived this Resolution of any binding character. But when

[1] LNOJ, December, 1931, 2307–9.

[2] E.g., Journal de Genève, 30 September 1931, for Martin's article, 'Un Grand Succès'.   [3] FRUS, 1931, III, 175–6.

[4] Geneva Special Studies, II, No. 11, 37. Cf. Journal de Genève, 18 October 1931; LNOJ, December, 1931, 2322–38.

[5] DBFP, VIII, No. 649; FRUS, Japan, 1931–1941, I, 27–9.

[6] LNOJ, December, 1931, 2338–62. For Martin's suggestions of collusion between Japan and the Western powers, see Journal de Genève, 23, 25 October 1931.

the Council then adjourned until 16 November, it had in effect staked its authority, together with that of the League as a whole, on securing Tokyo's compliance with its wishes.

Away from Geneva, the reactions of the press, of pressure groups and of private individuals in various Western countries would seem to have been even more cautious than was this new pronouncement on the part of the Council.[1] One could, of course, avoid uncertainty by exhibiting indifference to the whole affair, as the bulk of the Italian press were to do throughout (inclining towards Japan if anything).[2] Alternatively, one could unwaveringly proffer a single, neat interpretation, as did most of the French press in this period. From the outset, for example, Le Temps (which frequently reflected Government opinion) proclaimed that the League could only do more harm than good, and that direct negotiations alone could resolve an issue in which Japan, the bastion of order in the East, had much right on her side.[3] L'Echo de Paris was among several that followed this line, while Coty's Figaro and Léon Daudet's Action Française not only jeered at the League ('a large piece of cheese', Daudet called it), but found Japan's march towards destiny impressive. On the opposite wing, L'Humanité, needless to say, found incontrovertible evidence of an imperialist plot against the Soviet Union. In between, Léon Blum's Populaire called for swift action by the League,[4] but although Herriot's Radical-Socialist L'Ère Nouvelle and Daladier's La République were also critical of Japan, the former recognised the difficulties facing the League, while the latter, looking towards the Rhine, was quick to find reasons why France should not become involved.

As in the United States, no opportunity yet existed in France to debate the matter in the legislature. In Britain, on the other hand, there was at least an election in the offing, but Manchuria did not figure as an issue. Party divisions were being melted down and recast, and over foreign policy grew sharp and clear only some time afterwards. In the press, the Manchester Guardian and the New Statesman roundly condemned Japanese militarism,[5] but this did not exclude a readiness to believe that a settlement was near,[6]

[1] Apart from the primary sources cited below, reference should also be made to E. Tupper and G. McReynolds, Japan in American Public Opinion (New York, 1937), 283 ff.; Fleming, 375 ff.; Bassett, Democracy and Foreign Policy, passim; Geneva Special Studies, op. cit.

[2] See the summaries in DS 793.94/2118, 4622; 793.94 Commission/463. On 1 December 1932, the American Chargé in Rome was to describe public opinion there as 'tending to behold Japan in the light of an oriental Italy, materially poor and demographically rich, clamouring for an outlet which others will not let her have'. Ibid, 793.94 Commission/673. The German press exhibited considerable interest in the crisis, nationalist organs showing admiration for Japan, but the preponderant approach being one of sympathy for China. See, e.g., DS 793.94/5839; 793.94 Commission/478. For both countries, see also the Chatham House press files on the crisis.   [3] E.g., Le Temps, 19, 27 September, 12 October 1931.

[4] E.g., L'Humanité, 11 November 1931; Le Populaire, 15 October 1931.

[5] E.g., Manchester Guardian, 21, 22 September, 9 October 1931.

[6] See the changes of emphasis on the part of the Manchester Guardian, 1, 7, 15 October 1931.

and the subsequently-exasperated *Manchester Guardian* was ready to declare
on 24 September that the League 'must act with circumspection . . . (and) to
strengthen the forces which are striving for peace in Japan'. On 26 October,
the same paper thought that the League 'had done all it could for the
moment'. On the opposite side, a few papers like the *Daily Mail* and *Daily
Express* adopted an openly pro-Japanese stance, while the expatriate
lobbyist, O. M. Green, initially did the same in the *Daily Telegraph*.[1] *The
Times*, too, while deploring the methods adopted by the Japanese army,
recalled that their country, which in Manchuria had 'created a flourishing
oasis in a howling desert of Chinese misrule', had legitimate grievances in the
case. Thus, that army

> has for all intents and purposes become—after its initial well-prepared and
> warlike invasion—a militarily equipped police force in a disordered part of
> China where the Central Chinese Government can exercise little or no authority
> . . . It may not be inopportune to recall that in a district far less remote from
> Nanking the Chinese Government has so far quite failed to bring to justice the
> murderers of the Englishman, Mr. Thorburn, or to give any satisfaction to the
> British Government in spite of repeated diplomatic representations.[2]

Despite this sympathy for Japan's underlying grievances, however, even
business and residents' associations in China were not seeking to exert any
strong or unified pressure in a pro-Japanese direction in this period. Among
the British press at Shanghai, moreover, there were strong condemnations of
the 'cynically conceived acts' of the Kwantung Army that was now 'running
amok . . . (at a time when) the Chinese have displayed . . . remarkable
restraint',[3] while large firms contacted the Foreign Office in order to warn
against the likelihood of Japan's shutting the door to British trade in
Manchuria, as she had in Korea, if she were allowed to seize the area.[4] It was
The Times, too, that reminded its readers that

> the fundamental issue at stake is really of vital importance to future international
> relations . . . Are ultimatums and force to rule the relations between Sovereign
> States, or arbitration and judicial settlement? That is the immediate and funda-
> mental question; and the answer to be given to it may be of immense importance
> to the future stability of the world. That consideration must for the moment take
> precedence over the merits of the dispute itself.[5]

The L.N.U. could hardly have done better—indeed, they did not do better,
and hardly stirred in public, let alone mention the possibility of sanctions.
Prompted by Philip Noel-Baker, Gilbert Murray wrote to *The Times* to keep
Reading up to the mark,[6] but, like the *Manchester Guardian*, he was reason-

---

[1] See *Daily Telegraph*, 21 September 1931. Green had changed his emphasis by
the time he contributed to the *Sunday Times*, 27 September 1931.
[2] *The Times*, 21 September, 12, 21 October, 2, 7 November 1931. Cf. DBFP, VIII,
No. 473.   [3] *North China Herald*, 22, 29 September, 6, 27 October 1931.
[4] See Reichardt and Co. to Secretary of State, 24 September 1931; British
American Tobacco Co. to Pratt, 6 October 1931; John Swire and Sons to Secretary
of State, 28 January 1932; respectively, FO 371, F 5179/1391/10, F 5415/1391/10,
F 785/1/10.   [5] *The Times*, 16 October 1931.
[6] Noel-Baker to Murray, 11 October; Murray to Noel-Baker, 12 October 1931,
Murray Papers; *The Times*, 14 October, 1931.

ably satisfied by what had been achieved by the end of the period. 'Step by step, the Council has done extraordinarily well,' he wrote to Cecil, and although the problem was 'about as hard as one could possibly make it', the strength of the League was clearly 'quite at its maximum'.[1] Cecil himself, as will be seen below, was not displeased either. Thus, although the widespread pro-League sentiment of the public continued to set outer limits to what the Government might or might not do in the affair, there was also sufficient coolness, caution and disagreement to make it easy for policy-makers to shape in their own minds an image of that public opinion which coincided with their own views, formed by other and far more powerful factors.

In the degree of attention paid to public opinion there was to be a contrast between Britain and the United States, where the images held of it, however inaccurate, had long been 'the major limitation operating upon all American policy makers'.[2] Even so, American opinion exhibited several features similar to those in Britain, and in Washington, as in London, it was to play an essentially reinforcing role, especially where Hoover was concerned. Despite the goodwill towards China that existed from the outset[3] and despite a few early condemnations of Japan by individuals like Borah[4] and papers like those of the Scripps–Howard group, there was also much sympathy for the problems Japan was having to face in China and in general, demographic and economic terms.[5] 'There is here no such thing as an "aggressor" and a "non-aggressor",' wrote Walter Lippmann, setting out on a somewhat swerving course of commentary on the crisis. 'There are, if anything, two aggressors, the Chinese pushed into Manchuria by the pressure of their conditions, and the Japanese pushed by the pressure of theirs.'[6] Criticism of Japan did increase after the Chinchow episode, but conditions in Tokyo helped ensure that reports from there were usually close to Japan's own propaganda line.[7] Within the United States, pro-League groups produced no concerted call for sanctions,[8] and the numerous papers which approved the

[1] Murray to Cecil, 23 October 1931, Murray Papers.   [2] Osgood, 359.

[3] The genuine nature of this goodwill is not to be doubted, but in some quarters it was reinforced by dictates of self-interest. For example, the supplying of credits to China to enable her to purchase surplus American grain in the face of her severe floods was obviously of great importance to the desperate producers. This subject also had political implications. In a letter of October 1931, for example, that came before Hoover, it was suggested that, in the light of local surpluses and hardship, renewed credits to facilitate Chinese purchases 'would help immensely in insuring (that) Washington and Oregon go Republican.' Hoover Papers, Foreign Affairs, China, Misc. Early in September, the U.S. Farm Board had agreed to sell China fifteen million bushels of wheat on extended payment terms.

[4] Speech at inauguration of Borah Foundation, 24 September 1931, Borah Papers, box 328.

[5] E.g., New York Times, 24, 30 September, 6 October 1931; Sherwood Eddy in Problems of the Peace, 7th Series, 237. The New York Daily News expressed open support for Japan.   [6] Lippmann, Interpretations, 1931–3, 188–9.

[7] A valuable paper on 'U.S. Press Coverage of Japan, 1931–1941' was provided for the Hakone Conference by Ernest May.

[8] The failure of the Interorganization Council on Disarmament to reach a clear position on sanctions is traced in W. Cole's Hakone paper, 'The Role of Private Groups'.

Administration's policy of limited cooperation with Geneva remained cautious as to what could be achieved:

> It is disheartening to have to confess that the Powers are not in a position to do more, to vindicate law and order majestically and set justice upon her throne. They are not. The Manchurian issue lies beyond the present resources of our civilization, and the fact that the League, under the guidance of Secretary Stimson, has recognised this limitation is not a sign that diplomats lack good will, but that they are capable of acknowledging an unpleasant truth.[1]

So far, such American opinions had their parallels in Britain. Despite the odd Amery or *Daily Express*, however, there was nothing in the latter country to match the volume and ferocity of the anti-League, anti-involvement outcry in the United States. (The French Right provided some comparison.) Borah's condemnation of Japan was followed in the same speech by an even fiercer rejection of any risking of war in order to maintain peace; McCormick's *Chicago Daily Tribune* and Hearst's *San Francisco Examiner* were only extreme examples (the *Washington Post* was slightly more restrained in the same cause) of those who poured scorn on 'the worthless league of nations (that) reaffirms its futility every time it is confronted with an obligation out of its covenant', and attacked even the restricted cooperation symbolised by Gilbert's presence at the Council table.[2] 'The American people,' declared Representative Hamilton Fish, 'are not willing to be forced into a foreign war over disputes between nations halfway across the world, through the meddling and bungling of the State Department.'[3]

This cry to keep out at all costs was accompanied in some quarters by another feature that was again scarcely present in Britain: the perception of a direct, long-term Japanese threat to the United States and her possessions, and the desire for increased armaments to deter or prepare for such an eventuality. 'At any moment that our defences are vulnerable . . . Japan will not hesitate to strike'; 'Since (1921), lustful Japanese eyes have turned towards Magdalena Bay and Lower California'; 'In a world still warlike, let America forget about the fatuities of disarmament.'[4] Such views were not predominant in the country at the time, and outside the Navy were scarcely reflected in official circles. The disarmament cause, led by Borah and the peace societies, remained strong.[5] Yet coming events in the Far East were to contribute towards a growing anxiety. Even in 1933, suggestions of an eventual American–Japanese clash would still be widely discounted, but for some men a new question mark would by then hang over disarmament and Pacific relations alike.

[1] Lippmann, *Interpretations, 1931–3*, 189–90.

[2] E.g., *Chicago Daily Tribune*, 29 September 1931; *San Francisco Examiner*, 29 September, 14 October 1931; *Washington Post*, 20 September, 11, 12, 16, 18, 23 October 1931.

[3] *United States Daily*, 16 October 1931.

[4] Respectively, *Chicago Daily Tribune*, 23 September 1931; Senator Moses (of the Senate Foreign Relations Committee), quoted in *New York Times*, 14 November 1931; *San Francisco Examiner*, 25 September 1931; cf. *Washington Post*, 17 October 1931.

[5] See, e.g., Borah Speech, I October 1931, advocating further cuts in the Navy's budget. Borah Papers, box 328.

The shaping of policy: London, Paris and Berlin

Domestic opinion was not consciously taken into account, either in the Foreign Office or Cabinet, when shaping British policy in this period. As suggested above, however, it was not too difficult to form a picture of widespread sympathy for Japan's grievances and—even easier—of general opposition to anything in the nature of coercion. 'The bulk of "civilised" opinion,' Vansittart wrote a few months later '—and the uncivilised are untroubled by opinions—was with Japan.'[1] Soon afterwards, J. H. Thomas would likewise suggest that the Dominions' dislike of the sanctions provisions of the Covenant was 'very widely shared here',[2] while in the autumn of 1932 Hoare was to be 'sure that the great body of centre and right opinion . . . will not tolerate anything that can be construed into aggressive or hostile action against Japan'.[3] As the crisis drew to a close, Simon, too, in his tentative fashion, would be subscribing to the view that 'British public opinion hitherto had perhaps been somewhat pro-Japanese',[4] and although the President of the Board of Trade spoke on the same occasion of growing hostility in Lancashire towards Japan, he did so in the context of industrial competition, not military aggression. Even Cecil, anxious for loud public support, felt bound to acknowledge privately in 1932 that he found 'the richer class very unsound and even the poorer class very ignorant' over the crisis.[5] It could scarcely be said that the middle class either, however defined, had been straining to sacrifice itself on the barricades of collective security.

For the moment, certainly, the views of the bald-headed man on the back of the London omnibus were less significant in official eyes than the intentions of the generals in Tokyo or the temper of the Japanese populace as a whole. Early warnings that there were plans 'towards taking over in Manchuria' had been received in the Foreign Office with interest rather than anxiety from the middle of the summer onwards,[6] but once the Mukden incident occurred (the news reached Chang Hsueh-liang as he dined in Peking with Lampson and Admiral Kelly), Japanese actions and intentions received close scrutiny. Thereafter, the position of the Kwantung Army was usually known within a few days, as were individual incidents of aggression like the air attack on a Mukden to Tientsin train. It took rather longer to obtain information on the general state of order or disorder which figured so prominently in the Japanese arguments; by 9 October, however, it was learned from observers sent up from Peking that the Kwantung Army made

[1] CP 4 (32), CAB 27/476.
[2] Memorandum of 10 March 1932, CP 95 (32), CAB 24/228. Throughout the crisis, both Foreign and Dominions Office files, together with Cabinet conclusions, show that, while the Dominions were kept informed of Britain's general policy, they contributed almost nothing in the way of advice or even demands for discussion at government level. They *existed* as a defence responsibility, that was all. Delegates at Geneva and High Commissioners in London, however, were invited to air their views from time to time. In general, see DO 35/141, 144, 146, 147, 167 171, 178.
[3] Hoare to Simon, 11 September 1932, FO 800/287.
[4] Cabinet conclusions, 8 February 1933, CAB 23/75.
[5] Cecil to Noel-Baker, 7 March 1932, Cecil Papers, Add. 51107.
[6] E.g., DBFP, VIII, Nos. 491, 493, 494, 500.

no secret of preparing for 'further positive action' and, ten days later, that they were 'making preparations to stay in positions occupied for the winter'. The possibility of a Japanese-sponsored independence movement was also acknowledged, while from the spot Lampson's Military Attaché confirmed the Minister's initial diagnosis that they were witnessing 'a carefully worked plot and disguised scheme'.[1]

There was thus direct confirmation of at least the substance of the protest being made by Sze at Geneva, where he was already talking of 'the application of other articles of the Covenant'.[2] Nanking was also appealing to London to send observers, while offering reassurances that efforts were being made to curb anti-Japanese excesses in the rest of China, that war would not be declared, and that even a counter-attack on Mukden would be avoided in the interests of preserving a correct stance under the Covenant.[3] In addition, Eugene Chen, a prominent member of the Canton régime, pronounced himself to be in favour of direct talks with Japan.[4] Nevertheless, an unofficial suggestion from London that Nanking should not make troop withdrawals a prior condition for such negotiations produced consternation in Chinese Government circles,[5] and British diplomats, besides testifying to the spontaneity of anti-Japanese outbursts among the public, warned that 'if the League . . . does not produce an alleviation of the crisis, the Government will be discredited and either have to go or yield to popular clamour. Further, there may be an anti-foreign reaction . . . (and) chaos may ensue'.[6]

Apart from suggesting that there was a parallel between the present case and Britain's action at Shanghai in 1927, Tokyo's assurances to London were meanwhile much the same as those being expressed by Yoshizawa at Geneva: troop withdrawals were continuing, and a League commission of enquiry or observers would only serve to 'needlessly excite Japanese public opinion'.[7] On the other hand the 'fundamental principles' that Yoshizawa began talking about in public were soon known by the British delegation and others to include, not only mutual Sino–Japanese undertakings of non-aggression, an end to anti-Japanese agitation, and respect for China's territorial integrity, but also recognition by China of Japan's position and privileges in Manchuria under those agreements of 1915 which Nanking was determined to repudiate as having been extracted by force majeur.[8] From Geneva on 21 October, Reading confessed that the dispute was 'a tougher nut to crack than I anticipated when I left London'.[9]

[1] Ibid, Nos. 506, 511, 536, 544, 557, 578, 580, 581, 588, 597, 638, 641, 650.

[2] LNOJ, *December, 1931*, 2270, 2282, 2312, 2317.

[3] E.g., DBFP, VIII, Nos. 512, 556, 572, 610, 612, 626, 631, 641, 648, 653.

[4] Ibid, Nos. 553, 635.

[5] Ibid, Nos. 586, 599, 604, 634, 616. Lampson, having successfully appealed to London to withhold the suggestion, nevertheless passed it on unofficially, which Vansittart termed 'very odd diplomacy'. FO 371, F 5587/1391/10.

[6] See Lampson to Reading, 10 October 1931, DBFP, VIII, No. 603. Cf. ibid, Nos. 545, 547, 555, 565, 574, 591, 603, 609, 642.

[7] E.g., ibid, Nos. 519, 531, 542, 552, 620; LNOJ, *December, 1931*, 2267, 2279–81, 2289, 2314–5, 2347, 2350 and annex 1334.

[8] DBFP, VIII, Nos. 646, 653, 680.

[9] Reading to Vansittart, 21 October 1931, ibid, No. 672. Having failed in his technical arguments to prevent an American representative attending the Council

Lindley's advice from Tokyo was broadly in accord with Japan's own case, and from the outset, although he came in for some sharp criticism within the Foreign Office, he was to play an important part in shaping those considerations which were to dominate British policy throughout the crisis. Lindley saw himself as being in a country which, through little fault of its own, was thoroughly disorientated where international politics were concerned.[1] He also saw Britain as being entangled in a situation of general chaos throughout the world:

> 'The fact is,' he wrote privately a year later, 'that Wilson's doctrine of self-determination and the existence of the League of Nations have given such backward countries as China and Persia, as well as the newly constituted States, the idea that they can make themselves as intolerable as they like without suffering any of the consequences which would have followed such behaviour before 1914. The world is, in short, in the position of a country where duelling has been made illegal before the population have learned proper manners; and, however high-handed the Japanese have been, they have at least taught China that this sort of behaviour still brings unpleasant results.'[2]

His sympathies, therefore, were with Japan, as he made clear in this early period to both the Foreign Office and the King. 'The Chinese,' he wrote, 'have consistently attempted to undermine (the) Japanese position, which after all rests largely on treaty rights'; there was also 'the obvious probability that Japanese action in Manchuria will react favourably on British interests in China'.[3]

Lindley was soon to accept that the Mukden incident might well have been instigated by the Japanese, and that in Tokyo a desperate struggle was being waged by the Government to retain its authority. Nevertheless, his impression at this early stage was that action had been taken 'solely to force (the) Chinese Government to settle many long-standing disputes in (Manchuria)', and that whoever was directing Japanese policy 'would not be found unreasonable' if only the Chinese would have the sense to negotiate. The wide distribution of Japanese citizens in a disordered Manchuria provided a 'convincing explanation' for the delay in withdrawing troops to the railway zone, and if counsels of moderation were needed, it was in Nanking rather than Tokyo. Above all —and this note was resounding loudly in Whitehall long after the others had been forgotten or rejected—no Japanese government could now retreat over the issue, and would receive 'unanimous public support' for any action thought necessary to defend 'interests believed by all Japanese to be vital to the life of the nation'.[4]

(which the majority evaded by treating it as a procedural matter), Yoshizawa blocked all Briand's efforts to obtain sufficient reassurances to enable China to negotiate before a final withdrawal of Japanese troops.

[1] DBFP, VIII, No. 495.
[2] Lindley to Wigram, 26 October 1932, RA G.V, P 510/55.
[3] E.g., Lindley to Reading, 17, 20 September 1931, DBFP, VIII, Nos. 503, 509; Lindley to King George Vth, 30 September 1931, RA G.V, P 510/45.
[4] E.g., DBFP, VIII, Nos. 508, 516, 521, 531, 536, 550, 569, 570, 589, 595, 608, 637, 658. On 12 October, Lindley did concede that 'if America made serious threat of economic or financial hostility Japanese Government might be obliged to give way', but he withdrew even this qualification later. Ibid, No. 624.

As tension increased, Lindley was to feel that Tokyo had become 'a madhouse'—a description which, like the tone of some of his despatches, reminds one of Sir Nevile Henderson's feelings in Berlin some years later. Meanwhile in Peking, Lampson had long resigned himself to the confused Chinese political scene; yet for all China's faults, he now saw her as the injured party over Manchuria, a belief that was shared by Admiral Kelly, in marked contrast to the views of many senior officers in the West.[1] Lampson did urge restraint on the Chinese leaders, but he was unable to understand Lindley's suggestion that this was more needed than similar action in Tokyo. 'It is like counselling moderation to the hare with the hounds already close on his heels.'[2] Moreover he quickly raised a wider consideration, for which Lindley had little sympathy:

> 'Seen from this end,' he wrote on October 10, 'the whole structure of our post-war organisation seems at stake . . . If the League machinery and Kellogg Pact now fail, I submit that they and all their sponsors will suffer a set-back, (the) extent of which is hard to estimate . . . It seems to me imperative in all our interests that some form of definite action be (?taken) such as arbitration or (a) commission, or that the League unequivocally go on record as to what it holds to be the wrongs and rights of the case and should not wind up its endeavours in a colourless formula—viz., patience.'[3]

It was in keeping with the underlying ambiguity of British foreign policy as a whole, described in the previous chapter, that both Lindley's realpolitik and Lampson's wider view were to find expression in the line London was to pursue during the crisis. Priorities, however, were unavoidable, and for those inclined towards Lindley's thesis, despatches from Peking were not devoid of reinforcing material, especially when they accepted, well into October, that the safety of Japanese nationals outside the railway zone was 'by no means effectively assured'.[4] Even from Geneva, the consideration advanced by Lampson was being echoed with less than total vigour and clarity. Senior members of the League's Secretariat who were in China were emphasising, it is true, their belief that her cause was one of universal significance.[5] Drummond, too, was voicing his concern for the future and for the success of the Disarmament Conference, while in the light of his dependence on the major powers for both information and resources, any comment on his views must allow for the probability that they were conditioned to some extent by those of London, Paris and Washington.[6] It was he, however, who chose to

---

[1] See C. in C. China, 'Report of Proceedings', September 1931, ADM 125/69.
[2] Lampson to Reading, 10 October 1931, DBFP, VIII, No. 596. Cf. ibid, Nos. 510, 575, 581, 612.
[3] Lampson to Reading, 10 October 1931, ibid, No. 603. Cf. ibid, Nos. 522, 629.
[4] Ibid, Nos. 578, 650. Comfort of a different kind could be derived from reports from Moscow indicating the Soviet Union's likely passivity. Ibid, Nos. 525, 533, 549, 627, 671.
[5] E.g., ibid, Nos. 585, 618.
[6] E.g., ibid, Nos. 559, 567. In the files of the League there are a few reports from Paris and Berlin, and rather more from London. In a letter of 11 October, Massigli reported to Drummond that, according to French sources, 'la situation à l'intérieure de la Province est rendue grave par la présence de nombreux brigands et de déserteurs'. LN. Archives, R 1869.

withhold from the Council information that the Kwantung Army was staying put, in the hope of obtaining further news that 'would show a certain progress';[1] his own inclination, it seems, was towards circumspection and the avoidance of any pressure that might handicap Shidehara in his domestic struggle against extremists, and remarks of his to American diplomats will shortly be seen to reinforce such an interpretation.

From his place in the British delegation at Geneva, Cecil showed himself more ready than Drummond or the Foreign Office to remonstrate with the Japanese and to sustain the Chinese in the correctness of their position.[2] In his case, again, it must be recalled that once the Foreign Office had got a grip on the situation, his public utterances were bound to be conditioned to some extent by instructions from London. Even so, he was clearly less certain as to the right course than his memoirs were to suggest, and in the next chapter letters to close friends will be cited which overcome the problems of interpreting public statements. Nor has any evidence been found, either from the days in question or afterwards, to suggest that it was at the dictation of London that Cecil shifted his position at the Council between 22 and 25 September. On the former date, he emphasised the need for troop withdrawals on the lines of the draft Model Treaty (this was approved by the Government) and for taking the Greco-Bulgarian crisis as 'the locus classicus as to policy and procedure' (this was rejected in the Foreign Office, but only some time afterwards); on the 25th, however, he was agreeing publicly with Yoshizawa that 'primarily, the question of the dispute was a matter for the parties and not for the Council to deal with unless it came before the latter under Article 15', the present business being solely 'to safeguard the peace of nations'.[3] Indeed already, at a secret meeting on the 23rd, he had observed that Manchuria's 'remoteness from Geneva and the difficulty of communications must be taken into account. The Council had been well advised to act circumspectly'.[4] The *Manchester Guardian* had better reason than it knew for its comment soon afterwards that 'Lord Cecil's diplomacy at the last meetings was so extraordinarily diplomatic that he appeared in one speech to be undoing what he had achieved in another'.[5]

Like many others, Cecil had believed that matters were already improving by the end of September.[6] He was becoming more alarmed by 18 October, when he sat down with Massigli, Madariaga and Erik Colban of Norway to draw up a report on measures that the League might adopt should Japan

[1] DBFP, VIII, Nos. 573, 582, 585; FRUS, 1931, III, 260–1; Drummond's awareness of the problems of the Tokyo scene was sharpened by his Japanese Under Secretary-General, Sugimura Yotaro.

[2] See, e.g., Patteson to Reading, 24 October 1931, DBFP, VIII, No. 681; minutes attached to telegram from Mukden Chamber of Commerce to Cecil, 7 October 1931, FO 371, F 5502/1391/10. Cecil's views could have been included in the discussion of the debate within the Foreign Office. Unlike Cadogan, however, he was not a permanent official; therefore I have chosen to consider him alongside Drummond who also had links with, but was not of, the Foreign Office. Cecil's contributions in unofficial circles such as the L.N.U. will be noted separately.

[3] LNOJ, *December, 1931*, 2270, 2284; DBFP, VIII, No. 514.

[4] LN. Archives, R 6228.

[5] *Manchester Guardian*, 10 October 1931.

[6] DBFP, VIII, No. 539. Cf. Nos. 526, 540.

remain obdurate.[1] Yet even this document stressed the problems rather than the opportunities of further action—contrary to the impression later conveyed by Cecil in a passage in his memoirs which alleged that 'to (Reading) and his colleagues it seemed a matter of relatively small moment what happened in Manchuria'.[2] 'Apart from the Covenant,' the report admitted, 'it would seem doubtful whether such action as Japan has taken . . . would normally be regarded as an adequate reason for [a third party] interrupting diplomatic relations', and unless the American ambassador also were withdrawn 'the gesture would lose almost all its moral effect'. Similarly, a severance of economic relations 'would be quite useless without the association of the United States and probably Russia', and indeed any action under articles 10, 11, 15 or 16 would also require at least 'the benevolent neutrality' of the former. Cecil's main hope remained the one he had emphasised in 1919, and even there he was ready to display some caution:

> 'Let us remember always,' he observed at a public meeting of the Council on 24 October, 'that the chief . . . weapon at the command of the League is the support of the public opinion of the world. If the Council of the League were to go too fast, were to outstrip that opinion, it would not have its support. It is of the utmost importance that our deliberations—conducted with all the speed that is possible, no doubt—should yet be rather behind than in front of the opinion of the world.'[3]

Of Cecil's colleagues on the Council, Madariaga was the sharpest in questioning Yoshizawa's bland assurances.[4] From the other major powers, however, there was much of that circumspection of which Cecil approved. Grandi played little part in proceedings, although Italy, like France and Germany, was ready to join in common appeals for restraint. Over French policy in particular there hung questions that were likely to heighten any apprehension in London of being left in an exposed position vis-à-vis an irate Japan. Even Briand, Chairman of the Council after 13 October, could not dispel such fears, however much he might strive in public to emphasise what the League was achieving.[5] Quite apart from his own physical decline and private caution (which will appear more fully in the next chapter), his grip on the Quai d'Orsay was clearly limited. Assurances at Geneva, for example, that France would join in a remonstrance in Tokyo were followed by a delay that Vansittart felt obliged to put down to 'incompetence or illfaith', resulting in Britain's being 'manoeuvred into isolated action . . . which could only be interpreted by the Japanese Government as inspired by a less friendly feeling towards them than other countries cherished'.[6] From Paris,

---

[1] Ibid, No. 664. In discussing this memorandum with me, M. Massigli has recalled that he did at the time have 'the illusion', as he put it, that economic sanctions might be both practicable and efficacious. As he pointed out, an operation of such a kind was virtually unknown territory.

[2] Cecil, 225–6.

[3] LNOJ, December, 1931, 2360.

[4] E.g., ibid, 2352.

[5] Ibid, 2321.

[6] Vansittart to Tyrrell, 6 October 1931, DBFP, VIII, No. 563. Cf. ibid, Nos. 520, 528, 543; minute by McKillop on No. 529, FO 371, F 5131/1391/10.

Tyrrell wrote of 'the Léger influence in Far Eastern questions',[1] and while it was known that the French Ambassador in Tokyo believed that the Chinese 'deserved all they had got',[2] the Head of the Quai d'Orsay's Far Eastern Department informed a British diplomat that at Geneva Briand

> would not lose sight of the fact that the question now at issue ... could not be treated exactly as if it were a difficulty between two European Powers. It must be remembered that several Powers had the right, either by treaty or by custom, to send troops to China ... In the action which they had taken the Japanese had perhaps gone too far. None the less their action could not be treated as an act of war ... If the Council allowed itself to be influenced too greatly by the letter of its obligations under the Covenant, it might wreck the whole League organisation.[3]

So much was observed in London at the time, but it is worth turning aside briefly in order to dispel an idea that was not only widely entertained then, but has continued to be raised by historians since: that there existed a secret understanding between France and Japan, involving their Far Eastern possessions and their attitudes at the Disarmament Conference. The evidence available suggests that there was no such thing. In the records of the Quai d'Orsay, the Foreign Minister appears to have made no reference to the matter until January 1932, and when he and his senior officials then did so (in response to American press accusations in particular) it was to scornfully dismiss the idea in their secret telegrams.[4] Nor are there any indications to the contrary in the messages exchanged between the Quai and their Ambassador in Tokyo, Martel. But perhaps the most conclusive piece of evidence is the fact that, as will be related in due course, the Japanese were secretly to approach France for just such an understanding in the late summer of 1932, a move which would have been unnecessary had one already existed. (Not only was no mention then to be made on either side of a deal in the preceding period, but in private the Quai d'Orsay was to describe even the old 1907 agreement concerning spheres of interest as having only qualified validity.) What *did* exist was a determination to avoid becoming deeply involved in an anti-Japanese campaign at a time when a European crisis appeared to be not far away. Thus, when Massigli had cabled from Geneva on 24 September, asking for instructions and urging that any admission of weakness on the part of the Council would have grave repercussions, he was told that a démarche must embrace China as well as Japan.[5] This set the mood for the country's policy throughout the coming months.

If the French local interest in the Far East was obvious (and the Dutch,

---

[1] DBFP, VIII, No. 605. Alexis Léger, shortly afterwards Secretary General of the Quai d'Orsay, was Briand's Chef de Cabinet at the time. M. Léger, whose influence on French policy was to be considerable in 1932–3, has always declined to discuss this period with historians, French or otherwise.

[2] DBFP, VIII, Nos. 528, 636.

[3] Memorandum of 10 October 1931, FO 371, F 5689/1391/10.

[4] Berthelot to Claudel, 31 January 1932, AQD, T 74–6; Foreign Ministry to Claudel, 21, 23 February 1932, ibid, T 220–1, 223; Claudel to Foreign Ministry, 24 February 1932, ibid.

[5] Massigli to Foreign Ministry, 24 September; Foreign Ministry to Massigli, 25 September 1931, AQD, T 74–6.

too, were tiptoeing around with great care[1]), Germany, even without any territory of her own at risk, was also reacting with caution. By comparison with Paris, the policy of Berlin received little attention in London in this period—or, indeed, throughout the crisis—but the Auswärtiges Amt was only too content that this should be so. From the outset, the German desire was to remain as passive as possible, while hoping that the League's prestige could somehow be preserved. Various groups within official, as well as unofficial, circles—the army, business interests in China and Japan, and the Nazis, for example—were to display widely differing reactions to the new conflict;[2] but official policy sought to preserve both Germany's growing economic links with China and her good relations with Japan, who had already adopted a helpful stance over Memel and reparations and whose friendship was all the more attractive as the European scene darkened. The likelihood that France, too, was taking care to keep in with Tokyo provided added grounds for German caution.[3] Thus as early as 24 September the delegation at Geneva were being instructed to adopt a reserved attitude and to take no part in an anti-Japanese front;[4] they were again reminded of the need to be passive, before the new meetings in October.[5] As part of the balancing act, the German delegate (to Chinese alarm) was the only one to vote with the Japanese for submitting to legal experts the question of an American presence at the Council table, while he then voted with the majority in favour of the invitation to Washington.[6] The fate of the League remained a matter of concern—ironically, there were similarities with French fears from mid-1932 onwards in Berlin's anxiety lest Japan's example should encourage another power, i.e. France, to take the law into her own hands[7]—but strict neutrality was seen to rule out any initiative at Geneva.[8]

---

[1] See, e.g., DS 793.94/2289. The Dutch Minister of Colonies was reported as saying that the real danger in the Far East came from the Soviet Union, not Japan. For the brief, low-key references to the issue in the Dutch Parliament, where only a Communist member urged that Japan should be coerced, see *Rijksbegrooting voor het Dienstjaar 1932*, III, 22nd Session, 627–651.

[2] For example, the German Ambassador in Tokyo, Ernst Voretzsch, emphasised throughout that the bulk of foreign opinion locally was pro-Japanese, and that Japan was determined not to be thwarted. He also raised the possibility of closer German–Japanese cooperation, with economic advantages in mind. See, e.g., AA, serial K 2088/K 555771; serial L 1780/L 517580–3; serial 3088H/D 624337, 624344–6, 624458, 624479–80, 624502–3.

[3] See, e.g., German delegation to Foreign Ministry, 26 September 1931, AA, serial 3088 H/D 624273; Hoesch to Foreign Ministry, 4 February, 1932, ibid, D 624471–3. The reactions of the Soviet Union were also being carefully watched. See, e.g., AA, serial K 2088/K 555997–9.

[4] Bülow to Bernstorff, 24 September 1931, AA, serial K 2088/K 555438.

[5] Meyer memorandum, 12 October 1931, ibid, K 555855.

[6] See ibid, K 555965–6, 555983, 556003, 556013, 556049, 556068, 556086, 556089–90, 556097–8. Germany also sought thereby to prevent a precedent being set for majority decisions being taken in the Council on matters of substance.

[7] See, e.g., Bülow memorandum, 12 November 1932, ibid, K 557358–9.

[8] For a summary of Germany policy to date, see an Abteilung IV memorandum of 8 November 1932, AA, serial 5551 H/E 388036–61, which concluded: 'In

It was American, not German, policy which concerned officials in London, however. Here again the message received privately was above all one of caution. Washington would 'back the League wholeheartedly' in its search for peace, but it would frown on any action at Geneva, such as the despatching of a commission of enquiry, that would 'enable (the) military party (in Japan) to arouse national feeling and enlist national support' against Shidehara.[1] Nor should any attempt be made to transfer the initiative across the Atlantic.[2] Others must invoke the Kellogg Pact in the first instance, while they should remember that the State Department would have to pay close attention to the tendency of its public 'to revolt against close cooperation with the League'. 'Fear of exasperating sentiment in Japan' was also acknowledged by Stimson to be another of the constraining factors which had led him, for example, to seek to withdraw Gilbert from the Council's proceedings after only three days. In relaying such messages, moreover, the British Chargé d'Affaires in Washington judged the Secretary of State's apprehensions to be 'fully justified'.[3]

Within a few days of the Mukden incident, in other words, the Foreign Office was receiving ample confirmation of the image it already possessed of the limits and uncertainty of American cooperation. Meanwhile the only man in Whitehall who might at another time have sought strenuously to put a more optimistic interpretation on this aspect of the situation, MacDonald, was submerged with his Cabinet colleagues in the financial crisis and in the explosive question of whether and on what basis to call a general election.[4] After briefly noting on 22 September Reading's approval of Cecil's Geneva efforts, and his intention of keeping Washington informed,[5] the Cabinet did not discuss the Far Eastern crisis again until 11 November. No Cabinet committee was set up to watch the matter; scarcely a mention of it appears in the diaries and letters of senior politicians. On 9 October, MacDonald, who had been prodded by someone in Geneva (probably Drummond), did request Reading to join Briand out there and 'to take a leading part on a well thought out policy'.[6] What exactly Britain's line should be, however, was for the moment left entirely to the Foreign Secretary and his permanent officials.

chinesische-japanischen Konflikt hat die Reichsregierung stets eine streng neutrale Haltung eingenommen. Sie hat sich keiner gemeinsamen Aktion des Völkerbunds versagt, ist aber in der Erkenntnis der grossen Schwierigkeiten, die einer befriedigenden Lösung des Konflikts entgegenstehen, im Völkerbund für ein vorsichtiges Vorgehen eingetreten. Diese Haltung wird auch weiterhin für uns massgebend bleiben müssen.' In summarising German policy, I have also been helped by being kindly allowed to read the first chapter of an unpublished London University Ph. D. thesis by John P. Fox, 'The Formation of Germany's Far Eastern Policy, 1933–1936'.

[1] Osborne to Reading, 24 September 1931; Patteson to Vansittart, 17, 18 October 1931, DBFP, VIII, Nos. 524, 647, 654 respectively.
[2] Ibid, No. 643.
[3] Osborne to Patteson, 16 October; Patteson to Lindsay, 19 October; Lindsay to Patteson, 20 October 1931; ibid, Nos. 643, 660, 668 respectively.
[4] See Cabinet conclusions for 1, 2 and 5 October, CAB 23/68.
[5] Cabinet conclusions, 22 September 1931, CAB 23/68; DBFP, VIII, No. 515.
[6] DBFP, VIII, No. 593.

A policy was duly forthcoming, but it was scarcely one in which 'a leading part' was sought for Britain. Within the Far Eastern Department, a spate of early comments had all suggested that, in Wellesley's words, 'it would be the height of folly for us to interfere' if 'endless trouble and perplexity' were to be avoided.[1] Given Japan's existing rights in Manchuria, the dispute was seen, as Pratt put it, as 'utterly anomalous';[2] Tokyo's case was believed to be 'a much better one than her arbitrary action and ... bad showing ... at Geneva have allowed it to appear', while it was suspected that if the Kwantung Army immediately withdrew, 'the field would be open to every bandit leader who hopes to emulate the successful career of Chang Tso-lin'.[3] Admittedly, Nanking had behaved with 'commendable restraint' and must be handled as tactfully as possible in order to avoid 'something foolish and irremediable';[4] but as rumours of a secret deal between Canton and Tokyo suggested, anyone who sought to help the Chinese must expect double-dealing all round.[5] Japan, meanwhile, in Pratt's words, believed 'that her existence as a nation is at stake and ... will leave the League rather than submit to League intervention', in which event Britain and Geneva alike would suffer a serious blow.[6] 'Even on the extreme hypothesis,' added Douglas MacKillop, 'that (Japan) *actually annexed part of Manchuria*, we should not be demonstrably worse off.'[7] Vansittart, Wellesley and all the Department were agreed that 'the Chinese *must* negotiate with the Japs. [sic] about Japanese interests in Manchuria, or take the consequences'.[8] The only question was whether the Chinese could be expected to do this even before the Kwantung Army withdrew, and in this Pratt's view, supporting that of Lampson, eventually prevailed. One should avoid anything that entailed Nanking's 'complete capitulation', for this could create 'the grave danger that all traces of ordered government will disappear throughout China'.[9] Thus, while Nanking was pressed to show restraint, the suggestion that she should immediately negotiate was belatedly withdrawn;[10] while Japan was twice reminded privately of her obligations, she was assured that the initiative for an international démarche had not come from Britain;[11] while information from Manchuria was passed on to Drummond, it was carefully filtered beforehand, for 'fear of endangering our relations with either the Chinese or Japanese or both'.[12]

There remained, however, the wider problem that Lampson had raised

[1] See minutes on FO 371, F 4042, 5031, 5388/1391/10.

[2] Memorandum of 12 October 1931, DBFP, VIII, No. 621.

[3] See ibid, Nos. 505, 681, note; minutes on FO 371, F 6006/1391/10.

[4] Minute on FO 371, F 5611/1391/10.

[5] See Pratt memorandum, 19 January 1932, DBFP, IX, No. 95.

[6] E.g., Pratt memorandum, 12 October, cited above; minute on FO 371, F 5831/1391/10.

[7] Minute on FO 371, F 5179/1391/10, emphasis added.

[8] Minutes on FO 371, F 5168, 5263/1391/10; DBFP, VIII, No. 681, note.

[9] Memorandum of 12 October, cited above.

[10] See above, 142, note 5.

[11] See DBFP, VIII, Nos. 520, 523, 538, 587, 590, 620, 644, 646.

[12] Minute on FO 371, F 5397/1391/10. In effect this filtering was favourable to Japan. See the selection of material involved in DBFP, VIII, Nos. 557, 567 note, 573 note.

so forcefully, of maintaining the League. Over this, the ever-blunt MacKillop was untroubled, arguing that 'principles applicable to disputes between States in general do not by any means apply to disputes between China and another State', and that Japan, like Britain, must be allowed to act on the basis of that distinction. Wellesley, Vansittart and Eden agreed, the last-named adding on 6 October: 'There is I believe real danger in pressing the only available precedent too far. The Greco-Bulgarian dispute bears no true analogy to the Manchurian troubles truer than it would to any accen-tuation of our difficulties with China.'[1] Wellesley in particular was critical of what was being done at Geneva, the Council, as he saw it, making 'three supreme blunders: 1. To adopt a definitely anti-Japanese attitude from the start; 2. To invoke the assistance of the Americans on the Council; 3. To set a time limit within which the Japanese are to evacuate Manchuria'.[2]

In this, however, Wellesley was going counter to not only the attitude but the actions of his own Foreign Secretary. Reading clearly agreed with Cadogan, rather, that 'the League would be stultifying itself altogether if it did not insist on the principle of peaceful settlement'.[3] To Vansittart, he wrote privately that 'a failure by the League to find some way round the difficulty would be nothing short of a calamity . . . and might imperil any hopes we may have of making progress in the more immediate field of Europe . . .'[4] So much for Cecil's 1941 version. It was Reading, indeed, who at a secret meeting of the Council on 17 October stressed the need to look ahead to the moment 'when patience became feebleness', Cecil's contribu-tion merely being the observation that he did not believe the Japanese would withdraw until they had secured a railway agreement with the Chinese; nor did Reading privately raise any objection to Briand's draft Resolution (it needed to be strong, remarked the latter, for the sake of public opinion) that set a time limit for evacuation, the clause in question going through without discussion, in fact.[5]

By the time the Resolution was passed, even MacKillop and others in the Foreign Office were accepting that the League had done good work.[6] They could do so, of course, because it had not attempted coercion. Even Cadogan

[1] Minutes on FO 371, F 5217/1391/10. On the suggested parallel with Britain's action at Shanghai in 1927, accepted by McKillop but rejected (rightly, in strict terms) by others, see DBFP, VIII, No. 542, and the minutes on FO 371, 5325, 5334/1391/10.

[2] Minute on FO 371, F 5876/1391/10. Hankey held similar views. Referring to British representations to Japan, he wrote in his diary on 26 September 1931: 'Why do we do these silly things? This is one of the reasons why we are so mistrusted. We will poke our nose into everyone's business at the League.'

[3] Minute of 2 November 1931, FO 371, F 5217/1/10.

[4] Reading to Vansittart, 21 October 1931, DBFP, VIII, No. 672, note; FO 800/226.

[5] LN. Archives, R 6228. Briand displayed a certain optimism at these secret meetings. Japan might reject the League's proposals once or twice, he remarked on 18 October, 'mais une attitude éternellement négative lui sera impossible'.

[6] E.g., FO 371, F 6077/1391/10. It should be noted that Reading had been anxious to have Cecil with him at Geneva, and not, apparently, with the intention of using him as a cover for evasive action. Minutes by Cadogan and Vansittart, 9 October 1931, ibid, F 5649/1391/10.

did not suggest that article 16 should be invoked, and Reading joined
Vansittart, Wellesley and the rest in regarding any suggestion of economic
sanctions as dangerous in itself, premature in its implied judgement and
strenuously to be avoided. As Pratt minuted on the speculative paper by
Cecil, Massigli and others,

> This memorandum would seem to make clear that (the) Government should ab
> initio discourage the idea that the application of sanctions is even a remote
> possibility. The League would practically have to bring about a state of war in
> order to have an excuse for applying Article XVI. Moreover, . . . the United
> States at the first whisper of the word 'sanctions' would publicly dissociate itself
> from further cooperation with the League.[1]

On this last point, Pratt was undoubtedly correct. But although Wellesley's
deeper distrust of Washington was widely shared,[2] Reading was not alone
in the Foreign Office in believing in 'the necessity of doing everything possible
to secure the wholehearted cooperation of the United States Government'.
Delighted with Gilbert's presence at the Council, the Foreign Secretary
fairly leaped to attention when Colonel Stimson let it be known that he had
expected the League powers to invoke the Pact of Paris;[3] similarly, he
displayed the utmost consternation at the news that Gilbert might be speedily
withdrawn, successfully pleading with Stimson on the telephone that such a
move would be 'disastrous' for the matter in hand, for the League generally
and for the Disarmament Conference. (It might also lead to the fall of
Briand, he added.)[4] Satisfied that by 24 October the League 'had done its
utmost for the present', Reading believed, indeed, that hope of moving
Japan in the right direction must now rest in part on persuading the United
States 'to take matters up where the L. of N. has left it [sic]'.[5] Just how far
Washington would go in that respect would depend, however, not on pleas
from Geneva, but on the outcome of certain differences over policy that
were beginning to emerge around the bottom end of Pennsylvania Avenue.

The shaping of policy: Washington

Growing tension over Manchuria had not gone unnoticed in Washington
during the summer of 1931. Most American observers on the spot, however,
unlike several of their British colleagues, had doubted whether an explosion
was imminent: early in September, Nelson Johnson was describing a
Chinese official's story of Japanese plans to occupy the area within the next
three months as 'highly improbable' and 'fantastic',[6] while warning signs

[1] Minute of 27 October 1931, ibid, F 6091/1391/10. Pratt enclosed a *Times*
cutting which reported Borah's fierce opposition to any coercion. Cf. ibid,
F 5502/1391/10.

[2] 'The American's as usual unreliable', minuted one member of the Far Eastern
Department on DBFP, VIII, No. 660. FO 371, F5912/1391/10; cf. ibid, F5949/
1391/10.

[3] DBFP, VIII, Nos. 647, 654.   [4] Ibid, Nos. 660, 667.

[5] Ibid, No. 647; Reading minute of 28 October 1931, on FO 371, F 5950/1391/10;
Wigram memorandum, 24 October 1931, RA G.V, M 2333/1.

[6] Johnson to Forbes, 14 July 1931, Johnson Papers, vol. 13; FRUS, 1931, III,
1–3, 95–6; DS 793.94/1790.

in Tokyo did not disturb Cameron Forbes's concentration on his new
Embassy building and polo ponies. Even so, it was with some misgivings
that the Ambassador sailed home for leave on the day after the Mukden
incident, leaving Edwin Neville as Chargé d'Affaires.[1] Nor did it take
Johnson and Neville long to conclude that the affair had been instigated by
the Kwantung Army, Johnson more forcefully describing it as 'an aggressive act . . . apparently long planned . . . (that) must fall within any definition
of war'.[2]

A precise picture of developments was slow in coming, however. 'We
really don't know what is going on in Manchuria,' noted Stimson on 28
September, shortly before obtaining Japanese approval to despatch to the
area his Consul General in Harbin and a member of the Tokyo Embassy
staff.[3] From these men, together with Johnson and the Consul General in
Mukden, there followed a series of reports to the effect that the Japanese
were manipulating a separatist movement in Manchuria, were showing
little regard for 'modern conventions of ordinary humanity' (in their bombing of Chinchow especially), and, by 22 October, were displaying no sign of
intending to withdraw from the main centres of the territory. On the desirability of such a withdrawal, on the other hand, the diplomatic reports, like
similar British ones, were ambiguous. From Antung, for example, the two
special observers suggested that no adverse consequences would ensue;
from Newchwang, however, they described the danger of bandit attacks,
and on 13 October advised that '(the) complete withdrawal of Japanese
soldiers to (the) railway zone under present unsettled conditions would . . .
jeopardize not only lives and property of Japanese but also those of
foreigners and Chinese'.[4]

These developments on the ground had from the outset been accompanied by appeals from politicians and the Government in China. There
could be no doubting the urgency involved, despite private admissions like
the one by Sze, that it was not intended to press the matter of the Kellogg
Pact lest, by implication, a state of war were thereby acknowledged, thus
encouraging Japan to abandon all restraint.[5] The possibility of America's
convening a Nine Power Treaty conference was raised on several occasions,
for example, the argument being that such a gathering might provide China
with more redress than would the League, where Japanese influence was
strong.[6] The Chinchow bombing was also the occasion for renewed requests
and the suggestion that an American observer might sit with the Council at
Geneva;[7] at the same time criticism was being freely expressed in Nanking
of Washington's caution to date, and especially its opposition to a commission of enquiry.[8] When conveying such reactions, moreover, Johnson urged

[1] Forbes Journal, 2nd series, IV, 176; cf. ibid, 2nd series, III.

[2] Johnson to State Department, 21, 22 September; Neville to State Dept., 22
September 1931, FRUS, 1931, III, 2–5.

[3] Stimson Diary, 28 September 1931; FRUS, 1931, III, 85, 90–1.

[4] See FRUS, 1931, III, 106, 118–25, 128, 140–4, 167–8, 170–4, 196–7, 222–3,
237–40, 289–91; DS 793.94/2083.   [5] FRUS, 1931, III, 38.

[6] Johnson to State Dept., 19 September 1931, DS 793.94/1804; Gilbert to State
Dept., 19 September, Johnson to State Dept., 15 October 1931, FRUS, 1931, III,
17–19, 197–8.   [7] DS 793.94/2029.   [8] Ibid, 1944; FRUS, 1931, III, 104.

that it was vital to restore the confidence of the Chinese leaders in the value of international agreements, and that the signatories of the Kellogg Pact should pronounce on Japan's 'cynical disregard of (her) obligations'. In this, as in his desire to see pressure applied in Tokyo,[1] the Minister's views were in close accord with those of Lampson, as well as being far less detached than his suggestion a few months before that the United States should 'let Japan alone' in the Far East, even if the latter were to absorb Manchuria.

Johnson's attitude did not correspond, however, with that of the local American naval commander, Admiral Taylor, whose disillusioned views on the corruption of Chinese politics and society, cited earlier, were passed on to the President himself through the Chief of Naval Operations.[2] As for Neville in Tokyo, he was inclined to play down the whole affair, 'unfortunate and trying', as he described it in one report, 'but it does not amount to a world crisis'.[3] And although his alarm was thus far less than Lindley's, his advice was similar to the latter's: that Japanese opinion would not tolerate outside interference over Manchuria and that the Government would prove reasonable in those direct negotiations that were the only way to settle matters.[4] He was, in effect, seconding the messages being sent to Stimson by Shidehara, who offered frequent reassurances as to Japan's limited and defensive aims, her appreciation of United States efforts for peace, and the purely technical nature of her brief objection to an American presence at the League Council.[5]

Shidehara wanted time while he fought for his political existence (if there were any doubts on this last score, Debuchi Katsuji, the Japanese Ambassador in Washington, quickly dispelled them).[6] Drummond wanted information, advice, and support of a more open and positive kind. What was happening in Manchuria, and what were Stimson's views as to, say, the applicability of the Kellogg Pact? The Secretary General's own feeling was that the formal invoking of the Pact would entail 'grave practical disadvantages' of double jurisdiction with the Covenant (he recalled the Corfu episode as an unhappy precedent for such duplication); it would also involve the recognition of a 'resort to war', and that would in turn amount to 'a violation of the Covenant . . . with all that such violation entails under Article 16 and (where) the policy of the United States would be all important'.[7] This indication of apprehension at Geneva concerning coercion was not new. As early as 26 September, Gilbert had reported that the general opinion there was that military pressure was 'out of the question',

[1] FRUS, Japan, 1931–1941, I, 5; FRUS, 1931, III, 136–7.

[2] See above, 51–2; Taylor to Pratt, 6, 12 October, 5 November, 17 December 1931, Taylor Papers, box 1.

[3] FRUS, 1931, III, 200–1; Neville to Castle, 24 September 1931, Castle Papers, Japan.

[4] E.g., FRUS, 1931, III, 82–4, 279–80, 283; DS 793.94/2071.

[5] E.g., FRUS, Japan 1931–1941, I, 11–12, 22–3, 28–9; FRUS, 1931, III, 18–22, 67–9, 101–2, 240, 246; Stimson Diary, 28 September 1931.

[6] E.g., Hornbeck memorandum, 20 September 1931 (seen by Stimson, 24 September), DS 793.94/1888.

[7] FRUS, 1931, III, 164–5; DS 793.94/2058.

and that there was reluctance to contemplate any economic measures that would further dislocate international trade. Drummond himself, on 6 October, had agreed that 'in view of the present situation in the world, pressure through economic sanctions would be entirely out of the question', although he thought that a withdrawal of ambassadors was an alternative that would be very difficult for Japan to resist.[1] The cool approach of the Foreign Office in London was also reported to the State Department,[2] while Castle's comment on the openly expressed pro-Japanese views of the French Ambassador, Paul Claudel, was that they no doubt reflected 'the general French attitude'.[3]

Whatever the tactics to be employed, however—and Briand privately expressed his disappointment that the Nine Power Treaty had not been used as the basis for a settlement[4]—it was clear that Drummond and the major powers on the Council wanted the United States in at almost any price.[5] 'Never before have I seen here a situation so tense in which American cooperation is desired so earnestly,' reported Hugh Wilson on 22 September. In the eyes of Norman Davis, who was there on the following day, they were faced with a unique occasion 'loaded with dynamite and where there is . . . a great opportunity to do something perfectly wonderful . . . (that would also) save disarmament'. He and Wilson agreed that if the United States would join in the deliberations of the Council or its committee of five, as Massigli and others wanted, it 'would really solve the situation'. Alternatively, there was the request pressed upon Washington on the 22nd, 23rd and again on the 24th September, that America should participate in despatching a commission of enquiry.[6] Even after this had been turned down, Gilbert could report to Stimson that 'everything is going your way here',[7] and when Drummond hesitated over the wisdom of invoking the Kellogg Pact as the Secretary of State desired, Reading, Briand and others 'swept aside at once all of his opinions'. Like the others, moreover, Drummond was aghast when Gilbert reported that he was to be withdrawn from their discussions. According to the latter, the Secretary General 'almost broke down at the news', while one subsequent account had him in tears.[8]

In responding to this flood of appeals, information and advice that was well-nigh choking the channels of the State Department, Stimson and his

[1] FRUS, 1931, III, 70–1, 128–30.   [2] DS 793.94/1834, 2292, 2389.
[3] Ibid, 2369; FRUS, 1931, III, 111.   [4] DS 793.94/1971.
[5] Some of the smaller League states, however, feared that too high a price might be paid in terms of League solidarity, and looked with suspicion at the major powers' private negotiations with Washington. See DS 793.94/2362, and below, 231.
[6] FRUS, 1931, III, 37–9, 43–7, 57. On 25 November, Davis was to write to Lippmann of '(our) mistake in blowing hot and cold' with the League. Davis Papers, box 35. Yet in October, he had assured Stimson that he agreed with his policy entirely, and that a commission of enquiry would have had disastrous consequences. Stimson Diary, 8 October 1931. Stimson's tendency to bully ensured that men usually told him what he wanted to hear, but Davis himself was not always firm during these years.
[7] FRUS, 1931, III, 178–82.
[8] Ibid, 266–75; Gibson to Castle, 29 October 1931, Castle Papers, Switzerland; Pearson and Brown, 292–4.

officials, like their counterparts in the Foreign Office, were initially left with
a considerable degree of initiative by a preoccupied Government. An overburdened Hoover largely confined himself to supporting what his Secretary
was doing, and towards the end of the period the latter was describing him
as having been 'first rate throughout'.[1] Sufficient encouragement also came
from unofficial quarters for Stimson and others to believe that the public at
large would soon be delivering a forceful judgement on the crisis,[2] and by
13 October the Secretary was attributing what he thought was nervousness
on the side of the Japanese partly to the expression of American public
opinion.[3] Klots and Rogers, both of whom favoured a forceful policy,
encouraged him to hope for widespread support for openly associating with
the League Council, while Rogers reported after touring around that 'it was
rather general that (people) felt the responsibility of policing the world was
now on us and that we should build a big Navy'. 'The Manchurian matter,'
added Stimson, 'will certainly clinch these opinions'.[4] Individuals like Frank
Kellogg and Walter Lippmann, together with organisations like the L.N.A.
and Women's League for Peace and Freedom, were also expressing approval
for what was being done.[5] Representative Kent E. Keller of Illinois was
another who offered his advice—to the President, in fact—when recalling
America's diminishing 'trade and spiritual contacts with most of the vast
populations of Asia'. The least that should be done, he thought, was

> to serve special notice to Japan that America will not recognize any alienation of
> territory, or trade privileges with the Chinese peoples. It is the only open door
> we have left in the Orient . . . If we make such a declaration and stand by it,
> Japan will find a way to keep out of China. If we are too cowardly to do that,
> the door will largely be closed to us.[6]

William Borah, too, expressed his approval of the line Stimson was
taking, but that was before Gilbert took his seat with the Council and only
after the Secretary had emphasised that no one would be allowed 'to leave
the baby on America's doorstep'.[7] Moreover once it looked as if that might,
indeed, come about, and with the Geneva entanglement becoming more
evident, it was the harsher voices of Hearst, McKormick and their allies
which began to sound loudest in Washington, where the Cabinet showed
their alarm[8] and the limits set to policy by Hoover himself became more
apparent. At the same time, there remained a significant degree of sympathy
for Japan's position among senior members of the Administration. In
response to Admiral Taylor's latest account of Chinese chaos, for example,
the Secretary of the Navy, Charles Francis Adams, was soon to write that it
provided an excellent exposition of 'the reasons which make it clear that the

---

[1] Stimson Diary, 16 October 1931; cf. ibid, 22, 24, 30 September 1931.
[2] E.g., Hornbeck memorandum, 27 September 1931, DS 793.94/1945.
[3] Stimson Diary, 13 October 1931.   [4] Ibid, 10, 13, 15 October 1931.
[5] E.g., DS 793.94/1861, 1910, 1990, 2076; Stimson Diary, 6 October 1931; cf.
Rappaport, *Henry L. Stimson*, 41–2. Kellogg nevertheless found the Chinese
'somewhat lawless and undisciplined'. Letter to Johnson, 21 October 1931,
Johnson Papers, vol. 14.
[6] Keller to Hoover, 12 October 1931, DS 793.94/2138.
[7] Stimson Diary, 6 October, 1931.   [8] Ibid, 16 October 1931.

Japanese must have some satisfactory control over Manchuria'.[1] Hoover also was to find this particular letter of Taylor's 'illuminating',[2] and he shared the view, put to the press privately by Stimson, that Japan was 'our buffer against the unknown powers behind her on the mainland of China and Russia'.[3] Like Cecil, Stimson suspected the truth of Chinese statements;[4] like members of the Foreign Office, Hoover's friend and Secretary of the Interior, Wilbur, had 'fears and suspicions as to the duplicity on the part of various Chinese in dealing with the Japanese'.[5]

The same danger of American aid being manipulated by Chinese politicians for their private purposes was also appreciated within the State Department,[6] where William Castle was the leading advocate of restraint. While recognising that certain general principles were involved, Castle was inclined to believe by the end of this period that the United States 'might well have taken this more seriously than we should have done'. Japan was America's 'one useful friend in the Orient', and her 'oriental psychology' would ensure that offence would be taken if a commission of enquiry were sent to Manchuria; the main thing was 'to support Baron Shidehara to the limit' and avoid any precipitate action of the kind Stimson had taken over the Sino-Soviet clash in 1929.[7] The painstaking but vacillating Hornbeck,[8] who usually stood somewhere between Castle and the ginger-group of Stimson's closer associates, shared some of the former's views in this period, even to the extent of 'ruefully agreeing' when Castle suggested that Japanese control of Manchuria might prove the least of possible evils.[9] He, too, advocated support for Shidehara and the avoidance of anything that might increase Japanese 'suspicion, resentment and opposition',[10] while for the sake of both good relations with Japan and 'American domestic consumption', only the most limited cooperation should be extended to the League.[11]

[1] Adams to Taylor, 1 December 1931, Taylor Papers, box 1.

[2] Hoover to Adams, 28 November 1931, U.S. Navy Dept., General Records, Office of the Secretary, General Correspondence, EF 16/P9–2, 311128.

[3] Stimson Diary, 15 October 1931.

[4] Ibid, 28 September 1931.

[5] Wilbur to Chester Rowell, 6 January 1932, Wilbur Papers. In a letter to Hoover of 9 October 1931, Wilbur had urged the latter to maintain a position 'that will be recognised as a part of your general peace program and that will not imperil the whole of our question of disarmament.' Wilbur Papers.

[6] E.g., DS 793.94/2146.

[7] Castle to Neville, 20 October 1931, Castle Papers, Japan; Castle Diary, 29 September, 10 October 1931, cited in R. N. Current, 'The Stimson Doctrine and the Hoover Doctrine', American Historical Review, No. 59, 1953–4; FRUS, 1931, III, 63, 230–1.

[8] Clearly several of Hornbeck's forthcoming shifts of emphasis were due above all to changing circumstances. They were frequent enough to be worthy of a Simon, however.

[9] Castle Diary, 29 September 1931, loc. cit. Cf. the undated memorandum, 'The Case for Japan in Manchuria', Hornbeck Papers, box 242.

[10] Memorandum of 20 September 1931 (seen by Stimson, 24 September), DS 793.94/1889.

[11] Memoranda of 3 and 16 October 1931, (seen by Stimson, 5 and 19 October), ibid, 2144, 2245.

Reading, Briand and their colleagues might be well-intentioned, but they had little grasp of the Far Eastern question as a whole (in London, Pratt thought the same of Hornbeck), and, like Wellesley, he believed that they had blundered in pressing ahead with their invitation to the United States and in setting a deadline for a withdrawal of the Kwantung Army. In their refusal to comply with this last demand, he pronounced the Japanese to be 'sound';[1] in their insistence on their 1915 treaty rights they made 'interference and involvement by . . . other powers (a matter of) extreme delicacy'.[2]

Yet at the same time Hornbeck, like Pratt, recognised that there were also several considerations militating against a policy of passivity, and it is in the memoranda of these two men—Pratt's reflecting the greater ability—that the dilemma facing United States and British officials is most readily perceived. (Both men, it is worth recalling, and Pratt especially so, had more knowledge of China than did most of their London and Washington colleagues.) What was taking place in Manchuria, wrote Hornbeck, was of practical and moral concern to all states, and if matters were left simply to direct Sino-Japanese negotiations, that would not remove sources of irritation 'which would tend to lead sooner or later to a real war on a large scale'. The need, as he saw it by the middle of October, was to make a careful reappraisal of American policy after four weeks of hasty decisions and in the light of the double struggle that now existed: Japan versus China, and Japan versus the rest of the world.

> In the first of these contests, if China wins, China will be encouraged to persevere in the role of a trouble-maker; whereas if Japan wins, Japan will be encouraged to persevere in the role of a self-appointed arbiter of international rights in the Far East. In the second of these contests, if the world wins, China will have escaped some at least of the rightful consequences of her own weakness and obstreperousness; whereas if Japan wins, the principle of resolving international controversies without resort to force will have been given a terrific set-back.[3]

Stimson himself shared much of Hornbeck's uncertainty. To Castle's relief, his initial reaction to 'a very serious situation' had been one of caution, although this new problem, together with a spell of particularly stifling Washington weather, was not improving his temper.[4] Quickly accepting that the Kwantung Army was defying the Cabinet in Tokyo, he defined his problem as being 'to let the Japanese know we are watching them and at the same time to do it in such a way that will help Shidehara, who is on the right side, and not play into the hands of any Nationalist agitators on the other'.[5] Although accepting that 'a widely extended movement of aggression' had taken place, therefore, he suggested to Drummond that all provocative moves such as the sending of a commission of enquiry should be avoided: even if the Japanese Government consented to such a commission, its public would 'flare up' at the idea; if it withheld consent, the enquiry would

[1] Memoranda of 3, 16, 19, 20, 24 October 1931, ibid, 1978/5/6, 2325, 2330, 2340.
[2] Memorandum of 26 October 1931, (seen by Stimson, 27 October), ibid, 2447.
[3] See ibid, 1906, 2033, 2134, 2135, 2154, 2226, 2252, 2318.
[4] See Moffat Diary, 21 September 1931.
[5] Stimson Diary, 19, 21, 22 September 1931; FRUS, 1931, III, 15.

become 'to say the least, dangerous'. In any case, 'people in the Orient like to work things out by negotiation between the two parties'. There could thus be no American participation in a commission, and no acceptance of the 'rather wild propositions' put by Norman Davis on the telephone from Geneva ('the Secretary made short shrift of him and his ultra-League suggestions,' noted Moffat). When the League was 'bungling ahead', as Stimson put it, he would not risk appearing to be entangled in its actions and would not interfere with the normal workings of its machinery. Meanwhile the Nine Power Treaty and Kellogg Pact could be held in reserve, so that, through them, America could 'pull (the League) out if they got into trouble', perhaps by offering to act as a mediator.[1] At the same time, while privately exhorting Japan to show restraint,[2] the State Department also made re-assuring noises for her benefit. Castle told the press that it was understand-able that she would be slow to withdraw her troops until certain of the safety of her nationals; Stimson told Debuchi that he had advised the League that direct Sino-Japanese talks offered the best way out. 'It was better in inter-national relations,' the Secretary informed the Chinese Chargé on 8 October, 'to proceed on the assumption that a government will keep its pledges than on the suspicion that it will not'. As for the United States, she was 'playing no favorites'.[3]

This coolness on the part of Stimson, however, did not outlast the news of the bombing of Chinchow and of Japanese threats over the trade boycott. 'The situation . . . seems to be getting rapidly bad,' he noted on 8 October. 'I am afraid we have got to take a firm ground and aggressive stand toward Japan.' Three days later he was describing it as being 'high time that (the Japanese) got rounded up'.[4] Besides conveying his dissatisfaction, therefore, 'piercing questions', as he called them, were despatched to Shidehara on the subject of recent developments.[5] Equally, Hoover and his dubious Cabinet colleagues had to be convinced that vital principles were now at stake, even though, as he described it in an expressive metaphor, the post-1918 peace agreements 'no more fitted the three great races who were meeting in Manchuria than a stovepipe hat would fit an African savage'. As an addi-tional inducement, he reminded the President that 'if Japan (ran) amok, Congress (would) never let him cut a single dollar off on navies'.[6] Hoover responded, even to the extent of saying on 10 October that Gilbert should be authorised to sit with the Council when it next met;[7] Stimson could thus in

[1] Stimson Diary, 23, 24, 25 September, 1931; Moffat Diary, 23 September 1931; FRUS, 1931, III, 26, 43–52, 60.

[2] E.g., FRUS, *Japan, 1931–1941,* I, 5–8; cf. FRUS, 1931, III, 116–17.

[3] Castle press conference, 2 October 1931, DS 793.94/2022; FRUS, 1931, III, 108–9, 137–9.

[4] Stimson Diary, 8, 11 October 1931. Stimson was not, of course, in Lyndon Johnson's class as a user of cowboy metaphors, but such exotic language seems often to be followed by less than happy consequences for the United States. No doubt a similar pattern could be discerned in the use of cricketing metaphors in London.

[5] Stimson Diary, 10 October 1931; FRUS, *Japan, 1931–1941,* I, 17–21; FRUS, 1931, III, 22–3.

[6] Stimson Diary, 9 October, 1931.

[7] Ibid, 10 October 1931.

turn suggest to Drummond that the need was imminent to invoke the Kellogg
Pact as the basis for Gilbert's presence, reference to its second article being
seen as a warning over a possible future war, not as a recognition that an
act of war had taken place.[1] Delighted at being on the move, the Secretary
did not, apparently, acknowledge to himself that he was now adopting one
of those 'wild propositions' of Norman Davis's that he had abruptly turned
down a short time before. Instead, absorbed in the Manchurian question to
the exclusion of all others, he saw himself as 'making history'.[2]

Yet this did not mean that his reservations concerning the merits of the
dispute and possible means of dealing with it had disappeared. On 10 October, for example, in notes to China and Japan, he was still indicating that
both of them, and not Japan alone, had failed to observe their undertakings
embodied in the League Resolution of 30 September, while in private he
found in the five fundamental principles now being advanced by Japan as an
essential basis for a settlement 'nothing I could take exception to'.[3] 'Each
disputant,' he cabled to Drummond, 'has a good many and ever increasing
grounds for complaint against . . . the other'. Confident in his knowledge of
'Oriental psychology', he still believed on 16 October that neither party
wanted war, that direct talks (with or without observers) were the only
answer, and that 'what was needed was time and a chance to cool down'.[4]
As for one's own reaction, the Kellogg Pact could be invoked since it
involved 'no investigation, no argument, and no discussion', but even so the
League, not the United States, must take the initiative as otherwise 'it would
make us seem directly hostile to Japan and would inevitably provoke
hostility in Japan against us'; nor could there be any question of recognising
that an act of war had occurred, since that 'would open the whole question
of sanctions, with which we have nothing to do'.[5] Lest there should be any
misunderstanding, the Asiatic Fleet must be recalled from a cruise near
Japanese-held Manchuria, while Japan must privately be assured that the
'pressure' that had been mentioned in a recent note to Drummond referred
solely to 'the moral pressure of public opinion'.[6] If sections of the American
public, together with the Japanese, were hostile to Gilbert's presence with
the Council, then, as Castle and Hornbeck agreed, he should be withdrawn
as soon as possible; as we have seen, only the frantic pleas of Reading and

[1] FRUS, 1931, III, 154, 164–5, 167–8, 176–82, 198; DS 793.94/2032 A, 2042,
2071. Like Lampson, Stimson put forward the idea of neutral observers attending
Sino–Japanese talks.

[2] Moffat Diary, 9, 13 October 1931.

[3] Stimson Diary, 14 October 1931; FRUS, 1931, III, 152–3, 169.

[4] FRUS, 1931, III, 154, 211–12, 220–1; Stimson Diary, 17 October 1931. Noncommittal responses were also returned to China concerning the Nine Power
Treaty, partly in the reasonable belief that to invoke it would add to existing
confusion. FRUS, 1931, III, 208–9; DS 793.94/2246.

[5] Stimson Diary, 10 October 1931; Stimson to Gilbert, 12 October 1931, DS
793.94/2091 A–C; Stimson—Gilbert telephone record, 13 October 1931, FRUS,
1931, III, 178–82.

[6] Stimson Diary, 13, 15 October 1931; Castle memoranda, 14, 17 October 1931,
FRUS, 1931, III, 190–1, 219–20. Extra care was taken on the assumption that the
Japanese might well be decoding American diplomatic cables to Tokyo. See DS
793.94/2071, 2149.

his colleagues, together with some exchanges with a nervous and servile Gilbert himself ('It was nothing I did, sir.' 'I am always afraid you will confuse their views with mine.') got the decision reversed to the extent that he could remain, a silent listener, at the Council's 'damned table' during its public meetings only. The episode did nothing to alleviate Stimson's fear that, with its talk of deadlines, the League was in the process of mistakenly 'making a row' with Japan.[1]

The Secretary also had to reckon with Hoover, who even earlier had appeared to him not to be fully alert to the moral issues at stake and to be concerned mainly with avoiding any humiliation for the United States should Japan refuse to abide by 'our scraps of paper or paper treaties'. And although the President had stood firm when objections were raised to cooperation at Geneva, by 20 October he was talking sourly to Hugh Wilson of the penalties involved in anything of this kind; by early November he would be regretting that he had ever allowed the League connection to be made in the first place, and wanting 'to get completely out of it'.[2] He had been particularly disturbed when Stimson, on 17 October, had suggested the possibility of modifying America's 'old extreme doctrine of neutrality' should the League employ sanctions against an aggressor—a subject, it will be recalled, on which Stimson had already given MacDonald premature encouragement earlier that year.[3] It is important to note that the argument was not over the possibility of the United States instituting sanctions, Stimson himself still having major reservations on that score, and the division between him and Hoover being nowhere near as clear at this stage as the latter was to suggest in his memoirs.[4] But whereas Stimson wished at least not to actively undermine any moves the League might make in defence of its principles,[5] Hoover was quick to descry and avoid any involvement, however indirect, that might lead the country into war. His determination in this case was reinforced (there is no reason to believe that it would not otherwise have existed) by the gloomy estimates of his military commanders concerning a possible war with Japan, and, according to his memoirs, by a report from London through private channels to the effect that Britain was determined to avoid sanctions whatever might occur.[6]

Having therefore taken time off from the domestic crisis to ponder on this international one, Hoover put his views before his Cabinet ('shortly after mid-October' by his own account, but it may have been a little later) and summarised them in a memorandum thereafter. Japan's behaviour, he

[1] Stimson Diary, 16, 18, 19, 20 October 1931; Stimson–Gilbert telephone records, 16, 19, 20 October, FRUS, 1931, III, 203–6, 241–8, 266–75. Cf. Pearson and Brown, 289–90, and Stimson's later thoughts in Stimson and Bundy, 232.

[2] Moffat Diary, 20 October 1931; Castle Diary, 4 November 1931, cited in Current, 'The Stimson Doctrine'.

[3] Stimson Diary, 17 October 1931. See above, 115.

[4] Hoover, *Memoirs, 1920–1933*, 366 ff.

[5] See, e.g., Stimson's conversation with officials recorded in Moffat Diary, 17 October 1931. Cf. FRUS, 1931, III, 299.

[6] *Memoirs, 1920–1933*, 367–8. I have not been able to trace Hoover's private enquiry at the London end, nor his question to his Service advisers that he refers to. See above, 76.

acknowledged, was 'immoral', and her affront to the world and the United States 'outrageous'. But although she was bound to be absorbed or expelled by the Chinese in the end, she did have a good case in seeking to preserve order and her vital economic interests in a China over which there loomed the menace of bolshevism. As for the general principles of international behaviour that were involved,

> Neither our obligations to China, nor our own interest, nor our dignity require us to go to war over these questions. These acts do not imperil the freedom of the American people, the economic or moral future of our people. I do not propose ever to sacrifice American life for anything short of this. If that were not reason enough, to go to war means a long struggle at a time when civilization is already weak enough . . . [Cooperation with the League over conciliation] is the limit. We will not go along on war or any of the sanctions, either economic or military, for those are the roads to war.[1]

The matter was still not entirely closed to discussion. In the sphere of action, as opposed to words, however, the President had defined limits to United States policy that were to outlive his own tenure of office by several years.

Retrospect

These early weeks of the crisis have been examined in some detail, not merely because of the assertions made about them afterwards, but because of the strong hypothesis that, in responding to a new foreign-policy problem, officials, politicians and others are likely to be influenced over a long period by their initial definition of the situation.[2] (Thus, for example, the predominant images initially established will to some extent become self-preserving through their capacity as screens or filters for further incoming information.[3]) An initial question that arises is whether or not at this stage the definitions that were forthcoming warrant the application of the label, 'crisis'. The term has, of course, been used freely throughout the present work, and is a well-established piece of historical shorthand for describing a heightening of tension in situations as varied as developments in the Far East between 1933 and 1938, the Soviet Union's attempt to place missiles in Cuba, and Edward VIII's intention to marry Mrs. Simpson. Plainly, the subjective element is central, and in our case the attack in Manchuria presented Chang Hsueh-liang, say, with a 'crisis' of a different order to the one it created for Herbert Hoover. Indeed, if one applies the kind of criteria developed in recent years by political scientists,[4] the decisions taken in individual Western states were scarcely 'crisis' ones at all—although that would not be true for the League as an institution.

While a considerable degree of surprise was initially involved, it soon

---

[1] Ibid, 368–70; cf. Wilbur and Hyde, 600–1.

[2] See D. G. Pruitt, 'Definition of the Situation as a Determinant of International Action', in Kelman.

[3] See, e.g., Kelman, 134; Deutsch, *Nerves of Government*, 94.

[4] See C. F. Hermann, *Crises in Foreign Policy Making* (China Lake, California, 1965); cf. Kelman, 348; Hugo, *Appearance and Reality*, 88; C. Bell, *The Conventions of Crisis* (London, 1971).

became widely felt that the passage of time would ease the situation rather than worsen the circumstances in which major decisions would have to be made. Even those who placed a high or supreme value on upholding the League and its Covenant could reach a similar view in tactical terms. Moreover, as outlined in an earlier chapter, there existed initially not only confused but widely differing perceptions and priorities concerning international politics as a whole, a variety of cognitive maps upon which these new events would have to be placed and accorded their value. Incomplete information helped to perpetuate this degree of disagreement and confusion. An individual's immediate environment also appears to have contributed to the process, with diplomats of various nationalities in Tokyo tending to order their priorities nearer to each other's than to those of their compatriots in China, say, and with Reading, Pratt and Norman Davis, for example, displaying a shift of emphasis when in Geneva as opposed to their own capitals.[1]

For those who placed a high value on the maintenance of the post-war structure of international relations, Japan's action in Manchuria was generally seen to constitute a threat to the international community as a whole and to the League as an institution. It was possible, however, to avoid this conclusion by holding that the case was sui generis, while even Stimson, whose definition of the situation in this respect was fluctuating to a far larger extent than that of Castle or officials in the Foreign Office, was still far from setting up in his mind a closed image of Japan as 'an enemy'.[2] As far as a direct threat to one's own national possessions and material interests was concerned, this was scarcely perceived at all in Paris, London or Washington at this stage.[3] In part, this can be attributed to that mixture of history, personal experiences and other elements that help to make up a current image of another state and to guide one's expectations as to its future conduct.[4] Japan, as we have noted, had been seen by many politicians and foreign policy officials since the Washington Treaty as being reasonable and essentially friendly, however much her specific interests might diverge from one's own. Shidehara himself might now be in difficulties, but what has been termed the 'halo effect' of his past policies, as perceived in the West, could still affect outside attitudes towards his country, while the picture of a China in resentful chaos helped heighten the impression of the Japanese as being endowed with certain near-Western virtues. In addition, Western policymakers had invested a great deal, not only in terms of self-esteem but of self-preservation, in a non-threatening image of Japan; materially unprepared to face the consequences of a major error in that direction, their instinctive predilection for the more comfortable assumption was thus likely

[1] Would Reading, one wonders, have agreed to the deadline set by the League for a Japanese withdrawal if he had been working with Vansittart, Wellesley and others in London, and not Briand, Cecil, Cadogan and others in Geneva?

[2] See O. R. Holsti, 'Cognitive Dynamics and Images of the Enemy', in J. C. Farrell and A. P. Smith (eds.), *Image and Reality in World Politics* (New York, 1968).

[3] On threat perception generally, see, e.g., Kelman, 399 ff.

[4] See K. E. Boulding, 'The Learning and Reality—Testing Process in the International System', in Farrell and Smith; cf. Deutsch, 209.

to be all the greater. Such a process was also easier in that, while the evidence of Japan's *capability* of posing a direct threat to oneself could scarcely be doubted (though Stimson, for one, was not fully aware of the situation in this respect), that relating to her *intention* to do so still permitted of a wide range of interpretation.

In one sense, of course, such a failure to perceive a direct threat was in accord with the facts of the situation in Tokyo, where, as we have seen, no plans existed for an attack on Western possessions either singly or together. On the other hand it was significant for the longer view that there was also a widespread failure in the West to grasp either the extent of the political changes that were taking place in Japan, or the essential nature of the political culture involved. This was ultimately of far greater significance than, say, Stimson's short delay until 19 October in being able to note in his diary that 'the Japanese Government which we have been dealing with is no longer in control'. And even when some observers came closer to the reality of the situation—as did Lindley, for example—there remained a tendency—and again, Lindley provides an illustration—to regard what was taking place as a temporary aberration, and to suggest, as in the case of Germany later, that a sound and reasonable régime would soon be reestablished if no provocation were offered from outside. The failure also embraced those in unofficial circles who confidently asserted that a sufficiently clear display of 'world opinion' would send the Kwantung Army back to its billets. Not only did this belief rest upon a false picture of where initiative and control now lay on the Japanese side, but it assumed that the Japanese public, Colonel Itagaki, General Minami and others were essentially made in the mould of John Stuart Mill, possessing one's own hierarchy of values and a liberal, Western frame of reference.[1] In kind, in other words, the error was not dissimilar to that of believing in 1939 that Hitler could be placated with loans and large tracts of Africa, or, in 1969, that a high 'body-count', regardless of age, sex and intention, would help save South Vietnam for God, free enterprise and the Founding Fathers. Fundamentally, it arose from a failure of imagination.

For policy-makers in the West, the situation, if not directly threatening, was at least already perceived to be a complex one in terms of the tension between a large number of relevant desiderata. Even apart from the dilemma concerning the normative rules of international morality and the pragmatic ones of immediate self-interest, there arose major problems of balancing, for example, the need to retain China's good will against the desire not to antagonise Japan. To various unofficial commentators, the choices involved might appear simple, but to those at the main intersections in the web of international relations, the situation was rather the one that has been described in terms of domestic decision-making by Vickers:

> The more crudely simplified the objective, the more efficiently it is likely to be pursued. Given a single-valued objective and a repertory of 'means' assumed to be comparable simply by their cost in resources, it may be possible to demon-

[1] See De Rivera, cap. 9; cf. Hugo, *Britain In Tomorrow's World*, 122. This is not to say that Western governments and peoples had shown themselves as likely at all times to live up to this same, idealised portrait of liberal political man.

strate objectively which means is 'best'. But no political problem can or should be stated in these terms; the more truly we present to ourselves its multi-valued nature and the multi-valued effects of all the means by which we might pursue it, the more impossible it becomes to compare either the costs or the benefits of alternative solutions.[1]

In such circumstances, there is a familiar temptation to find comfort and certainty through analogy, to 'know' in this way the true nature of the present situation and the best course of action to adopt in order to solve its attendant problems and avoid its dangers.[2] As yet this had not occurred to any marked extent in the present case; but there were those in the Foreign Office in London, for example, who were already prepared to accept the parallel offered to them by the Japanese themselves—that of Manchuria in 1931 with Shanghai in 1927—and to be inhibited thereby, while Stimson on the other hand had powerful and painful memories of 1914 that might prompt him to speak out where Woodrow Wilson had remained silent. Meanwhile, there was in all Western capitals a strong disposition to avoid any lone initiative, and to order priorities—even if in the British and American cases this was scarcely done explicitly—in an essentially defensive fashion. Even among League stalwarts at Geneva and elsewhere, what stands out most in the confusion and uncertainty of the time is a search for constraints,[3] an attempt to define what is least unacceptable and what cannot immediately be done. One might continue resolutely to hope that the situation could be changed; but at the same time (some acknowledging it, some not, even to themselves) the notion is present that aspirations might have to be reduced.[4]

Could more have been attempted? It seems clear that a commission of enquiry, for example, might have been despatched far earlier than was to be the case, and probably would have been, had the United States lent its support to such a project at the outset.[5] A strong, joint démarche by the Western powers, perhaps even a withdrawal of ambassadors, was also practicable. At once, however, imponderables begin to appear, such as the reaction of the various publics in the West, and the evidence suggests that reluctance and discord might well have greeted more ambitious and apparently risky steps than the ones actually taken. Cecil himself recognised as much at the time, though not later. And even if the commission had been sent, or the démarche—even condemnation—delivered, would the desired result have been achieved? One cannot say that it would have been impos-

---

[1] Vickers, 104.

[2] See, e.g., Hoffmann, *Gulliver's Troubles*, 135 ff.

[3] See Huntington, *The Common Defense*, 250; Vickers 128-9, 138; Braybrook and Lindblom, passim.

[4] See J. Frankel, 'Rational Decision-Making in Foreign Policy', in *The Year Book of World Affairs* (London, 1960), 43.

[5] Under article 5, para. 2, a majority vote would have sufficed for items 'including the appointment of committees to investigate particular matters'. Had there still been difficulty, the Chinese could have appealed under article 15, whereby the Secretary General was bound to 'make all necessary arrangements for a full investigation' of the dispute.

sible. On the other hand, there is ample evidence from which to argue that, from the outset, there were too many groups within Japanese official circles who stood to gain from adopting a policy of fierce and scornful resistance to any concessions to Western pressure for any Tokyo administration making such concessions to long survive. Shidehara and others might have felt bound to order a complete withdrawal in the face of a threat of sanctions, but what then? It seems likely that the Kwantung Army would have pressed on in open defiance, and might well have received widespread backing in Japan. Even before the Mukden incident, public opinion and influential groups had been roused by propaganda teams from Manchuria. 'Powerful circles and figures behind the scenes, like the House of Peers Study Group and Impartial Club, Fukuda Masataro and Ito Myoji in the Privy Council, veered towards approval of a strong line. On 5 August . . . there were signs that a national movement was getting under way.'[1] The ruling Minseito party was itself split on the issue; the opposing Seiyukai had agreed in private that the Manchurian question 'could be settled only by the exercise of national power'.[2] Within the Navy and the Foreign Ministry—both long thought of by historians as centres of restraint—recent scholarship has demonstrated that powerful extremist factions were already at work.[3] Immediately after the Mukden incident, even the major liberal newspaper in Japan, the *Asahi Shimbun*, came out with a statement that the Kwantung Army had acted to protect the country's interests,[4] and while a public statement of intransigence by that Army on 4 October was received with enthusiasm, both Japanese and Western peace-workers were sending back to the West reports of the impossibility of stemming the rapid flood of excited nationalism.[5] Despite their differences, in retrospect it is the fundamental agreement between the military in Mukden and in Tokyo on what was at stake for Japan that stands out.[6] Where certainty is impossible, the present writer is inclined to agree with Professor Seki when he concludes that 'the efforts of Shidehara diplomacy to localise the outbreak were doomed to failure once military action broke out in Manchuria'.[7]

If it is doubtful whether any démarche by the League and United States would have brought success, the same consideration applies to the often-blamed unanimity requirement of article 11 of the Covenant and Japan's vetoing of the 24 October Resolution that laid down three weeks for a withdrawal of troops. Had the majority been able to make such a decision binding, would Japan have complied? If not, the same question would have had to be faced: what then? True, the debate over further measures had not yet

[1] Seki Hiroharu, 'The Road to the Pacific War', vol. 1, part 2.
[2] Ibid.
[3] Invaluable papers were prepared for the Hakone conference by Katsumi Usui on 'The Role of the Foreign Ministry', and by Asada Sadao on 'The Japanese Navy and the United States'.
[4] Hakone conference, proceedings.
[5] E.g., Gilbert Bowles to American Friends Service Committee, 30 January 1932, and Tano Jodai to Emily Balch, Jane Addams Papers, series 1, box 20. Both letters surveyed developments from September onwards.
[6] Shimada Toshihiko, 'The Road to the Pacific War', vol. 1, part 3.
[7] 'The Road to the Pacific War', vol. 1, part 2.

been fully joined in the West, but unless an answer was forthcoming that was both practicable and effective, then in a sense the unanimity requirement of article 11 had saved the League's face. Whatever the difficulties, however, there could be no ignoring the problem. The Kwantung Army was soon to see to that.

CHAPTER SIX

DETERIORATION: TO THE LEAGUE RESOLUTION OF 10 DECEMBER 1931

Developments in the Far East

ON 26 OCTOBER, the Japanese Government at last publicly revealed the five fundamental principles which must govern Sino-Japanese relations in the future. If the point relating to their own treaty rights in Manchuria was clearly the most contentious, that which pledged respect for China's territorial integrity already had a hollow ring as the Kwantung Army's promotion of local independence movements continued apace. A new Liaoning provincial government was established on 7 November, for example,[1] and a Self-Government Guiding Board for the whole area was set up around the same time. Speculation was particularly increased by the disappearance from Tientsin of Henry Pu-yi, heir to the Manchu dynasty, and his subsequent arrival in Mukden under the protection of the Kwantung Army.

With tension between local inhabitants and Japanese residents continuing to rise in other parts of China,[2] there was also renewed military activity in Manchuria in November. Some of it involved areas sufficiently far north to raise again the question of possible Soviet intervention. At the Nonni river, where, as we have seen, the retreating Chinese General, Ma Chan-shan, had destroyed the railway bridges in order to halt the Japanese-sponsored Chang Hai-peng, the Kwantung Army now intervened on the grounds of their country's interest in the line,[3] and demanded that the bridges be repaired. This was followed by an attempt by the Japanese themselves to do the work, and, amidst bitter winter conditions, the outbreak of fighting between their covering forces and Ma's troops on 4 November. On the 17th the former advanced northwards, beyond the Chinese Eastern Railway, and

---

[1] Its name was changed soon afterwards to Fengtien, as it had been known before the acceptance of union with China in the 1920s.

[2] There was now a widespread Chinese boycott of Japanese goods. In response, a meeting of 3,000 Japanese in the International Settlement at Shanghai on 1 November resolved 'that Japan severely punish China in order to promote the welfare of Japan and China by securing peace in the Orient', and that no Western interference be tolerated. FO 371, F6929/1391/10.

[3] The Taonan–Angangchi line had been financed by a loan from the S.M.R., and was an important route for transporting soya beans to the south.

two days later captured Tsitsihar, seat of the Heilungkiang provincial government. To general surprise, however, the Japanese began to withdraw within the week.

Meanwhile, far to the south in Tientsin, beyond the boundary of Manchuria, disturbances had occurred on 8 and 26 November which involved brief skirmishes between Chinese troops and the local detachment of Japanese soldiers who were stationed there under treaty arrangements. On the second of these occasions, units of the Kwantung Army in Manchuria had begun to move south-westwards towards Chinchow, bombing that town again and en route, it seemed, to aid their colleagues in Tientsin. As in the north, however, they halted, and on 29 November withdrew to the east of the Liao river without having entered Chinchow. An acrimonious dispute then arose concerning a Chinese proposal on the 23rd for the establishment of a demilitarized zone around Chinchow, with their own troops to be withdrawn to Shanhaikuan on the China-Manchuria border in return for a Japanese pledge not to advance. Despite Tokyo's acceptance in principle, no agreement was reached on the limits of the zone or the presence there of neutral troops or observers, as the Chinese wished. By 9 December, to the accompaniment of Japanese accusations of bad faith, the Nanking Government had withdrawn the whole idea.

One reason for Nanking's caution and final intransigence was the mounting pressure of public, and especially student, demonstrations against any concessions being made to the invader. Although the Fourth National Congress of the Kuomintang had recently proclaimed the unity of Nanking and Canton, faction fighting also continued and fed upon the confusion of the time. In the first week of December martial law was proclaimed in the capital, and both Alfred Sze in Geneva and Wellington Koo, the Foreign Minister, felt obliged to offer their resignations. Under Cantonese pressure, Chiang Kai-shek himself was to resign his offices on 15 December, with all his Nanking colleagues in the Government following a week later amid violent student attacks on official buildings in the city.[1]

Confusion was only slightly less apparent in Tokyo, where the Wakatsuki ministry, faced with a flight from the yen[2] as well as the Manchurian crisis, had resigned on 11 December. From late October, Shidehara had continued in muted form to try to get the army to accept a diplomatic solution to the conflict, while offering the world explanations which Wakatsuki despairingly described as 'rather flimsy, though still having some semblance of truth'.[3] Their discomfort was shared by Yoshizawa at Geneva, who had protested against the defiance of the League implied by the publication of the five principles, and had urged that attention be paid to 'the reasonable moral pressures of the Council'.[4] In addition, however—and it was vital to the degree of success which they did achieve—the civilian leaders received a limited measure of support from senior army officers in Tokyo who, to the anger of the Kwantung Army staff, invoked the right of supreme command

[1] See, e.g., *North China Herald*, 13 December 1931.
[2] Speculators were buying dollars in the expectation that Japan would follow Britain off gold, with a consequent depreciation of her currency.
[3] Harada Diary, quoted in Yoshizawa, 212–13.
[4] Ogata, 104, 109.

in their attempt to obtain the latters' obedience.[1] Still thinking in terms of allowing China at least nominal suzerainty over Manchuria, the General Staff above all remained unwilling to create a furore over possible Soviet intervention—in contrast to the Kwantung Army, which took secret assurances by Soviet officials in Harbin as proof that their tough policy was also a safe one. Therefore the order went out on 24 November[2] for a withdrawal from Tsitsihar 'immediately and irrespective of any circumstances'. Likewise, Itagaki and his enraged colleagues were told on the 27th to withdraw the force that was advancing on Chinchow.[3]

Although dramatic in themselves, however, these successes were only temporary. Already, faced with overwhelming public support for the army's actions, the Foreign Office had acknowledged in mid-November that a withdrawal of troops must be linked with the creation of an entirely new régime in Manchuria, and had instructed its diplomats on the spot to assist the new, and obviously manipulated, Committees for the Maintenance of Peace and Order. The Kwantung Army continued to draw up its own blueprint for a Japanese-dominated régime under which racial and social harmony would be achieved,[4] while Itagaki quietly slipped north to persuade General Ma, whom they had defeated in the advance on Tsitsihar, to accept the idea of an independent government for Heilungkiang.[5] Colonel Doihara Kenji, 'the Lawrence of Manchuria', was also active, defying orders by flitting into Tientsin to foment the riots there and engineer Pu-yi's removal to Manchuria.[6] In other words, whatever concessions they might make in their immediate design or overt methods, the Kwantung Army staff were not to be deterred in moving towards a solution 'that far exceeded the imagination and approval of military and civilian leaders in Tokyo'.[7] And while they received daily evidence of public support, their scorn for Shidehara and his colleagues was increased by the failure of the neutral-zone scheme, which Tokyo had been quick to adopt.[8] As for the idea of a League commission of enquiry (which the Japanese representatives, Yoshizawa and Matsudaira, finally put forward in public at a Council meeting of 21 November), the Commander of the Kwantung Army was apparently confident that it would be 'advantageous to make known the realities of the area to the League investigators'.[9] Tokyo was ready, in any case, to stipulate that its army's

[1] *Taiheiyo senso e no michi*, II, 49–64, 79–83.

[2] IMTFE, *Exhibits* 3422 L and M. Among civilian officials, the Japanese Consul at Tsitsihar opposed an advance. His colleague at Harbin, however, urged that the opportunity should be taken to defeat the Soviet 'enemy of humanity'. Ibid, *Exhibit* 700.

[3] Ibid, *Exhibit* 3422 N; Yoshihashi, 216–18. In Bergamini's version (op. cit., 449), the advance to and withdrawal from Tsitsihar was planned as a sop to the League.

[4] Ogata, 121 ff.

[5] IMTFE, *Proceedings*, 18,950 (Katakura testimony); cf. *Exhibits* 287, 3479 I and J. Ma was to join the Manchukuo régime, then revolt against it.

[6] Ibid, *Proceedings*, 3,969 ff. and 19,781 ff.; *Exhibits* 286, 289, 290, 294, 295, 299, 2196, 3479 H.

[7] Ogata, 132.   [8] *Taiheiyo senso e no michi*, II, 97–9; Takeuchi, 366–8.

[9] Ogata, 116. Crowley, 140, accepts what Matsudaira said at the time, that the proposal was entirely a personal suggestion. Nevertheless, the idea had obviously

freedom of action must not be curtailed by the proposal, and time was gained in which to erect the façade of an independent state. The need to hurry on with such work was appreciated by Itagaki and his friends, but the possible strictures of a League report were matters of indifference to them; like the General Staff in Tokyo, they also chose to interpret the League's forthcoming Resolution of 10 December as tacit recognition that an attack on Chinchow would proceed.[1]

Within the Cabinet itself, the Government's end was accompanied by intrigues that were aimed at the formation of a coalition with the opposing Seiyukai. It was a Seiyukai Prime Minister, Inukai Tsuyoshi, who took over from Wakatsuki, however, and although he had private hopes of re-establishing governmental control, the immediate prospects were slender. While Shidehara had departed in near-ignominy, the incoming War Minister, General Araki Sadao, was known as a vigorous exponent of the bushido tradition—the code of the warrior whose greatest glory was to die in battle for his divine emperor. Moreover, by the middle of December he and other army leaders in Tokyo had made it clear that the new Government must now reinforce the Kwantung Army to enable it to win control of North Manchuria; in addition, they approved the fostering of local independence movements, and suggested that if possible the Kwantung Army should also seize Jehol and the Shanhaikuan pass between Manchuria and North China.[2] In short, Western hopes that the affair might yet be settled peacefully and equitably were already doomed.

Public reactions in the West

The Council of the League had reassembled on 16 November in the Salle de l'Horloge of the Quai d'Orsay in Paris—Briand, desperately defending himself and his policies, not being able to leave that city for Geneva. Japan had not withdrawn her troops, but instead had rejected a Chinese offer, commended by Briand, to submit all matters of treaty interpretation to arbitration or judicial settlement under article 13 of the Covenant.[3] The atmosphere was thus a tense one from the first, and despite the past triumphs associated with the room where the Council met,[4] it was a setting that made some observers doubly uneasy. 'Dans ce palais du quai d'Orsay,' wrote William Martin, 'dont les murs sont si chargés d'histoire, on sentait comme un froid vous descendre sur les épaules: c'était toute l'ancienne diplomatie qui vous saisissait.'[5] Such sentiments were also strengthened by the greatly increased degree of official secrecy which from now on surrounded the Council's work.

been mooted in Manchuria and Tokyo some weeks before. *Taiheiyo senso e no michi*, II, 361–2.

[1] *Taiheiyo senso e no michi*, II, 99–102.

[2] Crowley, 152–3. In order to increase the army's grip on affairs, an imperial prince, General Kanin, was made titular head of the General Staff.

[3] For the exchange of correspondence after 24 October, see LNOJ, *December, 1931*, annex 1334.

[4] The Council had dealt with the Greco–Bulgarian dispute there, and the Kellogg–Briand Pact had been signed in the same room.

[5] *Journal de Genève*, 18 November 1931.

Only three secret meetings had been held by that body between March 1929 and May 1931; seven had taken place between the opening of the crisis and 24 October; now there were to be twenty-one up to 10 December, with only four public meetings in the same period, commencing on November 16 with a brief résumé of events to date.[1] Even the usual rumours and leakage of information only helped emphasise that several of the smaller states represented on the Council were unhappy at this degree of secrecy, as well as being impatient to reaffirm that Japan should withdraw her troops forthwith.[2]

As in the previous period, rumours also centred around the policies of the United States. In public, the State Department had continued to insist on the country's strict impartiality between Japan and China,[3] while it was known that Stimson had been given a reassuring answer by Shidehara when he had urged the withdrawal of troops.[4] The very moderation of this exchange helped stimulate speculation concerning a possible Japanese–American understanding,[5] and the *New York Herald Tribune* gave the pot a vigorous stir on 17 November by claiming to know 'on high authority' that Ambassador Debuchi had received assurances that the United States would take no part in economic sanctions, a withdrawal of diplomatic representatives, or any deadlines set by the League. A denial by Stimson did not remove anxiety;[6] nor did the presence in Paris of General Charles Dawes, banker, American Ambassador in London and formerly Calvin Coolidge's Vice President, a 'character' whose dogmatism passed for shrewdness in some corners of his native land. Dawes had been ordered to Paris on 10 November in order to be available for consultations with members of the Council on matters of mutual interest; unlike Gilbert at Geneva, however, he did not attend the Council's meetings, but remained in the Ritz, holding frequent interviews with representatives of the major powers and of the two disputants, including his friend Matsudaira Tsuneo, Japanese Ambassador in London. In some eyes, the General had in effect set up 'a rival League of his own'.[7]

Nevertheless, it was soon public knowledge that renewed Japanese military activity was disturbing Stimson as well as the men in the Salle de l'Horloge. News of the seizure of Tsitsihar burst 'like a bomb' in Paris, according to one eyewitness,[8] coming as it did on the heels of a strong warning from Sze that China would not negotiate until the Kwantung Army had withdrawn to the railway zone, and that she might soon invoke further articles of the Covenant: 'This is a life or death issue for the Chinese Government which has staked its political existence on the policy of relying on the

[1] LNOJ, *December, 1931*, 2362–4.

[2] *Geneva Special Studies*, vol. II, No. 12, 45, 53; Willoughby, 191–5; Toynbee, *Survey, 1931*, 504.

[3] E.g., Castle press conference, 31 October 1931, DS 793.94/2489.

[4] Stimson to Neville, 3 November; Shidehara memorandum, 9 November 1931, FRUS, *Japan 1931–41*, I, 34–5 and 39–40; Stimson press conferences, 6, 7, 11 November 1931, DS 793.94/2662, 2749, 2787/8; *New York Times*, 6, 7 November 1931.

[5] *Geneva Special Studies*, II, No. 12, 36.   [6] DS 793.94/2927.

[7] Fleming, 408.   [8] *Journal de Genève*, 20 November 1931.

League. It is also a life and death issue for the League and for the Disarmament Conference.'[1] News of the Japanese advance on Chinchow produced an even greater sensation, with the American press carrying reports of an angry Stimson declaring himself on 27 November to be 'at a loss to understand' the move in the light of assurances he had previously received from Shidehara.[2] A blight thus appeared to fall on the progress that had been made when Yoshizawa had proposed on the 21st that the Council should despatch a commission of enquiry, a step that had been incorporated in a draft resolution published on the 25th and welcomed by Stimson as one in which the United States, if invited, would almost certainly participate.[3]

Stimson's Chinchow outburst, together with subsequent appeals and recriminations over the neutral zone proposal, helped to heighten the relief when at last, in public sessions on 9 and 10 December,[4] there emerged a Resolution which could command the assent of all members of the Council. In this new document, the Resolution of 30 September (with its call for the speedy withdrawal of Japanese troops) was reaffirmed and both parties enjoined to refrain from any action which might aggravate the situation; at the same time all members were invited to continue to furnish information to the Council, which remained seized of the dispute, and a commission of five members, plus a Chinese and a Japanese assessor, was to proceed to the area to study and report on circumstances threatening to disturb the peace between Nanking and Tokyo. The commission, however, was not specifically instructed to lay down the basis for a settlement; nor, as Briand stressed in his covering observations, did its terms of reference embrace matters of direct negotiation between the two parties or the military arrangements of either. Nor did the Resolution as a whole attempt to set a new time limit for a withdrawal of troops, and Yoshizawa accepted it only on the understanding that it did not preclude military action against bandits as 'an exceptional measure called for by the special situation prevailing in Manchuria'. In return, Sze warned against further aggression being carried out on such a pretext, and declared that if Japan promoted 'so-called independence movements', China would hold her to be in breach of her undertakings.

Despite the relief of the occasion, Sze was clearly not the only member of the Council who retained serious misgivings. Madariaga, for example, passed some crisp and disapproving comments on the reservation made by Yoshizawa concerning bandits; Matos of Guatemala, Gonzalez-Prada of Peru, Garay of Panama and de Chlapowski of Poland all wished to reaffirm the basic principles of collective security and respect for treaties, which could not be made dependent on the will of one party to a dispute. Cecil, too,

---

[1] Sze to Briand, 18 November, LNOJ, *December, 1931*, annex 1334.

[2] The imbroglio can be followed in the Associated Press despatch of 27 November, which merged 'a general review from various sources' with Stimson's revelation of his enquiry to and reply from Shidehara. For the official press conference records, see DS 793.94/3064, 3065.

[3] LNOJ, *December, 1931*, 2364–71; Stimson press conference, 25 November 1931, DS 793.94/3041.

[4] LNOJ, *December, 1931*, 2374–83. There was much uncertainty over whether Dawes would attend the final session. He did not.

while recalling that, under article 11, the Council's task was one of 'mediation and persuasion' rather than 'arbitration or decision', was obviously anxious about the bandit proviso, and Briand, although asserting that there had been no 'resort to war' as set out in article 12, accepted that they were dealing with 'a special case' in ways which could not constitute a precedent. There could be no excuse for the use of force, however well-founded a state's grievances; but at least 'three months[1] have (now) been gained, and this is not only likely to bring about a calmer frame of mind, to arouse public opinion throughout the world and thus improve the psychological conditions of peace, but has made it possible to create machinery for the local organisation of peace'. On this note of troubled hope, and after paying warm tribute to its visibly declining Chairman, the Council dispersed. Its achievements were publicly welcomed by Stimson,[2] but its complete inability to commit or rely upon the United States was underlined on the same day by Hoover in a message to Congress.[3] Nor were there any signs that the Soviet Government intended to become involved in the matter, fierce criticism of Japanese imperialism continuing to be matched in the Moscow press by scorn for the puny efforts of the League.[4]

So much was public knowledge in the West, and in France the reactions to it showed little change from preceding weeks. In the Chamber, the only strong questions on the subject came from the extreme Left, where Doriot and other Communists warned that a situation akin to that in the Balkans in 1914 was developing, and pressed for swift action against Japan.[5] L'Humanité likewise continued to attack Japan, and also the League, which, under the guidance of the 'social-fascist' Briand, had joined Tokyo in working against the Soviet Union.[6] La République, Le Populaire and L'Ère Nouvelle also denounced the attack upon China, Herriot in particular applauding Briand's unsupported attempts to use the machinery of the League, while L'Oeuvre raised the seldom-heard cry of a long-term threat to French Indo-China.[7] Like much of the press in the smaller European countries,[8] these organs of the Left in France were also uneasy about the nature of the Council's final Resolution. They were outnumbered, however, by those who applauded the actions of 'our Japanese friends', as L'Avenir

[1] Briand was referring to article 12, under which parties to a dispute which was the subject of enquiry by the Council agreed 'in no case to resort to war until three months after the . . . report by the Council.'

[2] FRUS, Japan, 1931–41, I, 60–2.

[3] Congressional Record, 72nd Congress, vol. 75, 297–8.

[4] E.g. Izvestia, 4 November 1931; New York Times, 27, 31 October 1931.

[5] Annales de la Chambre des Députés, Novembre–Decembre, 1931 (Paris, 1933), 826, 4,202–7.

[6] L'Humanité, 11 November, 10 December 1931.

[7] La République, 11 November; L'Ère Nouvelle, 12 November; L'Oeuvre, 15 November; Le Peuple, 19 November; Le Populaire, 11 November 1931.

[8] See e.g., the Brussels paper Peuple, of 18 December 1931, which declared that henceforth no European state could rely on the League for protection against an aggressive neighbour. Not all papers of the French Left were unreservedly anti-Japanese, the radical-socialist Dépêche de Toulouse, for example (see the issue of 11 January 1932) viewing that country as a civilising influence in Manchuria.

termed them, and poured ridicule on the futile meddling of the League. A trumpeting chorus denounced the anarchy and Soviet-inspired bolshevism of China, hailed Japan as the civilised protector of Indo-China, and advised Briand to put an end to his foolish theorising about peace before he found, in the words of *Figaro*, a Hitlerised Germany enforcing its own kind of peace on the smoking ruins of France, 'notre belle pays, jardin du monde'.[1] The eloquent pronouncements of *Le Temps* on this subject have already been illustrated.[2]

In other countries, it was widely assumed at the time that the French Government looked to Japan to help prevent any significant disarmament measures emerging from the forthcoming conference, and that the French armament industry was busy manipulating its country's press in the same cause. The actual and less dramatic state of things has been outlined in the previous chapter,[3] but at least an outside observer would have been correct in assuming that domestic uproar awaited any French Government which tried to go so far as to take a prominent part in attempting to coerce Japan. Nor was there any substantial pressure pointing in the opposite direction within the United States, and this at a time when the new Congress assembled on the Hill ready and able to do battle with Hoover over taxation, expenditure and measures to relieve the fearful extent of social hardship. There was, it is true, an increasing amount of press criticism of Japan, particularly in the Mid-West, South and West.[4] East-coast papers, too, carried reports of the Kwantung Army's political manipulations, and condemned what the *Washington Post* called 'a deadly blow at the Chinese Republic'.[5] And while that same paper was suggesting that no one in Tokyo would dare defy an American protest based on the Nine Power Treaty, Walter Lippmann came out with the proposal that non-recognition was the simplest way in which the West could defeat a Japanese design which, 'as a matter of self-respect and self-interest', they were bound to oppose:

> They cannot and need not make threats. They have only to be patient and let public opinion become informed. For the Japanese objective is one which cannot be obtained without their help. Japan seeks a recognition of her treaty claims in Manchuria . . . She can get it only . . . from some kind of international conference in which the other Powers are represented.[6]

A few were urging more immediate measures: John Dewey's Independent Political Association, for example, wanted the American Ambassador in

[1] E.g., *L'Avenir*, 16 November; *Le Matin*, 16 November; *L'Echo de Paris*, 15, 19, 22 November, 10, 11 December; *Le Temps*, 21 November, 11 December; *Figaro*, 11 December; *Le Journal*, 12 December 1931.
[2] See above, 7.
[3] It is almost certain that sections of the French press were being manipulated by arms-manufacturing interests, but documentary evidence is hard to come by.
[4] Tupper and McReynolds, 304 ff.
[5] E.g., *Washington Post*, 5, 21, 27 November, 4 December 1931; *New York Times*, 19, 23 November 1931. The emphasis of comment tended to shift rapidly, however.
[6] Lippmann, *Interpretations, 1931–3*, 193–4; *New York Herald Tribune*, 1 December 1931.

Tokyo withdrawn,[1] while one group within the Washington Press Club defined the opportunity now facing Hoover in particularly dramatic terms.[2] Yet the forty-one peace organisations that petitioned the President on 24 November, although asking that Dawes should sit with the League Council, sought to halt the supply of American arms and loans to both Japan and China, an act which would have proclaimed a hatred of bloodshed rather than a readiness to punish the aggressor.[3] The L.N.A., too, after consulting with Arthur Sweetser, an American member of the League Secretariat, chose to express by shoals of telegrams their appreciation of Hoover's limited co-operation with the League, rather than to call for more vigorous action; individuals like Newton Baker and Raymond Fosdick did the same.[4] Meanwhile papers like the *New York Times* and *Washington Post* continued to print articles and editorials which suggested that right was by no means entirely on China's side, while the *Christian Science Monitor* openly supported Japan.[5] The Japanese, wrote Lippmann, 'confronted . . . with local corruption and disorder promoted from China proper and exploited as a method of disguised warfare . . . (have) by ordinary international standards been extremely patient under great provocation.' By setting up puppet governments their army was, 'in a word, carrying on not "a war" but "an intervention"', a procedure 'all the powers have in the past followed at one place and another, ourselves included, as in Nicaragua, Haiti and elsewhere'.[6] The same writer disapproved of the November deadline for withdrawal which the League had set, and privately thought that it had been 'probably illegal and certainly unwise' in inviting an American representative to sit with it.[7] As for Hearst, McKormick and their like, it need be said only that their outcry against the League—and, often, against any cuts in America's own military budget—became all the louder in this

---

[1] *New York Times*, 27 November 1931.

[2] As passed on to the Secretary of the Interior, Wilbur, by his executive assistant, the conclusion of this press group was: 'The hour for Herbert Hoover has struck. If he acts immediately he can insure his re-election and the peace leadership of the world. If he fails to act he will lose more heavily than in any situation that has yet arisen. The simple thing he could do is to declare a Japanese boycott . . . and invite the rest of the world to go along with him.' Du Puy memorandum, 19 November 1931, Wilbur Papers.

[3] Representative Hamilton Fish also introduced a resolution in December which sought to embargo arms to all belligerents. Among the anti-war groups, Dorothy Detzer stood out as an individual who was beginning to think of a financial and economic boycott. See her circular of December 1931, Detzer Papers, box 1.

[4] Clark Eichelberger to Sweetser, 12 November 1931, Sweetser Papers, box 31; Eichelberger to Newton Baker, 1 December 1931, Baker Papers, box 145; Baker et al. to Hoover, Baker Papers, box 100; Hoover Papers, China. Sweetser held the rank of counsellor in the Information Section at Geneva.

[5] See, e.g., Hallett Abend's article in the *New York Times*, 16 December 1931; *Washington Post*, 23 October, 17 November 1931; *Christian Science Monitor*, 5 December 1931.

[6] Lippmann, *Interpretations, 1931-3*, 195-8. Lippmann nevertheless wished Japan to gain 'no new advantages' as a result of her intervention.

[7] *New York Herald Tribune*, 6 December 1931.

period. The most that some would allow was that it was as well for honest and naïve Uncle Sam to have his blunt, no-nonsense Charlie Dawes around in Paris to make sure that he was not associated with 'the perfidy of the Council' or 'hoodwinked by the sinister moves made in Europe for the purpose of overreaching this country'.[1]

The possibility of an Anglo-Japanese clash at some future date still scarcely figured at all in British comment, but there, too, several papers continued to give prominence to Japanese grievances against China.[2] In private, some people were even more ready to indicate where their sympathies lay. 'Do what you can to help Japan in Manchuria!!' wrote Field Marshal Sir William Birdwood, former commander at the Dardanelles and now Master of Peterhouse, to his friend, the new Foreign Secretary:

> This I know sounds all wrong, perhaps immoral, when she is flouting the League of Nations, but 1. she has had great provocation, 2. she *must* ere long expand *somewhere*—for goodness sake let (or rather encourage) her to do so there instead of Australia's way, and 3. her presence fully established in Manchuria means a real block against Bolshevik aggression.[3]

Simon himself, while not accepting this argument unreservedly in private, maintained in the Commons that 'as long as there was any chance of the League operating usefully, they had to avoid taking up a position which might seem to prejudice or condemn'. For the Opposition, Lansbury agreed.[4]

To the *Manchester Guardian*, on the other hand, judgement against Japan now appeared long overdue. In this, the vital test for collective security, the British Government and League Council were alike failing in their duty, the 'miserable efforts' of the latter having 'made it contemptible in the eyes of the world'.[5] The commission of enquiry would not save China, and was probably intended only to save the Council's own face—a criticism which, surprisingly, was echoed in milder form by *The Times*, which referred to the commission's 'tardy mission' and 'modified terms of reference'.[6] The explanation of the *Manchester Guardian* school—that the major powers were happy to see China taught a lesson—was given a further gloss by William Martin in the *Spectator* of 19 December, to the effect that both Britain and France had in earlier years concluded secret deals with Japan which gave her a free hand in Manchuria:

> Lord Cecil, M. Briand and Mr. Stimson have all three had to fight their officials, and it cannot be said that they have emerged victorious. That is one of the

[1] E.g., *San Francisco Examiner*, 11, 12, 18, 24 November, 9 December 1931; *Chicago Daily Tribune*, 7, 8 November, 1 December 1931; *Washington Post*, 31 October, 1, 13, 20, 22 November, 23, 30 December 1931; *New York Herald Tribune*, 5 November 1931; National Patriotic League to Stimson, 3 November 1931, DS 793.94/2473.

[2] E.g., *Daily Telegraph*, 13 November 1931; *Evening Standard*, 16 November 1931; *The Times*, 16 November, 10 December 1931; *Observer*, 29 November 1931.

[3] Birdwood to Simon, 6 November 1931, Simon Papers (private collection), Foreign Affairs, 1931.

[4] *The Times*, 26 October, 2, 7, 23, 26, 28, 30 November 1931.

[5] *Manchester Guardian*, 8 December 1931; cf. ibid, 30 October, 4, 10, 11, 19, 27 November, 10 December 1931; Toynbee, *Survey, 1931*, 477–80.

[6] *Manchester Guardian*, 21 November 1931; *The Times*, 11 December 1931.

gravest factors of the whole affair . . . It proves that secret diplomacy is not dead, that its poison has not ceased to work.

When it came to suggesting what action should be taken, however, the critics showed far less confidence and clarity, as Bassett has already observed.[1] In Parliament, the question received little attention, and although Geoffrey Mander suggested a withdrawal of ambassadors followed by economic pressure and ultimately a blockade if Japan remained obdurate, no one took up the point.[2] The *Manchester Guardian* only tentatively and indirectly raised the possibility of economic sanctions, for which the Labour Party likewise showed little enthusiasm. As among the American peace societies, the idea put forward by Lansbury in the Commons and by the *New Statesman* on 19 December was for a ban on arms supplies to both parties in the dispute in order to avoid 'any further share in shedding this blood', despite the obvious fact that such a move would penalise an industrialised Japan far less than it would China. The same idea appeared on 24 November in a resolution of the L.N.U.'s Executive Committee, a body whose mild public performance (despite restless and crowded branch meetings) brought forth scathing comments from the *Manchester Guardian*.[3] Indeed, during a Union lunch on 10 December, at which Simon was the guest of honour, Gilbert Murray observed that the opinion of jurists was that it was not clear whether Japan 'had broken any particular clause of the Covenant', while on the following day Cecil, echoed by Grey, declared that 'the justification of the League was complete', it having 'laid the foundation for a better state of things' in the face of 'two great agencies of disorder . . .: Japanese militarism and Chinese anarchy'. 'When men like M. Briand, Señor Madariaga and Lord Cecil . . . come to us with a unanimous settlement,' wrote Murray, 'telling us that they have done their best, for my part, I believe them and am grateful to them.'[4]

It would not be surprising, of course, to discover that such statements had been designed simply to sustain hope and faith in the League, and that they had concealed a private impatience for swift and vigorous action against Japan. Cecil, after all, was to suggest as much in his memoirs, where he deplored the inactivity of the Foreign Office during this period when 'no honest man could doubt that Japan had "resorted to war" in breach of . . . the Covenant, or that members of the League were bound to take action under Article 16 to assist China'.[5] The implication appears to be that Cecil himself had been ready for even military action: '*Not only was force not used to restrain the aggressor*,' he wrote later, 'but the reason given for not using it reduced League action to fatuity or worse.'[6] Yet doubts which are aroused in the reader by the very confusion of these same memoirs[7] are

---

[1] Bassett, 13–57.   [2] *Hansard, House of Commons*, vol. 259, cols. 201–2.

[3] *Manchester Guardian*, 25, 30 November, 8, 11 December 1931.

[4] Ibid, 11, 12, 18 December 1931; *The Times*, 11, 12 December 1931.

[5] Cecil, 227–32. This passage, in the context of its paragraph, is clearly referring to the situation in the autumn of 1931, before the Lytton Commission was constituted.

[6] Ibid, 332; emphasis added.

[7] In one place, for example, Cecil implies that economic sanctions would have halted Japan, in another that a show of resolution by the West would have been

amply confirmed by the private correspondence that was circulating between Cecil and his L.N.U. colleagues at the time, and which makes Cecil's later writings appear not only tendentious but even at times vindictive.[1] Of Simon, for example, so soon to become the symbol of betrayal, Cecil was writing to Murray on 13 November that he was 'quite sound' on the Manchurian question; two weeks later he was dismissing a *News Chronicle* report 'which seemed to set up a kind of opposition between me and Simon' (over the desirability of encouraging L.N.U. pressure) as 'the very reverse of fact', whilst he termed Martin's *Spectator* article 'fantastic nonsense'. As late as April 1932, when suggesting to a friend that it had been 'too late for coercion' by February of that year, he was referring to his criticism of Simon 'so far as it goes, which is not very far'.[2] Even on the eve of the Paris meeting of the Council, on which Cecil was to centre this mild disappointment with the Foreign Secretary, he acknowledged to Murray:

> I rather incline to think that any violent or outspoken action on our part might be dangerous at this moment. The truth is that we must be content to move rather slowly because owing to the complex conditions of affairs just now we cannot threaten.[3]

A week later, while agreeing that the crisis was 'a very serious blow to the machinery which we have devised', he felt optimistic enough to add that, if the commission of enquiry were agreed to, 'that will be something and indeed perhaps in the long run more than anything else that could have been devised'.[4] The case could adequately be dealt with, he wrote on 28 November, 'on ordinary, straightforward lines'; overlooking his earlier desire to take as a model the Greco-Bulgar crisis (which had been dealt with under article 11), he now believed that, had the Chinese brought their case under article 15, 'we should have had an enquiry which would, by now, have been well on its way and we should have taken whatever measures were necessary to render an actual clash unlikely'.[5]

Cecil's close friend, Noel-Baker, was another who was now looking to article 15 for a solution. He, too, however, was not eager for sanctions, commending the consequences of the article to Murray as being '*not* (to) bring Art. 16 any nearer, but (to) put it off'.[6] Meanwhile Cecil argued to two other

sufficient, while in a third he accepts that 'force alone would have turned her from her purpose'. Ibid, 225, 227, 233, 332.

[1] This is not an adjective one would readily think of associating with so devoted a worker for peace, and no doubt Frances Stevenson's earlier description of Cecil as 'spiteful and malicious' was much coloured by local circumstances. A. J. P. Taylor (ed.), *Lloyd George: A Diary by Frances Stevenson* (London, 1971), 134. In the light of Cecil's memoirs and some of his private letters, however, Miss Stevenson's comment becomes more understandable.

[2] Cecil to Murray, 13, 28 November 1931, Murray Papers; Cecil to Murray, 24 December 1931, Cecil Papers, Add. 51132; Cecil to H. St. George Saunders, 11 April 1932, ibid, Add. 51100.

[3] Cecil to Murray, 13 November 1931, Murray Papers.

[4] Cecil to Murray, 21 November 1931, ibid.

[5] Cecil to Murray, 28 November 1931, ibid.

[6] Noel-Baker to Murray, 20 November 1931 (cf. also 18 November), ibid.

leading members of the L.N.U. who saw him in Paris on November 26
that there was a further reason for avoiding article 16:

'He personally thinks Japan is wrong,' reported one of Cecil's visitors to Murray,
'but that she cannot be charged with actually breaking the Covenant, though he
admits that she has acted against the spirit of it and that she *has* broken Art. 2
of the Kellogg Pact. But there has been no actual breach of any article of the
Covenant.' [At this point the writer had intervened to disagree and cite article
10.] 'Cecil says Japan can plead she has only acted to maintain order in same way
[sic] as we acted in Shanghai by sending in an expeditionary force. He agrees that
the Japanese military are in real control . . . (and) that Japan should withdraw,
but asks how it is suggested the League should turn her out. . . . As regards the
Disarmament Conference he said he does not think it will be affected by what's
happening and that it is in a way an argument for Disarmament.'[1]

It is conceivable, of course, that Cecil on this occasion was loyally striving
not to give his listeners fresh ammunition to use against the Government,
but the conversation chimes with his letters to both Murray and Simon. In
so far as there was calculation in the comments, Murray was probably
correct when he wrote of the incident: 'I am greatly disappointed about what
you tell me about Cecil's attitude. . . . I cannot help thinking that (he) is
influenced by his great desire to defend the League against the charge of
having failed completely.' [2]

Yet Murray himself was equally anxious to halt the fighting 'without
proceeding to the enormously heavy artillery of Article 16', suggesting to
Cecil as an alternative the forbidding of arms supplies to both combatants,
then prohibiting imports from them and the circulation of their bills of
exchange—an approach which Cecil was to condemn roundly in his
memoirs.[3] At bottom, however, all these men were still hoping that, as they
and others had proclaimed in 1919, the force of public opinion could itself
halt aggression. Thus Murray judged that 'the only chance of controlling
(Japan), without having to raise the question of absolute coercion, was to
show an overwhelming weight of public opinion against her breach of the
Covenant and Kellogg Pact'.[4] In Noel-Baker's view, the League was not
using 'the two main weapons which make up (its) strength—i.e. public
discussion and the supply of impartial information'. He was 'sure that once
the Commission was appointed and despatched . . . the Japanese would

[1] Vice Admiral S. R. Drury-Lowe to Murray, 26 November 1931, ibid. The
Admiral, who was a member of the L.N.U.'s Executive Committee, was accompanied by the Union's Secretary, Dr. Garnett. Interviews have confirmed my view
that, as when he was writing to his close friend, Murray, Cecil was likely to talk
frankly with Drury-Lowe.

[2] Murray to Drury-Lowe, 28 November 1931, ibid.

[3] Murray to Cecil, 25 November 1931, Cecil Papers, Add. 51132; Cecil, 235.
Murray was also in touch with Lippmann and others in America at this time.
Murray to Lippmann, 14 December; Lippmann to Murray, 24 December 1931,
Murray Papers. Of the other L.N.U. leaders, Grey was particularly cautious,
advising both Murray and Simon against any swift judgement or individual
initiative against Japan. Grey to Murray, 24 November 1931, Murray Papers;
DBFP, VIII, No. 789.

[4] Murray to Cecil, 9 November 1931, Cecil Papers, Add. 51132.

never dare to continue fighting . . .'[1] Cecil, too, deplored the undue secrecy of the Council's operations which, by baffling the public, had meant that the crisis, *quite unjustly as I think* . . . has done the League more harm than any other single event in its history'; had people been able to follow the steps taken by the Council, 'the great part of this discontent would vanish'.[2] 'Sooner or later,' he wrote privately, '(Japan) would have had to give way if public opinion had been strong enough.'[3]

The shaping of policy: London

In his capacity as substitute British representative on the League Council, Cecil still had a foot in the world of official advisers. And although his anxiety over the outcome of the crisis and his desire not to see the Chinese pushed into a disadvantageous settlement remained far greater than those of a good many (not all) permanent officials,[4] there, too, he appended much hesitation and qualification to what he had to say. He agreed, for example, that the Americans, whose active support was, he accepted, essential, 'preferred strong action to be taken by someone else rather than themselves'.[5] Article 15, he argued, would delay the possibility of having to consider article 16 and the 'extremely difficult and dangerous situation' which the latter would create, while he admitted that 'if Japan desires to establish what would be in effect a protectorate over Manchuria, she will not agree to any withdrawal of her troops until that has been accomplished'.[6] When declaring in secret meetings of the Council that it was difficult to say which party was to blame for the worsening situation, and that it was necessary to avoid offending Japanese susceptibilities,[7] it might possibly be that Cecil was constrained by verbal instructions from London. But when MacDonald, writing to thank him for his services on the Council, mentioned possible differences of opinion over policy, he replied:

> You speak of differences—but I am not conscious of any, more than must inevitably occur on such occasions—certainly there have been none to make it difficult for me to carry out the policy you and your colleagues decided on.

His collaboration with Simon, he wrote, had been 'close and cordial', and although he had decided not to accept an invitation to join the British

---

[1] Noel-Baker to Murray, 7 December 1931, Murray Papers.

[2] Cecil to Drummond, 18 December 1931, Cecil Papers, Add. 51112. Emphasis added.

[3] Cecil to Drummond, 31 December 1931, ibid.

[4] See, e.g., Cecil to Simon, 28 November 1931, Cecil Papers, Add. 51082; Cecil to Simon, 26 and 27 November 1931, DBFP, VIII, Nos. 782, 787, note, and 795; minutes of secret Council meeting, 7 December 1931, LN. Archives, R6228.

[5] DBFP, VIII, No. 795.

[6] Cecil to Simon, 13 November, 8 December 1931, ibid, Nos. 730, 831; Cecil to Simon, 19 November 1931, FO 800/285. Although disappointed by London's rejection of the possibility of sending British troops to a neutral zone at Chinchow, Cecil then admitted to Simon that he recognised the inadvisability of such a move. DBFP, VIII, No. 787; Cecil to Simon, 28 November 1931, supra.

[7] Minutes of secret Council meetings of 20, 27 November, 1 December 1931, LN. Archives, R6228.

delegation to the forthcoming Disarmament Conference, 'if I had to work only with you and him I should have no fear of serious disagreement'.[1]

Most of the other voices reaching London in private from Geneva and Paris were more cautious still. Cadogan, for example, while continuing to urge that the League must maintain 'the great principle (of) no settlement by force', accepted nevertheless that 'she may fail to enforce it', and did not suggest that sanctions should or could be applied.[2] Briand himself was 'very strongly against Article 15 being raised on the ground that it would bring us nearer to Article 16', and worked to this end in the Council's secret sessions. Startling results, he argued, could not be expected under article 11, but patience was needed 'pour accomplir une oeuvre d'apaisement. Si la Société intervient avec mesure, sans éveiller de susceptibilités, la situation s'en trouvera améliorée'.[3] Bülow's emphasis on the part of Germany was a similar one, while it was known that, behind Grandi's back, the Japanese were being offered encouragement in Rome.[4] From China (where he was staying with T. V. Soong), Dr. Rajchman of the League Secretariat continued to send forceful pleas on behalf of his hosts,[5] but from Tokyo Drummond's chef de cabinet, F. P. Walters, was despatching advice which not only contrasted with Rajchman's, but, as in Cecil's case, scarcely accorded with his later recollections and interpretations of the crisis:[6]

> He believes . . . that the resolution of 24 October led public opinion (in Japan) to support more strongly than before the military elements. He therefore suggests . . .
> 1. that it is of great importance that no appearance of haste should be given at the present Council Meeting;
> 2. that any suggestion that sanctions are to be applied should be avoided, as this only leads to the strengthening of the military elements; . . .
> 4. that the Council should, if possible, make a declaration that any essential treaty rights possessed by Japan in Manchuria must in future be respected.[7]

To Rajchman, Walters also urged the desirability of direct Sino-Japanese negotiations, in which he 'did not believe (the) Japanese would prove unreasonable'.[8]

As for Drummond himself, while he did not share this last opinion of

---

[1] MacDonald to Cecil, 19 December 1931; Cecil to MacDonald, 24 December 1931, 21 January 1932, Cecil Papers, Add. 51081. Cecil to Simon, 30 December 1931, Simon Papers (private collection), Foreign Affairs, 1931.

[2] See the notes printed with DBFP, VIII, No. 685.

[3] Ibid, No. 740; minutes of secret Council meetings of 19, 27 November, 5 December 1931, LN. Archives, R6228.

[4] DBFP, VIII, No. 743.   [5] Ibid, Nos. 687, 759, 762.

[6] In his *History of the League of Nations*, Captain Walters was to write that 'had the principal governments so desired they could have found unimpeachable grounds . . . (to) justify strong measures . . .' But 'the direct threat of sanctions . . . seemed to the chief Members of the Council too dangerous to be seriously considered'. Thus, after three months, 'the League had already suffered a severe loss of prestige and of public confidence'. pp. 478, 479, 482, 499.

[7] Drummond to Foreign Office, 16 November 1931, DBFP, VIII, No. 742, note; cf. ibid, No. 757.

[8] Lindley to Tyrrell, 28 November 1931, ibid, No. 797.

Walters', he, too, had no swift and simple solution to propose. Alone, apart from the Director of his Political Section, Sugimura,[1] the Secretary General was labouring behind the scenes to bring Japan and China closer together and to maintain the link between the League and the United States, drafting agendas, proposals and communiqués and excluding from the Council's secret sessions even his deputy, Joseph Avenol.

'Privé,' wrote Avenol in protest, 'en raison de sa nationalité, de la collaboration du Directeur de la Section Politique, vous avez assumé seul la totalité du travail relatif au conflict sino–japonais. Je crois pouvoir dire que votre décision, que d'ailleurs vous n'avez communiqué à personne, n'a certainement pas été occasionnée par les dispositions de vos collaborateurs toujours prêts à vous appuyer . . . J'étais venu ici [i.e. to Paris] avec l'espoir d'aider utilement à franchir un passage difficile. Depuis mon arrivée, je suis dans l'ignorance complète de vos actes et de vos desseins.'[2]

Drummond was, indeed, convinced of the need for the Council to work in the greatest privacy in order to avoid inflaming Japanese opinion;[3] similarly, he enjoined strict impartiality and prudence on all Secretariat officials in the face of Japanese criticism of Geneva's hostile bias.[4] At least, however, he had been ready to share with Avenol his own opinions and perplexity, in an exchange of letters during the first half of November.[5] For Avenol, there were special circumstances surrounding the Manchurian issue which disqualified it as a test case for the League, and which had also to be placed alongside the unlikelihood of any of the major powers' taking action against Japan. 'Les principes sont invariables mais les procédures sont flexibles.' In addition he was sceptical of the value of American co-operation, but the only alternative course of action he could suggest was to press Japan to clarify the issues she saw to be at stake and the conditions under which she would consent to return to the status quo. To this Drummond, on the other hand, could reasonably reply that at the Council meetings Yoshizawa simply evaded all such questions. Nor did he think it possible to expect China to acquiesce in Japan's demands, even though he believed that a thorough enquiry 'would prove the legitimacy of (the latter's) grievances'.

I feel that in the circumstances we must look upon the case from a more general standpoint, namely, whether it can be admitted that the occupation of territory is used as a weapon to enforce claims which have been contested by the other party for years past . . . If the League fails in this matter, not only is the value of

[1] See, e.g. ibid, No. 702, enclosure 2.
[2] Avenol to Drummond, 26 November 1931, LN. Archives, P34; cf. Barros, *Betrayal from Within*.
[3] Drummond to Cecil, 29 December 1931, Cecil Papers, Add. 51112; DBFP, VIII, No. 749.
[4] Meetings of 4, 11 November, 16 December 1931, *Directors Meetings, Papers and Confidential Circulars, 1931*, U.N. Library, Geneva.
[5] Drummond to Avenol, 6, 10, 13, 14 November; Avenol to Drummond, 7, 12, 14 November 1931, LN. Archives, P34. According to Drummond, the Chinese Government had at one point sent instructions to Sze to invoke article 15, while on another occasion the Japanese delegate had been authorised to state that a withdrawal of troops would not be made dependent on direct negotiations concerning wider issues.

the peace-keeping clauses of the Covenant destroyed . . . but also the success of the Disarmament Conference is seriously endangered, since if no security is afforded by the Covenant and other international conventions, each country can rightly say that she is bound to depend on her own armed forces.

But as to what could be done, Drummond 'did not see his way at all clearly'. None of the League powers, nor, he feared, the U.S.A., would wish to take action against Japan. Perhaps 'the delaying effects' of article 15 could be explored,[1] and he put this suggestion to London. At the same time, while insisting that the Chinese should not be forced into direct talks over Japan's five principles, he implored them to be accommodating over the question of a neutral zone, 'terrified' that Japan would withdraw her faint concessions in that matter if pressed too hard.[2]

With the Resolution of 10 December achieved, Drummond talked to his Directors of a satisfactory outcome for the League,[3] and indeed it was more than he had been able to hope for a month earlier, when he had submitted to the Foreign Office (in the face of their coolness, he had swiftly qualified his advocacy) 'a brilliant idea' by one of his staff for transferring the issue to the signatories of the Nine Power Treaty and hence, 'to some extent at any rate, taking the responsibility off the League's shoulders'.[4] In private, however, he was bitter at the limits which Britain in particular had placed upon League action:

'It is this,' he wrote to Cecil, 'that to my mind has really damaged the League. I can no longer confidently affirm to foreigners that a British Government will always scrupulously carry out all its engagements under the Covenant at whatever cost.'[5]

The general disappointment expressed here is understandable; the implications of the statement questionable. Had Drummond really believed until that moment—through Corfu, the rejection of the Geneva Protocol, the Italian–Yugoslav episode of 1927–8 and so forth—that Britain would carry out her obligations 'at whatever cost'? Did he not recall his own belief, in 1919, that without the United States the League could not become a major instrument for regulating conflict, or his own assurances to Balfour that the decision over sanctions would always rest in Britain's hands; his acknowledgement to Avenol that the United States would probably not join in sanctions, which, unless universally applied, would be 'worse than useless', or his avowal to Gilbert that in existing conditions economic pressure was 'out of the question'? For the Foreign Office and British Government there could be no mistaking the earnestness with which the

---

[1] According to Sweetser's rough notes of a secret Council meeting on 20 November, even Madariaga, while preoccupied with the principles at stake, observed that, given the American opposition to sanctions, the Council 'must go slowly' in order not to dissociate the League from Washington. Sweetser Papers, box 15.

[2] DBFP, VIII, Nos. 702, 708, 712, 742, 804, 811, 815, 819.

[3] Directors' meeting, 16 December 1931, loc. cit.

[4] Drummond to Cadogan, 11 November 1931, FO 371, F6544/1391/10; DBFP, VIII, No. 742.

[5] Drummond to Cecil, 29 December 1931, Cecil Papers, Add. 51112.

League's Secretariat and other champions desired to see it vindicated. The latter could not, however, alter the circumstances in the Far East; nor, when they cast their eyes down from faith to facts, could they point a sure way out of the dilemma.

When it came to this question of what could and could not be done, Drummond, Briand and Simon alike looked closely at the policies of the United States. In the foreground stood the homespun figure of Dawes, and there was little enough encouragement to be discerned in that quarter by anyone wishing to condemn and resist Japan. It was apparent from the outset that the General had considerable sympathy for the Japanese position in Manchuria, which, as he told Simon and his friend Matsudaira, was similar to the American one in Nicaragua—'that they were bound to make sure that there was order restored before they could withdraw.'[1] Dawes was genuinely anxious to see the matter brought to a rapid conclusion, and he was not indifferent to the prestige of the League; but his chosen means were to avert any public condemnation that might stiffen Japanese opinion.[2] Fulminating to his compatriot, Sweetser, about the incompetence of the Council ('I wouldn't even buy a gas company like that . . . Now get the hell out of here') and its desire for his presence at its meetings ('Go tell Briand I'm not going to come, and tell him quick!'),[3] Dawes also returned a blunt answer to Briand's query on 14 November as to America's attitude towards sanctions: 'My reply was that I had been informed that the U.S. would not join in the consideration of the question of sanctions *or in the enforcing of them* if hereafter imposed by the League . . .'[4] And although his pressure helped bring the Chinese to accept the Resolution of 10 December, his private utterances were not conducive to achieving a swift peace. 'The Chinese are altogether too cocky,' he apparently told Matsudaira. 'What you people need to do is to give them a thoroughly good licking to teach them their place and then they will be willing to talk sense.'[5]

This last and somewhat unsubtle observation was not known in London; even so, however, there was a clear impression of American caution, despite Stimson's démarche over Chinchow and rumours that he might even be

[1] Simon to Lindsay, 11 November 1931, DBFP, VIII, No. 723; cf. ibid, No. 728. In his memoirs Dawes repeated that 'from the first . . ., from the standpoint of realities, the argument seemed to be with Japan'. *Journal as Amdassador*, 424–5. In the Dawes Papers, whose value is in inverse proportion to their bulk, there are the contemporary notes on the Paris episode on which the published *Journal* was based. They add a few details and nuances only.

[2] E.g., DBFP, VIII, No. 740, note.

[3] Sweetser Papers, box. 15.

[4] Dawes, *Journal as Ambassador*, 415–16; emphasis added. From Dummond's remarks during secret Council meetings, it appears that Briand may have kept this remark largely to himself. E.g., minutes of 20 November, LN. Archives, R6228.

[5] Ferrell, *American Diplomacy*, 146; I have not been able to trace this in the Dawes Papers, however. On 6 December, Dawes wrote despairingly to Owen Young: 'When our end of the board goes up, the other end of the board in Manchuria goes down, and vice versa.' Dawes Papers.

trying to upstage the League by telling Nanking that only the Council's timidity was preventing action being taken.[1] At the end of October, for example, Drummond had passed on from an 'absolutely certain' source what was said to be the State Department's view, that delay would be inevitable and an immediate Japanese withdrawal dangerous.[2] Soon afterwards Castle was observing to the British Ambassador that the League had unduly favoured China in the dispute,[3] while when Stimson, on Simon's orders, was questioned directly about sanctions, he was 'completely noncommittal'. There was thus no reason for Lindsay to amend his initial impression (which was backed also by second-hand reports) that sanctions 'would be entirely abhorrent to the United States Government and that if others had recourse to them (that Government) would formally dissociate itself'.[4]

If Stimson was choosing to let the picture of American policy appear blurred round the edges, the same was still true of information coming in to London from Nanking and Manchuria.[5] There was no ambiguity, however, about the Chinese Government's extreme reluctance to accept a commission of enquiry unless a time limit for evacuation were set at the same time;[6] nor did British observers on the spot mince matters in reporting that in Chinchow there was 'no disorder or brigandage or excuse apparently for (the) advance of (the) Japanese', against whom there was a feeling of 'passive resentment' and by whom atrocities had probably been committed during the early stages of their campaign.[7] Lampson, for his part, was also blunt in his advice as matters came to a head before 10 December. Local passions, which were at 'white heat', severely restricted Nanking's freedom of manoeuvre; therefore, he argued, any attempt to press China to abandon what she saw as vital interests in Manchuria would be disastrous for Britain and the League alike.[8] Lindley, on the other hand, was by now still more vehement in urging that any suggestion of putting pressure on Japan should be avoided at a time when the moderates in Tokyo had their backs to the wall. 'The whole country,' he reported, 'believes that Japan is altogether in the right and we do not think that (the) Government would heed any threat, even if the United States joined the Council in making one.'[9] If further negative reinforcement were needed, he found it in the widespread Japanese press attacks upon Britain for allegedly seeking to curry favour with China

[1] See DBFP, VIII, Nos. 719, 762, 766, 802.

[2] Drummond to Cadogan, 30 October 1931, ibid, No. 694.

[3] Lindsay to Reading, 2 November 1931, ibid. No. 700. Cf. Nos. 701, 709.

[4] Lindley to Simon, 9 November; Simon to Lindsay, 10 November; Lindsay to Simon, 10 November; Lindsay to Vansittart, 18 November 1931; ibid, Nos. 714, 717, 719, 748.

[5] For example, there were reports of intrigues between Cantonese politicians and the Japanese. Ibid, No. 727.

[6] Ibid, Nos. 765, 771, 772, 774, 779, 791, 818.

[7] E.g., FO 371, F7043 and 7456/1391/10.

[8] DBFP, VIII, Nos. 687, 747, 814, 820, 823, 830.

[9] Lindley to Simon, 9 November 1931, ibid, No. 714. Cf. Nos. 686, 693, 721, 726, 736, 813. Lindley wrote to King George V on 13 November to describe the League Resolution of 24 October as 'exceedingly imprudent'. RA G.V, P510/46.

at Japan's expense—and this when America was still being held up to view
as an understanding friend.[1] Lindley also found positive backing in various
official assurances in Tokyo,[2] and although he had no doubts by late
November that the military were now in control there,[3] this did not lead
him to revise his belief that an annexation of Manchuria was not intended.
The army's object, he suggested, was to oust Chang Hsueh-liang; if the
latter departed and China agreed to direct talks, then a settlement might well
be effected.[4]

Within the Foreign Office, however, this reading of the situation by
Lindley was not accepted in toto. To Pratt, for example, it was clear that
the Kwantung Army 'intended to hold on to all it had got' and that puppet
governments were being established,[5] while Simon himself indicated to the
Cabinet that 'some sort of protectorate, at any rate in Southern Manchuria',
was quite possibly part of Japan's plan.[6] Yet no one doubted the solidarity
of Japanese public opinion or the danger of external criticism adding fuel to
the blaze.[7] Nor did anyone question Pratt's observation that Japan believed
her stake in Manchuria to be vital to her existence, or his conclusion that
'she has got to remain there' if chaos and misrule were to be avoided—and
perhaps ruin and bolshevism in Japan itself.[8]

'There exists a widespread feeling,' wrote Simon for the Cabinet, 'which I believe
to be justified, that although Japan has undoubtedly acted in a way contrary to
the principles of the Covenant . . ., she has a real grievance against China and the
merits of the matter are complicated by a further consideration. This is not a
case where the armed forces of one country have crossed the frontiers of another
in circumstances where they had no right to be on the other's soil.'[9]

Add to these aspects the continued belief, not that Japan harboured any
present aggressive designs against Britain,[10] but that, in Pratt's words, 'a
really hostile Japan might inflict serious injury on British interests in

[1] DBFP, VIII, Nos. 682, 698, 731.
[2] E.g., ibid, Nos. 728, 734, note, 749, 764, 827.
[3] Lindley to Tyrrell, 20 November 1931, ibid, No. 756. Cf. No. 760.
[4] Lindley to Reading, 30 October, 5 November; Lindley to Simon, 13, 14
November, 11 December 1931, ibid, Nos. 693, 710, 732, 735, 836.
[5] FO 371, F6246, 6267/1391/10; cf. F 807/1391/10. Wellesley, too, recognised the
unreliability of Japanese versions of their troop movements, though when talking
to the French Ambassador he was ready to record one such suspect statement as 'a
fact'. DBFP, VIII, Nos. 716, 722.
[6] Simon memorandum, 23 November 1931, DBFP, VIII, No. 769; Cabinet of
10 December 1931, CAB 23/69.
[7] See, e.g., Pratt minutes and memoranda, FO 371, F 6439 and 7102/1391/10;
Cadogan memorandum, ibid, F 6489/1391/10.
[8] Pratt memorandum, 27 October 1931, DBFP, VIII, No. 685. Cf. FO 371,
F 6387/1391/10. For other Foreign Office views on the affair, the Chinese and Dr.
Rajchman, see FO 371, F 6237, 6470, 6557, 6759, 7213/1391/10, and DBFP, VIII,
No. 811. For views of the Soviet Union's passive policy, see FO 371, F 6357, 6407/
1391/10.
[9] DBFP, VIII, No. 769.
[10] See, e.g., the minutes dismissing the notion that the Japanese military might be
trying to stir up trouble in India, FO 371, F7217/1391/10.

Shanghai' without even having to resort to military action, and the conclusion followed that economic sanctions against her were 'neither possible nor desirable'.[1] Cadogan might dispute Pratt's assertion that the Covenant scarcely applied in such a case, but as we have seen he did not resist the establishment of this major limitation on what could be done.

Yet it was also accepted by many officials that the League Council must remain seized of the dispute (Vansittart dismissed Drummond's Nine-Power-Treaty scheme as one that would look like 'helpless abdication' on the part of Geneva[2]), and despite the influence of Pratt and Wellesley,[3] Simon was at one with Cadogan in recognising the damage which could be done to the League if the question were simply allowed to drag on. 'If the matter is one which League authority cannot clear up it is a pity', he wrote to MacDonald:

> But it would be much better I think for the League to face that fact, if it is a fact, and to tell Japan that whatever may be her economic or practical case the League cannot as a League confirm the continuance of Japanese troops on Chinese territory and regrets that it is not possible owing to Japanese opposition to reach a unanimous and effective conclusion . . . That is not satisfactory, but . . . it is better than pretending (what nobody believes) that the League is really in a position to control the situation.[4]

The immediate disadvantage of losing favour with Japan, he told the Cabinet, must be weighed against 'the general risk, in which we share, that the League, in refusing to reaffirm its true function, will lose so much respect as may yet be accorded it in the face of its failure to enforce its demands upon the parties'.[5] There were to be those later, of course, who would maintain that Simon himself was preventing the League from controlling the situation. Even if they could now demonstrate how success could have been achieved, however, it would be difficult for them to dispute the Foreign Secretary's concern for that organisation's future existence.

Simon's submissions, together with the likelihood that Japan would ignore the deadline set by the League on 24 October, brought the attention of the Cabinet as a whole back to the dispute. Even now the matter was overshadowed by tariffs, the Round Table Conference on India[6] and the need to hammer out some sort of policies on reparations, debts and disarmament. Few Ministers had given Manchuria much thought, while MacDonald, who had kept himself informed, took the somewhat dismissive line of blaming Japan and China alike, 'neither (of whom) will meet the Council in the

[1] DBFP, VIII, No. 685. Cf. ibid, Nos. 720, note, and 746.
[2] FO 371, F6544/1391/10.
[3] Simon's engagement diary for 7 November suggests that one of his first acts as Foreign Secretary was to obtain a briefing from Wellesley on the situation. Simon Papers (private collection).
[4] Simon to MacDonald, 17 November 1931, DBFP, VIII, No. 746; cf. ibid, No. 745, for Simon's excessively juridical approach to finding a solution.
[5] Cabinet conclusions, 25 November 1931, CAB 23/69.
[6] See, e.g. Cabinet conclusions for 13 November 1931, ibid; MacDonald's closing speech to the Conference, 1 December 1931, Cmd. 3972. On 1 January the Congress Party were to announce a resumption of civil disobedience; Gandhi was imprisoned three days later.

spirit of the League', which would therefore, he argued, have to restrict its intervention in order not to expose its weakness further still.[1] On 11 November, however—a significant date for those haunted by the thought of another war—everyone had to consider the matter.[2] In doing so, the Cabinet set its seal on major limits to British policy not unlike those being established in Washington by Hoover's own Cabinet memorandum, although where the President tended to see too little at stake for his country in the area, the British Government saw too much for theirs. The outcome was the same, nevertheless: the acceptance that it was not worth the heavy cost of using coercion to impose one's will upon Japan. The two Western powers also shared a distrust of each other's policies. 'It would be wrong to assume that (the United States) would participate in putting pressure on Japan,' reported Simon, and he went on to warn that China 'had only to prove the violation of Articles XII, XIII and XV of the Covenant to commit members of the League automatically to sanctions'.[3]

> As had been shown at the time of the Corfu incident, however, it was not a practicable policy in a case of this kind to impose the sanctions provided for in Article XVI, which would involve the imposition of very drastic reductions on trade . . . The withdrawal of Ambassadors . . . would be equally unwise. The only way to exercise any influence on the Japanese Government was to keep a representative of high standing at Tokyo. A third suggestion, that an international force . . . should be sent to Manchuria, appeared inapplicable, since the Japanese were entitled to police the South Manchurian Railway.

Simon's argument—including his Corfu precedent, which could now help painlessly contract one's area of doubt—was accepted without question by his colleagues, who also approved the line that he should follow at the forthcoming session of the Council:

> The League of Nations should be upheld. The Cabinet recognised, however, *inter se*, that the sanctions provided for in Article XVI were not suitable and could not in practice be applied in the present case. In the interests of the League itself, therefore, every effort must be made to avoid the Chinese appeal being shifted from Article XI to Article XVI. If necessary, it must be impressed on the Chinese delegate that he must assist the League and not throw the responsibility on to the other members of the Council . . . In a word, the policy . . . should be one of conciliation, with an avoidance of implied threats.

As Simon himself scribbled it down on a scrap of paper at the time:

> Policy—conciliatory to Japan.
> To China—Don't rely solely on others: play your own part. Don't seek to transfer to Art. 16.
> To Japan: We don't *want* to apply sanctions.[4]

The Foreign Secretary was also asked to avoid giving the Japanese press further excuses for 'placing the odium for the initiative on this country';

[1] MacDonald to Murray, 28 December 1931, 4 January 1932, Murray Papers.
[2] CAB 23/69.
[3] This interpretation might appear to conflict with Drummond's 1921 note to Balfour and MacDonald's analysis of 1930, both cited earlier. But then one must ask who and what is involved in the word 'prove'.
[4] FO 371, F 7596/1391/10.

in addition it was indicated that he, rather than Cecil, should put Britain's case before the Council.

In effect, the Cabinet had thus endorsed the policy already established within the Foreign Office. It had also, without any detailed examination of the practical problems—economic and, potentially, military—involved in this particular case, reaffirmed the traditional attitude of British governments towards the League. Its conclusion that the need was for China to help the League, rather than vice versa, will be seen by some as realism, by others as an outrageous betrayal; but as an earlier chapter has attempted to show, the accompanying desire that 'the League of Nations should be upheld' reflected ambivalence and confusion, not cynicism. The same characteristics were exhibited in the brief moments that the Cabinet devoted to the subject after 11 November. A week later it merely noted a progress report from Paris; a week after that, however, it accepted Simon's new submission that, whatever the Council's current impotence, it should reaffirm 'the fundamental principle upon which it has been attempting to build . . . an organisation for the preservation of peace'—though approval was given only on the understanding that the British representative should not take 'a special and separate attitude' over the matter.[1] In none of these meetings was there any suggestion that a direct, long-term threat to British possessions was perceived, nor was there any discussion of broader implications, or of the need for contingency planning. Even the C.I.D. at its meeting on 7 December did not examine either the immediate Far Eastern situation or its possible consequences.[2] A diplomatic dilemma, not a military danger, was how the affair was perceived in this period. As it was, the only wound suffered by H.M. Forces in the vicinity was self-inflicted.[3]

The Cabinet's 11 November decision did not alter the direction of day-to-day policy, although it enabled Simon to inform Drummond on his arrival in Paris that 'no sanctions whatever' could be contemplated.[4] Already, the

[1] Cabinet conclusions of 18, 25 November, 10 December 1931, CAB 23/69; DBFP, VIII, Nos. 769, 775.

[2] CAB 2/5. This meeting was attended by representatives of Australia, New Zealand, South Africa and the India Office, together with the Director of Military Operations and Intelligence.

[3] On 9 November, in bad visibility and with her Captain soon seasick, the sloop H.M.S. Petersfield left Shanghai, carrying the C. in C. China, Admiral Sir Howard Kelly, together with Lady Kelly, their daughter and amah. After a series of incidents in which the Admiral forcefully intervened in the pilotage and navigation of the ship, he retired on the night of 11–12 November, leaving the watch-keeping officers uncertain as to the rigidity of his instructions concerning the ship's course. Although these officers believed the ship to be standing into danger, therefore, they chose not to disturb the Admiral. Then, in the immortal words of the latter's subsequent report: 'At about 0245 . . ., practically in agreement with her position by Dead Reckoning, the ship took the ground on Tung Yung Island.' The Petersfield was a total wreck, and her Captain and Navigating Officer—not the C. in C.— were severely reprimanded. Accounts of the incident are to be found in ADM 125/71 and the Kelly Papers, vol. 7, 96–113, and vol. 41. Former or serving commanding officers of H.M. ships are warned that they read them only at the risk of some degree of stress.

[4] DBFP, VIII, No. 773.

Foreign Office was screening information passed on to the Secretary General in order to minimise its anti-Japanese element.[1] Both in London and Tokyo, Japanese diplomats were assured of Britain's friendly feelings towards their country (Reading had even admitted that Britain might find herself in the same position as Japan 'if any question arose affecting our particular position and our obligations under the Covenant'),[2] while over such issues as the despatch of observers or of troops to supervise the proposed neutral zone around Chinchow, individual initiatives were shunned. 'We should have more to lose than any other Power,' minuted Wellesley, 'as the whole of our policy in the Far East rests very much on Japanese goodwill.'[3]

Within the limits set by the Cabinet, however, other considerations continued to play some part in shaping policy. Like everyone else in the game, Simon tried to use his own public as a lever, even though 'the extremely large and important body of public opinion supporting and deeply interested in the League', which he cited when urging the Japanese to make concessions, could scarcely match the value of ferocious Japanese—or Chinese—nationalism.[4] At the same time, unilateral pressure upon China was avoided for fear of invoking her hostility, and if others looked like making concessions in that direction, London rushed to do the same.[5] In Paris, too, Simon repeatedly emphasised to his colleagues on the Council the need 'solemnly to reaffirm the principles of the League' and to make clear in the forthcoming resolution that the appointment of a commission of enquiry did not provide grounds on which Japan could delay her withdrawal of troops.[6] Astonishingly enough (in view of the recent Cabinet decision), the Foreign Secretary apparently went even further in private conversation with Dawes on 19 November, suggesting that, should the Chinese invoke further articles of the Covenant, and should a commission of enquiry prove ineffective, then the League 'should proceed under Article 16'. 'He is inclined to think, in other words,' reported Dawes, 'that the League should go to the limit of its powers irrespective of whether the probabilities favour success or not.'[7] Given Dawes's own views, it is unlikely that on this occasion Simon was indulging in his tendency to adjust his pronouncements to suit the opinions of a forceful listener. More probably, the explanation lay in his genuine concern for the standing of the League, together with his desire to

[1] Vansittart minuted on 13 November: 'Most of our information is surely very anti-Japanese. I don't think it would be wise to produce it at this juncture.' 'I agree,' added Eden. 'We are sufficiently suspect—however unjustly—as it is.' FO 371, F 6423/1391/10. For an example of the toning down of a report before passing it on, see ibid, F 6314/1391/10. A reply by Simon in the Commons on the subject was carefully amended to allow for this kind of procedure. Ibid, F 7414/1391/10.

[2] DBFP, VIII, Nos. 707, 724; cf. FO 371, F 6756/1391/10.

[3] FO 371, F 6979/1391/10; cf. ibid, F 6932/1391/10, and DBFP, VIII, Nos. 688, 722, 765, 779, 787, 790, 792, 822.

[4] DBFP, VIII, Nos. 683, 689, 707, 749, 752, 753; FO 371, F 6681/1391/10.

[5] E.g., DBFP, VIII, Nos. 786, 793, 799, 801.

[6] E.g., minutes of secret Council meetings, 18, 23 November 1931, LN. Archives, R 6228.

[7] Dawes to Stimson, 18 November; Dawes–Stimson telephone record, 19 November 1931, FRUS, 1931, III, 486–98.

fish again in the muddy waters of Washington for some clear statement of the limits and possibilities of American policy. His bold observation did not mean, however, that the restrictions set in London on British policy had been changed. Nor did it alter the outcome of the dialogue that was taking place on the same subject between Hoover and his Secretary of State.

The shaping of policy: Washington

Simon got on well with Dawes, the latter in turn considering the Foreign Secretary's appointment to be a strong one and admiring his common sense and clarity of thought.[1] As in the preceding period, Washington could not doubt the eagerness with which the British representative or his main colleagues on the League Council desired American assistance and even leadership,[2] while Dawes himself, though anxious to minimise his contact with the League in order to forestall 'unjustified attack by foes in the Senate',[3] felt at one point that perhaps he should, after all, attend Council meetings. (He then reversed this opinion, but still believed that America should step in and 'clear up this situation' by publishing the facts of the case for the public to judge.)[4] Meanwhile a sympathetic Nelson Johnson continued to transmit the increasing despair and resentment of the Chinese Government at American and League passivity,[5] and from Manchuria itself there came fairly frequent reports of the political, as well as the military, activities of the Kwantung Army.[6]

Both from Europe and the Far East, however, considerations still arose which could be taken as pointing in the direction of continued caution and equivocation. For all his musing over article 16, for example, Simon did not give Dawes a precise statement of his Government's position concerning sanctions. (No one, it seems, wished to confess his unpreparedness to make sacrifices in the cause of justice and virtue; hence, to the detriment of Anglo-American relations, direct speaking on the subject was avoided, even in private, by both parties.) On the other hand, besides conveying his own unrealistic and legally-preoccupied ideas for a settlement,[7] the Foreign Secretary did reveal that he thought the time limit which had been set for a Japanese withdrawal by Reading and the Council had been a mistake.[8] The basic caution of British policy was clear enough, as was that of France, where both Briand's hesitations and Berthelot's 'more or less frankly pro-Japanese' attitude were noted and reported to Washington.[9] With Laval's Government seen as being in a precarious position[10] and both diplomats and

[1] See DS 841.00/1197; cf. ibid, 841.00/1211, and Atherton to Castle, 1 December 1931, Castle Papers, England.

[2] E.g., FRUS, 1931, III, 352–4, 476–7.

[3] Ibid, 452; DS 793.94/2639, 3095½. 'If I run around making a spectacle of myself,' Dawes declared to Stimson, 'I won't do any good.'

[4] FRUS, 1931, III, 444–5, 499–502.

[5] E.g., ibid, 562, 647–8, 673; DS 793.94/2697; Johnson to Peck, 3 November 1931, Johnson Papers, vol. 14.

[6] E.g., FRUS, 1931, III, 363–4, 449, 451.

[7] Ibid, 460–2.   [8] Ibid, 426–7.   [9] Ibid, 387–9, 444–5.

[10] E.g., DS 851.00/1112.

the Paris press revealing their interest in anything that might make the Disarmament Conference 'doubly impossible', as Claudel put it,[1] the rumours of a secret Franco-Japanese understanding continued to spread.[2] The Dutch, too, went on opposing any thought of coercion, their Foreign Minister observing that the League 'had not had sufficient regard to the susceptibilities of the Japanese', and the administration in Batavia working hard to prevent any anti-Japanese outbursts among the local Chinese.[3] From Canada, also, much sympathy for Japan was reported.[4]

Meanwhile, of course, the Japanese continued to supply their own private assurances of good intentions, including the one from Shidehara to Forbes on 24 November 'that the Premier, the Secretary of War, the Chief of Staff and he are agreed that towards Chinchow there shall be no hostile operations, and orders have been issued to that effect'.[5] (When Stimson as good as revealed this undertaking to the press, Shidehara was angered at what he saw as a breach of confidence; Stimson blamed inaccurate press reports, but also Forbes's lack of clarity when drafting his despatch; Forbes, while contrite to Stimson's face, privately blamed the latter for 'failing to understand the situation and making an unmitigated mess of that particular episode'.[6]) There was also a convincing display of annoyance from Tokyo over the affair of the Chinchow neutral zone, a reaction which commanded some sympathy in Washington when the confusion involved was traced to the French Ambassador in Tokyo, who had mistakenly given Shidehara to understand that the Chinese proposal for such a zone was a firm one, just when Nanking was attaching to it new conditions.[7] At the same time Shidehara's desperate struggle for survival was being openly admitted by Matsudaira and others;[8] even liberals in Japan were reported by a newly-returned official of the Institute of Pacific Relations to be supporting the actions of the Kwantung Army.[9] From Tokyo, Forbes's Counsellor, Neville, was urging (in vain) that Stimson's stronger protests to Shidehara be toned down, while the Ambassador himself, privately incensed at the Secretary of State's 'offensive and insulting' habit of using him as a mere 'errand boy', cited virtually all foreign diplomats in the city as being agreed on the folly of trying to put further pressure on Japan.[10] He

[1] FRUS, 1931, III, 385–7; cf. DS 500 A15 A4/515.
[2] E.g., Castle Diary, 15 December 1931, cited in Rappaport, *Henry Stimson*, 78.
[3] DS 793.94/2752, 3018, 4566.
[4] Ibid, 3229, 3978; cf. ibid, 4225, 4505.
[5] Forbes to Stimson, 24 November 1931, FRUS, *Japan, 1931–41*, I, 50; cf. ibid, 39–40; FRUS, 1931, III, 596–8; DS 793.94/2588.
[6] Forbes to Stimson, 28 November, 9 December; Stimson to Forbes, 28 November, 1931, FRUS, *Japan, 1931–41*, I, 51–4, 57–8; Stimson to Forbes, 30 November 1931, FRUS, 1931, III, 595–6; Forbes to Stimson, 2 December 1931, DS 793.94/3058; Forbes, Journal, 2nd series, III.
[7] FRUS, 1931, III, 562, 580, 590–2, 605–6, 629–30, 657–61; FRUS, *Japan, 1931–1941*, I, 58–9; Dawes, *Journal as Ambassador*, 428–9; cf. DS 793.94/3058 $\frac{3}{7}$, $\frac{4}{7}$, 3138 for accompanying rumours and recriminations.
[8] FRUS, 1931, III, 446–7, 450, 478, 582.
[9] DS 793.94/3228; cf. FRUS, 1931, III, 513.
[10] FRUS, 1931, III, 366–7, 452; Forbes, Journal, 2nd series, III, November 4; 2nd series, IV, pp. 16, 41. Forbes had already tendered his resignation, but had

also continued to suggest that the Japanese case was a strong one, with no disadvantage likely to accrue to China if she accepted Tokyo's five fundamental points.[1] As with Admiral Taylor's letters that were circulating in Washington, or Lindley's that were going to Buckingham Palace, such reports from the Far East at least helped ensure that those in élite circles who were inclined to look upon Japan with some indulgence had fresh ammunition with which to support their case.

Again, it was Castle who most consistently represented this viewpoint within the State Department, believing as he did that the affair was still being allowed to generate too much excitement.[2] His support for Hoover's notion of seeking to satisfy both Japan and China by replacing Chang Hsueh-liang with a new 'viceroy' or governor-general appointed by Nanking ('it would be very difficult for the Japanese to refuse to recognise him, and it would immediately assert the authority of Nanking in Manchuria') suggested that Castle, like the President and many others, had not yet fully grasped the reality of the situation;[3] at the same time he remained decidedly cool towards cooperation with the League, whose activities he regarded with a certain wry cynicism,[4] and Drummond rightly observed that he was helping to impart confusion to what was heard by others of American policy. Castle was not alone among State Department officials in advising restraint, however, while John V. A. MacMurray, the country's former Minister in Peking, was also making known the view that China was merely 'reaping where she had sown'.[5] Hornbeck, too, fairly spewing forth memoranda, joined Castle in opposing any entanglement in a commission of enquiry, even recommending a policy of 'let it alone' as regards any further Japanese advances that might be made on the pretext of pursuing bandits:

> 'Japan has assumed control (in Manchuria),' he wrote. '. . . The powers cannot put Japan out. They must and will permit her armed forces to remain there—for some time at least . . . (and) to try to impose upon them restraint in the form of pledges . . . is to attempt the impracticable. The Japanese will not assent. If they did (it) would further complicate the situation.'[6]

Klots and Rogers, on the other hand, continued to advocate a strong anti-Japanese line, the former, for example, supporting the idea of again seating an American with the League Council.[7] Surrounded by divided

---

been asked to remain at his post for a while longer. Repercussions of Forbes' criticisms of Stimson's policy will be found in the Hornbeck Papers, box 167.

[1] FRUS, 1931, III, 375–80.

[2] Castle Diary, 10 December 1931, cited in Rappaport, *Henry Stimson*, 77; Castle to Stimson, 30 October 1931, DS 793.94/2509.

[3] Hoover to Stimson, 12 November 1931, FRUS, 1931, III, 431–2; Castle to Stimson, 4 December 1931, DS 793.94/3101.

[4] E.g., Castle to Gilbert, 28 November 1931, Castle Papers, Switzerland; DS 500 A15 A4/649½: 'If French soldiers chase bandits in Yunnan, will the League call a special session to consider the matter?!'

[5] Moffat Diary, 13 November 1931.

[6] Hornbeck memoranda, 20, 30 November, 1, 3 December 1931, DS 793.94/2891, 3011, 3012, 3032, 3116; Castle Diary, 20 November, 1931, cited in Rappaport, 72.

[7] Castle Diary, 10 November, cited in Rappaport, 68; Stimson Diary, 7 November 1931.

counsellors, therefore, Stimson himself displayed much uncertainty over what should be done. Before the new Kwantung Army advances in November he had believed that the Chinese trade boycott was 'likely to bring Japan to her knees', and after the Chinchow scare he still thought that Tokyo would 'go ahead and make a settlement'.[1] After all, American disapproval was, he was sure, a formidable weapon—'The Japanese Army has been as hardboiled as an Easter egg,' he wrote on 17 November, 'and if finally our views have to be publicly stated, they will be sufficiently forcible to crack the egg'[2]—and he was encouraged to believe that it was his own remonstrances which had produced the 'wonderful news' that Tokyo would agree to a commission of enquiry.[3] Yet the Secretary's moments of optimism were short-lived, and he was rapidly coming to take a more serious, if unstable, view of the situation than either Forbes or Castle. By mid-November he was concerned at the prospect of puppet governments giving Japan de facto control of Manchuria;[4] after the ensuing military advances, he saw matters as now being 'in the hands of virtually mad dogs', with the Japanese army, backed by a chauvinistic public, 'running amuck' in the belief that it could 'go ahead and defy the whole world'.[5]

Such a conclusion, however, only left Stimson more restless and uncertain still. 'I don't know what can be done,' he noted privately on 16 November, 'except to watch the thing go through to its conclusion'. Nor was the problem simply a practical one, for it was now that those underlying issues relating to national interest, sovereignty and international morality began to thrust themselves at the Secretary—or, in part, were thrust at him privately by friends like Elihu Root and Major General William Lassiter. In proposing that the United States ought to show some appreciation of Japan's position, for example, Root suggested that 'Manchuria occupies very much the same relation to (her) that Cuba does to (us)'.[6] 'Must we not realize,' asked Lassiter, 'that every nation, when faced with intolerable disorder, will take some measures to cure them [sic] . . . We ought to measure our words (to Japan) very carefully because tomorrow we may be up against the same sort of conditions ourselves. It is Japan's problem and she must work it out just as we would have to if we got involved in Mexico.'[7] Root's letter troubled Stimson. In response to Lassiter's, he acknowledged the validity of the General's point, not denying that the United States might behave in such fashion in Latin America, but claiming, rather, that 'China is not Mexico', and that in a phrase already quoted, one had to bear in mind the American 'foothold in the minds of the Chinese people which is pregnant with possibilities for good, provided we do not forfeit it'.[8] He still believed

[1] Stimson Diary, 30 November 1931; Stimson memorandum, 29 October 1931, FRUS, 1931, III, 342–3.

[2] Stimson to Dawes, 17 November 1931, FRUS, 1931, III, 470–1; cf. 477.

[3] Stimson Diary, 20, 21 November 1931.

[4] FRUS, 1931, III, 434; Stimson Diary, 4, 17 November 1931.

[5] Stimson Diary, 6, 19, 26, 27 November, 6, 11 December 1931.

[6] Root to Stimson, 20 November 1931, Stimson Papers, box 303.

[7] Lassiter to Stimson, 8 November 1931, ibid.

[8] Stimson to Lassiter, 12 November 1931, ibid; Stimson Diary, 7, 14 November 1931.

that some clear response to Japan's actions was called for, and that meant resuming his debate with Hoover.

Stimson had pondered on the possibility of invoking the Nine Power Treaty, but recognised its lack of sanctions.[1] He therefore began to look at some form of economic pressure, even though he had agreed with Lassiter early in November that one must rule out any suggestion of an embargo, and with Hoover that 'a blockade (could) lead to war. It is almost a belligerent step'.[2] His mind was still far from made up, but the thought was there that the Japanese army would respond 'only through suffering and not by the sanctions of public opinion'.[3] With Castle, Rogers, Klots and Hornbeck, he discussed the matter at length on 6 December,[4] Castle strongly opposing a boycott of Japan's goods on the grounds that she would probably then blockade China and head for a direct collision with the United States. Rogers and Klots, on the other hand, supported the idea of economic pressure, as did Hornbeck, despite his recent advice against meddling. (He might have argued that this was not 'meddling'.) Hornbeck's memorandum on the subject was in fact the first such study to be made since the crisis had begun, and is doubly of interest in the discrepancies between its conclusions and those arrived at soon afterwards in a more detailed British analysis. The paper is also worthy of note in the light of the confident predictions its author was to make about Japanese reactions to American pressure in 1941.[5] On this occasion Hornbeck assumed (as did few, if any, Western diplomats in Tokyo) that Japan would submit to economic coercion without blockading China or taking some more violent action, while he also advanced a most dubious hypothesis—very much that of the academic rather than the politician—about the favourable reactions to be expected from the American public. In brief, the memorandum argued that an 'economic boycott' [i.e. not a blockade] was desirable in order to vindicate the United States before history and the League of Nations, although the League itself should initiate the proposal; that it would be approved by Congress and by a public that was convinced of Japan's wrongdoing and of the reasonableness of the League and American case; that even if the League members alone took such a step it would have 'considerable effect'; that the United States' economy would not be hit unduly hard if she participated; and that Japan's economy would suffer such damage that 'within six months the Government would have to make terms with the Powers'.

Stimson accepted, and even enlarged upon, this version of the effects of a boycott. The analysis showed, he wrote, 'that (Japan) could not stand it more than a very few days or weeks'. Even so, he thought it too vigorous a move, and continued to reflect on the need for patience 'in a desperate situation (where) many people are . . . urging drastic steps or words upon me'. Perhaps a boycott of Japanese goods by private individuals would have

[1] Stimson Diary, 8 December 1931; DS 793.94/2711 A.
[2] Stimson Diary, 7 November 1931.   [3] Ibid, 27 November 1931.
[4] Ibid, 6, 8, 9 December 1931; Castle Diary, 7 December 1931, cited in Ferrell, *American Diplomacy*, 148; Hornbeck memorandum, 6 December 1931, DS 793.94/4314; cf. memorandum estimating Japan's military strength, July 1931, Hornbeck Papers, box 228.
[5] See below, 390.

some effect; alternatively, it might be sufficient if the United States and the rest of the world were to declare their refusal to recognise any Sino-Japanese treaty or arrangement made under military pressure, as Bryan had done over the Twenty-One demands in 1915. Despite his thoughts on the need to inflict 'suffering', Stimson believed that such an act of non-recognition would have 'a very potent effect', and Castle supported the idea too; Hornbeck, tenaciously inconsistent as ever, came round to it as well after first dismissing it as having achieved nothing in 1915. The proposal was shelved for the time being since the League Resolution of 10 December was now imminent, and with the thought that a new declaration might make the Japanese recalcitrant over subsequent negotiations.[1] It remained attractive, however, not least because it had originated with the President (perhaps prompted by Representative Keller; Lippmann's public advocacy was to come soon afterwards), in whose mind it had become a possibility replacing that of withdrawing Ambassador Forbes in protest.[2]

The strain on Hoover in this period was intense. Nevertheless he managed to discuss Manchuria with Stimson in most weeks, and supported the latter in Cabinet when he resisted Pat Hurley's argument that since Japan was going to take her slice of China whatever the United States said, any interference would simply invite a rebuff.[3] On the other hand the President, like Hurley, was not inclined to see the setting up of puppet governments in Manchuria as a diplomatic defeat for America, and was quickly exasperated when the Chinese expressed their justified misgivings over the proposed commission of enquiry.[4] And although he continued to back Stimson's policy of limited co-operation with the League, even to the point of giving Dawes discretion to sit with the Council if he thought it necessary, his initial apprehension did not diminish as the opening of Congress drew nearer.[5] Similarly, although he did now accept Stimson's proposal for non-interference in any League blockade and approved the idea of a boycott by individual citizens, there remained his underlying conviction that any official sanctions 'would be provocative and lead to war'. The narrow limits of his consent were thus scarcely changed.[6]

[1] Stimson Diary, 9 November, 2, 3 December 1931; Castle Diary, 9 November 1931, cited in Current, 'The Stimson Doctrine', loc. cit.; DS 793.94/2888, 3005, 3117; drafts in Hornbeck Papers, boxes 243, 320.

[2] Stimson Diary, 7, 9 November 1931; Hoover, *Memoirs, 1920–1933*, 373 (where his proposal is misdated).

[3] Stimson Diary, 13 November 1931; cf. Lohbeck, *Hurley*, 96. Hoover was also reluctantly accepting the arguments of both Hurley and Stimson for deferring Philippines independence: Stimson Diary, 27 October 1931; Stimson to Hurley, 29 October 1931, Stimson Papers, box 302; Joint Board to Secretaries of War and Navy, 23 October 1931, Joint Board, 305. See above, 54–7.

[4] Stimson Diary, 17, 21 November 1931.

[5] Ibid, 9, 16, 20 November, 10 December 1931; Castle Diary, 4 November, cited in Current, 'The Stimson Doctrine'; Rappaport, *Henry Stimson*, 69.

[6] Stimson Diary, 7, 19, 27 November, 6 December 1931; Castle Diary, 7 December, loc. cit.; Hoover, *Memoirs, 1920–1933*, 366, 370. In his *Far Eastern Crisis*, published in 1936, Stimson was to provide an opportunity for those eager to misread and to conclude that Britain alone had prevented the general application of

It is not surprising, in view of the foregoing exchanges, to find that American policy as carried out in this period manifested much ambivalence and confusion. To some extent, of course, its changes reflected a worsening in the external situation, as well as a degree of that balancing and appeasing which are essential to a constructive and realistic conduct of affairs; at the same time, however, they arose from Stimson's uncertainty, the growing differences between him and the President, and, at a deeper level, that ambiguity over the national interest in the Far East that has been explored in an earlier chapter. Thus, China must not be coerced by Japan into ratifying the latter's disputed treaty rights in Manchuria,[1] but she could be pressed to accept a commission of enquiry without accompanying guarantees of a Japanese withdrawal, must be restrained at the Council meetings in Paris, and was ignored in her appeals for a Nine-Power-Treaty initiative from Washington.[2] Japan, on the other hand, must be privately warned of American displeasure at her army's behaviour and general intransigence (with the addition of a public rebuke in the case of Chinchow, regardless of what harm it might do to Shidehara);[3] American impartiality must be maintained, however, and isolated initiatives avoided over such matters as local observers.[4] After an initially adverse reaction and a pause of some days, the League Council's plans and new draft resolution could be approved and a place accepted on its commission of enquiry;[5] but in its early sessions the Council must be held back from any hasty action against Japan, while domestic hostility to the League must not be resisted too strenuously. Above all, the message sent to Paris on 19 November would not be revoked: 'We do not ourselves believe in the enforcement of any embargo by our own Government . . . We believe an embargo is a step to war.'[6]

Stimson summarised his own endeavours and motives in a seventeen-page

sanctions. In discussing the book with Hoover before publication, Stimson suggested that it would be better to make no reference in it to the former's opposition to sanctions in the autumn of 1931, lest this be blamed for the failure to halt Japan. He argued that, since the American decision had been concealed until the summer of 1932, 'it could not have played any part in the League's decision' against sanctions. Stimson to Hoover, 6 June 1936, Hoover Papers, Stimson file. In the light of the clear intimations given to Briand and Drummond at the time, Stimson's assertion was on factual grounds, let alone others, absurd. As suggested below, the pattern of mutual influence was in fact a complex one.

[1] FRUS, 1931, III, 470–1, 477.

[2] Ibid, 543–4, 547–8; DS 793.94/2892, 2893.

[3] Stimson Diary, 28 November 1931; FRUS, *Japan, 1931–41*, I, 44–6, 48–9, 50–1, 54–6; FRUS, 1931, III, 534–5, 629–30, 637–41.

[4] E.g., FRUS, 1931, III, 362–3, 368–70.   [5] Ibid, 507–12, 514, 559–60.

[6] Ibid, 407–14, 452–7, 488, 502, 507–12; Stimson Diary, 6 December 1931. Stimson did come to feel that Dawes was overdoing his doggedly independent line in Paris, and was 'playing with a little too much finesse' (!). Stimson Diary, 25 November 1931; DS 793.94/3095½. When Sweetser visited Washington in December, he bitterly revealed to Moffat and others how Dawes had boorishly alienated foreign statesmen in Paris. Encouraged by Hornbeck, he then repeated this to an infuriated Stimson. 'He is a loose-tongued, rather dangerous person,' noted the Secretary afterwards. Moffat Diary, 23 December 1931; Sweetser to Mrs Sweetser, 24 December 1931, Sweetser Papers, box 15; Stimson Diary, 22 December 1931.

letter to Root on 14 December.[1] He did not blame Japan for protecting herself against what Root had described as 'the dagger aimed at her heart', and his respect for her civilian leaders had prompted him to exercise restraint as long as possible. Nor had he forgotten the need to avoid 'getting entangled in League measures'. Despite its over-zealous actions early on, however, he believed that the League had helped prevent an openly-declared Sino-Japanese war, and if Japan remained obdurate he believed that the United States would have to join in with some form of protest or initiative of her own. So far, the writer might have carried the President with him. Elsewhere in the letter, however, when Stimson recapitulated the considerations which had weighed with him in what he had done, he began to move into some areas which were largely foreign to Hoover, and where the two men were to find the gap widening between them in the coming year. Indifference, wrote the Secretary to his old mentor, would have dismayed the organised peace movement in the United States and weakened all it stood for; it would have also destroyed China's faith in the United States, causing 'an almost irreparable loss to the future interests of this country in the Far East'. On reading this, Root may well have recognised some of his own teachings—and those of Theodore Roosevelt—coming back to face him.

Retrospect

Despite briefly successful restrictions on the Kwantung Army's operations, the near-impotence of the civilian Government in Tokyo had been confirmed in this period, and the basis laid for permanent Japanese control over at least the southern part of Manchuria. Protests and appeals from the West and the League had at times increased the urgency with which Shidehara strove to keep the affair within bounds, but in this, as in the maintenance of the Minseito Government in power, no decisive or lasting effect in the required direction was achieved. (If anything, it could be argued that Western interventions hastened that Government's fall.) Amid this scene, Western observers in Tokyo were virtually unanimous in continuing to argue that any suggestion of trying to coerce Japan would only provoke a fierce and united reaction. Several of those on the spot, however, and many more in the West itself, still failed to grasp the full extent of the aims of those who were in effect leading Japanese policy by the nose through their activities in Manchuria. There was also continuing confusion as to whether one was or was not in the presence of 'a war'—Stimson was by no means alone in believing that such an eventuality had been avoided[2]—since neither side declared this to be the case or even broke off diplomatic relations. In several quarters, indeed, China was soon to be criticised for her very passivity, even though some of those, like F. P. Walters, who were to level the accusation had at the time approved when the League and the United States urged China to exercise the greatest restraint.[3]

[1] Elihu Root Papers, box 147.

[2] Cecil also saw the matter in these terms, for example; cf. *North China Herald*, 15 December 1931.

[3] This is not to suggest that, had they received orders to fight, Chang Hsueh-liang's troops would have achieved any great success.

Confusion was also one major feature, together with caution, of the attempts by more zealous League supporters to suggest what could be done to bring matters to a satisfactory conclusion. Such understandable reactions were to be largely forgotten, however, by the time it came to writing of the crisis in retrospect. The process is not uncommon. 'If messages or memories about past events do not directly reinforce a strongly held image, they may be selectively screened or distorted until they do so.'[1] Meanwhile the League's Council had salvaged further time and a semblance of authority from the wreck of the 24 October Resolution, but its underlying impotence and loss of prestige could not be disguised. The British Government was soon to be blamed for this unhappy state of affairs, and it had, indeed, now set firm and narrow limits to the means by which an attempt could be made to uphold the Covenant. Nevertheless, and however brusque and haphazard the process of decision involved, the acceptance in London of a lack of immediate coercive power over Japan had been realistic, and the more careful analyses that were provided later would merely reinforce what had been this almost instinctive recognition of the situation. Hoover had re-acted in similar fashion for the United States, and a circular process had been taking place whereby Washington and the League powers could each point to the unwillingness of the other to put pressure on Japan when justifying its own decisions to avoid such action. Much facile recrimination could thereby be exchanged later in memoirs and so-called works of history, but one can only speculate whether, had Britain, say, pushed the League into sanctions, the United States would have followed, or vice versa. Other elements in the situation would inevitably have been changed thereby, so that any firm conclusion is doubly impossible. One can observe the deep-seated opposition on each side to running any of the risks associated with coercion; perhaps one might also tentatively suggest that, given on the one hand the various European desires to achieve a modification of American policies over debts, tariffs and international security, and on the other the wide-spread belief within the American body politic that Europe was the source of all pestilence; given also the contrasting degrees to which the League and American positions were *seen* to be involved, then the likelihood of the League falling into line behind the United States over sanctions would have been greater than the other way round.

Mutual perceptions of reluctance and even hostility towards forceful action were only one of the common features to be found in the various leading Western states. In Paris, Berlin, London and Washington no one had the slightest desire to bell the cat, especially since it was strongly suspected that their fellows might then privately seek to improve their own place in that dangerous animal's affections. In retrospect, it is similarities such as this, not differences, that stand out in those British and American policies which have so often been contrasted. Within each group of policy-makers there were strong reasons for wishing to be able to ignore the conflict in the Far East, although each was persuaded that the proclaimed new ethic of international relations, if no other reason, made this impossible. Within each of them, too, there was considerable sympathy for Japan's

[1] Kelman, 145.

case, though not her methods, while by early November each had ruled out the use of economic and military sanctions against her. 'Realism' was no more the exclusive property of one group than 'idealism' was of the other, while on all sides men were reaching for precedents and analogies with which to orientate themselves in a confused situation. Differences did exist, of course—in Washington, for example, perceived domestic opposition to entanglements was more powerful a factor than were images of British opinion in London. The most significant contrast, however, lay at the level of aspirations, where the broad consensus in Whitehall was beginning to show up against the nascent but profound split between Stimson and Hoover. The roots of this contrast have been examined in Part One of this study; its implications were to become clearer in the summer of 1932. Meanwhile in neither capital was there yet a strong perception of even an indirect threat to the country's local material interests, nor an acute sense of having little time in which to make major decisions. The Japanese now proceeded to oblige with both.

CHAPTER SEVEN

THE FOUNDING OF MANCHUKUO AND WAR IN SHANGHAI

Developments in the Far East

IN THE early part of 1932, Chinese politics appeared to be plunged into new depths of confusion. Between February and April, Communist forces were threatening Hankow and Amoy, and were to hold Changchow until the summer; the Kiangsi Soviet Republic (where Mao Tse-tung was entering a brief period of eclipse vis-à-vis other party leaders) also remained a major preoccupation for the Nationalist Government.[1] Meanwhile thousands of refugees and hundreds of square miles of devastated land were still remaining in the wake of the autumn's floods, while in many areas—there were some which provided a tranquil contrast—banditry was a feature of everyday life. In Nanking itself, Chiang Kai-shek wasted little time in beginning to recover his recently-abandoned influence over the central Government, which thereupon lost its brief basis of reconciliation between the main Kuomintang factions. The Cantonese Eugene Chen and Sun Fo resigned as Foreign Minister and President of the Executive Yuan respectively, and during an abortive and muddled attempt at the end of January to transfer the capital to Loyang, other ministers simply gave up and walked out. 'Nanking seems an empty shell,' reported one paper. 'It might almost be suggested that any group who cared to walk into the offices today and assume the duties of government might be presented at once with full permission to do so by the men lately installed there . . .'[2] By the middle of March, Chiang Kai-shek had resumed his place as military dictator in the guise of Chairman of the Kuomintang Military Affairs Commission. His writ still covered only a restricted part of the country, however, while the régime was as bankrupt financially as it was of creative concern for the mass of the Chinese people.

In this condition, which was a gift for her detractors, China now had to face a renewed Japanese offensive in Manchuria and a savage battle at Shanghai. At Geneva, she desperately invoked articles 10 and 15 of the Covenant on 29 January, and on 12 February asked for the issue to be

---

[1] See, e.g., Fitzgerald, *Birth of Communist China*, 71 ff.; S. Schram, *Mao Tse-tung* (Harmondsworth, 1966), 154 ff. Details of the Chinese political and social scene can be obtained from the Quarterly Political and Intelligence Reports of British Consuls, FO 371, files 16189, 16190, 17066; cf. Toynbee, *Survey, 1932*, 408–21.

[2] *North China Herald*, 19 January 1932. Chen was succeeded as Foreign Minister by Lo Wen-kan. Before the Shanghai crisis, Sun Fo was apparently in that city, negotiating with the Japanese. Bergamini, 466.

transferred from the Council to the Assembly; for her own part, and despite the large number of men she had under arms, it appeared to be the boycott of his goods which could hurt the Japanese invader most.[1] In the short run, however, a boycott could anger but not stop him, and although further public assurances of moderation were forthcoming from the new Premier in Tokyo,[2] more belligerent utterances by General Araki and the Kwantung Army were suggesting that a new offensive was imminent almost as soon as the League Council had dispersed from Paris.[3] It was in fact 23 December when the advance began, proclaimed as a drive against bandits, and with the Chinese troops withdrawing immediately towards the Great Wall, Chinchow was taken on 3 January. A greater surprise was then provided by another advance far to the north, into the Soviet-dominated area of Manchuria. In the wake of fighting between rival Chinese generals and on the pretext of protecting Japanese lives in Harbin, the Kwantung Army seized trains, advanced up the C.E.R. from Changchun, and occupied Harbin on 5 February. Chinese troops continued to operate as guerillas, especially in Kirin province, around the Sungari river, and along the C.E.R. itself,[4] but in the following months the Japanese pushed out again to Hailun in the north and to Hailin and beyond in the east. Already, on 18 February, new Chinese local authorities—Hsi Hsia of Kirin, Tsang Shih-yi of Fengtien, Ma Chan-shan of Heilungkiang, and others—announced the setting up of a new, independent Manchu–Mongolian state. On 9 March this new state of 'Manchukuo' was formally inaugurated, with Henry Pu-yi at its head as 'Regent'. By the end of April the Lytton Commission (as the League's new investigating body was now commonly known) could state in its preliminary report: 'The Chinese Government does not now exercise authority in any parts of Manchuria.'[5]

Although Japan's formal recognition of Manchukuo was not yet forthcoming, her control there was as evident as the exhilaration of her military and public alike, while the possibility of having to face a clash with the West over the matter was openly talked about and grimly accepted.[6] This new triumph did not stabilise the country's internal political situation, however, despite the overwhelming victory obtained by the ruling Seiyukai party at a

[1] According to Japanese sources, Japan's export trade in February 1932 was, in comparison with the figures for a year earlier, 96 per cent less in Central China, 97 per cent less in the South and 72 per cent less through Hongkong. *Manchester Guardian*, 14 April 1932; cf. *Japan Advertiser*, 29 December 1931.

[2] See, e.g., IMTFE, *Exhibit* 243; *Manchester Guardian*, 29 December 1931.

[3] See LNOJ, *February 1932*, 284–6; *Manchester Guardian*, 31 December 1931. For a summary of ensuing operations, see *Lytton Report*, cap. IV.

[4] An illustration of the continuing struggle faced by the Japanese was to be witnessed by a member of the League Secretariat accompanying the Lytton Commission, Adrianus Pelt, as he travelled alone back to Europe in the early autumn of 1932, along the C.E.R. to the Trans-Siberian Railway. At one remote stop, a procession of Chinese appeared alongside the train, carrying on a pike the head of the local Japanese consular official.

[5] See IMTFE, *Exhibits* 2425, 2429; *Lytton Report*, cap VI; LNOJ, *Special Supplement No. 101*, annex IV.

[6] E.g., IMTFE, *Exhibit* 3167; Ogata, 146; *New York Times*, 26 February 1932.

general election on 20 February.[1] The nationalist extremist, Mori Kaku, was busily conspiring to bring down Inukai's Government; General Araki openly sympathised with militants among the younger officers; during February, Baron Dan Takuma, head of the Mitsui business empire and much admired in the West, was assassinated, as was one of the recent Wakatsuki Cabinet. Inukai himself was to be murdered by young officers soon after this period, on 15 May.[2] By then his hopes of re-establishing governmental control of policy had come to nothing, like his private attempts to negotiate with Nanking a settlement that would maintain at least a semblance of Chinese sovereignty over Manchuria.[3] Those few statesmen who had voiced their fears for 'Japan's credit with the League of Nations and the great powers'[4] had fallen silent, and before the end of December the Cabinet itself had approved both the seizure of Chinchow and the reinforcing of the Kwantung Army.[5] Meanwhile the latter continued to press ahead with their blueprints and political preparations,[6] while bluntly presenting their intentions to politicians and imperial advisers in Tokyo.[7] Both Araki and Minami spoke to similar purpose in the presence of the Emperor himself.[8] Yoshizawa, en route from Geneva and Paris to the Foreign Minister's desk in Tokyo, stopped off in Manchuria to assure General Honjo that the clouds had now lifted from his mind and that he would strive to help the General achieve his desires.[9] On 28 January the General Staff in Tokyo approved Honjo's plans for an advance on Harbin, while the Cabinet, having decided early in March to set up the new state of Manchukuo, agreed on 11 April, 'regardless of the consequences', to organise that state in such a way as to achieve, together with Japan itself, 'a self-sufficient economic unit'.[10] The Great East Asian Propaganda Society, formed in Mukden in the same month, with Honjo and Itagaki among its officials, put it more forcefully (although its words were not published until the following year):

> The ultimate purpose of Manchukuo . . . is the creation of a foundation so as to successfully serve the allied and friendly Nippon in her struggle against the Anglo–Saxon world, as well as against Comintern aggression. In this holy struggle, all the peoples of East Asia must join to form the united front of the common fight with the oppressors.[11]

The Japanese commitment to take and hold Manchuria was now irrevocable. Yet the establishment of the new puppet state there had been overshadowed in Western eyes by the outbreak of Sino–Japanese hostilities at

[1] Ogata, 147 ff.; Crowley, 168 ff.; Storry, *Double Patriots*, 118 ff.
[2] See Byas, cap 1.   [3] See Crowley, 151 ff.
[4] Minutes of the Privy Council, 9 December 1931, IMTFE, *Exhibit 2205A*.
[5] IMTFE, *Exhibits* 188, 706; *Japanese Monographs*, No. 77.
[6] See IMTFE, *Exhibits* 245, 3296A; *Judgement*, part B, cap. V, 586 ff.; Ogata, 127–8.
[7] E.g., Kido Diary, 11 January 1932, IMTFE, *Exhibit* 2191.
[8] IMTFE, *Exhibits* 2251, 3174.
[9] Ibid, *Proceedings*, 19,003 ff. (Katakura testimony).
[10] Ibid, *Exhibits* 223, 226, 3422–O; *Taiheiyo senso e no michi*, II, 102–13, 150–70, 177–9; Crowley, 191.
[11] IMTFE, *Proceedings*, 7,606–8.

Shanghai, the centre of Western and above all British interests in China. Here, most dramatically, West met, or more often failed to meet, East: in the foreground, the office blocks and hotels of the International Settlement, the pomp and bustle of the Bund and Broadway river front; in the rear, the mazy poverty of Chinese suburbs like Chapei; 'a combination of luxury and squalor', in the words of the British Commander in Chief,[1] and one even more marked than that of Manhattan and Harlem forty years later. Here it now appeared that the Japanese were launching an assault on the heart of China, planned in conjunction with the Manchurian operation and intended as a prelude to similar attacks on all of the country's major ports. As usual, Tokyo protested through all possible channels that its forces were acting only defensively, as those of Britain had done in 1927;[2] to most Western observers, however, it seemed of more significance that on 8 February the Japanese Foreign Ministry unofficially aired a sinister scheme for establishing de-militarised and neutral zones round all the main ports of China.[3] Moreover there were also signs of impending action by Japanese troops at Tientsin, while at Nanking, where there were 3 Japanese cruisers and 4 destroyers, one of these ships loosed off several rounds into the city on the night of 1 February, causing a rash of dug-outs to appear thereafter.[4] A wholesale offensive against China was thought by many to be imminent.

This time, however, there was some truth in Tokyo's protestations, and the political position can briefly be summarised before the Shanghai fighting itself is outlined. At Nanking, the firing appears to have arisen from a Japanese belief that they were themselves being fired upon. As for Shanghai, both the Government and senior officers in Tokyo were embarrassed by the episode, which was seen as likely to hamper activities in Manchuria, increase Anglo–American accord against Japan, and weaken the local Chinese leader, Wang Ching-wei, who was a strong and not notably anti-Japanese rival of Chiang Kai-shek's.[5] Once the local Japanese commander had precipitated matters, however,[6] and an early attempt to secure the good offices of the Western powers had failed, the aim adopted was that of a quick victory, but a limited one; and although successful Chinese resistance then led to a greatly increased military commitment in order to save face, the intention remained that of reaching a settlement which would preserve Western, as well as Japanese interests, and thus win Western approval.[7] In other words, the contrast with the value placed upon Manchuria, and with the aims

[1] Kelly Papers, vol. 7, 39.
[2] See IMTFE, *Exhibits* 2416, 2417; *The Times*, 6, 8, 27 February, 1932.
[3] See DBFP, IX, No. 393.
[4] *Manchester Guardian*, 17 February 1932.
[5] See Ogata, 143 ff.; Crowley, 166 ff., and the selective memories of Shigemitsu, *Japan and Her Destiny*, 76 ff.
[6] It seems likely that Rear-Admiral Shiozawa was eager to show that the navy could deal with the Chinese as effectively as the army was doing elsewhere.
[7] *Taiheiyo senso e no michi*, II, 134–5, 141–5. The Western offer of good offices was probably rejected because it implied some blame for Japan, and suggested that Manchuria, too, would have to be discussed. From Shanghai, Admiral Nomura informed Tokyo of the desires of local British and American subjects for a speedy military decision, and suggested that this would be reflected in the policies of London and Washington.

adopted there, was a distinct one which entirely invalidates the later arguments of Cecil and others, noted earlier,[1] that Western firmness alone caused the Japanese to withdraw from Shanghai, and could easily have brought about a similar retreat in Manchuria.

This conclusion holds good even though, as no one was aware at the time, the incident which sparked off the Shanghai battle had been plotted by a Japanese military aide who was attached to the local Consulate-General. Tension in the city had been mounting for some time, as the Chinese refused to touch Japan's goods, demanded total resistance to her in Manchuria, and made abusive remarks in the press against her Emperor. On 18 January, at the secret instigation of Major Tanaka (who apparently was prompted by Itagaki among others to divert attention from the vital work being done in Manchuria), five Japanese, two of them monks, were beaten up by workers from a Chinese towel factory.[2] In the early hours of the 20th, a Japanese mob then set fire to this factory, and went on to attack a nearby police post, stabbing its Chinese constables and leaving them for dead.

> In the afternoon, above 1,000 Japanese met in their club in Boone Road where fiery and excited speeches were made, expressing indignation over attacks on the Japanese priests (one of whom died on Sunday) and the insult to their Emperor. A resolution was passed calling upon their Government to despatch additional warships and military units to Shanghai for the complete suppression of all anti-Japanese movements ... About half those present then marched to their Consulate-General to present Mr. Murai with a copy of the resolution ... The Consul-General attempted to appease them but they were dissatisfied and decided to march on the headquarters of the Japanese landing force. On the way a riot commenced ...[3]

Murai did take action himself, however, and later on the same afternoon of the 20th demanded from the Chinese Mayor of Shanghai[4] a formal apology for the events of the 18th, together with compensation, the arrest of those involved, and the immediate dissolution of all anti-Japanese organisations. These terms were followed by a warning from the local Japanese Commander, Rear-Admiral Shiozawa, that if they were not complied with he would 'take appropriate steps to protect the rights and interests of the Japanese Empire'.[5] Four days later a cruiser, an aircraft carrier and 4 destroyers arrived to reinforce Shiozawa's existing 3 cruisers and 3 destroyers, and when the Mayor, while conciliatory, delayed his full acceptance of the Japanese demands, he was presented with an ultimatum expiring at 6 p.m. on 28 January.[6]

The Mayor gave in, and, before the deadline, furnished what the Japanese civil authorities on the spot deemed to be a satisfactory reply.[7] Already,

---

[1] See above, 134.

[2] *Taiheiyo senso e no michi*, II, 118–20. Cf. Bergamini, 437, 457, 463 ff., where it is again suggested that the Emperor was involved, and that 'a fake war' was planned at Shanghai in order to give the League the satisfaction of a Japanese withdrawal.

[3] *North China Herald*, 26 January 1932; cf. DBFP, IX, Nos. 97, 103.

[4] I.e., of the city beyond the International Settlement.

[5] DBFP, IX, No. 118.　　　　　　　　　　[6] Ibid, Nos. 127, 135, 147, 375.

[7] Ibid. Nos. 140, 148. The reply is printed in *China Year Book, 1931–1932*, 649.

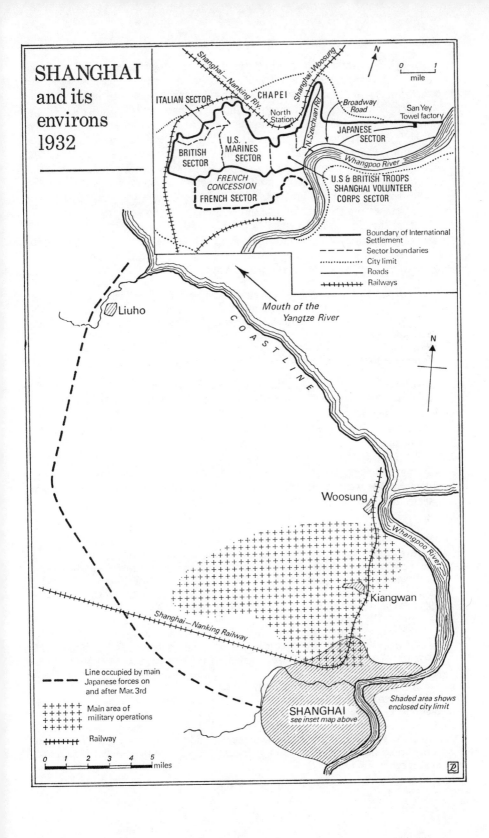

SHANGHAI and its environs 1932

CHAPEI

ITALIAN SECTOR

North Station

BRITISH SECTOR

U.S. MARINES SECTOR

FRENCH CONCESSION
FRENCH SECTOR

Shanghai – Nanking Riv.

Shanghai – Woosung

N. Szechuan Rd.

Broadway Road

San Yey Towel factory

JAPANESE SECTOR

Whangpoo River

U.S & BRITISH TROOPS SHANGHAI VOLUNTEER CORPS SECTOR

N

0   1
mile

——————— Boundary of International Settlement
– – – – – Sector boundaries
················ City limit
——————— Roads
++++++++ Railways

Mouth of the Yangtze River

C O A S T L I N E

Liuho

N

Woosung

Whangpoo River

Kiangwan

Shanghai – Nanking Railway

Line occupied by main Japanese forces on and after Mar. 3rd

+ + + + +
+ + + + +   Main area of
+ + + + +   military operations
+ + + + +

++++++ Railway

0   1   2   3   4   5
————————— miles

SHANGHAI
see inset map above

Shaded area shows enclosed city limit

however, Shiozawa was talking openly of his determination to send his marines into the Chinese suburb of Chapei in order to protect the Japanese who were living there;[1] now he was provided with a cover of legality by the Municipal Council of the International Settlement under its British Chairman, Brigadier-General Macnaghten. Alarmed at the growing tension, with Chinese troops preparing positions beyond the Settlement and refugees streaming in in anticipation of a battle in the Chinese part of the city, the Council declared a state of emergency as from 4 p.m. on Thursday the 28th.[2] A contingency plan thereby came into operation, under which regular and volunteer units of both Japan and the Western powers were to take up their allocated sectors for the defence of the Settlement; in some cases, including those of the British and of the Japanese, these sectors spilled into Chinese territory.[3] Shortly before midnight on the 28th, therefore, with an outward semblance of righteousness, Japanese forces advanced down the North Szechuan Road into their salient in Chapei:

> For some time previously, Japanese marines had been lined up outside the barracks adjacent to Hongkew Park, with seven formidable armoured cars and 20 motor lorries in readiness to transport them... The pavements were crowded with Japanese residents... At zero hour the first four lorry loads moved off... amid wild cheers from the onlookers, while Japanese photographers took an endless series of flashlight photographs ...[4]

Armed civilians went with the marines, and together, spraying the road and adjoining buildings with machine-gun fire as they went, they sought to push beyond their allotted perimeter. Units of the Chinese 19th Route Army were waiting. In this bizarre fashion, the savage and destructive battle of Shanghai had begun.[5]

The 19th Route Army owed its allegiance to Wang Ching-wei, not to Chiang Kai-shek, and was to receive only token assistance from the latter's divisions that were stationed further inland. Yet its tenacious resistance was to win the admiration of all observers and do much to restore Chinese morale

---

[1] Ferrell, *American Diplomacy*, 175. P. J. Treat, in his article, 'Shanghai, January 28th, 1932', *Pacific Historical Review*, September 1940, suggests that Shiozawa did not have aggresive intentions. Contemporary accounts now available, however, leave little doubt that areas beyond the allotted perimeter were scheduled for attack by the Japanese from the outset, and that their advance was conducted in the most provocative manner. E.g., DBFP, IX, No. 375; FRUS, 1932, III, 595–6; 'The Road to the Pacific War', vol. 1, part 3.

[2] DBFP, IX, No. 158.

[3] The history of the defence scheme, which had been drawn up in this foolish fashion *after* the outbreak of fighting in Manchuria, can best be followed in FRUS, 1932, IV, 65–6, 85–91, 224–6. Its changes of perimeters had not been notified to the Chinese.

[4] *Manchester Guardian*, 29 January 1932.

[5] The course of the fighting can be followed in the four reports of the League of Nations' Consular Committee, LNOJ, *March 1932*, annexes III, VIII, XI; LNOJ, *Special Supplement No. 101*, annex VI; also in the *Lytton Report*, cap IV; in the published British and American documents, and in numerous press reports, of which those in the *New York Times* (Hallett Abend) and the *North China Herald* are especially useful.

after the Manchurian fiasco.[1] Moreover, this resistance was displayed in the face of virtually unchallenged Japanese control of the air, and of a ruthlessness of the Condor–Legion variety that was displayed under the eyes of Western officials and press correspondents. ('One of the popular night amusements,' noted Admiral Kelly, 'was to go to the top of the tower of the Cathay Hotel, an American-dimensioned building, to watch the war in which one was practically taking part.'[2])

> 'For terrifying ghastliness', wrote one correspondent, 'the aerial bombardment of Chapei is . . . appalling beyond appreciation except by those who had seen the same in the European war . . . Opening from a fair height, the Japanese aviators came in lower and lower until at the time they bombed the Railway Station they could have been little more than 300 feet up. They were so low that they leaned over the sides of their machines as they were manoeuvring into position, waved their hands to the watching Volunteers below, then banked, circled, flew over their targets, and could not possibly miss their objectives . . .' 'Outer Chapei is ruined. Larger buildings, with few exceptions, last night were bare and gaunt walls, their interiors a seething mass of glowing embers, reflecting against the night sky. Houses by the hundreds are a wreck and a ruin . . .'[3]

Heavy artillery and tanks were soon adding to the destruction. Amid the smouldering ruins of no-man's-land, Chinese civilians wandered, dazed, under a reign of terror, wantonly picked off by the advancing Japanese[4] in a manner to which the world has subsequently become more hardened, thanks to the further exploits of the Japanese themselves, the Americal Division, and others. The Settlement itself was used by the Japanese as a springboard for their attacks and for landing reinforcements, while at times Chinese shells, aimed at the enemy's ships in the Whangpoo river, flew overhead in the other direction. On the night of 16–17 February, two British sailors from H.M.S. Suffolk were killed in this way, and on the 22nd the Italian cruiser Libia received four hits. New contrasts were being added to that city of contrasts, as the Dean of Canterbury found when he arrived soon after the fighting had died down:

> To enter Shanghai today is to enter a strange world. An endless line of battleships flying flags of many nations strung together stem to stern up the fairway of the river, grey and murderous but with a clean-cut beauty of their own, leads one to Shanghai. A tragic world it is, and yet ludicrous, too, as in those tales of a London or Brussels citizen wandering around sightseeing while Wellington won Waterloo. Tourists hustle among the ruins with cameras, and from their Buick cars hoot the conquering Japanese soldiers to one side. A warship flying the flag of Japan coals in the very heart of the city, while a Chinese sailor on my river steamer dips the Union Jack as she passes by.[5]

[1] E.g., Lytton Report, 87; China Weekly Review, 13 February 1932; North China Herald, 5 April 1932. On the subsequent clash between the 19th Route Army and Chiang Kai-shek see, e.g., D. Wilson, The Long March (London, 1971), 53.

[2] Kelly Papers, vol. 7, 139–40.

[3] North China Herald, 2, 9 February 1932; cf. Manchester Guardian, 19 March 1932.

[4] E.g. New York Times, 24 February 1932; China Weekly Review, 12 March 1932.

[5] Manchester Guardian, 31 March 1932. By 'battleships', the Dean meant warships. General McCoy wrote to his sisters on 9 April describing the ruins of Chapei

By the time this was written the Japanese had at last won the bitter struggle for the main suburbs of Shanghai. Their marines (about 2,000 in all) had earlier made little headway when a tenuous cease fire was arranged on 29 January,[1] but an artillery duel had been resumed on 1 February, to the accompaniment of Japanese demands for a complete withdrawal of Chinese troops to a distance soon named as twenty kilometers. Two days later Japanese ships and aircraft had commenced a bombardment of the Woosung forts, where the Whangpoo joined the sea,[2] and on 7 February four army battalions had begun arriving from Japan to attack the same area. A further 12,000 troops were landed at Woosung and in the Settlement on the 14th, and following the presentation of an ultimatum demanding a general Chinese withdrawal a new assault was launched in the Kiangwan–Woosung locality. Again, however, the Chinese slowed down the enemy, and yet more troops began arriving from Japan on 29 February—bringing the total to around 50,000—together with the highly-placed General Shirakawa to take over supreme command. Two divisions, landing at Liuho, higher up the mouth of the Yangtze, turned the flanks of the Chinese, who at last began to withdraw on 2–3 March. This new thrust had wrecked cease-fire talks between the two sides which had been arranged on the British flagship, *H.M.S. Kent*, on 27 and 28 February,[3] but it enabled the Japanese to feel that their prestige had been restored, and the Chinese to bow to force majeure. A cease fire was thus agreed on 3 March. Three weeks later, with Japanese troop withdrawals already under way, Sino–Japanese talks on Shanghai commenced their long crawl towards a final settlement, in accordance with the wishes of the League Assembly in far off and peaceful Geneva.

Public reactions in the West

In the public eye, it was the United States of the Western powers that reacted most vigorously to these dramatic new developments in the Far East, despite Washington's continued declaration that the country was impartial as between the two contestants.[4] Notably, the Japanese occupation of Chinchow was followed on 7 January 1932 by the promulgation of what became known as 'the Stimson doctrine' of non-recognition. In notes to China and Japan, the United States Government informed them that it was unable

> to admit the legality of any situation *de facto*, nor does it intend to recognise any treaty or agreement entered into between those Governments, or agents thereof, which may impair the treaty rights of the United States or its citizens in China,

and the untouched Settlement: 'Thinking of New York, the Bronx might have been destroyed without Manhattan showing signs of war.' McCoy Papers, box 8.

[1] See Kelly Papers, vol. 7, 131–5.

[2] The second report of the League's Consular Committee stated: 'Since 3 February, a state of open war exists . . . The offensive is entirely in the hands of the Japanese.'

[3] See Kelly Papers, vol. 7, 152–60. The new Japanese Admiral, Nomura, got on excellently with his Western naval colleagues, and his letter setting out Japan's terms for a cease-fire is preserved in the Kelly Papers, vol. 41.

[4] See e.g., *U.S. Daily*, 11 January 1932; *New York Times*, 22 March 1932.

including those which relate to the sovereignty, the independence, or the territorial and administrative integrity of the Republic of China, nor to the international policy relative to China commonly known as the open door policy; and that it does not intend to recognise any situation, treaty or agreement which may be brought about by means contrary to the covenants and obligations of the Pact of Paris . . .[1]

As Stimson recalled at the time,[2] the Bryan note of 1915 furnished this new document with a healthy American ancestry. From Tokyo, however, it evoked only a sarcastically-phrased official denial of territorial ambitions, together with unanimous denunciation in the Japanese press,[3] while in London the Foreign Office merely issued a statement on 9 January to the effect that the British Government, having already noted Japan's assurances concerning the maintenance of the 'open door' in Manchuria, saw no need to do more than ask for a confirmation.[4]

On the other hand the Shanghai explosion was very different, creating immediately a great deal of public anxiety on the part of the British, as well as the American Government. On 31 January, for example, statements from both Downing Street and the White House announced that military and naval reinforcements were being hurried to the International Settlement;[5] it was also made known that the two governments, together with the main European powers, were pressing Japan to accept a cease-fire, perhaps with the establishment of a neutral zone, and that subsequently they were both protesting against the military use and endangering of the Settlement. Even so, Simon and his colleagues continued to recall in Parliament Japan's assurances, and sharply rejected any suggestion that the time to think of sanctions under article 16 might be at hand ('most improper and highly dangerous,' Hailsham termed them). It was stressed that no premature judgement could be made whilst the dispute was under juridical consideration by the League. 'Our aim all the time,' declared Baldwin, 'is to bring about a peaceful settlement . . . and to avoid embroiling ourselves with either side'.[6] It all looked very pale stuff when set alongside the scarcely-concealed anger of Stimson, and above all his open letter to Senator Borah, dated 23 February, in which he forcefully reiterated America's non-recognition policy, invited other states to subscribe to it, and warned that, should the Nine Power Treaty be disregarded, then the United States would

---

[1] FRUS, *Japan, 1931–1941*, I, 76. Also, on 27 January, the U.S. Government published a White Paper, 'Conditions in Manchuria', containing a selection of diplomatic correspondence since the Mukden incident. This was in accordance with a Congressional resolution of 17 December. See *Congressional Record, 72nd Congress*, vol. 75, 672.

[2] DS 793.94/3508.

[3] FRUS, *Japan, 1931–1941*, I, 76–7; Takeuchi, 372.

[4] DBFP, IX, No. 66, note; on 16 January a further press release indicated that the Japanese Ambassador had conveyed 'express assurances' concerning Manchuria.

[5] Ibid, No. 208, note; FRUS, 1932, III, 148.

[6] See the contributions of Ministers in the Commons between 8 and 29 February, *Hansard, House of Commons*, vol. 261, cols. 480, 671, 827, 1265, 1612, 1830; vol. 262, cols. 178–83, 360–2; and of Hailsham in the Lords, *Hansard, House of Lords*, vol. 83, cols. 638–48.

have to reconsider the military agreements which had been reached at the same time.[1] To many contemporaries, this letter appeared to be a prelude to action against Japan. It thus tended to obscure Hoover's earlier statement that the United States was not going to get involved in a war,[2] as it did the American refusal to send a representative to sit again with the League Council, and the State Department's anxious (and false) denial of all knowledge of the appeal to Japan which that Council, minus the disputing parties, had despatched on 16 February.[3]

This 'appeal of the twelve'—which recalled Japan's 'very special responsibility for forbearance' and her obligations under both article 10 of the Covenant and the Nine Power Treaty[4]—constituted the only major public initiative taken by the Council during its largely abortive series of meetings between 25 January and 29 February.[5] It was not that there remained any uncertainty as to the seriousness of the situation. The alarm of the *Journal de Genève* was by no means untypical, when the paper declared on 31 January: 'C'est la guerre. Pour la première fois depuis 1918, ce mot redoutable qu'on a si souvent proféré comme une menace, redevient une réalité.' This image, however, served only to heighten the frustration at Geneva, especially at such moments as the eve of the expiry of the Japanese ultimatum at Shanghai on 19–20 February. Paul-Boncour, newly installed as the Council's chairman, might ask Japan's Sato Naotake whether there was not 'an appalling inconsistency' between his country's protestations and the major battle which was developing, and J. H. Thomas, substituting for Simon, might cry out for a halt to 'war in everything but name'; but apart from setting up a consular committee to report from the spot, and blessing the negotiations being conducted by the powers, there was apparently little the Council could do but listen to Sato and W. W. Yen, the new Chinese representative, accusing each other's country of internal anarchy and external aggression. The League, confessed Paul-Boncour on 9 February, had achieved 'very inadequate results', and ten days later he was admitting that a 'powerless' Council was 'unable to accomplish its chief task—namely, to prevent hostilities'.

Already, however, these proceedings were becoming overshadowed by the forthcoming special session of the Assembly, to which China, over Japan's protests, had referred the dispute after invoking articles 10 and 15. Yet by the time the Assembly met on 3 March and elected Hymans of Belgium as its president, the final Japanese assault at Shanghai was itself providing the basis for a cease-fire.[6] Moreover when the Chinese delegate asked the Assembly to bring about a withdrawal of invading forces, to recognise that the Covenant had been broken, and to declare China free of responsibility for what had occurred, he still expressed the hope that such a 'mobilization

[1] FRUS, *Japan, 1931–1941*, I, 83–7. Cf. Stimson press conferences, DS 793.94/4257, 4259, 4262, 4406, 4484, and *Journal de Genève*, 29 January 1932.

[2] See Stimson Diary, 29 March 1932.

[3] Stimson and Castle press conferences, 3 and 18 February 1932, respectively, DS 793.94/4121, 4367.

[4] LNOJ, *March, 1932*, appendix XII; DBFP, IX, No. 471.

[5] LNOJ, *March, 1932*, 325–72, 917–20.

[6] LNOJ, *Special Supplement No. 101*, 11–89. Paul-Boncour's opening report to the Assembly makes interesting reading.

of moral forces' would prove sufficient to bring the conflict to an end. It was scarcely a major breakthrough, therefore, when a Resolution was adopted on 4 March which called for a cease-fire and for negotiations with the aid of the powers on the spot, leading to a withdrawal of Japanese forces.

Nevertheless the meeting of 4 March did witness the beginning, in dramatic fashion, of a revolt by many smaller states against what they believed to be the unprincipled temporising of the major League powers. Several eye-witnesses recorded the scene as an unforgettable one when Hymans, exasperated by a succession of Japanese amendments to the draft resolution, called upon the representatives of other states to express their opinions:

> A silence followed, so tense as to be almost painful ... During this moment it looked as though no one was going to speak: every delegate was waiting for every other one. Then at last Motta rose amidst a burst of applause, and by this single action the conscience of the Assembly was unloosed.[1]

Giuseppe Motta, President of the Swiss Confederation, was on home ground, sustained by roars of applause from the public galleries, and then from the Assembly itself. Seconded by Benes, he made a simple assertion that went to the heart of the issue: 'The principle of the withdrawal of the Japanese troops must not be questioned ... China demands it as a natural right.' For three days thereafter, broken only by Sunday the 6th and by the sadness which greeted the news of Briand's death, Motta's lead in calling on the major powers to defend the very existence of the League was followed by a stream of delegates, among them Braadland of Norway and Löfgren of Sweden, Erich of Finland and Munch of Denmark, Restrepo of Colombia and Costa du Rels of Bolivia; Politis of Greece, de Zulueta of Spain and Sepahbidi of Persia; the delegates of Salvador, Haiti and Panama; Te Water for South Africa and Sean Lester for Ireland. For the Netherlands, Beerlaerts van Blockland was more restrained, while the Aga Khan for India pronounced the first requirements of the time to be 'patience and understanding'. Yet even the delegates of the four major European powers, led by Simon on 7 March, firmly endorsed the principles of the Covenant, however much they might emphasise that the immediate task under paragraph 3 of article 15 was mediation. We have already seen that when Simon—who by now was widely distrusted at Geneva[2]—declared that 'it would be far better for the League to proclaim its principles, even though it failed to get them observed, than to forsake those principles by meaningless compromise', he was not being insincere; when he ventured to propose, however, that changes brought about by means contrary to the Covenant and Pact of Paris should not receive the endorsement of League Members, the influence of Stimson and of his Geneva audience was evident.

It was thus with Simon's encouragement that the Resolution of 11 March

---

[1] Sweetser to Hornbeck, 24 March 1932, Sweetser Papers, box 15; cf. St. G. Saunders to Cecil, 7 March 1932, Cecil Papers, Add. 51100.

[2] Early in March, for example, Captain B. H. Liddell Hart in Geneva noted: 'In the eyes of most foreign representatives here, Britain has come to be viewed as manoeuvring to shield Japan for the benefit of her own interests, regardless of justice. I doubt if the old idea of "perfide Albion" has ever been more widespread.' Noel-Baker to Cecil, 7 March 1932, Cecil Papers, Add. 51107.

was shaped and approved by the Assembly.[1] It affirmed that the Covenant was 'entirely applicable' to the Sino–Japanese dispute and that it was contrary to the spirit of the Covenant for a settlement to be sought through military pressure, referred also to the Pact of Paris, and set forth the principle of non-recognition as suggested by Britain's Foreign Secretary. A committee of nineteen[2] was also set up to follow and report on the execution of this and previous Resolutions, to endeavour to find the basis for a settlement of the dispute, and to draft a report for the Assembly. With Washington publicly approving what had been done,[3] the League had once more been resolute, on paper at least, while the Shanghai cease-fire also gave cause for satisfaction. On 6 March, William Martin could write: 'L'Assemblée a sauvé l'honneur de la Société des nations.' But could it save Manchuria?

Partly obscured by the drama of Shanghai, the founding of Manchukuo had created scarcely a ripple in France. The centre and right-wing press had continued either to defend Japan's actions or at least to advise that the new régime in Manchuria must be accepted as a fait accompli.[4] Daladier's *La République* also suggested that, legality apart, the creation of a new, stable state was a welcome event, and that even if Peking itself were taken by the Japanese it would be of no concern to France.[5] Meanwhile the League's efforts continued to be widely derided as futile meddling, several commentators, for obvious reasons, drawing the conclusion that only a permanent international force could give some meaning to collective security.[6] Stimson's non-recognition notes also came in for scorn.[7]

The Shanghai episode did create much greater concern, despite continued sympathy for Japan's initial grievances.[8] But if the bombing of Chapei increased anti-Japanese sentiment generally, it appears to have been the direct threat to the local French Concession which particularly stimulated the press,[9] and the outcome in many cases was a heightened sense of dilemma rather than a resolute call for a change of policy. Herriot, soon to face the

[1] Japan abstained on the grounds of the inapplicability of article 15; the Chinese delegate abstained for lack of instructions, but affirmed his support later.

[2] The Committee consisted of Hymans, the twelve Council members (Japan and China apart), and Switzerland, Colombia, Czechoslovakia, Portugal, Sweden and Hungary. It was widely believed—unjustly it seems—that Simon had conspired to keep Te Water of South Africa (who was openly hostile to Japan) off the Committee. See Te Water to Dominions Office, 15 March 1932, and Price to Dominions Office, 14 March 1932, DO 35/178.

[3] FRUS, *Japan, 1931–1941*, I, 213.

[4] E.g., *Le Temps*, 20 February, 22 March 1932; *Le Journal*, 30 December 1931; *Le Matin*, 30 December 1931.

[5] *La République*, 20 March 1932; cf. *Manchester Guardian*, 1 February 1932.

[6] E.g. *Le Temps*, 29 December 1931, 3 January, 7 March 1932; *L'Echo de Paris*, 3 January, 17 February 1932; *Le Matin*, 23 February 1932.

[7] E.g. *Le Temps*, 23 January 1932.

[8] E.g. *Le Temps*, 26 January, 17 February 1932; *Le Journal*, 30 January 1932; *L'Action Française*, 5 February 1932. For the increased anxiety in the Dutch Parliament, see *Rijksbegrooting voor het Dienstjaar 1932*, III, 50th Session, 1613.

[9] E.g. *Le Temps*, 5 February 1932; *La République*, 15, 20 February 1932.

problem as premier, expressed this in *L'Ère Nouvelle* on 28 January, when he described France as 'suspended between an international policy, in this case sterile, and a national policy which is impossible for anyone wishing to behave loyally. M. Paul-Boncour finds himself, after Aristide Briand ... faced with almost irreconcilable contradictions.' In the Chamber, too, where foreign policy debates were almost exclusively concerned with Europe, Herriot could warn against allowing the Covenant to be undermined, but could offer no recipe for restraining Japan.[1] Moreover the bulk of the press still averred that none of the powers—including the United States, who might encourage others to become involved—would take action, and that France should do no more than defend her own possessions. From their different starting points, for example, both Coty's *Figaro* and Daladier's *République* concluded that to do more would be to invite trouble in Indo–China.[2] (If there was going to be a war, the expectation was that it would be a Soviet–Japanese one.[3]) Meanwhile rumours increased of a secret Franco–Japanese understanding, and of large-scale bribery of the French press by the Japanese and by French arms manufacturers, the sharp rise in the value of shares of firms like Hotchkiss and Creusot being noted in the same connection.[4] Given the volatile state of French politics and the country's growing European preoccupations, at least it seemed clear that no government could embark upon sanctions against Japan without the likelihood of being overthrown, and with the May elections drawing near it was doubly unlikely that risks of any kind would be taken.

In Britain, the public outcry against Japan in this period was much greater than in France. Paradoxically, however, and quite apart from other considerations, a parliamentary situation that was the reverse of the French one helped make it unlikely that official policy would be significantly deflected as a result. Among the press, the *Morning Post* continued to support Japan throughout,[5] while *The Times*, in rejecting the need for non-recognition notes of the Stimson variety and explaining the early rumblings in Shanghai, asserted that so long as the 'administrative integrity' of China remained a fiction the Japanese were bound to act to protect their interests in that country, as Britain had done in 1927.[6] These arguments were also being

---

[1] *Annales de la Chambre des Députés, janvier-mars, 1932* (Paris, 1934), 239–40, 313–6, 471 ff.

[2] E.g. *La République*, 30 January 1932; *Le Figaro*, 6, 14 February 1932; cf. *L'Echo de Paris*, 29 January, 27 February 1932; *Le Temps* 17, 23, 28 February 1932; *Le Matin*, 31 January 1932; *Journal des Débats*, 30 January 1932; *Journal du Commerce*, 11 February 1932.

[3] In this period, the Soviet press was accusing Japan of anti-Soviet activities in alliance with the Russian émigrés in North Manchuria, and warned of the likelihood of war. See, e.g., *Izvestia*, 24 January, 4 March, 15, 18 April 1932; *Manchester Guardian*, 1 February 1932; *New York Times*, 8, 29 February 1932.

[4] See e.g., *Manchester Guardian*, 1, 8, 29 February 1932; *The Times*, 27 February 1932; *Le Populaire*, 5, 26 February, 4 March 1932; cf. Roy Howard to Lowell Mellett, 10 March 1932, Newton Baker Papers, box 122, and for further second-hand evidence of Japanese bribery of the French press, a State Department memorandum of 27 January 1932, DS 793.94/3753.

[5] E.g., *Morning Post*, 18 February 1932.

[6] *The Times*, 11, 19, 29 January 1932.

echoed by expatriate groups in Shanghai itself, together with their spokesmen in London. On 1 February, for example, the Joint Committee of the Shanghai British Chamber of Commerce and China Association urged that a neutral zone of ten or fifteen miles radius should be permanently established round the city, a proposal that received little sympathy when forwarded to the Foreign Office, but one that may well have encouraged the Japanese to release their ballon d'essai on the same subject a week later. The same Committee returned to the attack in March:

> We have good reason to believe that the Japanese . . . are genuine in their dis-claimer of any territorial or political ambitions in this area and would welcome the co-operation of the British and American Governments in achieving a reasonable solution, whether by establishing a demilitarized zone . . . or by simple extension of the existing Settlement . . . Unless we are mistaken the British Government attitude is to continue the policy of conciliation of Chinese Officialdom at all costs which has been largely responsible for the outbreak of Sino–Japanese conflicts . . . Unless this attitude can be converted into one more positive, . . . the whole advantage of the situation created by the Japanese dominating position around Shanghai will be lost.[1]

Individual members of the China Association were writing to London in a similar spirit ('the Japanese are "pulling the chestnuts out of the fire" for us'), while the observation of the Vice-Chancellor of Hong Kong University that the Japanese 'were not so accustomed to turning the other cheek to the Chinese smiters as we poor British' also found its way to the Foreign Office.[2]

Yet the need to preserve Chinese good-will continued to act as a modifying consideration, and there were those on the spot who disagreed outright with the idea of seizing the opportunity of China's misfortunes to put pressure on her local authorities.[3] Moreover, the destruction of Chapei called forth strong denunciations among the British in Shanghai and from China-lobbyists in London.[4] Like the *Observer*, *The Times* also swung round to hold Japan solely responsible for the loss of life in the burning suburb and to censure conduct, 'naval, military and political, (that) has cast doubts on the good faith of the Japanese Empire'.[5] Both papers urged the closest co-

[1] China Association to Foreign Office, 2 February; China Association to Secretary of State for Foreign Affairs, 18 February; Shanghai Joint Committee to China Association, 11 March; China Association to Foreign Office, 14 March; C. W. Orde to China Association, 9 April 1932; China Association, *General Committee Papers, July 1931–December 1932*; cf. FO 371, F 865, 1606 and 2166/ 1/10, F2671/65/10; Teichman, 166.

[2] R. E. Wilson to H. E. Arnhold, 11 February 1932. China Association, *General Committee Papers, July 1931–December 1932*; FO 371, F 3038, 3076, 3336/1/10; cf. ibid, F 15/1/10, and Tientsin British Residents Association to Simon, 27 January 1932, FO 800/286.

[3] See the correspondence in March between O. M. Green and the Shanghai Joint Committee, China Association, loc. cit., and *North China Herald*, 22 March 1932.

[4] Letters from O. M. Green, *The Times*, 3 February 1932; *North China Herald*, 2, 23 February 1932.

[5] *The Times*, 30 January, 1, 3, 5, 6, 18, 26 February 1932; *Observer*, 31 January 1932.

operation with the United States to meet the emergency, whilst the *Manchester Guardian*, convinced that another 1914 was dawning in Asia, severely condemned MacDonald's Government for lacking the zeal being displayed in Washington.[1] The similar applause for the United States of Toynbee, Gooch and other scholars has already been noted.[2]

The desire to see an end to the fighting was deep and widespread, being intensified by specific episodes such as the Japanese bombing of a camp of flood-refugees. On the means that could or should be adopted to bring this about, however, there was scarcely any more clarity or agreement than before. Among those offering an answer were the hundred and more people (writing from Welsh guest-houses, Oxford colleges, northern industrial towns) who informed the League Secretariat of their readiness to enrol in the Peace Army that was being proposed by Dr. Maude Royden and others, and of their willingness to lay down their lives if necessary when that army interposed itself between the combatants.[3] The *New Statesman*, the Independent Labour Party and the General Assembly of the Church of Scotland, for their parts, were now advocating an embargo on arms supplies to Japan,[4] although there remained much confusion as to whether an embargo should be sought for punitive purposes, or to diminish the scale of slaughter—the L.N.U., for example, again petitioning the Government to halt shipments to both Japan *and* China. The *New Statesman*, the *Economist* and the National Joint Council of the T.U.C., Labour Party and Parliamentary Labour Party also called for the application if necessary of financial and economic sanctions against Japan, a possibility that aroused much evasiveness and hostility. In the Commons, for example, although Geoffrey Mander and Seymour Cocks continued to put questions on the desirability of proceeding to article 16 of the Covenant, they received little support and from Lansbury only meandering references to 'some of the powers that we believe to rest in the Covenant'.[5] The *Manchester Guardian* wrote of the need 'to exert real pressure in one form or other', but shied away from any prospect of war, which, even with American participation, would resolve itself into 'a mere clash of interests'.[6] Most of the press, together with the many individuals who wrote to recall the horrors of 1914–18, rejected the idea of sanctions out of hand, as did ex-premier Billy Hughes of Australia.[7]

As for the L.N.U., it had at last moved beyond the restrained concern that Murray was still expressing as late as 6 January[8] to call for some form of sanctions and a declaration of non-recognition; in a covering statement which accompanied the Executive Committee's resolution of 12 February, Cecil, Murray, Sir Arthur Salter and J. W. Hills, M.P., stressed the unique

[1] *Manchester Guardian*, 29 January, 5, 6, 22, 29 February 1932.
[2] See above, 9–10.   [3] LN. Archives, R 1871, 5706.
[4] *Manchester Guardian*, 3 March 1932; FO 371, F 1759/37/10; C. Thorne, 'The Quest for Arms Embargoes', in *Journal of Contemporary History*, October 1970; Bassett, 160–1.
[5] *Hansard, House of Commons*, vol. 261, cols. 1265, 1612–14; vol. 262, cols. 175–8.
[6] *Manchester Guardian*, 5, 6 February, 14 March 1932.
[7] E.g., *The Times*, 23, 24, 27 February, 11, 23 March 1932; *Manchester Guardian*, 19 February 1932.
[8] *The Times*, 6 January 1932.

opportunity which existed for cooperating with the United States, and their repeated appeal in *The Times* of 18 February brought support from Harold Laski, J. E. Neil, R. H. Tawney, Leonard Woolf and others in the *Manchester Guardian* of 2 March. To a meeting on 27 February, Cecil declared that 'from 3 February Japan was, in the ordinary sense of the word, the aggressor', while elsewhere Wickham Steed and Geoffrey Mander emphasised the long-term threat to Australia and New Zealand in consequence of the American–Japanese conflict which would inevitably follow Japan's domination of China and the Pacific.[1] Salter—until recently the Head of the League's Economic Section—was also writing to Simon to urge joint League–United States sanctions, arguing that Japan was 'happily more susceptible than almost any other country to the threat of isolation and the severance of economic relations'.[2] In addition, Simon agreed to receive a small but formidable Union delegation (it included Toynbee, Salter and Zimmern) on 16 February, which rehearsed their Committee's resolution and left a memorandum on future policy composed by Murray. 'He told us he was convinced, even passionately convinced, that ours was the right policy,' reported the Union's Secretary to Murray afterwards, but the Foreign Secretary had not indicated what risks the Government were prepared to run.[3]

One major qualification which Murray had attached to his suggestions was the need for active American assistance in any coercive measures. (With an optimism that was not shared even by the Union's ex-Service advisers,[4] he declared that, given American and French co-operation, 'Japan cannot openly resist'.) Without such assistance, he recognised that 'we must submit to the naval superiority of Japan. But we should say so, and not attempt to cover our humiliation by hypocritical defences that deceive no one'. Murray had also accepted the need to avoid 'proclaiming policies for which the public is not prepared',[5] and while in private he admitted that that public would not support a British lead in imposing a blockade on Japan, he also hoped that the latter would not be expelled from the League, even if she remained recalcitrant. 'Government action', he believed, 'should be as polite as possible and avoid threats,' any resort to boycotts or blockades being in his eyes 'a mark of failure'.[6] (It was thus with genuine relief that in March he would privately offer Simon his 'warmest congratulations' on helping to bring Britain and the League 'almost out of the wood in the Far East' by mobilising a world opinion 'which proved, in conjunction with other things,

[1] Ibid, 29 February, 1 March 1932; *Manchester Guardian*, 13 February 1932.

[2] Salter to Simon, 2 February 1932; FO 371, F 590/1/10.

[3] FO 800/286; Garnett to Murray, 16 February 1932, Murray Papers. Simon also asked that the Union should cease making representations direct to the Japanese Embassy.

[4] Murray had been advised by senior ex-Service officers in the Union that a blockade would bring Japan down, but only after Shanghai and Hongkong had been lost. Murray to Stevenson, 5 February; Murray to Dickinson, 17 February 1932, Murray Papers.

[5] *Manchester Guardian*, 9 February 1932.

[6] Murray to Cecil, 12 February; Murray to Rich, 27 February; Murray to Drummond, 16 March 1932, Murray Papers.

irresistible'.[1]) As it was, Murray's own attempt to organise a private boycott of Japanese goods in February had rapidly come to nothing in the face of evasion by Lansbury and others. Cecil privately believed such a scheme to be 'useless' since the amount of goods involved was negligible, while on the issue as a whole, as noted earlier, he now found that 'the richer class is very unsound and even the poorer class is very ignorant'. The inherent rightness and power of public opinion was clearly taking time to emerge, although with characteristic muddle Cecil was writing to a friend a few weeks later that, for all the Government's feebleness, 'that does not mean that in the last stage it may not have been desirable to proceed by way of an unofficial boycott'.[2]

Despite his mounting anger and frustration, in fact, and despite the greater freedom of public expression open to him after the beginning of February, when he ceased to substitute for Simon on the League Council, Cecil's inner uncertainties continued in this period. He was sure that the Japanese were bluffing when they talked of leaving the League or reacting fiercely to sanctions, 'fear of every shadow, not the desire to shield Japan', being what he condemned as the root of British policy. To Austen Chamberlain, however, he revealed that he had 'for a long time believed that economic blockade was impracticable except as a part of belligerent action', and that any 'strong action' would require the participation of the United States and perhaps even the Soviet Union.[3] (Again in muddled fashion, he added that this necessity did not alter Britain's 'broad obligation to carry out the undertakings we have given under the Covenant'. Under paragraph 1 of article 16, of course, these included the undertaking to '*prevent* all financial, commercial or personal intercourse between the nationals of the covenant-breaking State and the nationals of any other State, whether a Member of the League or not'.) Before March was out, in any event, Cecil was turning his attention almost exclusively towards disarmament. 'It is as much as you can do to get the ordinary [L.N.U.] branch secretary to understand one set of points,' he wrote to Noel-Baker soon afterwards. 'If you ask him to understand two he will either muddle them both or drop one of them.' He added a consideration that might have come from Simon: 'I should prefer now to defer any very strong action about Manchuria until the Lytton Commission has reported. Indeed, I do not quite see how you could justify to practical people action before that.'[4] Noel-Baker himself had been striving from

[1] Murray to Simon, 16 March 1932, Simon Papers (private collection), Foreign Affairs, 1932.

[2] Murray to National Peace Council, 2 February; Murray to Lansbury, 3 February; 'F.W.' to Murray, 2 February 1932, Murray Papers. Cecil to Noel-Baker, 25 February, 7 March 1932, Cecil Papers, Add. 51107; Cecil to St. G. Saunders, 11 April 1932, ibid, Add. 51100.

[3] To Simon, Cecil again admitted that Britain had to have 'the full co-operation of the United States'. If that were not forthcoming 'it would be better for us to wash our hands of the whole business'. Such are the privileges of non-responsibility. Cecil to Selby, 20 February, Cecil to Simon, 25, 26 February 1932, FO 800/286.

[4] Cecil to Noel-Baker, 12, 22 March, 25, 29 April 1932, Cecil Papers, Add. 51107; Cecil to Austen Chamberlain, 13 January 1932, ibid, Add. 51079; *The Times*, 23 February 1932. Cecil's semi-official submissions to the Foreign Office from Geneva will be noted below.

Geneva to keep the Union up to the mark, although his emphasis varied between seeking a withdrawal of ambassadors and embarking upon a major sanctions campaign.[1] At times, even his ardour was tinged with despair. Drummond, he wrote, was making known his belief that both condemnation of Japan and action against her were undesirable, while Avenol was asserting that the Lytton Report would reveal that it was right for Japan to maintain control over much of Manchuria. Even Lytton himself, he thought, might 'need some stuffing put into him'.[2]

However much Noel-Baker might strive, and for all the public horror at Japan's Shanghai attack, it was a foregone conclusion that the L.N.U. would not speak with a single and mighty voice. Grey, as Cecil's fellow President, expounded to an Albert Hall meeting on 7 March his belief that war was unthinkable and that the League, faced with an untypical situation, had achieved as much as was possible.[3] Austen Chamberlain, who, as we have seen, had reluctantly consented to join the Union's Executive Committee (a year later, he would be describing it as 'comprising some of the worst cranks I have ever known, led by Cecil', whose methods were 'nearly always wrong and his judgment wholly unreliable'[4]), also believed that Chinese anarchy 'presented a problem which really was not contemplated by the framers of the Covenant'. Japan's actions were reducing the widespread sympathy she had commanded at the outset, but still the British public would not support a policy more active than the one Simon was pursuing—a policy for which Chamberlain declared his 'wholehearted approval' in the Commons. To Murray, the former Foreign Secretary repeated one of the main beliefs which had guided him during his days in office:

> Now the strength of the League is not in its sanctions, which without the active and belligerent support of the United States are unworkable, but in ascertaining facts, focussing the moral opinion of the world on the issue, and thus bringing to bear a world opinion which renders conciliation effective.[5]

Among these various L.N.U. opinions, belief in the need to secure American participation in any economic measures against Japan was thus one common feature. But here only a single suggestion of hope arrived in the shape of a cable to Murray on 25 February from Raymond Rich, of the League of Nations Association in New York:

SORRY UNABLE TALK TODAY DESIRED EXPLAIN SERIOUSLY UNFAVOURABLE REACTION HERE TO REPORTS BRITAIN WILL

[1] Noel-Baker to Murray, 17, 28 March 1932, Murray Papers; Noel-Baker to Cecil, 2 March, 20, 26 April 1932, Cecil Papers, Add. 51107.
[2] Noel-Baker to Cecil, 2 February, 7, 18 March 1932, Cecil Papers, Add. 51107.
[3] *Manchester Guardian*, 8 March 1932.
[4] Chamberlain to Tyrrell, 13 February 1933, Austen Chamberlain Papers, AC 40/5–9; Chamberlain to Lady Chamberlain, 22 March 1933; ibid, AC 6/1/902–1062. Cecil was equally exasperated with Chamberlain. 'His power of doing nothing,' he wrote to Murray, 'amounts to genius.' The situation when the two had been government colleagues in the 1920's was thus renewed.
[5] Chamberlain to Murray, 11 February 1932, Murray Papers; Chamberlain to Cecil, 11, 18, 20 January 1932, Cecil Papers, Add. 51079; *Hansard, House of Commons*, vol. 162, col. 183.

OPPOSE ECONOMIC PRESSURES ARTICLE SIXTEEN STOP LARGELY DESTROYS OTHERWISE EXCELLENT PROSPECTS AROUSE NATION WIDE DEMAND AMERICA CONCUR ECONOMIC MEASURES STOP HAVE POSITIVE HIGHLY CONFIDENTIAL INFORMATION IF LEAGUE LEADS WE MUST AND WILL FOLLOW . . .[1]

Even Cecil remained sceptical, however, not believing 'that any suggestion for economic pressure has ever come from the American Government', while Murray replied that the British public would want America to do the leading, even if it were wise to threaten, which he doubted.[2] Moreover, Murray's caution was endorsed by one of the leading figures of the American peace movement, James Shotwell of the Carnegie Foundation, who had written to the former on 15 February to suggest that 'any interference (with the Japanese) now would only intensify their emotions'. Viewing matters from an America 'almost completely submerged by a rising tide of nationalism', Shotwell had added:

> Under the circumstances obtaining here now, I don't see any chance of peace forces taking an aggressive stand. They have lost courage and leadership. Their councils are confused. The extremists are becoming more extreme, and the middle-of-the-way people are frankly turning their interests from idealism to domestic economic questions.[3]

If Shotwell, not Rich, was right—and by this is meant the contemporary Shotwell, not the subsequent pedlar of myths[4]—then the frustrated and confused cries of the leaders of the League movement in Britain might well have been directed, by their own reasoning, against the American public, or the depression, or man's incapacity to live up to the ideal of collective security, rather than against their own Government. And Shotwell was indeed right.

The excited cable from Raymond Rich was part of a new surge of activity on the part of those few enthusiasts in America who sought action of some kind in defence of the post-1918 peace agreements. In January, for example, Representative Morton Hull's Resolution for placing an embargo on arms

[1] Murray Papers. Rich was also Director of the World Peace Foundation. For an exchange on the same subject between Roy Howard and Beaverbrook, see Newton Baker Papers, box 122.

[2] Cecil to Murray, 25 February; Murray to Rich, 27 February 1932, Murray Papers.

[3] Murray Papers.

[4] A few years later, Shotwell was to put a rather different complexion on American public opinion at this time: 'The conception of permanent peace between civilized nations became more and more real in the thinking of American people. . . . It was because of this new outlook that the Oriental war became a matter of such general concern to the American public. For its judgement against Japan, which was almost universal, was chiefly due to the fear that the violation of the Pact (of Paris) and the Covenant endangered the structure of that international relationship which is the heart of the program of the new era.' *On the Rim of the Abyss*, 224. As with Cecil's later writings, here was a myth in the making, and one so flattering to the idealised public which read it.

supplies to a violator of the Kellogg Pact had come before the House Foreign Affairs Committee; in March, following the abandoning of that attempt, Hull was to try again with a bill to forbid loans to an aggressor, but that, too, would wither away in committee, as would Senator Capper's arms-embargo effort in April.[1] Yet here again, as in Britain, the notion of a punitive embargo was entangled with that of cleansing one's hands of 'blood money', or of avoiding all risk of becoming involved in a war. The Peace Section of the American Friends Service Committee thus wanted both some form of anti-Japanese boycott and an embargo on arms to Japan and China together;[2] some individual members of the Women's International League For Peace and Freedom also came to support the idea of a boycott, but only with 'many qualms', in Emily Balch's words, lest they should 'stir up a mass movement of hatred and war spirit', and only on the reassurance from the American Boycott Association that there was 'no danger of precipitating a war with Japan'.[3]

The Boycott Association sought to bring Tokyo to accept arbitration by shunning Japanese silk goods in favour of woollen or cotton articles from elsewhere;[4] meanwhile the Directors of the L.N.A. (whose membership overlapped with that of the former body) appealed for whole-hearted American cooperation with the League in defence of civilisation,[5] and on 19 February Hoover was presented with a petition signed by Lawrence Lowell (the President of Harvard), Chester Rowell and other leading civic and academic figures, who urged that the United States should join the League in applying economic sanctions if Japan were to be found guilty of violating the Covenant.[6] One signatory of this petition was Newton D. Baker, a former Secretary of War and a leading candidate for that year's Democratic presidential nomination. And it was behind his signature that there lay the occasion for Rich's excited assertions concerning the Administration's willingness to follow the League over sanctions—a minor episode in itself, but one worth briefly recounting in order finally to remove the confusion which it helped create and as an example of the distortions that can easily attend the efforts of enthusiastic international pressure-groups in a crisis situation.

Rich had telephoned Baker on 17 February, asking if the latter's name could be added to Lowell's petition, and on the same day Baker replied in the affirmative by telegram.[7] He made no conditions for signing, and his papers

[1] See, in general, Divine, *The Illusion of Neutrality*, 26.

[2] DS 793. 94/4800, 4801. One American businessman, on the other hand—and several more in Germany were openly saying the same thing—urged that a wholesale war would lift America/Germany out of the depression. Ibid, 4059, 4453.

[3] Emily Balch to Jane Addams, 29 January, 16, 24 February; American Boycott Association circular, 2 March 1932, Jane Addams Papers, series 1, box 20; Dorothy Detzer to W.I.L.P.F. officials, 10 February 1932; American Committee on the Far Eastern Crisis (R. Rich) to Balch, Balch Papers, box 3; Detzer to Madam Chiang Kai-shek, 20 February 1932, W.I.L.P.F. Papers, American Section, Correspondence, box 5.

[4] Tupper and McReynolds, 327–37; *Washington Post*, 20 February 1932.

[5] *New York Times*, 12 February 1932.

[6] *Congressional Record, 72nd Congress*, vol. 77, 4586–8; cf. DS 793.94/4121.

[7] Newton Baker Papers, box 199.

contain no other communication on the subject at the time; yet on the following day Rich—who may of course have spoken again by telephone to Baker—engineered an interview with Stimson in order to obtain for his friend an assurance that the Administration would not be embarrassed by the petition in question. Following this interview, Rich began to glow with optimism, ready to proclaim not only to Murray but also by telephone to Arthur Sweetser in Geneva that the State Department awaited only a lead from the League before imposing sanctions, and that France had intimated to the United States that she herself might propose action under article 16. Again, on the 25th, Rich repeated this message to Geneva, although Sweetser, Norman Davis and other recipients were as sceptical as Murray and Cecil.[1] There the matter faded away, only to be revived in the following May when Walter Lippmann, who at the time was keen to see Newton Baker secure the Democratic nomination, sought Stimson's version of the affair in order to protect Baker from Republican criticism of his having signed the February petition, 'Mr. Baker's friends (being) under the distinct impression that the State Department encouraged this expression of American opinion'.[2] Stimson's lengthy response was not accurate in every respect,[3] but the Secretary's account of his interview with Rich on 18 February tallied with his diary entry for that day. He had told Rich then that he had no objection to a private boycott, but he had also pointed out that no League initiative over sanctions appeared likely; after the interview, he had noted: 'Rich is one of the peace people and has the rather narrow view that they have. It is very curious now to have a peace man trying to urge action which normally leads to war.' A week later, when Hugh Wilson had telephoned from Geneva with a report of Rich's 'fantastic' messages to Sweetser, Stimson had again noted: 'It shows what a crazy zealot can do.' Baker himself immediately accepted the Secretary's version of what had occurred.[4]

Of course Rich and his friends were by no means alone in their sense of outrage at what was taking place in Shanghai, and while almost the entire press dismissed Manchukuo as a transparent fiction, Stimson's non-recognition note and Borah letter came in for extensive approval. Criticism of China's political chaos was not stilled,[5] but Lippmann was only one of the commentators who believed that the Secretary of State's pronouncements might help bring eventual victory for international order out of present humiliation and defeat at the hands of Japan.[6]

[1] Telephone records, 24, 25 February 1932, Norman Davis Papers, box 17.

[2] Lippmann to Stimson, 16 May 1932, Newton Baker Papers, box 149.

[3] He declared, for example, that he 'had been in full agreement with the essentials of the President's position' in firmly opposing an official boycott as likely to lead to war.

[4] Stimson to Lippmann, 19 May 1932; Baker to Lippmann, 26 May 1932, Newton Baker Papers, box 149; Stimson Diary, 18, 26 February 1932. Rich's version of the Hoover Cabinet's opinions was equally inaccurate: cf. FRUS, 1932, III, 428. It is, of course, quite possible that he was encouraged by someone in the State Department other than Stimson.

[5] E.g., *New York Times*, 6 May 1932; and on the Chinchow episode, see the approach of the *New York Herald Tribune*, 21 December 1931.

[6] Lippmann, *Interpretations, 1931–3*, 200, 203–8; cf. Lippmann to Stimson, 22 December 1931, Stimson Papers, box 303; *New York Herald Tribune*, 9 January

Yet at the same time the vehemence of anti-League sentiments in other quarters was if anything increased by the apparent dangers of the moment, with reports of British duplicity available to add fuel to the flames.[1] Newton Baker himself now reluctantly accepted that there was insufficient public support to make American entry into the League practicable in the foreseeable future, while in February his nomination rival, Roosevelt, came out strongly against any such possibility—to the disgust of his wife among others.[2] Moreover, many of those who approved of non-recognition were also extremely vocal in their opposition to sanctions or any risk of war. Congressmen privately pressed such views upon the State Department;[3] Borah, echoed by various patriotic societies, denounced sanctions as 'the best way to advance the cause of war between this country and Japan';[4] Representative Fish and Senator Dill sought legislation that would halt arms supplies to all belligerents in order to keep the United States away from trouble.[5] The banker, Thomas Lamont, was at one with the peace-lobbyist, Dorothy Detzer, in warning against any move towards military action,[6] and the pro-League Scripps-Howard press, as well as that of Hearst and McCormick, did the same.[7] 'The power does not exist to prevent or restrain a determined aggression like that of Japan in Manchuria,' concluded Lippmann: there should be no withdrawal of ambassadors, no embargo on arms to Japan, no economic sanctions. 'A war with Japan,' he wrote, 'would create stupendous misery and vindicate no principle whatsoever'. Moreover, if the safety of the International Settlement at Shanghai required support for the Japanese demand for a withdrawal of Chinese troops, then the West should provide that support, 'ignoring all sentimental considerations'.[8]

In mythology, of course, (often masquerading as 'history'), opinions such as these were to become virtually the exclusive property of Simon, the City, and others who lurked in London to betray man's progress towards universal peace. In fact, realism and uncertain idealism, coloured by a general defensiveness of spirit, existed widely on both sides of the Atlantic. In each

1932; *New York Times*, 9 January, 25 February, 12 March 1932; *Washington Post*, 17, 19 January, 25 February 1932; *Chicago Tribune*, 9 January 1932; Tupper and McReynolds, 313–14, 339.

[1] E.g. *Washington Post*, 22, 28 February 1932; *San Francisco Examiner*, 17 February 1932; *New York Times*, 28 January 1932.

[2] Baker to Howard, 22 January 1932, Newton Baker Papers, box 122; Baker to Nash, 25 February 1932, ibid. box 145; *Washington Post*, 3 February 1932; J. P. Lash, *Eleanor and Franklin* (New York, 1971), 346–8.

[3] E.g., DS 793.94/4436.

[4] Coalition of Patriotic Societies to Borah, 22 February and Borah to Coalition, 23 February 1932, Borah Papers, box 332; Borah press statement, 20 February, 1932, ibid, box 341.

[5] *Congressional Record*, 72nd Congress, vol. 75, 4654; cf. *U.S. Daily*, 8 February 1932, and Divine, 28 ff.

[6] DS 793.94/4802, 4803½.

[7] E.g., *Washington Post*, 4, 9, 31 January, 23, 24 February 1932; *Chicago Daily Tribune*, 25, 26 February 1932; *San Francisco Examiner*, 15 January, 25 February 1932; Tupper and McReynolds, 324; cf. the House speech of Representative Loring Black, *Congressional Record*, 72nd Congress, vol. 75, 4818.

[8] Lippmann, *Interpretations, 1931–3*, 200–1, 202–3, 205–7.

country, domestic preoccupations continued to overshadow even the most dramatic international events (in parts of the United States, for example, police were fighting with the unemployed, and killing some of them, while pre-election skirmishing embraced such rousing issues as the Eighteenth Amendment); in Shanghai itself, many American residents, like their British neighbours, were eager to seize the chance to extend the boundaries of the Settlement and put the Chinese in their place.[1] And despite Stimson's public pronouncements, there continued to be much in common between the immediate Far Eastern policies of the two governments, Toynbee, Gooch and other observers notwithstanding.

London and Washington: information and advice

Over Shanghai, as never at any other time during the Far Eastern episode of 1931–3, the men responsible for British and American policies were faced with a crisis situation. Although attention was already focussed on the area in general, the sudden outbreak of major warfare in the city came as a surprise; moreover the fighting was seen as constituting a major threat to Western possessions, lives and interests which were valued far more highly than anything touched by the Manchurian campaign, while events demanded that significant decisions be made within a matter of days or even hours. A harsher light than before was thus thrown upon Western policies. Dilemmas which had been merely observed now had to be faced; latent conflict between various desiderata had to be recognised, and choices made, rather than avoided or concealed. At the same time, from behind these immediate issues longer-term ones also showed through more obviously than before, that is for those with the will, time and ability to see them. These weeks also witnessed a new frequency and urgency in Anglo–American exchanges concerning Far Eastern policy, just as they formed the subject of later recriminations. France and Italy might send cruisers to Shanghai, but the nub of the Western response centred around those moments when Britain and the United States reached out towards one another, yet did not embrace. In order to emphasise and analyse this aspect of the situation, therefore, the formulation of policy in London and Washington will be brought together on a comparative basis before the chapter is concluded with a narrative of the major decisions and exchanges involved.

Where domestic opinion was concerned, the broad contrast between the two capitals which was noted earlier continued to hold good in this new situation. The comments of officials already quoted[2] indicate the convenient, though no doubt sincere, belief within the Foreign Office and Government that events in Shanghai had diminished, but not removed, an underlying sympathy for Japan's case among the British public, despite the efforts to the

---

[1] See Johnson memorandum, 11 March 1932, Nelson Johnson Papers, box 36; cf. Dr. Blakeslee's subsequent observation on the attitude of American businessmen whom he met in the Far East when there with the Lytton Commission: '(It) seemed to depend on whether or not they could make money out of Manchukuo. . . . On the whole they gave me the impression of having more sympathy with Manchukuo than any other of the groups we interviewed.' FRUS, 1932, IV, 149–65.

[2] See above, 141.

contrary of the L.N.U. At the height of the crisis the tendency was to assume that people's concern was primarily for the safety of British lives and property on the spot,[1] while the overriding criterion of self-preservation tended to reduce all non-official submissions to minor significance, as will be seen below. Nationalist fervour among the Japanese and passivity among the Americans still outweighed indignation—usually of a limited-liability variety —among the British. In Washington, on the other hand, with the presidential election now only months away, both Hoover and Stimson were frequently looking over their shoulders at what in their different ways they saw as the limits imposed by Congress and the country. Where Borah, especially, was concerned, Stimson went out of his way to ensure that he was 'not likely to get an attack from behind'.[2] He wrote to MacDonald: 'I cannot adequately describe the intensity of the wave of isolationism that has swept over the country during this gloomy autumn and is now reflected in Congress.'[3]

Obviously there were similarities too, not least in the way in which members of the British Government, like Hoover, were quick to emphasise isolationist tendencies in their own country and in each other's. Where flows of information and advice from the Far East were concerned, the two capitals also had much in common. Each received advance warning of the seizure of Chinchow, and, early in the new year, of the setting up of some form of separate, puppet régime for Manchuria as a whole.[4] Each was also aware of Inukai's private attempts to come to an arrangement with the Nanking Government, as well as receiving the usual assurances over Japan's lack of aggressive intent.[5] It was towards London in particular, however, that Tokyo displayed its eagerness for some kind of co-operation among the powers to meet any unilateral termination of extraterritoriality on the part of China, a prospect which alarmed Lampson for its likely repercussions among the Chinese.[6] Even so, Lampson, like his American colleague, Johnson, was also ready to place some emphasis on one possible inter-pretation of Japan's intentions that carried with it a certain reassurance for Western governments—that aggression in Manchuria was primarily an anti-Soviet move.[7] And while neither Lampson nor Johnson subscribed to the belief of their opposite numbers in Tokyo that Chinese anarchy had provided Japan with good reason for her intervention ('she has put herself squarely in the wrong,' wrote Forbes at the end of January, 'and yet it seems clear that what Japan is doing is necessary and (that) . . . it could only have been done

[1] E.g., minute by Orde on DBFP, IX, No. 410, FO 371, 1255/1/10.

[2] Stimson Diary, 9 January 1932.

[3] Stimson to MacDonald, 27 January 1932, Stimson Papers, box 304.

[4] E.g. DBFP, IX, Nos. 9, 31, 50; FO 371, F 7722/1391/10, F 231 and 236/1/10; FRUS, *Japan, 1931–1941*, I, 70–5; FRUS, 1931, III, 684–6; FRUS, 1932, III, 386–7; DS 793.94/4362. Bassett's suggestion (*Democracy and Foreign Policy*, 113) that the puppet-nature of the Manchukuo régime could only be a matter of speculation is untenable.

[5] DBFP, IX, Nos. 68, 84, 90, 98; FRUS, 1932, III, 3–4.

[6] DBFP, VIII, Nos. 484, 485, 489; ibid, IX, Nos. 109, 110. Simon had briefly and tentatively raised the possibility in December of talks among the powers on extraterritoriality.

[7] DBFP, IX, Nos. 91, 119; FRUS, 1932, III, 26–7.

by force'),[1] they did not dispute the warning that, if provoked, the army might soon seize complete control in Japan, and that sanctions could well lead to war.[2]

Both Ministers in China, moreover, were having to report the extensive political confusion which existed in that country, however much Lampson, especially, might attribute it primarily to the Japanese incursion in Manchuria; also, in the lull which followed the seizure of Chinchow, both tended to treat excited Chinese talk of further and imminent danger with some scepticism.[3] It was mainly to the United States that the politicians in Nanking were looking for advice and assistance; yet before the Shanghai fighting Johnson's interpretation was that these men were exaggerating domestic dangers in order to push the powers into mediation, and thus to avoid the onus of having to meet Japan's demands on their own responsibility. The sudden contrast between this and Johnson's warning of impending disaster during the coming crisis was to reflect an element of instability in the sender, and not merely changed circumstances. 'China is too weak to maintain her sovereignty in Manchuria,' he was writing in January, and in private he agreed with his Dutch colleague that the West should not become involved in what looked like the makings of a new Sino–Japanese quarrel in Shanghai. Yet at the same time—there was no outright contradiction but rather an uncertainty as to where to place his emphasis—he was bitterly noting that 'if Japanese activities in Manchuria . . . are not war, then the Kellogg Pact has become a hideous farce', and was deploring what amounted almost to 'Western approval of what they have been doing'.[4] By contrast, Admiral Taylor was not at all equivocal:

> 'There is no doubt in my own mind,' he wrote to the Chief of Naval Operations at the end of January, 'that (Japanese) control will be to the advantage of all Chinese in Manchuria but the official parasites. . . . The boycott, to me, is an evil thing as carried out . . . News has just come in of the outbreak in Shanghai, and I can imagine the Japanese have been pushed beyond the limit. It would be interesting to be there, but were I to go there is little doubt that the Chinese would broadcast the idea that it was to support them against the Japanese, and in my opinion they have had enough support already.'[5]

Taylor's British colleague, Admiral Kelly, was generally more sympathetic to the Chinese, as we have seen. But he, too, formed the initial impression that, for all their brutality, the Japanese were justified in their early actions at Shanghai.[6]

[1] E.g. DBFP, IX, Nos. 23, 24, 115; FRUS, 1932, III, 109–15. Lindley was now aware of the role of 'a clique of utopian colonels'. Despite his sympathy, Forbes was becoming irate over Japanese intransigence; he added, however, that 'an orderly China would be a tremendous field for foreign salesmanship—bringing back to the world, perhaps, good times'.

[2] E.g. FRUS, 1932, III, 108–9; ibid, 1932, IV, 672–7; DBFP, IX, Nos. 29, 30, 33, 43.

[3] See DBFP, IX, Nos. 51, 71, 87, 89, 96.; FO 371, F 121 and 135/1/10.

[4] Johnson to Mrs. Archbold, 6 January 1932, Johnson Papers, box 5; Johnson note, 28 January, ibid, box 36; FRUS, 1932, III, 14–15, 26–7, 55–7, 65–6, 91–2; DS 793.94/3267, 3912.

[5] Taylor to Pratt, 23 January 1932, Taylor Papers, Box 1.

[6] C. in C. China to Admiralty, 28 January 1932, FO 371, F 722/1/10.

As tension and then the battle itself built up in that city, little time elapsed—far less than in Manchuria—between an event taking place and a reasonably accurate description of it arriving in the West.[1] On occasions, indeed, as over the Japanese ultimatum which expired on 19 February, officials in London and Washington were prepared for a new offensive before the troops had left their trenches. Even so, there remained no clear and agreed version as to who had been responsible for the conflict in the first place. Nor was there unanimity among Western observers in the Far East as to Japan's intentions or the source of greatest danger to Western possessions. The alarm of the moment helped create new divisions of opinion, as well as emphasising existing ones.

Both British and American officials in China were now quick to warn of a possible disintegration of the Nanking Government as one consequence of these new events. Lampson, hastily returning from the start of a trans-Siberian journey home on leave, arrived at the scene of the fighting on 12 February, and plunged into an attempt to arrange a cease-fire. He made no secret to Johnson or the Foreign Office of his indignation at the atrocities being committed by the Japanese,[2] while his desire to protest at such moves of theirs as the landing of fresh troops on the quays of the Settlement was sharpened by fear of a general anti-foreign reaction on the part of the Chinese. Johnson expressed the same fear more dramatically, in a telegram to Washington in which he urged dissociation from the 'sinister' idea put out by the Japanese Foreign Office concerning the possibility of setting up demilitarised zones round major Chinese ports. 'I am certain,' he added, 'that the time is ripe for another disaster similar to the Boxer uprising unless we walk carefully with these sorely exasperated people.'[3] It followed that the two Ministers were also in accord in rejecting the proposals of expatriates for enlarging and entrenching the privileges of the Settlement whilst the Chinese were reeling.[4]

At once, however, there arose a related and immediate issue over which there were sharp differences of opinion, not between Lampson and Johnson, but among local Western officials generally: was it desirable, in the interests of the safety of the Settlement, that the Japanese should gain a military victory and push back the 19th Route Army? According to a Japanese source, both the American and British Consuls-General, Cunningham and Brenan, had openly expressed such a desire, as well as their sympathy for Japan's grievances, at a meeting with reporters on 29 January.[5] And whether such a major indiscretion was intended or committed, even, Japanese on the spot certainly derived the impression that their efforts would command Western approval. Moreover Brenan was soon and more properly repeating

[1] For examples of warnings before the full conflict, see DBFP, IX, Nos. 97, 100, 103, 105, 111, 127, 135; FRUS, 1932, III, 39, 41, 66; DS 793.94/3618, 3624, 3673; Stimson Diary, 23 January 1932.

[2] See DBFP, IX, Nos. 144, 307, 435, 436, 450, 451, 452.

[3] Johnson to State Department, 9 February 1932, FRUS, 1932, III, 256–7.

[4] Lampson to Johnson, 8 February 1932, Johnson Papers, box 15; Johnson memorandum, 11 March 1932, ibid, box 36; DBFP, IX, No. 583; ibid, X, No. 20; FRUS, 1932, III, 506–8, 526–7.

[5] *Taiheiyo senso e no michi*, II, 139–40.

such views to London. He, Cunningham, and the commander of the British troops were agreed, he reported, that a victorious Chinese army might invade the Settlement, while an outflanked one might be driven back into that same preserve. Therefore,

> we must desire (a Japanese victory) . . . I am not interested to rescue China from a position to which she has been brought largely by her own folly. One cannot forget that all foreigners and especially British have suffered in recent years from (the) utter incompetency and unjustifiable pretensions of Chinese nationalism. Provided therefore that the Japanese avoid interference so far as possible with the municipal administration and policing of the Settlement there is something to be said for letting them settle their accounts with the Chinese if they can, and secure terms that may be of benefit to other nationals.[1]

With this 'too local and too dogmatic' view, Lampson expressed his immediate and strong disagreement: he did not believe that a victorious Chinese army would invade the Settlement, nor could he see anything but trouble stemming from another Japanese triumph.[2] Yet it was the opinion of the Consuls-General, not that of the Ministers, which commanded the support of the British, American and French admirals who were now on the spot, and they, too, made known to their respective capitals this desire for 'a substantial Japanese victory'.[3]

Whatever one's view of the requirements of immediate self-interest, there was also the major question of what intention lay behind the new assault by the Japanese. One could desire their victory without being satisfied as to their motives, for it was Brenan who, on 1 February, described their attitude as 'not (being) that of men who desired a peaceful solution'. Their designs in Shanghai, he suggested, were 'deeper than at first thought', perhaps extending as far as the seizure of a large area from which to trade and exert pressure on China.[4] Cunningham likewise reported to Washington that the Japanese were insincere when they talked of peace: 'the mask has been discarded,' he telegraphed on 20 February, while Admiral Taylor discerned the presence of 'a long-standing plan'.[5] Yet there were also enough asides or private appeals coming from various Japanese to convince some observers that the conflict had taken Tokyo, if not the local commander, by surprise, and that what was being sought was an opportunity to disengage without loss of face.[6]

Something of each of these interpretations found its way into the opinions

[1] Brenan to Holman, 8, 9 February 1932, DBFP, IX, Nos. 376, 395.

[2] Lampson to Brenan, 9 February 1932, ibid, No. 410.

[3] Vansittart to Patteson, 11 February 1932, ibid, No. 425; Taylor to Pratt, 20 February 1932, Taylor Papers, box 1; Kelly Narrative, Kelly Papers, vol. 7, 136.

[4] Brenan to Lampson, 1 February 1932, DBFP, IX, No. 228.

[5] Cunningham to State Department, 10, 20 February 1932, respectively DS 793.94/4101, FRUS, 1932, III, 405–6; Taylor to John Taylor, 21, 27 March 1932, Taylor Papers, box 1. Taylor believed that the staunch Chinese resistance at Shanghai had 'engendered the idea that they are as good as the foreigner, which will make the old policy of bluff harder to carry on'. Another bad result had been the growth of communism, he wrote.

[6] E.g., DBFP, IX, Nos. 333, 502; FRUS, 1932, III, 286, 317–19, 412; cf. Castle memorandum, 23 February 1932, FRUS, *Japan 1931–1941*, I, 198–200.

of Lindley and Forbes in Tokyo itself, as they sought fervently to restrain their own governments. Japan, they argued, might well be happy to see the Shanghai affair brought to an end, but she would not be deterred from achieving this on the basis of an immediate military victory. Repeated Western protests would thus serve only as irritants, while more than ever before the suggestion of economic sanctions might result in war. If Forbes appended a few more qualifications than did Lindley, he never doubted this general thesis, quoting Lindley's views in support of his own and privately agreeing with his Military Attaché that the situation was 'heading right straight for war'. With Neville's encouragement, he even had the temerity to suggest that he and his senior Western colleagues saw the effect of Stimson's prize letter to Borah as being 'extremely injurious'. 'My relations with Stimson,' he noted later, 'were extremely difficult and getting more so.'[1] Lindley also was being blunt in his reporting—so much so that on one occasion he drew down upon his head a stern reprimand from Wellesley, who redrafted part of a despatch for him rather than let it stand in the files in its original form which would give needless offence to others.[2] The Ambassador's premise remained as before: 'There is no limit to the damage Japan can do to our interests in the Far East if we fall foul of her, and . . . there is no limit to the injury she will do them in that event.' 'The Japanese,' he wrote to the King, 'would prefer to go down fighting if they are to go down at all . . . They are immensely strong locally . . . so that the war would be bound to be a long one. During the interval it is not impossible that complications with Russia or Germany might put an entirely new complexion on the affair.' There would be no yielding over Manchuria; therefore to link that issue with the Shanghai one would be folly. Meanwhile if there were even a suggestion of resorting to article 16, the result was likely to be a military dictatorship in Tokyo and an assault on Western possessions. If he could privately tell the Japanese Government that sanctions had been ruled out it would ease the situation; as it was, he telegraphed on 4 February, 'a single false step (might) precipitate catastrophe'.[3]

Mingled with these varying interpretations and prescriptions from the Far East (the location and function of the author often being of more account, it would seem, than other factors such as nationality or personality) came pressing requests and advice from European states and Geneva. It was for Britain especially, of course, that the dilemma involving the League now became more acute than ever. Cecil's growing anxiety, for example, while privately conveyed to Stimson during an exchange of appreciation at the end

[1] FRUS, 1932, III, 202, 314–5, 442–3; DS 793.94/4692, 4727; Forbes Journal, 2nd Series, IV, 45 ff.; Neville to Castle, 28 February, 26 March 1932, Castle Papers, Japan.

[2] The trouble concerned a despatch in which Lindley was scornful of the failure of Reading and Cecil, in the early stages of the crisis, to heed his advice not to antagonise Japan, and expressed his vehement disagreement with Wellesley's observation that Britain might find herself dragged into war with Japan. 'The tone of this despatch is most reprehensible,' minuted Wellesley, and Vansittart: 'Sir F. Lindley is asking for trouble.' FO 371, F 3374/1/10, and DBFP, X, No. 64.

[3] DBFP, IX, Nos. 274, 300, 319, 321, 344, 350, 396, 439, 441, 445, 620, 629; Lindley to King George V, 31 March 1932, RA G.V, P510/49.

of January,[1] was primarily directed at Simon, for whom he again briefly deputised on the League Council. From there he warned of the likely consequences of allowing Japan to create in Manchuria 'a second Egypt' (an interesting description): the League's authority would be rendered bankrupt in Asia and impoverished in Europe; France could not be answered when she contended that the Covenant alone did not provide security; Indian unrest would be exacerbated by this triumph of Asia over the West. Therefore if Japan persisted with her 'deliberate and well thought-out plan', American participation should be obtained in diplomatic and economic sanctions—not a blockade or military measures, which were 'quite impracticable'—and Simon himself should come to Geneva in order to emphasise Britain's concern for what was at stake.[2]

The general mood of unhappiness at the League was brought out all the more by the opening of the Disarmament Conference there on 2 February: Arthur Henderson, in his inaugural address, might 'refuse to contemplate even the possibility of failure', but the gunfire in Shanghai provided its own mocking response. Washington, like London, was well aware of this mood and of the details of Council sessions, thanks to Sweetser and Wilson. But although Drummond and others appealed for Stimson's advice and for close Anglo–American cooperation,[3] this last suggestion for a special Anglo–Saxon partnership also gave rise to sourness among some League members. The Belgian Ambassador in London, for example, spoke to Vansittart of the resentment which would be felt in Europe if there were any more 'clumsy attempts of the United States Government to draw us into exclusive action with them in the Far East', an observation that was deemed sufficiently important for it to be circulated to the Cabinet. American diplomats at Geneva were also aware of these sentiments.[4]

The attitude of France, in particular, was now giving rise to as much uncertainty and speculation in diplomatic as in press circles. Laval having formed his new Ministry without Briand on 13 January, he had then fallen from power by 16 February on an adverse vote in the Senate, and it was not until the 20th that André Tardieu was able to cobble together a new combination from the same, centre-right groups, with himself as Minister for Foreign Affairs. In addition, however, reports were coming in to Washington and London of much coolness among French diplomats over both Stimson's declarations of principle and the more practical efforts being made in Shanghai itself,[5] and Simon was only one of those who were now privately saying that some form of understanding probably existed between Paris and

[1] FRUS, 1932, III, 85–6, 94–5.

[2] DBFP, IX, Nos. 132, 204, 266, 267, 283, 347; Cecil to Simon, 12 January, 1 February 1932, FO 800/286. Cecil withdrew from the Council on Simon's arrival, on 6 February.

[3] See FRUS, 1932, III, 73, 176–8, 285–6, 301–5, 402–3, 430–2, 456–7, 475–7; DBFP, IX, No. 159. Reports of private Council meetings and informal talks can be found in ibid, Nos. 122–490, passim; for an interesting survey of the League scene by Hugh Wilson on 30 March, see DS 793.94/4948.

[4] DBFP, IX, No. 267 and FO 371, F 640/1/10 for Vansittart's minute; Vansittart to Simon, 30 January 1932, CP 54 (32), in CAB 24/228; FRUS, 1932, III, 273–4.

[5] See FRUS, 1932, III, 4–5, 21–2, 35–6, 411–12; DS 793.94/4256.

Tokyo.[1] Nevertheless, discreet enquiries by the State Department failed to reveal any secret French Government loans or arms-sales to Japan, and Stimson eventually accepted that the indignant denials of duplicity which he received through the French Ambassador, Paul Claudel, were genuine.[2] He was right to do so, for now, as earlier, there was in fact no collusion, and Paris dutifully joined the other capitals in urging moderation upon the Japanese.[3] Even so, the submissions of their Ambassador in Tokyo—that it was important to tread softly with Japan, especially in view of the Disarmament Conference—were being received with sympathy by officials in the Quai d'Orsay,[4] and when Massigli in Geneva told Sato that the Council was not likely to take further action until the Lytton Report had been received, he was echoing the private anxiety of Laval that this should be so.[5]

No other state counted for much in terms of possible immediate influence on British or American policy. Italy and Germany made the appropriate, soothing noises when required, but, like the Dutch, they also made no secret of their distaste for any idea of coercion, and followed Britain in declining to subscribe to Stimson's non-recognition note of 7 January.[6] In Berlin, in fact, there remained a strong desire to stay out of the affair altogether;[7] yet already the Japanese Ambassador in Moscow was musing aloud to his German colleague on the possibility of closer cooperation between their two countries, with perhaps a cancellation of Japan's reparations claims against Germany in return for the latter's friendly understanding over the Far Eastern conflict. The Auswärtiges Amt made no positive response to this— but it was careful not to dismiss abruptly such a notion either.[8] Meanwhile in London, as Eden was forced to reveal in the Commons, the Dominions were 'being informed' rather than consulted over British policy.[9] Individuals occasionally made their voices heard—the Aga Khan suggested that the League was 'a dangerous institution for the British Empire to be influenced by in this conflict',[10] while Te Water, as noted, spoke forcefully in the opposite sense—but the single major summary of Commonwealth opinion that was

[1] DS 793.94/3524, 4255.

[2] Ibid, 3489, 4328A, 4347, 4412, 4544, 4608; FRUS, 1932, III, 157–8, 166–7, 428; Stimson Diary, 20 February 1932.

[3] E.g., Foreign Ministry to Martel, 30 January 1932, AQD, T 33–6.

[4] Martel to Foreign Ministry, 11 January 1932, to which is attached a docket with the comment: 'Je souscris.' AQD.

[5] In the Quai d'Orsay there is a draft letter—it was not sent, it seems—from Laval to Paul-Boncour, dated 8 February 1932, setting out the dangers of the Council acting on article 15 in such a way as to provoke on Japan's part 'une réaction inconsidérée telle que son retrait de la Société des Nations'. Massigli to Foreign Ministry, 3 February 1932, AQD.

[6] See FRUS, 1932, III, 6, 23–4, 31, 48; DS 793.94/4282, 4797; cf. FO 371, F 2219/1/10.

[7] E.g. Michelson memorandum, 5 February 1932, AA, serial K 2088/K 559464–6. The Japanese were showing particular concern at this time over the role of German advisers to the Chinese army.

[8] Dirksen to Bülow, 23 February, Bülow to Dirkson, undated, 1932, AA, serial K 2088/K 560402–5 (also serial K 2264/K 625486–7).

[9] Hansard, House of Commons, vol. 261, col. 827; cf. DBFP, IX, No. 271.

[10] DBFP, IX, No. 520.

presented to the Cabinet derived from a British initiative, and as will be seen below was formulated by the Dominions Secretary, Thomas, simply to reinforce a decision that had already been taken on other grounds. Even had there existed, which there did not, a desire in Commonwealth capitals to play a forceful role in helping to shape policy, it is doubtful whether much encouragement would have been forthcoming. As various unofficial pressure groups were finding, too much was seen to be at stake for anyone outside Whitehall to get much of a hearing.

London and Washington: disposition[1] and debate

It will be seen that in several respects not only the information but the advice being received in London and Washington was remarkably similar. Yet often the responses of the two sets of policy-makers were to be different, at least up to a certain level of perceived risk, and an understanding of this and other features of the day-to-day reactions to the new crisis requires an initial comparison of the general orientation of these men as it was emerging from discussion within official circles.

To a considerable extent, of course, it is sufficient to refer back to those features of British and American policies which were brought out in the first part of the book. It also requires only a brief reminder—but an important one—of the extent to which domestic matters continued to overshadow everything else in this period. For Hoover and his colleagues the recession was blacker than ever, with Stimson, for example, privately describing the country early in February as being 'in an emergency like war'.[2] For Mac-Donald's Cabinet, the financial situation was showing some improvement; but already the tariff issue was producing threats of resignation from Samuel and others, as Neville Chamberlain prepared a major protectionist announcement for delivery in the Commons early in February—'the greatest day in my life ... Father's triumph.' For a time the cracks were papered over, thanks to Hailsham's proposal that the rule of collective Cabinet responsibility should be relaxed in this instance, and to Simon's plea that an open split would undermine Britain's influence on European affairs and her 'new status' in American eyes. The forthcoming Ottawa Conference promised to tear apart this uneasy compromise, however, while less seriously Jimmy Thomas, no doubt remembering the verbal rough-house in which he had been involved during the Imperial Conference of 1930, was going round muttering about resigning on the grounds that the Canadians were conspiring to 'do him in'.[3]

With the Cabinet thus preoccupied, it continued to be the Foreign Office that shaped the main features of Britain's Far Eastern policy, despite a greatly increased degree of Ministerial involvement and decision-making at the height of the crisis over Shanghai. And within the Foreign Office, the

[1] On the question of predisposition and consensus formation within an organisational context, see De Rivera, caps. 3 and 8.
[2] Stimson Diary, 7 February 1932.
[3] Neville Chamberlain Diary, 22 January 1932; Neville Chamberlain to Ida Chamberlain, 23 January, 6 February 1932, Neville Chamberlain Papers; Cabinets of 21, 22 January 1932, CAB 23/70.

dominant image of China was even more than before one of a country in chaos, fought over by politicians who in many cases were untrustworthy. This is a simplification of the various views that were held, but simplification was notably present at the time.[1] From January into the summer of 1932, internal minutes sounded a gloomy refrain: 'The puppet Govts. in Manchuria are probably the stablest elements in China!'; 'It is clear that there is now nothing resembling a real Govt. in China'; 'To the Chinese mind appearance is more important than reality . . . (but) it is obvious that the area wherein the Chinese Government exercises real authority is shrinking rapidly'; 'I doubt if we shall see a stable central government in China in our lifetime.'[2] Anyone who tried to support China's cause was thought likely to find himself lost in a maze of deceit, while contrary to several reports from British observers and to the subsequent findings of the Lytton Commission, it was accepted as 'certainly true' that the Chinese in Manchuria, having suffered oppression and misgovernment under their previous rulers, were not opposed to a Japanese take-over.[3] Indeed, both Pratt and Wellesley, probably the two most influential members of the Foreign Office in terms of Far Eastern policy, remained convinced that in Manchuria, in the words of the former, 'the Chinese were almost entirely in the wrong' over the basic issues, having by 'corruption, incapacity and blind conceit' threatened to ruin a region of great potential wealth, and having set out to sabotage Japan's treaty rights by devious means.[4]

There was thus an initial readiness within the Foreign Office to accept that the Japanese might have good grounds for exasperation in Shanghai as well. The intensified trade boycott was seen as causing them to 'suffer grievously', in Simon's words,[5] and with the attacks on Japanese citizens in mind, Pratt felt at the beginning of the new crisis that 'the distinction between (Britain's) case in 1927 and the Japanese case in 1932 is so fine that it does not seem advisable . . . to join in a démarche'.[6] Similarly on 29 January Wellesley, while admitting in an internal minute that the Japanese appeared to have put themselves in the wrong (a view which Pratt, too, soon came to accept), conveyed advice to the Prime Minister's Private Secretary which the latter noted as pointing in a far-from-condemnatory direction:

[1] Reasons obviously varied, but it may be suggested that where options are seen as being severely limited by certain overriding factors, subordinate considerations will tend to be simplified in a direction conforming to what is perceived to be the dominant requirement.

[2] Minutes by Orde and Pratt, FO 371, F 159, 209, 4967 and 5127/27/10; but cf. F 3622/10/10. Baldwin once remarked that he didn't like the Chinese. Jones, *A Diary*, 93.

[3] Pratt, minute and notes, 19 January 1932, DBFP, IX, No. 95; cf. FO 371, F 7043/1391/10, and *Lytton Report*, 108 ff.

[4] Unless otherwise stated, the opinions of Pratt and Wellesley set out in this section are taken from the following memoranda: by Pratt, n.d. (probably 31 January) and 1 February 1932, DBFP, IX, Nos. 216, 238; by Wellesley, 1, 6 February 1932, ibid, Nos. 239, 256. No. 216, conflated with para. 4 of No. 238 together with No. 239, were circulated to the Cabinet as CP 65 (32), CAB 24/228.

[5] DBFP, IX, No. 153.

[6] Pratt memorandum, 26 January 1932, ibid, No. 120.

He thinks it a case for keeping very cool heads, and that it is not unlikely that Japs. will have not a bad case. Under the state of emergency declared by the *Municipal Council* the Japs. were *bound* to man their sector. While proceeding to do so they were attacked (according to their account) . . .[1]

Even when Japanese excesses had become indisputable, it was to be Brenan's emphasis on the immediate danger to the Settlement from the Chinese, and hence on the need for a local Japanese victory, that was readily accepted in London, rather than the more balanced view of Lampson.[2]

Here, then, was one element in a screen of images and priorities which ensured a greater degree of receptivity for pro-Japanese than for pro-Chinese information and advice. The contrast was not an unqualified one, however, particularly where longer, rather than short-term, perspectives were involved. Pratt and Wellesley, for example, both recognised the danger of an anti-foreign outburst in China, and while there was always the chance that specifically anti-Japanese sentiment might push more business in Britain's direction, it was agreed that no unnecessary risk should be run of alienating the people who were potentially one's major customers in the East. Therefore there must be no attempt to deprive China of her one, boycott weapon before she negotiated with the Japanese, and no further talk of discussions with others, including Tokyo, concerning extraterritoriality.[3] The Japanese idea of creating demilitarised zones round Chinese ports was likewise scornfully dismissed as contravening all the tenets of the new morality of international relations,[4] and in the face of the expatriate clamour for a heavy-handed extension of the privileges of the Shanghai Settlement, Lampson was given prompt and firm support for his determined resistance:

> 'British policy aims at holding the scales evenly between China and Japan,' telegraphed Simon, 'and the real interests of the British Community in the International Settlement are best served by this course . . . It would be a very short sighted view to imagine that Chinese acquiescence can be gained by taking sides against them.'[5]

In other words, during the Shanghai crisis the British approach towards China retained the main features already noted in preceding years.[6] Marked by short-term pessimism yet also by a certain long-term hope, it was essentially concerned with Britain's material interests, and this itself was sufficient to require that some heed be paid to Chinese susceptibilities. For Stimson, too, in this period, material gain remained a significant consideration, as he revealed in inimitable fashion during one of his attempts to make Simon aware of the consequences of acquiescing in Japan's seizure of Manchuria:

[1] FO 371, F 601/1/10; PM/1/116.
[2] Vansittart to Patteson, 10 February 1932, DBFP, IX, No. 404; FO 371, F 1255/1/10.
[3] Vansittart minute, 4 February 1932, FO 371, F 894/1/10; cf. ibid, F 466/5/10 and DBFP, IX, No. 137.
[4] Minutes by Orde, Wellesley and Vansittart, FO 371, F 1252/1/10; cf. DBFP, IX, No. 408, notes.
[5] Patteson to Lampson, 10 March 1932, DBFP, X, No. 51; cf. ibid, Nos. 20, 48, 78, 112, and FO 371, F 1019/1/10.
[6] See above, 44–50.

We should lose the moral issue in it and we should arouse the nationalists to probable aggression against foreigners in China. There is a very real direct cash value to all of us in the policy towards China.[1]

There were also present several other considerations of a practical and self-interested nature when State Department officials were discussing Chinese matters. Privately, for example, Stimson acknowledged that there might indeed be a danger of the 19th Route Army being pressed back into the Settlement, while Castle, who believed Japan's anti-boycott grievance to be a legitimate one, noted that American lives and property were 'seriously endangered in all probability more from the Chinese than the Japanese'.[2] When trying to curb the Japanese, care was also taken not to impair one's own local rights, lest the United States should wish to take action against the Chinese in defence of her nationals in Shanghai,[3] and over extraterritoriality in general there was no serious thought of initiating further concessions to meet Chinese nationalist impatience. In December, in fact, the idea of preparing for 'simultaneous and identical or similar action' on the part of all the relevant powers—including Japan—had been entertained in Washington, just as it had been briefly in London.[4] What is more, the Japanese notion of demilitarised zones in China, so abruptly rejected in London, was thought by Hornbeck and others in the Far Eastern Division in Washington to 'have merit', although Stimson, backed by Hoover, was to reject suggestions from the same quarter that the opportunity should be seized to 'smooth off some of the problems' of the Shanghai Settlement at least.[5] Among the many myths surrounding the period, few have a more stale smell on examination than the ones concerning America's unique and flawless disinterestedness towards China when propagated by members of the State Department who had been specially concerned with the area. Nevertheless, the presence of a strong disposition to look for immediate material benefits was accompanied by a powerful, sustained, and, according to his own lights, genuine concern on the part of Stimson for the spiritual and political destiny of China, albeit under American patronage. It was this, for example, that made him so receptive to Johnson's warning of a possible repeat of the Boxer rising, an outcome which he appeared to find more credible than that of a Communist triumph in China, which troubled Hoover among others.[6]

Whatever one's reasons for looking closely at the Chinese side of the Shanghai imbroglio, however, it was to Japan and her intentions that the gaze of officials was drawn back time and again. In this respect, the sympathy

[1] Stimson–Simon telephone record, 15 February 1932, FRUS, 1932, III, 341.

[2] Stimson Diary, 4 February 1932; Castle Diary, 25 January, 2 February 1932, cited in Current, loc. cit.

[3] FRUS, 1932, III, 120–1.   [4] FRUS, 1931, III, 928–31.

[5] Stimson Diary, 7 March 1932; Hornbeck memorandum, 10 February 1932, DS 793.94/4169. Hornbeck's readiness to hope for 'enlarged, special municipalities under joint Sino-foreign control or supervision' is yet another piece of evidence which suggests an inadequate grasp of the situation in the Far East at that time.

[6] Stimson Diary, 25 February 1932; Stimson memorandum, 11 March 1932, FRUS, 1932, III, 566–7. Stimson's readiness to receive Johnson's message recalls, on a wider scale, the receptive climate in Washington that awaited Kennan's 'long telegram' in 1946.

for Japan's tribulations in Manchuria which many Foreign Office officials shared with Sir Francis Lindley did not mean that the Ambassador's other promptings were accepted uncritically in London, any more than they were by Lampson and Cecil. It was felt, rather, that Lindley lacked perspective, 'treating our policy too much in isolation' and 'not taking sufficiently into account the many extraneous factors which so largely have to determine the course of action at Geneva'.[1] Vansittart, Wellesley and Simon all commented in this vein at one time or another. Nor did Lindley's analysis of the considerations which underlay Japanese policy command full acceptance. To him, despite Japan's obvious demographic and economic problems, the question was at bottom a political one, with Manchuria itself representing 'a political ideal . . . of a bulwark against Russian and Chinese influence' even more than it did a source of raw materials. For Wellesley, on the other hand, long preoccupied with this subject as we have seen, it was now economic considerations which not only should lie at the heart of policy (Lindley did not disagree there), but actually did so. Thus in the Far East he located the root of the trouble in 'the increasing economic disequilibrium between Japan and China', one consequence being that if China were to close its doors to Japan the latter 'would be forced to fight for her very existence'; this was the aspect of international relations which the League should examine above all others, and not only in the Far East.

Wellesley's assumptions were apparently shared by most of his colleagues in the Foreign Office who joined in this particular debate—which is hardly surprising in the circumstances of the period. His conclusions also carried weight, amounting as they did, in Vansittart's words, to 'a powerful and reasoned statement, at least to a large extent, of a case for Japan'.[2] Yet it will be seen below that, however much senior officials might attempt to grapple with the question of underlying causes or of long-term probabilities, these matters received scant attention at Cabinet level. For a tariff-orientated Government approaching the Ottawa Conference, such an exercise would no doubt have been especially uncomfortable where Wellesley's theses were concerned, quite apart from being by nature foreign to the hand-to-mouth process by which British policy tended to be conducted from on high.

Senior officials also disagreed with Lindley in one other important respect. Whereas he asserted that by her own volition Britain could ensure that there would be no clash with Japan in the future, even Wellesley was ready to acknowledge 'that we may be dragged by events along a path which may end

[1] FO 371, F 3374/1/10; cf. ibid, F 1443/1/10.

[2] Wellesley memorandum, 6 February, loc. cit., and Vansittart minute, FO 371, F 1033/1/10; Lindley to Simon, 28 April 1932, DBFP, X, No. 284, and minutes on FO 371, F 4400/1/10. Vansittart finally brought the discussion on Lindley's despatch to an end with the observation: 'Novalis affirmed that to philosophise is to generalise; and the older I get the more I mistrust that ancestral pastime, whether applied to nations, sexes, "or any other adversity". . . .' A strange comment from the writer of the 'Old Adam' series of memoranda and, later, of *Germany's Black Record*. For all the qualifications which might be made concerning the substance of the debate stimulated by Wellesley, it did represent an attempt to grapple with problems in a way which Vansittart's epigrams did not. There are times when this gifted man appears almost as an amateur within the Foreign Office.

in war with her'. 'A Far East where Japan was dominant . . .', noted Pratt, 'and also perhaps contemptuous of Great Britain would not be a favourable sphere for the development of British trade and industry'. 'If Japan continues unchecked . . . ultimately we will be faced with the alternatives of going to war with (her) or retiring from the Far East. A retirement from the Far East might be the prelude to a retirement from India.' Vansittart agreed, adding that Britain's position in the Middle East might also be shaken by such an outcome: '*We* are incapable of checking Japan in any way if she really means business and has sized us up, as she certainly has done.'[1] Fears such as these were compounded by the belief that at Shanghai Japan was pursuing what Simon termed 'an ambitious plan', an interpretation which coexisted uneasily with the more comforting one offered by Lindley, that she had probably stumbled into a situation where her prestige was at stake and was bound to restore face before accepting a settlement.[2] Whichever the case, there was virtually unanimous acceptance in Whitehall that the Japanese armed forces could, and if thwarted quite possibly would, wreak almost limitless damage to Britain's Far Eastern interests, borne along by the fever of 'something like a fascist movement' into 'a policy of adventure far exceeding anything which we have witnessed as yet'. Thus when Lindley suddenly warned that 'a false step might precipitate catastrophe', his lack of global perspective mattered little by comparison with what was accepted as his local knowledge. Vital interests were seen as being in jeopardy. It was a price that had not been contemplated when, for example, officials had emphasised in 1931 the desirability of seeking the close friendship of the United States.[3]

There, too, the possibility that Japan might strike out at those who sought to thwart her—perhaps even by means of a surprise attack on the main American fleet—began to trouble Stimson's restless and sleep-starved thoughts during the closing stages of the Shanghai fighting.[4] In the longer run, the possibility, even likelihood, of an eventual Japanese–American war has already been observed as a view held in some quarters of the U.S. Navy in particular, and in the State Department Hornbeck was referring to the same possibility during January, suggesting that the United States could diminish it

(a) by not standing conspicuously ahead of the other powers in advocacy of principles which Japan does not allow to stand between her and her 'destiny';
(b) or by always being more strong at sea than is Japan.[5]

For Stimson, this sense of impending crisis had already been heightened by the fall of Wakatsuki and Shidehara, and by the occupation of Chinchow,

[1] Pratt memoranda, loc. cit., and minutes attached.
[2] Simon to MacDonald, 29 January 1932, DBFP, IX, No. 153; Wellesley and Vansittart minutes, FO 371, F 713 and 1572/1/10; Simon–Stimson telephone record, 11 February 1932, FRUS, 1932, III, 278–84; Londonderry to Baldwin, 22 February, 10 March, 1932, Baldwin Papers, vol. 118.
[3] See above, 123.
[4] Stimson Diary, 1, 2 March 1932; cf. Miller memorandum, 2 March 1932, Hornbeck Papers, box 251.
[5] Memorandum of 12 January 1932, DS 793.94/3610 ½; cf. memorandum of 28 March 1932, Hornbeck papers, box 423.

which he saw as 'bringing the Manchurian matter up to a final climax'.[1] He was thus far more alert than, say, Pratt or Wellesley to the possibility of major trouble emerging from the clashes between civilians at Shanghai in the middle of January, quickly assuming that Japan's hope was to get China to declare war and thus provide grounds for a full-scale blockade of all her ports.[2] Suggestions from Forbes that Tokyo was basically anxious for a settlement were given little credence by Stimson's officials,[3] while within the Cabinet both Hoover and Hurley also believed that a far-reaching Japanese plan was being unfolded.[4]

Even now, however, the upshot of such gloomy speculation was not a clear and agreed definition of the situation in American policy-making circles, nor even a steady appraisal of Japan's intentions. Whatever local expansion by the invader might follow, Hoover had not altered his opinion that no vital American interest was involved, and while Castle admitted that 'nobody could blame (the Secretary) for his fury against Japan',[5] there continued to be a marked difference of emphasis where he and Stimson were concerned. Stimson's own volatility (together with the usual patchy reporting by Forbes[6]) was helping to produce swift and radical changes of interpretation. As he admitted to Hugh Gibson, the Secretary was 'not in a very pacific frame of mind', and memories of 1914 and of the shame he had felt then at President Wilson's aloof silence came crowding in upon him.[7] Yet he was beset by uncertainties which he could not readily relieve or resolve by taking action, and it was thus all the easier for his darkest estimates to alternate with much lighter ones as some new piece of evidence passed before his gaze. On 11 January, for example, he now thought that the Japanese Government was 'getting more conciliatory'; on 1 February he judged that it had 'got the bear by the tail and can't let go, and is trying to get help to get out of the situation without losing too much face'; by mid-March, after swinging back to the opposite view, he was once again accepting that it did, indeed, wish to get out of Shanghai.[8]

As in the case of immediate policy towards China, there was, then, a significant degree of similarity between the confused British and American attempts to establish the significance of Japan's actions. The same was true in another area which has been examined in detail earlier:[9] that involving the means and options open to the West in order to meet this new situation.

[1] Stimson Diary, 11 December 1931, 2 January 1932.

[2] Ibid, 25 January 1932.

[3] Ibid, 11 February 1932; FRUS, *Japan, 1931–1941*, I, 191–3. On February 5 Hornbeck confidently predicted that 'if Japan occupied Chapei she would not give it up'; on 7 March, he declared: 'I shall not be at all surprised if we hear within a few days of attacks by Japanese forces upon such points as Hangchow, Soochow, Chinkiang, Nanking and Hankow.' Memoranda in Hornbeck Papers, box 382.

[4] Stimson Diary, 27, 29 January, 8 March 1932.

[5] Castle Diary, 3 February 1932, cited in Ferrell, *American Diplomacy*, 178.

[6] See State Department to Forbes, 3 February 1932, FRUS, 1932, III, 196.

[7] Stimson Diary, 8 February 1932; Stimson–Gibson telephone record, 8 February 1932, FRUS, 1932, III, 251–2.

[8] Stimson Diary, 8, 11 January, 1, 14 February, 15 March 1932.

[9] See above, 59ff.

Here again, however, one also comes across a feature which began to emerge during the 1931 stages of the crisis. Not only were there certain strong, underlying similarities between London and Washington, but also differences which reflected in part the further contrast noted earlier, between the consensus of opinion among senior British policy-makers, and the cleavage that existed within the ranks of their opposite numbers in the United States.

In Whitehall, the two most detailed studies of the military and economic resources immediately available in the Far East were not distributed until the Shanghai crisis had passed its peak and the major decisions had in essence been taken. (Such a pattern is at least as common as the ideal one of first gathering 'all the facts', and then basing decisions upon them. The setting in hand of a military survey of the Czech problem in March 1938, when the British Government's policy was in effect already decided, provides a further example. What Chamberlain sought then was supporting, not challenging evidence.) These two studies—one on the military balance; one on economic sanctions—will therefore be considered at a later stage, but the attitudes that they were to bring out had clearly existed throughout the period. Over sanctions and article 16, for example, there had been if anything a strengthening of the widespread antipathy which was noted in the years before 1931. Thomas was one who gave vent to this, in a memorandum for the Cabinet on 10 March in which he cited his own trade-union experience of the superiority of conciliation over compulsory arbitration, together with the abiding hostility of the Dominions to sanctions; the present crisis, he submitted, had merely demonstrated once more that these provisions of the Covenant were 'an embarrassment and a hindrance to the preservation of peace rather than a help'.[1] Hankey was another who was expressing such ideas at this time:

> 'For my part,' he wrote to a friend, 'I am undismayed by the breakdown of the beliefs [concerning the League] to which you refer . . . From the earliest days when a League of Nations was mentioned I have held that any attempt to enforce sanctions must fail. My own conception has always been a League to maintain peace by conciliation and not by force . . . In the circumstances I am very glad that the utter futility of the present Covenant has been demonstrated in the Far East, where by a reasonably adroit policy we should be able to avoid the consequences falling on ourselves, instead of in Europe, where we might get involved. After the present failure, following Corfu and Vilna, no one is ever likely to believe in sanctions, and they will become more and more a dead letter. Personally I would like to see them got rid of.'[2]

In the Foreign Office, it had been accepted from the outset that in the Sino–Japanese dispute 'a conciliatory way out is the only one', and a brief study which was prepared in December recalled that, during the Corfu incident, economic sanctions had been 'found to be impossible without setting up the elaborate war-time machinery'. Moreover, without full American participation such measures would be futile, and all the signs were that no such participation would be forthcoming; even a withdrawal of Britain's ambassador would only harm her own position and reduce the prospects of success at the Disarmament Conference. Simon agreed, while

[1] CP 95 (32), CAB 24/228.
[2] Hankey to Sir Edward Harding, 23 February 1932, CAB 21/368.

Pratt filled in some of the commercial and financial costs that would attend an attempt to employ sanctions.[1] Sir Arthur Salter's letter referred to earlier, in which the writer urged a resort to economic coercion, was therefore given short shrift. 'Sir A. Salter is not talking practical politics,' minuted Vansittart. 'I do not agree,' wrote Wellesley, 'that even if America were prepared for drastic action, which she is not, it would be wise to jeopardise our interests in the F(ar) E(ast) by allowing ourselves to be tied to the chariot wheels of America unless there is some counter-balancing advantage of a very substantial kind.' Eden, following suit as usual in this period, added that Salter's memorandum was 'academically valuable but practically useless. He overestimates Japanese susceptibilities to League opinion. Collective offensive action—which sanctions imply—even if desirable, is, we know, unobtainable'.[2]

These conclusions rested upon the belief, shared, it would seem, by the entire Cabinet, that in Vansittart's words 'we cannot contemplate, in any circumstances, the severance of economic and diplomatic relations unless we are also eventually prepared for war'. And war, he accepted, would mean that 'our trade and influence in the Far East (would be) obliterated and . . . both Hong Kong and Singapore (lost) without possibility of defence'.[3] In so far as this belief rested upon a forecast of Japanese reactions to a hypothetical situation, it could be tested only by taking the risk itself; where it rested upon an estimate of Japan's military capability it was on firmer ground, though unsubstantiated; where it involved the measure of Britain's own military resources there was little room for doubt or argument.[4] In this connection, on 1 February the First Lord of the Admiralty, Eyres-Monsell, gave MacDonald, Baldwin and Simon one each of the few copies of a 'most secret' memorandum which had been prepared the day before by the Navy's Director of Plans. Its answer to the question of what would happen if Britain opposed a Japanese intention 'to press matters to extremes' was unequivocal:

(a) At Shanghai and Tientsin five battalions of infantry are isolated and surrounded by vastly superior Japanese forces.
(b) At Shanghai 3 8″ cruisers . . . are exposed to attack by overwhelmingly superior forces.
(c) In the Yangtze one 6″ cruiser, 2 sloops and 12 gunboats are isolated and exposed to attack by superior forces.
(d) Hong Kong has been denuded by 5 out of 6 of the battalions which, even if supported by 5 squadrons of aircraft, are needed for its defence: no aircraft are, however, available. [The guns, mines and anti-submarine defences of the island were also non-existent or 'quite inadequate.']
(e) Singapore. The garrison is inadequate and coast defences are virtually non-existent. The anti-submarine defences are also non-existent. A squadron of

[1] DBFP, IX, No. 216; FO 371, F 7730/1391/10 and F 655/1/10.
[2] FO 371, F 590/1/10.
[3] DBFP, IX, Nos. 216, note, 267, note; Jones, A Diary, 30.
[4] This is not always so, of course. The delightful habit of Italian officials under Mussolini of preserving their reputation by moving planes from one aerodrome to another to be counted twice in their country's armaments' inventory led to only one, rather special, example of ignorance or misperception of one's own strength.

torpedo-bombing aircraft is stationed (there) but is believed to lack an adequate supply of torpedoes and to possess no bombs suitable for attacking heavy ships.

(f) Trincomali is completely undefended . . . (Our forces in the Far East), even if they themselves avoided destruction, could not prevent the capture of Hong Kong and Singapore and the destruction of the oil fuel reserve at Trincomali by the Japanese before the arrival of the main fleet [from the West] . . . This would leave the Japanese undisputed masters of the China Seas.[1]

It is important to recall the high-charged atmosphere which was engendered in policy-making circles by knowledge of this kind, coupled with a pessimistic uncertainty as to Japan's intentions. On 2 February, for example, Baldwin described the situation to a friend as 'a nightmare; I daren't express my feelings on what is happening as it might be dangerous'.[2] In a handwritten note to Simon on the same day, the King observed that he had 'not given up hope that war (might) be prevented'.[3] 'There is grave risk of war with Japan arising out of the present situation at Shanghai,' telegraphed Admiral Kelly on 1 February, although Vansittart thought that this was being 'alarmist' and an angry Chief of the Imperial General Staff revealingly described the cable as 'very wicked . . .; the sentiments contained therein ought never to have been mentioned'.[4]

This dominant view of the capabilities and possible reactions of the Japanese when matched against Britain's own resources was the main factor in setting the outer limits to the country's policy during the period. This did not entail, however, calling a halt to attempts to safeguard British interests or to end the fighting. For example, despite Admiral Kelly's objections to 'locking up' several of his ships at Shanghai, reinforcements were speedily despatched to the city, as we have seen.[5] And while British officials on the spot continued to take the lead in attempts to bring about at least a truce, Simon in London, unhappy at the timid way in which Wellesley and others had handled the Chinchow episode, now authorised numerous protests to Japan, some of them, as will be observed in the following narrative, couched in strong terms.[6]

Yet the limits remained. There could thus be no suggestion of threats or of a judgement on the merits of the dispute, and no leadership in what might be construed as an anti-Japanese movement. Public protests should likewise be eschewed, since they were likely to achieve only an increase in Japanese irritation. 'Japan is not going to be deflected from her purpose by notes, however strongly worded,' wrote Vansittart on 10 February, 'and in her present temper . . . a note of the kind advocated by Mr. Stimson might well sting her into going further than she otherwise would'.[7] The League 'should be upheld', as the Cabinet had earlier declared—as we have seen, even Londonderry, for all his ineptitude in arriving at the Disarmament Con-

---

[1] Simon Papers (private collection), Foreign Affairs, 1932.

[2] Davidson Papers, cited in Middlemas and Barnes, 727.

[3] Simon Papers (private collection), Foreign Affairs, 1932. The writer may have had in mind a full-scale Sino-Japanese war.

[4] FO 371, F 896/1/10.   [5] Ibid, F 722 and 833/1/10.

[6] See, e.g., DBFP, IX, Nos. 16 and note, 21 and note, 85, 139, 142, 154.

[7] Ibid, No. 419; cf. Nos. 400, 508.

ference in a bomber, was writing privately from Geneva in this period that it was 'of the highest importance that we should maintain the League and it depends on Britain whether (it) will develop ... or languish'.[1] In this instance, however, preserving the League meant preventing it from attempting more than it could possibly achieve, a belief that was all the easier since the British and League contexts of policy could merge effortlessly in the mind. (The League could also be used as a dumping ground for lesser but embarrassing questions, such as that of an arms embargo.[2]) As for the desirability of enunciating some legal or moral principle, the Foreign Office might well have quoted Castlereagh's response in 1820 to a Russian desire to invoke general principles as grounds for suppressing a revolt in Naples:

> The British Government do not regard mere declarations as of any real or solid value independent of some practical measure actually resolved upon; and what that measure is that can be genuinely and universally adopted against bad principles overturning feeble and ill-administered governments, they have never yet been able to divine.[3]

The reference to 'bad principles' and 'ill-administered governments' might have made the quotation a particularly tempting one at the time for some junior official—or Vansittart; no one produced it, however, partly, no doubt, because it would have been superfluous. Autopsies would reveal that the approach in question is embedded, like some benificent Strontium 90, deep in the bones of most of those who are professionally concerned with British foreign policy. Raymond Aron would call it 'style'.[4]

Here again, when it came to the options open to the West, there are similarities to be observed in Washington in this period. Within the State Department, for example, both Castle and Hornbeck had opposed making any representations that might irritate Japan in the period before she took Chinchow, and had been reluctant to see lone American initiatives thereafter.[5] In the Cabinet, Pat Hurley continued to insist that the United States should either 'put up or shut up'—which amounted to saying shut up.[6] As for Hoover, while he was prepared to contemplate certain modest forms of protest (at one stage he avowed that a withdrawal of ambassadors, coupled with non-recognition, would have 'an enormous controlling effect upon an Oriental nation like Japan'), his mind remained 'as much closed as possible' in the belief that economic sanctions would probably lead to war, and that 'to get into war with Japan on this subject would be folly'.[7] Before Shanghai, Stimson, too, shied away from the idea of a naval demonstration as being

[1] See above, 109.
[2] See, e.g., the minutes printed with DBFP, IX, No. 427.
[3] C. K. Webster, *The Foreign Policy of Castlereagh, 1815–1822* (London, 1934). 283–4.
[4] Aron, *Peace and War*, 290 ff.
[5] Hornbeck memoranda, 15, 21 December 1931, 12 January 1932; Castle memorandum, 17 December 1931, respectively DS 793.94/3383, 3313, 3610 ⅞, 3384; Castle Diary, 12, 15, 16, 19 February 1932, cited in Current, loc. cit.
[6] Stimson Diary, 26, 29 January 1932.
[7] Ibid, 26 January, 2, 20, 21 February 1932; cf. Hoover, *Memoirs, 1920–1933*, 375.

too strong, while continuing to turn down Chinese suggestions for a Nine-Power-Treaty conference. Despite his own hesitations over the subject, he reiterated to friends and to his officials in Geneva alike that American policy was set upon avoiding 'the dangers of a boycott'. As he informed Hugh Wilson on 26 February:

> I see no reason to believe that this country has reversed its former sentiment against the use of sanctions of force in international controversies. While much public sentiment has undoubtedly been excited by the invasion of China at Shanghai, I have no reason to believe that a proposal to enforce an economic boycott against Japan today would command any substantial support in Congress . . .[1]

It was Wilson, rather than Prentiss Gilbert, who had been briefed to keep in touch with the League during the new crisis—to the chagrin of the latter, for there was a distinct social and professional tension between the two men. Here, too, however, limits were marked out from the beginning: no one would attend Council meetings, no invitation to attend the special session of the Assembly was wanted, and the Consul-General in Shanghai could only co-operate with, not join, the special League committee set up there.[2] In terms of the fighting itself, there was a strong inclination among some American policy-makers to withdraw into a passive attitude. One reason for doing so, in Stimson's eyes, was the need to preserve the country's dignity in the face of Japanese non-co-operation,[3] a stance which it was no doubt pleasant to be able to afford, but which did nothing to help curb the Japanese, while it reinforced other indications that the United States would run no risks on the part of China or the sanctity international agreements. From Washington, as from London, the message went out that every care should be taken to avoid 'giving any impression that the American Government is taking sides as between China and Japan'.[4] And just as Simon tried to prevent the L.N.U. and others from angering the Japanese, so Stimson worked privately to prevent Congress from debating that resolution of Representative Hull's which envisaged an embargo on arms-supplies to a violator of the Kellogg Pact, on the grounds that 'it would be very dangerous to have it brought up just now (when) . . . everybody would discuss Japan'— and that such an act might disrupt American–Japanese trade.[5]

Yet besides these self-imposed limitations on Washington's policy, there were other speculations which restlessly reappeared among certain officials, and helped create, not further similarities, but differences with London. A hankering after some form of coercion still existed here and there, for example, with Hornbeck and others continuing to glance at the idea in January and February. 'This Division,' wrote Hornbeck on 12 February,

[1] Stimson Diary, 14 January 1932; Stimson to Henry Fletcher, 27 February 1932, Stimson Papers, box 305; FRUS, 1932, III, 452–3; DS 793.94/3655, 3886.
[2] FRUS, 1932, III, 43, 70, 123–4, 452–3.   [3] E.g., ibid, 221–5.
[4] E.g., ibid, 120–1, 290–2, 553; FRUS, Japan, 1931–1941, I, 200–1.
[5] Stimson to Linthicum, 2 February; Rogers to Linthicum, 18 February 1932, DS 811.113/153, 156A, 158, 167; Stimson Diary, 21 January, 13 February 1932; cf. Detzer, 141–2, and her comment: 'Mr. Stimson's bearing toward ordinary folk always seemed infected with a lofty, papa-knows-best attitude.'

'does not believe that Japan would reply to a severance of economic relations by "a general declaration of war against all powers involved" '.[1] Assistant Secretary James Rogers was also exploring the possibility of a 'sliding scale' of sanctions late in February,[2] while both he and Hornbeck—together with Lippmann outside the Department[3]—had continued to be drawn to the idea of some kind of declaration concerning the treaties which Japan was breaking. Rogers agreed with Stimson that if Japan refused America's terms for mediation at Shanghai, it was best to terminate dealings and leave her to 'sizzle in pretty sharp disapproval', and Hornbeck looked to 'the moral effect' a Nine Power Treaty declaration might have on China as well as Japan; Klots, too, was pondering in this period on the need to spell out the moral basis of United States policy as being 'in accordance with the most enlightened Occidental theories of democracy and self-determination'.[4]

This general inclination matched Stimson's own. In December he had been thinking of lambasting the Japanese verbally should they enter Chinchow, and in January of privately closing the American money market to them; thereafter he became still more preoccupied with the need to guide American public opinion, to hearten the Chinese and to cow their foes by 'putting the situation morally in its right place'.[5] Moreover where the idea of non-recognition was involved, he even received the support of Castle and of Hoover himself, the President, indeed, being shyly and not unfairly insistent thereafter that the so-called 'Stimson doctrine' (with its attendant political credit) should be more openly linked with his own name.[6]

Stimson's thoughts went further still, however, dwelling also, as they did, on America's destiny in the Western Pacific and on the swelling movement in Congress and the country to end her rule in the Philippines.[7] Was not 'the whole trouble with Japan and her intransigence . . . based upon her belief that we do not wish to remain a Far Eastern power . . .'?[8] At a deeper level, what assumptions could one make concerning the relationship of ends to means in the quest for a new world order? The Secretary had found himself less and less certain. Behind his dogmatic diplomacy in this Shanghai period

[1] Wallace memorandum, transmitted by Hornbeck, 5 February; Hornbeck memoranda, 27 January, 12, 28 February 1932, respectively DS 793.94/3719½, 3754, 4170, 4479½.

[2] Moffat Diary, 25 February 1932.

[3] On 22 December 1931, Lippmann wrote to Stimson to suggest that, should the Japanese take Chinchow, he should organise a declaration of non-recognition by the remaining Nine-Power-Treaty signatories. 'I think then we could afford to sit and wait, leaving Japan on the defensive. Time would work against her, and so would economic circumstances, and it would be fair to hope that the military party would eventually be overthrown . . . Since all resort to force is barred to us, any measure short of it but in that direction should be avoided. . . .' Stimson Papers, box 303.

[4] Stimson Diary, 5 February 1932; Hornbeck memorandum, 19 February, and Klots memorandum, 10 March 1932, respectively DS 793.94/4441, 4903½.

[5] Stimson Diary, 8 February 1932; Castle to Lamont, 12 February, Lamont to Castle, 15 February 1932, Castle Papers, Japan; DS 793.94/3607, 3876.

[6] Stimson Diary, 23 February, 12 March 1932; Castle Diary, 18 February, 1, 8 April, 1932, cited in Current, loc. cit.

[7] E.g. Stimson Diary, 10 February 1932.   [8] Ibid, 3 February 1932.

lay doubt, not assurance. In January he had revealed some of this to Pierrepont Moffat and other officials:

> Had the theory of offensive defense gone by the board? Did the Kellogg–Briand Pact so change human nature that only the defense of one's actual territory was essential?... He, for one, was by no means sure. He had had to unlearn a great deal of what was axiomatic in his youth, and did not have very clear-cut convictions as to the new order.[1]

The same questions reappeared as the main Japanese assault at Shanghai drew near, though now there was the suggestion of an answer:

> The whole situation is beginning to shake me up and get me back to a little bit nearer my old view that we haven't yet reached the stage where we can dispense with a police force; and the only police force I have got to depend on today is the American Navy. Pretty soon I am going to tell the President so.[2]

'Tumultuous changes in my mind and attitude' were taking place, he noted.[3] Meanwhile, if economic sanctions with military backing were ruled out, at least one need not neglect 'the importance of having Japan fear this country'. The main U.S. Fleet should therefore be left in Hawaiian waters after its exercises there, as part of the bluff that some firmer action might be forthcoming.[4]

Here, in the military sphere, one encounters a further and final contrast, between the reasonably accurate and wholly pessimistic assessment of the Far Eastern balance that was entertained throughout by all senior British officials and Ministers, and the more comfortable illusions that were retained by Stimson until the crisis was well advanced. The Secretary had discussed the situation with Pratt and other admirals at earlier stages, but it was only on 19 February that he decided 'to make a tabulation of real guns and see what our strength is'. By 8 March he had arrived at answers which 'very much alarmed' him, the Navy, he discovered, being 'down to the danger point' and 'more unequal than I had thought to meeting Japan'. His reaction was to urge that something be done to repair the worst deficiencies, a complete contrast to Hoover's response that it was 'all the more reason for not having an offensive Navy'.[5]

Over Shanghai it was Hoover's reactions, not Stimson's, that ultimately set limits to American policy, but it was Stimson's restlessness which did most to prompt those declarations that so caught the eye of the world. The moment had now arrived which was foreshadowed in theory in the first part of this book:[6] the United States, having less, materially, at risk in the area than Britain, in Stimson's mind at the time also possessed the power to keep Japan in her place. These two factors made it all the easier to talk loudly; the 'real nobility' of America's Far Eastern policy, the memory of 1914 and the new morality of international relations made it imperative to do so. The consequences were to deceive many intelligent and attentive people in the West, but not those who controlled the policies of Japan.

[1] Moffat Diary, 4 January 1932.   [2] Stimson Diary, 18 February 1932.
[3] Ibid, 19 February 1932.   [4] Ibid, 26, 29 January 1932.
[5] Ibid, 10, 30 January, 19, 20, 29 February, 2, 8 March 1932; table of U.S. and Japanese naval strengths, n.d., Stimson Papers, box 304.
[6] See above, 58.

London and Washington: interchange and decision

Challenged by Japan more directly than before, or so it seemed, Britain and the United States quickly looked to each other for sympathy and support. It has already been observed that Stimson and MacDonald, in particular, were likely to react in this way, and while even Hoover had his satisfactory memories of the 1929 talks with MacDonald, together with his vision of 'the Anglo–Saxons' saving civilisation, across the Atlantic Simon and Londonderry were among those who joined the Prime Minister in acknowledging the need to keep in step with Washington.[1] From the British point of view, indeed, the case for doing so could easily be argued in terms of unadulterated self-interest. Unless the United States eventually stood by her, as Vansittart bluntly remarked, Britain 'must eventually be done for in the Far East', while Lindsay more sentimentally suggested that there could be no thought of 'coming down on the non-American side of a fence' for the first time since 1812.[2] If other arguments were needed, then those relating to debts and disarmament stood close enough to hand in these early months of 1932.

Even so, the mutual suspicions which were noted as existing on the eve of the Manchurian affair[3] had not abated. Few men in Washington shared Stimson's eager belief in a natural community of interests, and Lindsay was merely preaching to the converted in Whitehall when he now admitted that the Americans were 'dreadful people to deal with (who) cannot make firm promises but jolly you along with fair prospects and when you are committed . . . let you down'.[4] Wellesley, Vansittart and Simon had all been saying the same thing, reinforced in their conviction by Lindsay's current reports of the underlying passivity of America's Far Eastern policy. 'You will get nothing out of Washington but words,' observed Baldwin at the height of the crisis. 'Big words, but only words.'[5]

On each side distrust went deep. Compounded by frustration and failure it was to help produce in 1934 and '35 those recriminations that were alluded to in the first chapter of the book. From Stimson, there would come then the private accusation that during the Shanghai crisis Britain had thwarted his hopes of 'stopping Japan in her career or at least bringing her into a [Nine-Power-Treaty] conference in which the voice of reason might ultimately prevail, preferring to take refuge in the inconspicuousness of League action among the flock of European nations'; from the Foreign Office would come private denials, as well as Pratt's public rebuke which was cited earlier.[6] The

---

[1] Londonderry to Baldwin, 22 February, 1932, Baldwin Papers, vol. 118; DBFP, IX, No. 153, note.

[2] DBFP, IX, Nos. 238, note, 665.

[3] See above, 123.   [4] DBFP, IX, No. 665.

[5] E.g. ibid, Nos. 42, 81, 102, 138, 153, note, 239; Jones, *A Diary*, 30.

[6] The 1934–5 fracas can be traced in the following sources: Norman Davis Papers, box 17, for Davis to Hull, 11 December 1934, Stimson to Davis, 13 December 1934, Phillips to Davis, 12 December 1934, Stimson to Lothian, 15 March 1935, Davis to Armstrong, n.d., Foreign Office memorandum, 30 April 1935; Lothian Papers, General Correspondence, for Sinclair to Lothian, 12 December 1934 and 11 May 1935, Stimson to Lothian, 27 June 1935. (I am grateful

following summary of the exchanges and policy decisions of the two countries will show that in these subsequent arguments neither side had a monopoly of right.

The brief flurry over Stimson's non-recognition note of 7 January provided a foretaste of troubles to come. Restless after the fall of Chinchow, the Secretary had surprised and then won the support of both his officials and Hoover with the draft which he had first composed four days earlier. The major European ambassadors were given some general idea of what was afoot, and on the 6th an invitation to join in the declaration arrived in the Foreign Office in London.[1] As Pratt admitted later, it was not accorded much significance at the time, being seen as a futile gesture which would only irritate Japan; hence the clumsy press communiqué (drafted by Wellesley), and a more amiable note to Washington which nevertheless amounted to a refusal to act as required.[2] At the time, neither Hornbeck nor Stimson himself was particularly surprised, each commenting privately on the troubles which were plaguing 'poor old England' and cramping her diplomatic style. If there was a degree of bitterness over the matter later on, it was the blandly offensive *Times* leader of 11 January[3] rather than the official exchanges that gave an edge to hindsight.[4]

The assumption that it was necessary to put some water in Stimson's wine still held good in the Foreign Office on 26 January, when the Secretary suggested the need to warn Japan not to send troops into the Shanghai Settlement, and to despatch American and British reinforcements to the area. Within the State Department and Administration, this growing anxiety of Stimson's had not at first found a responsive audience; in London, his view of the situation was agreed by Pratt and Wellesley to be 'almost entirely imaginary . . . (and designed) to rush us into hasty and ill-considered action which would have gravely aggravated the situation in the Far East'. At the same time, however, they acknowledged 'the delicate problem . . . of how to avoid rebuffing America without incurring the hostility of Japan'.[5] Simon in particular was more alert to this consideration than were his officials, and in

to Donald Watt for providing me with copies of this Lothian material.) Reverberations of the affair were still to be heard in 1943: see material in the Hornbeck Papers, boxes 181, 289, 351. See above, 10.

[1] Stimson Diary, 3, 4, 5, 6 January; Castle Diary, 7 January 1932, cited in Current, loc. cit.; FRUS, 1932, III, 1–2; Lindsay to Selby, 24 December 1931, FO 800/285. In general, see R. A. Hecht, 'Great Britain and the Stimson Note of 7 January 1932', in *Pacific Historical Review*, May 1969; Pratt, *War and Politics in China*, 225–8.

[2] DBFP, IX, Nos. 53, 58, 61, 66; minutes by MacKillop, Orde and Wellesley, FO 371, F 97/1/10. Senior members of the British Embassy in Washington made no secret of their disappointment at London's cool response.

[3] See above, 215.

[4] Castle memorandum, 11 January, Hornbeck memorandum, 12 January 1932, respectively DS 793.94/3488, 3610⅜; Stimson Diary 7, 9 January 1932.

[5] Stimson Diary, 25, 26 January 1932; FRUS, 1932, III, 61–3; DBFP, IX, Nos. 114, 120, 128.

accordance with his suggestion to the Cabinet he softened the somewhat blunt draft reply to Stimson that had been put before him, tactfully raising the difficulty of the 1927 precedent, and suggesting that a call for restraint should be addressed to both parties rather than to Japan alone. The Foreign Secretary's anxiety increased when he learned, late on the 28th, that this reply had not been delivered by Lindsay to an already-impatient Stimson, the Ambassador feeling that the Secretary's latest promptings might be thought to require a more positive British response. On the 29th Simon took to his bed with a temperature and pains in the head.[1]

His own view of the situation was already drawing closer to Stimson's, however. He had been much alarmed by a paper left at the Foreign Office by a member of the Japanese Embassy on the afternoon of the 28th; this mentioned the possible need 'to take drastic measures' at Shanghai, and Simon had promptly conveyed his concern to Tokyo. His preoccupations were also set out on paper for the Cabinet when it met on the morning of the 29th, and although no decisions were taken on this occasion, Vansittart, presumably with the approval of MacDonald or Baldwin, sent instructions later in the day for Admiral Kelly in the 8" cruiser Kent to proceed to Shanghai from Batavia; this had been done, he wrote, 'both with an eye to possible criticism here in the event of danger to our interests increasing, and also with an eye to the United States'. Washington was also invited to follow a sharp protest that was despatched from London to Tokyo on the same day: Stimson himself could scarcely have bettered its reference to 'a strong "prima facie" impression of (an) attack [at Chapei] that was both unprovoked and indefensible . . . upon a cosignatory of the Kellogg Pact and a fellow member of the League of Nations'. In the event, Lindley (like Sir Nevile Henderson on one occasion at Nuremberg in 1938) chose to omit the sharper passages of this communication when delivering it, but Stimson, like Simon, was not to know that at the time, and was greatly pleased by the response he was now getting.[2]

Moreover, on 30 January Stimson was informed of a further British protest which had been sent to Tokyo following the arrival of reports which appeared to make nonsense of Japanese assurances and to suggest that British lives and property were now in serious danger. An unconfirmed Reuter's report which was sent round to MacDonald on the same day also held out the even more alarming prospect that the Chinese Government were about to declare war on Japan. In these circumstances it was not apathy that caused Mac-Donald to ask for time to consider Hoover's suggestion, telephoned to him

[1] DBFP, IX, Nos. 136, 153; FO 371, F 490/1/10; CAB 23/70. Further anxiety was occasioned by a description in The Times of Stimson's anxiety over Britain's slow response. On the other side, Atherton later suggested to Washington that the British were tapping his telephone line. The writer has found no evidence to support this idea, but that does not mean it was wrong.

[2] DBFP, IX, Nos. 143, 154, 155, 156, 162, 191; CAB 23/70; FO 371, F 722, 762, 833/1/10; Stimson Diary, 29 January 1932. The record of Vansittart's briefing of Atherton was circulated to the Cabinet at Simon's suggestion, in order 'to comfort them'—further evidence of the strong desire to stay in line with the U.S. The Kent arrived in Shanghai on 5 February.

by Stimson, for an appeal by the King and the President to the heads of state of China and Japan.[1]

Sunday, 31 January, saw the policy-makers in each capital—and the change was the more marked in London—working in a new atmosphere of tension and crisis-perception as news came in from Shanghai of the likely breakdown of the brief truce which had been arranged. (The only hopeful sign came from Tokyo, where the Minister for Foreign Affairs had put out feelers for obtaining the good-offices of the Western powers in halting the conflict.)[2] Belying Whitehall's reputation for week-end somnolence, Mac-Donald, Simon, Neville Chamberlain, Eyres-Monsell, Vansittart and the Chief of the Imperial General Staff, Field Marshal Milne, met at 10 Downing Street in the morning and concluded that the situation was one of 'immense peril to the entire . . . foreign community' in Shanghai. As noted earlier from the press communiqué, reinforcements were agreed upon in the shape of the cruiser Suffolk from Hongkong, followed by the cruiser Berwick with artillery and infantry on board, the troops to be used to help set up a neutral zone if such a possibility still existed. Meanwhile in Washington Admiral Taylor's Asiatic Squadron, with marines embarked, was despatched to Shanghai from Manila, the main U.S. Fleet already being scheduled to gather at Hawaii for a joint Army–Navy exercise in that area between 6 and 13 February. The other similarity between the responses of the two capitals concerned Hoover's 'heads of state' proposal, which both sides were rejecting independently of each other. In Washington it was thought that the situation was now changing so rapidly as to make it inappropriate; in London, as MacDonald indicated to Stimson on the telephone, the draft appeal was not much liked, as containing too one-sided an appeal on behalf of China and including Manchuria, as well as Shanghai, in its terms. For the moment, therefore, further protests against Japan's military use of the International Settlement were the only additional steps agreed upon.[3]

At least there had been a common zeal and basic agreement in the last forty-eight hours or so. On the following day, however, 1 February, there appeared the first suggestion of a difference of emphasis between the two sets of men. Ironically it was MacDonald who, with Brenan's latest assessment to hand, warned Stimson on the telephone that the Japanese appeared to have sinister intentions, while the Secretary of State chose rather to dwell upon Tokyo's desire for the West's good offices. When it came to laying down the conditions upon which the two countries would provide

[1] DBFP, IX, Nos. 178, 186, 190, 195, 196; FO 371, F 708, 718, 865/1/10; PM/1/116; FRUS, 1932, III, 124–8; Stimson Diary, 30 January 1932.
[2] DBFP, IX, Nos. 198, 205, 207, 211, 213, 215; FRUS, 1932, III, 143, 149; FRUS, Japan 1931–1941, I, 169–71.
[3] DBFP, IX, Nos. 200, 201, 202, 208; FO 371, F 770, 773, 1004/1/10; C. in C. China, Report of Proceedings, 31 January to 29 February 1932, ADM 125/70; China Station Records, ADM 125/111; King George V to MacDonald, 31 January 1932, RA G.V, K 2344/2; Butler to Baldwin, 31 January 1932, Baldwin Papers, vol. 118; Stimson Diary, 31 January 1932; FRUS, 1932, III, 128–9, 136–40, 142–3, 147; FRUS, Japan 1931–1941, I, 168–9, 171; Joint Board Records, 350/491, 500. In the American manoeuvres off Hawaii, the carriers Lexington and Saratoga achieved a successful surprise attack on the islands' defences.

those good offices, however, it was Stimson who wished to make them as comprehensive and rigorous as possible, above all by specifying that Sino–Japanese negotiations, with neutral observers or participants, should seek 'to settle all outstanding controversies . . . in the spirit of the Pact of Paris and the (League) resolution of 10 December without prior demands or reservations'. In the Foreign Office, this attempt to link Manchuria with Shanghai was thought to be crude and unwise; but although Stimson agreed to remove from the document a demand that the Kwantung Army should halt in Manchuria, it was substantially his draft that was agreed upon and forwarded to Nanking and Tokyo, with the hope that France and Italy would also subscribe to it.[1]

The emerging contrast between the British preoccupation with the immediate, local danger and Stimson's with the Far Eastern conflict as a whole became clearer on 2 February, when Japan rejected the fifth point of the West's conditions, concerning the talks on 'all outstanding controversies'. To Stimson, supported by Hoover, this was a crucial matter; to the British Cabinet's ad hoc Far Eastern Committee, meeting for the first time in the Prime Minister's room in the House of Commons,[2] Tokyo's acceptance of the first four conditions for good-offices 'was deemed fairly satisfactory', especially since, as the Committee were reminded, there was nothing Britain could do without immense risk to prevent the Japanese from obtaining even a permanent settlement of their own at Shanghai if that was their intention. The Committee agreed, however, 'that the most important thing at the present time was to work as closely as possible with the United States'—a desire that had not yet run up against a danger and consideration of greater size. In his subsequent telephone conversation with Stimson, therefore, Simon did not attempt to insist that the fifth of the conditions should be abandoned, although significantly his own notes of the talk, by implying that some reconsideration of the matter might prove necessary, stopped short of the agreed position as it was recorded in the State Department. Also significant for the future was Stimson's adamant approach, compared to signs of the nervousness which lay behind Simon's own, cool exterior. 'Don't worry,' scribbled Baldwin to the Foreign Secretary. 'We shall support you whatever you do provided you don't do some damned fool thing of which I hope and believe you are incapable!'[3]

---

[1] DBFP, IX, Nos. 225, 228, 235, 236, 237; Stimson Diary, 1 February 1932; FRUS, 1932, III, 153–5, 158–65; FRUS, *Japan 1931–1941*, I, 174–5.

[2] Its members were MacDonald, Baldwin, Simon, Hailsham, Londonderry and Eyres-Monsell. Eden attended this first meeting. Hankey, inevitably, was secretary. MacDonald had an eye operation on the following day, when Baldwin took over the running of the Government. It will be seen, however, that MacDonald remained involved in Far Eastern decision-making from his nursing home. On this, the factual details and inferences offered in Middlemas and Barnes, 726–7, are, in most cases, wrong.

[3] DBFP, IX, Nos. 242, 243, 245, 247, 249, 252, 254, 255, 257–261, 271; CAB 27/482; Baldwin to Simon, 2 February 1932, Simon Papers (private collection), Foreign Affairs, 1932; Stimson Diary, 2 February 1932; FRUS, 1932, III, 179–84; FRUS, *Japan 1931–1941*, I, 175–6. Baldwin's remark to Simon recalls his later treatment of Hoare.

The transatlantic gap widened a little more on 3 February as reports multiplied of the dangers at Shanghai. In Washington Stimson was becoming more impatient and musing on the need to demonstrate America's determination to remain a Far Eastern power; even Castle, while restraining the Secretary and privately admitting to Lindsay that he thought 'a good deal would have been accomplished if the Japanese accepted the [West's] first four points', also aired the possibility of a substantial part of the British Fleet moving to Singapore as a demonstration parallel to that being made by the U.S. Fleet at Hawaii. (In his report, Lindsay omitted this notion; in his, Castle revealed nothing of his admission over the four points.) By contrast, the mood in London was predominantly defensive, with the Cabinet agreeing to damp down awkward questions in the Commons and Simon preparing to dissuade the Council of the League—which Britain was glad to see considering the issue—from making 'provocative declarations'. Lindley's dramatic, 'single-false-step' telegram, in particular, had led to a rapid application of brakes in all directions.[1]

During the next two days, 4 and 5 February, Japan's continued intransigence over the basis for mediation—an attitude which showed up all the more by the side of China's acceptance of all the West's conditions and her assurance that she did not intend to declare war—drove Britain and the United States still further apart. While Stimson began to draw back from taking any more initiatives on the spot, for fear of impairing his country's dignity and principles alike, the arrival of fresh Japanese troops at Shanghai made London all the more anxious to keep negotiations going.[2] The tone of British protests at these latest developments was now moderated, as Vansittart admitted, in the light of Japanese irritation, while modified versions of the conditions for mediation were drawn up for Stimson's inspection: should not Manchuria be left on one side? Could not the Lytton Commission take the place of the neutral observers previously proposed? Might not the Commission also act as an intermediary between China and Japan on the boycott issue? Stimson was unimpressed. It would be a serious mistake to intrude into the boycott question, which was vital for China, while to omit references to Manchuria would enable the Japanese to infer a tacit acquiescence in the conquest they had made. The next move should be left to Tokyo.[3] The Secretary repeated this argument to Simon by tele-

[1] DBFP, IX, Nos. 269, 272–4, 279, 280, 289, 434; CAB 23/70; Simon to King George V, 3 February 1932, RA G.V, K 2343/4; Stimson Diary, 3 February; Castle Diary, 5, 6 February 1932, cited in Ferrell, *American Diplomacy*, 180; FRUS, 1932, III, 194, 196–7, 199–200, 210, 316, 334; FRUS, *Japan, 1931–1941*, 1, 177–9.

[2] Further alarm in London was created by Admiral Kelly, who had suddenly informed the Japanese Commander that if the latter's planes continued to fly over British ships, he would shoot them down. Lindley, on hearing the news, rushed to the telephone to urge restraint on Kelly in this, 'a week of the acutest anxiety of my life'; Vansittart, together with the Admiralty, was likewise astonished, and an admonishment was duly sent off; Kelly himself drafted a telegram demanding to know of London 'who was going to conduct the business, (them) or the man on the spot', but decided not to send it. Kelly Papers, vol. 7, 129–30; FO 371, F 1152/1/10; DBFP, IX, Nos. 349, 350.

[3] DBFP, IX, Nos. 295, 306, 312, 317, 318, 322, 323, 326, 330, 335, 341; FO 371, F 1087/1/10; Stimson Diary, 4, 5 February, 1932; FRUS, 1932, III, 209, 211–13,

phone on the 6th, the Foreign Secretary now having arrived in Geneva to spread his counsels of caution. Stimson did agree that it might be best 'to keep . . . the League quiet' and to stay away from article 16 of the Covenant, but for the rest the conversation consisted mainly of separate statements, with little movement towards common ground. 'We must keep something or other going,' pleaded Simon; 'We are concerned,' pronounced Stimson, 'with the public opinion of this country on the moral issue towards Japan', and although he promised to delay such a move, he made clear his desire to issue a public statement concerning America's position. In the light of later events it is important to observe that this was the main impression left upon Simon, that Stimson was thinking of a pronouncement *'for the purpose of vindicating to his own public their moral position'*. When the Secretary later produced his proposal for a joint démarche, he had thus already helped to condition the Foreign Office to perceive it in a way which diminished its intended international significance. Meanwhile he noted hopefully: 'Sir John was very amenable to my suggestions.'[1]

It was during the following days that the conviction grew among Western residents and officials in Shanghai that the main immediate danger was of a Chinese incursion into the Settlement, an opinion which was endorsed in London, as we have seen, but which scarcely fitted into Stimson's current view of the situation. Similarly, although Anglo–American cooperation on the spot was close, Consul-General Brenan's instructions looked hopefully for some implementation of Japanese assurances, while those sent from Washington for Cunningham stressed the necessity of not giving offence to China.[2]

9, 10 and 11 February saw those responsible for British policy being forced towards a choice which it was fundamental to their view and approach to avoid, and which was to haunt the country's defence and foreign policies for years to come: the choice between alienating Japan and cooperating with the United States. For Stimson was now on the rampage, embarking upon a week in which, according to Castle, he occupied himself exclusively with the formulation of some kind of démarche based upon the Nine Power Treaty, an idea which he first broached to Hornbeck on the 9th. The arrival of Johnson's 'Boxer-rising' telegram later in the same day spurred him on in the belief that some form of gesture must be made, but he had moved already by taking up the matter of a démarche with the British Ambassador,[3] whose

216, 219–25, 228–9. Lindley's request that he should inform the Japanese that sanctions would not be employed was refused, but he dropped a broad hint to a senior Japanese official all the same, rather as Nevile Henderson was to tell the Germans that Britain would not fight for Czechoslovakia. DBFP, IX, Nos. 346, 381.

[1] DBFP, IX, Nos. 348, 360; Stimson Diary, 6 February 1932; FRUS, 1932, III, 234–40, 242–3.

[2] DBFP, IX, Nos. 372, 384, 399, 422; FRUS, 1932, III, 242–3. On the question of arms sales, see DBFP, IX, No. 427.

[3] Johnson's 'Boxer Rising' telegram was received in the State Department at 8.35 p.m. on the 9th; Lindsay despatched his account of his Nine-Power-Treaty talk with Stimson at 8.5 p.m. Nevertheless Stimson later saw Johnson's despatch as 'the chief compelling motive' behind his letter to Borah. FRUS, 1932, III, 440–2.

account of the conversation arrived in the Foreign Office on the morning of the 10th. 'No such shock as events at Shanghai,' Stimson had declared, 'had been administered to the cause of international morality since August 1914 ... It seemed to him that the moment might be approaching when a very strong indictment should be addressed to the Japanese Government ... based mainly on Articles 1 and 7 of the Nine Power Treaty ... (together with) a passage in the sense of his note of 7 January . . .'[1]

At this point, and in the light of later recriminations, several aspects of the situation need to be recalled. First, as suggested earlier, there lay behind Stimson's outward confidence a great deal of uncertainty:

> 'I am afraid it is rather doubtful,' he wrote in his diary for the 10th,' whether we shall be able to secure Great Britain to join with us in this appeal under the Nine-Power-Pact. I am even doubtful whether it should be made in this form. I am only clear that something along this line ought to be done according to the best of our lights.'

Second, when musing aloud to Simon, Stimson had emphasised the need to give a lead to American public opinion. Third, it is clear that in his talk to Lindsay Stimson made no mention of a conference. The Ambassador specifically asked him whether he contemplated 'anything further than a note', and recorded that in his reply the Secretary still talked only of 'a remonstrance'; moreover Stimson's own summary confirmed this: what he was considering was 'a statement'. Finally—and again the two records agree—Stimson clearly allowed for the possibility that 'he might go on alone', a course which he was to rule out in high dudgeon when, as he noted in his diary on 19 February, 'the dangers of making a move under the Nine Power Treaty . . . (were becoming) more and more evident'.

There was thus some reason for senior Foreign Office officials to accord less weight to the proposal from the outset than Stimson had intended. Such a reaction also fitted into their established pattern of giving mental priority to messages from Lindley in Tokyo, however quickly they might dismiss some of the more extreme views of the Ambassador or his hosts. As it was, Wellesley described Stimson's proposal as 'thoroughly ill-advised and impulsive . . ., typically American and intended for home consumption'. 'Indictments must wait till the danger is less acute,' added Vansittart. 'We have been trying to keep the League from going off the deep end. The same tactics should now be followed in regard to Mr. Stimson.' He repeated this view by telegram to Simon in Geneva: 'We should refrain from joining the United States in a "very strong indictment" at this juncture.'

Meanwhile at a meeting on 10 February, and apparently without Stimson's latest communication being known, the idea was being implanted in the minds of the British Cabinet as well that the American Secretary of State was designing a pronouncement for domestic purposes above all. Thomas had been speaking on the telephone to Simon in Geneva, and the latter had summarised for his colleague the conversation which he had held with Stimson on the 6th. The Dominions Secretary thus relayed to the Cabinet the news that 'Mr. Stimson had contemplated the publication of a statement

---

[1] Stimson also aired his idea to the French Ambassador; from Paris there was a long diplomatic silence, however. FRUS, 1932, III, 287–9, 373–4.

prepared more especially for consumption in the United States . . . but . . . had agreed to refrain for the moment'. It was therefore in this light that the proposal itself, which had in fact arrived in the Foreign Office at 9 o'clock that morning, would come to be viewed; in addition, the Cabinet would have in mind the other part of Simon's message, that 'in private conversations with the American delegates [at Geneva] it had become clear that the United States intended to keep out of the [Shanghai] matter as far as possible'. As if to emphasise this last point, Washington's instructions to Consul-General Cunningham to dissociate himself from Japan's insincere peace negotiations were relayed to the Foreign Office on the 11th. By contrast, and for want of any other resource, British hopes were increasingly placed in those talks, especially since Lampson would shortly be arriving in Shanghai to bring to bear his considerable skill as a negotiator.

In retrospect, it seems evident that a clear British intimation to Stimson at this point that they could not join him in any denunciation of Japan would have saved much subsequent misunderstanding and resentment. While the dilemma was recognised, however, there was still too high a value placed on cooperation with the United States for such a choice and decision to be an easy one, and the temptation to go on straddling the widening gap proved too great. Worse still, Simon in Geneva, who had probably not yet received Vansittart's warning on the matter, gave Stimson some encouragement when the latter telephoned him at 5 p.m., Geneva time, on the 11th. The different emphases of the two men were again apparent (Stimson also suggesting that British representatives in Shanghai might have contracted 'cold feet' or be 'pro-Japanese'); but, having listened to the Secretary's Nine-Power-Treaty idea, Simon felt able to say that 'in principle, subject to thinking it over', he believed that 'the British Government will be glad to stand side by side with you. Our interests are essentially the same and in any case we both of us want to support the Nine Power Treaty. That is my first impression.' The Foreign Secretary had correctly reserved his final judgement ('tentatively he was with me,' noted Stimson in his diary), but he had aroused the other man's hopes. Given Stimson's mood, it was unfortunate.[1]

Uneasiness on both sides, but not clarity between the two, increased during the following three days. Simon had obviously become aware of the views held in London by the time he next spoke to Stimson on the telephone from Geneva at 5 p.m. on 12 February, and he began by raising various difficulties over the idea of a joint declaration: Britain's membership of the League, his desire to await Lampson's judgement, and his hopes that a local settlement might still be achieved. He also warned that he must consult MacDonald before making a decision, and that he would be 'averse to anything that amounted to an indictment on one side, because it would be prejudging and the League would very much object to it'. For 'the League' read 'the British Government'; nevertheless, to Stimson's question (which is missing from the British record): 'You see no reason why, on the general sharp issue of keeping alive the Nine Power Treaty, your country should not stand with us?', Simon replied that he saw no reason at all. Stimson was already

[1] DBFP, IX, Nos. 397, 400, 419, 422, 423; FO 371, F 1156/1/10; CAB 23/70; Stimson Diary, 9, 10, 11, 19 February 1932; FRUS, 1932, III, 261, 278–84, 290–2.

suspicious of the Foreign Secretary's intentions, however. He recalled that MacDonald had told him when they met in 1931 that Simon was 'apt to change'; now Hugh Wilson passed on to him by telephone an account of what the Foreign Secretary was alleged to have said to the Anglo–American press association in Geneva shortly before, that 'it would seem the Covenant was drawn up without considering the ultimate necessity of the expansion of any certain nation', and that 'boundaries were bound to change from time to time'. 'Was China a country,' he was reported as asking, 'or rather a geographical phrase?' If Simon did, indeed, speak in this vein, it was extra-ordinarily maladroit. It was also naïve of him to think that he could get away with the attempt, which he made before the League Council on the same day, to blur the sharp but disappointing fact that the United States was reducing its efforts over the local negotiations in Shanghai.[1] Stimson therefore took two steps to circumvent so sinuous a negotiator. By means of a telephone message via Atherton in the London Embassy on the 13th he sought the aid of MacDonald, who sent a reassuring reply; and in a cable to Johnson in Shanghai he tried to have Lampson surreptitiously influenced in favour of a Nine Power Treaty declaration, hoping to reach Simon himself by this round-about route.[2]

For all his efforts, however, Stimson's draft statement which he had now despatched to London was too close to an indictment of Japan to be acceptable there. By now Lindley had been consulted, and had reported that the Tokyo ambassadors of all the major powers were agreed that any such démarche would be most unwise; in addition, Simon talked with Laval on his way through Paris from Geneva to London, and although no record of what was said appears to have survived in either the British or French archives, it would be surprising if the French Premier did not then express a strong distaste for Stimson's proposal. Moreover by the time the Foreign Secretary arrived back in Downing Street on the evening of the 14th, the most urgent requirement appeared to be to try to prevent the Chinese from making trouble at Geneva by their attempt to convene a special Assembly, not to placate Stimson.[3]

Yet the Secretary's proposal still had to be answered, and Monday, 15 February, was the day when the issue was at last faced by the British Government and a general agreement reached—it can scarcely be described as a

---

[1] Simon was clearly uneasy over this, for he clarified the American position to the Council on the 13th and showed the text to Wilson. In October, however, he was to repeat the process, suggesting 'by mode of expression or manner' that there was a closer understanding with Washington than was the case. FRUS, 1932, III, 301–5, 324; ibid, IV, 317–22.

[2] Lampson reported on 21 February that Johnson had been 'sounding him out' on the advisability of a declaration based on the Nine-Power-Treaty and Kellogg Pact. Vansittart replied on the 23rd that 'no such suggestion' had been made to London by the U.S. Government. Unless he believed that communications to China were being intercepted, it is difficult to see what Vansittart hoped to gain by thus deceiving one of his own, senior men in the field. DBFP, IX, Nos. 534, 550.

[3] DBFP, IX, Nos. 431, 432, 441, 445, 456; Stimson Diary, 12, 13 February 1932; FRUS, 1932, III, 294–8, 301–5; FRUS, *Japan 1931–1941*, I, 80–2; DS 793.94/4144$\frac{1}{2}$; cf. Stimson, *Far Eastern Crisis*, 164.

clear-cut decision—that to sign, alone with the United States, the kind of document that Stimson had in mind was undesirable. As a significant moment of choice in Britain's foreign policy, and as the central point in a notorious exercise in international communication, the process involved in this agreement deserves a certain amount of detailed attention. From the outset, of course, the final outcome was implicit in the policies and priorities which had been adopted up to this point of the crisis. In addition, however, it seems that even within the limited perspective of these few days, the decision itself was as good as taken before the responsible Cabinet body met in order, theoretically, to perform that act. Senior officials in the Foreign Office, as we have seen, were already convinced that to sign with Stimson would be folly, and on the morning of the 15th Simon conveyed this view to MacDonald in the Park Lane nursing home where the latter was recuperating from an eye operation. For all his private assurances to Washington, the Prime Minister was at one with the Foreign Secretary on the matter, and it appears likely that they agreed on the possibility of using the League Council as a place where one could sidestep Stimson's oncoming rush. At some time that afternoon, and almost certainly before Simon contacted Stimson again, the Foreign Office dictated by telephone to Cadogan in Geneva the text of an appeal to Japan by the Council, including a reference to article 10 of the Covenant.[1]

The decision having virtually been pre-empted internally, it was now blurred externally. At 4 p.m. and in Atherton's presence, Simon telephoned Stimson. Sketching the idea of a League statement that would refer to article 10, he emphasised British doubts as to the wisdom of including Manchuria in any declaration if speedy results were to be obtained in Shanghai. On the question of whether Britain would join the United States in signing a single document he hedged however, allowing ambiguity to creep in in a way which was unlikely to have been fortuitous in one so precise: 'Whether or not we actually join you in your declaration or press on the members of the League to make a League declaration won't matter so much as long as we do it together.' And when Stimson repeated his preference for a separate, Anglo–American declaration, in addition to anything which the League might put out, Simon's response, although properly cautious, revealed his undue readiness to accommodate what he had to say to the desires of a listener, together with a tendency to invoke the limitations placed upon him by his Cabinet colleagues in a manner which went beyond what was necessary and smacked of an unwillingness to face personal responsibility ('I will discuss it with my colleagues . . . The only thing I have to be careful of is that I must

---

[1] The transactions between London and Geneva on 14 and 15 February are inadequately documented in the Foreign Office archives, but the approximate timing and content of this particular telephone call can be deduced from DBFP, IX, Nos. 456 and 459. Cadogan appears to have conveyed Simon's text to Drummond, discussed the situation with the latter, and despatched his response by 3.45 p.m., London time. Simon also discussed the situation with the King on the 15th, who recalled his friendship with members of the Japanese royal house and offered 'to use his influence with the Emperor of Japan in the hope of easing matters in China'. Nothing appears to have come of the idea. Wigram memorandum, RA G.V, M 2333/6.

not seem to desert the Council of the League, but I don't mind doing it so far as I am concerned . . . Of course I have to see what my colleagues say about it . . .'). Stimson, by contrast, was becoming increasingly assertive and all too ready to identify himself personally with what was, technically, a proposal from one government to another. (In the second conversation of the day, for example, he is recorded as saying: 'I think you will have to sign two papers. I think it is very vital . . . I should feel very badly if you did not accept . . .') The transatlantic telephone is obviously not the best of settings for an exchange of views, but neither man can be said to have executed his diplomacy with skill. Stimson scarcely strengthened his credit in British eyes by remarking, in connection with his additional proposal for joint representations in order to reserve the West's legal position over damage sustained within the Shanghai Settlement, that he didn't want to do it 'if it required much initiative on the part of (the United States)'. An American note on this last subject would be sent to Tokyo to await the arrival of a similar British one for joint delivery. Meanwhile he would await a counter-draft from London of the proposed Nine-Power-Treaty declaration. It would not, he hoped, 'be too damned friendly'.

At 5.15 p.m., Simon joined Chamberlain, Hailsham, Thomas, Eyres-Monsell and Hankey for a meeting of the Far Eastern Committee at MacDonald's nursing home. In theory the decision on whether to sign with the United States was now to be taken, but while Simon was handing round copies of Stimson's draft at the beginning of the meeting he also mentioned as a possibility the alternative, League course of action which he and MacDonald had in fact already set in motion. Thomas helped by stepping in to suggest that America would in any case merely issue her declaration and then 'wash her hands of the whole affair', leaving Britain to bear the brunt of any hostile Japanese reaction; in addition he agreed with the Foreign Secretary that 'none of the Powers at Geneva meant business [either]; they wanted to find a way out'. Yet contrary to what has often been supposed, Simon himself was not for placating Japan at any price, even if he was convinced that Stimson's alternative went too far in the opposite direction. He was 'rather opposed' to the idea of leaving Japan alone over the matter, for then 'she would think that we had been afraid to make representations and would ignore us. On the whole, therefore, if America insisted on making a declaration, he thought we should have to make one also.' Hailsham—shortly afterwards to be dismissed by Atherton in a report to Stimson as 'the apotheosis of [pro-Japanese] die-hard Tory opinion'—supported Simon's judgement. He believed that 'public opinion would insist on something being said', and he attached the greatest importance to keeping on 'our present good terms with America'.[1] On the other hand Eyres-Monsell echoed Thomas on the subject of American unreliability, while Hankey, invited to speak in his capacity as Secretary to the Committee of Imperial Defence, emphasised 'the gravity of the situation and the great desirability of avoiding any action that might provoke hostilities'. To thrust the point home he invited his listeners to draw an ominous inference from an enquiry which had

---

[1] At Geneva in the Spring, Stimson was surprised to hear Hailsham repeat these views. FRUS, 1932, III, 734–5.

recently been made by a Japanese official, as to whether Japanese refugees from Hongkong could take shelter with the Portuguese in Macao in the event of an emergency. Meanwhile Chamberlain said little, but revealed his anxiety over the risk of stirring Japan into action; to this extent he faintly foreshadowed his advocacy in coming years of an understanding with that country.

On this occasion, however, there was no careful examination of long-term prospects and alternatives of the kind which senior Foreign Office officials had been attempting in the preceding weeks; only the thought of immediate dangers and a search for a way out of the unexpected dilemma which Stimson had created. As might have been expected in a somewhat insecure group where power was diffused, it did not take long for those present to move from their various starting points towards the compromise and alternative already trailed before them by Simon, in the vain hope that the problem would then go away. Thomas agreed that it was necessary 'to keep in step with the United States'; Simon declared that he 'could not associate himself with any document lecturing the Japanese on the Manchurian episode', nor would he push the Japanese into reminding Britain 'of what we did in 1927'; MacDonald summarised the general belief that even if the Japanese chose to return 'an insulting reply', nothing more than paper flourishes would emerge from Washington. 'He would ask (Stimson) point-blank whether in that event he would send his whole fleet into Chinese waters. There was no doubt he would reply in the negative.' In the circumstances, he concluded (the Committee having come to where he and Simon had arrived that morning), the best plan was for the League Council to draft a report referring to the Covenant, the Nine Power Treaty, and the Kellogg Pact. 'The Report could then be sent to the Assembly for its guidance. Japan could not possibly object to that. If (she) was not seeking trouble that would get us out of the difficulty.' The very vagueness of the decision was evidently one of its chief merits, given the value which was still placed on Anglo–American cooperation. In April, meeting Stimson in Geneva, MacDonald contorted himself even further by declaring that he was horrified to hear of it when the indignant Secretary revealed the difficulty he had experienced with the Foreign Office during these February negotiations; he, MacDonald, having been in his hospital bed at the time, had known nothing, he said, of the decision to avoid the American proposal. Stimson swallowed it on that occasion. Meanwhile, still on 15 February, it was Simon's turn to face up to the Secretary's frustrated ardour once more.

The two men were linked by telephone at 6.30 p.m., London time, and again Simon swayed to the other man's breeze. He opened well enough, in accordance with the sense of the meeting he had recently left: Britain, he revealed, while acting 'in accordance with (America's) general scheme', would 'probably have to do it . . . through or in connection with the League'. This was then modified, however, to the words: 'I am not decided whether we can actually join you on the same piece of paper or not'; and under further pressure for co-signature, this in turn gave way to: 'I will mention it to the Prime Minister because several of us here think that if we could be parties to both documents it would be the best way.' Stimson, for his part, was unyielding, recalling the way in which previous warnings by Western

diplomats in Tokyo had not been fulfilled (he did not recall that the hypothetical situation on which most of those warnings had been based had not
been arrived at), as well as invoking the international ideals and national
cash benefits that were at stake. It was also Stimson, however, who recalled
the awkward precedent of 1927, and who mentioned the desirability of
getting France and Italy to join in the Nine-Power-Treaty declaration—a
line of thinking which Simon was to seize upon as his final means of
prevarication.

There matters rested for the moment. At midnight, London time, however,
Atherton was on the line to Stimson with indications that the latter's hopes
might not be realised. The Chargé d'Affaires (as Atherton then was) had
recently dined with Simon, and at some time during the evening the Foreign
Secretary had passed on the news that the Council of the League were to
meet the next day in order to draft an appeal to Japan which would recall her
obligations under article 10. 'This was the first he had heard of this. It came
to him entirely as a surprise and he wanted to know whether (you) had any
suggestions.' To what seems to have been a barely-disguised ploy on the part
of Simon,[1] Stimson replied that the Council's proposal seemed all right to
him; he was less calm, however, when Atherton went on to report that some
members of the Cabinet—'soft and pudgy', Stimson called them in his diary
—did not wish to sign alone with the United States, and that Britain would
probably do so only if the other signatories of the Nine-Power-Treaty would
do the same. Simon had therefore announced that he was leaving for Geneva
'with the purpose of trying to round up the members of the Treaty to go into
action with us'. Having wavered away from the conclusions of the Cabinet
Committee, the Foreign Secretary, it seems, had decided—or more likely had
had it decided for him—that he must revert to evasion.[2]

There would be no Anglo–American démarche, although the demise of
the idea was drawn out by hope on Stimson's part and, even now, by the
strenuous avoidance by Britain of any blunt rejection. When a highly-valued
and long-term policy goal has to give way to one that is more highly valued
still in the short run, it is tempting, though not necessarily wise, to allow
proposals concerning the former to fade away in neglectful silence rather
than to kill them in the presence of witnesses.

From London the League alternative was finally arranged on 16 February
by sending to Geneva a new draft appeal which included references to the

[1] Simon's 'surprise' cannot have been occasioned by the news of the planned
appeal, nor by the reference to article 10, both ideas having been formulated in
London. That leaves the timing of the meeting as the cause, which is technically
possible (in the Cabinet Committee, Simon had talked of a meeting towards the
end of the week), yet scarcely sufficient reason for seeking Stimson's opinion. Was
Simon trying to suggest that the other members of the Council were whisking
Britain along at a pace which would preclude a separate but simultaneous signing
with the U.S.A.? If so, he did not succeed, while Washington soon knew that it
was the other members of the Council who, at a private meeting on the 16th, were
surprised by Britain's suggestion for the inclusion of article 10 in their appeal.
DBFP, IX, Nos. 456, 459; FRUS, 1932, III, 351–2.
[2] DBFP, IX, Nos. 455, 458; CAB 27/482; Stimson Diary, 15 February, 21 April
1932; FRUS, 1932, III, 335–49. Cf. Wilson, *Diplomat Between Wars*, 276–8.

Kellogg Pact and Nine-Power-Treaty, together with an avowal of non-recognition. This document, adopted by 'the twelve' almost in its entirety, did contain, as MacDonald had suggested, 'a good deal of the substance' of Stimson's proposal (the Secretary himself even judged that the League had gone ahead 'rather drastically' in the matter), although it was couched in the form of a friendly appeal and pronounced no verdict against Japan. The text was given to Atherton by Vansittart during the afternoon of the 16th, together with the Foreign Office's 'tentative criticisms' of Stimson's Nine-Power-Treaty draft. As expected, the British alternative left Manchuria on one side, while its final paragraph implied that all signatories of the treaty should 'associate themselves with the American démarche'. Hints and implications were indeed as much as Washington was ever to be given on the matter, and although later in the day Atherton could tell Stimson that there was now 'quite a different tenor' in London, he had to talk of 'inferences' and his 'impression' that Britain would demand that only certain of the Nine Power signatories, and not all of them, should join in the declaration. Again it was only an impression, though a predictable one, that Atherton had obtained from Simon over dinner that the problem lay, not in any un-willingness on the Foreign Secretary's part, but in the difficulties of a coali-tion government. On one change, however, Atherton could be precise. Contrary to what Simon had indicated on the telephone that morning, he had now learned from Vansittart that Britain would not be making a further representation to Japan over damage inflicted within the Shanghai Settle-ment, as this would detract from the broader pronouncements which were being made and would unnecessarily inflame matters in Tokyo.

Stimson was scarcely concerned over this last matter, having himself doubted the wisdom of such a move when Hornbeck had pressed it on him.[1] But the Nine-Power-Treaty news was a shock. He thought that Britain had 'let America down', and Atherton could tell Vansittart so. His means of trying to put pressure on the policy-makers in London, however, demon-strated his gross over-estimation of the value put by others on such state-ments of principle by the United States at moments of immediate danger. The threat that Atherton was told to convey to Vansittart, that America would 'very seriously question the advisability of going alone on this paper at all', carried no weight at the time, as Atherton must have gathered when he saw the Permanent Under Secretary that evening. Vansittart did not say so bluntly of course, any more than Atherton repeated Stimson's remark about being let down; nor did Vansittart's record of their talk indicate conclusively whether or not Britain was demanding that all signatories must join in the proposed démarche. Privately, however, he wrote to Simon:

[1] Having already sought the company of France and Italy over a legal-rights protest, Stimson felt bound to continue with it. On 18 February, however, the proposal was dropped on the grounds that there appeared to be a chance of agreement at Shanghai, and that a further protest would be used to their advantage by extremists in the forthcoming Japanese general election—roughly the arguments used in London, in fact. Shortly afterwards the Western Ministers in China, including Lampson, reserved their countries' legal rights over Shanghai without any fuss. DBFP, IX, Nos. 506, 509, 525; FRUS, 1932, III, 373–4, 398.

Whatever the U.S. Government do, or don't do, I don't think *we* can now multiply representations to the Japanese Government in order to get the U.S. Government in on a Nine-Power-Treaty basis. This situation is too dangerous for that. The League action should suffice us for the nonce. Of course I did not say this to Mr. Atherton.

'I'm afraid America is "too proud to"—do anything,' minuted Simon that evening. On each side of the Atlantic there was now a clear but exaggerated image of the other government as being timid, rigid and uncooperative.[1]

Even now Stimson did not entirely give up hope, being cautioned by Hornbeck not to push the British Government too fast, trusting in the eventual soundness of British public opinion to overcome the wretched Tories, and pondering on the possibility of exerting pressure through the Dominions. He even sent a revised draft of his declaration to Atherton, with orders to deliver it if circumstances appeared favourable, but the latter wisely held on to it and thus avoided further embarrassment. Hoover was still prepared to issue a statement without Britain, but wanted France, at least, in as a partner. Stimson, his anxiety mounting lest a cease-fire were established at Shanghai 'without America having said her word on the morality of this great situation', began to move off in search of an alternative vehicle for such a pronouncement. The latest and equivocal Parliamentary performances of Simon and Hailsham speeded him on his way.

In the Foreign Office, despite an awareness of the need to associate the United States with any further protests that might have to be made, all minds were fixed upon the forthcoming major battle at Shanghai. Rejecting Lampson's advice for once, Simon informed the Cabinet on 17 February that 'from the point of view of the security of the Settlement it appeared better that the Japanese should succeed than the Chinese'. At the same time, and with Cabinet approval, every effort was made to reassure Japanese diplomats as to the friendly nature of the Council's recent appeal, since, as Simon put it, 'it was impossible for this country to assume the burden of Japanese resentment'. A sense of helplessness pervaded all discussions. China could not be pushed to accept the latest Japanese ultimatum, but until Japanese honour was satisfied the battle would have to take its course; preparations could be made to evacuate British women and children from Shanghai, but at Geneva nothing could now be done to prevent the Assembly from meeting as China desired. The mood was reflected in one of Neville Chamberlain's weekly letters to his sisters:

'I wonder what has been happening at Shanghai since last night', he wrote on 20 February. 'It seems almost impossible for the Settlement to escape without serious damage to property and perhaps loss of life. And we are not in a position to do much to help, while if we got into a real quarrel with Japan she could blow our ships out of the water one by one as they tried to get out of the Whangpoo.'[2]

[1] DBFP, IX, Nos. 465, 468–71, 474; Stimson Diary, 16 February 1932; FRUS, 1932, III, 350, 352–6, 362–3.
[2] DBFP, IX, Nos. 480, 481, 483, 484, 485, 508, 509, 522; CAB 23/70; CAB 27/482; FO 371, F 1391, 1398, 1443, 1572/1/10; Neville to Ida Chamberlain, 20 February 1932, Neville Chamberlain Papers; Stimson Diary, 17–21 February 1932; FRUS, 1932, III, 373, 383–5, 388–90, 398, 402; DS 793.94/4255, 4438.

Stimson did not feel helpless, however. Aided and encouraged by Rogers and Klots,[1] he began shaping his open letter to Senator Borah, successfully resisting for the moment Hoover's strong inclination to reveal at the same time that the only sanction the United States would contemplate using was that of public opinion. The Secretary had to admit to Lindsay that this was the case, however, while his attempt in a telephone conversation on the 24th to make Simon realise that his new letter was in one sense a rebuke to the British Government fell a trifle flat. In the Foreign Office, indeed, the document was at first seen as little more than a pointless reiteration of the January non-recognition note, and, since it did not seek to lay down that *all* treaties arrived at by the use of force should be regarded as invalid, it was thought to be insignificant in terms of international law.[2] Vansittart did believe that it might be wise to humour Stimson in some small way, but it was Simon who now showed the most concern to restore confidence and cooperation between the two countries, especially when Lindsay spelt out the resentment which was felt in Washington.[3]

American diplomats in London and Geneva remained deeply suspicious of the Foreign Secretary ('he would like to be all things to all people,' wrote Atherton), but they acknowledged to an equally-suspicious Stimson that he did appear to be trying, even to the extent of pushing the League Assembly towards its own declaration of non-recognition. Privately, too, Simon was recording for his officials his hope of thus

> deserving and obtaining American cooperation in supporting moral principles, while at the same time paying full regard, as we are bound to do, to our own necessities and to the warnings of Sir F. Lindley which British policy will not dream of disregarding.

To Hugh Wilson, he avowed on the same day that 'he had not confided his thoughts to London . . . (and) that even if some declaration to the contrary had been made' (Eden, bland in private over the founding of Manchukuo, had taken the same line in the Commons) 'it should be disregarded as he himself was directing foreign policy'. To a friend, however, Simon confided his exasperation that

> everybody [at Geneva] conspires to blame . . . our unfortunate country while at the same time expecting our unfortunate country to undertake every sort of burden, leadership and responsibility. And . . . while America is careful to keep out of the League, her representatives are sitting in the stalls and are a little

---

[1] In his draft autobiography, Hornbeck was to display resentment against historians who had denied him a major role in shaping the Borah letter. Hornbeck Papers, box 496. He certainly was involved, but Stimson found the other two more congenial as companions and helpers.

[2] At Geneva on 7 March, Drummond warned Simon that they must be on their guard against a likely attempt by 'the South Americans' to use the occasion to secure a statement that intervention by one country in the affairs of another could never be justified. Drummond recalled that the U.S.A. had resisted such a proposal at the Pan–American Conference in 1928. DBFP, X, No. 29.

[3] DBFP, IX, Nos. 560, 574, 577, 578, 590, 608, 621, 665; FO 371, F 1719/1/10; Stimson Diary, 21–27 February 1932; MacArthur to Stimson, n.d., Stimson Papers, box 304; FRUS, 1932, III, 432–6, 440–2, 449.

disposed to enquire why the Christians in the arena do not attack the lions more vigorously.

Encouraged by Matsudaira, he set about trying to revive the idea of the West using its good offices over Shanghai, envisaging a Sino–Japanese conference in that city, assisted by the major powers and aimed at restoring peaceful conditions. Stimson also approved the attempt, subject to the emphatic reservations that the business of the conference must be restricted to Shanghai, that China must enter it of her own will, and that it must entail no impairment of the principle of non-recognition as applied to Manchuria. By 2 March, the Foreign Secretary felt able to report to his Cabinet colleagues that British prestige at Geneva was high.[1]

It was an extremely rose-tinted view of the situation, and before the Assembly's Resolution of 11 March went through, those responsible for British policy were to experience one final spasm of anxiety. Simon himself admitted that as his major speech to the Assembly on 7 March drew near he felt 'a bit rattled', as Baldwin put it (the latter told Vansittart that the Foreign Secretary ought to get on with his job unaided, but that if help were really needed it would be sent).[2] On the 8th, the Cabinet's Far Eastern Committee met again under Baldwin's chairmanship and with a Foreign Office memorandum before them which surveyed the possibility that the League might proceed from article 15 to 16.[3] Everyone agreed that sanctions remained out of the question, and it was now that Hoare revealed his discovery that 'the Indian exports to Japan were double the imports from Japan'. Vansittart, who had been invited in Simon's absence, believed that if the Japanese became still more intransigent 'it would be impossible for Sir John . . . to resist animadversions being passed on them by the Assembly (or to) avoid associating himself with them'; it was agreed, however, that Simon should 'not go beyond strong regrets', and on the following day the Cabinet as a whole endorsed this position. If facts justified it, the League 'could state in clear terms that the Japanese action was reprehensible', but an attempt to institute sanctions would have consequences far more disastrous than the alternative of a present diminution in the League's prestige. The conclusion reached was that 'the sanctions provided for in Article XVI of the Covenant had proved throughout a handicap to the League and more especially to those nations who might be called upon to apply them'.[4] Hankey happily pressed home the point by circulating on the same day, 9 March, the detailed report on the same subject of a sub-committee of the C.I.D. In this, while Japan's vulnerability in terms of her exports was

---

[1] DBFP, IX, Nos. 603, 606, 612, 657, 667; ibid, X, Nos, 8, 9, 26; FO 800/286; CAB 23/70; CAB 27/482; ADM 125/70; Simon to Geoffrey Shakespeare, 7 March 1932, Simon Papers (private collection), Foreign Affairs, 1932; Eden to Simon, 26 February 1932, ibid, Personal Correspondence, 1932; Stimson Diary, 27 February, 3, 4 March 1932; Atherton to Castle, 23 February (seen by Stimson, 8 March) and 7 March 1932, Castle Papers, England; FRUS, 1932, III, 458–63, 465–71, 475–7, 501–4, 508–9, 511–5, 524–5, 528; FRUS, Japan, 1931–1941, I, 208.

[2] Baldwin to MacDonald, 8 March 1932, MacDonald Papers, RM 1/48.

[3] CAB 27/482; DBFP, X, Nos. 33, 34.

[4] CAB 23/70.

admitted, a substantial over-estimate[1] was presented of the stocks of vital raw materials which she had probably built up in order to be able to face an emergency. Moreover, the report continued, in order for Japanese exports to be crippled, the full cooperation of the U.S.A. would be essential, and even then a considerable amount of evasion could be expected; meanwhile Australia and India would suffer particularly hard in return, and in general 'the nations of the Commonwealth, including Colonies, would be the first to be affected by the application of economic sanctions, whose double-edged effect would be immediate and severe'.[2]

Amid this chorus of caution, the one note of uneasiness was now belatedly sounded by MacDonald, who was still removed from the centre of affairs. On a telegram despatched to Simon on 7 March he minuted: 'I am not sure but that circumstances now call for a more definite attitude on our part— nearer to the U.S.' He expanded these thoughts in a note which he sent to Hankey and Baldwin after reading the minutes of the Far Eastern Committee's meeting of the 8th:

> I am not too happy about the recent change in the Jap.—Shanghai position. Japs. (I judge from the press) not straight: League being fooled: Powers hope to blame us and hold up to opprobrium: Some of our Press anxious to do same: If this were to happen we lose prestige at Geneva and the East. Should be quite firm but not censorious nor blustering on last demands of Japan . . . We should not take up a kind of defensive or apologetic position, nor one which can be represented by hostile minds as equivocal to League's position . . . A permanent representative (at Geneva) is desirable owing to new developments re. Japan but not owing to Disarmament, regarding which we need not trouble very much for the immediate future unless there are happenings of which I am ignorant.[3]

For the moment, however, it appeared that the Assembly's new Resolution was enough to satisfy not only MacDonald but a large and diverse number of interested parties. As we have seen, Simon returned from Geneva to receive a warm private tribute from Gilbert Murray as well as the plaudits of his Cabinet colleagues. After he had gently prodded Hugh Wilson, who in turn prodded Stimson, he also got an appreciative letter from the Secretary of State, and in return sent his own somewhat glutinous gratitude for close Anglo–American cooperation. Norman Davis, who was on his way back to America from Geneva, testified that 'largely on account of your ability and efforts . . . it does look to me as if we were on a way to a final solution of the controversy'. From Tokyo, the Japanese Foreign Minister transmitted his 'deep gratitude for your friendly and helpful attitude', attributing to this consideration Japan's passive acceptance of the final Assembly Resolution. Herbert Hoover, too, when reminded by Stimson, found time for a little

---

[1] E.g., it was believed that for Japan 3 million tons of oil would prove adequate for two years of war and that in 1930 she had stocks of about 2 million tons, a figure which had probably been increased subsequently. In fact, as noted earlier, Japanese sources show oil stocks at the end of 1931 to have been a mere 83,000 kilolitres (c. 72,000 tons) and a year later 88,000 kilolitres (c. 76,000 tons). In 1941, the Japanese were to estimate their war-time needs as being over 8½ million tons for two years.

[2] CP 92 (33), CAB 24/228.

[3] Butler to Vansittart, 10 March 1932, MacDonald Papers, RM 1/48.

enthusiasm for what had occurred. Most people in the West had already turned their minds back to other matters.[1]

London and Washington: aftermath

The shock of the Shanghai episode lent impetus to the movement which was already growing in Whitehall for a change in the assumptions on the basis of which British defence policy was conducted. According to Vansittart, he had already decided in 1931 that the Ten Year Rule was no longer tenable (a somewhat odd remark in the light of the conclusion to the Foreign Office survey of that year, on which a renewal of the rule had been based), while Hankey conveyed to MacDonald his impression 'that most members of the Cabinet think that the assumption is now out of date'.[2] Hankey himself had chaired a sub-committee of the C.I.D. which investigated the situation in the Far East, its report being circulated on 17 March, together with the Chiefs of Staff Annual Review for 1932.[3] The two documents delivered a severe and urgent warning. On the Far East, the vast deficiencies which in outline had already been brought to the attention of leading Ministers were now set out in detail. As the Chiefs of Staff concluded:

> The position is about as bad as it could be ... In a word, we possess only light naval forces in the Far East; the fuel supplies required for the (thirty-eight-day) passage of the Main Fleet to the Far East, and for its mobility after arrival are in jeopardy; and the bases at Singapore and Hong Kong, essential to the maintenance of the fleet of capital ships on arrival ... are not in a defensible condition. The whole of our territory in the Far East, as well as the coastline of India and the Dominions and our vast trade and shipping lies open to attack ... We have no hesitation in ascribing this highly dangerous weakness mainly to the assumption that at any given date there will be no major war for ten years.

Recalling that the crisis of September 1931 had arrived out of 'a relatively clear sky', the Chiefs of Staff now argued that no ten-year type of guarantee could ever be valid, a point which Hankey illustrated in an appendix by means of historical examples. They appealed for a lead to be given that would overcome the public's 'general ignorance of the facts and spirit of complacent optimism', and concluded in dramatic, if unstylish, fashion: 'Recent events in the Far East are ominous. We cannot ignore the Writing on the Wall.'

It has already been emphasised that the men who composed these documents were casting anxious eyes at the future of their Services as the Disarmament Conference got under way. Despite the obvious inclination to overstate the potential enemy's capacity and preparedness, however, it cannot be said that the facts of the situation were significantly distorted. The Chiefs of Staff were not, after all, ascribing to Japan the immediate intention

[1] DBFP, X, Nos. 62, 71, 82, 86, 92; CAB 23/70; Stimson Diary, 11 March 1932; FRUS, 1932, III, 567–8; Simon to Stimson, 15 March 1932, Stimson Papers, Box 306.

[2] Vansittart to Hankey, 20 February and Hankey to MacDonald, 25 February 1932, CAB 21/368.

[3] CP 104 (32), CAB 24/229.

of attacking the British Empire, but as one of their proper functions were emphasising the likely consequences should such a possibility materialise. The validity of the warning becomes more apparent still when seen in the light of the time-scale within which decisions could produce tangible resources for defence and foreign policy. On the day that these reports were circulated, for example, the Board of Admiralty concluded that it would take five years from the date of authorisation to complete even the truncated scheme for equipping and preparing the Singapore base.[1] In an equally important sphere, the Principal Supply Officers' Committee of the C.I.D. were warning of the lengthy period which it would take to restore to British industry an adequate armament-building capacity, the preparations for such a transition being in their opinion 'behind those of the other principal Powers, including the United States of America'.[2]

At its meeting on 22 March, with Simon concurring for the Foreign Office, the C.I.D. accepted that the existence of the Ten Year Rule was now dangerous, and transmitted to the Cabinet the Chiefs of Staff recommendation for its cancellation. (In passing, the Committee also accepted the recommendations of the advisory committee on economic sanctions against Japan. 'In view of the present circumstances,' observed MacDonald, 'no action was likely to be called for, though this Report might be useful for future record'.)[3] On the following day the Cabinet 'did not dissent' from the Ten-Year suggestion, and although some confusion ensued as to whether this had amounted to a decision to terminate the rule, it is clear that this is what had been intended. Formal cancellation was forthcoming in November 1933, when the Cabinet set up a Defence Requirements Sub-Committee of the C.I.D. to examine Britain's resources in a world which by then had grown more menacing still.[4]

In all this there was, as yet, no serious conflict among senior officials and Ministers over Britain's Far Eastern Policy. There was present, however, one of the elements of what was soon to become a major dispute concerning this area. As in the 1902 decision for an alliance with Japan, and as was to be the case throughout the 1930s, the voice of the Treasury was a powerful one— all the more so now, following the cataclysm of 1931 and in the persons of Warren Fisher as Permanent Under Secretary and Neville Chamberlain, potentially the most powerful member of the Cabinet, as Chancellor. Chamberlain did not now dissent from the need to abandon the Ten Year Rule, but in a memorandum of 17 March he warned:

> The fact is that in present circumstances we are no more in a position financially and economically to engage in a major war in the Far East than we are militarily. It would seem, therefore, that ... we must for the time being be content with applying such deterrents as may be available ... What has to be considered ... is one set of risks balanced against the other, and the Treasury submit that at the present time financial risks are greater than any other that we can estimate.[5]

[1] Board minutes, 17 March 1932, ADM 167/85; cf. memorandum of 8 March, ADM 167/86.
[2] Ninth Annual Report, 1931-2, P.S.O. 350, Weir Papers.   [3] CAB 2/5.
[4] CAB 23/70; Hankey to MacDonald, 16 January 1933, CAB 63/46; Cabinet Conclusions of 15 November 1933, CAB 23/77.
[5] CP 105 (32), CAB 24/229.

In arriving at its quasi-decision on the Ten Year Rule, therefore, the Cabinet dutifully recorded 'that this must not be taken to justify an expanding expenditure by the Defence Services without regard to the very serious financial and economic situation that still obtains'. If one were to add to this consideration the thought that, with European tension growing, one might bridge the gap between commitments and resources by means of an understanding with Japan (a variation on the 1901–2 debate, in other words), together with the sour reflection that only 'big words' could be obtained from the United States, and the stage would be set for a major policy debate and dispute.

Even this nascent argument, however, was to be concerned with the means to be adopted in pursuit of a broadly agreed end: the preservation of the British Commonwealth and Empire as it stood.[1] In Washington, on the other hand, the Shanghai crisis left behind it, newly-churned in its wake, contrasting ideas which again concerned not only the means but the very ends of American policy in the Far East, and even wider. Many believed that the previous weeks had been dangerous ones for the country. Elihu Root, for example, told Stimson that he thought he had 'taken great chances', while the Secretary of the Navy, Adams, wrote to Admiral Taylor that 'it wouldn't have taken much hard luck or hasty judgement to have developed a war between Japan and ourselves';[2] Hoover's own disquiet over the same possibility had several times threatened to undermine Stimson's efforts to bluff Tokyo over the cost that the United States was prepared to pay in the dispute. However, whereas Stimson took this recent tension as a starting point from which to move closer to the belief long held by senior officers of the U.S. Navy, that an eventual conflict with Japan was well-nigh inevitable, Hoover for his part drew back from any such notion. In his diary, Stimson noted that 'during the course of . . . rivalry (over the Open Door) it is, in my opinion, almost impossible that there should not be an armed clash between two such different civilizations', and in Cabinet he warned that the President 'had better keep his powder dry'. Hoover responded with something about phantasmagoria,[3] and, as already observed, was not unhappy at the Navy's lack of a full offensive capacity. Among State Department officials, too, there were contrasting currents of opinion. Castle, Moffat and Pierre Boal (Moffat's predecessor as Chief of the West European Division) were among those who were uneasy at the implications of Stimson's restless outbursts over Far Eastern affairs, the Secretary's approach being seen by Moffat as 'daily bringing us nearer to the anti-revisionist school' so far as disarmament and the European peace treaties were concerned. Hornbeck, on the other hand, submitted with good reason that America's failure to build her navy

---

[1] It may rightly be argued that the retreat from India was already in progress. At this stage, however, there was no thought of being able to abandon Britain's defence obligations there, any more than for the Commonwealth. On 23 March, for example, the Cabinet approved a C.I.D. recommendation to the effect that it was inconceivable that any effort would be spared in the future to secure India's safety.

[2] Stimson Diary, 21 March 1932; Adams to Taylor, 11 May 1932, Taylor Papers, Box 1.

[3] Stimson Diary, 9 March, 5 April 1932.

up to the level permitted by treaty had upset those naval ratios which had been envisaged at the Washington and London conferences, and that failure to remedy this situation would cause Britain

to doubt the will or ability of the United States to do its part in maintaining the régime . . . then established. Will it not encourage the Japanese Government in the assumption that, if the United States Government has neglected the naval instruments for support of American Far Eastern policy, the American Government may also be induced to modify or abandon the objectives of that policy? . . .
Unless the United States is prepared to maintain its relative naval strength in the Pacific must we not expect to be forced to modify our policies . . . in favour of those Powers which are prepared to maintain their naval forces up to the limits contemplated in international agreements?[1]

The question linked itself to the ones which Stimson had been asking himself about the means of maintaining the new morality in international relations; these in turn raised the issue of the degree and method of co-operation that should be envisaged between the United States and the League. In this and other ways, the crisis which had just occurred on the western shores of the Pacific was joined to the series of problems with a mainly European context which were facing the West in the spring and summer of 1932.

Retrospect

Over Shanghai, the commitment of the Japanese military, Government and people as a whole was of a different order to the one that they brought to the Manchurian issue. Once face had been saved by a local victory, a settlement of the affair lay squarely within the country's policy. To many foreign eyes, however, the assault on the city represented not only the most barbaric but also the most sinister of the Japanese moves since September 1931. Public condemnation of Japan reached new heights in the West, although even now there remained deep divergences of opinion as to her intentions, her likely response to various forms of pressure, and the price that could or should be paid in order to bring her to submit.

For those responsible for British and American policies, it was a crisis situation, and in several instances one can observe examples of that phenomenon whereby a person's range and clarity of thinking diminishes as the stress rises beyond a certain, stimulating level.[2] In Stimson's case, for example, he developed something of a fixation over the necessity for and efficacy of a major pronouncement of principle; in London, the 'burden of resentment' which might fall upon Britain if she spoke out of turn began to assume greatly exaggerated proportions. In each case, of course, there were other considerations which were being taken into account. Within limits, for example, opinion at Geneva was capable of modifying the tactics of the British Government, and while Simon's traditional and European-centred picture of Britain 'holding the scales evenly between China and Japan'

[1] Ibid, 8 March 1932; Moffat Diary, 28 January, 24 February, 4 March 1932; Castle Diary, 4 April 1932, cited in Current, loc. cit.; Hornbeck memorandum, 30 March 1932, DS 500 A4/628.
[2] See Kelman, 499; De Rivera, 150 ff.

hinted at power, influence, and immediate disinterestedness which the country did not possess, even so, Chinese susceptibilities were not entirely overlooked.

The dominant factor, however, remained the widespread perception in official circles in the West of a united and determined Japanese people, set upon defying the world if necessary in pursuit of a vital interest. An acceptance of this factor, coupled with that of Japan's overwhelming military preponderance in the area, brought home to policy-makers as never before that gulf between their Far Eastern commitments and their resources which was explored in the first part of this book. There were some exceptions, but in general it was believed that one was faced with the choice between what amounted to acquiescence, practically speaking, or the readiness to mount a high step on to an entirely new level of exchanges where the likely costs outweighed the value of what was immediately at stake. As far as purely verbal reactions were concerned, of course, Stimson's two major public pronouncements stood out on their own, although eventually followed by the firm League Resolution of 11 March. From the moment when he was far quicker than the Foreign Office—or his own officials—to perceive that trouble was coming at Shanghai, Stimson's screening of incoming messages was based on a different order of priorities from the one which obtained in London; hence the differing responses to largely similar information and advice, while behind the contrasting priorities themselves lay such factors as national history, aspirations, style and resources which were examined earlier, as well as the influence of personality. The contrast was emphasised, on Britain's side, by her very uncertainty as to America's degree of engagement, and hence, in Vansittart's words, her acceptance of an inability to do more than 'live from hand to mouth'.

It has also been suggested, however, that there were again many underlying similarities between the policies of the two countries. Indeed, paradoxically there were too many such similarities, especially in terms of the risks to be run, for complete confidence and cooperation to be established between the two, an inherent source of tension in their relationship which was aggravated by the need, in the age of Kellogg and Covenant, to turn a face of selfless idealism to the outside world. Yet even had Britain joined in Stimson's Nine-Power-Treaty démarche, what might have been achieved? The chances of the Shanghai fighting being halted would not have been drastically improved, and indeed it might have made the Japanese all the more determined not to appear to give way to external pressure; nor is there any evidence to suggest that it would have made Tokyo more compliant over Manchuria. At the probable price of suspicion and resentment among certain League states it would no doubt have warmed Anglo–American relations; but it would be difficult to argue that it would also have led to any greater readiness on the part of the United States to engage herself in the Far East in the following years to an extent which would have enabled Britain to resolve her own major dilemma of global defence.

Among Western officials and military planners, there were those who were prompted by the crisis to peer into the future of international relations in the Far East. On a few occasions, as when Wellesley foresaw the possibility of Japan embarking on 'a policy of adventure far exceeding anything which we have witnessed as yet', the forecasts made were to bear a fairly close relationship to the events of later years. In general, however (and it was true of Wellesley, as of Hornbeck, who was also warning of the undemocratic impulses behind Tokyo's policy), there remained a failure to appreciate the full extent of the long-term changes that were taking place in Japanese politics. Moreover, there were remarkably few attempts by members of the British and American Governments to project their own policies forward into various hypothetical situations in the Far East. One observes, rather, a characteristic which has been noted among American officials in 1940–1: 'the paradox of pessimistic realism coupled with loose optimism in practice.'[1] Where there were exceptions, they arose less from careful analysis than from the 'loose pessimism' of Stimson and American admirals when they thought of war with Japan as being somehow written in the destiny of the two nations.

Coupled with inadequacies in the formulation of policy, and like them due in part to the stress of events, there were also several instances when its execution was poorly handled. The particular case of the Stimson–Simon exchanges requires no further comment, beyond the final one that in subsequent years Stimson was wrong in claiming that he had proposed a conference, but right in his conviction that the British had deliberately evaded and procrastinated over his request for a joint démarche. Nevertheless there were a good many other instances when politicians and diplomats resorted to evasion or outright deception at the time, both among themselves and with their publics. Pace the spiritual heirs of Woodrow Wilson, it would be unrealistic to expect international politics to be conducted always without resort to such tactics; pace Lord Cecil, the diplomacy of the Shanghai crisis could not, with any hope of success (measured, say, in Cecilian terms of defeating aggression), have 'proceeded always frankly and in the public view', while by comparison with, say, Suez or Vietnam, the deception of the public which was involved was pale indeed. The disadvantages are obvious of the League's asking the United States as Paul-Boncour later suggested it should have done: 'Sans vous nous ne pouvons rien; si nous agissons, que ferez-vous?'[2] But although some of the reasons are evident enough—not least the heightened tension between the private limiting and the public idealising of policy—was not evasion sometimes carried to excess? Would the British aim of keeping the United States in play, for example, have been less well served had the limits to British policy been frankly exposed and explained to Stimson? In seeking to bluff the Japanese, did not Stimson himself permit a blurring of communications with those whose cooperation he sought, and did not London sometimes fail to press those questions which would have enforced a measure of clarification?

Whatever the errors and anxieties of the past weeks, it seemed to many by the middle of March that a large measure of success had been achieved in the end. Yet, obscured by the drama of Shanghai, a new and nominally independent régime now claimed to rule Manchuria, where the Japanese determination to stay put was quite different from their approach over

[1] R. Wohlstetter, *Pearl Harbor, Warning and Decision* (Stanford, 1962), 69.
[2] Paul-Boncour, *Entre Deux Guerres*, vol. 2, 203.

Shanghai. And while within Western administrations it had now largely been established what would *not* be done to meet a continuing challenge to international agreements in the Far East, no alternative had been produced beyond the satisfying but as yet unproductive one of non-recognition. In the hope that circumstances would somehow improve, one could only wait for Lytton.

CHAPTER EIGHT

WAITING FOR LYTTON

Developments in the Far East

Quo Tai-chi (Chinese Vice-Minister for Foreign Affairs):

'I suppose that we might save the situation in this way by adding the words: "which they expect will be completed in—or not later than—" to the end of the Japanese declaration.'

[Sir Miles passes formula to Shigemitsu Mamoru (Japanese Minister to China) who studies it and passes it back to Sir Miles, who hands it to Quo.]

[Silence.]

Rear-Admiral Shimada: 'We Japanese are of such a peculiar character that if six months should be stipulated [for withdrawal], we might feel we had to stay that long, although perhaps wishing to get out sooner.'

[Long Silence.]

Quo (to Shigemitsu): 'Another formula for solving it would be for you to send me a confidential note defining the term "temporarily" in Article III as meaning—.'

[Silence.]

Lampson: 'Could you not consider Mr. Quo's wording?'

[Long Silence.]

Lampson: 'Where are we?'
Lieutenant-General Uyeda: 'We seem to be discussing the number of months, but for my part we cannot name any time.'[1]

Thus, in a style reminiscent, if not fully worthy, of Vladimir and Estragon, representatives of Japan and China grappled from 24 March onwards with the task of restoring peaceful conditions to Shanghai. From time to time there were renewed exchanges of fire between the two armies, and in the city itself, where a modified boycott of Japanese goods continued, Japanese troops were involved in some ugly incidents. Much alarm was also aroused on 29 April, when, at a Shanghai parade to mark the Japanese Emperor's birthday, a Korean independence-fighter threw a bomb which cost Shigemitsu a leg, General Uyeda part of a foot, and Admiral Nomura the sight

[1] Notes of meeting of 4 April 1932, Johnson Papers, box 36.

of one eye. Despite this, and urged along by Lampson, Johnson and their French and Italian colleagues, the negotiations creaked towards agreement, finally overcoming the main obstacles of China's desire for a time-limit for their opponents' withdrawal and Japan's attempt to create a permanent de-militarised zone round the city. From Geneva, the League Assembly's Committee of Nineteen tried to help by empowering its Consular Commission to declare when conditions warranted the complete withdrawal of Japanese troops, but on all sides it was acknowledged that the successful conclusion to the talks on 5 May owed more to Lampson than to anyone else. Japanese troop withdrawals were completed by July 17 with little incident.[1]

In many minds, however—and the Japanese were obviously anxious that it should be so—this was not the end of the matter. During the League's discussions on Shanghai in February and March there had emerged the idea of an eventual 'round table conference' on the problems which underlay the immediate conflict there, and although the Resolution of 11 March had not specifically provided for such an event, the hazy expectation persisted that it would occur, whatever the location, membership and agenda.[2] Nothing happened. All that the world could see were talks between local Chinese authorities in Shanghai and members of the Settlement's Municipal Council, which approached agreement on such matters as the roads leading out of the International area, but which then became paralysed through the intransigence of Japanese members of the Municipal body.[3]

Meanwhile new alarms were sounded in July and August over the barren, mountainous province of Jehol which bordered and was loosely associated with Manchuria, and which would constitute an important strategic position in any Japanese defence scheme against both the Soviet Union and attacks into Manchuria from North China. A Japanese officer was captured by troops of the local ruler, Tang Yu-lin; the Kwantung Army, claiming that Jehol belonged to Manchukuo, made threatening noises; Chang Hsueh-liang moved units of his depleted army towards the southern borders of Jehol.[4] Again, however, nothing happened for the moment, and attention was drawn away to Peking itself, where the guard of the Japanese Legation began conducting exercises in a provocative manner (invading the garden of an American Marine officer, for example, and in the words of the British Chargé d'Affaires, 'uttering their tiresome yells and popping at each other from behind the bushes'), thus suggesting that they planned to seize

---

[1] The problems encountered during the talks and the efforts of the Committee of Nineteen can be followed in DBFP, X, Nos. 141–324, passim, and LNOJ, *Special Supplement No. 101* (Geneva, 1932); the text of the final agreement is printed in Cmd. 4077 (1932). On Japanese troop withdrawals, see DBFP, X, Nos. 341, 370, 387, 425, 536. Lampson received strong support from Mr. (later Sir Eric) Teichman, Chinese Secretary of the British Legation. On the close cooperation between Western diplomats and commanders, see the narrative in the Kelly Papers, vol. 7, pp. 10, 68, and vol. 8, p. 1.

[2] The resulting confusion was well exposed in the *North China Herald*, 17 May 1932.

[3] See DBFP, X, Nos. 346, 407, 569, 604, 634, 660.

[4] See ibid, Nos. 538, 540, 544, 549, 550, 568, 586, 611, 665.

the city by a coup de main in the event of renewed Sino-Japanese fighting away to the north.[1] To add to the Nanking Government's troubles, a boundary dispute with Tibet also flared up at this time, involving the rivalry between the Dalai Lama and the Chinese-supported Panchan Lama,[2] while nearer at hand nationalist extremists gave vent to violent dissatisfaction over what they saw as the régime's feeble response to the Japanese attacks.[3] Little impression was being made by Chiang Kai-shek on the Communist forces, who advanced to threaten Amoy;[4] in the south, the Canton faction maintained a surly independence while finding time for their own internecine struggles, which led to fighting in the Chefoo area;[5] to complete the confusion, Wang Ching-wei and the whole Nanking Government resigned early in August amid renewed animosity between the civilians and Chiang Kai-shek, while Marshal Chang Hsueh-liang followed shortly afterwards.[6]

In Manchuria, the Japanese were also experiencing some discomfort, having to engage in what promised to be a long fight with Chinese troops and irregulars to the north and north-west of Harbin, and unable even to prevent guerillas from making lightning raids on Mukden itself.[7] The Manchukuo régime nevertheless continued to consolidate its power, and by the end of July had forcibly ejected the existing Commissioners of Customs in the region, securing for itself that vital source of revenue (about $20 million annually), together with the proceeds of the salt gabelle.[8] Meanwhile, despite the usual disclaimers, the new coalition government in Tokyo, led by Admiral Saito Makoto in place of the murdered Inukai, showed every sign of continued and resolute support for these Manchurian developments, a hard-line policy seeming all the more likely as a result of the retention of Araki as War Minister and the introduction of Count Uchida, a former president of the South Manchurian Railway, as Minister for Foreign Affairs. On 15 September, defiance was given formal shape when Japan recognised the new State of Manchukuo. In return she accepted the position of guardian and adviser, as personified by General Muto Nobuyoshi, who arrived in Mukden as Special Ambassador and Commander of the Kwantung Army rolled into one.

In private, the staff of that Army had been adamant that the seal of formal recognition should be placed upon their work,[9] and even before Inukai was murdered on 15 May, the Cabinet in Tokyo had been moving in the required direction. By August, with liberalism a spent force in the country and the energy of radical conservatism[10] surging forth, the choice had been made. The Japanese people, declared Uchida to the Diet on 25 August, were 'solidly determined not to concede a foot, even if the country turned to scorched earth'. Two days later the Cabinet agreed to take early steps to replenish armaments and prepare emergency economy and mobilisation

---

[1] E.g., ibid, Nos. 582, 584, 593, 600, 614, 662.
[2] For a summary, see ibid, No. 571.
[3] E.g., ibid, No. 316.   [4] E.g., ibid, Nos. 256, 615.
[5] E.g., ibid, Nos. 318, 352; Kelly Papers, vol. 8, p. 23; FO 371, file 17060.
[6] E.g., DBFP, X, Nos. 588, 596, 607.   [7] E.g., ibid, Nos. 329, 371, 508, 638.
[8] E.g., ibid, Nos. 49, 166, 446, 452, 471, 495, 520, 580.
[9] See IMTFE, *Exhibits* 226 and 227; *Taiheiyo senso e no michi*, II, caps. 6 and 7.
[10] Some would say fascism. See above, 36.

measures. If the League intervened over Manchuria the Japanese delegates would withdraw from its proceedings, and if any form of pressure were exerted the country would leave the League altogether. This did not mean that the politicians were planning to fight the West. Nor were the Staffs of the Army and Navy, who agreed that Britain's position 'in Shanghai, Canton, and other places along the Yangtze River and in South China' should be respected. The Kwantung Army, too, accepting the War Minister's judgement that 'under the present circumstances of complete Conservative control, the anti-Japanese forces of the Liberals and Labourites can almost be disregarded', suggested that in the interests of Anglo-Japanese friendship 'consideration should be given to guaranteeing the security of India' (shades of 1905), with a similar approach to be made to the French over Indo-China.

Even from the United States, against whom the Cabinet nevertheless directed various contingency preparations to be made, no immediate trouble was expected, with various sops such as investment opportunities in Manchukuo being devised in order to make doubly sure. And while the Kwantung Army and Araki alike believed that 'a Japanese-Soviet war in the future was inevitable', even that eventuality did not appear to be imminent. 'Indications are,' the Privy Council were told on 15 September, 'that our country's recognition of Manchukuo, although it will . . . cause for a time no small shock to the world, will not bring about any international crisis.' 'In fact,' added Uchida—presumably he was being inventive—'when Ambassador Debuchi recently approached the American Government authorities and informally asked if they would protest in case Japan should recognise Manchukuo, they replied that they had not the slightest intention of making a protest or convening a Nine-Power Conference, inasmuch as there was no hope of such a conference reaching a conclusion.' Thus, conscious and yet unconscious of what they were doing, as Maruyama and others have pointed out, the new leaders of Japan pursued what they saw as the nation's destiny.[1]

Public reactions in the West; the Lytton Commission and its Report

Among the major powers, the Soviet Union clearly had as much cause as any for alarm at the extension of Japanese control over the whole of Manchuria. Soviet diplomats and newspapers made no secret of their apprehension, and a rapid military build-up was reported to be taking place in the regions adjoining Manchuria and Inner Mongolia. It was still equally evident, however, that the Soviet Government was straining to avoid a confrontation, and negotiations for a non-aggression pact with Japan (Moscow had, in fact, proposed such a pact in December 1931, and Tokyo rejected the idea only a year later) were widely rumoured; also, in August, a new fishing agreement was concluded between the two countries. As the Foreign Office and State Department appreciated, Japan did indeed have

[1] IMTFE, *Exhibits* 223, 233, 241, 2210, 2211; Ogata, 160–70; Maruyama, 26 ff.; Storry, *Double Patriots*, 118 ff.

little to fear immediately from that quarter, despite moves by China to step in with her own non-aggression pact with Moscow.[1]

In the West, there was little open condemnation of Japan during that summer. The main exception was provided by Stimson, in a speech to the Council on Foreign Relations in New York on 8 August. In this the Secretary hypothetically but unmistakably referred to 'a nation which sought to mask its imperialistic policy under the guise of defence of its nationals', proclaimed his belief that under the Kellogg Pact there could be no neutrals, no failing 'to denounce (those wrongdoers) engaged in armed conflict . . . as lawbreakers', and declared that the United States could not avoid its obligation to consult with other signatories of the Pact on such an occasion.[2] As if to add weight to his warning, it had already become known that the Scouting Force of the U.S. Fleet would be staying in the Pacific after the spring manoeuvres, and not returning to the Atlantic as planned.

Yet although Stimson had travelled to meet MacDonald and other European leaders at Geneva during April and May, no concerted Western reaction to Far Eastern developments was visible, beyond a continued refusal to acknowledge the Manchukuo régime's announcements of its existence. Meanwhile back in the United States William Castle, known to be a confidant of Hoover's, had taken the opportunity of Stimson's absence to make some speeches of his own, in which he emphasised that his Government would have nothing to do with an official economic boycott of Japan since such a move 'implied a blockade and (there was) no measure more certain to lead to war'. Hoover himself, while accepting the idea of international consultation, emphasised America's freedom of action, or rather inaction, in his major speech at the Republican Party Convention.[3] A shrinking disposition had also been manifested by the House of Representatives in April, when it had voted overwhelmingly and after only a cursory debate to grant complete independence to the Philippines in eight years time. The rest was silence, broken only by reminders from London in particular of the need to await the findings of the League Commission. Lytton and his colleagues had been granted an extension of the six months laid down in article 12 of the Covenant for the presentation of a report,[4] and were now toiling around the area of conflict.

Victor Alexander George Robert Bulwer-Lytton, the second Earl, son of a Viceroy of India, himself a former Governor of Bengal and a man of commanding aspect and temper, had been his Government's second choice as the British member of the Commission, and on personal grounds had

[1] See DBFP, X, Nos. 149, 184, 216, 270, 362, 367, 381, 413, 423, 609, 657; *Izvestia*, 15, 18 April, 15 May 1932; Erickson, 357–63; Karl Radek, 'The War In the Far East: A Soviet View', in *Foreign Affairs*, July 1932.

[2] *Foreign Affairs*, vol. 11, No. 1, *Special Supplement*, and FRUS, 1932, I, 575 ff.

[3] DS 793.94/5201; DBFP, X, No. 330; cf. *U.S. Daily*, 2 May 1932, for a similar speech by Hornbeck.

[4] LNOJ, *Special Supplement No. 102*, (Geneva, 1932), 16.

accepted the job only at the second time of asking.[1] Throughout the Commission's existence there was to be no doubt as to who was chairman; but there could be no doubt, either, of Lytton's immense capacity for work,[2] nor of his forthright loyalty to the ideals of the Covenant, as might have been expected from a member of the L.N.U.'s Executive Committee and a recent member of the British delegation to the League Assembly. In personality and approach, Lytton was thus far removed from his French colleague, General Henri Claudel, a member of the Conseil Supérieur de la Guerre, recently Inspector-General of Colonial troops, and, so many of the party believed, under orders from Paris to see that no trouble was created for France by any provocative condemnation of Japan.[3] Like most or all of Lytton's party, it seems that Claudel accepted from the outset that without Japanese support the Manchukuo régime would never have existed; but with what one American member of the group described as 'his treaty-port mind', the General's inclination was to shrug off this state of affairs with the observation that, like it or not, the illegitimate child now existed, and would therefore have to be accepted. It did not help that Claudel spoke nothing but French, a tongue that Lytton managed only with difficulty. 'As the days passed,' wrote an American adviser, 'the two men misunderstood each other more completely, and the gulf between them continually widened'. The German member, Dr. Heinrich Schnee, a former Governor of German East Africa with administrative experience in the Pacific as well, had a precise, pedantic mind, but lacked the imagination or flexibility to help smooth things over between his two warring colleagues. Such a role was more possible for Count Luigi Aldrovandi, a former Italian Ambassador in Berlin who had left there in 1929 under a cloud and had not held a diplomatic post since, but whose tact and command of French helped prevent Claudel from retreating into totally negative isolation. Aldrovandi was less significant, however, than the remaining member of the Commission, Major-General Frank Ross McCoy of the United States Army. Like Lytton, McCoy had not been a first choice (Walter Hines and Henry Fletcher had been invited before him), and his active-list status, together with experience which included the supervision of a presidential election in

[1] DBFP, IX, Nos. 6 and 40, notes. In the section that follows I have made use of a lengthy letter written by Dr. Blakeslee to Hornbeck on 14 September 1932, a copy of which is in the Stimson Papers, box 310; of details contained in the State Department files designated 793.94 Commission; of the McCoy Papers, as cited separately, together with the extremely detailed 'Military Narrative' of the Commission's work and interviews which was compiled for McCoy by his military aide, Lt. (now Major-General) William Biddle and is in the McCoy Papers, box 76 (cf. material in boxes 77 and 78); of Nelson Johnson's letters to Hornbeck of 13 June, 16 and 30 August 1932, Johnson Papers, box 15; and of the voluminous though generally unexciting material concerning the Commission's formation and work contained in the League of Nations Archives, R1875 and S29–50. As acknowledged earlier, I am also much indebted to Adrianus Pelt and General Biddle for discussing these matters with me at some length.

[2] Lampson's impression, indeed—though not correct—was that 'Lord Lytton virtually is the Commission'. FO 371, F5292/1/10.

[3] If Claudel was given written instructions, however, no trace of them appears to have survived in the Quai d'Orsay archives.

Nicaragua, as well as much work in the Philippines, had prompted both Briand and Avenol to suggest that Latin American members of the League might look askance at his selection.[1] Nevertheless McCoy's quick grasp of affairs and clarity of thought were to win him the admiration of his colleagues, a position of esteem which helped him when it came to moderating some of Lytton's more aggressively forthright drafting. In the opinion of more than one observer, the achievement of a unanimous report owed more to McCoy than to anyone.

It is important to note—and here one sees a reflection of the essence of the League itself—that this was a Western Commission, composed of men who, however divergent their particular views, had all but one been engaged in careers which underlined the assumption of the universal significance and leadership of Western civilisation. It is not surprising, then, that such an assumption was to be manifest in their final report. Meanwhile as they embarked upon their task they were accompanied by Yoshida Isaburo, Japanese Ambassador to Turkey, as one assessor, and by Dr. Wellington Koo, a former Chinese Premier, as the other. Robert Haas led the Secretariat staff, seconded by Adrianus Pelt; both McCoy and Claudel took military aides (Lieutenant William Biddle in the case of the former), and the Hon. William Astor went as Lytton's secretary. Experts of various kinds were gathered in ambulando, including Dr. George Blakeslee, who had recently been assisting the State Department on Far Eastern affairs, Dr. de Kat Angelino, who was a historian summoned from the Dutch East Indies, and Dr. Walter Young of the New York Institute of Current World Affairs.

By the time that the Europeans in the party had sailed to America and, together with McCoy, had crossed that Continent, much time had elapsed since the League Council's Resolution of 10 December, and it was 29 February, 1932, when they reached Tokyo. There were various and good technical reasons for this measured progress, but at times a certain lack of urgency was felt by McCoy amongst others. Naturally, none of the Commission arrived with his mind a tabula rasa, nor did they lose touch with their own capitals during their stay in the Far East. Schnee, for example, had at the outset been appointed only with much reluctance by his Government in the face of private Japanese pressure for Germany not to participate—the Tokyo press argued that it was unlikely that an objective view would be taken by anyone from a country with such a growing economic interest in China as Germany had—and while in the Far East he was reminded by Berlin of the need to avoid anything in the nature of an initiating or eminent role.[2] (Some possible advantages to Germany of such caution were suggested

[1] Stimson Diary, 21, 22, 26, December 1931; DS 793.94/3322. McCoy had been General Wood's military aide in Cuba and the Philippines, and had held a similar post with Theodore Roosevelt. He had several friends among élite circles in Japan from his stay there in 1923 in command of the American earthquake-relief mission. Despite the differences of personality and opinion that have been noted, McCoy could write to his sisters on 4 March 1932: 'We live and work together like warm friends.' McCoy Papers, box 8.

[2] See AA, serial 3088H/D624426, 624432, 624438-9, 624447, 624520, 624522-5; ibid, serial K2088/K558578, 558666-8. The Japanese had privately proposed as an alternative German member of the Commission Dr. Solf, a former ambassador in Tokyo.

in May, when the Japanese Ambassador in Moscow again aired the idea of a German-Japanese understanding, perhaps embracing the Soviet Union as well, while in September Tokyo's Ambassador in Berlin was pointedly asking what German policy would be towards Manchukuo. As before no positive response was made, but State Secretary von Bülow was at least interested to the point of 'awaiting more concrete Japanese proposals before we seriously consider how far we can go along with them'.[1] Lytton himself had not received any special briefing in London—when Astor arrived at the Foreign Office before his departure and suggested some 'coaching' for the chairman concerning the British interests that were involved he received a negative and distinctly cool response[2]—but analyses of the situation by Wellesley and others were passed on to him during the summer. As with all the Commissioners, Lytton was also able to avail himself privately of reports by his country's diplomats on the spot.[3] McCoy, for his part, was given a tour d'horizon by Stimson before leaving (the Secretary's views were also passed on to Lytton[4]) and had lengthy discussions with American diplomats in China and Japan. The State Department's Blakeslee, as we have seen, was also on call.

In return, the Commissioners and various assistants saw to it that their views, as well as progress, were known at home. A notion of Astor's for a Sino-Japanese alliance, for example, which was apparently entertained by Lytton, found its way to Washington, as did reports of the puppet-like nature of Manchukuo and of major incidents such as the Commission's interviews with the Japanese Foreign Minister.[5] By 22 July, McCoy was able to inform Stimson by letter that the final report would be 'in harmony with American policy' (one wonders what would have happened if the evidence available had pointed strongly in a different direction), while Blakeslee's summary of that report was in the Secretary's hands on 26 September.[6] In London, meanwhile, MacDonald was among those who saw an account by Astor of the widespread hostility in Manchuria to what was, in effect, a Japanese tyranny,[7] while early in July both Stimson and Simon,

---

[1] Dirksen to Bülow, 5 May; Bülow to Dirksen, 11 May; Neurath memorandum, 14 September 1932, respectively AA, serial 4620/E199703–9; serial K2264/K625519–20; serial 3088H/D623135–6. Bülow wrote: 'Auch darin stimme ich völlig mit Ihnen überein, dass für uns keine Veranlassung vorliegt, uns zurzeit als Vermittler zwischen Japan und Russland aufdrängen zu wollen. Ich empfehle deshalb, zwar Unterhaltungen mit Hirota über diesen Gegenstand nicht auszuweichen, sich aber weiterhin rezeptiv zu verhalten. Wir können und müssen m.E. erst abwarten, ob die Japaner mit konkreteren Vorschlägen an uns herantreten, bevor wir uns ernstlich überlegen, wie weit wir auf dieselben eingehen können.'

[2] Orde minute, 22 January 1932, FO 371, F477/1/10.

[3] See, e.g., DBFP, IX, No. 356, note; ibid, X, Nos. 197, 208, 209, 521, 572.

[4] Stimson Diary, 20 January 1932: FRUS, 1932, IV, 200–1; DS 793.94 Commission/46A, 160, 186, 5047.

[5] See, e.g., Grew Diary, 12 July 1932; FRUS, Japan, 1931–1941, I, 95–8; FRUS, 1932, III, 632; ibid, IV, 149–65, 214; DS 793.94 Commission/180, 292½.

[6] McCoy to Stimson, 22 July 1932, Stimson Papers, box 309; Stimson Diary, 26 September 1932.

[7] FO 371, F5564/1/10; Butler memorandum, 22 July 1932, MacDonald Papers, RM 1/48.

as well as Drummond, were able to read Lytton's own lengthily-expressed conviction that although 'the chaotic condition of China of which Japan complains is largely of her own making', it would be fatal for the rest of the world to try to coerce the wrongdoer:

> The fact is that Japan (has) bitten off more than she can chew and if left alone circumstances will be too strong for her. With a hostile China boycotting her trade, with a hostile and resentful population in Manchuria and continual guerilla warfare, the draining on her resources will be terrific and already her economic position is on the verge of collapse. If resisted, her people will unite and suffer any amount of hardship and privation, but if left alone—disgraced, humiliated, but unchallenged—with no fruits to show for their violence, the liberal opinion in Japan will begin to assert itself and the military party will be criticised for the mess they have got the country into . . . Our only chance is to avoid coercion. Will you [i.e. his sister, Lady Balfour] help to make people realise this at home?[1]

It will be seen below that this sanguine belief of Lytton's—and McCoy broadly shared it[2]—that Japan, if left alone, would suffer and accept the error of her ways, came to be widely held among leading diplomats and politicians in the West. In part it sprang from an understandable failure to appreciate the full nature and extent of political developments in Japan; in part, as with Cecil's earlier belief in the coercive powers of public opinion, it rested upon an assumption that the Japanese and their leaders would eventually react in an idealised Western fashion to the facts of the economic balance sheet and the disapproval of others. It was also a comforting conclusion to be able to draw in a frustrating situation where immediate remedial action appeared to be out of the question. As Verba has observed, 'individuals do not have a clear set of value preferences that exist independently of the situation and can be matched against a variety of alternatives to see which gives the best value outcome. Instead one's values depend in part upon the situation one is facing, and what is attainable in that situation. In actual policy decisions . . . means and ends are not isolated from each other or handled independently'.[3]

During the spring and summer of 1932 the Lytton Commission covered thousands of miles as it sought to establish the background to the crisis and the nature of events since the previous September. In Shanghai they surveyed the ruins of Chapei, but decided not to become involved in the peace talks which were then being prepared;[4] at Shanhaikuan, on the border between China and Manchuria, Lytton observed the makings of another military

[1] Enclosure in Ronald to Drummond, 23 June 1932, DBFP, X, No. 449.

[2] Stimson Diary, 31 December 1932, 14, 18 January 1933. Shortly before his assassination, Baron Dan appears to have urged similar considerations upon his friend McCoy, who broadly accepted them. See also McCoy to Mrs. Reid, 17 June 1932, McCoy Papers, box 29.

[3] S. Verba, 'Assumptions of Rationality and Non-Rationality in Models of the International System', in K. Knorr and S. Verba, (ed.), *The International System* (Princeton, 1961), 110.

[4] DBFP, X, Nos. 91, 111, 113, 115, 124. On meeting the Kuomintang leaders, McCoy wrote to his sisters in a letter of 9 April 1932: 'They are a brilliant lot of revolutionists and Chiang (Kai-shek) much the best of the lot, a Cromwellian character.' McCoy Papers, box 8.

clash.[1] Within the domain of Manchukuo itself, where the authorities allowed Wellington Koo to accompany the Commission only after strenuous protests by Lytton, Drummond and others,[2] the party was spied upon and heaped with false evidence. Messages from frightened Chinese would appear in the hands of hotel staff, and clandestine meetings were arranged to enable opponents of the Japanese to put their case. Despite the watchfulness of his 'advisers', Pu-yi himself managed on one occasion to convey the helplessness of his position, by means of a Chinese member of his staff who spoke in German to Adrianus Pelt in the presence of uncomprehending Japanese officials. Various Japanese attempts to obtain a sight of the Commission's forthcoming conclusions were also foiled—for a time at least, once by Robert Haas's simple strategem of hiding false copies of draft papers in his hotel room, while leaving the genuine copies blatantly and decoy-like in full view.

In Japan the Commission were treated with courtesy, but Uchida was adamant that his country would recognise the new régime in Manchuria and that no outside interference would be tolerated.[3] The final task of drafting was then undertaken in Peking, where Chinese officials appeared to accept that the League was unlikely to be able to force the evacuation of Japanese troops. Despite having to retire to hospital for some weeks with a high fever, Lytton tried to insist that he should absorb the drafts prepared by various experts and then write the whole report himself, but in the event the final document was the work of several hands.[4] At the end of August, with Claudel resisting anything which smacked of a condemnation of Japan, it seemed that unanimity was out of the question, but McCoy, Aldrovandi, and to a lesser extent Schnee[5] helped avert a breakdown. Claudel for his part felt able to report to the Quai d'Orsay that he had succeeded in preventing Lytton from declaring Japan to have been the aggressor on 18 September 1931, and that he and Aldrovandi had inserted a passage to the effect that the Commission's suggestions for the future would remain of value, even if Japan were to recognise Manchukuo. The Report, he believed, was nevertheless more favourable to China than Japan, and he feared that the latter might well leave the League if she were blamed for what had occurred:

> Je dois ajouter que, du point de vue de sa défense nationale, les garanties stratégiques en Mandchourie, qui tiennent tant de place dans les préoccupations japonaises, n'ont été, à mon avis, que très insuffisamment prises en considération dans le rapport.[6]

McCoy, on the other hand, thought that the Japanese 'would be pleased

[1] DBFP, X, No. 401.

[2] Ibid, Nos. 216, 244, 299.

[3] See Lindley to Simon, 13 July 1932, DBFP, X, No. 524; cf. ibid, Nos. 419, 443, 455, 528, 533; Massigli to Quai d'Orsay, 23 July 1932, DDF, I, No. 57; cf. ibid, No. 2.

[4] Haas, for example, wrote one portion, whilst Blakeslee and other advisers had a large hand in others. There is no truth, however, in the suggestion sometimes made that Blakeslee wrote the entire Report himself.

[5] See AA, serial 3088H/D624527–8.

[6] Wilden to Paul-Boncour, 3 September 1932, DDF, I, No. 140.

with the tone of the Report'.[1] As for Lytton, he spent many hours awake during the night of 3–4 September, considering whether to publish separately a reservation to the effect that the artificial and Japanese-controlled nature of Manchukuo deserved greater emphasis; in the morning, however, he signed the Report as it stood, as did his colleagues.[2] He then left for Europe by sea, taking one copy of the document with him, while Haas carried another by a separate route. Pelt took a third on a lengthy and eventful journey through Mukden, Harbin and the Soviet Union. Whilst waiting for transportation through the beleaguered north-west of Manchuria, he was invited to play goalkeeper in a football match between some Japanese soldiers and a group of their new Chinese satraps. The Lytton Report, eagerly awaited by the world's politicians and by all supporters of the League, lay in the goal behind him, sewn into the lining of his raincoat.

The Report of the Lytton Commission was, and remains, a document remarkable for its thoroughness and its attempt to do justice to all parties to the dispute—thus rapidly becoming a cornucopia of comfort to men of many persuasions. Its overriding limitation was the one already referred to: the Western assumption that the disruptive problems of China must be resolved 'by following lines similar to those followed by Japan', and by learning from, rather than resisting, those who had brought the blessings of modern civilisation to her shores.[3] Within this framework (and with emphasis on the current communist menace to orderly government), the Report acknowledged the damage which Japan above all had sustained as a result of the ferment in China; it also set out those Japanese privileges and contributions which had enabled the Manchurian economy to sustain a rapidly increasing population and which gave the case its uniqueness, as well as describing the Kuomintang as 'the real organising, driving, coordinating factor' in Chinese anti-foreign propaganda and the boycotting of Japanese and other goods.[4]

On the other hand, the Commission found that for all their malpractices and inefficiency the Chinese themselves had begun to make a significant contribution to the development of Manchuria, a region whose independence, as declared in the past by Chang Tso-lin, had 'never meant that he or the people of Manchuria wished to be separated from China'.[5] Moreover, they concluded, the operations of the Kwantung Army had been instituted on 18 September 1931 in a way which, whatever individual officers might have thought at the time, 'could not be regarded as measures of legitimate self-defence'; had been guided thereafter 'by essentially political considerations'; and had led to the creation of a régime 'which cannot be considered to have been called into existence by a genuine and spontaneous independence movement'. The Government of Manchukuo, for which 'there is not

---

[1] Johnson to Stimson, 31 August 1932, FRUS, 1932, IV, 219–21.

[2] See DBFP, X, Nos. 631, 654, 712, together with main sources cited at the beginning of the section.

[3] *Lytton Report*, part B, cap. 1.

[4] See, e.g., ibid, 38, 116, 119–20.   [5] Ibid, 28–9.

general Chinese support', thus owed its existence to two factors above all others: 'the presence of Japanese troops and the activities of Japanese officials, both civil and military.'[1] Without these it would not have come into being, and in the interests of all parties it should now be removed. No solution could be found, however, by a mere return to the status quo. Under Chinese sovereignty, therefore, Manchuria should be governed by an auto-nomous régime with 'an adequate number of foreign advisers . . . of whom a substantial proportion should be Japanese'. Japan's economic interests in the area, together with those of the Soviet Union, should be rendered secure, while the powers should assist in the reconstruction of China and the maintenance of her territorial and administrative integrity. In conclusion, it should be remembered that

> the interests of peace are the same the world over. Any loss of confidence in the application of the principles of the Covenant and of the Pact of Paris in any part of the world diminishes the value and efficacy of those principles everywhere.[2]

The contents of the Report became public knowledge on 3 October, nearly ten months after the League's decision to set up a commission of enquiry. At Geneva the Committee of Nineteen had to await the formal observations of the Council on the document, although they took the opportunity to associate themselves with the regret at Japan's recognition of Manchukuo which had already been forcefully expressed by Eamon de Valera, the Council's new chairman.[3] The Japanese delegation were meanwhile seeking a delay until mid-November to enable the Report to be studied before a debate took place,[4] thus adding to the frustration and impatience which was building up in the corridors and cafés of the city. Adrianus Pelt found on his return there was now a greater degree of acceptance among his colleagues of the Secretariat that little hope existed of shifting Japan by means of sanctions, but at least a clear declaration of Japan's guilt was looked for. Arthur Sweetser told Hugh Wilson that the Secretariat wanted to see her expelled from the League altogether.[5]

In the Japanese press the Report was universally condemned.[6] In Western countries, on the other hand, it was accorded widespread praise, with the bulk of the American press hailing it as fair, penetrating, and an indictment of Japan.[7] In Britain *The Times* and others were careful to emphasise that a basis for conciliation had now been provided, and the degree of enthusiasm attained by the *Manchester Guardian* was not common; the L.N.U. resolved that the Report should be accepted as it stood, but added at this stage only that 'the combined weight of world opinion' should be brought to bear in

[1] Ibid, 71, 97, 107–8.

[2] Ibid, 126–37.

[3] LNOJ, *November, 1932* (Geneva, 1932), 1731; DBFP, X, No. 725. Cf. E. Benes, 'The League of Nations: Successes and Failures', in *Foreign Affairs*, October 1932.

[4] See DBFP, X, No. 713.

[5] Disarmament Diary, 24 September 1932, DS 500 A15A4/1469½.

[6] Takeuchi, 399.

[7] See Tupper and McReynolds, 350 ff.; DS 793.94 Commission/433; the press of 3 October 1932, in particular.

order to bring the two contending parties into conference.[1] Much of the
German press was sympathetic towards China; in Italy, however, the event
was almost ignored, while there was little comment in the French press,
individual papers underlining merely those portions of the Report which
proved to their privileged readers the truth of whatever had been revealed
to them for months past.[2]

From the end of the Shanghai fighting up to that moment, Far Eastern
matters had attracted little popular attention in any country. For those
concerned with international affairs, disarmament and reparations had
claimed priority, with the Ottawa Conference also in the running; for the
great majority there continued to be more pressing matters nearer home—
the continuing fight over the budget between Hoover and Congress, for
example, or the arrival in June of thousands of bonus marchers in Washington, from where they were finally removed by tanks and infantry; the selection of Roosevelt over Al Smith for the Democratic ticket, or the agonies
of wet versus dry.[3] Most of the American press, it is true, took notice of
Stimson's 8 August speech, and, with the obvious isolationist exceptions,
expressed cautious approval;[4] in seeming contrast, reports of the British
Government's lack of zeal against Japan were given some prominence
during September.[5] When the American Boycott Association continued its
efforts, however, or Nicholas Murray Butler and others advocated arming
the Kellogg Pact with sanctions, they were completely overshadowed by
those who were determined that no risks of any kind should be run. 'Very
frankly,' wrote the pro-League head of the Scripps–Howard press in a
private letter, 'my interest in the Nine Power Treaty is entirely secondary to
my interest in keeping the United States out of war with Japan.'[6] Earlier, of
course, he had unflinchingly called upon Britain to stand firm behind
Stimson's Borah letter.

There were those like James Shotwell whose concern for world peace was
to find expression in specific proposals concerning Manchuria; the schemes
produced were constructive, civilised—and in practical terms irrelevant.[7]
In Britain as well, the *Manchester Guardian*, while continuing to criticise the
Government's Far Eastern policies, chose to link its demand that the
League should indict the aggressor with the suggestion that, in order to
revive the Disarmament Conference, the major powers should impose upon
themselves 'so large a reduction (in armaments) that Germany could rightly

[1] See Bassett, 262 ff., and the press of 3 October.
[2] See, e.g., DS 793.94 Commission/446, 455, 478, 581. There was no debate on
the Report in the French Chamber.
[3] See, e.g., *Washington Post*, 14, 16, 28, 30 May, 7, 17, 30 June, 1, 11 July 1932;
Lippmann, *Interpretations, 1931–3*, 26 ff.
[4] Tupper and McReynolds, 345 ff.; *New York Times*, 9 August 1932; *Chicago
Daily Tribune*, 29 August 1932; *San Francisco Examiner*, 16 August 1932.
[5] E.g., *New York Times*, 19 September 1932.
[6] Howard to Newton Baker, 17 September 1932, Baker Papers, box 122.
[7] Thus in 1937, Shotwell suggested that the way to success over Manchuria lay
through 'the elimination . . . of questions of prestige', concentration on 'questions
of welfare affecting the peoples in dispute', and 'League forebearance rather than
the forceful assertion of its authority.' *On the Rim of the Abyss*, 256 ff.

be asked to content herself with the recognition of her title to equality, combined with a diminishing disparity in force'. Thus, in East and West alike, 'the supremacy of the moral authority of the League' would be maintained.[1] Again, it was scarcely such as to cause General Araki, Colonel Itagaki and their colleagues much loss of sleep. Similarly when G. P. Gooch at a conference in Geneva deplored Britain's timidity and hailed America's leadership over the Far East, the most he could advocate for the future was resolute non-recognition of Japan's conquests.[2]

In L.N.U. circles, too, confusion continued to accompany a deeply-felt concern. It was not difficult to find individuals whom one could blame for their contribution to the wretchedness of the situation. Cecil and Noel-Baker alike deplored MacDonald's clumsiness and his absurd amour-propre.[3] At Geneva, Noel-Baker was also horrified at the way in which the Secretary General was attempting, as he saw it, to stifle radical criticism of Japan:

'Drummond's share in all this business has been quite lamentable,' he wrote to Cecil at the end of April. 'He is almost as Japanese as the Japanese and has consistently brought pressure to bear on the Chinese to surrender ... and in everything has made himself the spokesman and agent of Simon's policy ... Even his best friends are terribly worried about him. And unfortunately everybody has begun to say that it is because he is financially obliged to try to get an embassy out of Simon next year. I only repeat this because it is common talk and it has distressed me more than anything for a long time.'

Drummond was, indeed, striving, as he wrote to a friend in the Foreign Office, 'to prevent the extreme people here from recrimination or threats which will only stiffen the Japanese and make them more united'. Moreover he had also written to Simon in January stating his intention to resign the Secretary Generalship in 1933, and asking to be considered for 'any suitable appointment' after that event—an unfortunate position in which to place himself as a leading international civil servant with a substantial period of service remaining. On the other hand, there is no reason to believe that Drummond's deep concern for the principles at stake over Manchuria, so forcefully expressed in his correspondence with Avenol during the previous autumn, was not genuine. In addition, one has to return again to the point that he could work only within limits that were largely imposed by the major powers of the League, and that while there may well have been a serious misjudgment involved, it was by no means absurd in those circumstances to seek above all to avoid an outright and irrevocable confrontation with Japan.[4]

It was Simon, however, who was by now becoming the main target for criticism from within the ranks of the L.N.U. During the summer and autumn, even Austen Chamberlain judged the Foreign Secretary to be

[1] *Manchester Guardian*, 26 September 1932; cf. ibid, 30 March, 23 April, 5 May 1932.

[2] *The Problems of Peace* (7th Series), 5 ff. and 256 ff.

[3] Noel-Baker to Cecil, 26 April 1932, Cecil Papers, Add. 51107; Cecil to Murray, 3 October 1932, ibid, Add. 51132.

[4] Noel-Baker to Cecil, 18 March, 30 April, 1932, Cecil Papers, Add. 51107; Drummond to Simon, 7 January 1932, ibid, Add. 51112; Drummond to Ronald, 23 June 1932, FO 800/287.

friendless, '(without) any policy beyond drifting' and thus unable to give clear guidance to British delegates at Geneva, whom Chamberlain found 'ill at ease, hesitating and floundering'.[1] Alternatively, of course, one could indulge in the pastime of criticising each other, and Chamberlain himself now became something of a catalyst in this respect. 'Austen's power for doing nothing amounts to genius,' wrote Cecil privately, and Murray responded that 'the real mischief done by people like (him) is that while saying that public opinion is the only weapon that the League can use, they themselves undermine public opinion'. On his side, Chamberlain remained ready to support Simon's Far Eastern policy in the Commons, ferociously condemning the Union's Secretary for passing on critical branch-resolutions to the Japanese Embassy, and, with Simon's help, fighting those like Cecil who were increasingly attracted to the idea of a League air-force as an instrument of collective security and national disarmament.[2]

There remained as before, however, the question of what could or should be done to defeat Japan. Konni Zilliacus and others still believed that, given guidance, 'the moral force of public opinion . . . (could) operate effectively'; after Stimson's arrival in Geneva, Noel-Baker believed that the Secretary was ready for a withdrawal of ambassadors and was 'already considering economic action as the next step after that'; Cecil declared that Japan's talk of leaving the League was 'pure bluff', though perhaps it would be best if she were expelled. He wished he 'felt free to say exactly what I think', and was troubled, à propos disarmament, by suggestions that the Americans would now wish to retain all their capital ships in order not to weaken themselves against Japan. Murray, faced with Lytton's letter warning against any hint of coercion, accepted privately that their absent colleague's views 'ought largely to determine our policy', but before long he was writing publicly of possible 'diplomatic and economic' measures.[3] It needs to be emphasised that confusion of this kind derived in part—though only in part—from a lack of detailed and up-to-date information. In official circles, on the other hand, where information and advice were floating around in profusion, some clear answers to the Far Eastern dilemma had by now assumed unshakable proportions. As developments in the earlier periods had suggested, they were largely of a negative kind.

[1] Austen to Lady Chamberlain, 6 July, 16 September, 5 October 1932, Austen Chamberlain Papers AC6/1/774–901.

[2] Cecil to Murray, 23 March, Murray to Cecil, 23 March 1932, Murray Papers; Austen Chamberlain to Ida Chamberlain, 29 May, to Hilda Chamberlain, 5 June, to Lord Cranborne, 12 May, to Simon, 30 May, 14 November 1932; Simon to Chamberlain, 24 May 1932, Austen Chamberlain Papers, AC 5/1/569–682 and AC 39/1–6.

[3] Cecil to St. G. Saunders, 23 March, to Noel-Baker, 25, 27 April 1932; Noel-Baker to Cecil, 20, 30 April 1932; Zilliacus to Cecil, 11 May 1932, Cecil Papers, Add. 51100, 51107; Murray to Cecil, 18 June 1932, Murray Papers; *Manchester Guardian*, 9 September 1932.

The shaping of policy: Washington, London and Paris

All three main Western governments and foreign offices were engaged in what was essentially a holding operation over the Far East during the summer of 1932. This common feature did not disguise the continuation of important differences of emphasis, however; nor did it produce a clear harmonising of policies for the crucial stage which lay ahead, following the presentation of the Lytton Report. One of the easier problems, despite the time it absorbed, was the matter of a Shanghai round-table-conference. At Geneva and in the three Western capitals the Japanese lost no opportunity to press their eagerness for such a gathering, which should deal, they suggested, with matters such as boycotting, and which by implication should take the form of a get-together of the extraterritorial powers in order to protect their interests against the unruly Chinese.[1] Not surprisingly, the proposal was loudly supported by British and American citizens living in Shanghai,[2] who in turn were bitterly resented by the Chinese and their Government for this attempt to capitalise on the country's misfortunes. The Nanking régime swiftly made it clear that they would condemn any conference held in their absence, would enter it themselves only if they had agreed the agenda beforehand, and would insist on Manchuria as well as Shanghai being discussed.[3] Moreover Western diplomats on the spot, immersed as they were in the frustrations of the Shanghai peace talks, were firmly opposed to any appearance of seeking to coerce China in this other matter.[4] Even Lindley in Tokyo was moved to acknowledge the strength of Chinese objections,[5] while in the Foreign Office it was regarded as 'unthinkable', in Pratt's words, 'that we should seek to take advantage of Japan's use of force in order to obtain political benefits, either for the International Settlement or for Great Britain'. Hence the need was 'to talk (the proposal) out of the realm of practical politics'.[6]

In short, and in contrast to the situation as it had been seen in February, the immediate threat that Japan was likely to pose if disappointed over this matter was not thought sufficient to outweigh the long-term disadvantages of alienating China. The reaction of the State Department was broadly similar, although, as in London, there was a desire 'to keep the Japanese in play', with Stimson being anxious to miss no opportunity for bringing the two combatants together, perhaps on a Nine Power Treaty basis.[7] In Paris,

[1] See DBFP, X, Nos. 6, 206, 289, 342; FRUS, 1932, IV, 69; DS 793.94, Shanghai Round Table file.

[2] DBFP, X, Nos. 134, 369, 457; FRUS, 1932, III, 622-3, 682; ibid, 1932, IV, 149-65.

[3] See DBFP, X, Nos. 52, 175, 177, 426; DS 793.94/5316.

[4] See, e.g., DBFP, IX, No. 643; ibid, X, Nos. 134, 351; FRUS, 1932, IV, 18-19; DS 793.94/4526.

[5] DBFP, X, Nos. 372, 382.

[6] Pratt to Orde, 10 March 1932, ibid, No. 55; Pratt and Wellesley minutes of 17 and 19 May, 1932, FO 371, F 4184, 4185, 4252/1/10.

[7] See, e.g., Hornbeck memorandum, 16 May 1932, DS 793.94 Shanghai Round Table/11; FRUS, 1932, IV, 16-17, 19-21, 25-8.

too, it was accepted that there could be no conference which excluded China.[1] Following a series of exchanges between themselves, therefore, the three Western powers, together with Italy, gently placed sandbags round the Japanese proposal by suggesting that the scope of the possible conference, which must include China, should be thoroughly discussed through individual Japanese ambassadors in the West.[2]

On this matter, Anglo-American cooperation had held firm. It was also eventually agreed—despite a fondness for the idea on the part of Hornbeck —that a proposal to neutralise Peking and its environs in order to diminish the ill-effects of any Sino-Japanese fighting that might take place south of the Great Wall had better wait upon such an eventuality.[3] On the other hand the entrenchment of the new Manchukuo régime was not a problem of this easier, hypothetical kind. Drastic changes were actually taking place, and to do nothing smacked less of shrewdness than of tacit acquiescence. Even so, the temptation to adopt a passive stance was again a strong one, since there was far more at stake here for both Japan and China than there had been over the proposal for a Shanghai conference. China in particular brought pressure to bear on the West over the matter of customs and salt-revenue seizures, while Japan's determination over the matter was in no way concealed by her disclaimers of responsibility. The details of the lengthy exchanges between Washington and London on this subject can be reduced to a summary of the contrasting positions that were adopted, and which were but extensions of those which had been developed during the fighting in Shanghai. To Stimson, overcoming the inclination of his Far Eastern Division to proceed more quietly, it appeared essential to register publicly 'the unrest of the world in relation to the Chinese Customs, Salt, and Postal Administrations', by means, perhaps, of similar and simultaneous statements by the Western powers. In the Foreign Office, on the other hand (where this last notion was termed 'a fatuous production'), priority was given to private endeavours to maintain the integrity of the Chinese Maritime Customs Administration, whose operational efficiency had been built up by Britons and whose revenues were essential to the Chinese Government. However, just as Stimson on his side was by no means indifferent to Japan's ill-will, so there was a limit to Simon's desire to avoid friction with that country, and when at the end of June Japanese officials were flagrantly involved in Manchukuo's seizure of the Customs at Dairen, it was the British Foreign Secretary who proposed that vigorous representations should be made to Tokyo. The State Department, while still hankering after something 'on the broader basis of the principles involved', happily complied.[4]

This joint move, needless to say, failed entirely to prevent the loss of the Customs to China. Nor did it provide an answer to the underlying question of how to respond to the establishment of Manchukuo as a government and

[1] DBFP, X, No. 365.

[2] Ibid, Nos. 353, 366, 385, 405; FRUS, 1932, IV, 32–3, 69–70.

[3] See DBFP, X, No. 734; FRUS, 1932, IV, 250–3, 280–1; DS 793.94/5476, 5497, 5499, 5586, 5595.

[4] See Stimson Diary, 28 April, 25 June 1932; FRUS, Japan, 1931–1941, I, 89–90; FRUS, 1932, III, 654–5, 660–2; ibid, 1932, IV, 47, 108–10, 115–16; DBFP, X, Nos. 170–525, passim.

to the likelihood of its formal recognition by Japan. From the beginning of the period rumours had been plentiful that Japan would leave the League if she were arraigned over Manchuria, and early in April Tokyo officially warned that, with her national existence at stake, Japan would at least with-draw her delegation from the Assembly if, for example, a time limit were set for the removal of her troops.[1] Before the summer was out Uchida was also emphasising his intention to conform to the wishes of the Army in matters of foreign policy, while by 10 September he had removed any last doubts that recognition of Manchukuo would soon be forthcoming.[2]

Against this background, Western diplomats and commanders in the area were practically unanimous in warning that the Japanese meant what they said and would fight rather than give way. Meanwhile Lampson, who never lost sight of the consequences for China of what was taking place, had at last managed to reach Britain for some leave, where, paradoxically, his advice probably carried less weight than it had done from the other side of the world. By his own account he found everyone except Simon and the King gloomily uninterested in what he had to say:

> 'Frankly,' he wrote back to Nelson Johnson, 'I was amazed at the blank pessimism of it all! The F.O. was like the tomb: everything economic was going to the devil and that was all there was to it! I refused to be infected . . . (but) the really [word unreadable] thing is the complete indifference of everyone towards China and Chinese affairs! No one here cares a twopenny d—n about it.'[3]

Johnson himself continued to exhibit a moody ambivalence towards events. Convinced that there was occurring in China 'a renaissance that will take years to complete its force', and that in Manchuria Japan had 'ruined what might have been a very fine case (by) its initial handling', he nevertheless accepted that the Manchurian issue was 'settled to all intents and purposes', with annexation by Japan as the final outcome. 'Nothing short of superior physical force,' he wrote to a friend, ' . . . or an economic cataclysm in Japan itself is calculated to compel (her) to leave.'[4] He now concluded that the affair 'declared in clarion tones that the world is not yet prepared for the kind of international philosophy upon which some of the modern treaties have been worked out'; therefore, he argued to McCoy and the State Department, the Lytton Commission should avoid creating un-necessary and futile controversy by making specific recommendations—or, if it had to make them, should do so in a form 'which could be filed and forgotten'. At the same time the United States should go out of its way 'to show the Japanese the appreciation which we actually do have of the principal difficulties which they have encountered in Manchuria'.[5] As he admitted to Hornbeck, it was a view similar to that of General Claudel,

[1] DBFP, X, Nos. 143, 147, 161, 162; FRUS, *Japan, 1931–1941*, I, 87–9.

[2] DBFP, X, Nos. 445, 545, 669, 686; FRUS, 1932, IV, 143–8, 240–3; DDF, I, No. 211.

[3] Lampson to Johnson, 30 June 1932, Johnson Papers, box 15.

[4] Johnson to Grew, 7 June, to Hornbeck, 29 June, to Bickel, 29 November 1932, Johnson Papers, box 15; cf. FRUS, 1932, IV, 33.

[5] Johnson memorandum, 25 March; Johnson to Stimson, 22 June, 15 July 1932, FRUS, 1932, III, 631; ibid, 1932, IV, 98–9, 142–3 respectively.

although he preferred to see it acted upon in private rather than in public.[1] Japan should be given 'a helping hand' since 'a broken Japan can be of no service to us ... (and) if she is forced to turn away from us altogether she will so hurt our prestige and position in Asia that some day or other we will feel it necessary to fight in order that that prestige may be re-established'.[2]

This is an interesting thought. Johnson, like Stimson, was in other words beginning to muse on the possibility of a war between Japan and the United States which the latter would feel obliged to enter for reasons going well beyond her immediate material interests or her own direct safety. Yet at the same time Johnson was unable to resolve the conflict within his mind between the advisability of accepting Japan's fait accompli and the need to speak out on behalf of the sanctity of international agreements; between his belief, expressed in the summer of 1931, that the United States need not and should not get herself involved over Manchuria, and the feeling that unless she plunged into Far Eastern politics more decisively, affairs would drift on to disaster. Thus within the space of a single week early in September he wrote of his 'earnest hope that we would not become involved in the situation', and then suggested that America's position 'demands that we take a lead'.[3] The fact that he saw a distinction between the context of Manchuria and that of the Far East as a whole helps to explain, but does not satisfactorily resolve, the contradiction.

Johnson's naval colleague, Admiral Taylor, together with Britain's Admiral Kelly, was likewise convinced that no protests would now shift Japan from her course.[4] The French Minister in Peking, Wilden, was another who agreed. He, too, recalled the sacrifices Japan had had to accept in the past, and dismissed Stimson's declarations as futile; his blunt conclusion was that the task facing Western diplomats now consisted of finding some means of accepting what had been done while at the same time concealing the defeat which was involved.[5] From Tokyo, the new American Ambassador, Joseph Grew, subscribed broadly to the same thesis. Although he approved Stimson's policy—in so far as he could divine what it was—Grew privately expressed 'a good deal of sympathy (for) the Japanese argument of self-defence—not legally but practically ... It was probably their only practical method to get results. I don't blame their utter exasperation with the Chinese'. 'No treaty,' he believed, 'which runs counter to the inexorable facts of history and economic necessity can in any case wholly restrain (Japan's) penetration in Manchuria ... She is there to stay unless conquered in war.' Echoing Hurley, the Ambassador accepted that the United States must 'like it or fight', which he assumed meant 'like it'. Economic

---

[1] Johnson to Hornbeck, 30 August 1932, Johnson Papers, box 15.

[2] Johnson to Hornbeck, 13 September 1932, ibid.

[3] Johnson to Stimson, 1, 7 September 1932, FRUS, 1932, IV, 219–21, 229–31. 'China,' declared Johnson, 'is at present a disorganised country unable to meet the obligations of statehood ...'

[4] Taylor to Pratt, 10 June 1932, Taylor Papers, box 1; Annual Report, C. in C. Asiatic Fleet, July 1932 to June 1933, U.S. Navy Department General Records, FF6/A9–1/30710; Report of Proceedings, C. in C. China, October and November 1932, ADM 125/70.

[5] Wilden to Paul-Boncour, 2 September 1932, DDF, I, No. 139.

sanctions must therefore be ruled out, while 'mere moral ostracism on the part of the nations (would not) materially affect the situation'.

'Nations as such,' he observed in his diary, 'have no conscience if their people believe, rightly or wrongly, that aggression is essential to their self-preservation. The moral disapproval of others may change their conception of what constitutes justifiable aggression, but only if that disapproval threatens to entail social or economic disadvantages or losses of a practical and material nature.'[1]

Grew believed that somehow Japan would manage to stay in the League of Nations; throughout the summer, however, he warned Washington that her people were 'calm and self-confident', ready to face any economic sanctions and solidly behind the Government's Manchurian policies. As the outcry against Stimson's speech of 8 August sounded around him, he went so far as to recall the war psychology that had been fostered in Germany before August 1914.[2]

Like many other Western observers, and encouraged in this by Shidehara, Grew could console himself with the thought that the pendulum of Japanese politics was bound to swing back eventually 'to a normal position'.[3] Lindley travelled even further along this attractive road, believing that if the Manchurian issue could be got out of the way then 'the ultra-patriotic fervour from which we are suffering might well die down rapidly and be replaced by the sweet reason of disillusion'.[4] Early in May he had 'no reason to doubt that . . . the progress of the Fascist movement in this country . . . is on the wane',[5] and even managed to construe the unease he saw at the murder of Inukai as going 'some way to allay fears of unlimited Japanese aggression', with the militarists now 'on the defensive'.[6] 'It is impossible,' he wrote, 'for those living in Japan to subscribe to the belief that these people are fundamentally militaristic'.[7] If opposed or condemned over Manchuria, however, they would rise as one man against anyone who sought to stand in their way; ultra-nationalism would triumph; Britain would lose a bulwark against disorder in the Far East. Swiping at the naïve follies of Reading and Cecil, and also, privately, at Lampson's short-sighted encouragement of China to rely upon the League, Lindley poured out his warnings to the Foreign Office and to the King as before.[8]

[1] Grew Diary, 28 September 1932; FRUS, *Japan, 1931–1941*, I, 99, 102; FRUS, Grew's Counsellor, Neville, returned from leave in China at this time, delighted to be back in 'the orderliness and refreshingness of Japan' after that 'cesspool'. Ibid, 3 November 1932.

[2] Grew Diary, 28 September 1932; FRUS, *Japan, 1931–1941*, I, 99, 102; FRUS, 1932, IV, 76–8, 132–3, 240–3.

[3] Grew Diary, 24 October 1932.

[4] Lindley to Simon, 1 April 1932, DBFP, X, No. 163.

[5] Lindley to Simon, 12 May 1932, ibid, No. 336.

[6] Lindley to Simon, 26 May 1932, ibid, No. 374.

[7] Lindley to Simon, 30 August 1932, ibid, No. 639.

[8] DBFP, X, Nos. 63, 79, 102, 125, 162, 357, 462, 736; Lindley to King George V, 7 July 1932, RA G.V, P510/52; Lindley to Wellesley, 14 April 1932, FO 371, F4190/3163/10. Pratt minuted on this last document: 'This letter does not add to one's confidence in Sir F. Lindley's judgement. The criticisms of Sir M. Lampson are particularly ill-founded.'

There were some who continued to place the emphasis of their advice elsewhere. Cecil, for example. who in the autumn was once more a delegate to the League, raised the possibility of 'moral pressure, such as excluding Japan from the League or withdrawing Ambassadors'.[1] Above all, Stimson was again pressing for a firm public condemnation of Japan's breaches of international morality, and at Geneva in April conveyed what Simon described as his disappointment that Britain had hitherto 'not been ... sufficiently strenuous' in this respect.[2] Thereafter he sought to furnish London with further proof of Japan's guilt, and, as the delivery of the Lytton Report drew near, emphasised his concern that Britain should ensure for it a clear and bold reception within the League.[3] But would the United States herself undertake any more than she had in the past? In London, the answer appeared to be a decided negative. Reports might arrive that the U.S. Navy looked to an eventual war with Japan, but so, too, did ones which confirmed that the American press and public thought only of peace.[4] Castle's speeches were also carefully noted, as was his closeness to Hoover, while Lindsay's own conviction remained that nothing in the nature of sanctions could be expected.[5] Lindley passed on similar information from Grew, and even Stimson himself, when put in a corner by Simon during their Geneva talks, admitted that 'nothing beyond protest could be done'.[6] On a report of one of the Secretary's later messages of exhortation, in which he had nevertheless confessed that the election campaign 'inevitably imposed a kind of moratorium on action in international affairs', Pratt minuted: 'This seems to confirm our belief that Mr. Stimson does not propose to take a particularly strong line.' Simon obtained the same impression from Senator Reed when the latter visited Downing Street in September.[7]

Most Foreign Office officials thus felt all the more free to concentrate on what Pratt described as 'the realities of the situation in the Far East and not solely juridicial considerations'.[8] In this vein the same writer had already observed that Japan 'was going to succeed in Manchuria as she has ... in Korea'. 'It is good for the world at large,' he added, 'that (she) should succeed in her Manchurian programme—now that she has definitely embarked on it', and he also kept open the possibility of Britain's recognising Manchukuo should the latter 'definitely establish its independence'. Japan, he

---

[1] Cecil to Foreign Office, 12 October 1932, DBFP, X, No. 745.

[2] Simon to MacDonald, 16 April 1932, ibid, No. 228.

[3] See ibid, Nos. 409, 664, 697, 710; FRUS, 1932, IV, 44, 228.

[4] DBFP, X, Nos. 157, 361. In connection with the U.S. Navy's desire to prepare for war, unofficial hints were transmitted via Lindsay concerning the possibility of certain British naval bases being exchanged for debt cancellation. The Foreign Office dismissed the idea as one that was not taken seriously in either country, but as seen above, 117, n. Castle himself had had a hand in it not long before.

[5] Brand to Simon, 17 May 1932, FO 800/286; Lindsay to Simon, 23 March, 6 April 1932, DBFP, X, Nos. 132, 179.

[6] DBFP, X, Nos. 228, 448.

[7] Pratt minute, 2 September 1932, FO 371, F 6828/1/10; Simon minute, 17 September 1932, DBFP, X, No. 674, note.

[8] Minute of 3 October 1932, FO 371, F 7103/1/10.

believed, 'did not want to break with the West if she could avoid it'; therefore she should be given no cause for doing so.[1] Vansittart, Wellesley and Eden agreed. Eden wrote: 'We, with vital interests at stake, must continue to moderate the zeal of those who have none.'[2]

In public, therefore (as distinct from private exhortations against such a step), there would be no denunciation of Japan if she recognised Manchukuo.[3] Even so, Simon and Vansittart in particular recognised that a Far Eastern policy dictated solely by self-interest was, in the latter's words, 'not at this time a practicable one'.[4] Legal opinion within the Foreign Office was that Japan's recognition of the new régime did amount to a breach of the Nine Power Treaty, and Vansittart accepted that in the circumstances it was 'inconceivable both on the grounds of obligation and expediency' that Britain should follow suit 'in any visible future'.[5] Simon above all, the overriding dangers of the Shanghai period behind him, intelligently sought once more to bear in mind a number of desiderata:

> 'Let us try to keep in touch and in line with the U.S. while pursuing the policy indicated,' he minuted. 'For ourselves, the controlling considerations must be (1) be faithful to the League and act with the main body if possible (2) do not take the lead in an attitude which, while necessarily futile, will antagonise Japan seriously (3) be fair to both China and Japan (4) work to keep Japan in the League.'[6]

There can be no doubt that the Foreign Secretary was being sincere when he wrote to Cecil in June of the need for 'a judicious mixture of the new League methods and "the old diplomacy"', although such a course was not calculated to win him friends in either camp.[7]

Simon maintained his intention to 'be fair to China', despite pressure in an opposite direction from another part of Whitehall. This was not the Dominions Office—again, those countries were being informed rather than consulted[8]—but Sir Samuel Hoare's India Office. Hoare wrote to Simon in September to suggest that the bulk of the British public would not tolerate any hostility towards Japan, and also to declare that he himself shared the Aga Khan's suspicions regarding 'a so-called democratic China'.[9] At the same time, and during the following months, Hoare was pressing for diplomatic support and if necessary increased arms supplies to be given to the Dalai Lama to enable him to resist any encroachment by China on his

[1] Minutes of 26 May, 30 May, 31 March, 28 September 1932, respectively FO 371, F 4235, 4432, 2886/1/10 and DBFP, X, No. 619, note.

[2] Minutes of 27 August and 28 September 1932, DBFP, X, No. 545, note. Cf. ibid, No. 745, note.

[3] See, e.g., ibid, Nos. 677, 703.

[4] Minute of 5 October 1932, FO 371, F 7103/1/10.

[5] Memoranda by Becket, 28 September, and Orde, 30 September; minute by Vansittart, 5 October 1932, DBFP, X, Nos. 719, 724.

[6] Minutes of 7 October and 17 September 1932, respectively FO 371, F 7103/1/10; DBFP, X, No. 674, note.

[7] Simon to Cecil, June 1932, FO 800/287.

[8] See, e.g., DBFP, X, No. 626.

[9] Hoare to Simon, 11 September; Aga Khan to Hoare, 6 September 1932, FO 800/287.

authority in Tibet proper, and also to preserve his rights in Inner Tibet. As a Foreign Office official noted, 'the Government of India are very naturally anxious to make as full use as possible of an opportunity of strengthening their position (in Tibet)', their main aim being to exclude any external influence that might create trouble on the Indian frontier.[1] Indeed, there were those in the Foreign Office itself who showed scant sympathy for China's claims in the area, or for her alarm at reports of British arms supplies and of the presence in Tibet of 'a certain Colonel Lawrence' who was said to be on a secret mission for the Government of India.[2] In Vansittart's opinion the Chinese were hypocritically infringing in Tibet principles of the very kind that they cried out to be upheld in Manchuria, while the Head of the Far Eastern Department believed that the interests of Britain and India in the region outweighed any disadvantages that might arise from Chinese displeasure.[3]

Others saw the matter less simply, however, and Vansittart's chosen parallel was not the only one that was proffered. Earlier in the year, for example, Wellesley had accepted that the difference between Japan's position in Manchuria and Britain's in Tibet was one only 'of degree'; even this view, however, did not remove the consideration that was pointed out by another official in October, that 'theoretically the Chinese, as Suzerain Power, have more right to intervene in Tibet than we have'.[4] Might not Britain's critics at Geneva seize upon this as the reason—false though it was —for her not denouncing Japan? The point was taken, in some measure at least, and as the Tibetan issue dragged on into the spring of 1933 the Foreign Office, with Lampson's encouragement, declined to press China to negotiate, as the India Office desired.[5] Moreover, while the image of China which was held by Hoare and those like him undeniably contributed to the setting of British Far Eastern policy, there appears to have been no conscious linking of the Manchurian issue with Indian matters by the remainder of the Cabinet during this period. Even implications that such a connection existed (as suggested at the time by Arnold Toynbee[6]) are hard to come by in the official and private correspondence of Baldwin, MacDonald and others who were struggling to find a way through the communal and constitutional deadlock with India. The same holds true of Simon, whose past services had given him a special interest in the subject,[7] while in response to Hoare's

[1] India Office to Foreign Office, 1 August, 16, 21 September 1932, FO 371, F6172, 6831, 6884/7/10; Government of India to Foreign Office, 14 February, 1933, ibid, F 1064/16/10.

[2] 'Colonel Lawrence' was, in fact, Lt. Col. J. L. Weir, Political Officer in Sikkim, who had been invited to Tibet by the Dalai Lama. See FO 371, F 6133/7/10, F 1356/16/10.

[3] See FO 371, F 6884, 7440, 7513/7/10. On Chinese anxieties and the shaping of Britain's response, see DBFP, X, Nos. 605, 606, 613, 648, 714, 717, 720, 729, 738, 739.

[4] DBFP, IX, No. 635; Mallett minute, 21 October 1932, FO 371, F7441/7/10.

[5] See, e.g., FO 371, F 865 and 1661/16/10.

[6] Toynbee, *Survey, 1931*, 39; *Survey, 1932*, 523-4.

[7] See, e.g., the discussions of the Cabinet Committee on India, CAB 27/520; the discussions of the Cabinet itself on 15 June 1932, CAB 23/71; MacDonald correspondence on India in RM 1/109 and 2/25; Simon's correspondence on India from

submission concerning British opinion and the Far East the Foreign Secretary recalled that there was also a substantial section of the public, epitomised by the L.N.U., who were indignant at what Japan had done. 'I am sure you will agree with me,' he added, 'that we must avoid getting into a position of antagonism and keep in the middle of the road'.[1]

This attempt of Simon and his officials to balance between Japan and China was made all the easier in their eyes by the wide-ranging content and emphasis of the Lytton Report itself (not that this was thought likely to commend the document in Tokyo).[2] Like the *Manchester Guardian* or *Journal de Genève*, one could select from it evidence to reinforce one's existing image of the situation, and for Pratt, speaking for many of his colleagues, this meant that 'though it may be difficult to defend the methods employed by Japan . . . if one looks to the substance below the surface, the balance of right inclines to her side'. The key passage of the Report, he believed, was the one which declared that this was no simple case of one country violating the frontiers of another; this in turn should 'very considerably modify' the application of the non-recognition principle, and must remove all grounds 'for treating Japan as the criminal in the dock. There can be no question of sanctions or of driving Japan from the League'.[3] Beyond this, the Report also provided that 'breathing space' which was desired by everyone—even Lampson, whose interpretation of the document diverged from that of Pratt.[4] 'It is more than admirable,' wrote Vansittart, '—it is useful, for it provides us with a position at Geneva that is relatively comfortable compared with that which we have hitherto had to occupy. Its main desiderata—reconstruction and reconciliation—will take, and give, time.'[5]

This cautious line which the Foreign Office intended to follow was fully appreciated in Paris.[6] So, too, was the Japanese desire to forestall any possibility of a strong Western alignment against them, for between July and the publication of the Report they made a determined effort to reach a secret understanding with France. General Koiso, the Vice-Minister of War, began the play on 8 July, when he approached de Martel, the French Ambassador in Tokyo, with talk of Japan's need for loans and of the common interest of their two countries in ensuring stability in the Far East. Colonel Kobayashi, military adviser to the Japanese delegation at Geneva, followed this up the next day by suggesting to Massigli that military circles in Tokyo were keen for a rapprochement which would also give France certain obvious benefits: 'Il donnerait à la France une garantie contre la Russie; il assurerait la sécurité de l'Indochine . . .' Massigli stalled politely and returned no encouragement to the suggestion that General Claudel might be sent instructions to favour Japan in his work for the League

March to August 1932, Simon Papers (private collection), Personal Correspondence, 1932; Hoare's India correspondence, Templewood Papers.
[1] Simon to Hoare, 13 September 1932, FO 800/287.
[2] See DBFP, X, Nos. 720, 730; FO 371, F 7243/1/10.
[3] Pratt memorandum, 10 October 1932, FO 371, F 7304/1/10; cf. DBFP, X, No. 746.
[4] Lampson to Pratt, 15 October 1932, FO 371, F 7573/1/10.
[5] Minute of 2 November 1932, ibid, F 7127/1/10; cf. DBFP, X, No. 713.
[6] See DDF, I, Nos. 106, 121.

Commission.[1] Koiso nevertheless returned to the charge with a distinctly interested de Martel soon afterwards, and Matsuoka Yosuke, on tour in Manchuria, did the same with the French Consul in Harbin.[2] Finally, Araki himself took a hand in a carefully recorded conversation with Admiral Berthelot, the French C. in C. in the Far East, on board the cruiser *Amiral Primauguet* at Tokyo on 6 September. French opinion, as epitomised by General Claudel, had exactly understood Japan's problems, said the War Minister. Together, the two countries could further both their own interests and the cause of world peace.[3]

The existence of these approaches was not revealed to the Americans until October, although Stimson and his officials had long before shown their concern at rumours that something was afoot.[4] Both Berthelot of the Quai d'Orsay and Herriot, Prime Minister since mid-Summer, went out of their way to reassure Washington that France would not weaken the front—such as it was—against Japan,[5] and in private the Japanese had, indeed, been turned away. Both Martel and the very differently inclined Massigli were left in no doubt as to the position regarding the advances they were receiving: 'Inacceptable; éludez toute réponse.' France's continuing desire for friendship with Japan could be emphasised, although their special Far Eastern agreement of 1907 was held to have lapsed in various respects;[6] where the French position concerning the League and the Nine Power Treaty was concerned, however, there must be no ambiguity.[7] The opinion of the Quai d'Orsay was that to recognise Manchukuo would be to offend against the Covenant and Washington treaties and to act against the interests of France,[8] and Herriot unhesitatingly agreed. Japan should be given time to study the Lytton Report if she wanted it, but on the principles at issue France would stand firm. This did not mean that she would take the lead, however, any more than would Britain.[9]

One particular query to arrive in Paris from Tokyo had concerned the Soviet Union: what did Herriot think of a possible Soviet-Japanese non-aggression pact, towards which Matsudaira, for one, was favourably inclined? Herriot privately noted that such a pact would increase Soviet freedom of action in Europe, as well as that of Japan in China; he therefore suggested that the observation should be let drop in passing that the advantages were more apparent for the Soviet Union than they were for

[1] Massigli to Paul-Boncour, 9 July, 1932, DDF, I, No. 3, and notes.
[2] Martel to Paul-Boncour, 19 July; Reynau to Paul-Boncour, 8 August 1932, ibid, Nos. 37, 93; Martel to Paul-Boncour, 8 July 1932, AQD, T 352–355.
[3] Berthelot procès-verbal, 6 September 1932, DDF, I, No. 148.
[4] See FRUS, 1932, IV, 67–9, 71–2, 215–19, 234–5, 295–6.
[5] Ibid, 239–40; DS 793.94/5563; Stimson Diary, 15 April 1932.
[6] See Paul-Boncour to Wilden, 10 October 1932, AQD, T181–2: 'La note secrète concernant le Foukien a été expressément considérée par les deux Gouvernements comme ayant pris fin. Quant au projet d'engagement portant désintéressement respectif au Yunnan et au Foukien, ébauché en 1917, il n'a jamais été réalisé. Aucun de ces documents ne concernait d'ailleurs Mandchourie, ni Mongolie.'
[7] DDF, I, Nos. 3, 8.
[8] Note by the Direction Politique, 11 September 1932, ibid, No. 168.
[9] See FRUS, 1932, IV, 295–6; DS 793.94/5563.

Japan.[1] Yet Herriot was now moving towards the conclusion of his own non-aggression pact with Moscow which was signed on 29 November,[2] while Stimson's eyes, too, like those of the Chinese leaders, were turning in the same direction. If the United States accorded recognition to the Soviet Union, reasoned the Secretary, she might thereby forestall a possible Soviet-Japanese pact or Moscow's own recognition of Manchukuo. The mighty Borah, who had long advocated such a step in the face of howls from the Daughters of the American Revolution and other such defenders of the faith, urged Stimson on. In the end the latter dropped the idea, however. He knew that Hoover and Castle were strongly opposed to any such move, and he also decided that it would smack unduly of expediency, thus forfeiting the 'moral standing' that the United States had obtained over the Far Eastern dispute.[3]

This was only one of the lesser problems that were troubling Stimson that summer. He was far more disturbed by the 'lunatics' in Congress who were calling for the Philippines' independence and thus, as he saw it, 'playing ducks and drakes with our Japanese policy'.[4] The British attitude was equally distressing. True, MacDonald, Simon and the rest had all reassured him that they agreed with his policies when he had met them in Geneva, where, after an impatient glance at the laborious proceedings of the Disarmament Conference, he had directed affairs from a luxurious villa overlooking the lake ('I sent for Simon . . . ,' he noted on 19 April.)[5] Later, however, there was mounting evidence that neither the Foreign Office nor the Cabinet intended taking any risks with Japanese opinion. 'The role I think they would like to play,' wrote Atherton at the end of August, 'is that of "honest broker" between Japan and the League, and Japan and the United States. In the Cabinet the only friendly feeling in general to the United States one can count on (and I do not except Simon) is the varying influence of the Prime Minister.' And even MacDonald, in an interview in which he had faced Atherton with some uncomfortable questions concerning what measures the United States might be expected to take, had left no doubt as to his intention to avoid the merest whisper of sanctions.[6]

Stimson found representatives of the Dominions more cheering, and there was indeed much concern in Australia and New Zealand, as well as in the obvious case of Canada, to maintain good relations with the United States.

[1] See DDF, I, Nos. 171, 182, 210, 270.

[2] See ibid, II, No. 48; Herriot, *Jadis*, vol. 2, 354; Duroselle, 223 ff.

[3] Castle Diary, 7 September 1932, cited in Current, *Secretary Stimson*, 110; Borah to Stimson, 25 August 1932, Borah Papers, box 332 (and material in ibid, boxes 339, 352); Stimson to Borah, 8 September 1932, Stimson Papers, box 310.

[4] Stimson Diary, 6 April 1932. Cf. Johnson to Castle, 14 April 1932, Castle Papers, China.

[5] Stimson Diary, 16, 21, 25 April 1932; cf. FRUS, 1932, III, 734–5, and Klots to Hornbeck, 24 April 1932, Hornbeck Papers, box 267.

[6] Atherton to Castle, 30 August (seen by Stimson, 9 September), 1932, Castle Papers, England; Atherton to Stimson, 4 April 1932, FRUS, 1932, III, 664–6; Stimson Diary, 29 March 1932. Cf. FRUS, 1932, IV, 206, 244–5; DS 793.94 Commission/315. Hornbeck believed that there existed a group of financial and industrial leaders in Britain who 'gave direction to her foreign policy'. DS 793.94/5579.

As will be seen later, however, even Canada was not yet prepared to fly in the face of her own inclinations, as well as those of Britain, in order to achieve a complete alignment with the U.S.A. in public, and Stimson was naïvely optimistic in his assessment of the situation. One trivial incident can serve as an illustration. When he was in Geneva, the Secretary had retailed his difficulties and differences with the Foreign Office to two Dominions representatives whose profound sympathy over this matter he found 'refreshing, like the traditional British Dominion attitude towards the United States, and bucked me up a good deal. It was like talking to your own country [sic]'.[1] In the case of one listener, South Africa's Te Water, the sympathy was genuine. His companion, however, was Sir Thomas Wilford, New Zealand's High Commissioner in London, who was privately to reveal his actual views on the situation to Wellesley some months later:

> He was most strongly convinced that it was to the interest of not only New Zealand but of the Empire as a whole to back Japan in the present dispute with China . . . (because) Japan was the strongest Power in the Far East and constituted . . . a grave military menace to the security of Australia and New Zealand (and because) Japan was our chief bulwark against what was possibly the principal danger to the world at the present time—namely the spread of communism.[2]

Meanwhile, Stimson was delighted above all with the morally sound attitude of the smaller states at Geneva. Drummond, too, impressed him, although the latter bemoaned the difficulties that were being created by League enthusiasts, 'our unwise friends'. There was agreement all round, however, that further action must await the presentation of the Lytton Report,[3] and the Secretary returned home to prepare to back up the League when the time came; with Hoover's approval, he also briefed his friend, Senator David Reed, so that the latter could help stiffen the line being taken at Geneva when he was there in the autumn.[4] In addition he obtained Hoover's agreement to the lengthening of the Scouting Fleet's stay in the Pacific,[5] but this bluff had already been rendered transparent by those no-sanctions speeches of William Castle, which a somewhat nervous Hoover confessed he had authorised in order to forestall any possible Japanese attack on American ships or possessions.[6] There remained the idea which took shape in Stimson's mind during the summer as he talked to Borah,

[1] Stimson Diary, 19 April 1932.

[2] Wellesley memorandum, 28 November 1932, DBFP, XI, No. 77. It must be emphasised that Wilford was not speaking for his Government nor for those elements in New Zealand politics who were shortly to direct their country's policies—over Abyssinia, for example, towards a staunch defence of the League.

[3] Stimson Diary, 16 April 1932; FRUS, 1932, III, 734–5: ibid, 1932, IV, 122–3; DS 793.94/5525½. Cf. Stimson, *Far Eastern Crisis*, 199 ff.

[4] Stimson Diary, 15 July, 11 August 1932; FRUS, 1932, IV, 180–2; DS 793.94 Commission/334A. Cf. Hornbeck's views in DS 793.94/4943.

[5] Stimson Diary, 19, 20 May 1932; Adams to Taylor, 20 May 1932, Taylor Papers, box 1. For a Japanese reaction, see FRUS, 1932, IV, 197–8.

[6] Stimson Diary, 3 April, 16, 19 May 1932; Moffat Diary, 4 May 1932; Castle Diary, 2, 15 May, 23 June 1932, cited in Current, 'The Stimson Doctrine'; Hoover, *Memoirs, 1920–1933*, 376; cf. Grew Diary, April 1932.

Shotwell and others, of making a speech that would proclaim America's international commitment through the Kellogg Pact, and thus 'rally the European countries round the Pact so that when the issue with Japan comes up they will support us intelligently on this central element'.[1]

Once again, however, Hoover set limits to what could be done. Rejecting some of the key passages of the draft speech which Stimson had submitted to him, the President insisted (in his particular brand of English):

> If there is no chance under the Kellogg–Briand Pact to clash with the League of Nations, it means there must be commitment upon our part not to clash with any action in force which they might impose. I cannot believe that we should pledge the American Government to such policies . . . I am intensely sorry that I cannot agree on this point.[2]

'The President has been an enormously stabilising influence,' wrote Castle later. 'He has probably more clearly seen the danger [over Japan] than anyone, and has prevented things coming out of the State Department which might have been so irritating as to be disastrous.'[3] On his side, Stimson was appalled at what he took to be Hoover's obsequiousness towards the Hearst press, and was unreceptive to the desire of his now desperately-campaigning leader that he should weigh in with some speeches attacking Roosevelt. Already, in July, the two men had acknowledged that they were 'very far apart' over foreign policy as a whole,[4] and Stimson was becoming an increasingly isolated figure within the Administration generally. When the Lytton Report arrived, the absorbed silence which descended upon the second floor of the State Department was followed by delighted enthusiasm on the Secretary's part (Castle, too, approved of the Report, though he saw it through different and more Pratt-like eyes). When Stimson eagerly read out portions of the document to the Cabinet, however, 'they did not take any great interest'.[5]

Nevertheless, as in earlier stages of the crisis, Stimson's restless inclination to go beyond the limits set by the President should not be allowed to

[1] Stimson Diary, 5, 11 June, 14, 20, 25 July 1932. An early draft of the speech can be found in box 304 of the Stimson Papers.

[2] Hoover to Stimson, 28 July 1932, Stimson Papers, box 309; cf. Stimson Diary, 27, 28 July 1932; Castle Diary, 20 August 1932, cited in Current, *Secretary Stimson*, 109. Hoover was objecting to a draft passage which referred to possible League moves against an aggressor, and in which Stimson proposed to say: 'Under such circumstances no American Government of whatever party would undertake to hamper the efforts of the League to preserve peace; on the contrary every consideration would urge it to follow the precedent of cooperation just as it was established last autumn . . . [Between the actions of the League and the obligations of the U.S.A. under the Kellogg Pact] a clash could not conceivably arise.'

[3] Castle to Johnson, 21 December 1932, Johnson Papers, box 15.

[4] Stimson Diary, 12 July, 6, 9 September 1932.

[5] Ibid, 26 September, 3 October 1932; Moffat Diary, 3 October 1932; Castle Diary, 5 October 1932, cited in Current *Secretary Stimson*, 111; FRUS, 1932, IV, 287. Stimson was nettled by an article of Lippmann's which suggested that there might be some conflict between the Report's recommendations and America's nonrecognition policy. See Stimson Diary, 5 October 1932; Stimson to Lippmann, 4 October, and Lippmann to Stimson, 12 October 1932, Stimson Papers, box 311.

obscure those other limits within which he himself was content to operate. When seeing Debuchi after his speech of 8 August, for example, he took care to protest that he had no desire to annoy Japan or to question her rights in Manchuria, while he instructed Wilson in Geneva to discourage all idea of American leadership being available in the forthcoming confrontation over the Lytton Report.[1] Even allowing for the particular views of the writer, there remained a basic truth in Castle's explanation to Wilson of why the Secretary was anxious to see the League condemn Japan without help from Washington:

'Of course,' wrote Castle, 'his reason is that he does not want the United States to be put in a position where Japan will blame us for opposing their ambitions, at the same time feeling that the rest of the world might have been friendly.'[2]

Nor did Stimson's concern for China produce much in the way of tangible assistance for that country. According to Castle again, his inability in this respect distressed the Secretary,[3] but it was always as an ideal, rather than as a living body of people, that China excited Stimson's enthusiasm. When Nanking asked for surplus American military supplies, they were turned away; when they sought a team of American aviation experts (Britain was prepared to send such a mission), McCoy and the State Department hastened to have the idea ruled out on the grounds that it would probably provoke Japan.[4] The Chinese were likewise told that no loans could be provided, were given advice that amounted to 'grin and bear it', and were reminded not to infringe any of their treaty obligations.[5] Their suggestions that Washington might call a Nine Power Treaty conference were also turned down, and although Stimson and Hornbeck did have such a move in mind should the Lytton Report not bring Tokyo to reason, the Secretary had already had to admit to Simon that a conference would have to await the moment 'when Japan does get ready to talk'.[6] Chinese régimes of whatever hue have seldom had reason to place strong faith in the United States, and Stimson's period of office was no exception. The blunt Foreign Office view that practical foreign aid for China must await her achievement of stable government may have been harsh and was certainly not irrefutable, but it stopped short of hypocrisy.[7]

China, then, would receive no practical assistance from the governments of the West. Any discomfort this might have caused in London, Paris or Washington was minimised, however, just as inactivity against Japan could

---

[1] FRUS, *Japan, 1931–1941*, I, 100–2; FRUS, 1932, IV, 271–2.

[2] Castle to Wilson, 15 August 1932, Castle Papers, Switzerland. Of course Stimson was also anxious to get Britain to speak out, and he always had Hoover's restricted approval in mind. Throughout the crisis, however, his own instinct was for the 'deus ex machina' role which was noted in an earlier chapter.

[3] Castle Diary, 14 July 1932, cited in Rappaport, 167.

[4] See FRUS, 1932, III, 643, 668–9, 680; ibid, 1932, IV, 55–6; DBFP, X, Nos. 400, 610, 732.

[5] FRUS, 1932, IV, 165–9.

[6] Stimson Diary, 28 April, 20 July 1932; DS 793.94/5603; FRUS, 1932, IV, 232–4.

[7] See DBFP, X, Nos. 205, 527 and notes, 530.

be partially justified, by a growing acceptance of the belief which has already been noted in the minds of the Lytton Commission and many Western diplomats in the Far East, that the Japanese would fall upon hard times as a result of their wrong-doing. Within the Quai d'Orsay it was observed that with her finances burdened by galloping inflation and her exports crippled by the Chinese boycott, Japan's position was already gravely compromised.[1] In the Foreign Office, a few mental gymnastics were required before the same stance could be adopted—images involving a Manchurian population hostile to Japan and a Manchurian drain on Japanese finances had to replace those previously held, of a people welcoming the bringers of stability and a land whose possession was essential to the well-being of the Japanese economy—but the comfort of the new position was too attractive to resist (no doubt fresh evidence also played its part), and Pratt and Wellesley duly slipped into it. Eden and Simon appear to have followed along.[2] For the benefit of L.N.U. members and, perhaps, of his own peace of mind, Gilbert Murray was also publicly declaring that 'the collapse of Japan's policy was inevitable'.[3] Meanwhile Stimson's economic advisers had been telling him for some time that Manchuria would not provide the benefits Japan was looking for (Hornbeck, like Wellesley, saw economic motives as being at the bottom of it all), and that Tokyo's financial difficulties would increase. Unlike more prosaic minds in the Foreign Office, the Secretary also believed that 'world opinion' would continue to exert strong pressure in the same direction; together with China's own resistance, these factors 'would make it almost imperative that (Japan) should listen to reason'. Like his friends across the Atlantic, therefore, he could fall back on the belief that time was on his side.[4] Scarcely anyone suggested that if Japan were, indeed, eventually driven into a corner economically, she might strike out in other directions rather than submit.

Retrospect

By its recognition of Manchukuo, the Japanese Government had set the seal on the compromise solution to the Manchurian problem which the Kwantung Army and General Staff in Tokyo had eventually agreed upon in the late autumn of 1931. With the publication of the Lytton Report, on the other hand, the League, and above all its leading Western members, was brought to the point where the requirements of the Covenant made it impossible to delay a pronouncement much longer in the hope that the dilemma would be resolved in some other way. The Report itself was, inevitably, something of a compromise, but within its own framework of Western standards and assumptions it was both thorough and fair. Its con-

[1] DDF, I, No. 168; cf. ibid, No. 309. The new belief also made it easier to accept the now clear signs that Western commercial interests in Manchuria were going to suffer under the new régime.

[2] See, e.g., DBFP, X, No. 508, note, and the minutes on FO 371, F 4235, 4236, 5030, 5542, 5564/1/10. Cf. DBFP, X, Nos. 380, 531, 581, 623, 629.

[3] Manchester Guardian, 9 September 1932.

[4] Stimson Diary, 14 March, 28 April 1932; Stimson to Reed, 11 August 1932, Stimson Papers, box 309; DS 793.94/5567. Cf. DS 693/326.

structive proposals for a settlement were likewise earnest and well-intentioned; yet like those of various individual commentators, they bore scant relation to the aims and force of Chinese nationalism, and none at all to the self-confident beliefs of those who were now directing Japanese policy. Meanwhile American and British policy-makers underlined again what they could and would not do to affect the outcome of the crisis, to their increasing mutual distrust, even though the French attitude was being given at least a greater appearance of firmness by Herriot.

Where the Far Eastern problem was concerned, the passage of time was now generally thought likely to produce its own effortless solution. In other matters, however, it appeared to be working against both the separate interests and mutual understanding of the United States, Britain and France. In addition, it was impossible entirely to divorce these other issues from Far Eastern affairs, or vice versa. During the summer and autumn of 1932, all were woven into the complex and shifting pattern that constituted the triangular relationship among the three countries. It is time, therefore, to pick up this relationship where it was left at the end of chapter four, and to observe how, in the new situation, many of those concerned were being forced to reconsider the very nature of the League and collective security, together with the price to be paid in the search for peace.

CHAPTER NINE

THE WEST IN DISARRAY

Disarmament, reparations and debts: public manoeuvres in the West

BEFORE examining the painful formulation of British, French and American policies over these issues, and above all the complications that were introduced by the Far Eastern crisis, a brief outline of developments as seen by the public may help to establish some landmarks in what was and remains a confusing scene. Since any outline of this kind is inevitably shaped to some degree by the views that its writer has already formed on the subject, one general opinion should also, perhaps, be stated at the outset. It is that amidst the confusion of 1932, the questions being posed and answers attempted by those responsible for Western policies were of great significance for international politics in the later 1930s. No student of those following and more dramatic years can achieve an adequate perspective if he does not frequently cast his eye back to the dilemmas of the period which immediately preceded that convenient but in some ways misleading line drawn across European history by the arrival of the Nazis in power in January 1933.[1]

At the end of chapter four, the Disarmament Conference was left poised at its inauguration on 2 February, 1932, surrounded by the hopes and petitions of millions. During the following months, however, Western publics, as much as their politicians and military establishments, were to adopt separate and particular stances over the matter. 'The Germans demanded payment in the coin of French and Polish disarmament; the French in the coin of British and American commitments; the British in the coin of French disarmament and American commitments—and so on through the whole catalogue of sovereign self-centred nations.'[2] When Cecil eventually offered to join the fray at Geneva, it was in order to help lead his own public, as well as to try to impart momentum to the Conference itself on

---

[1] Toynbee, *Survey, 1932*, 45–300, remains a valuable guide, and there is an outline of disarmament developments in DBFP, III, 506. No adequate study has yet been written, however, of international politics in the West in this crucial period, despite the wealth of primary sources now available. That the perspective of the later 1930s should extend even earlier than 1932 goes (almost) without saying.

[2] Toynbee, *Survey, 1932*, 174–95.

this issue by which he believed the League 'would more or less stand or fall'.[1] Herriot, who, over both armaments and debts, was at least emotionally inclined to lead the French people beyond the limits suggested by immediate self-interest, had fallen from power by the end of the year. In the United States, where Congress begrudged the country's disarmament delegation every dollar of its expenses, both President and State Department perceived an increased resolve on the part of their own public to put America first whatever the consequences, and therefore were encouraged to react to the international situation very differently from the ever-eager Norman Davis and his colleagues in Geneva:

> 'It is clear,' wrote the State Department's chief disarmament official, 'that the Delegation does not yet appreciate the change of feeling which has swept over this country since last January; the growing concern over the situation in the Far East and the possible repercussions on our policy; the growing feeling that our Navy is improperly equipped to carry out our policies; the visible change in attitude on the part of the Secretary and higher Departmental officials, and finally the diminishing in strength of the pacifist groups.' 'Basically, the Geneva [delegation's] recommendations relate to conference strategy, the Washington answer is motivated by the state of public opinion at home.' 'Hoover looks at (proposals) from the point of view of political expediency rather than success in negotiations.'[2]

Meanwhile at the Conference itself each of the Western powers put forward schemes which, while proclaimed as the path towards universal peace, strongly reflected the special interests of their authors. Tardieu, then the principal French delegate, was early in the field with a plan to place civil aviation, heavy bombers and certain land and sea forces at the disposal of the League, together with increased powers for the Council to ensure mutual assistance against aggression. 'The present conference,' declared the French document, 'offers the best opportunity that has ever occurred to make a definite choice between a League of Nations possessing executive authority and a League of Nations paralysed by the uncompromising attitude of national sovereignty. France has made her choice. She suggests that the other nations should make theirs.'[3] And if this proposal echoed the Bourgeois Plan and Treaty of Mutual Assistance,[4] the idea of qualitative disarmament (which the French rejected, essentially because it promised to rule out the possibility of their attacking Germany's western frontier in order

[1] See, e.g., Cecil to Simon, 25 May 1932, FO 800/286; Cecil to Noel-Baker, 26 May, 21 July 1932, Cecil Papers, Add. 51107; Cecil to Murray, 3 August 1932, Murray Papers. Cecil also urged Hoover to send Stimson to the Geneva Conference, a move which had already been decided upon. Cecil to Hoover, 23 March; Hoover to Cecil, 3 April 1932, Hoover Papers.

[2] Moffat Diary, 11, 13, 22 April 1932. Cf. ibid, 4, 5, 28 March, 12 May 1932. While the British Government paid up more readily for its disarmament delegation, it was led by Chamberlain into a campaign to reduce the overall expenditure of the League. See, e.g., Cabinet Conclusions of 13 April 1932, CAB 23/71.

[3] *League of Nations, Conference For the Reduction and Limitation of Armaments: Conference Documents*, vol. I (Geneva, 1932), 113–16. For further Conference details see these League publications, which will not be cited individually hereafter.

[4] See above, 104.

to aid the Czechs and others in the east[1]) was also familiar. It was now revived in April by Hugh Gibson, for the United States, when he called for the abolition of 'aggressive weapons'—which in this case were held to include tanks and heavy mobile guns, but not, apparently, battleships or aircraft carriers.[2] Details of the ensuing debate and of the public positions adopted (to the British, for example, the submarine was a manifest evil; to the French and Japanese, a protector of the innocent) can be left aside; it was soon evident that the vital discussions were not those within the Conference itself, but the private ones between MacDonald, Stimson and other political leaders. Litvinov's proposal for complete all-round disarmament produced a frisson, nothing more, and was quite eclipsed by the drama of 22 June, when the Conference was faced, out of the blue, with a new plan devised by Herbert Hoover.[3] In this the President proposed that land forces above a 'police' minimum should be reduced by a third, with bombers, tanks, large mobile guns and chemical warfare to be abolished or prohibited; numbers of battleships should be reduced by a third, as should those of submarines, while cruisers, aircraft carriers and destroyers should be reduced by a quarter. Scarcely had the shock been absorbed when a British counter-proposal was on the table, calling for reductions in the size and armament, rather than in the numbers, of warships; it also asked for the abolition of submarines, but only of those tanks over twenty tons; for unspecified limitations on the weight and numbers of bombers, rather than their complete removal; and for a manpower ceiling that would still permit the maintenance of order throughout the Empire.[4] Not surprisingly, scant progress had been made by the time the Conference adjourned on 23 July after passing a resolution which embodied little more than hope, and existing plans were then overshadowed by the announcement by Germany that she would cease to participate in the Conference until given satisfaction over her claim for equality of rights with other countries.[5]

There ensued much public pronouncing and private conversing. At the end of July Germany proposed confidential talks with France, which the latter rejected on 11 September. The British Government declared its own position shortly afterwards, reaffirming the validity of all parts of the Versailles Treaty, but hoping that talks could dispose of questions of status as a preliminary to tangible arms reductions.[6] After much skirmishing over their location, such discussions finally took place early in December in Geneva, where Britain, France, Germany, Italy and the United States agreed on the 11th that Germany should return to the Conference and join

[1] On this, and qualitative disarmament in general, see Liddell Hart, cap. 8.

[2] FRUS, 1932, I, 76–83. Cecil also favoured the approach of banning those weapons 'without which in modern conditions aggression is impossible'. *News Chronicle*, 12 February 1932.

[3] See FRUS, 1932, I, 186 ff.; DBFP, III, appendix V.

[4] Cmd. 4122, 1932. The proposal was for battleship reduction from 35,000 tons displacement and 16″ guns to 22,000 tons and 11″; for cruisers, from 10,000 tons and 8″ to 7,000 tons and 6·1″; for aircraft carriers, from 27,000 tons to 22,000 tons. Destroyer reduction was made dependent on the abolition of submarines.

[5] See DBFP, III, Nos. 265, 267, 269, 270.

[6] DBFP, IV, No. 92.

in a solemn renunciation of force by European states; in return, it was accepted that the Conference would seek 'equality of rights in a system which would provide security for all nations'.[1] Even now, however, only a faint hope was aroused, for the Germans had already rejected the latest French plan which had been announced by Herriot in October and tabled by Paul-Boncour early in November. Under this scheme, there would be a 'progressive equalisation of the military status' of the various European countries on the basis of short-service armies, with automatic mutual assistance requirements for continental European states only, but with British (and, through her positive neutrality, American) assistance being counted on to render article 16 of the Covenant fully effective.[2] Matters were then complicated still further by the Japanese, who in December produced proposals which included the abolition of aircraft-carriers, the retention of submarines as a defensive weapon, and new battleship totals for the United States, Britain and Japan of 11, 11 and 8 respectively.[3]

Continuing gloom over the Disarmament Conference mingled at the end of the year with despair over the disunity which Britain, France and the United States were displaying at the same time over the question of intergovernmental debts. In American eyes, especially, the two issues were linked within the framework of persistent European delinquency. In Congress and the press, it was loudly being suggested that when an armed continent sought remission of the debts which it had contracted during its last blood-letting, it aeserved a contemptuously unyielding response from the Great Republic.[4] William Borah declared that debts should be discussed only as part of a drastic operation to draw out the poison of reparations and armaments from the European body politic, and the President's financier friend, Thomas Lamont, spoke in similar vein;[5] several of the incoming Democrats were also sour over the matter, though few could outdo Hoover in this.[6] It will be recalled that Pierre Laval had failed to secure concessions over debts during his visit to Washington in the autumn of 1931—although the joint communiqué issued at the end of his talks with Hoover had been so worded as to allow the interpretation that the question would be open to reconsideration should progress be made over reparations and disarmament. Moreover, when Congress were ratifying the Hoover moratorium soon afterwards, they 'expressly declared it to be against their policy that any of the indebtedness of foreign countries to the United States should be in any manner cancelled or reduced'.

In Paris and London, however, transatlantic debts were regarded as being closely bound up with war reparations from Germany, and when, following the report of a committee of financial experts at Basel, Berlin announced its

[1] Ibid, No. 219.　　　　　　　　　　　[2] DDF, I, No. 331.
[3] See DS 500 A15A4/1690; DBFP, X, No. 733.
[4] See, e.g., DS 500 A15A4/1284; *Washington Post*, 3 February, 4 April, 14, 24 November 1932.
[5] See Borah speech of 19 April 1932, Borah Papers, box 10, together with correspondence in ibid, box 331; Lamont speech of 22 June 1932, and speech of Senator Arthur Robinson of 26 August 1932, Hoover Papers.
[6] See, e.g., Cordell Hull, *Memoirs*, vol. 1, 171. On Hoover's views, see above, 118–9.

intention of bringing these payments to an end, Laval in turn warned that France 'would sacrifice no credit without a matching remission of debts'.[1] British proposals for European discussions on the reparations issue early in 1932 thus foundered on French intransigence,[2] and it was not until 16 June that such a conference convened at Lausanne under the chairmanship of MacDonald, whose own Government was advocating the cancellation of all claims within Europe prior to separate debt negotiations with the United States. A compromise ensued—but also a remarkable achievement for European diplomacy, and for MacDonald in particular—in the form of the Lausanne Agreement of 9 July: reparations were to be abolished, but only on the payment by Germany of a final, lump sum in bonds.[3] After many rumours, however, it was belatedly revealed that a condition had also been added in the form of a 'Gentleman's Agreement' between signatories that ratification would await a satisfactory settlement between them and their creditors; American suspicions of a plot against their country were further aroused by the publication at the same time of an Anglo-French agreement to exchange information, to cooperate over disarmament and a projected world economic conference, and to avoid trade discrimination harmful to each other.[4] Hoover promptly showed his disquiet by publishing a letter to Borah—by now a well-nigh indispensable method of informing the world of American policy—in which he affirmed that the United States would not 'be pressed into any line of action . . . by a combination [of her debtors], either open or implied'. In November the President's suspicions were confirmed when, in separate notes, Britain and France requested that their debt repayments, due to be resumed on 15 December, should be suspended pending a review of the subject. The United States refused. After further exchanges[5] the British Government paid up (in all, £200 million more than the sum originally borrowed had now been returned), but with the warning that this was to be regarded as an 'exceptional and abnormal' transaction that in no way committed the country to a resumption of payments on the old basis. Herriot, after a valiant attempt to make a similar, conditional payment for France, was submerged by the resentment of the Chamber against the apparent inflexibility of the American response. His Government fell on the issue on 14 December.[6]

Further tension among Western governments was thus added to the ill-feeling already being engendered by rising tariff barriers. Franco-American relations were notably poor in this last respect,[7] while the British Government, despite its proclaimed intention of fostering world trade by a growth

---

[1] DS 500 A15A4/740; cf. DBFP, II, pp. 246–99.

[2] See DBFP, II, pp. 300–82, and ibid, III, Nos. 37, 50, 60–6, 76.

[3] DBFP, III, appendix III.   [4] Cmd. 4131, 1932.

[5] See Cmd. 4192, 4203, 4210, 4211, 4215, 4216, and 4217, 1932; FRUS, 1932, I, 731–68.

[6] See DDF, I, No. 321 and ibid, II, Nos. 27, 35, 55–7, 69, 77, 79, 102, 104, 107. Belgium was among other states which refused payment.

[7] In April, Pierrepont Moffat noted that, at a time when improved relations were being sought with France in other spheres, 'the powers that be' in Washington were working on retaliatory trade restrictions against that country, with no consideration for their effect on policy as a whole, Moffat Diary, 14–17 April 1932.

in purchasing power, had aroused much resentment in August by concluding the Ottawa Agreement on increased Commonwealth trading preferences. In addition, the course of international relations had been affected to a significant degree by the year's list of political casualties, where Herriot's was only one of the last and more illustrious names. His arrival in power early in June, following the brief Tardieu Government of February to May, had symbolised an increased readiness within France to seek a lasting European settlement by means other than those of intransigent nationalism. Yet the pronounced swing to the Left in the elections of 1 and 8 May had not brought Herriot and the Radicals firm support from Blum and the Socialists, and the latter were soon criticising the Government's disarmament and reparations policies for being insufficiently conciliatory, the opposite fault to the one being proclaimed by the Right. Mounting financial difficulties also beset Herriot and his colleagues, whose future in office was already uncertain when they made their major gesture of European reconciliation at Lausanne.[1] Even before their arrival in power, the chances of agreement with Germany had declined with the resignation of Brüning at the end of May, and the speed with which von Papen's Government raised the new demand for 'equality of rights' after the Lausanne Agreement produced a further shock in Paris.[2] In the opinion of the British Ambassador, Herriot's successor, Paul-Boncour, was prepared for more drastic disarmament measures than Herriot had been, and certainly as late as March 1933 he was to propose reductions in the French armed forces.[3] But in December Schleicher had succeeded von Papen, and in January 1933 Hitler arrived in the German Chancellery.

In the White House, Herbert Hoover still presided over the fortunes of America, but under notice to quit after his overwhelming defeat by Roosevelt on 8 November. The bitterness of the preceding campaign and Hoover's conviction that his successor would jeopardise the very social and political structure of the country[4] did not bode well for cooperation between the two men in the months before Roosevelt's inauguration; soon, despite a joint statement in January on debt negotiations, there was ample public evidence of the coolness and distrust that in private were helping to take the life out of American policies.[5] Growing fears that the incoming President might devalue the dollar, together with an unemployment total now approaching the thirteen million mark, rendered bold international initiative on the part of the United States all the more unlikely. Meanwhile, amidst all this political carnage, the National Government in London survived. As with the Abbé Sieyès, that might have seemed a sufficient achievement in itself at the time, and the financial position of the country was also appearing more healthy.

[1] See Herriot, *Jadis*, vol. 2, 275 ff. and 302 ff.; Soulié, *La Vie Politique d'Edouard Herriot*, 351 ff., 371 ff.; Paul-Boncour, *Entre Deux Guerres*, vol. 2, 213 ff.; Colton, *Léon Blum*, 79 ff.; DS 851.00/1181, 1189, 1190, 1191, 1194; DS 500A15/1404, 1408.

[2] See the valuable testimony of Thanassis Aghnides, file 2, 8 ff., Carnegie Foundation, European Centre, Geneva.

[3] DBFP, IV, No. 266; cf. ibid, No. 64.

[4] See, e.g., Stimson Diary, 5 August 1932; Lyons, *Hoover*, 305 ff.; see above, 81.

[5] See, e.g., Stimson Diary, 22, 23 November, 17, 21 December 1932, and below, 350.

But despite this, and for all Baldwin's loyalty to him, MacDonald's position had been made more anomalous still in September by the resignation from the Government over the Ottawa tariffs of Samuel, Sinclair and Snowden. The Prime Minister was now almost alone within a Tory Administration, and his health had deteriorated further.[1] Baldwin, too, was obviously tired, while Simon's excess of intelligence and good intentions over decisiveness were being shown up by his very appreciation of the growing complexity of the international scene. Protection and financial recovery were proving something of a triumph for Neville Chamberlain, but for the moment his influence on foreign affairs was still mainly of the negative kind to be expected from Chancellors of the Exchequer,[2] and did not give to British policy a direction that the outside world could readily perceive. Leadership, like hope, appeared to be more scarce a commodity in the West in the winter of 1932 than it had during the meetings in the Genevan spring. Many answers had been proffered to the question of how to achieve peace, security and international harmony; few of them had been compatible.

Internal debate, international argument, and the Far Eastern factor

The growing clamour of German nationalism, together with further evidence of that country's breaches of the disarmament section of the Versailles treaty, preoccupied both Tardieu and Herriot in this period,[3] and belligerent anti-French noises were also being made in the officially-inspired Italian press.[4] At Geneva in the summer, a friend observed to Herriot: 'Je vois dans le miroir de Macbeth revenir la guerre.'[5] Nor did Herriot find much else to comfort him during this visit to the headquarters of the League, being startled at the transformation that had taken place since his previous term of office in 1924. Privately, he noted:

> Nos ex-ennemis sont entrés dans la Société des Nations, chacun avec sa clientèle. Les ex-alliés sont dissociés. Les États-Unis sont présents à la Conférence, avec le désir évident de désarmer l'Europe mais de réserver tous leurs privilèges. La Tour de Babel ... voilà mon impression d'arrivée ... L'abstraction peut seul réunir des éléments si divers. Toute réalité les divise.[6]

What could France hope for, then, from Britain and the United States? Tardieu had raised the prospect of Anglo-French cooperation on a wide range of matters, and in private conversation with Simon had recalled the Lansdowne–Delcassé entente of 1904.[7] Herriot, too, with his own memories of 1924, sought to renew close relations with MacDonald. He was aware,

---

[1] MacDonald underwent a second eye operation in May 1932.

[2] There have been obvious exceptions to this: Macmillan's influence before Suez, for example—though in its way that was negative enough for a generation of Chancellors.

[3] See, e.g., DDF, I, Nos. 53, 102, 118; DS 500A15A4/1033; DBFP, IV, No. 90; Duroselle, 210 ff.   [4] See Herriot, *Jadis*, vol. 2, 343.

[5] Herriot private papers, quoted in Soulié, 379.

[6] Herriot private papers, quoted in ibid, 377.

[7] Simon memorandum, 12 March 1932, DBFP, III, No. 236.

however, that there were many in France who doubted the latter's good intentions towards their country,[1] and that over the German question in particular the Prime Minister's attitude was at best an equivocal one. To 'wipe the slate clean' of reparations might sound attractive, for example, but as Herriot asked, 'who pays the sponge?'[2] De Fleuriau, the Ambassador in London, wrote during June of 'la tendance présente des Anglais à suivre le principe de moindre résistance',[3] and in October, following talks in Downing Street, Herriot himself admitted to his colleagues that he had been shocked by the British insistence on further land disarmament and by their gullibility where Germany was concerned. In this respect he believed that it was the United States that was the better friend of France.[4]

Nevertheless, to Pétain's question: what guarantees can Britain and the United States offer us?, Herriot was obliged to admit that on the American side, too, there were serious limits to what could be expected. Following Laval, Tardieu had sought in vain for some token of commitment on Washington's part where problems of European peace and security were concerned.[5] French diplomats were repeatedly warning that, whatever his personal inclinations, Stimson had very little freedom of manoeuvre in such matters, and that over both armaments and debts there was a strong anti-French element in American public opinion.[6] The suspicion also existed that the United States, together with Britain ('la manoeuvre anglo-saxonne' was what the Minister of Marine called it), sought to force France into making sufficient concessions to Italy to enable Rome and Paris belatedly to adhere to the London Naval Agreement.[7] Even so, and in the face of extensive hostile comments on the plan from many shades of French opinion,[8] Herriot believed that only a broad acceptance of Hoover's new disarmament proposals would enable France to find some way of maintaining her military position vis-à-vis Germany: 'Il est bien certain que, si nous pouvions nous rapprocher de la proposition Hoover, nous pourrions espérer un engagement de principe visant le maintien du *statu quo* actuel.' Thus, while the new French scheme of the autumn of 1932 was put forward as a maximum demand, it not only sought to take account of American—and British—susceptibilities over written commitments, but was envisaged as possibly leading to a compromise based on the Hoover plan.[9]

---

[1] See Soulié, 371.   [2] Ibid, 362.   [3] Herriot, vol. 2, 315–16.
[4] Procès-verbal of the commission for Disarmament Conference preparations, 18 October 1932, DDF, I, No. 250. The continuation of this vital meeting is recorded in ibid, Nos. 268, 272, 273, and the decisions of the Conseil Supérieur de la Défense Nationale on 28 October 1932, in No. 286.
[5] See, e.g., FRUS, 1932, I, 34–9, 54–9; DS 500A15A4/1005¼.
[6] DDF, I, Nos. 6, 10, 16, 96, 104, 198; ibid, II, No. 10.
[7] DDF, II, Nos. 43, 44; cf. ibid, No. 39.
[8] See, e.g., DS 500 A15A4/1153, 1178.
[9] See DDF, I, Nos. 250, 273, 286; ibid, II, Nos. 28, 59, 60, and the somewhat differing emphases in Herriot, vol. 2, 332–3, Soulié, 375 ff., and Paul-Boncour, vol. 2, 223 ff. It should be noted that contemporaries in a position to observe these matters closely recall Herriot as being less resolutely adventurous in private than his emotional good-intentions might lead one to expect. On the other hand he did do battle in Paris for an unpopular cause, and eventually fell from power in consequence.

Such optimism, or desperate hope, on Herriot's part was all the more remarkable in that France was also seeking concessions from the United States over debts, a suggestion that had again been sharply rejected in January, when Laval had advanced it for the final time.[1] The possibility which existed of working more closely with Britain over this matter was by no means an asset for France in American eyes, and Herriot always accepted that in the higher interest of a disarmament-cum-security agreement, the debt instalment that was due in December would have to be paid if Washington remained adamant.[2] Nevertheless it could be hoped that the sacrifice which France had made at Lausanne would stand to her credit, and that following the electoral defeat of Hoover her requests might be met in a more imaginative and liberal spirit.[3]

Meanwhile domestic political anxieties dogged Herriot and eventually, while enhancing his stature internationally, brought him down.[4] As already suggested from the outwardly visible signs, MacDonald was in scarcely more comfortable a position, defensively hinting to the King that he might resign,[5] aware that, despite Baldwin, there were a good number of prominent Conservatives who wished to throw him over,[6] and apparently 'expressing great concern that (he was) being driven into supporting a Tory and anti-Labour policy'.[7] As noted earlier,[8] the Prime Minister's close involvement in foreign affairs during the year had also, from personal rather than political causes, led to strained relations with Simon, while in a wider context the wranglings which took place at Ottawa brought home to the whole Cabinet, in Chamberlain's words, 'how thin the bonds of Empire had worn'.[9] Nor was there unanimity in Whitehall itself when it came to assessing the present and possible future policies of Germany. The well-known anxieties of Vansittart on this subject have perhaps obscured the warnings that were being uttered by others: Hankey, for example, who judged the Foreign Office to be 'defeatist' over German armaments demands,[10] and within the Cabinet Hailsham above all, who repeatedly expressed his disquiet on the grounds that 'Germany alone desired her armaments not for defence, but for aggression'.[11] MacDonald, on the other hand, was impressed by Germany's 'strong psychological position', and believed that no one could 'rightly

[1] See Stimson Diary, 17 January 1932.
[2] See, e.g., Soulié, 387.   [3] See, e.g., DDF, I, No. 313.
[4] For accounts of Herriot's battle over debt-payments, see Herriot, vol. 2, 355 ff.; Soulié, 409 ff.; DDF, II, Nos. 102, 104, 107; DS 851.00/1203.
[5] Wigram memorandum, 4 May 1932, RA G.V, K2344/29.
[6] See James, *Memoirs of a Conservative*, 379–80.
[7] Snowden to MacDonald, 29 August 1932, MacDonald Papers, RM 5/53; cf. the further exchanges, bitter on Snowden's part, in this file; also Neville to Ida and Hilda Chamberlain, 12, 18, 25 September 1932, Neville Chamberlain Papers; Jones, *Diary*, 56; Cabinet of 27 September 1932, CAB 23/72; Simon to Runciman, 16 September 1932, Simon Papers (private collection), Foreign Affairs, 1932.
[8] See above, 94.
[9] Cabinet of 10 August 1932, CAB 23/72; cf. Neville to Ida and Hilda Chamberlain, 11, 21 August 1932, Neville Chamberlain Papers, and Baldwin Papers, vol. 98, passim.   [10] Hankey Diary, 23 October 1932.
[11] See, e.g., Cabinets of 30 September, 31 October 1932, CAB 23/72. But cf. DBFP, III, appendix IV.

resist (her) claim that the Treaty of Versailles must in some respects be reconsidered'.[1] Simon, too, was anxious above all to keep the Germans in play. He was another who found their moral claim to be 'very strong', and felt that if France proved intransigent Britain should make her own declaration cancelling the arms clauses of the Versailles document; after all, he argued, if 'disarmament propagandists' in Britain were given the evidence that existed of Germany's intention to rearm, they would only blame it on the unreasonable treatment which had been handed out to that country.[2]

Not surprisingly it was the MacDonald–Simon line that was adopted as British official policy, for the alternative of moving towards an acceptance of the French position was ruled out, even by those who strongly distrusted Germany. MacDonald continued to blame years of French stupidity for the current unrest, and bluntly emphasised to French leaders the gap between the views of London and Paris.[3] Although members of the British Government recognised that their opposite numbers across the Channel were anxious for a closer understanding,[4] the two French disarmament plans of Tardieu and Herriot were dismissed out of hand. As Hankey set out at length and MacDonald emphasised to his colleagues,[5] the Tardieu scheme, like those of Bourgeois and others, rested on an entirely different conception of the League to Britain's, while in private talks at Geneva both Stimson and the Dominions' representatives agreed that the plan was 'quite unworkable'.[6] For all Herriot's efforts to skirt round the British aversion to commitments, his own November proposal was likewise rejected by Vansittart, the Admiralty, the Army Council, Hankey and others as seeking to resurrect the substance of the Geneva Protocol. 'Plus ça change, plus c'est la même chose,' wrote Hankey.[7] Herriot and Paul-Boncour were soon made to realise that they would receive no encouragement in London, where the official response was thus the same as it had been earlier in the year to the idea of a 'Mediterranean Locarno'.[8] Throughout the discussions on how to get Germany back into the Disarmament Conference, it was MacDonald,

[1] Notes of MacDonald–Herriot meeting, 13 October, and MacDonald to Herriot, 10 October 1932, MacDonald Papers, RM 1/255.

[2] Cabinet of 11 October 1932, CAB 23/72, and memorandum of 5 April, DC(M) (32)10, in CAB 27/509. In the Commons on 10 November, Simon proposed that states should sign a solemn affirmation not to use force to settle their present or future difficulties. Any disregard for such a pledge 'would mobilise world opinion'. So much for Kellogg—and for the Manchurian experience. *Hansard, House of Commons*, vol. 270, cols. 545–8. In a memorandum placed before the Ministerial Committee on the Disarmament Conference on 15 September 1932, Simon also argued that it was extremely possible that the Conference might fail, and that 'any blame for failure should . . . tend to be shifted elsewhere'. CAB 27/505.

[3] See MacDonald to Cecil, 13 September 1932, MacDonald Papers, RM 6/13; MacDonald–Paul-Boncour conversation, 22 April 1932, ibid, RM 1/250.

[4] See, e.g., Neville to Hilda and Ida Chamberlain, 19 June, 4 July 1932, Neville Chamberlain Papers.

[5] Hankey note of 16 March 1932, CAB 27/509; minutes of Disarmament Committee, 21 March 1932, CAB 27/505.

[6] See record of talks of 23 April 1932, DBFP, III, No. 240, and of 29 April 1932, MacDonald Papers, RM 1/250.

[7] DC (M) (32), 26–29, in CAB 27/509.   [8] See above, 121.

the balancer between the two Continental powers as he saw it, who extracted concessions from an unhappy yet dogged Herriot, never vice versa.[1]

There was no doubt that MacDonald, together with Baldwin and Simon, was desperately anxious to achieve a measure of disarmament as part of general conciliation in Europe, if necessary at French expense. When it came to what Britain herself could or should contribute in that direction, however, a good many voices were raised in opposition within the Government, among its advisers, and from the ranks of the Empire and Commonwealth. Leaving aside the details of the internal debate, broadly speaking it was the three above-named Ministers who in Cabinet displayed the greatest concern to bring about some positive British contribution that might save the Disarmament Conference from failure.[2] On the opposite side, the specific objections which they encountered from the three Armed Services were sometimes backed up from other quarters as well. There was widespread sympathy, for example, for the Admiralty's insistence that the principle of international arms inspection should be rejected since it would 'lay bare our weakness'; similarly, when Londonderry and the Air Staff opposed the abolition of bombers (a weapon, they argued, which 'in the long run would prove our best defence'), they were joined by the Governments of India and South Africa, as well as by the King, before whom MacDonald was particularly pusillanimous over this issue of military aviation. In short, it was far easier to agree on the demerits of schemes which had emanated from Paris than it was to produce a significant contribution of one's own, while as one result of the consequent turmoil not only the Service Ministers but also Baldwin and Hankey among others were increasingly alarmed at the glaring deficiencies that were being shown up in the country's defence capability.[3]

Baldwin's thoughts at this time dwelt increasingly upon the likely horrors of aerial bombardment in any future war, together with the financial agony that would be involved in major arms increases. Searching around within the dilemma of whether to look to one's own defences or make a last attempt to obtain an international agreement on arms reduction, he was thus all the more ready to examine even apparently radical notions if they offered any

[1] See record of talks, 2 December 1932, DBFP, IV, No. 204.

[2] Neville Chamberlain produced a scheme for disarmament by stages, each stage to be dependent on German good behaviour. See Cabinet of 31 October 1932, CAB 23/72, and Neville to Hilda and Ida Chamberlain, 30 October, 5 November 1932, Neville Chamberlain Papers. 'It amuses me,' he wrote, 'to find a new policy for each of my colleagues in turn.' Simon, meanwhile, declared to his colleagues that, like America, Britain 'was not a European state.' Committee meeting of 21 March 1932, CAB 27/505.

[3] The points made above can be followed in detail in, e.g., Wigram memoranda of 6, 10 June, 9 August 1932, RA G.V, K2353/1 and 8; King George V to MacDonald, 20 June 1932, ibid, K2353/2; Hankey to Batterbee, 2 March 1932, CAB 21/368; report of Cabinet Committee on Disarmament, 11 January 1932, CP 5 (32), CAB 27/476; minutes of the Committee of 5 April, 6 June 1932, CAB 27/505; Cabinets of 10 February, 4, 11 May, 1, 7 June, 12 July, 9 November 1932, CAB 23/70-72. It is worth noting that Murray and Cecil accepted that Simon was more concerned than most of his colleagues to achieve progress in disarmament. E.g., Murray to Noel-Baker, 2 July 1932, Murray Papers; Cecil to Simon, 25 May 1932, FO 800/286.

prospect of lasting safety. One such idea, although it never fully materialised as a serious proposition in the international arena, became in this period something of a catalyst in Anglo-American relations where the Far East and disarmament were concerned. Technically, Baldwin's starting point was the link between the size of capital ships and their need for protection against submarines and aircraft:

> If, therefore, it was possible, by abolishing military and naval aircraft, to make an offer greatly to reduce the size of Capital Ships in return for the abolition of submarines, great results might be achieved. A reduction in the size of the Capital Ship would affect coast defences and the size of new docks, and if submarines were abolished, he gathered that the abolition of the laying of contact mines in the open sea would also be acceptable to the Navy. His proposal opened up the prospect of great economies at a time when the world could not afford their [sic] existing expenditure, and he thought the time was not far distant when the nations might be willing to listen to such proposals.[1]

In this form, Baldwin's idea was to find partial expression in the official British proposals that were put to the Geneva Conference in July. In private, however—and the Admiralty do not appear to have been informed—he was pondering something more spectacular still: the complete abolition of capital ships as part of a package that would also include the abolition of submarines, military aircraft, aircraft carriers and 'aggressive weapons' such as heavy mobile guns and tanks. Capital ships, he told Simon, Norman Davis and Hugh Gibson, 'were an insurmountable obstacle to securing action in regard to other categories which we all desired . . . and the prohibitive costs of replacing these vessels doomed them to early disappearance . . .'[2] Such a scheme stood virtually no chance of acceptance in the summer of 1932, although in passing it may be observed that its adoption in its entirety might well have greatly increased the security of Britain and her overseas possessions. What it required immediately, however, was the support of the United States—just as that country's good offices were soon to be thought essential to help get Germany back to the Geneva Conference.[3] Like the French, the Americans were required to cooperate; but like the French, they made things more difficult by producing a plan of their own that was unacceptable in London.

In Whitehall, as in the Quai d'Orsay and various quarters of the State Department,[4] it was widely assumed that Hoover's dramatic arms plan was fundamentally a domestic political manoeuvre. MacDonald himself described it as 'a political manifesto called a disarmament proposal'.[5] Yet

---

[1] Cabinet of 11 May 1932, CAB 23/71.

[2] Mellon to State Department, 13 May 1932, FRUS, 1932, I, 121–5; cf. DS 500 A15A4/1030, 1037. [3] See DS 500 A15A4/1491, 1508. [4] See above, 82–3.

[5] MacDonald to Baldwin, 24 June 1932, Baldwin Papers, vol. 119. Admiral Sir Frank Field (First Sea Lord) wrote to Chatfield on 12 August 1932 of 'Hoover's electioneering stunt'. Chatfield Papers. Simon wrote to MacDonald on 18 July 1932 of 'the now familiar operation by our American friends of suddenly producing a complete resolution of their own as an ultimatum and announcing that nothing less would satisfy the peace-loving sentiments of Hoover in particular and the great American people in general'. FO 800/287. Gibson and Davis were well aware of the difficulties caused by Hoover's abrupt method.

while he accepted the Admiralty's contention that the American scheme 'was open to very grave objections from every aspect' and that by reducing her numbers of cruisers and capital ships it would cripple Britain's imperial defences, the Prime Minister sensibly went out of his way to prevent his colleagues from rejecting the President's proposal in abrupt fashion. Over this, as over the rumours of an anti-American front at Lausanne, he worked hard to soothe both Stimson and the United States delegates at Geneva.[1] Simon and Hankey helped by impressing upon Baldwin and the Cabinet that 'if we can show ourselves forthcoming to the American proposals, we shall create a much better atmosphere for the discussion of the American debt . . .'[2] Yet the debt question, too, brought with it disagreements within the Cabinet. Chamberlain, who was determined to work for cancellation and not to settle with Washington behind the back of France after the Lausanne agreement, distrusted the resolve of both MacDonald and the Foreign Office over the matter. 'My Treasury people,' he wrote privately, 'are in a terrible stew about leaving negotiations in the hands of the F.O. as they say they always run away the minute the Yanks say Boh.'[3] Neverthe-less, while he 'intensely disliked' the payment that was eventually made in December, Chamberlain came to accept Baldwin's argument that a final gesture of this kind was necessary to preserve Britain's good name. Hail-sham, Runciman (President of the Board of Trade) and Cunliffe-Lister (Colonial Secretary), on the other hand, advocated an outright refusal to pay.[4]

To MacDonald's distress, the debt issue, together with the conflicting requirements of the two countries over naval disarmament, helped signific-antly to increase the degree of anti-American feeling which has already been seen to have existed throughout Whitehall. 'I am fed up with America!!' wrote Londonderry in June. 'A real good bludgeon is all that they under-stand and require!!'[5] Baldwin's exasperation was also growing,[6] while Neville Chamberlain wrote to his sister: 'I find it hard to control my feelings about the Americans. They havn't a scrap of moral courage about any of their prominent men (they have no leaders). Even the P.M. is furious with them at last and all the more because he has so long believed that they

[1] Cabinets of 24, 27, 30 June, 6 July 1932, CAB 23/71, 72; Gibson to Stimson, 26, 28 June 1932, DS 500 A15A4/1185, 1190; Davis to Stimson, 16 July 1932, ibid, 1323½; MacDonald to Davis, 17 November, 4 December 1932, Norman Davis Papers, box 40; MacDonald to Stimson, 12 November 1932, Stimson Papers, box 309; Stimson Diary, 29 November 1932.

[2] Cabinet of 24 June, 1932, CAB 23/71; Hankey to Baldwin, 27 June 1932, Baldwin Papers, vol. 119.

[3] Neville to Ida Chamberlain, 19 November 1932, Neville Chamberlain Papers.

[4] Neville to Ida and Hilda Chamberlain, 11, 20 June, 4, 10 December 1932, ibid; Cabinets of 28, 29 November, 7, 13, 21 December 1932, CAB 23/73. Chamberlain wrote that he would have resigned rather than betray France by a separate deal with the Americans. He disliked the outcome because 'the longer they go without payment the more easy it will be for them to accept the prospect that there never will be any payment'. MacDonald, too, 'did not contemplate a second payment'.

[5] Londonderry to MacDonald, 21 June 1932, MacDonald Papers, RM 3/5.

[6] On 7 October 1933, Neville Chamberlain was to write in his diary: 'S.B. says he has got to loathe the Americans so much that he hates meeting them.'

would behave like gentlemen out of personal regard for himself.' In response to a similar outburst from Austen, he repeated his 'disgust' for a people '(who) continually talk about their friendly feelings (and) give us endless advice as to the way in which we may profit by their friendliness; but (who), when it comes to the point, never translate into practice any of the hopes which they have inspired'.[1] Even MacDonald was nettled, as Chamberlain saw, and in a letter to his friend Lamont suggested that the Americans had 'come into the world with your pockets . . . (but) not with your heads'.[2] Britain would give way over this one debt instalment, as Herriot had felt obliged to give way to Britain over Lausanne and the return of Germany to Geneva; in neither case, however, were relations thereby improved.

In Washington, Stimson in particular viewed with alarm the mounting strain between the United States and her two war-time allies:

'These thoughts (of friendship) have been particularly poignant to me during the past two weeks,' he wrote to MacDonald early in December, 'when I have sometimes wondered whether a cruel fate was going to shatter the structure of good will between our two nations which you and I have worked so hard to build up since 1929.'[3]

The Secretary was also distressed by the fall of Herriot, whose enhanced stature as a result of Lausanne and his debt endeavours he contrasted privately with Hoover's, and for whom he sought recognition in the Senate through the help of Borah.[4] Stimson did not believe that the outright cancellation of inter-allied debts was practicable, and he resented Neville Chamberlain's clumsy public statements on the subject; but throughout the year he wished that 'the doubting and recalcitrant elements' in the United States could be brought to see the need for a more wise and generous policy over these matters, and he winced at Hoover's belligerent suspicions of an anti-American front at Lausanne. Privately, Stimson thought that Mac-Donald had achieved 'a magnificent piece of work' at that conference. 'Over here,' he wrote apologetically to the Prime Minister, 'the combination of continued . . . depression with the intense politics of a presidential campaign . . . make it impossible to expect fairness and a poised judgement in respect to the actions of our sister nations . . .', and he was privately 'disgusted' with what he saw as the narrow view taken by his colleague Ogden Mills at the U.S. Treasury. Borah, too, despite Hoover's fears, was delighted with the Lausanne Agreement, and wrote to tell MacDonald so.[5]

[1] Neville to Hilda Chamberlain, 26 November 1932, Neville Chamberlain Papers; Austen to Neville and Neville to Austen Chamberlain, 8 and 9 December 1932, Austen Chamberlain Papers, AC 39/1–6.

[2] MacDonald to Lamont, 17 November 1932, MacDonald Papers, RM 6/13. Cf. MacDonald to Zimmern, 27 July 1932, ibid, RM 2/24.

[3] Stimson to MacDonald, 4 December 1932, Stimson Papers, box 312.

[4] Stimson Diary, 4, 15 December 1932; Stimson to Borah, 16 December 1932, Borah Papers, box 345; Claudel to Herriot, 17 December 1932, DDF, II, No. 117.

[5] Stimson Diary, 26 December 1931, 17, 27 May, 8, 18, 19, 20 June, 11–14 and 26 July 1932; Stimson to MacDonald, 20 July 1932, Stimson Papers, box 309; Borah to MacDonald, 15 August 1932, MacDonald Papers, RM 6/13. Cf. Borah speeches of 23 July and 3 August 1932, Borah Papers, box 341, and correspondence in ibid, box 334. Cf. Hoover–Lamont correspondence, Hoover Papers, and Borah's draft

For all the private congratulations, however, a willingness to seek a comprehensive settlement of the debt question never came near to being incorporated in American policy. Stimson, as well as Hoover, had preferred to try to split Britain from France on the issue, employing for this purpose inspired statements by Senator David Reed, in addition to private messages of his own to London.[1] (He did at least have the grace to admit that he was proposing to the British Government 'an extremely difficult task ... of carrying cooperation with the French Government just to the point where it suited themselves and then breaking it'[2]) Following the 'bombshell', as he called it, of the November requests for suspension of the next debt instalment, Stimson continued to clash strongly with Mills and Hoover over the American response: both of them, he noted, were 'thinking of this matter inevitably in terms of politics, the President to protect his record in the past, and Mills to protect his future'. He could only moderate the tone of what was said to Europe, however, not change its direction.[3]

American officials were also looking for links between, on the one hand, the reparations and debt policies of London and Paris, and on the other their manoeuvrings over disarmament. Did the Anglo-French accord at Lausanne, for example, signal a disguised league for the defence of the Royal Navy and the French Army? Conversely, Stimson had come to accept the need for the Hoover disarmament initiative to be launched in June, partly in order to help forestall a united front at Lausanne against the U.S.A.[4] Here again, however, as in London, it was easier to sit in Washington and dismiss what was unacceptable in the schemes produced by others than it was to agree on a formula of one's own—a situation which we have seen was reflected at the outset of the Disarmament Conference by the frenzied, last-minute throwing together of a set of proposals which Gibson could trot out in order to placate the peace groups in America.[5] Nothing in the nature of a commitment in Europe could be entertained, as Stimson reiterated to all and sundry during his stay in Geneva;[6] even a consultative pact was acknowledged by State Department officials to be 'a political impossibility'.[7] Thus Herriot's plan, like Tardieu's before it, was dismissed as being 'still based entirely on the old idea of force', even though Stimson, unlike Hoover, was by now alarmed at the resurgence of 'the old Prussian

proposals of October concerning the conditions under which debts might be cancelled, ibid.

[1] See Reed's speeches of 12, 14 January, Hoover Papers; Stimson Diary, 10, 24 January, 29 April 1932; Stimson to MacDonald, 27 January 1932, Stimson Papers, box 304. Cf. Simon to MacDonald, 2 June 1932, Simon Papers (private collection), Foreign Affairs, 1932; Simon to Tyrrell, 9 June, and to MacDonald, 10 June 1932, FO 800/287; Atherton to Castle, 3 May 1932, Castle Papers, England.

[2] Lindsay to Simon, 1 June 1932, DBFP, III, No. 117.

[3] Stimson Diary, 10, 12, 16, 18–21, 23, 28 November, 1–3, 11, 13, 16, 17, 21 December 1932; Moffat Diary, 3 December 1932; draft notes in Stimson Papers, box 311; FRUS, 1932, I, 731, 754–78.

[4] Stimson Diary, 21 June 1932; Moffat Diary, 22 June 1932; DS 500 A15A4/1126, 1140½, 1319; Davis to Roosevelt, 18 November 1932, Davis Papers, box 50.

[5] See above, 122.

[6] E.g., Stimson Diary, 20, 23 April 1932.

[7] Moffat Diary, 29 June 1932; cf. Stimson Diary, 4 November 1932.

spirit' in Germany.[1] The British proposals put forward early in July were likewise rejected instantly in so far as they threatened to reduce the size, and hence the cruising radius, of American warships.[2]

The major shock in Washington had been created earlier, however, by Baldwin's musings on the possible abolition of capital ships, a notion so appalling as to be concealed from inquisitive American admirals (several would undoubtedly have died of apoplexy on the spot) and one described by Castle as a Tory scheme to 'again make Great Britain mistress of the seas'.[3] Reassurances were soon received that nothing more than private and tentative speculation had been involved, but Hoover remained alarmed lest a bold British plan of this kind should steal the limelight at Geneva; he therefore began to think of forestalling matters by producing a dramatic and vote-catching scheme of his own, while Stimson, too, believed that Baldwin had created 'a major emergency'.[4] Again, however, the two men parted company at this point. Even earlier, the State Department had looked askance at various disarmament ideas emanating from the White House;[5] now, when Hoover listened to the calls of economy, isolation and votes, Stimson looked to the battleships of the U.S. Navy as holding the situation in the Pacific. Yet the most the Secretary could do was to modify Hoover's original idea of proposing 40 per cent naval reductions, and on 24 May the President still produced a draft scheme for 30-per-cent cuts which Stimson privately described as something 'from Alice in Wonderland'.[6] Hoover hesitated for a short while, even though he was as usual supported by Castle. Then, fearing a public attack by Borah and determined to demonstrate before the Lausanne Conference was concluded that Europe could save vast sums through disarmament rather than through debt cancellation, he suddenly plunged ahead in the latter part of June, taking with him a much-troubled Stimson and a somewhat distraught delegation at Geneva.[7]

---

[1] Stimson Diary, 4, 7, 15, 18, 20 September, 20 October 1932; Moffat Diary, 17, 20, 27 September, 14 October, 15 November 1932; FRUS, 1932, I, 388; DDF, II, No. 5; DBFP, IV, No. 205.

[2] Stimson Diary, 7 July 1932; FRUS, 1932, I, 305–8.

[3] Stimson Diary, 14 May, 7 June 1932; Moffat memorandum, 23 June 1932, Moffat Papers, vol. 22; Davis to Stimson, 24 May 1932, Davis Papers, box 54; Castle memorandum, 25 May 1932, DS 500 A15A4/1075½; FRUS, 1932, I, 153–7; Simon to Lindsay, 8 June 1932, FO 800/287.

[4] FRUS, 1932, I, 158–60; DS 500 A15A4/1112; Stimson Diary, 15 May 1932.

[5] Moffat Diary, 31 March 1932.

[6] See Stimson Diary, 22–4 May 1932; Hoover memorandum, 24 May, Castle memorandum, 25 May 1932, FRUS, 1932, I, 180–6. Cf. Castle Diary, 23 June 1932, cited in Current, Secretary Stimson, 108, and material in Stimson Papers, box 308.

[7] See Stimson Diary, 18–21 June, 25 July 1932; Hoover to Stimson, 17 November 1932, Stimson Papers, box 312; Moffat Diary, 18 June 1932; telephone records, Washington–Geneva, Davis Papers, box 20; FRUS, 1932, I, 186 ff. On the often diverging views of the Geneva delegation, see, e.g., Swanson to Robinson, 7 March 1932, Davis Papers, box 20; Davis to Baker, 16 June 1932, ibid, box 3; Davis to Hull, 23 June 1932, Cordell Hull Papers, box 32; Wilson to Stimson, 14 December 1932, Hugh Wilson Papers; DS 500 A15A4/899, 941, 1065, 1083; note of Mac-Donald–Davis conversation, 18 October 1932, MacDonald Papers, RM 1/258.

Baldwin had thus unwittingly prodded Hoover into proving his zeal for disarmament; Hoover thereby spurred the British Government into producing its own display of good intentions. By making public their conflicting desiderata over naval armaments in particular, these gestures worsened relations between the two countries, and the private talks on the subject which ensued made scant progress.[1] In Washington—where Hoover's francophobia also found continued expression in this period[2]—suspicions of the British Government matched the exasperation that was now flowing in the opposite direction. From London, Atherton described 'the Die-hard Tory group' as being dominant; various reports also depicted MacDonald as fading (the Prime Minister unwittingly encouraged this by privately suggesting that all British moves which America disliked were none of his making), with the majority lapsing into a mood of weary cynicism.

'They are far more deeply exhausted from the war than we have appreciated,' wrote Norman Davis. 'The period of expansion, or imperialism, is over; they seem to be shrinking, contracting into the Empire. No more troubles, no more adventures, no more entanglements. Manchuria is an unpleasant subject, best not to talk about it; they have already more than they can carry. England today is profoundly conservative, even Tory . . .'

The sense of faltering partnership weighed heavily on Stimson's mind. By the autumn he was himself weary and again not sleeping well. 'The world was crumbling in all directions and falling about his shoulders.'[3] Toynbee's 'annus terribilis' was past, but to the Secretary, as to Toynbee himself and many others, it now seemed that there could be worse to come.[4]

Over reparations, debts and disarmament there were thus major conflicts among the desiderata of the three Western powers in 1932. The roots of this situation have been explored earlier in the book, and only two further features need to be brought out here. One is the tension which existed *within*

[1] See Cabinets of 6 July, 4 August, 11 October 1932, CAB 23/72; Woodley conference memoranda of 20, 21 September 1932, Davis Papers, box 17; memoranda of naval conversations, 7 October–4 December 1932, ibid, box 20; DS 500 A15A4/ 1515.

[2] E.g., Stimson Diary, 3 June 1932. As the debt conflict came to a head, officials in Washington were wont to await encounters between Hoover and Ambassador Paul Claudel with no little relish.

[3] Atherton to Castle, 23 August 1932, Castle Papers, England; Stimson–Gibson telephone record, 7 July 1932, Davis Papers, box 20; Davis to Hornbeck, 17 September 1932, ibid, box 11; Sweetser to Davis, 1 October 1932, ibid, box 11; Atherton to Davis, 31 October, ibid, box 2; Davis to Stimson, 4 December 1932, ibid, box 20; DS 841.00/1225; DS 500 A15A4/1240½; Moffat Diary, 13, 30 September 1932. For further (and not always accurate) portraits of leading figures in London, see DS 793.94/5624, and DS 500 A15A4/982½.

[4] In his *Survey, 1933* (London, 1934) Toynbee quoted Ismet Paça: 'This century is very pitiless; and, as the years pass, the brutality of the times is . . . becoming uncontrollable, as though it were going to pass over every boundary.' Toynbee wrote that 'the clear lesson for the detached observer was a crushing refutation of the creed of Humanism which has inspired the march of Western Civilization for more than four hundred years'. Op. cit., 3–4.

that entwined collection of goals and means which is loosely described as the 'policy' of each member of the triangle—a tension to be explained only partly by the obvious differences to be found between, say, admirals and treasury officials in each capital. This feature was least prominent in the case of France, who most perceived herself to be in need of the good-will and assistance of the other two. Her alignment with Britain over debts, however, did not square with her quest for American sympathy over finance and security, while it was in this period that the conflict already noted became more prominent, between France's role as champion of the League and of the small, successor states in central and eastern Europe, and her manoeuvrings as a Great Power outside and above the Genevan arena that was so dear to Benes and others.[1] For Britain, too, her debt policy, and especially her eventual loyalty to France on that issue, sat uneasily alongside her desire for American assistance over European problems, while her anxiety to make France more amenable over reparations and disarmament was at odds with the determination not to pay for this in the one reassuring currency that France desired. (One feature of Britain's inter-war appeasement recipes was that it was usually others—France, Czechoslovakia, Poland, Portugal, Abyssinia, China—who were expected to foot the bill for the ingredients.) As for the United States, she continued to preach military disarmament and the payment of debts while practising what amounted to economic warfare, and to urge Anglo-French cooperation in achieving European reconciliation while endeavouring to drive the two countries apart over debts. Like Britain, she desired influence without responsibility and a reduction of armaments without a diminution of her own power.

The second feature to be noted is the influence on relations within the Western triangle of states and developments lying outside it, and above all the varying perceptions of these developments which existed in London, Paris and Washington.[2] Germany supplies one obvious example; Japan and the Far East, the one which, in the context of the present study, must be examined in more detail. At Geneva, especially, a sense of general interaction between the Far Eastern crisis and disarmament was inescapable:

'The reverberations of the fighting around Shanghai echoed and re-echoed in Geneva,' wrote Arthur Sweetser, 'unsteadying everyone's mind from the original purpose of disarmament . . . I do not imagine that at a distance you can possibly sense the extraordinary interplay back and forth between one set of meetings seeking almost hopelessly to stop the march of war in the East and the set of meetings seeking almost equally helplessly to bring the nations into a mood to reduce their armaments.'[3]

Norman Davis, League disarmament officials and others spoke in the same sense.[4] To Noel-Baker, the entire outcome of the Conference was jeopardised

[1] See DDF, II, No. 118, and above, 40–1.

[2] For a discussion of similar features concerning a bilateral relationship, see R. Morgan, 'Washington and Bonn', in *International Affairs*, July 1971. Cf. Wolfers, 'Stresses and Strains in "Going It With Others" ', in *Discord and Collaboration*.

[3] Sweetser to Hornbeck, 24 March 1932, Arthur Sweetser Papers, box 15.

[4] See Aghnides report, 23 March, and Drummond's of 11 June 1932, *L.N. Directors' Meetings and Papers, 1932*, U.N. Library, Geneva; Davis press conference, 28 March 1932, DS 793.94/4970.

by the Japanese manoeuvrings over various kinds of weapons, and Cecil, too, while believing that 'a way could be found to bring (Japan) to reason', was impressed by the connection; their friend Murray, although diverging from Cecil over the need for a separate League force, also drew his arguments from the current Far Eastern case.[1] In addition there was much speculation in the press concerning these matters, the suggestion being made, for example, that the United States might have promised to help France resist Germany's claim to equality of rights in return for support against Japan in Manchuria.[2]

From the point of view of the policy-makers themselves, the interweaving of issues was more complex still, but for the sake of clarity the process can be divided into the impact made by Far Eastern events on debts and disarmament, and vice versa. In Washington, as we have seen, events pushed Hoover and Stimson wider apart on disarmament as the latter became what one admiral described as 'the real defender of the Navy' in anticipation of a possible conflict with Japan.[3] There followed not only the inevitable rejection of Japan's naval proposals at the Disarmament Conference,[4] but an over-reaction to Baldwin's apparent threat to those American battleships that Stimson believed were 'preventing Japan from running completely amuck'.[5] The country's own naval proposals were likewise drafted with an eye to the military balance in the Pacific. As Norman Davis was to put it in the following year (Frenchmen, upbraided by America for always looking at Germany before they made a move, would have enjoyed reading the letter):

> The attitude of Japan has had a vital bearing on our action as regards armaments. When we have discussed a treaty of universal application, there has always been a certain unreality as far as the United States is concerned because we know that we cannot accept a treaty limiting American armaments unless the same type of limitation applies to Japan, and that the measures of limitation which are now envisaged for a universal treaty will be essentially unacceptable to Japan.[6]

There was thus an awareness on the part of some American diplomats of the realism and pursuit of national interest that underlay the policy of their own country, as it did that of others. And in this respect, Far Eastern events did more than confirm Stimson in his inclination to look with sympathy on the reparations and debt difficulties of Britain and France. They also fostered a significant shift of opinion within the State Department, and one which, despite Hoover, Borah and others, made itself felt in Geneva: a move away from an optimistic, reforming approach to such issues as disarmament, the Versailles Treaty and international conciliation, and towards a conservative

[1] Noel-Baker to Cecil, 20, 26 April 1932, Cecil Papers, Add. 51107; Cecil to Murray, 17 September 1932, ibid, Add. 51132; Murray to Lee, 29 August 1932, Murray Papers.

[2] E.g., *The Times*, 21 September 1932; DS 033.1140/Reed.

[3] Stimson Diary, 25 July, 16 September 1932; Moffat Diary, 29 March, 3 June 1932.

[4] Stimson Diary, 20 October 1932; Moffat Diary, 8 December 1932; Tuleja, 80 ff.

[5] Stimson Diary, 14 May 1932.

[6] Memoranda of State Dept.—U.S. Navy talks, 30 March and 20 September 1932, Davis Papers, boxes 20 and 17 respectively; Davis to Stimson, 16 April 1933, DS 500 A15A4/1815.

caution that was much closer to the approach of France. Certain important
comments of Pierrepont Moffat on this change have already been noted,[1]
for as Chief of the disarmament section and then of the West European
Division he was well placed to observe what was taking place and to speculate on the connection between this and what he saw as 'a noticeable increase in the isolationist sentiment in the country' since January 1932:

> 'Little by little,' he noted in August, 'the "revisionist" sentiment which I found
> so strong throughout the Department last summer has been giving place to the
> idea that the maintenance of the status quo is of supreme importance in the
> present world situation.'[2]

Japan's challenge to the treaty system in the Far East thus helped to
diminish what sympathy there was in Washington for the growing claims of
Germany in Europe, while bringing out the Administration's ambivalent
approach to naval disarmament. In the reverse direction, the proposals
which Hoover nevertheless insisted on producing at Geneva underlined
what was already fairly apparent: that Stimson's muscle-flexing over the
Far East remained little more than a charade. Together with the President's
debt policy, the American plan also diminished whatever chance Stimson
had of achieving at least the appearance of a united Western front in the
face of Japanese expansion.

In London, Far Eastern events were seen both as confirming the wisdom
of existing assumptions regarding the future development of a major international organisation, and as revealing the inadequacy of such an organisation in terms of providing national security. In the former context, they made
doubly certain that French proposals for endowing the League with greater
authority and even a military capability of its own would meet with instant
rejection. Hankey, for example, was quick to suggest that developments in
Shanghai and Manchuria confirmed the lesson of Corfu, that article 16
could not be applied to a major power,[3] and there was a chorus of agreement
at an important meeting of the Cabinet's Disarmament Committee which
was held on 21 March to discuss the latest French proposals. Thomas, for
one, repeated his earlier arguments about the futility of sanctions without
the United States, and pointed out that only if sanctions were abandoned
altogether might that country be 'brought in to the principle of the League'.
'There could be no doubt,' added Simon disarmingly, 'that the effect of
sanctions was definitely to diminish the influence of the League, particularly
because Japan, who would respect the views of the Great Powers, would say
at once, if they attempted to threaten her, that they had no intention of
carrying out their threats ... The whole situation might have been very
materially changed if it had not been that the question of sanctions was
always lurking in the background.'

> 'The fundamental difference,' concluded MacDonald, 'lay in the fact that in our
> view the League was an instrument created for handling situations on a con-
> ciliation basis and that the League should create a moral force strong enough to
> override attempts to obtain satisfaction by resort to arms. France, on the other

[1] See above, 305.   [2] Moffat Diary, 30 August 1932.
[3] Memorandum of 16 March 1932, CAB 27/509.

hand, held the view that there could be no security . . . unless there was an armed man by your side to ensure it.'[1]

The Prime Minister repeated the argument to both French and American representatives at Geneva, using the Far East as evidence. To Paul-Boncour, he observed that there could be no question of allowing the smaller states to commit those 'who would have to pay the piper'; from Stimson, he forced the admission that Washington, too, had ruled out the use of economic sanctions as being 'a warlike act'.[2]

Yet at the same time the so-called French thesis of needing more 'armed men by your side' was precisely what a good many of MacDonald's advisers and colleagues were themselves now seeking, again brandishing the Far Eastern crisis to support their case. If what had occurred served as a reminder of the world-wide nature of Britain's commitments—and hence the apparent folly of undertaking new ones in Europe—it has been seen that events also brought home to many people in Whitehall what the Services had been saying for years: that the country's military resources were grossly inadequate for meeting those existing obligations. 'If the Japanese ever "ran amok",' observed Baldwin to the Committee of Imperial Defence, 'we would in present circumstances be helpless'.[3] Following the shock of the Chiefs of Staff report in March, a flurry of further studies provided the pieces from which a detailed picture of the military situation began to emerge. Even the Treasury acknowledged that there would have to be some spending at Singapore and other ports, although its response fell far short of what the Services held to be the minimum needed for security, whether over details such as the provision of a second aerodrome at Singapore, or over major estimates such as the one noted earlier from the Admiralty of £22 to £23 million to give the Fleet full operational capability.[4] And while this new emphasis on defence requirements increased the dilemma over a British initiative at Geneva, in naval and Far Eastern terms, as seen above, it drove London apart from Washington. Indeed, where modes of naval disarmament were concerned, it was Japan, the newly-perceived menace, rather than the United States, the hoped-for ally, whose position appeared the closer to Britain's.[5]

There obviously remained strong considerations, of which debts were only

---

[1] CAB 27/505.

[2] Notes of MacDonald—Paul-Boncour conversation, 22 April 1932, Mac-Donald Papers, RM 1/250; DBFP, III, No. 240.

[3] C.I.D. Minutes for 9 June 1932, CAB 2/5.

[4] See, e.g., Hankey to Batterbee, 21 March 1932, CAB 21/368; Air Staff memorandum, 23 March 1932, CAB 27/509 ('Should we refrain . . . from bombing Japanese transports and warships which might be about to attack Singapore before the arrival of our main fleet?'); report of C.I.D. sub-committee on coastal defence, 11 July 1932, CAB 24/231; memorandum by First Sea Lord on Singapore, 11 July 1932, CAB 24/232; memoranda of Secretary of State for Air and First Sea Lord, 8 September and 3 October 1932, respectively, CAB 24/233; Cabinet of 11 October 1932, CAB 23/72; First Sea Lord review, 14 November 1932, ADM 167/87; First Sea Lord to Chancellor of Exchequer, 14 December 1932, ibid.

[5] First Lord memorandum, 24 August 1932, DC(M) (32) 16, CAB 27/509; Cabinet of 24 June 1932, CAB 23/71; DBFP, X, No. 625.

one, for not flinging away American good-will over the Far East. Nevertheless, difficulties over debts and disarmament helped prepare the way for a contrary inclination concerning Far Eastern policy itself. The growing bitterness which has been illustrated, and which was particularly strong in the Treasury and Service Departments, contributed significantly to the belief which became pronounced in 1933 and 1934, that it was high time to stop alienating Japan simply for the sake of placating a moralising, jealous, and unreliable United States.

In Paris, as in London, Far Eastern developments suggested the need to avoid offending Japan unless a major quid pro quo were obtained from across the Atlantic, for example over Germany's claim to 'equality of rights'.[1] On the other hand there could be no mistaking Stimson's keen desire for a clear anti-Japanese line on the part of France.[2] Moreover Norman Davis, Hugh Wilson and others, backed by various press reports and commentaries, went out of their way to emphasise that such a policy might well be decisive in swinging American opinion behind France in a European context, with appropriate action to follow on the part of the Government in Washington. Massigli reported Wilson as putting the matter in the following terms:

> La politique du Japon en Mandchourie est aussi intolérable que peut l'être la violation des clauses militaires du traité de Versailles. Si la France, lorsqu'il s'agit d'application du traité des neuf puissances, garde le souci de ne compromettre ses relations avec le Japon, les États-Unis, de leur côté, auxquels les armements de l'Allemagne importent peu, n'ont pas intérêt à nuire à leurs rapports avec le Reich.
>
> C'est pourquoi l'attitude de la délégation américaine dans la question de l'égalité des droits dépendera finalement, dans une large mesure, de la position qu'adopteraient les puissances européennes et, en particulier, la France, à l'égard des traités qui règlent le statut politique et territorial en Extrême-Orient.[3]

Tokyo's approaches for an understanding helped to push France further into a corner. For all her distant menace in the Far East, Japan could offer far less than Herriot persisted in hoping for from the United States where Germany was concerned, and debt considerations pointed in the same direction. 'Au moment où se pose la question des dettes de guerre,' wrote Massigli in this context, 'nos relations avec l'Amérique sont pour nous d'une suprême importance'.[4] Herriot's own inclination, together with the manifest difficulty of supporting contrary principles in different parts of the world, ensured that the required shift in at least the emphasis of French policy was forthcoming, to be widely commented upon in the press as well as in diplomatic circles.[5] One result was to isolate Britain as the main, timorous if not

[1] See DDF, I, Nos. 202, 209, 286. Earlier in the year, reports had reached Washington that the French Government was only too glad to see the U.S. involved in Far Eastern difficulties, since this would enable Paris to speak out more boldly over debts. DS 851.00/1137, 1138.

[2] E.g., DDF, I, Nos. 78, 96.

[3] Massigli to Herriot, 22 September 1932, DDF, I, No. 202. Cf. ibid, Nos. 195, 206; FRUS, 1932, I, 34–9.

[4] Massigli to Herriot, 9 July 1932, DDF, I, No. 3.

[5] E.g., New York Times, 19 September 1932; News Chronicle, 17 September 1932; Davis to Hornbeck, 17 September 1932, Davis Papers, box 11.

pro-Japanese, villain of the piece in the eyes of many League supporters in Europe and the United States.

Retrospect

Of the three Western powers in the summer and autumn of 1932, it was France who most perceived herself to be in need of concessions from the other two, and whose policies were accordingly most subject to amendment, even if the ensuing changes seldom went very deep.[1] This feature embraced the ending of reparations and the granting in theory of equality of rights to Germany, as well as the refusal of comfort to Japan, and should not be lost sight of beneath the view commonly held at the time—and it was not without some substance—that it was French intransigence above all that was to blame for the failure to achieve success in the desperate search for disarmament and conciliation during that year. In particular, the results of the May elections, coupled with external developments, prompted France to move closer to the United States; in return, despite increased sympathy on the part of the State Department in general, she obtained little more than warm intentions and fair words from Stimson, and certainly not the concessions over debts and security that Herriot hoped for. Where debts were concerned, it was rather the Anglo-French side of the triangle that was strengthened, although here, too, France received little, security-wise, in return for her concessions at Lausanne and in bringing Germany back to the Disarmament Conference. Meanwhile such improvement as there was along the Anglo-French axis was achieved partly at the expense of the Anglo-American one, where the inter-weaving of Western and Far Eastern issues increased distrust in both directions. Britain still paid some heed to the susceptibilities of the United States, and Stimson—far more shrewd and realistic over European than over Asiatic affairs—would have liked to reciprocate to a greater degree than Hoover, Congress and the American public allowed. As it was, it was the United States of the three countries that made the fewest concessions, while moralising the most.

At the end of 1932 the debt question was still there to sour Western relations. Despite Germany's return to the Conference, significant arms reductions appeared further off than ever. MacDonald and Simon in London and Hornbeck in Washington were among those considering the possibility of strengthening the representation of their respective countries at Geneva by means of having permanent missions there (a development which Drummond was resisting vigorously where the small states were concerned).[2] On all sides, however, it was acknowledged that the League of Nations had

[1] It could be said, for example, that there was little *practical* change in French Far Eastern policy. And there are those who would argue that it was Léger (now Secretary-General of the Quai d'Orsay) rather than Herriot who guided that policy.

[2] See Cabinet of 13 December 1932, CAB 23/73; MacDonald to Baldwin, 3 December 1932, Baldwin Papers, vol. 118; MacDonald to Simon, 26 October 1932, and 3 January 1933, Simon Papers (private collection), Foreign Affairs, 1932, 1933; Tyrrell to Simon, 3 January, 1933, ibid; MacDonald to Simon, 23 December, Simon to MacDonald, 30 December 1932, FO 800/287. MacDonald thought that

suffered a severe loss of prestige during the year.[1] Apart from the lack of progress over disarmament, it was the unresolved Far Eastern question that was mainly responsible. And with the Lytton Report now on the table, this issue was about to build up to its second and final climax.

Eden did not yet have the weight to assume permanent leadership at Geneva; he put forward his son's name for consideration, Tyrrell that of Austen Chamberlain. See also Sweetser to Davis, 2 September 1932, Davis Papers, box 62; Shotwell to Davis, 29 November 1932, ibid, box 53; Hornbeck memorandum, 22 March 1933, Hornbeck Papers, box 276; Green memorandum, 13 April, 1933, ibid, box 176; Hornbeck–Gilbert correspondence, ibid, box 177. On Drummond's views, see V-Y Ghébali, *Les délégations permanentes auprès de la Société des Nations* (Geneva, Carnegie Foundation, 1969).

[1] See, e.g., *The Problems of Peace, 7th Series*, passim.

CHAPTER 10

A LEAGUE CONCLUSION AND THE DEPARTURE OF JAPAN

Developments in the Far East

FAR FROM enjoying undisturbed the fruits of its conquest in Manchuria, the Kwantung Army in this period continued to find itself engaged in far-flung and inconclusive attempts to prevent Chinese irregulars and bandits from disrupting communications, especially in the north and north-west of the country.[1] Public attention was now focussed on an area further south, however, where the Great Wall marked the boundary between Manchuria and North China. Here, where the Mukden-Peking railway crossed this line at Shanhaikuan, an incident on 1 January 1933 led to a brief flurry of renewed fighting, with the Japanese occupying Shanhaikuan itself two days later and pursuing the Chinese towards Chinwangtao ten miles away, a coaling port where there were important British economic interests centred around the Kailan Mining Administration. More significantly, the new move left the Japanese poised for action within the vital strategic triangle bounded by Shanhaikuan, Luanchow and Hsifengkow, the occupation of which up to the Luan river would seal off a major alternative route into Manchuria, as well as providing a preliminary base for the occupation of Jehol province to the north.[2]

From the outset the Japanese had maintained that Jehol fell within the jurisdiction of Manchukuo, and it was true that under both Chang Tso-lin and Chang Hsueh-liang the region had been loosely controlled from Mukden; as noted earlier, its contiguity with Chahar and Inner Mongolia also made its fate a matter of particular concern to the Soviet Union. Bold promises of a great patriotic war to defend the province now issued from the Chinese, and although Chiang Kai-shek continued to direct his own efforts against the Communists in Kiangsi, around 200,000 troops under Chang Hsueh-liang had been gathered in Jehol by February 1933. On the 23rd of that month the Japanese issued an ultimatum, rejected by Nanking on the following day, demanding the acceptance of Manchukuoan sovereignty over the region; in the face of a swift pincer movement by Japanese forces who, though better armed, amounted to less than a quarter of their number, the Chinese then

[1] See, e.g., DBFP, XI, Nos. 1, 8.

[2] See, e.g., ibid, Nos. 167, 168, 172, 174, 281. 'Shanhaikwan' is an alternative spelling.

retreated in confusion, with Jehol city falling on 4 March and a firm line of resistance being established only back around the passes through the Great Wall.[1] The damage done to the standing of China in Western eyes was considerable.[2] In addition, there was mounting anxiety at the possibility of a Japanese descent into the region of Peking and Tientsin—perhaps, some thought, with the intention of installing Pu-yi on the throne of China to which he had once been heir. Particular attention was paid to the rights which Japanese troops, as well as those of the West, already enjoyed in this area.[3]

The Jehol fiasco also created further confusion on the Chinese political scene, where a great deal of bitterness was now being directed against Britain for what was claimed to be her shielding of Japan from the condemnation of the world. Simon's major speech at Geneva in December provided the chief occasion for this hostility, with the existence of a secret Anglo-Japanese understanding over Tibet and Manchuria being claimed as a fact, as some Foreign Office officials had gloomily foreseen.[4] The futility of relying on the League as a whole was also the subject of much press and Kuomintang comment.[5] At the same time her resumption of diplomatic relations with the Soviet Union in December suggested that China could find an alternative friend—even if that friend continued to sit on the fence where the Far Eastern conflict was concerned, its press ready to condemn Tokyo's imperialism, but its Government, for example, permitting the conclusion of a new agreement for the delivery of oil to Japan.[6] Meanwhile the policy that China herself should pursue towards Japan formed one of the issues in her own continuing faction-fights. There were those who advocated coming to an understanding with the invader, and rumours of secret negotiations had frequently to be denied;[7] on the other hand the extent of anti-Japanese feeling made the cry of outright resistance a more attractive one politically, and provided ready ammunition for the Canton régime of Marshal Chen Chi-tang to use against Nanking and Chiang Kai-shek. Relations were also strained between Chiang and T. V. Soong, Minister of Finance and Acting Chairman of the Executive Yuan, while the Jehol affair completed the reduction in stature of Soong's friend, Chang Hsueh-liang. In Fukien, Kiangsi, Hupeh and Hunan the Communists remained

---

[1] See, e.g., ibid, Nos. 368, 378, 379, 412, 419, 448.

[2] Scornful press comments were numerous. On a despatch reporting the large-scale desertions from the Chinese Army, Vansittart wrote: 'The Chinese appear to be nearly related to the Oxford Union.' FO 371, F 1434/18/10.

[3] See, e.g., DBFP, XI, No. 288. Under the Boxer Protocol of 1901 the Japanese had the right to station a Legation guard at Peking, a garrison at Tientsin and a railway guard along a section of the line from Peking to the sea. The Chinese for their part were forbidden to station or march troops within twenty Chinese li (6⅔ miles) of Peking, or within two miles of the Peking–Tientsin railway.

[4] See, e.g., DBFP, XI, Nos. 101, 113, 114, 265, 271, 273, 275, 277, 280, 290. The anti-British agitation began to die down in February (see ibid, No. 315), although the Tibetan issue remained unresolved. See ibid, Nos. 9, 12, 14, 21, 157, 269, 296.

[5] See, e.g., ibid, No. 139.

[6] See ibid, Nos. 109, 123, 242 and in particular Ovey to Simon, 25 October 1932, ibid, No. 18.

[7] See, e.g. ibid, Nos. 65, 457, 464.

powerful, and in Szechuan continued to win ground.[1] As Japan embarked upon the final presentation of her case at Geneva, there appeared to be strong evidence for her contention that China did not constitute an organised state as contemplated by those who had framed the League Covenant.

In Japan itself public opinion still showed no lessening of support for what was being done in Manchuria. The growing likelihood that the League would formally condemn these acts created what one observer described as 'public frenzy and excitement', together with talk of the need to face economic sanctions or even war if necessary; that Japan should defy her accusers and leave the League was almost unquestioned in public.[2] In January 1933 a protocol of alliance with Manchukuo demonstrated the Government's own determination not to turn back, with Mukden's subsequent promise of an 'open door and equal opportunity' in the economic development of the new state being plainly at variance with the special position already accorded Japan.[3] A Foreign Exchange Control Law, following the Capital Flight Prevention Law of 1932, also testified to Japan's preparedness to fight for her economic and financial survival.[4] Following an adverse vote in the Assembly of the League, the country duly withdrew from the proceedings at Geneva on 24 February 1933, and on 27 March formally notified Drummond of her intention to leave the organisation entirely.

Publicly, then, the policy of the Japanese Government appeared to be clear and decisive. Privately, too, Cabinet members braced themselves for the international crisis that might lie ahead.[5] Rather than becoming more coherent in this situation, however, the policy-making process in Tokyo was now rapidly taking on those features of confusion and fissiparity—'a system of irresponsibility', as one scholar has described it[6]—that were to last into the Pacific war. Over Jehol, for example, suggestions for restraint came from the Foreign Office and Navy, lest the League and Soviet Union be needlessly antagonised; but Araki, while promising that operations would not go beyond Shanhaikuan, obtained Government authorisation for the move which the Kwantung Army was already determined upon.[7] Araki also maintained a strong line in public against any League interference, while helping to ensure that the Cabinet decided on 19 February to leave that organisation if it censured Japan (both senior civilian Ministers and Matsuoka at Geneva were still hoping not to have to adopt this course); in addition, he obtained the rejection of certain softening phrases that were

[1] See, e.g., ibid, Nos. 15, 495 and appendix; also, for local conditions, the Quarterly Political and Intelligence Reports of British Consuls and Consuls-General, in FO 371, files 17066, 17067.

[2] Takeuchi, 415–17. Stimson in particular was popularly blamed in Japan for foreign criticism of the country, and the Democratic electoral victory in November was greeted with much satisfaction.

[3] See the 'Economic Construction Programme for Manchukuo', promulgated on 1 March 1933; IMTFE, *Exhibit* 442.

[4] IMTFE, *Proceedings*, 8,480–1.

[5] See, e.g., records of the Cabinet meeting of 22 December 1932, IMTFE, *Exhibit* 234.

[6] Ogata, 192; cf. Crowley, 180, and below, 373–4

[7] See IMTFE, *Proceedings*, 19,499 ff.; *Exhibits* 230, 3378A; *Taiheiyo senso e no michi*, II, cap. 7; Crowley, 183–4.

suggested by the Emperor for inclusion in his Edict on the country's with-drawal.[1] Meanwhile hostility towards the Soviet Union in Army circles constituted a complicating factor during the negotiations with Moscow over a possible non-aggression pact, and although one senior Foreign Office official thought it 'absolutely necessary to strengthen Soviet-Japanese relations now, not only for obtaining oil, but for securing our rear', the Soviet proposal was ultimately rejected as being 'untimely'.[2] Thus, when the break with the League took place, the future direction of Japanese policy remained a matter of some confusion in Tokyo, as well as one of intense speculation in the West.

Public reactions in the West

The regular Assembly of the League had gathered at Geneva in September 1932 in an atmosphere of gloom. 'Let us be frank with ourselves,' declared de Valera in his opening speech as chairman of the Council:

> There is on all sides complaint, criticism and suspicion. People are complaining that the League is devoting its activity to matters of secondary or very minor importance, while the vital international problems of the day . . . are being shelved or postponed or ignored. People are saying that the equality of States does not apply here in the things that matter . . . Finally, there is the suspicion that little more than lip service is paid to the fundamental principles on which the League is founded . . . We are defendants at the bar of public opinion with a burden of justification upon us that is almost overwhelming.[3]

De Valera repeated his warning, with particular reference to 'an intolerable defiance of public opinion', when, following the delay granted to Japan, the Council itself met between 21 and 28 November to consider the Lytton Report. That body did little to restore the confidence to which its chairman had referred, however, being content to listen to the usual exchanges be-tween the Chinese and Japanese representatives, now Wellington Koo and Matsuoka Yosuke respectively, and being reminded by the latter of Austen Chamberlain's note to Kellogg in 1928 concerning 'certain regions of the world . . . of special and vital interest' to Britain.[4] Lytton, who had been invited to appear in order to answer questions, added nothing to his Com-mission's Report, which the Council then passed on without comment to the special Assembly, which technically had remained in being since the previous March.[5] The Committee of Nineteen also survived from the spring, although, as Motta tartly observed, its presence within the Assembly 'did not release States Members of the Council from the obligation incum-bent on all other States to form a definite opinion on the dispute and state their views on the way in which it should be settled'.[6]

[1] See IMTFE, *Exhibits*, 2427, 3164A; Takeuchi, 412; Ogata, 174–5.
[2] Togo Shigenori, report 'On the Foreign Policy of Japan vis-à-vis Europe and America Following Withdrawal From the League of Nations', April 1933, IMTFE, *Exhibit* 3609A; cf. *Exhibits* 745, 746, 747, 2253.
[3] LNOJ, *Special Supplement No. 104* (Geneva, 1932), 24–6.
[4] LNOJ, *December, 1932*, 1870–77, 1891–98, 1901–12.   [5] See above, 212–4.
[6] LNOJ, *Special Supplement No. 111* (Geneva, 1933), 18–21.

Motta's remark reflected a feature of the autumn's meetings that was widely remarked upon: the distrust, disappointment and even scorn of representatives of several of the smaller states for the major powers on the Council, and for Britain in particular.[1] In the summer of 1933 Sean Lester of Ireland was to comment publicly on this split, and in private he had tried to strengthen the final report being drafted by the Committee of Nineteen for presentation to the Assembly in February.[2] The same sentiments were revealed during the Assembly's meetings between 6 and 9 December in the speeches of Benes, Unden, Madariaga and Motta, and above all in the draft resolution—'the hoisting of a flag', Lester later called it—that was put forward in the names of Switzerland, Spain, Ireland and Czechoslovakia, and that sought to have Japan's actions condemned and the non-recognition of Manchukuo reiterated there and then.[3] Such impatient anger naturally received the warm approval of the Chinese delegation; from Matsuoka it drew forth warnings on the folly of precipitate action, as well as reminders of such past actions by Western powers as those of Britain in Shanghai in 1927 and of the United States in Nicaragua.

The exasperation of many League supporters reached a peak during the speeches made by delegates of the major powers on December 7. In his address to the Assembly, Paul-Boncour chose to emphasise that 'a whole host of complexities' had been encountered in Manchuria 'such as could not be matched in any other part of the globe'; in his, Neurath for Germany quoted the Lytton Report's conclusion that this was no simple case of frontier violation or a declaration of war; Aloisi for Italy, in one of his rare contributions, described 'world public opinion' as demanding 'a solution based on realities', rather than the establishment of 'academic principles'. It was Simon's address above all, however, which aroused the greatest indignation and subsequent controversy. Speaking impressively as usual— one critical observer found himself 'paralyzed for the moment' by the flow of the argument[4]—the Foreign Secretary referred to this reported division in the ranks of the League when he proclaimed Britain's continuing loyalty to that organisation:

> There is no difference in this connection . . . between what are sometimes called the small States and the great Powers. There is a difference, no doubt, in the way that the great Powers, by the very circumstances of their position, may have upon their shoulders the greater responsibilities and the largest risks, but, so far as the desire and the determination to act as loyal Members of the League of Nations are concerned, for all of us alike the Covenant . . . is our constitutional law . . . We are not at liberty to disregard it. We are bound to sustain it.

[1] See, e.g., Toynbee, *Survey, 1932*, 488 ff., *Journal de Genève*, 13 December 1932.
[2] Lester to Hymans, 30 January 1933, LN. Archives, R3624; *The Problems of Peace, 8th series* (London, 1934), 120 ff.
[3] See LNOJ, *Special Supplement No. 111*, annex X. For the Assembly speeches of December 6–9, see ibid, 32–75. The final resolution of 9 December is given in annex XI. The session of the 9th also approved the appointment of Avenol to succeed Drummond on the latter's retirement on 30 June 1933. See Barros, *Betrayal From Within*, cap. 1.
[4] Fleming, *The United States and World Organization*, 446, note. The speech is described and defended in Bassett, 281 ff.

It was not this passage that remained in the minds of most of Simon's listeners, however, nor his observation that Japan had 'not employed the methods of the League' in her dispute with China. It was rather his continued emphasis on conciliation as opposed to condemnation (in other words, his contention that section 3 of article 15 was not yet exhausted, and that the time had not yet arrived to proceed under section 4), and above all the way in which he dwelt upon those faults on the part of China that the Lytton Report had found deserving of note. Conditions in Manchuria and most of China, he remarked, 'made sorry reading'; with that, his protestations of loyalty, like his constructive suggestion for inviting the United States and the Soviet Union to join the Committee of Nineteen in its task of conciliation, were quite overshadowed. Matters were made worse in the eyes of his critics by Matsuoka's widely reported aside that the Foreign Secretary had succeeded in saying in a short space of time what he himself had been trying to get across for ten days.[1] Commonwealth collusion appeared proven when Bruce of Australia followed on by deprecating 'the rigorous and censorious application of theoretical and dogmatic principles'; Cahan, the Canadian Secretary of State, then completed matters by expressing 'more or less personal' doubts as to whether China fulfilled the conditions necessary for admission to the League as a responsible state.

The indignation of Benes, Madariaga and others was apparent. At the same time it should be noted that the representatives of some small states chose to speak with caution—Politis of Greece, for example, expressed the hope that section 4 of article 15 could still be avoided—and that a secret meeting of ten such states on 5 December failed to agree on the prompt condemnation of Japan that was advocated by Benes.[2] It was also reported that Madariaga and others were apparently contemplating a bargain whereby the Assembly would merely reaffirm its Resolution of the previous March in return for Japan's agreement to examine the concluding chapters of the Lytton Report in company with China, the Committee of Nineteen, the Soviet Union and the United States.[3] Even Yen of China, although he asked for a report under section 4 of article 15, a demand for the withdrawal of Japanese troops and a declaration that the Tokyo Government had violated the Covenant, did not seek the swift application of article 16, while the radical leaders among the smaller states likewise stopped short of calling for immediate economic sanctions. Clearly, this failure to advocate forceful measures must be attributed in part to the knowledge that support would not be forthcoming from those powers, including the United States, whose participation would be essential to success. In addition, however,

---

[1] Matsuoka subsequently wrote Simon a treacly note claiming to have been misreported: 'What I did say to a friend was: "It was a fine, judicious speech, so ably condensed. Why, it would take me ten days to draft, and yet I wouldn't be able to make such a fine speech." ' Simon Papers (private collection), Foreign Affairs, 1932. It is important to note that Benes, in his speech, had also recalled some of China's shortcomings, and had suggested that her anti-foreign propaganda and boycotts 'should be condemned'.

[2] Pratt memorandum, 5 December 1932, DBFP, XI, No. 88. On the division of opinion within Sweden, for example, see ibid, No. 152.

[3] Wilson to Stimson, 2 December 1932, FRUS, 1932, IV, 381–2.

there appears to have been an increased awareness that Japan was not going to back down before 'world' opinion or verbal censure, and a matching caution when it came to suggesting alternative and potentially more dangerous courses of action. Such an interpretation is reinforced by an examination of the subsequent and private proceedings of the Committee of Nineteen (which the Assembly on 9 December requested to study the Lytton Report and to submit proposals for a settlement), together with those of its own drafting committee on which Britain and France were joined by Switzerland, Spain, Czechoslovakia and Belgium. Despite the fact that some members of the Committee were anxious, in the words of a British observer, 'to lay down principles and pass to an immediate judgement against Japan',[1] the majority were prepared to explore further the possibility of conciliation,[2] only the Irish representative, it seems, objecting to a draft of the final report which failed to state unequivocally that Japan had broken articles 10 and 12 of the Covenant.[3]

This is not to say that tension did not continue to exist at Geneva, nor that Britain's own policy, as expressed by Eden on the drafting committee, did not respond to it in some degree. It is not true, however, that the smaller states were ready to go to any lengths to compel Japan to give way and thus preserve the League as a bulwark for the future. As for the efforts of the Committee of Nineteen and its drafting body, the details need not be recapitulated here (they were not publicly available at the time, though as usual leaks and rumours abounded). One difficulty lay in Japan's objection to the idea that the United States and Soviet Union should be invited to participate in the task of conciliation, and on this point it was agreed that that intention could be abandoned if Tokyo made concessions on other, major issues. These centred around the draft resolution and 'statement of reasons' that were adopted by the Committee, and in particular around the refusal contained in the second of these documents to accept the Manchukuo régime as part of a final settlement. Despite the submission by Japan of counter-proposals up to the last moment, negotiations inevitably foundered on this point. Hymans, the Committee's chairman, had made every effort to avoid such an outcome; so had Drummond, who, with Sugimura, continued to play a major role behind the scenes and in doing so incurred the largely unjustified accusation of the *Manchester Guardian*, *Le Populaire* and others, that he was both exceeding his competence and helping to shield Japan.[4]

[1] Patteson to Vansittart, 13 December 1932, DBFP, XI, No. 110. The meeting referred to took place on 12 December.

[2] See, e.g., Patteson to Simon, 19 January 1932, ibid, No. 220.

[3] See Pratt memorandum, 30 January 1933, ibid, No. 260; Lester to Hymans, 30 January 1933, LN. Archives, R 3624. At one point Madariaga suggested that a time-limit should be established for compliance with the League's proposals for a settlement. DBFP, XI, No. 295. On the question of whether Japan should be explicitly declared to have broken the Covenant, Dr. Madariaga has written to me: 'I remember only that Lester and I were in complete agreement, and if he often spoke alone, we thought and voted together. So, I surmise that such was the case on this particular point. Proof, however, I have none.'

[4] See *Le Populaire*, 15 January 1933; *Manchester Guardian*, 14, 16, 23 January 1933. Cf. DBFP, XI, Nos. 191, 203, 217, 223, 226, 227, 229, 237, 247, 248, 264, 297, 298; minutes of the League Directors' meeting, 17 January 1933, loc. cit. For

On 15 February, the Committee resolved that their attempts at conciliation were exhausted and that their final report should be published two days later as provided for under section 4 of article 15 of the Covenant. After seventeen months, the League was about to reach a conclusion.[1]

The draft report that now came before the Assembly incorporated the substance of the Lytton Commission's findings, while recommending a settlement based on a large measure of autonomy for Manchuria under Chinese sovereignty, a non-aggression treaty between China and Japan, and temporary international cooperation in the internal reconstruction of China. Japan's rights in Manchuria should be recognised; Manchukuo should not. On the conflict itself, the report concluded that 'before 18 September, 1931, certain responsibilities would appear to lie on one side and the other', but that 'no question of Chinese responsibility can arise for the development of events since (that date)'. Japan's military actions thereafter could not be regarded as measures of self-defence, while it was in her hands that there lay the real power behind the so-called independent state of Manchukuo. Nevertheless, Japan was not explicitly declared to have broken the Covenant. By this means, the logic of proceeding to article 16 was avoided, just as it had been up till then, in terms of international law, by the failure of both parties to declare war or their intention to make war.[2] Instead, it was 'pointed out' that under article 10 Members were pledged to respect each other's territorial integrity and political independence, and that under article 12 they were bound to submit disputes that were likely to lead to a rupture to arbitration, judicial settlement, or the Council. Likewise, the major conclusion of the report, while clear enough, also contained an important qualification:

> Undoubtedly the present case is not that of a country which has declared war on another country without previously exhausting the opportunities for conciliation provided in the Covenant . . .; neither is it a simple case of the violation of the frontier of one country by the armed forces of a neighbouring country. . . . It is, however, indisputable that, without any declaration of war, a large part of Chinese territory has been forcibly seized and occupied by Japanese troops and that, in consequence of this operation, it has been separated from and declared independent of the rest of China.

At the tense and crowded Assembly meeting of 24 February,[3] the Chinese delegation welcomed this report and accepted its recommendations. At the same time, and no doubt to the discomfort of some present, they emphasised that this could not be considered the end of the matter, and that in Jehol a

---

tributes to Drummond in the Assembly, see LNOJ, *Special Supplement No. 111*, 75–7.

[1] The Committee of Nineteen's draft report and 'statement of reasons' are printed in LNOJ, *Special Supplement No. 112* (Geneva, 1933), annex V, and correspondence relating to its drafting in annex VI. The private proceedings of the Committee can be followed in DBFP, XI, Nos. 98–365, passim, and FRUS, 1932, IV and 1933, III, passim. The Committee's final draft report was broadcast in morse from the League's new wireless station near Geneva.

[2] See Quincy Wright, 'When Does War Exist?', in *American Journal of International Law*, vol. 26 (1932), 362–8.

[3] See LNOJ, *Special Supplement No. 112*, 11–28.

new threat appeared imminent, against which the Covenant provided 'all the sanctions' that might be required. Matsuoka, on the other hand, speaking with great earnestness, urged the Assembly not to adopt the report, 'for the sake of peace in the Far East and for the sake of peace in the world'. Japan's record was one of working for order and stability. Now, in close proximity to the chaos of China and the menace of the Soviet Union, 'we look into the gloom of the future and can see no certain gleam of light before us'. What did the League propose to do about the anarchy which prevailed under the fiction of a responsible government in Nanking? In Manchuria, which was vital to Japan, international supervision had been proposed, but 'would the American people agree to such control over the Panama Canal Zone? Would the British people permit it over Egypt?'

A few, brief speeches followed, then the vote. Japan alone opposed the motion; Siam abstained;[1] the remaining forty-two states agreed to adopt the report. Matsuoka rose again, and in a brief statement that impressed its gravity on all present[2] declared that, while Japan would still endeavour to cooperate with the League for the preservation of world peace, he regretted that she could no longer do so as regards her dispute with China. Abruptly motioning his delegation to his side, he then left the hall.

These developments at Geneva provided almost the only public reactions of the Western powers in this period, still absorbed as they were with domestic and other international difficulties. In the United States, for example, with unemployment still rising, a new banking crisis sprang up in February as Roosevelt's inauguration drew near and the country moved closer to going off gold. (Pierrepont Moffat noted in his diary on 20 February that Washington was 'almost hysterical in its fear for our financial and economic future'.) In France, Paul-Boncour, who had succeeded Herriot as Premier, lasted only until 28 January, and was followed in turn by Daladier. The Disarmament Conference, which resumed in February, showed no likelihood of resolving the central Franco-German deadlock or of reaching an agreed definition of the term 'aggression', and awaited the final major attempt to revive it by MacDonald in March. With new tariffs and other measures of economic nationalism clogging the exchange of goods, a world conference on the subject was planned for the summer, but war-debts were excluded from its draft agenda on American insistence, while for all his fair words the incoming President of that country was (rightly) not wholly trusted to adopt a wide view in practice.[3]

Over the Far Eastern dispute, Roosevelt did imply that he would continue the policy of the Republican Administration by proclaiming in January that the United States 'must uphold the sanctity of international treaties'.[4]

[1] On Siam's motives for abstaining, see DBFP, XI, Nos. 472, 473. The Assembly went on to appoint an advisory committee 'to follow the situation', consisting of the members of the Committee of Nineteen, plus Canada and the Netherlands, and with invitations to be issued to the United States and the Soviet Union to cooperate in its work.   [2] See, e.g., Wilson, 281.

[3] These issues can conveniently be followed in outline in Toynbee, *Survey, 1933.*
[4] FRUS, 1933, III, 102; *New York Times.* 17 January 1933.

Stimson himself welcomed the Assembly's vote of 24 February to the extent of declaring that the United States was 'substantially in accord' with the League over the facts of the case, and in agreement with its principles advanced as the basis for a settlement'.[1] Beyond this, however, the period following the publication of the Lytton Report was marked by almost complete silence on the subject from Washington, and the one official move that in theory might have had some bearing on the issue, a request by Hoover for the power to impose an arms embargo on belligerents, swiftly became bogged down in the interest-ridden mire of Congressional committees.[2] As if to add further embarrassment, Senator Thomas Schall listed the extensive strategic supplies that continued to flow into Japan from the United States.[3] Meanwhile French policy, although remaining firm in support of the Covenant, continued to show no sign of initiative. The one surprise move in public, in fact, came from London of all places, when, on 27 February, Simon announced that pending international discussion licences would be suspended for the export of arms from Britain to both Japan and China.[4] Even this step, far from being a punishment of Japan, was evidently no more than a gesture, and on 13 March Baldwin announced that it had been withdrawn for lack of support abroad.[5] League supporters were left to draw what comfort they could from the Assembly's pronouncements and Japan's departure.

Britain's abortive embargo nevertheless deserves some further attention, for whatever its apparently futile nature, it constituted a direct response to members of the public who were seeking support for the post-war system of international obligations.[6] Various and discordant calls for an arms embargo of some kind have been noted earlier, in connection with the Shanghai crisis,[7] and their volume, though not their harmony, reached a new level as the Assembly prepared to make its final decision and fighting was resumed, this time in Jehol. It was not that Britain was the major arms supplier to the area. The battle for orders among European firms was a fierce one, especially in China,[8] with French manufactures coming in through Indo-China and aeroplanes being supplied by Italy and by Heinkel of Germany. Weapons for the Far East were also being shipped out of Hamburg from the Czech Skoda works (a trade which Benes apparently felt unable to stop), while several other German firms besides Heinkel were selling to both belligerents, despite denials by their Embassy in Tokyo. In the United States, as Senator Schall and others had revealed, private firms continued to supply planes, weapons, and explosives, and arms were also said to be entering China from the Soviet Union. Oil supplies also continued

---

[1] Stimson to Wilson, 25 February 1933, FRUS, *Japan, 1931–1941*, I, 115–16.

[2] See below, 345–6

[3] *Congressional Record, 72nd Congress*, vol. 76, 5446.

[4] For the details of the debate of 27 February, referred to again below, see *Hansard, House of Commons*, vol. 275, cols. 34–156.

[5] Ibid, col. 1592.

[6] For a more detailed study, see Christopher Thorne, 'The Quest for Arms Embargoes: Failure in 1933', in *Journal of Contemporary History*, vol. 5, No. 4, 1970. Cf. Bassett, 383 ff.

[7] See above, 217.   [8] See, e.g., FRUS, 1932, IV, 588.

to flow into Japan from the Soviet Union, the United States and the Dutch East Indies.[1] In fact in 1932 British arms sales as recorded by the Board of Trade had amounted to only £500,000 to Japan and under £100,000 to China, with licences issued in February 1933 also covering only small amounts of material.[2] As noted earlier, however, the British Government was alone in having to issue a licence for each sale of this kind, and was therefore vulnerable to the demand that it should give a lead to other states.

It was this situation, together with the widespread distrust that had been engendered by Simon's performance at Geneva, which critics of the Government now set out to exploit. The T.U.C. General Council and Labour Party National Executive, for example, proposed on 22 February an embargo on arms to both combatants—a 'no-blood-money' decision, in other words, which they promptly and characteristically mixed with a punitive one by calling for an economic boycott against Japan alone if she refused the League's proposals. The *Daily Herald*, too, wanted to see an arms embargo against both states, then changed to a demand for one against Japan alone. The *News Chronicle*, *New Statesman* and *Manchester Guardian* were now more consistent in the latter cause, and while Lord Lytton himself spoke ambiguously on the matter, even *The Times*, after some wavering, appeared to support an embargo on arms to Japan in a leader of 25 February, as did a small group of Conservatives in the Commons.[3]

The main mover outside official circles, however, was Gilbert Murray, who had abandoned his earlier desire for an embargo on arms to both countries, and who now led the L.N.U. in a search for some gesture, at least, by which faith in collective security could be reaffirmed in an otherwise highly frustrating situation. In December, amid the repercussions of Simon's speech at Geneva, Murray had written to the Foreign Secretary to warn him

> that opinion in the Union is greatly worked up over the Japanese crisis. They fear that you are going too far in the direction of conciliation . . . and that any failure to stand firm for the Lytton Report and the non-recognition of Manchu-Kuo will result in a betrayal of the League and the whole new order in international politics . . . Cecil and I used strong influence with the Council to prevent some public message of the sort being sent to you . . . Letters of indignation are pouring in daily.[4]

The outcome of the letter was an invitation to Murray to call on Simon at his home in Oxfordshire at the end of the month, when the Foreign Secretary went out of his way to reassure his visitor that the Government would not default over the Lytton Report, but also to explain the constraints within which British policy had to be formulated. Simon followed this up with a letter to the same effect, enclosing a copy of the remarks he had recently addressed to representatives of both China and Japan concerning Britain's

[1] See, e.g., FRUS, 1932, IV, 70; ibid, 1933, III, 285; DS 793.94/4606, 4652, 4726, 4823, 5767; Pearson and Brown, 353. In Germany, the Foreign Ministry was largely ignorant of the arms sales to China being promoted by the Defence Ministry.

[2] Minutes of the Disarmament Committee of the Cabinet, 22 February 1933, CAB 21/379; *The Times*, 14 March 1933; *Manchester Guardian*, 17 April, 1933.

[3] See *Journal de Genève*, 16 February 1933; *Manchester Guardian*, 18, 20, 24, 25, 27 February 1933; *The Times*, 22, 24, 25 February 1933.

[4] Murray to Simon, 14 December 1932, FO 800/287.

readiness to pronounce on the merits of the dispute if conciliation failed.[1] 'It is a relief to me to see your letter,' Murray replied, 'and I shall now be able to reassure many of my friends on the Left, of course without quoting or hinting at my authority.'[2]

Within a few weeks, however, Murray had become convinced of the need for 'a great national agitation against the supply of arms to Japan',[3] and was again warning Simon of the mounting feeling in the Union's Executive Committee. With the implied threat that those on 'the Left' still favoured a resort to article 16, he described the Committee as a whole as desiring a strong line on non-recognition, a denial of financial aid to Japan, and an arms embargo against that country. 'The feeling on this [last] point is extremely strong,' he added.[4] On 31 January he followed this with a visit to the Foreign Secretary, accompanied by Austen Chamberlain. Chamberlain also favoured an embargo, although he soon came to believe that, however unfair it might seem, such action would have to embrace China as well as Japan, for fear of the 'very dangerous complications' that might otherwise arise.[5] 'Gilbert Murray goes with me to ginger me up,' he wrote to his wife, 'and I go with him to tone him down and we both go to keep the Union from taking violent courses'.[6] On the day after the interview he reported that he thought he and Murray could 'hold the Union Committee with the material given us and prevent any follies', while Simon from his side wrote to say that he was setting out to explore the arms question further, 'one of the most *intractable* of subjects'.[7] Murray speeded him on his way on 13 February by sending a resolution from his Committee that urged the Government to secure international agreement for the banning of arms supplies to any disputing state which refused to accept a League decision or report,[8] and in *The Times* on the 25th he applied the suggestion to Japan by name.

The Government's limited response in the shape of its two-nation embargo was publicly welcomed by Cecil, Murray and the Union as an interim measure that they hoped would be followed by similar international action against Japan alone. Stafford Cripps was among those who spoke in the same sense in the Commons, while pacifists like Maude Royden rejoiced, even while recognising that China, with its inadequate domestic arms-industry, was being unfairly penalised.[9] Lord Davies, leader of the Welsh branch of the L.N.U., however, condemned the embargo as 'a cowardly and futile effort to avoid "trouble"'; the right-wing press meanwhile attacked it for endangering relations with Japan; business interests in China regretted

[1] Simon to Murray, 29 December 1932, Murray Papers.

[2] Murray to Simon, 30 December 1932, ibid.

[3] Murray to Davies, 27 January 1933, ibid.

[4] Murray to Simon, 21, 26 January 1933, FO 371, F 881/33/10.

[5] See Austen to Lady Chamberlain, 24, 25, 28 February, 1 March 1933, Austen Chamberlain Papers, AC 6/1/902–1062.

[6] Austen to Lady Chamberlain, 30 January 1933, ibid.

[7] Austen to Lady Chamberlain, 1 February 1933, ibid; Simon to Murray, 1 February 1933, FO 371, F 881/33/10.

[8] Appendix to Simon memorandum of 18 February 1933, CP 42 (33), CAB 24/238.

[9] See Royden to Murray, 28 February 1933, Murray Papers; *Manchester Guardian*, 28 February, 4 March 1933; *The Times*, 28 February, 1 March 1933.

the damage it was likely to cause to Anglo-Chinese trade.[1] There was little outcry when the new measure was lifted only two weeks later;[2] the Government could claim, after all, that it had sought international action, as so many of its critics had demanded, while the swift end to the fighting in Jehol seems to have reduced the pressure on a good many consciences.

The reasons for this brief and limited measure of success by the Union will emerge later in the chapter, when the private reactions within Whitehall are examined. Here it can be suggested that an arms embargo of some kind was an attractive target for the L.N.U. in the first place, partly because it represented a highest-common-factor among the senior ranks of that earnest but often unharmonious body. In the early part of 1933, fierce disagreements over disarmament and a League force—matters which had important implications for the Far Eastern issue as well—were reaching a climax, with Austen Chamberlain straining to resign from the Executive Committee. His exasperation with Cecil, Garnett and others has been illustrated earlier,[3] and he was now frequently and wearily complaining to friends of the uphill task of introducing an element of realism into the Union's thinking. In turn, Cecil came to believe that there was a serious danger that Chamberlain might paralyse the Union's work altogether.[4]

In addition, there remained deep divisions over the Far Eastern question itself, although as before there was a substantial amount of common dissatisfaction with others. MacDonald, for example, was now generally despaired of as having sold out to the Tories, a charge he bitterly rejected in private correspondence, demanding—and not obtaining—proof of the pro-Japanese Tory conspiracy whose existence was suggested to him.[5] Simon continued to attract widespread criticism, including that of Austen Chamberlain, who thought he 'played too much for safety and inspired no confidence in anyone',[6] while Drummond again came in for unfavourable comment, especially from Noel-Baker in Geneva.[7] More positively, there

[1] See *The Times*, 1 March 1933; *Daily Telegraph*, 28 February, 1933; British Chamber of Commerce, Shanghai, to China Association, n.d., China Association, General Committee Papers, 1933. Cf. FRUS, 1933, III, 219.

[2] Individuals did express considerable disappointment. See, e.g., Adams to Baldwin, 13 March 1933, Baldwin Papers, vol. 120. Murray attributed the revocation to a flood of new arms orders. Murray to Crozier, 24 March 1933, Murray Papers.   [3] See above, 220, 287.

[4] See Austen to Lady Chamberlain, 3, 16 February, 2, 3, 22 March 1933, Austen Chamberlain Papers, AC 6/1/902–1062; Chamberlain to Tyrrell, 13 February, 12 April; Murray to Chamberlain, 1, 4 May 1933, ibid, AC 40/5–9; Cecil to Murray, 23 March 1933, Cecil Papers, Add. 51132; Chamberlain to Murray, 24 March, 15 April 1933, Murray Papers.

[5] Slater to MacDonald, 25, 28 February, 2 March; MacDonald to Slater, 1, 3 March; Murray to Cecil, 7 March; Murray to Slater, 8 March 1933, Murray Papers.

[6] Austen to Lady Chamberlain, 20 January 1933, Austen Chamberlain Papers, AC 6/1/902–1062; cf. Cecil to Murray, 5, 26 January 1933, Murray Papers and Cecil Papers, Add. 51132, respectively.

[7] See Noel-Baker to Cecil, 5 November 1932, Cecil Papers, Add. 51107; Noel-Baker to Murray, 28 December 1932, Murray Papers. Noel-Baker also warned that Germany appeared ready to do a secret deal with Japan. Notes of 23 November 1932, Cecil Papers, Add. 51107.

was general acceptance by February 1933 that it was best that Japan should go from the League, even the ailing Grey subscribing to this view.[1] But beyond this, what should be done? Among the Union's branches, there were those who asserted that their leaders in London were being altogether too restrained, while within the headquarters itself some of the staff were moved to protest that too much caution and too little principle were diminishing public confidence in League and Union alike, 'particularly among the younger generation'. Lord Davies in Wales was notably keen to call for the application of article 16 if Japan remained intransigent, producing a resolution and petition to this effect from among his local branches.[2]

Cecil, meanwhile, who was emotionally inclined in a similar direction, remained confused intellectually, and in his public speeches, which were generally restrained, declined 'to define what (measures) he had in mind' should one party to the dispute defy the pressure which he still relied upon, of 'the overwhelming majority of civilised public opinion'.[3] Austen Chamberlain, for his part, went on supporting Simon's policy in Parliament, as well as working to prevent the Union's Committee adopting binding or hard-line resolutions;[4] on the same Committee, Lytton himself, who as noted above recognised the possible need to avoid an arms embargo on Japan alone, was nearer to Chamberlain's position than to Cecil's, while still greatly overrating the power of sweet reasonableness where Japan was concerned.[5] In the Commons debate of 27 February, Geoffrey Mander, who was a member of the Union and one of the few tenacious Parliamentary critics of Government policy, suggested a withdrawal of ambassadors from Tokyo, but admitted that 'he did not think military action of any kind could be used with effect, or should be used in (this) particular dispute',

[1] Grey to Murray, 21 February 1933, Murray Papers. Grey died in the following September.
[2] See, e.g, Hon. Sec., Fleetwood branch to Murray, 9 January; Carruthers to Murray, 24 January; Davies to Murray, 11, 26 January; memorandum to Murray from Eppstein, Freshwater (future Secretary of the Union), Miller and Thomas, March, n.d., 1933, Murray Papers; cf. *Manchester Guardian*, 19 January 1933.
[3] See *The Times*, 11 January 1933; *Manchester Guardian*, 12, 16 January 1933; Cecil speeches of 2, 29 November 1932, *Hansard, House of Lords*, vol. 85, cols. 988–90; vol. 86, cols. 126–8.
[4] See debates of 10 November 1932 and 27 February 1933, *Hansard, House oj Commons*, vol. 270, col. 556, and vol. 275, col. 67; Austen to Lady Chamberlain, 8, 9 February 1933, Austen Chamberlain Papers, AC 6/1/902–1062.
[5] See, e.g., Austen to Lady Chamberlain, 12 January 1933, ibid; Murray to Cecil, 22 March, and Cecil to Murray, 23 March 1933, Cecil Papers, Add. 51132. In October, Lytton had told Simon and Norman Davis that he believed Japan would eventually give way if the West told her 'in a friendly but firm way' that they would not condone or recognise what she had done. FRUS, 1932, IV, 316–17, and DBFP, XI, No. 23. After the vote of 24 February, Lytton suggested to Simon that the League should explore the possibility of itself establishing an effective government in Manchuria, a proposal that Vansittart correctly described as 'made in happy disregard of reality'. Lytton's ideas were attracting similar comments among his senior L.N.U. colleagues. Lytton to Simon, 28 February 1933, and Vansittart minute of 2 March 1933, FO 800/288.

and that technically article 16 did not apply since there had been no declaration of war. His Union colleague, the Conservative Vyvyan Adams, also pronounced an economic blockade to be 'one of the cruellest devices ... (which would) probably inflict upon the Japanese women and children, perfectly innocent most of them, ineffable hardship'.

As for Murray, having already absorbed Lytton's advice on the need to avoid provoking extremists in Japan any further,[1] he now accepted most of the limitations on British policy that were outlined to him privately by Simon—an example of the common phenomenon of an unofficial lobbyist being made use of by his official contact as much as, if not more than, the other way round.[2] After his meeting with the Foreign Secretary at the end of 1932, for example he accepted 'that with her trade disappearing, her unemployment increasing and her currency off the gold standard, Great Britain simply dare not shoulder the responsibilities which she undertook when she was a strong power'.[3] Thereafter he worked to secure from his Executive Committee a moderate resolution that would 'not say beforehand what ought to be done if Japan refused to come into conference because that seemed like assuming wrong action on her part' (a truly Simonian formulation); he also declined to sign Lord Davies's petition on the grounds that he was 'not in favour at present of the application of Article XVI—at any rate not in its entirety', because of the danger of 'directly provoking war with Japan'. In addition—and at the Foreign Secretary's prompting—he wrote privately to the Editor of the *Manchester Guardian* to suggest that the the paper's League correspondent 'showed prejudice against Simon and the Council and the Powers that Be in Geneva'.[4] Murray still distrusted the Government's policy, and intensely disliked the situation as a whole; he was not the man, however, to lead a campaign on the basis of crude slogans and facile solutions.

Beyond the Union, the *Manchester Guardian*, *Economist* and *New Statesman*, there was little sustained criticism of the way in which the crisis was being handled. Attlee described Japanese policy as 'a militarist try-on' and Lansbury became less obscure in his acceptance that coercion might prove necessary, but the Labour Party displayed no lasting zeal in this direction, despite its mention of possible sanctions in mid-February.[5] Among prominent Liberals, Samuel was opposed to the use of trade embargoes as a weapon;[6] in the Commons, Seymour Cocks spoke of the grave threat now posed by Japan to Britain and the Dominions in the Far East, but Amery

---

[1] See Murray to Noel-Baker, 7 October, Lytton to Murray, 16 October, Murray to Tsurumi, 6 November 1932, Murray Papers. At the request of a liberal friend in Japan, Murray got Grey to express appreciation of Japan's difficulties in an Armistice Day speech.

[2] See, e.g., Milbrath, 'Interest Groups and Foreign Policy', in Rosenau, *Domestic Sources of Foreign Policy*, and R. Bauer, et al., *American Business and Public Policy* (New York, 1963).

[3] Murray to Cecil, 4 January 1933, Murray Papers.

[4] Murray to Davies, 13, 27 January; Murray to Madariaga, 25 January; Simon to Murray, 18 January; Murray to Crozier, 23 January 1933, Murray Papers.

[5] See Bassett, 551 ff.

[6] Samuel to Murray, 30 May, 1933, Murray Papers, and Bassett, 558.

offered an alternative interpretation by dismissing 'the worship of un-realities' at Geneva, and observing, Matsuoka-like, that 'our whole policy in India, our whole policy in Egypt, stand condemned if we condemn Japan'.[1] *The Times*—and, in Shanghai, the *North China Herald*—approved Simon's cautious policy (including the final British vote to uphold the principles of the League),[2] and while there was no mass support for those like the *Daily Telegraph* and expatriate groups in China who continued to lean in a decidedly pro-Japanese direction,[3] there is little evidence to suggest that the electorate as a whole were prepared for major sacrifices in the cause of forcing Tokyo to submit.

The same observation continues to hold good of France and the United States, and indeed there was not even a debate in the French Chamber on these final aspects of the crisis. In *Le Populaire*, Blum called for an initiative on the part of Paris to save the League, breaking off diplomatic relations with Japan if necessary, while the Radical-Socialist *République* demanded sanc-tions of some kind to force Japan to retreat.[4] Britain's brief arms embargo came in for much criticism on the Left as penalising China rather than Japan,[5] *Le Temps*, too, being cool towards it, although in this case the motive was a desire to see the whole issue buried and forgotten. As with more blatantly pro-Japanese papers like *L'Echo de Paris*, *Le Temps* also expressed grave disquiet at Tokyo's departure from the League,[6] but in general French attention was by now firmly fixed across the Rhine.

The British embargo also received a bad press in the United States. Lippmann had dismissed any such move some time before, Borah now condemned it as dangerous and unfair to China, while the *New York Times* and others described it as ineffective and deviously conceived.[7] Meanwhile there were still a few internationalist editorials appearing in favour of some kind of commercial or financial sanctions aimed against Japan alone,[8] and there was widespread approval—in the mid-West, as well as elsewhere—

---

[1] See the debates of 10 November 1932, and 27 February 1933, loc. cit. In an address to the Anti-Socialist Union, Churchill observed that the League, with 'great work to do in Europe', would be well advised not to tangle with Japan, whose problems in China and as a neighbour of the Soviet Union should be appreciated. *The Times*, 18 February 1933.

[2] E.g., *The Times*, 8 December 1932, 6, 14, 25 February 1933; *North China Herald*, 9 November, 21 December 1932, 18 January, 8 February 1933. A strong *Times* leader on 6 February calling for the principles of the Covenant to be upheld had been requested by the Press Department of the Foreign Office. FO 371, F860/33/10.

[3] See *North China Herald*, 30 November 1932, for a report on the London Committee of the Shanghai Residents Association and the China sub-committee in the House of Commons.

[4] E.g., *La République*, 5 January 1933; *Le Populaire*, 9, 31 December 1932, 3, 22 January, 15 February 1933.

[5] E.g., *Le Populaire*, 27 February, 1 March 1933.

[6] E.g., *Le Temps*, 5, 17 January, 13, 24, 28 February 1933; *L'Echo de Paris*, 5 January, 24 February 1933.

[7] Lippmann, *Interpretations, 1931–3*, 207; *Manchester Guardian*, 28 February 1933; *New York Times*, 2 March 1933.

[8] See Borg, *The United States and the Far Eastern Crisis*, 88–9.

for the League's February Resolution.[1] Despite this, however; despite reports from North China of the possibility of a full-scale war, protests against the menace of cut-price Japanese trade competition, and warnings of an Asiatic threat to the position of the white man in the Pacific,[2] there was even so a general decline in interest and a rise in equanimity.[3] (One newsman attributed this in part to China's Jehol performance: 'If she doesn't want to save herself, why should others worry?')[4] Sanctions were still widely believed to be 'a logical prelude to war';[5] papers like the *New York Times* and individuals like James Shotwell offered the comforting thought that time would bring about Japan's inevitable downfall;[6] 'Strongest popular motive here,' confessed Shotwell in a telegram to Gilbert Murray, 'avoid war with Japan', adding later that 'the country is so absorbed in its internal troubles that the problem of peace and war seems unreal and far away'.[7]

In several quarters, nevertheless, there was increased unease over what had occurred, in some cases involving criticism of the policies which Stimson had followed. The *New York Times*, for example, while deploring Japan's methods, declared that 'China does not answer to the definition of a "nation" as countenanced in the Covenant of the League',[8] and Newton Baker felt that the United States could have found more ways of helping Japan to escape from her difficulties:

> 'I think we may fairly say,' he wrote to Shotwell, 'that the flip of a coin threatens to decide whether Japan shall disappear as a great power. That I should profoundly regret. I cannot forget that Japan was the one Oriental Power with largeness of mind enough to remodel its own civilization in order to live cooperatively and helpfully with the nations of the Western World . . . while Chinese mobs, under the direction of their Government, were chasing and killing "foreign devils" throughout the length and breadth of China . . . The punishment ahead of (Japan) bids fair to be tragically severe.'[9]

Lawrence Lowell, President of Harvard, was especially and publicly critical

---

[1] Tupper and McReynolds, 357; Fleming, 458–94; e.g., *Washington Post*, 25 February 1933.

[2] E.g., *New York Times*, 20, 21 February 1933; *Washington Post*, 21 October 1932, 14 February 1933; *Chicago Daily Tribune*, 11 November 1932.

[3] See Tupper and McReynolds, 357–63.

[4] B. D. Hulen to Johnson, 10 August 1933, Johnson Papers, box 18.

[5] E.g., *Chicago Daily Tribune*, 26 February 1933.

[6] See *New York Times*, 11 February 1933; Shotwell to Baker, 12 January 1933, Newton Baker Papers, box 208.

[7] Shotwell to Murray, 6 March, 28 April 1933, Murray Papers. Both Shotwell and Baker felt that they could best work for peace from outside the leadership of the L.N.A., whose presidency Baker declined at this time. Baker to Shotwell, 10 December 1932, Baker Papers, box 208. Meanwhile the Women's International League for Peace and Freedom despairingly tried to exercise continued moral pressure—for example through the Japanese Ambassador. See W.I.L.P.F., U.S. Section, Correspondence, note of 31 December 1932.

[8] See *New York Times*, 23 February, and a letter in the issue of 4 March 1933.

[9] Baker to Shotwell, 14 January 1933, Baker Papers, box 208. Baker found the idea of a Japanese–American war 'utterly unrealistic.' Baker to Howard, 3 August 1933, ibid, box 122.

of Stimson's non-recognition pronouncements, for without some form of practical sanction behind them they amounted, he believed, to no more than futile irritants.[1] Professor Edwin Borchard of Yale, whose approach was very different to Lowell's, was another who regretted what he saw as the unrealistic and moralising basis of the Secretary's policy,[2] while in more restrained terms the financier Thomas Lamont urged Stimson not to inflame Japan any further.[3]

Related side-issues now attracted as much attention as the Far Eastern dispute itself. The arms-embargo legislation that was eventually sought by Hoover in January, 1933, was approved by Borah—once it had been made clear that there was no intention of making use of it in punitive fashion or over the current Sino-Japanese affair—as well as by peace-workers like Dorothy Detzer; even so, it was fiercely and successfully opposed by arms-manufacturing firms and their agents in Congress.[4] More significantly, and overriding both the pleas of Stimson and Hoover's attempted veto, Congress forced through a bill in January to give the Philippines their independence after a ten-year period of home rule.[5] Like Britain, the United States appeared quite unready to challenge a triumphant Japan in the Western Pacific.

The shaping of policy: Washington

The passing of the Philippines independence bill was a bitter moment for Stimson. As foreshadowed in previous years, he saw it as both a blow to the political equilibrium in East Asia and a negation of his vision of a widening circle of American commerce, Christianity and civilisation. Of all the cries against the move which were submitted by members of the Administration, his was the loudest; had he been a private citizen, he told Elihu Root, he would have made it stronger still.[6] Towards the end of 1932, with his conscience troubling him over his earlier opposition to such legislation, he had also worked hard to convince Hoover of the need to obtain from Congress the power to halt arms supplies to belligerents (growing troubles in South America added a further incentive for doing so). The President agreed, then changed his mind under indirect pressure from the Army and the direct appeals of Colt and other arms firms that had contributed to Republican

[1] *Boston Herald*, 8 January 1933; cf. Shotwell, *On the Rim;* Lowell to Baker, 31 October 1932, Baker Papers, box 147.

[2] Borchard to Borah, 18 February 1933, Borah Papers, box 344; cf. Lattimore, *Manchuria*, 291.

[3] Lamont to Stimson, 4 October 1932, DS 793.94 Commission/449½.

[4] See Borah to Borchard, 17 February 1933, Borah Papers, box 344; DS 811.113/201, 203, 206, 224, 229, 332; Moffat Diary, 23 December 1932; Divine, *The Illusion of Neutrality*, 32 ff.

[5] For an outline, see Toynbee, *Survey, 1933,* 544–74. The Philippines Legislature refused this bill, which lapsed in 1934, whereupon a new bill was passed and accepted.

[6] The January 1933 memoranda on the Philippines of Stimson, Hurley, Hyde and Chapin are filed together in the Hoover Papers, Philippines. The draft of 30 December 1932, prepared for Stimson by his military aide, Regnier, is in the Stimson Papers, box 313; Stimson to Root, 4 January 1933, Root Papers, box 151.

funds; with the help of Castle, who had initially opposed the idea, Stimson got Hoover to switch back again, but for all his subsequent efforts, public and private, he could not shift the Congressional opposition of Senator Hiram Bingham and others, even though he emphasised that no embargo would be risked over the Far Eastern crisis.[1] Britain's own, two-nation embargo was futile in the Secretary's eyes, and he let it be known indirectly that he also opposed the bolder step of applying such measures to Japan alone, since that would lead to her blockading China, and to 'complications' with the West. Simon 'emphatically agreed'.[2]

By now, however, the Foreign Secretary's most effusive assurances could not dispel the suspicion with which he was regarded in the State Department. For all his subsequent explanations, Simon's main speech to the League Assembly in December convinced Stimson and his officials that he was up to no good, a belief that was reinforced by Gilbert's report that at Geneva the struggle was now seen in terms of Britain versus the League, rather than the League versus Japan. The speech there of the Canadian Secretary of State made matters worse for Stimson, since only the day before his comfortable image of reliably pro-American Dominions had been confirmed by a message from the Canadian Prime Minister to the effect that his country would follow the Secretary's lead over the Far East. Simon, too, had sent assurances through Norman Davis that Britain regarded recognition of Manchukuo as being out of the question; but his argument that conciliation proceedures must be exhausted before judgement was delivered appeared like backsliding to an impatient Stimson. Reports from United States diplomats might suggest that the Foreign Secretary, like MacDonald and Vansittart, did care for Anglo-American relations. As before, however, they also indicated that Baldwin was lukewarm and his Tory colleagues not even that. Chamberlain, in particular, was found to be unhelpful—'cold-blooded, hard-headed, and utterly Conservative-minded'. 'Every time (he) makes a speech,' noted Moffat, 'Anglo-American relations suffer a setback.'

'In conversations,' reported Atherton shortly after the Assembly's February vote, 'it is frequently brought out that the British Cabinet is increasingly conscious of England's political responsibilities as a European nation and, after surveying the field of Anglo–American cooperation, has reluctantly come to the conclusion that while Anglo–American aims may coincide in their general outlines, any policy of effective cooperation is practically unobtainable in view of conflicting interests.'[3]

Other information reaching Stimson from Europe helped to confirm him in the unhappy belief that the nations of the League were 'like a flock of

[1] See Stimson Diary, 9 November, 21, 23 December 1932; 15 February 1933; Stimson to Horner and Daggett, 30 January 1933, Stimson Papers, box 314; Moffat Diary, 21–23 December 1932; 1, 10 January, 7 March 1933; Hornbeck memoranda, 7 March 1933, DS 893.113/1168, 1467; DS 811.113/189A, 194, 195, 221; Pearson and Brown, 355–6; Divine, loc. cit.

[2] Stimson Diary, 24 February 1933; FRUS, 1933, III, 204–5, 217–18, 231–4.

[3] Atherton to Hull, 9 March 1933, DS 841.00/1233; also Stimson Diary, 6, 9 December 1932; Moffat Diary, 3 January, 1 February 1933; Davis to Stimson, 28 November 1932, Norman Davies Papers, box 2; Davis to Roosevelt, 15 October 1932, ibid, box 50; FRUS, 1932, IV, 317–22, 388–90, 399–402, 403–4, 417–18, 420–2;

sheep (who) tend to scatter when the shepherd does not keep them in the herd'.[1] Drummond, increasingly gloomy and, it was thought, probably influenced by the Foreign Office, spoke privately of the need to head off the radicals at Geneva and of his belief that the Nine Power Treaty would prove a better basis on which to handle the dispute—doubly so since he judged that Japan could not easily be proved to have broken the Covenant in a technical sense. It was no surprise, then, when Sweetser described the need for a clear statement of America's position as urgent.[2] Meanwhile the Italians were obviously indifferent to the whole affair and the Dutch cautious in the extreme. Davis thought that the Germans would stay in line, however, and above all the French now appeared to be much firmer. By early February the news from Geneva was more reassuring (the draft report of the Committee of Nineteen produced something like euphoria in Sweetser, who, like Cecil, Lytton and others, implicitly assumed that a deeply ingrained Western liberalism underlay Japan's current bad behaviour), and the final Resolution pleased Stimson greatly. Even so, events had done little to foster a sense of united Western endeavour, while within the State Department there remained the suspicion, for example, that 'the "League" would like to increase the British (and European?) influence in China and back the American Advisers off the map'.[3]

Information and advice reaching Washington from the Far East itself had also continued to make the whole problem appear as intractable as ever. While China called for the United States to speak out clearly in her defence, and talked of leaving the League in disillusionment, Japan, despite her usual assurances, remained adamant over Manchuria, on which issue she, too, would leave the League if necessary.[4] Senior American diplomats on the spot once more confirmed the dangers of the situation. Nelson Johnson, although not unhopeful for the long term, admitted that China remained a shambles politically, and while he believed that Japan would hesitate before going into North China itself, he expected a new and major explosion to be set off by

ibid, 1933, III, 18–19, 64–5, 137–9; DS 793.94/474; DS 793.94 Commission/653. Lord Lothian told Stimson at the time that Simon was regarded in Britain as 'a great barrister without a brief in the Foreign Office'. Stimson Diary, 25 February 1933. In November, General McCoy went to London 'to do a little missionary work'. McCoy to Miss McCoy, 4 October 1932, McCoy Papers, box 8.

[1] Stimson Diary, 12 January 1933; cf. ibid, 12, 15 December 1932.

[2] Gilbert to Stimson, 31 October 1932, FRUS, 1932, IV, 322–5; Gilbert to Stimson, 12 January 1933, DS 793.94 Commission/760; Davis to Roosevelt and Stimson, 10 January 1933, Davis Papers, box 50.

[3] Stimson Diary, 7, 11, 20 February 1933; Moffat Diary, 18 February 1933; FRUS, 1932, IV, 337–8, 362, 375–6; ibid, 1933, III, 86–7; DS 793.94/5637; DS, 793.94 Commission/532, 595, 695, 924. Sweetser believed that 'if the present draft report is adopted, the whole moral situation throughout the world will have changed . . . My own belief is that the minute the report is drafted it will be like a fresh breeze blowing through the world making people believe at last they can breathe freely again . . . It is just inconceivable to me that, if the report is allowed to simmer quietly for some time, it will not penetrate so deeply into the minds of people both in Japan and in other countries as to force some kind of change'.

[4] See FRUS, 1932, IV, 349–52; ibid, 1933, III, 21–3, 27–9, 115–16; FRUS, *Japan, 1931–1941*, I, 107–12.

'active young minds on both sides'.[1] From Tokyo, Joseph Grew also believed that Japan would be reluctant to move south of Manchuria, or even into Jehol, and that she had no wish to leave the League. He, too, however, reiterated in a stream of despatches that no concessions could be expected over Manchuria, that the country was ready to fight rather than submit to coercion, and that gradual, moral pressure offered the only hope of obtaining an eventual improvement as Japan's financial and other difficulties increased.[2]

Either explicitly or by implication, the views of several career-diplomats like Grew were increasingly diverging at this time from the course which Stimson had set—on the surface, at least—during the previous twelve months or so. In part, this arose from increased anxiety that, in Johnson's words, 'everything should be done to prevent any actual hostilities between ourselves and the Japanese'.[3] This preoccupation could coexist, as it did in Johnson's case, with an acceptance of the need to 'appeal to the conscience of the world at large'.[4] More frequently, however, it could lead, as it did with Grew, to a dislike of statements that might further inflame Japanese opinion and strengthen the hand of extremists.[5] Hugh Wilson, with whom Grew kept in fairly close touch, declared privately that for this reason he felt like bursting into tears when he saw a tendency in the opposite direction:

'Mr. Stimson,' he wrote, '. . . had every legal right to take and maintain the position which he did . . . But you know and I know that the endeavour to place humanity within a rigid framework of legal restriction has never yet succeeded . . . We could have done most of the things we did do, but we could have done them with an understanding of the real difficulties under which Japan was labouring . . . We need not have done any of these things in such a way as to make us . . . the leaders in what Mr. Stimson called "mobilizing world opinion against Japan".'[6]

[1] See Johnson to Stimson, 13 February 1933, FRUS, 1933, III, 70–2; Johnson to Grew, 19 January 1933, Johnson Papers, box 17; Johnson to Hornbeck, 28 March 1933, ibid, box 18. For Admiral Taylor's increasing disillusion with China, see Taylor to Taylor, 18 April 1933, Taylor Papers, box 1; Taylor to Johnson, 4 May 1933, Johnson Papers, box 19.

[2] E.g., FRUS, 1932, IV, 381–2; ibid, 1933, III, 225; FRUS, Japan, 1931–1941, I, 110–11; Grew Diary, 3 December 1932, 27 January 1933; Grew, Ten Years In Japan (London, 1944), 44, 61, 69–71, 74–5; Heinrichs, American Ambassador, 172 ff. On the 'closing door' in Manchuria, see FRUS, 1933, III, 166.

[3] Johnson to Castle, 15 November 1932, Castle Papers, China. In the spring of 1933, reports reached Washington that senior French officials (no doubt they had an eye on the Disarmament Conference) were saying that they expected a Japanese attack on the Philippines and other American possessions. FRUS, 1933, III, 155–7, 241. The U.S. Navy and State Department continued to be concerned with the fate of Japan's League mandates in the Pacific. See, e.g., memorandum of 2 February 1933, Johnson Papers, box 18, and material in the Davis Papers, box 20.

[4] Johnson to Hornbeck, 20 December 1932, Johnson Papers, box 15.

[5] E.g., Grew to Stimson, 8 October 1932, Grew Papers, vol. 57 (and Grew, op. cit., 66 ff.).

[6] Wilson to Grew, 27 December 1932, 22 March 1933, Hugh Wilson Papers. Cf. Wilson to Grew, 10 December 1932; Wilson to Davis, 22 February 1933; Wilson to Hull, 29 March 1933, ibid.

Like Grew, Wilson believed that the League's final report and recommendations were unrealistic, however well-intentioned,[1] while both men retained much sympathy for the role that they expected Japan to play in the years ahead. Grew noted:

> Japan will in all probability eventually guarantee to Manchuria an administration of peace, safety and prosperity which that unfortunate country has never before experienced . . . and furthermore Japan is acting as a staunch buffer against the spread of bolshevism eastward which is an item worth considering. If Japan deserves merit for nothing else, we must at least give her credit for the fight she is putting up against communism which is now overwhelming China like a forest fire and would rapidly overrun Manchuria too if the Japanese hadn't taken a hand.[2]

Outside the Foreign Service (where financial pressure and structural inefficiency were continuing to impair morale[3]), Admiral Taylor was another who believed that Stimson's lawyer-like concern to win a verdict rather than to nurture a long-term policy had had dangerous results;[4] the Army's Chief of Staff, General Douglas MacArthur, for his part saw 'little likelihood of any belligerent outbreaks which might involve the United States in the Pacific', and even in Europe believed that 'no serious war is likely within any measurable period of time'.[5] Meanwhile in the State Department itself, where Castle, as noted earlier, regarded Hoover as having prevented some dangerous follies on Stimson's part,[6] Hornbeck was now aware that there was little point in talking of the swift effectiveness one could expect of economic sanctions. Instead, in his stiff manner, he privately reiterated the party line about 'a crystallized public opinion (that) will ultimately become of sufficient strength substantially to deter powers from the use of force in their relations with other powers'. For the moment, however, he believed that only the threat of sizeable military intervention by other powers could prevent a probable extension of Sino-Japanese hostilities, although whether this situation also presaged a threat to the United States he was not entirely clear. In late December he saw the likelihood of a Japanese attack on the United States or the Soviet Union as 'daily diminishing'; by mid-March he was declaring that 'a war between Japan and the United States within the next four years is a possibility of such reality that the factors which may bring it about . . . need to be given constant attention'. What was now apparent to him was that 'neither words nor formulae, neither rules nor regulations nor resolutions nor law nor treaties are decisive when a country is embarked upon a course such as Japan has followed'. Therefore the United States should not get involved as a go-between for China, and should keep

---

[1] See Grew Diary, 23 February 1933 (and Grew, op. cit., 76 ff.).

[2] Grew Diary, 27 January—10 February 1933.

[3] See above, 87–9, and Moffat Diary, 6 May, 1933; Wilson to Hornbeck, 18 January 1933, Hugh Wilson Papers; Davis to Castle, 27 September 1933, Castle Papers, Switzerland; Grew to Nye, 13 December 1933, Grew Papers, vol. 56; J. W. Pratt, *The American Secretaries of State and Their Diplomacy*, XII, Cordell Hull (New York, 1964), 23–4.

[4] Taylor to Taylor, 25 February 1933, Taylor Papers, box 1.

[5] MacArthur to McCoy, 28 October 1932, McCoy Papers, box 28.

[6] See above, 300. Cf. Castle Diary, 8 November 1932, cited in Rappaport, 187.

away from any decisions of the League that might involve trouble with Japan in the future.[1]

Nor were the brave days of Stimson and his *cercle intime* from the previous year recaptured in this twilight period of the Secretary's tenure of office. Klots gave another two cheers for non-recognition, but it was a final gesture before disappearing back into private life in January.[2] Stimson himself was weighed down with difficulties on all fronts and had lost some of his former bounce (by February, Moffat thought he was 'one step ahead of a complete breakdown'[3]). After the strain of the election—strain arising from within his own Party rather than from attacks by the Democrats—he found himself caught up in those wrangles with Hoover and Mills over debts which were noted in the previous chapter, and also in some tense and rancorous manoeuvring between the President and his successor—for example, over whether to hold talks with the European debtor nations. During the course of these exchanges, Stimson was happy to be used by the charming and ever-concurring Roosevelt as an alternative contact to the sour and mistrustful Hoover. It did nothing to improve the Secretary's own relations with the latter.[4] At the same time he found himself having to defend his non-recognition policy against Lowell and others, enlisting Lippmann's aid in this cause and employing General McCoy to talk on his behalf to people of influence in New York and elsewhere.[5]

Over the Far East, as well as over debts, Stimson found that Roosevelt's ideas appeared to be closer to his own than did Hoover's. The two men met at Roosevelt's home at Hyde Park on 9 January, and the President-elect's only criticism was that his visitor's non-recognition policy could have been developed earlier. He agreed that in the long run China would successfully resist the invader, who would be forced to give way by economic difficulties, and assured the Secretary that he would not undermine any policy statement the latter might wish to make on the issue.[6] With Roosevelt's approval

[1] Hornbeck to Johnson, 14 November 1932, Johnson Papers, box 15; Hornbeck memoranda, 5, 10 January 1933, FRUS, 1933, III, 16–17, 43; Hornbeck memoranda in DS 793.94/5810, 5901; DS 793.94 Commission/718½; DS 711.94/804. One relatively junior member of the Far Eastern Division was bold or naïve enough to take up again the economic sanctions issue in this period. DS 793.94 Commission/479½.   [2] Klots memorandum, 31 December 1932, DS 793.94/5663⅜.

[3] Moffat Diary, 1 February 1933; cf. Stimson to McCoy, 13 April 1933, McCoy Papers, box 30.

[4] See Stimson Diary, 23, 24 December 1932; 20–23 January 1933; Castle Diary, 10 January 1933, cited in Ferrell, *American Diplomacy*, 242, and ibid, 24 January 1933, cited in Current, *Secretary Stimson*, 124; Hoover memoranda, January, n.d., and 15, 27 January 1933; Davis to Stimson, 28 December 1932; Roosevelt to Stimson, 24 December 1932; Roosevelt to Hoover, 4 January 1933; Stimson memorandum, 15 January 1933, Stimson Papers, box 314; Hoover to Roosevelt, 20 December 1932, Hoover Papers; Davis to Hull, 3 February 1933, Hull Papers, box 32; MacDonald to Roosevelt, 10 February, Roosevelt to MacDonald, 20 February, 1933, in E. Nixon (ed.), *Franklin D. Roosevelt and Foreign Affairs* (Cambridge Mass., 1969), vol. I; cf. H. Feis, *1933: Characters in Crisis* (Boston, 1966).

[5] Stimson Diary, 5, 23, December 1932; 9 February 1933; Stimson to Lippmann, 12 January 1933, Stimson Papers, box 314.

[6] Stimson Diary, 9 January 1933.

Stimson was therefore able to inform London that no change in United States policy need be anticipated under the new Administration, while Roosevelt himself, prompted also by Sweetser's appeal for clarity from Geneva, made the public statement noted earlier, on the need to uphold international agreements.[1] By way of contrast, Stimson and Hoover had their final argument on the subject (memoirs apart). At this time the President was again active in obtaining the testimony of his colleagues—'to put away for use many years hence'—as to his paternity of non-recognition, a child not yet as sickly as it was to appear when those many years had gone by.[2] He remained adamant, however, that no sanction could be invoked beyond that of public opinion, and on 24 February, alarmed by one of Grew's despatches warning of Japan's readiness to resist coercion, proposed to Stimson that a statement welcoming the League's new Resolution should also emphasise America's refusal to contemplate anything forceful. Once more, however, the latter persuaded the President not to weaken Washington's façade of unbending and formidable disapproval.[3]

Stimson himself was still pondering on what sanctions were appropriate in international relations 'after we reach the point where public opinion will not be effective'.[4] To suggest, however, as some have done, that he was now convinced of the desirability of applying economic, and then if necessary military, coercion is to impute certainty and clarity where there remained doubt and confusion. This was also the case in purely military terms, for it is apparent from his own account of the talk with Roosevelt on 9 January that Stimson still had a very incomplete grasp of the strategic situation in the Pacific. Where Japan was concerned politically, he knew that he wanted the League to accept the Lytton Report with all speed, followed by the non-recognition of Manchukuo by name, and the whole topped off with a suitable dash of rhetoric (he privately complained that the proposals of the Committee of Nineteen were 'unemotional'). To this end he could continue to prod France and above all Britain, with the threat that unless he were fully satisfied the United States was unlikely to participate in the work of any League conciliation committee that might be set up.[5] Besides having to admit once more, however, that 'no positive action' in the nature of sanctions could be contemplated by his Government,[6] he also declined all opportunities of taking a local initiative over the confrontation around Shanhaikuan and the borders of North China, the State Department's line

[1] Ibid, 13, 17, 19 January 1933; Davis to Roosevelt, 10 January 1933, in Nixon, op. cit.

[2] E.g., Hoover to Wilbur, 13 January, Wilbur to Hoover, 26 January 1933, Wilbur Papers, I-D/231.

[3] Stimson Diary, 24 February 1933; Hoover to Stimson, 24 February 1933, FRUS, 1933, III, 209–10.

[4] Stimson Diary, 14 February 1933.

[5] E.g., ibid, 16 December 1932; Castle Diary, 2 December 1932, cited in Rappaport, 192; Stimson to Davis et al., 21 November 1932, Davis Papers, box 17; FRUS, 1932, IV, 385–6, 405–6, 415–17, 424–8; ibid, 1933, III, 54–6; DS 793.94 Commission/449½; DS 793.94/5625½; Stimson, Far Eastern Crisis, 220 ff.

[6] Wilson to Stimson and Stimson to Wilson, 7 February 1933, FRUS, 1933, III, 152–4.

being that since Simon was so keen on conciliation, he should get on with it there and then.[1] In part, this passivity had the positive purpose of preventing the League's position being undermined, for example by an invocation of the Nine Power Treaty, and of preserving American influence for the moment when Japan would finally agree to talk with China without conditions.[2] Yet in part also, Stimson was merely adopting once more the stance he had taken up during the Shanghai fighting, of 'sitting pretty in an off-side position', as he now complacently put it,[3] and reading moral lessons to those immediately engaged in the consequences of what was happening.

As before, such a policy entailed little or nothing in the way of practical assistance for the Chinese.[4] In private, moreover, several of Stimson's thoughts on the situation now bore a far greater resemblance to those of Simon than he would have cared to recognise or admit. Together with McCoy, for example, the Secretary believed that 'moral pressure' still offered the most effective means of shifting Japan,[5] while when Lippmann revealed his worries (they were shared in London) as to how long non-recognition would have to be kept up, Stimson accepted, as did Simon, that the matter would have 'to be worked out by evolution'.[6] In order not to anger Japan, he modified an article that he had drafted on the Far Eastern question, and sat down with McCoy to try to work out 'whether there was not some way by which we could hold out a friendly hand to Japan in an attempt to show that there was nothing personal to her in what we had done . . .'[7] He also asked Hornbeck to explore the possibility of getting the American immigration laws amended in a way that would 'ameliorate Japanese opinion'.[8]

It is all the less surprising, therefore, to find Paul Claudel reporting to Paris as early as October that Stimson had admitted that the moment had perhaps come 'de laisser parler les sentiments de raison et de conciliation', and that Hoover had apparently described China's provocation of Japan as revealed by Lytton as 'intolerable'.[9] There was a great deal of sense in these thoughts and explorations of Stimson's—constituting as they did a certain private acknowledgement of realities which, by leaving immediate matters to the League, one could happily combine with the public role of keeper of the world's conscience. He was also prepared to oppose the President at this time when the latter, ready once more to yield to the industrial paymasters of his party, was all for sending a cruiser to Liberia in order to cow the

[1] See ibid, 30, and Stimson Diary, 3, 14 January 1933. For Stimson's private warning to Debuchi, see FRUS, *Japan, 1931–1941*, I, 107–8.

[2] See Stimson to Davis, 14 November 1932, Davis Papers, box 2.

[3] Wilson–Stimson telephone record, 15 December 1932, FRUS, 1932, IV, 424–8. Cf. Moffat Diary, 23 February 1933.

[4] See, e.g., FRUS, 1932, IV, 591–5; ibid, 1933, III, 39–42, 81–2.

[5] Stimson Diary, 14 January 1933. He later acknowledged this misjudgement: Stimson and Bundy, 261–2.

[6] Stimson Diary, 30 December 1932. Cf. Hornbeck memorandum, 15 February 1934, Hornbeck Papers, box 319.

[7] Stimson Diary, 18 January, 15 February 1933; cf. Stimson to Grew, 21 January 1933, Grew Papers, vol. 65.

[8] Stimson to Hornbeck, 1 February 1933, Hornbeck Papers, box 402.

[9] Claudel to Herriot, 14 October 1932, DDF, I, No. 242.

government there, who were making things difficult for the all-powerful Firestone company.[1]

Nevertheless, Stimson had still not established in his mind a clear relationship between power and morality in international relations. Where Far Eastern affairs were concerned he retained a strong streak of almost romantic idealism, while in wider terms he had not lost the tendency to assume an inherent, disinterested righteousness for American policy which contrasted with the selfish villainy of others. He was horrified, for example, when, during the clash between Peru and Colombia over Leticia, and apparently because of her ties with Peru, Britain suggested that Leticia should be turned over to Brazil pending negotiations between the disputing parties. 'The proposal,' he noted, 'certainly shed a lurid light on the difference between British Foreign Office diplomatic policy and similar American policy.'[2] It was an effortless assumption for him that his own presence in Nicaragua some years before, or his avowal that the United States must if necessary enforce order in the Caribbean in her own interest,[3] were part of a different order of things. Likewise, he now declared to Roosevelt that before recognising the Soviet Union it should be established that she would abide by the fundamental principle of non-interference in the internal affairs of other countries;[4] yet almost certainly it would not have occurred to him that there were implications of interference behind his own remark in this period concerning the corrupt, brutal and illegal régime in Cuba that was providing a haven for American business: 'I do not approve of Machado or what he (is) doing; . . . (but) at least he (is) able to hold the country safe and suppress revolutions.'[5] The same would have applied to his desire to see China develop in the American image, her religion and politics, like her machinery, imported from an alien civilisation. To Stimson this was not interference but evangelical and profitable charity. Since his arrival in office, the Secretary's grasp of European affairs had substantially increased; in Asia, his distorted vision of the future remained unchanged, only now there were moments when he believed that Japan would have to be fought along the road to achievement. In over-all terms, and diametrically opposed to Hoover's nascent concept of 'fortress America', he had also found new grounds for thinking that perhaps the United States and its Navy would have to police the world.

The shaping of policy: London, Paris and Berlin

Stimson's impatience over the proceedings at Geneva was unmistakable to Simon and his officials by the end of December 1932; so, too, was his refusal to take any further initiative himself.[6] There were some grounds, however, for the slight puzzlement with which such messages were initially received

[1] See, e.g., Stimson Diary, 17, 26 January, 1, 7 February 1933; Moffat Diary, 17, 21, 24 January, 4 February 1933; Moffat memorandum, 21 January 1933, Moffat Papers, vol. 22. On the Liberian episode in general, see also material in the Detzer Papers, box 2.   [2] Stimson Diary, 31 January 1933.
[3] See above, 117.   [4] Stimson Diary, 9 January 1933.
[5] Ibid, 10 January 1933. Cf. G. Kolko, *The Politics of War* (London, 1969), 473.
[6] See, e.g., DBFP, XI, Nos. 92, 118, 121, 125, 141, 195, 206, 272, 335, 341, 408.

in London. Early signs had suggested that a final search for conciliation on the basis of the Lytton Report would command Washington's approval, while the visiting Norman Davis (who had nothing to suggest when asked what further measures might be adopted against Japan, and who was opposed to expelling her from the League) had specifically enquired whether it was not possible for the League 'to allow time for the cooling off process'.[1] In addition, relations with the United States were again bedevilled in the New Year by the debt issue, which once more appeared to have its links with Far Eastern matters.[2] As the Cabinet faced the question of what to do in June, when another payment was due, and whether they should risk a Ministerial visit to the perplexing Roosevelt,[3] anti-American sentiments continued to be strongly expressed. Neville Chamberlain, bent upon 'educating' the incoming President and his public, felt himself 'to have the misfortune to be dealing with a nation of cads', and his Permanent Under-Secretary was said to hate Americans as much as Vansittart loathed Germans.[4] Simon, encouraged by Vansittart, was still concerned to maintain an understanding with Washington; MacDonald again went furthest in this respect, telling the King that the handling of the debt issue 'may well determine Anglo-American relations for a century', and once more clearing his own Far Eastern role with Stimson by a process of disloyalty to his colleagues—this time to Simon in particular.[5] Before the summer was out, however, even the Prime Minister was again to be disillusioned by his American friends.[6]

MacDonald also continued to devote himself in this period to 'the chief endeavour of keeping clear of European entanglements', blaming a stubborn France for having raised the 'Frankenstein' of German nationalism, while admiring 'the widespread spiritual development' and 'regeneration of Italy under the Fascist régime'.[7] Over the Far East, however, where Italy revealed herself to be uninterested and disillusioned with the League in its extra-European form,[8] it was the French who conveyed their readiness to stand

[1] Pratt memorandum, 26 October, and record of conversation, 26 October 1932, ibid, Nos. 22, 23; cf. ibid, No. 27.   [2] See ibid, No. 429, and ibid, V, No. 531.

[3] See, e.g., Cabinets of 30 January, 13 February, 5 April 1933, CAB 23/75; Ministerial Conversations on War Debts, 6–8 February, 10 March 1933, CAB 27/548.

[4] Neville to Hilda Chamberlain, 8 January, 4 February 1933, Neville Chamberlain Papers; Jones, A Diary, 129.

[5] MacDonald to King George V, 13 February 1933, RA G.V, K2366/10; cf. ibid, 6 April, 1933, K2366/18; Stimson Diary, 15 July 1933.

[6] See the letters concerning Roosevelt's wrecking of the World Economic Conference in the MacDonald Papers, RM 6/114, RM 1/67, and RM 1/82.

[7] MacDonald to King George V, 13 March 1933, RA G.V, K2353/19; Cabinet of 22 March 1933, CAB 23/75. Cf. Ministerial Committee on Disarmament, proceedings, CAB 27/505 and CAB 21/379. It was in this period, surveying the darkening European scene, that Vansittart feared a return to 'the pre-war condition of the balance of power—but even worse'. Minute of 26 February 1933, Vansittart Papers. MacDonald believed that if the Disarmament Conference failed, the Cabinet would have to be warned that there might be war in two years time. Baldwin and Austen Chamberlain were others who were extremely alarmed.

[8] DBFP, XI, Nos. 179, 306.

by the Lytton Report, and perhaps even to intervene diplomatically on the basis of the Boxer Protocol to try to restrict the skirmishes on the North-China border.[1] There were, indeed, several similarities between the formulation of Far Eastern policy in London and Paris in this period. In the Quai d'Orsay, as in the Foreign Office, suggestions were heard that the Chinese leaders might secretly be doing a deal with Japan, advice was again received from Tokyo that the Government there would fight rather than submit to sanctions, and the conviction was established that nothing in the way of practical assistance could be expected from the United States.[2] At the same time, the pressure of the majority of states at Geneva for a resolution that would uphold the Covenant was acknowledged to be not only irresistible but valid: France possessed important interests in the neighbourhood of Japan, advised the Far Eastern department in Paris, but she had an even greater stake in the maintenance of the post-war system of international undertakings. In this connection, China's argument at the Disarmament Conference that the League as it stood was inadequate for the provision of security brought exclamations of delight from Paul-Boncour as he annotated the reports from Geneva.[3] France, therefore, would continue strenuously to deny rumours of her collusion with Japan, and would endorse the draft report of the Committee of Nineteen. On the other hand she would take no separate initiative—to halt arms supplies, for example, would resist any suggestion of resorting to article 16, and would privately assure Tokyo of her lasting friendship.[4]

The Quai d'Orsay's reasoning behind this policy is of particular interest for its long-term projections.[5] As elsewhere, there was a continuing belief that growing economic difficulties would make Japan more ready to discuss the Manchurian question, while there remained much sympathy for her grievances against the nationalist excesses of China. In this latter connection, moreover, French officials were ready to adopt an ambivalent attitude of the kind that Wellesley in London had seen to be a feature of Japan's own policy in the area:[6]

> Il serait en outre dangereux d'encourager toute solution qui comporterait la réorganisation, avec ou contre le Japon, d'une Chine homogène, et disciplinée, qui constituerait un danger immédiat à la frontière même de l'Indochine.

[1] Ibid, Nos. 36, 184, 187, 207.

[2] See DDF, I, No. 233; ibid, II, Nos. 222, 286, 297, 337. On the debt issue, see ibid, II, Nos. 317, 321, 326, 328, 338, 348, 371.

[3] See Massigli to Paul-Boncour, 10 January, 11 February 1933; note of La Sous-Direction d'Asie-Océanie, 15 January 1933, DDF, II, Nos. 183, 291, 198 respectively. Cf. ibid, Nos. 7 and 400.

[4] See ibid, Nos. 12, 136, 199, 234, 261, 352, 353, 383.

[5] See the memoranda of 15 January and 6 March 1933, DDF, II, Nos. 198, 375; cf. ibid, No. 393.

[6] 'In these circumstances it is not difficult to understand why Japan does not want a well-ordered and united China, nor a completely chaotic China, but something between the two . . . This attitude of mind is a very intelligible one. How, for instance, would Great Britain welcome a united and hostile Europe, which is comparable to China both in population and area?' Memorandum of 6 February 1932, DBFP, IX, No. 356.

This desire to have things both ways where China was concerned was, as we have seen, a not-uncommon feature in the West. League and Foreign Office officials had urged her not to exacerbate the crisis by taking up arms against Japan, then proclaimed that her very feebleness provided a major reason for not being able to help save her; Stimson wanted a new China, but one beholden to the United States; in Paris and London, as in Tokyo, there were many impatient demands for an end to the country's political chaos, but also disquiet at what a truly united China might portend.

There was an additional reason for the Quai d'Orsay's caution, however. It was now recognised that Japan herself constituted a serious threat to French possessions, experiencing as she was a major demographic, economic and social crisis, and having absorbed the advantages of Western technology without 'des disciplines morales et intellectuelles de l'Occident'. Worst of all, might not Japan turn towards Germany and seek there an understanding to the mutual political and economic benefit of the two countries? Matsuoka's visit to Berlin early in March, like Germany's massive soya-bean purchases from Manchukuo, were viewed with much uneasiness in Paris. In London, the alarming prospect of a Tokyo–Berlin axis was as yet scarcely even considered, but the French were right to sense this as a possibility, however distant. The thought was already being expressed in direct fashion, for example, by the Japanese Military Attaché in Berlin:

> Japan was now at a decisive turning point in her entire policy which could also be important for Germany . . . The trend in Japan that was pro-German and had always demanded that one stand by Germany in her fight against the Versailles Treaty had so far been confronted by a very strong trend that was orientated towards France. Now the way was becoming clear for cooperation with Germany. From now on Japan did not need to take any more account of France and could fight against Versailles together with Germany.[1]

No response appears to have been made to this overture, which was clearly designed to affect the vote at Geneva on 24 February. Senior officials in Berlin were anxious to avoid Japan's departure from the League, but they were also continuing to emphasise in private their desire to see that organisation retain its prestige,[2] and when the Resolution finally came before the Assembly, Nazi Germany, as she now was, duly joined in the censure of her future ally. The country's expanding investments and trade in China— promoted by German military advisers among others—had to be considered, after all.[3] Yet Berlin was also aware of the new business opportunities that were opening up in Manchukuo as well,[4] while from China itself the German Minister, Trautmann, advised that 'the League of Nations melody is played out politically. From this it follows that we, too, should be as reserved as possible at Geneva . . . We ought, above all, to keep aloof from matters of armaments, for that is an annoyance to Japan'.[5] Manufacturers like Krupp were accordingly warned not to do anything to offend Tokyo

[1] Foreign Ministry memorandum, 20 February 1933, DGFP, I, No. 28.

[2] See, e.g., AA, serial L1780/L518518–20; serial 3147/D664258–9.

[3] See DGFP, I, Nos. 156, 412; AA, serial 3088H/D624603–4; serial 4619/ E197580, 197601; Bloch, 24–33.   [4] See DGFP, I, No. 50.

[5] Trautmann to Bülow, 24 August 1933, ibid, No. 410.

when expanding their interests in China.[1] For some years, the Third Reich would continue to balance delicately between the two Far Eastern powers, as Berlin had sought to do throughout the 1931–33 episode. China as a potential source of economic benefits had much in her favour; yet as a Foreign Ministry survey observed in the summer of 1933, 'as a Great Power and factor in world politics Japan will ... be able by her attitude, particularly where the Soviet Union is concerned, to exercise a strong influence on international affairs, and thus on Germany's political situation'.[2] It was a consideration which boded ill for France and Britain alike.

British policy-makers in this period continued to be faced with their own dilemma between not provoking Japan and not losing the friendship of China. Basically, the response was to carry on with Simon's attempted balancing act, but during these final months of the crisis there was a shift of emphasis on the part of certain individuals within the Foreign Office, as never before since September 1931. The reason for this change, and for the very limited effect it had on Government policy, deserves more attention than does the reiteration of previous arguments, however powerful, which will be compressed accordingly.

Communications and advice from Japan come within this latter category. Before the end of November, the Japanese had made it plain that they would leave the League if formally censured for their actions in Manchuria, and their insistence that the Manchukuo régime must stay did not waver throughout Matsuoka's attempts to devise some compromise formula which would be acceptable to the Committee of Nineteen.[3] Lindley, as before, lent emphasis to this consideration. Still privately fulminating against a Government which chose to follow the fatuous and dangerous advice of Cecil rather than his own (an extraordinary interpretation of British policy), despairing of the future of the Empire in a world of unruly and upstart states,[4] the Ambassador nevertheless provided London with a picture of the Japanese political scene that was reasonably accurate at the time, if not in its estimation of the future. The Government in Tokyo, he believed, were anxious to avoid a breach with the West, and were not seeking a full-scale war with China; ultimate control, however, still rested with the military, and if it were felt necessary to leave the League or fight against economic sanctions, then as before the public would respond as one man.[5] Before too long, economic difficulties would bring failure, and then public opinion would begin to turn against the Army; but in the meantime external criticism would only harden that opinion in its present form, just as the Jameson Raid 'only received popular support in England because of the Kaiser's telegram'. In order to save itself from total failure, therefore, the League should merely accept the factual portions of the Lytton Report and recommend direct

---

[1] See ibid, Nos. 436, 463.

[2] Memorandum, 'Die Lage im Ferren Osten', 5 July 1933, AA, serial K2049/539174–193. Cf. K. Drechsler, *Deutschland–China–Japan, 1933–1939* (Berlin, 1964).

[3] See DBFP, XI, No. 72, and on Japan's various manoeuvrings and assurances, ibid, Nos. 3–356, passim.

[4] Grew Diary, 22 February 1933; Lindley to Wigram, 26 October 1932, 7 January 1933, RA G.V, P510/55 and P510/57 respectively.

[5] See DBFP, XI, Nos. 4, 27, 49, 64, 67, 72, 348, 351, 393, 404, note, 414, 437, 560.

Sino-Japanese negotiations; Britain, for her part, should reveal that sanctions had been ruled out. Reaching a somewhat hysterical note on the day of the Assembly's vote, the Ambassador found himself 'faced with the imminent danger, if not actual probability, of the supreme failure of not having prevented a disastrous and avoidable conflict with the country to which I am accredited'.[1]

Lindley's was the most insistent, but by no means the only voice heard in Whitehall in favour of putting friendship with Japan before all other considerations. In a memorandum which also warned against European entanglements and advocated a role for Britain 'as a balancing force to maintain peace', the Chief of the Imperial General Staff, Field Marshal Milne, emphasised the need to retain Japan's assistance against 'the insidious activity of Soviet Russia . . . with India as a major objective in her plans':

> To thwart Japan in her present mood, which should be regarded only as a passing phase, might well result in forcing her deeper into the mire and might even lead to the complete collapse of authoritative government in that country . . . Though we do not wish and in fact are morally unable to condone Japan's disregard of her obligations . . . and cannot even justify the methods she has thought fit to employ, it must remain beyond dispute that the extension of Japanese control in Manchuria would be less inimical to the British Empire than the inevitable alternative—an increase of Soviet influence.[2]

The former First Lord of the Admiralty, Lord Bridgeman, was writing to Baldwin in a similar sense, although making the United States, rather than the Soviet Union, the villain of the piece. Japan, he wrote, was Britain's 'natural ally', and under men like Saito, whom he knew well, 'there is no reason to be afraid of excesses on (her) part'.[3] Bridgeman's successor, Eyres-Monsell, did not advance this argument in so blunt a fashion, but in Cabinet he always inclined strongly against any antagonising of Japan, and the implications were clear enough when he warned that the Navy was unprepared, that no new basis of planning had yet been adopted in place of the Ten Year Rule, and that when the Government chose to defer to the Treasury's vetoes on expenditure it must also assume responsibility for a perilous situation.[4] What little expression of Commonwealth opinion there was[5] tended in the same direction. In anticipation of his speech at Geneva, the Canadian Secretary of State set out his opposition to any hasty censure on Japan, while the New Zealand High Commissioner's trenchant views on

---

[1] Ibid, Nos. 4, 333. Lindley was forced to acknowledge, however—and in this the cautious estimates of his experienced Commercial Counsellor were decisive— that at the time Japan's economy had a healthy look. See ibid, Nos. 62, 68.

[2] Memorandum of 28 October 1932, CP 362 (32), CAB 24/234.

[3] Bridgeman to Baldwin, 9 October 1932, Baldwin Papers, vol. 118.

[4] See, e.g., Board of Admiralty minutes, 19 January, 1933, ADM 167/88, and relevant memoranda in ADM 167/89; Eyres-Monsell memorandum, 8 February 1933, CP 25 (33), CAB 24/237; Cabinet of 15 February 1933, CAB 23/75.

[5] See, e.g., DBFP, XI, Nos. 58, 63, 66, 343. On 5 November 1932, the C.I.D. considered a report on the defence of Australia, but neither in that body nor the Cabinet was Dominion opinion of direct and significant influence in this period. CAB 2/5.

the need to support Tokyo have been cited already.[1] In the later case, indeed, Wellesley and Orde found themselves having to dissuade the High Commissioner from seeking his Government's permission to vote on the Japanese side when the time came, soothing him with the thought that an alien doctrine like communism was unlikely to take hold in China as he feared it would.

From Tokyo and the Antipodes the advice was to pursue the line of immediate safety and self-interest; from senior League officials in Geneva it was for caution at least. For all his dependence on the views of member states, Drummond himself remained strongly inclined against any confrontation that might lead to Japan's departure, as he had indicated to diplomats from the United States. From him, too, there came the argument that financial difficulties would soon produce a more reasonable outlook in Tokyo; meanwhile he would like to see the Assembly adopt only the factual sections of the Lytton Report, and then play for time by passing on the remainder of the document to a committee which would include the United States and the Soviet Union, as well as the remaining signatories of the Nine Power Treaty.[2] Haas, back from his work with Lytton, was another who agreed on the need for a leisurely programme, while Frank Walters was looking ahead to a massive League effort to help provide the financial and administrative basis for a strong central government in China.[3]

This last proposal was regarded as impracticable in the Foreign Office, and an even more ambitious scheme devised by Dr. de Kat Angelino (the Dutch Adviser to the Lytton Commission) for 'League organisation, control and supervision' in China was peremptorily dismissed as resembling the ideas 'put forward from time to time by the extreme die-hard element among the club-bar politicians of Shanghai'.[4] Here there remained one of the major considerations that were working in the opposite direction to those noted so far: the mounting despair and resentment of China. True, Lampson in Peking, like so many others, believed that 'time (and population) will be on her side and she can afford to wait';[5] true, he was also chary of getting involved in mediating between her and Japan over the new, North-China skirmishes, while the Chinese themselves were prepared to admit in private that they entertained little hope of practical assistance from the League.[6] But the Nanking Government did desire at least a clear statement of Japanese guilt, and let it be known that in this respect they shared the bitterness of their press and public over Simon's equivocal performance at

[1] Price to Clutterbuck, 5 December 1932, DBFP, XI, No. 89. See ibid, No. 77, and above, 299.
[2] Drummond to Simon, 24 October, 2 November; Drummond memorandum, 7 November 1932, ibid, Nos. 17, 32, 37.
[3] Ibid, Nos. 26, 32, 151.
[4] Ibid, No. 26, note, and Pratt minute, 21 January 1933, FO 371, F 311/33/10. Angelino's scheme appears to have been endorsed by Drummond and Walters. As before, Drummond's inclination was to express enthusiasm for the proposal of another when forwarding it to London, and then to back-track hastily when doubts or opposition were expressed.
[5] Lampson to Pratt, 15 October 1932, DBFP, XI, No. 10. Cf. ibid, No. 461.
[6] See ibid, Nos. 16, 180–2, 190, 199, 205, 234, 425, 455.

Geneva in December.[1] Lampson, too, believed that the League should not shirk its duty to pronounce against Japan—by March he would be sourly reflecting that China had been encouraged to rely for support where none would be forthcoming—and that above all, Britain should beware of provoking a lasting reaction against herself:

> Our moral and material positions in China are possibly at this moment at stake. If we seem in any way to condone injustice or try to shield Japan the effect might well be deplorable and world-wide.[2]

In the Foreign Office it was now the interplay of forces from these three directions—Japan, Geneva and China—that most absorbed the attention of senior officials. (Stimson's nagging was devalued by his country's obvious passivity, and by now was almost assumed as a constant, to be considered but not given any special weighting.) That Japan would refuse to yield over Manchukuo and that her public were solid on the matter was not doubted, nor was there any thought of being able to prevent the conquest of Jehol; even over North China, it was accepted that one would have to take Tokyo's assurances as the best that could be obtained in the circumstances, and that mediation would become possible only if both sides expressed a clear desire for it. Privately, Japan should be urged to prevent a breakdown of negotiations at Geneva and to halt her troop movements; economic sanctions remained unthinkable, however, while even a withdrawal of ambassadors would only remove channels of potential influence just when they were most needed. As Pratt summed it up, Japan's departure from the League would weaken the moral authority of the organisation, remove all hopes of progress over disarmament, and foreshadow a series of Shanghai-like conflicts around centres of British commercial interest in North China. Cadogan, who was less alarmed than Pratt at the prospect of Japan's departure from Geneva, nevertheless agreed that no effort should be spared to obtain a settlement based on conciliation and section 3 of article 15, and that it 'might be all for the best' if sanctions were to be erased from the Covenant and the League rebuilt on a regional basis in the future. Eden was another who accepted the need for caution, displaying in private a certain long-suffering amusement where the Geneva radicals were concerned. The way Simon saw it in December, the thing to do was to avoid any pledges of perpetual non-recognition, 'keep out of the limelight, take no unnecessary responsibility, and let things drag on till the end of January'.[3]

[1] See ibid, Nos. 140, 228, 246.

[2] Lampson to Simon, 6 February, 11 March 1933, ibid, Nos. 293, 448; cf. ibid, Nos. 10, 230. Over Tibet, too, Lampson urged that Britain should pay heed to Chinese susceptibilities. Ibid, No. 296.

[3] The exchange of ideas and proposals within the Foreign Office becomes so dense in this period that for this and the following paragraphs an all-embracing reference is almost the only one that is practicable. The argument is based upon internal reports and minutes printed in DBFP, XI, Nos. 17, note, 54, 85, 129, 155 and note, 173 and note, 202, 260, note, 264, 270, 271, 309, 324, 371, note, 402, note. Expressions of opinion by Simon are printed in ibid, Nos. 23, 53, 92, 142, note, 149, 285, 294, 309, note, 321, 342; see also Simon to King George V, 19 November 1932, RA G.V, K2353/16. Fuller minutes than those printed, and others not printed at all, will be found in FO 371, F 7699, 7868, 8687, 8873/1/10; ibid, F 74,

By the time the end of January arrived, however, Japanese stubbornness, Chinese anger and pressure at Geneva were combining to bring about a re-examination of priorities, rather as the fighting at Shanghai and the initiatives of Stimson had done a year before. Moreover, within the limits set by the refusal to contemplate sanctions, there was already sufficient complexity—even ambiguity in some respects—about Foreign Office opinion to make it susceptible to pressures of this kind. Lindley, as we have seen, had always been regarded as narrowly dogmatic; Pratt had not been entirely unmindful of those forces within China which he had known at first hand; Simon had genuinely desired to see the League maintain its principles, even if on this occasion they could not be vindicated in practice. All these elements were among those which now began to show through more strongly than they had done at the end of 1932. The urgency of Lampson's advice helped. So, too, it appears, did a factor that was noted earlier with reference to Lord Reading and J. H. Thomas among others: the effect upon a politician or official of a change of environment. When Simon was at Geneva for any length of time, the emphasis of his ideas, already finely balanced, tended to alter;[1] with Eden and Pratt, the change was even more marked, as seen if one compares some of the memoranda they composed in or on return from Geneva with the minutes which they had written in Whitehall when deprecating a firm stand or British leadership of the League during the first year or so of the crisis. Of course circumstances themselves had changed, and the factor suggested here cannot be measured at all precisely or claimed to have been decisive. There can be no doubt that it existed, however, or that there now began to emerge a significant new emphasis in which Wellesley, who did not have experience of service either in China or Geneva, played little part.

Like Vansittart's forthcoming warnings concerning Germany, Lindley's cries from Tokyo were now suffering from their very volume and frequency. 'Like all good diplomats,' wrote Simon charitably, 'he is a perfect chameleon

392, 715, 730, 1936/33/10; ibid, F 65, 194/18/10; ibid, W 13584/13584/98. On the questions of warning Japan and mediation, see DBFP, XI, Nos. 165, 190, 193, 206, 211, 236, 313. Eden's views are contained in letters to Baldwin, 10, 22 February 1933, Baldwin Papers, Vol. 129; his pleased comments on one of Matsuoka's attacks on Madariaga (whose name Eden misspelt) are contained in a letter to Simon, 9 December 1932, Simon Papers (private collection), Foreign Affairs, 1932. There was some disagreement on what attitude the Soviet Union would take if invited to cooperate in conciliation. E. H. Carr, for example, believed that she would 'take a reasonable and even helpful part in the proceedings'. Wellesley, in particular, showed interest in Japan's intentions towards Moscow, while the presence of Litvinov at Geneva in December encouraged some people to hope for his country's cooperation over the Far East and other matters. See DBFP, XI, Nos. 326, 466.

[1] This was not a universal characteristic, and some politicians reacted strongly against the conditions at Geneva. In February 1932, for example, Hoare had returned 'very glad to have escaped from its curiously artificial and neurotic atmosphere'. Hoare to MacDonald, 4 February, 1932, Templewood Papers, box VII. MacDonald, too, disliked Geneva as 'a perfect hot-bed of intrigue and a forcing-house of rumour'. MacDonald to King George V, 29 June, 1932, RA G.V, K2354/3.

at taking colour from the ground he rests on',[1] and like his senior officials the Foreign Secretary had little hesitation in rejecting the Ambassador's pleas that opinion in Nanking and Geneva should virtually be disregarded. 'Sir F. Lindley hears only one son de cloche,' minuted Vansittart. 'It is rather astonishing that he cannot appreciate the need for treading very warily in this matter.' Contrary to what Lindley asserted, there was 'not the faintest "probability . . . of a disastrous and avoidable conflict" with Japan', and the Permanent Under Secretary agreed with Pratt and Cadogan that 'it would be far better that (Japan) should go than the League should swallow its pride and its principles to keep her'.

'Presumably,' he wrote, 'Japan will huff out of the League . . . What then? Why should anybody's withers be wrung—if we are prudent. Japan is at present a wholly unfit member of the League . . . From *our* point of view Japan will always be a nuisance and a danger *in* the League; for she is not housebroken, and in every show-down between the League and Japan, public opinion will always, and rightly, push us towards the League. A risky prospect. I would of course prefer that Japan should be reasonable and stay in the League, but if—or as— she won't, why worry too much, unless we have been fools enough to take the lead in provoking her . . .'

It will be seen that this change of emphasis since the autumn of 1931 involved the unconscious amending of various component images—including that of public opinion, for example, which Vansittart had earlier sum- marised as being essentially pro-Japanese[2]—and that, as with Stimson in a different context, the change represented in part an adjustment to an apparently unalterable situation. Meanwhile Pratt, while still opposed to a dramatic expulsion of Japan from the League, was moving even further than Vansittart. From suggesting early in December that Britain 'should avoid taking a prominent . . . part' at Geneva, he had come to argue by the end of that month that

A false step now, or even the appearance of any hesitation, might arouse the abiding hostility of the Chinese and seriously compromise our position both with the League and in America. The good-will of Japan—even if we are able to retain it—would hardly suffice to save our extensive interests in China. It would certainly not provide us with any compensation in Manchukuo or anywhere else.

At the beginning of February, writing from Geneva, he now went so far as to advocate a step that he and other British policy-makers had shunned throughout the crisis:[3] a major initiative in an anti-Japanese direction, although one with the important proviso that it should be prefaced with a

[1] Simon to Baldwin, 20 December 1932, Baldwin Papers, vol. 118.

[2] See above, 141, and on changes in values related to changes in circumstances, above, 281. Another change concerned the 'open door' in Manchuria. At the outset, much play had been made in the Foreign Office with Britain's concern for its maintenance, and Japan's assurances to that effect. When it became clear that the door was rapidly being shut (see, e.g., FO 371, F 8275/1/10), the matter was accorded a lower priority, by what seems to have been an almost unconscious process. A similar development occurred in Washington.

[3] Simon's sponsorship of non-recognition in the Assembly in March 1932 could be advanced as an exception, but the initiative on that occasion had essentially been Stimson's.

declaration that the powers did not intend to apply sanctions. Concluding that 'the Assembly would be well-advised to declare unequivocally that Japan had broken the Covenant'—something that most of the smaller states represented on the Committee of Nineteen had chosen not to demand —Pratt asked, and answered, the question of what course Britain should follow in these circumstances:

> The choice before us appears to be, either we can side more or less silently with the majority on the side of caution, or we can openly advocate a bolder policy. If we adopt the latter course, our line would be to state plainly that Japan had broken Articles X and XII of the Covenant and that we would not recognise Manchukuo; we would also condemn China's anti-foreignism and the boycott . . . The danger of such a course [apart from the matter of sanctions, to be openly rejected] is that we would run the risk of offending both Japan and China. Japan, however, will probably not resent a judgement couched in plain language more than one wrapped in diplomatic phrases . . . As regards China, . . . if we take the lead in advocating (non-recognition) we shall establish ourselves firmly in her good graces. Finally, the bold course would seem to be the only one calculated to rehabilitate the League in world opinion, and by openly advocating such a course we should place ourselves in a brilliant—and not really dangerous— position.

Whether such a declaration—in effect, that a case for applying article 16 had arisen but that the powers were not going to do so—would have rehabilitated either the League or Britain as firmly as Pratt expected is open to doubt. The proposal itself did constitute a new development for the Foreign Office, however (Cadogan had come nearest to it in the autumn of 1931), and was accompanied by similar proposals for clear speaking from Eden, who was now a member of the Committee of Nineteen's drafting body. 'It is news indeed,' he commented on one of Lindley's outbursts, 'that the League has from the first adhered too strictly to its principles. I should rather fear that the criticism of history might be that, had the League at the outset shown the measure of firmness its report eventually contained, the later stages might have been avoided.'

Simon did not go so far: for one thing—and he was not alone in this—he did not trust the other powers to follow a lead of the kind that Pratt was advocating, and thus saw the likelihood of Britain finding herself isolated in an anti-Japanese position. He also continued to insist that it would be totally unrealistic to bind future British governments to perpetual non-recognition, regardless of changing circumstances, while his notorious speech at Geneva on 7 December had been prompted by the belief that the necessary balance was being tipped by other speakers 'so universally hostile to Japan and so one-sided in their references to the Lytton Report that the Great Powers had to intervene'. Nevertheless, for all his self-congratulation that his contribution on that occasion had 'steadied the tone of the debate and relieved tension which was near to breaking point', he could not remain unaware of or indifferent to the fierce resentment which he had thereby aroused. Moreover it was consistent with his attitude throughout that he should still be ready to see Japan depart rather than have the League abandon its principles, principles, he now repeated, which Britain could not throw over 'merely because Japan would prefer this'. 'As regards breaches of the Covenant,' he wrote, 'this is a legal question. If it is clear that the facts established by the Lytton Report involve this conclusion, the conclusion must be accepted.' His own reading of that document and of the Assembly's final report enabled him to accept the more comfortable interpretation that this was not a straightforward case of international aggression, but this did not mean that he was indifferent to preserving good relations with China, and to the end he continued to return to his metaphors of the 'even balance' variety:

> 'We really can't do more than we have done to conciliate Japan', he wrote to Baldwin. 'I have got into hot water with the Chinese for going so far. And, after all, British trade with 400 million Chinese would be in jeopardy from a Chinese boycott. So we ought to keep in the middle of the road and give no handle to Uncle Sam.'[1]

This intention of the Foreign Secretary's suited at least two of his senior colleagues. Baldwin wrote back to him in similar vein of 'keeping the ship on an even keel . . . I want to avoid a Chinese boycott or (sic) a war with Japan. I have faith you will avoid both'.[2] MacDonald meanwhile described himself to Norman Davis—again the approach was a negative one—as being 'very anti-Japanese and likewise very anti-Chinese. He could not forget what China had tried to do to England [sic: it is the American who is reporting the conversation] a few years ago, and he realised Japan was acting outrageously'.[3] On the other hand when the Cabinet as a whole were faced with alterations in emphasis on the part of the Foreign Office, they were strongly inclined to underline the need for caution and to stress once more the limits which had been established in London from the early months of the crisis. The inertia-tendency of all British policies goes a long way to account for this reaction. The Foreign Office had itself played a major part in marking out those limits in 1931, and the sudden and fearful shock of Shanghai had scored them more deeply still into the Cabinet's collective mind. The recent flood of bad news from Europe and the Service Ministries pushed the process even further, and the defensive mood that had prevailed since the peak of the financial and political crisis completed it. There would be no shift in the basic British position, and, within that, only modest changes of emphasis once all attempts at conciliation had clearly failed. (Pratt's final proposal did not even get as far as the Cabinet.) When Simon, in a characteristically perceptive and inconclusive memorandum, set out the various and often-conflicting desiderata to be borne in mind, it was his final sentence that the Cabinet picked out for emphasis in its own Conclusions: 'We must not involve ourselves in trouble with Japan.'[4]

Nevertheless the Government had one brief concession to make beyond its vote in the Assembly on 24 February, in the form of the embargo on arms

---

[1] Simon to Baldwin, 20 December 1932, Baldwin Papers, vol. 118.

[2] Baldwin to Simon, 21 December 1932, Simon Papers (private collection), Foreign Affairs, 1932.

[3] Davis memorandum, 2 April 1933, Davis Papers, box 9.

[4] Cabinets of 23, 30 December 1932, 19 January, 8, 22 February 1933, CAB 23/73–75. Hankey's own inclinations may also have helped produce the emphasis which was recorded in the Conclusions.

supplies to the Far East. It was a gesture made in response to the demands of what some members of the Cabinet saw as a substantial and committed section of public opinion, led by Murray and the L.N.U., who now sought some means of expressing their anger at the way in which the hopes of 1919 had been dealt their most severe blow to date. The idea of an embargo was supported by Thomas and received at least emotional approval from MacDonald; it had been introduced in the first place by Simon, a pillow on which, as we have seen, Murray had recently sat fairly hard, but it was finally pushed through by the strong man of the Cabinet, Neville Chamberlain. The episode is thus all the more interesting for having brought together the fading remnants of Labour's Union of Democratic Control pioneers,[1] the still-hopeful Liberals like Murray who had fought Germany to fashion from victory a better world, and the rising Conservative who was stubbornly to cling to a similar hope when it had long passed to defeat.

The full details of the Cabinet's discussions on the issue can be read elsewhere.[2] Significantly, Simon opened matters on 22 February with the submission that to do nothing was a course 'he did not think parliamentary and public opinion would tolerate'—a tribute to Murray in particular, with his scarcely-veiled threat of extremists in the L.N.U. who, unless given some satisfaction, would mount a campaign for invoking article 16 of the Covenant. The moral aspect of the situation also hovered over the ensuing debates, it being recognised and recorded that supplies to Japan alone ought to be stopped 'if practical considerations could be disregarded'. MacDonald's long-standing dislike of the arms trade showed through at times, while Chamberlain bluntly described it as 'a beastly business' and suggested that even if Britain's own armaments industry declined, the country could always obtain supplies from the United States in an emergency. The Chancellor of the Exchequer, who was well placed to withstand suggestions that an embargo would damage the country's economy, was also clear in his own mind that 'we cannot fold our arms like those smug Americans and say we cannot help it if our people *will* sell ammunition and machine guns'. Other states might display a bad conscience, but the decision to impose the embargo 'was not taken to please them but to satisfy our own people'.

Chamberlain got his way, as Baldwin told him, 'by knowing his mind and sticking to it'. For a limited period, during which negotiations would be conducted to see if others would join in, arms supplies to China and Japan would be halted—an unfairness to the former, but the best that could be done when the alternative of penalising Japan alone was believed likely to lead to her blockading China. Many of the Cabinet were unhappy at even this modest decision, however. Hailsham at the War Office, Eyres-Monsell at the Admiralty, Runciman at the Board of Trade and Betterton at the Ministry of Labour had all opposed it, for obvious reasons, and were joined by Cunliffe-Lister, the Colonial Secretary. (Eyres-Monsell's most dramatic

---

[1] See above, p. 107.

[2] Thorne, 'The Quest For Arms Embargoes', loc. cit.; Cabinets of 22, 27 February, 5, 6, 13 March 1933, CAB 23/75; Simon memorandum, 24 February 1933, CP 48 (33), CAB 24/238; Hankey Diary, 4–6 March 1933; Neville to Hilda and Ida Chamberlain respectively, 25 February, 4 March 1933, Neville Chamberlain Papers.

intervention was to warn that the Admiralty believed that the Japanese had contingency plans for an attack on Singapore, and possibly a force standing by to execute it in the event of a confrontation with Britain. There does not appear to have been truth in the suggestion.) The permanent officials of these Ministers, together with those at the Foreign Office, were also solidly against the move according to Hankey, who himself led the fight against it outside the Cabinet on the grounds that export orders were essential to help build up Britain's sickly arms industry now that new threats were looming up in Europe.[1] MacDonald havered; Baldwin observed only that he saw no way out of a difficult situation; Simon, to the disgust of at least one close observer, changed his mind twice within the space of a few days as he was 'got at' by one side and then the other. 'The trouble with the Cabinet,' wrote Chamberlain to one of his sisters, 'is that no one has any fixed ideas. They agree with me and then go back on it and then agree again and then go back again. Only Jimmy Thomas remains faithful.'

The opposition helped see to it that, once born, the embargo rushed to its end. It had in any case been only a gesture; the Chinese and most delegates at Geneva were far from pleased by it, as was Stimson. The majority of the states that were approached for possible co-operation were evasive—the Dutch, for example, stipulated that they would have no part in an oil embargo—and although the French Government were not entirely discouraging, their Ambassador in London was highly sceptical in private.[2] Lampson disliked what had been done as much as did Lindley,[3] while from Geneva Simon and MacDonald, like Eden before them, reported that there was no sign of agreement on the question. Hence, after only two weeks, and with the dissident Ministers having kept up their pressure meanwhile, the embargo was lifted.

At least the public conscience appeared to have been eased somewhat—as in the case of Abyssinia later, it seemed that this required little more than a gesture or two. A new Far Eastern issue was rapidly growing up, however, which touched, not the conscience, but the public purse, especially in Lancashire, and which was again closely to involve Neville Chamberlain. With a depreciated yen and low wage-rates to help her, Japan was swiftly expanding her trade—in volume it increased by about 16 per cent during 1933— at a time when world trade as a whole was stagnating.[4] Faced with such a threat, the platitudes of politicians on the need to revive the inter-

[1] On the state of the British arms industry, see the C.I.D. minutes for 6 April 1933, CAB 2/5, and reports of the Principal Supply Officers Committee, PSO 350, 404. Later that year, a Cabinet Committee on the Private Arms Industry reported on the seriousness of the situation, and, with many a glance at Geneva and the L.N.U., the Cabinet agreed to facilitate export orders unless there were 'exceptional circumstances'. CP 289 (33), CAB 27/551.

[2] For the diplomatic exchanges involved, see DDF, II, No. 383; DBFP, XI, Nos. 256–430, passim.

[3] See, e.g., DBFP, XI, Nos. 402, 415, 432. Lampson wrote to Admiral Kelly on 1 March 1933: 'It is becoming a little hard always to be labouring along trying to wipe out the results on our position *here* of an act of foolishness at home! . . . *No* one else will follow our lead, and the thing is ineffective from the word go—in fact it's all too d—d silly!' Kelly Papers, vol. 41.

[4] For a valuable outline, see Toynbee, *Survey, 1933*, 98–105, 438–9.

national flow of goods were as nothing compared to the demand of domestic industries for protection. A reaction of this kind was already well advanced in the United States, while following the Ottawa Conference the Government of India had raised its tariffs against Japanese cotton goods. Now the Secretary of State for India and the President of the Board of Trade brought before the Cabinet in London the demands of the Lancashire textile industry for yet more protection in the Indian and other imperial markets, as well as at home.[1] They received an immediate and sympathetic hearing. In April the Government of India, with Cabinet approval, gave notice that it intended to denounce the Commercial Convention of 1904 which governed its trade with Japan, and in May London informed Tokyo that in a year's time the West African colonies would be excluded from the Anglo-Japanese Commercial Treaty of 1911. One observer commented that it seemed that measures of economic warfare were in order for the defence of immediate national self-interest, but were thought too dangerous to employ in the cause of the League.[2] The contradiction was not peculiar to British policy, of course; rather, it was inherent in the accepted rules of the international game at the time, when economic aggression was marked off in men's minds from its military counterpart even more clearly than was still to be the case forty years later. For those who were in despair at Britain's Far Eastern policy, a more ready source of indignation was supplied in April, when a trade embargo was brought in against the Soviet Union following the trial and sentencing there of the Metropolitan Vickers engineers who had been accused of espionage.[3] Economic sanctions thus remained a weapon to be used under certain circumstances—de Valera's Irish Free State was the other recipient of such treatment in these years—but not where they were thought likely to be ineffective, or expensive, or the cause of a heavy blow in return.

Retrospect

Following the publication of the Lytton Report the Japanese rounded off their conquest of Manchuria, although without quelling all resistance to their rule. They were now poised to move north-east and north-west against the Soviet Union, or south into the heart of northern China. The likelihood and direction of such further moves depended to a considerable extent on political developments in Tokyo, but over Manchukuo there was no thought of retreat. It was also clear that, whatever now occurred, the presence of the Soviet Union, diplomatically active as well as militarily on guard in the area, would again be a major factor in the situation.

By its vote of 24 February 1933 the League had at least saved its honour, and a fraction of its morale, Drummond and others having underestimated the consequences of further procrastination in this respect, however reasonable their desire to try to avoid Japan's departure. But the organisation had preserved little of its credibility—or whatever had remained of it in terms of

---

[1] See Cabinet of 8 February, 8, 29 March 1933, CAB 23/75; DBFP, XI, Nos. 396, 453, 499, 513. [2] Toynbee, loc. cit.

[3] See DBFP, VII, pp. 423–91. The embargo was lifted on 1 July, when the two imprisoned men were released.

action against a major power after America's refusal to join and the gentle handling of Italy over Corfu. Among League supporters in Britain, especially, and in several of the smaller member states, this came as a doom-laden revelation; and yet in this last phase of the crisis, as in the earlier ones, few of them had shown themselves to be ready for major national and personal sacrifices in order to achieve anything more (members of Maude Royden's Peace Army being among the obvious exceptions). Even among those who regularly followed international affairs, attention was already turning elsewhere, and to Europe in particular, the comforting thought now being widespread in official and non-official circles alike that before long Japan would both suffer for her actions and react with reason and restraint to that suffering when it came.

For the present, however, there remained in all three Western capitals the expectation of a belligerent reaction on the part of Japan should coercion be attempted. As before, this was the argument which silenced all others and set narrow limits to one's responses. Thus there continued to be more in common between the policies of the three countries than admirers of Stimson, in particular, recognised at the time; this included a strong desire to make things up privately with Japan, and in this period there was in American Far Eastern policy a marked degree of that passivity which was to be its chief feature in the ensuing years. In London, Pratt had come up with his late suggestion for plain speaking and British leadership at Geneva. It could be argued that this would have been more useful earlier in the dispute, when hopes of success had not disappeared and Stimson was less soured by his experiences; on the other hand the belief in the need to strive first for conciliation had not been an unreasonable one (however misguided, some might say), while the need to admit one's inability to impose sentence when now bringing in a verdict of guilty might have shaken the League as much as Drummond's plan to put off the verdict itself for as long as possible.

As one French diplomat had bluntly remarked, the League, together with the leading Western powers, had already suffered a defeat over Manchuria. What had been done in this final period was largely a matter of disguising the fact as best as possible. Policies had been adjusted; but so, too, in many instances, had images and interpretations, in order to maintain a tolerable degree of harmony with what was now seen to be feasible in the circumstances. If politics is the art of the possible, much of foreign policy consists of redefining the bearable.

PART THREE
RECAPITULATION

CHAPTER ELEVEN

AFTERMATH AND PROGRESSION

Developments in the Far East

REGARDLESS OF League resolutions, the swift Japanese triumph in Jehol proved only the prelude to a final flurry of fighting in an area of far greater concern to the Western powers. Towards the end of March there were frequent skirmishes along the Great Wall between Shanhaikuan and Hsifengkow, with the Chinese, anxious to restore their tattered morale and reputation, claiming major victories over small Japanese units that had been installed to cover the passes. In their turn, the Kwantung Army announced their refusal to tolerate the presence of Chinese troops in the Shanhaikuan—Hsifengkow—Luanchow triangle. After making an attack to clear this area and then withdrawing, they found the enemy reoccupying it and thereupon launched a new and heavy assault on 7 May, driving south towards the Luan river. Japanese planes appeared over Peking, where a direct attack was now expected as Chinese troops abandoned Miyun and other towns not far to the north. With a major victory within their grasp, however, the Japanese pulled up, and negotiations between military commanders—the Chinese delegates fearing for their lives at the hands of enraged compatriots—led to the signing of a truce at Tangku on 31 May. Chinese forces were to withdraw from a broad zone stretching up to the Wall from just north of Peking and Tientsin, leaving it to be controlled by their police only; once the Kwantung Army were satisfied by means of aerial and other observation that this had been carried out, they, too, would withdraw to the Wall. The North-China plain now lay under permanent Japanese threat, and the objectives defined by the Army leaders in Tokyo at the end of 1931 had been achieved.[1]

In desperation, Chinese politicians had been calling for intervention by the West, but widespread rumours also continued to circulate concerning moves to achieve a secret Sino–Japanese understanding. Nothing of the kind emerged in the spring of 1933, but the visit to China in March of Yoshizawa Kenkichi, the former Japanese Foreign Minister, suggested that there were those in Tokyo who might be ready to pursue this goal. Such a proposal, however, served only further to divide those who held power in Nanking, already at odds over whether to fight on or seek an armistice. Canton

---

[1] Detailed accounts of the fighting and truce are contained in, e.g., *The Times* and *New York Times*, together with British and American diplomatic reports. See, e.g., DBFP, XI, Nos. 435–592, passim.

watched and accused as before; Chang Hsueh-liang having resigned after the Jehol débâcle, soon departed for Europe; T. V. Soong, en route to the World Economic Conference in London, was seeking help in the United States.[1] In the ensuing months some of the surviving war-lords in the country were curbed, while Nanking was soon announcing victory over the Communists as well, as the latter were forced to abandon their Kiangsi Soviet in 1934. Nevertheless the nature and structure of Kuomintang rule almost guaranteed that defeat would succeed victory. Following their Long March, the Communists were securely ensconced in Shensi by 1936; at the end of the year, moreover, Chang Hsueh-liang, now restored to his command, made his presence felt by holding Chiang Kai-shek captive in Sian until the latter agreed to come to terms with the Communists and to combine with them in active resistance to the Japanese.[2] With the Communists in turn having agreed to recognise Chiang Kai-shek's authority, it was a Republican China superficially united as never before that faced full-scale war with Japan in 1937; despite another resolute stand at Shanghai, however, that city, together with Nanking, Hankow, Canton and the North-China plain were soon lost to the invader, and from its Chungking retreat the Kuomintang régime thereafter preferred discretion to defiance. Further north, the Communists chose to fight on, and in doing so strengthened the basis of their own eventual accession to power—a double defeat for those in the Japanese Army who had included among their aims in 1931 the removal of the 'Red Menace' from neighbouring areas of the Asiatic mainland.

Meanwhile the Soviet Union had passed through a period of great anxiety on its eastern frontier following the Manchurian crisis. For some time it appeared that a conflict with Japan might break out over the Chinese Eastern Railway, and Soviet endeavours to improve their military preparedness continued apace. In 1935, however, after nearly two years of negotiations, Moscow agreed to sell the railway to the new rulers of Manchuria. The move looked like appeasement of the invertebrate variety and the Red Army did not like it, but the commercial and strategic value of the line had sharply declined, and it made sense to remove such a source of friction at a time when signs of a German–Polish rapprochement in the West suggested increased danger on that front, and perhaps even a massive German–Polish–Japanese encirclement aimed against Soviet territory and power.[3] By the same token, the improvement of relations with France and the Little Entente, accompanied by entry into the League, took on a new urgency for Moscow, while as the threat from Hitler's Germany reached a new peak in 1938 a further reminder of the two-front danger was provided by a short but fierce battle with the Kwantung Army at Lake Khasan, on the borders of Manchuria, Korea and the Soviet Maritime Provinces.[4] On that occasion Soviet troops secured a remarkable victory, despite the contemporary activities of the NKVD; Stalin nevertheless needed a success of another kind, which he duly obtained with the signing of a Soviet–Japanese Neutrality Pact in April 1941.[5] Even this was little enough guarantee that the Kwantung Army would

[1] See, e.g., ibid, Nos. 439, 448, 533, 547, 570.
[2] See, e.g., Fitzgerald, 79 ff.; D. Wilson, *The Long March* (London, 1971).
[3] See Erickson, 357–401.
[4] Ibid, 494–9.   [5] Ibid, 577.

not attack at a time of its own choosing, but in fact the Pact held until the Soviet Union herself broke it in 1945—the flimsy legal justification for doing so being supplied by those who, from Washington, had proclaimed themselves to be fighting to uphold the sanctity of international agreements.[1] This blow fell at a time when Tokyo's last hopes were pinned upon securing Soviet mediation with the Western powers, and as Stalin's mechanised units raced into Manchuria through the depleted remnants of the Kwantung Army, another of the aims of 1931 lay shattered.

By then, of course, Japan's renewed assault in China had long been merged into a struggle which embraced vast areas of the Pacific and South-East Asia. This development as relating to Japanese policy between 1933 and 1941 has now become a matter of fruitful debate after many years of the orthodoxy of long and clearly-planned Japanese aggression, as handed out by the Far Eastern war crimes tribunal.[2] Numerous and important new studies have been emerging from Japan itself, and while most conclusions must remain tentative for some time to come, it does seem clear that considerable revision and qualification of the traditional interpretation is called for. As Richard Storry wrote as long ago as 1957, the events of 1931 to 1941 were 'not the product of a single grand conspiracy',[3] and the lack in 1933 of any clear and agreed notion of future steps and their likely consequences has been described above. In part, this can be ascribed to those mental processes depicted by Maruyama and others, and embracing what to the Western mind appears as illogicality, wishful-thinking and a refusal to follow questions to a conclusion. In part, too, it arose from the lack of a coherent structure of decision-making and executive responsibility; while this did not produce a clear civilian-military dichotomy thereafter, it did enable the Army and Navy to influence and interpret policy in directions that suited their own sectional interests.[4]

Among the discordant voices to be heard in and after 1933, those of some (by no means all) officials of the Foreign Ministry were raised on the side of caution. In a survey made in the spring of 1933, for example,[5] the Director of its European–American Bureau advised that 'a Japanese–American war should by all means be avoided', and that 'any idea of trying to monopolise the Pacific is equally unrealistic whether considered from an American or Japanese standpoint. It is to be expected as a matter of course', he continued, 'that the United States would not countenance the establishment of a Japanese hegemony over all the Far East.' 'Reckless adventure' should therefore be avoided, and in addition an accommodation should be sought with Britain and France concerning China. Dutch fears, too, should be allayed, and the writer was pleased to note that, on Dutch initiative, negotiations were already proceeding towards the conclusion of a treaty of arbitration

[1] Butow, *Japan's Decision to Surrender*, 84 ff., 155–8.

[2] See above, 5.

[3] Storry, *Double Patriots*, 298–9.

[4] Maruyama, 87–9; Iriye, *Across the Pacific*, 207–9; Hosoya Chihiro, 'Retrogression in Japan's Foreign Policy Decision-Making Progress', in Morley (ed.), *Dilemmas of Growth*; Ogata, 195; Crowley, 195, 378, 385, 396.

[5] Togo memorandum, IMTFE, *Exhibit* 3609A. Togo later became Foreign Minister. See his book, *The Cause of Japan* (New York, 1956).

and mediation.[1] Meanwhile there also remained some factions within the Japanese Navy (though again they were by no means dominant) who emphasised the need to avoid a confrontation with the Western powers,[2] and the Cabinet had done the same in an official foreign-policy programme in the autumn of 1933.[3] Even in the discussions that led to approval being given to the notorious 'Fundamental Principles of National Policy' in 1936 (the document envisaged the eradication of the Soviet menace to the north, the securing of self-government for North China, and an advance into the South Seas), the Inner Cabinet agreed that any southward extension of power must be achieved 'gradually and peacefully'.[4] The accepted significance for foreign policy of the bloody army coup of the same year, known as the 26 February incident, has also come to be questioned.[5]

During this period, that element of Japan's ambivalent policy which involved eventual rapprochement and pan-Asian comradeship with China continued to be sincerely believed in, and it is now evident that in 1937 neither the Kwantung Army nor the Government in Tokyo sought to bring about the Marco-Polo-bridge skirmish which triggered off the war against China; indeed, the Army's General Staff were beginning to think of accepting the lasting tenacity of Chinese nationalism in the area, and of reducing their own anti-Kuomintang activities.[6] Moreover, although the Anti-Comintern Pact had already been signed with Germany in 1936, it was remarkably lacking in specific commitments, even against the Soviet Union whom the Japanese had hoped to restrain by its signature; and even when the idea of an actual alliance with Germany had become more attractive from 1938 onwards (especially as a means of holding the Soviet Union in check while the China war was being won), the Navy refused until 1940 to come out openly in such a clear anti-British direction. Thereafter there was increased momentum towards a move to the south and against Britain in particular, but as was noted earlier, there remained in 1940 no plans for the seizure of American possessions, the Dutch East Indies, Australia, Burma or India,[7] and the Army still believed and asserted that war with the United States should be avoided. Only in the spring and summer of 1941, with both Britain and the Soviet Union under great pressure and the small likelihood of being able to divorce the United States from Britain, France and the Netherlands in a Far Eastern context becoming more apparent, was the idea accepted of a war against all the Western powers in the area, and plans made accordingly. Even then policy-making in Tokyo retained its cloudy and sinuous characteristics, and although finally it was agreed that there was no acceptable alternative to fighting, no one could assert that Japan would win the war that was now to be launched at Pearl Harbour.[8]

[1] Cf. DBFP, XI, Nos. 475, 532, 544.   [2] See Crowley, 287.   [3] Ibid, 191.
[4] IMTFE, Exhibits, 216, 704, 979.
[5] Crowley, 249. Cf. Maruyama, 26 ff., and Storey, Double Patriots, passim.
[6] 'The Road to the Pacific War', vol. II, part 2; Crowley, 380. Earlier, the Army had continued to hope to attract American capital into Manchukuo. Hakone Conference, proceedings.
[7] See above, 67.
[8] See above, 63; Ike, Japan's Decision For War, passim, and R. J. Butow, Tojo and the Coming of War (Princeton, 1961).

This all-too-terse reminder that for Japan the transition from 1931 to 1941 was by no means a straightforward and clearly planned one will be placed alongside a further consideration in the final chapter, concerning the part played by the Western powers in helping to bring about the conflict that ultimately took place. Nevertheless it is important at this stage not to lose sight of those trends which survive even major revisions relating to individual episodes of Japanese policy.[1] For underlying all the confusion and disagreements in Tokyo after 1933, there remained a widespread belief that stability in East Asia required Japanese domination over China and a readiness to defeat if necessary the forces of both the Soviet Union and the Western powers in that part of the world. To this end, economic and strategic autonomy must be achieved, while in general terms, as one of the leading 'revisionist' historians himself has put it, one consequence was that

> an inordinate emphasis on the subject of 'national defense' served to rationalise aggression and authoritarianism as the best ways to overcome the challenge posed by the demands of total war and two strategic enemies endowed with plentiful natural resources.[2]

More specifically, it meant that a statement like the 'Amau doctrine' in 1934, which suggested that Japan alone bore responsibility for maintaining peace in Asia, did represent a genuine conviction and intention, just as, within the Foreign Ministry, one of the more moderate figures like Shigemitsu Mamoru could write of the need to base such a claim 'on the rationale of actual power'.[3] Where North China was concerned, only briefly and belatedly was there a reconsideration of the intention, spelt out by the War Ministry and Army General Staffs in July 1933, to 'destroy the actual influence of the Nationalist Party and extend this tendency to the South ... (and to) eliminate from the civil and military heads of the Nanking Government pro-European and -American elements, replacing them by pro-Japanese and -Asiatic ones'.[4] The sudden flare-up of hostilities in 1937 was, indeed, unlooked for; but soon the Cabinet in Tokyo were set upon making it the occasion for a war of chastisement, and then a war of annihilation, in which the question of Sino–Japanese relations would finally be settled—settled on Japanese terms, that is, rather as Hitler proposed to settle relations with Poland on German terms early in 1939.[5]

As for strategic autonomy, where was this to be found? Not within the Japan–Korea–Manchuria bloc, for despite considerable industrial development in Manchuria after 1933 (especially in metals, engineering and chemicals), that much-prized land did not provide the amount of raw materials, in oil, for example, that optimists had hoped for, any more than it proved to be an attractive outlet for Japan's swelling population.[6] The virtually

---

[1] On similar considerations relating to German policy and the war in Europe, see E. M. Robertson, *Hitler's Pre-War Policy and Military Plans* (London, 1963) and Thorne, *The Approach of War*.
[2] Crowley, 394. Cf. ibid, 299.   [3] Ibid, 189–90, 196–7.
[4] IMTFE, *Exhibit* 3607A; cf. Crowley, 195, 202, 210, 229.
[5] See Crowley, 301 ff., especially 340, 350, 372.
[6] In 1931, 240,000 Japanese civilians were living in Manchuria and in 1939, 837,000; of the latter figure, however, under 70,000 were agrarian colonists, despite

inescapable logic of the quest for autonomy lay, rather, in an extension of Japanese power and dominion southwards, towards the tin, rubber, and above all oil of the Dutch East Indies and Malaya. It was this goal that was particularly attractive to the Navy, in which an anti-Western and pro-German faction was by now of strong account and which, for all its hesitations, had subscribed long before 1941 to the need to 'correct the dominating policies' of those Western powers in the Far East; it was also the Navy which had set out to ensure that no new naval agreement was reached with the West in 1934–5, and whose Chief of Staff was by 1941 advocating war with the United States even before the latter placed an embargo on her export of oil to Japan.[1] Immediate American involvement in any fighting, although quite possible, may not have been the certainty that Tokyo was coming to accept, as was noted earlier;[2] but in this southward drive by Japan lay at least the immediate cause of the Pacific war. This is not to say that such a war had long been 'inevitable', or that the Western powers were simply its passive and blameless victims.

Links between the approach of war in the Far East and developments in Europe already existed, not only in Japanese eyes, but in the global defence preoccupations of Britain, for example, and Germany's readiness to proclaim Japan as an ally.[3] As late as the outbreak of the Sino–Japanese war in 1937, German policy had continued to balance between those two countries, but thereafter the clear inclination had been towards Japan, with de jure recognition being accorded to Manchukuo on the way. As in the case of German–Italian friendship, a certain difficulty might have been expected to arise from Nazi racial doctrines; Hitler, however, merely pronounced his certainty that 'Japan's greatest victory would not affect the civilisation of the white races in the very least'. What the two allies could and did share, despite their particular emphases, was a determination to create a disciplined society that would contrast with the decadence of the United States and the European democracies. From the new centres of national and racial regeneration, the liberal West and its proclaimed ideals of international harmony appeared not the wave of the future but an ebbing past.

extensive schemes to promote such settlement. In 1941 Manchuria was producing 20·7 million tons of coal per annum (just under 9 million tons in 1931) and 1·4 million tons of pig iron (673,000 tons of iron ore in 1931); but the production of crude oil and synthetic oil from coal had not been successful. Germany's own quest for autarchy had damaged the Manchurian soya-bean trade, although this was revived somewhat by the German–Japanese–Manchukuoan trade agreement of 1935. See Jones, *Manchuria Since 1931*, cap. V et seq.; Allen, *A Short Economic History of Japan*, 143 ff.; Mitsubishi Economic Research Bureau, *Japan's Trade and Industry* (London, 1936), 625–6.

[1] 'The Road to the Pacific War', vol. IV, part 2; Asada Sadao, 'The Japanese Navy and the United States', Hakone conference paper.

[2] See above, 76.

[3] See E. L. Presseisen, *Germany and Japan: A Study in Totalitarian Diplomacy, 1933–1941* (The Hague, 1958); T. Somer, *Deutschland und Japan zwischen den Maechten, 1935–1940* (Tuebingen, 1962); Drechsler, *Deutschland–China–Japan, 1933–1939*.

The League and public opinion in the West

On 27 March 1933 the Japanese Government gave notice of its intention to withdraw from the League of Nations, a step which, as some hopefully noted, required under the Covenant two years to become effective and the fulfilment by that time of all Japan's obligations arising from her various international undertakings.[1] If this was all but meaningless, it was now scarcely of greater significance that she did not choose to leave the Disarmament Conference; more to the point, however, was her determination not to surrender those Pacific islands that she held under League mandate, a situation which Geneva eventually accepted. Meanwhile the League's Advisory Committee on the Sino–Japanese dispute had met, without the Soviet Union which had declined membership in moderate terms, and with Hugh Wilson as the non-voting representative of the United States, whose Government took care to emphasise that his presence at the table did not commit it to anything.[2] The Committee then set up sub-groups to examine various problems such as arms supplies, then rapidly gave up the attempt to disguise the fact that it was moribund.

League officials did make strenuous efforts to mount a technical assistance programme for China, but its very existence was enough to arouse Japanese anger (especially where it again involved Dr. Rajchman, whose passionate advocacy of the Chinese cause has been noted earlier), and for his part the new Secretary General, Joseph Avenol, was only too happy to divest the League of any such political embarrassments.[3] Avenol, indeed, went further than merely restricting Rajchman's activities in his desire to preserve relations with Tokyo, if necessary at China's expense, and in his acceptance of what he termed the 'infinite fact' of the seizure of Manchuria, against which he had detachedly watched the Assembly 'pit their finite wills'.[4] Even so, that same Assembly, urged on by stalwarts like William Jordan of New Zealand, chose in 1937 to condemn Japan's new attack upon China as a breach of the Kellogg Pact and Nine Power Treaty, and in 1938 went so far as to authorise the application of sanctions against Japan should members individually so decide.[5] By then, however, such pronouncements, like the League itself, were almost without significance. Even before 1933 had passed, Lytton had privately confessed to McCoy: 'It looks very much . . . as if our work has been wasted.'[6]

In the political tasks to which it was committed, and particularly those concerning disarmament and security, the League had been faced with one setback after another following its condemnation of Japan in February 1933.

---

[1] LNOJ, *May, 1933* (Geneva, 1933), 657–8.

[2] LNOJ, *Special Supplement No. 112* (Geneva, 1933), 98–100; FRUS, *Japan, 1931–1941*, I, 119.

[3] On the aid programme to China, see LN. Archives, files R5680–5685; S706–7; S713–17; R3309; also the report by R. Haas on his mission to China, 1935. Cf. Walters, 331–4, 738; Barros, *Betrayal From Within*, 40 ff.

[4] Barros, *Betrayal*, 45–7; Wilson, *Diplomat Between Wars*, 281.

[5] Walters, 734–8.

[6] Lytton to McCoy, 3 October 1933, McCoy Papers, box 30.

Despite a last major effort by Britain to save it by means of a draft convention complete with actual figures for military establishments, the Disarmament Conference hastened downhill and was to all intents finished when Germany left both it and the League in the following October.[1] With Mussolini's proposal for a four-power pact, the nineteenth-century concept of a European concert, so obnoxious to the smaller League states, came briefly to the fore; it, too, came to nothing, however, and thus eased matters between France and her allies.[2] The World Economic Conference, convened by the League in June, had already foundered on Roosevelt's refusal to participate in currency stabilisation, despite his preceding appeal to all heads of state not to permit failure in this sphere and that of disarmament. One consequence was yet a further deterioration in Anglo–American relations.[3] Tension also continued to exist for some time between the United States and the League over the Chaco war between Bolivia and Paraguay, where intervention from Geneva was being hampered by the separate manoeuvrings of Washington.[4]

More hopeful signs were not entirely lacking. Among them was one in which Simon clearly enjoyed being able to play a part: the settlement through League channels of an Anglo–Persian oil dispute in 1933 on a basis that greatly increased Persia's share of the profits made within her territory. In the following year, the Soviet Union became a member of the League,[5] and Drummond was not alone when, writing to a friend from his new post as British Ambassador to Italy, he proclaimed his continued optimism over the future of the organisation. 'I am quite clear,' he added, 'that (Mussolini) is now really anxious to strengthen the League, because above all he wants peace and quiet.'[6] Unfortunately, however, this proved to be one of the many myopic judgements that Drummond was to make in Rome (Mussolini had already removed Grandi as his Foreign Minister in 1932 partly because of the latter's pro-League inclinations[7]). By the time the League had moved in 1936–7 into its new headquarters on the hill overlooking the Lake of Geneva—an imposing edifice, perhaps, but one whose main halls were significantly designed for declamation rather than discussion—Italy had helped finally to shatter its political credibility. In the Abyssinian crisis, unlike its Manchurian predecessor, the Council and Assembly agreed to act under article 16 of the Covenant. For Britain, Hoare as Foreign Secretary made what seemed to be a resolute and unqualified declaration of the kind not heard from Simon, and few doubted—rightly so—that if they possessed

---

[1] See DBFP, IV, Nos. 278, 290, 294 and appendix IV; Toynbee, *Survey, 1933*, 224–31.

[2] See, e.g., DBFP, V, pp. 56–156; DDF, III, passim; Walters, 544–6.

[3] See, e.g., Toynbee, *Survey, 1933*, 35–81; Walters, 517–23. For the preceding visits of MacDonald and Herriot to Washington, see DBFP, V, Nos. 545, 549, 550; DDF, II, Nos. 317, 321, 328, 348, 392; ibid, III, No. 195. When Stimson met King George V soon after the breakdown of the Economic Conference, the latter exploded with anger at Roosevelt's action. Stimson Diary, 20 July 1933.

[4] See Walters, 524 ff.   [5] Ibid, 579 ff.

[6] Drummond to Sweetser, 27 January 1934, Sweetser Papers, box 31.

[7] On this and the development of Mussolini's ideas in this period, see G. W. Baer, *The Coming of the Italian–Ethiopian War* (Cambridge, Mass., 1967), cap. 1.

the requisite determination Britain and France could cut off both the cam-paigning Italian army and the bulk of its country's oil supplies. Yet by the summer of 1936 all was despair and disillusion once more. Haile Selassie had lost his kingdom and at Geneva had shamed the Assembly, where only a few delegates—those of South Africa and New Zealand among them—continued to resist the abandonment of sanctions. In 1937 Mussolini, too, left the League, recognising Manchukuo in the process; Britain nevertheless was to recognise the Italian Empire in Abyssinia not long afterwards.[1]

The painful progress of the League which followed, through Spain and Central Europe to the final gesture of expelling the Soviet Union for its attack on Finland, need not be recounted. During this phase there was much discussion of possible amendments to the Covenant, while in the shape of the new and enforced emphasis on the organisation's potentialities in the social and economic spheres, significant preparations were made for those develop-ments which subsequently took place under the United Nations.[2] The central, collective-security function of the League was now openly aban-doned, however. In 1936 Neville Chamberlain had called for regional arrangements as an alternative, and in February 1938 he announced that smaller states should be under no illusion that they could find shelter within the articles of the Covenant. In the autumn of that year the Assembly formally accepted Britain's proposal that members should no longer be bound to apply either economic or military sanctions.[3]

This withering away of the League caused much distress among those sections of the British public that had reposed so much hope in its success. The major domestic landmarks to be encountered in this context—the dram-atic government defeat in the Fulham by-election of 1935 and the results of the Peace Ballot in the same year, for example—are well known, so much so that there is a certain amount of myth-clearing to be done.[4] Here, however, attention must be confined to the immediate repercussions of the Far

[1] On the Abyssinian episode, see Baer; A. J. Barker, *The Civilising Mission* (New York, 1968); Middlemas and Barnes; Warner; Barros, *Betrayal*; Walters, 623 ff.; A. Marder, 'The Royal Navy and the Ethiopian Crisis of 1935-6', *American Historical Review*, vol. LXXV, No. 5, 1970. I have also benefited from an un-published paper by Dr. David Carlton on 'The Dominions and British Policy in the Abyssinian Crisis', written for a seminar at the Institute of Commonwealth Studies, London, of which I was a member.

[2] See V-Y. Ghébali, *La Réforme Bruce, 1939–1940* (Geneva, Carnegie Endow-ment, 1970); Walters, 687 ff., 709 ff., 749 ff.; Barros, *Betrayal*, cap. 5.

[3] Walters, 778–83.

[4] See, e.g., R. Heller, 'East Fulham Revisited', *Journal of Contemporary History*, vol. 6, No. 3, 1971. In general, see Angell, *After All*; Martin, *Editor*; H. Nicolson, *Diaries and Letters, 1930–1939* (London, 1966); H. Dalton, *The Fateful Years* (London, 1955); *History of the Times*, vol. IV (London, 1952); M. Gilbert, *The Roots of Appeasement* (London, 1966) and *Plough My Own Furrow*; A. L. Rowse, *All Souls and Appeasement* (London, 1961); K. W. Watkins, *Britain Divided* (London, 1963); E. R. Gannon, *The British Press and Germany, 1936–1939* (London, 1971); N. Thompson, *The Anti-Appeasers* (Oxford, 1971); R. Eatwell, 'Munich, Public Opinion and the Popular Front', *Journal of Contemporary History*, vol. 6, No. 4, 1971, and the Gallup Poll on the Danzig issue printed in later editions of my *Approach of War*.

Eastern crisis and to the broad outlines of the debate on general issues to which that event had helped give rise. In the summer of 1933 and beyond, leading members of the L.N.U. continued to deplore what had occurred over Manchuria and to call for a firmer British response in future. Cecil, for example, declared in the Lords that the Government's actions had been 'lacking in firmness and consistency', a charge which he increased to one of 'poltroonery or worse' in the *League Year Book*.[1] In particular he protested to the Foreign Office at the sending to Manchukuo of a mission from the Federation of British Industries, while again assuring Vansittart and others that Japan would not react violently to a cutting off of her exports.[2] This exasperation was partly fostered by his being deceived into believing that American cooperation, which he admitted to be a sine qua non for any action, might well be forthcoming—the dangerously optimistic Norman Davis 'warmly agreeing' in May 1933 that an embargo on Japanese trade would be the right move, and stating, according to Cecil's record, that 'he believed that in this matter the President was of the same mind'. Davis strongly denied that the United States would not take practical steps in the matter, short of war—though he rapidly hedged when Cecil suggested that the President should therefore take the initiative.[3] A further flurry of public anger was occasioned by remarks that were ascribed to Lindley in the Canadian press as he passed through that country on his way to Britain for a period of leave, and in which the Ambassador's sympathy for Japan's case appeared to have got the better of his discretion.[4] Meanwhile at Geneva, where Philip, Noel-Baker saw 'the policy of organised international co-operation (to be) in grave danger', Gilbert Murray issued a call 'to keep faith' in dark times.[5]

Although European events soon overshadowed all others, the plight of China was not entirely forgotten by League supporters in Britain,[6] and the

[1] *Hansard, House of Lords*, vol. 87, cols. 872–86; *League Year Book, 1933* (London, 1933), Foreword. Cf. FO 371, F 5162/33/10.

[2] Cecil to Eden, 30 July; Wellesley to Cecil, 3 August; Cecil to Wellesley, 10 August 1933, Cecil Papers, Add. 51083; DBFP, XI, No. 553.

[3] Cecil memorandum, 12 May 1933, Cecil Papers, Add. 51101. In 1937 Cecil talked to Roosevelt about the latter's 'quarantine' speech. The President admitted that he had had to reply to a question from Paris that the U.S.A. could not stand by France against Japan if she resumed arms supplies to China. Cecil memorandum, November 1937, ibid, Add. 51131.

[4] See *Hansard, House of Commons*, vol. 278, col. 340; DBFP, XI, No. 562.

[5] Noel-Baker memorandum, 5 July 1933, Cecil Papers, Add. 51108; Murray, 'A Survey of Recent World Affairs', in *Problems of Peace, 8th series*. Cf. the correspondence of Garnett and others, *New Statesman*, 11 November 1933 et seq.

[6] With the advent of the Sino–Japanese War in 1937, the L.N.U., Union of Democratic Control and other bodies attempted to organise a private boycott of Japanese goods. During the Anglo–Japanese confrontation at Tientsin in 1939, it would appear that a substantial proportion of the public were prepared for a show-down with Japan: a Gallup Poll of 9 July 1939, asked: 'How far should Britain go at the present time to defend her interests in China? Fight Japan if necessary? Forbid all trade between Britain and Japan? Supply credits and munitions to China? Withdraw our Ambassador as a protest? Do nothing?' To this somewhat

Manchurian episode helped to provoke a debate in which familiar questions were raised once more: in a world of sovereign states, how should the national interest be defined and what priority should it be accorded? What price could or should be paid in striving to prevent another war, especially if one might end up by helping to bring about the very outcome one sought to avoid? How was one to define an act of aggression, and to what extent could states be expected to bind themselves beforehand to defend the victim of such an act? Even before the shock of Abyssinia a new note of caution, as well as confusion, was noticeable in such discussions. A booklet on *Economic Sanctions* that was issued by the L.N.U. in 1934, for example, emphasised that 'a system which provided for the use of economic sanctions alone and . . . not for co-operation in armed resistance must be considered inadequate', while a more detailed analysis of the practical and psychological difficulties involved in the application of sanctions was to emerge a few years later from the work of a study group at Chatham House.[1] In other discussions held at Chatham House in the summer of 1936, Sir Arthur Salter, his confident call for the economic coercion of Japan in 1932 well behind him, now recognised that 'from the start we should have faced the fact that it is no use whatever to think of imposing any kind of sanctions against an aggressor unless you are prepared if necessary to support that pressure by the use of armed forces'.[2] At the same time Arnold Toynbee, Harold Nicolson, Gathorne Hardy and others who were present on that occasion leaned heavily towards giving the League an openly European bias. 'You can cut out Asia,' suggested Gathorne Hardy; if Japan attacks China, observed Nicolson, 'it is horrible but it is not going to ruin Western civilisation'. Seldom had the essence of the League, as conceived by many of the liberal and intellectual Left in Britain, found more blunt expression.[3] Toynbee and Nicolson were also among those in the gathering who admitted, in the former's words, 'that we have hardly begun to face up to the implications of the aim we . . . set ourselves (in 1919)'. As H. G. Wells waspishly put it: 'It is very interesting that in 1936 you have got a Committee sitting to find out what the League of Nations is about, because there was just such a Committee in existence eighteen years ago.'[4]

crude set of alternatives (seeking a single preference), the percentage responses were:

	Fight	Forbid	Supply	Withdraw	Do Nothing
Government Supporters	22	37	15	9	17
Opposition Supporters	25	38	15	9	13
All	22	37	17	9	15

[1] R.I.I.A., *International Sanctions*.

[2] R.I.I.A., *The Future of the League of Nations* (New York, 1936), 65–6.

[3] Ibid, 99–100, 121, 131. For a Foreign Office memorandum of July, 1936, examining possible reform of the League, see FP (36) 5, Vansittart Papers.

[4] *The Future of the League*, 14–16, 159. For examples of confusion and self-

In the same year, 1936, even Cecil privately admitted by implication that he had been mistaken in what had been his fundamental assertion during the Far Eastern crisis:

'I put aside, personally,' he wrote to Eden, 'all hope of maintaining peace by objuration or appeals or even the unassisted influence of world opinion. These influences which have ultimately great power in international affairs have never yet succeeded in preventing a war which had been determined upon by any powerful country . . . If we are to give the new system [of maintaining peace] fair trial . . . we must be as ready to make sacrifices for (it) as we used to be to make sacrifices for matters of "honour and vital interest".'[1]

As for Murray, while remaining privately cautious over the idea of imposing economic penalties on Japan[2] he was shocked by the criticisms of the sanctions provisions of the Covenant that were made in his inaugural lecture at Aberystwyth by Professor E. H. Carr, formerly Assistant Adviser on League Affairs in the Foreign Office. It pained Murray all the more that it was from a Chair founded in the name of Woodrow Wilson that Carr now repudiated 'the whole League principle', as Murray saw it. How, he demanded, was the expansion of Germany, Japan and Italy to be resisted if sanctions were abandoned? Carr responded that in his view article 16 was based upon the fallacy 'that economic sanctions can be compulsory and military sanctions optional'. Since 1932 it had seemed clear to him that without a readiness to resort to force all talk of economic coercion was pointless; now what he hoped for was 'a universal, sanctionless League—the League of Art. 11. After all that *was* the League in the days of its greatness— the period from 1925–30 . . . By trying to get more you have broken the League altogether'.[3]

The greatest confusion of all centred around that earnest area where belief in collective security mingled with socialism and pacifism.[4] Kingsley Martin, who was subsequently to acknowledge this feature of the 1930s, provided an outstanding example of it in the post-Manchurian period. Having supported the idea of sanctions in that earlier crisis, he now opposed their use over Abyssinia on the grounds that a war against Italy on this issue would be no more than an imperialist squabble, and that 'Abyssinia will go down the drain whatever you and I do or say'.[5] He was supported by Bertrand Russell on somewhat different grounds, ones which left the principle of collective security with a distinctly tattered look, but which came close to what had been the Government's position in 1931–3:

I am against a League war in present circumstances, because the anti-League forces are strong . . . If the League were strong enough, I should favour sanctions

contradiction on the part of Churchill and others, see Thompson, *The Anti-Appeasers*, 82, 110.

[1] Memorandum on League Policy, 26 May 1936, Cecil Papers, Add. 51083.
[2] Murray to Lauterpacht, 29 January, 3 February 1934, Murray Papers.
[3] Murray to Carr, 5 December; Carr to Murray, 8 December 1936, Murray Papers.
[4] See, e.g., 'The Pacifist's Dilemma', *New Statesman*, 28 October 1933.
[5] Martin to Zilliacus, 1935, n.d., Kingsley Martin Papers.

because either the threat would suffice or the war would be short and small. The whole question is quantitative.[1]

Leonard Woolf, on the other hand, one of the men who had done most to propagate the League ideal during the Great War, remained both more resolute and less confused than Martin and many others:

'I have always been clear,' he wrote to Martin, '... A, that the use of (the League) system may lead to sanctions and sanctions may lead to war and that in a world of capitalist, imperialist, nationalist states and governments, the use of force by the League to resist a clear case of aggression may degenerate into something difficult to distinguish from any other capitalist, imperialistic, nationalist war. B, that an international system which makes the elimination of war practically a certainty in the next two or three hundred years is practically out of the question; that the more or less firm establishment of the League system would make war more improbable; that capitalism is one of the chief ... long-term causes of war; that the League without socialism will not prevent war permanently and that socialism without the League or a League will not prevent war.'[2]

It is well known that in this area of peacekeeping, defence and the just war, experience had wrought great changes in men's minds by the time a Labour Government found itself in office in the post-war world. Clement Attlee's approach to the problem was not now that of the man who in one breath had condemned Britain's failure both to disarm and to coerce Japan over Manchuria; the victor in the East Fulham by-election ended his career as Minister of Aircraft Production. With one notable exception,[3] leading

[1] Russell to Martin 7 August 1935, ibid.

[2] Woolf to Martin, 29 September 1935, ibid.

[3] Philip Noel-Baker remained—and remains—convinced that Arthur Henderson was correct when he told him that had he, Henderson, still been Foreign Secretary, he could have removed the Japanese from Manchuria by the pressure of world opinion. I am most grateful to Mr. Noel-Baker for spending many hours in expounding this view to me, and for the following summary which he wrote to me on 15 September 1971:

'I do not think anything useful could have been done about Manchuria unless the Prime Minister and Foreign Secretary had gone to the League Council or Assembly (preferably the Assembly) and had said that they were ready to stay in the Assembly as long as was required to ensure the withdrawal of Japanese troops from Manchuria. They would, of course, have taken their stand on the principles of the Covenant, declaring that if the Covenant were sacrificed once it might be sacrificed again, and that the end would be another world war. They should, of course, have done everything in public debate.

'The main weapon which the community of mankind possesses to restrain militarist aggression is that of world opinion mobilized as it only can be under the leadership of the top statesmen of important countries. If the British Prime Minister and Foreign Secretary had done what I suggested in 1931, they would have had the support of every Prime Minister in the Commonwealth, beginning most importantly with Smuts [Smuts was not, in fact, Prime Minister in 1931. C.G.T.] ... They would have evoked such a storm of popular support in every continent that diplomatic and then economic sanctions would most certainly have been made effective. If in fact the Japanese militarists had been able to keep their hold and make a war, the war would have been fought in Asia instead of in Europe and in conditions infinitely more favourable than those which we faced in 1939.'

advocates of some kind of action against Japan in 1931-3 had also modified
their views to a considerable extent by then. Cecil, for example, had in 1941
called for a League based on 'a confederation or confederations of geographi-
cally related powers', with article 16 of the Covenant to be clarified in the
sense of making joint action against an aggressor 'preventive rather than
penal and . . . only obligatory if it is reasonably likely to be successful'.[1]
Towards the end of his life, Gilbert Murray came to echo those reflections of
Carr's which had so disturbed him in 1936, acknowledging on radio that
economic sanctions 'only worked as a threat when the victim was very weak',
and that they were at the mercy of a counter-threat to treat such measures as
a war-like act; within the limits of peaceful action, he concluded, it was
'impracticable . . . for even a unanimous Council to compel any moderately
effective free nation to do something which it is determined not to do'. What
he now saw as the collapse of liberal, European civilisation had been 'a
terrible shock', as if a veneer had been peeled away to reveal the true, underlying nature of 'la bête humaine'. 'The civic monk,' commented Madariaga,
'has become a sage—through disenchantment.'[2] Madariaga himself, while
perhaps not disenchanted, had already written:

> Sanctions are based on a false analogy between inter-individual and international
> relations. A man is attacked in the street. A policeman and half a dozen zealous
> citizens rush to defend him, collar the bully and land him in gaol. Can this scene
> be transferred to international life? Evidently not. Nations cannot 'rush' . . .
> They are determined by the natural laws of their place to do certain things and
> avoid others . . ., organisms whose life oozes through frontiers . . . It follows
> that sanctions—even so-called economic sanctions—hurt the punishing nation
> as much as—at times even more than—the punished . . . Publicity is the strongest
> force to coerce small nations and the only force to coerce big nations.[3]

If he read this, or, from the shades, listened to Murray's broadcast, even
Simon might have smiled.

The morality of international politics and coercion had troubled Frenchmen far less than the British in the 1930s, and after 1945 they had other
subjects for agonising reappraisal. Following Japan's departure from the
League, Germany had absorbed their attention (one scholar has suggested
that not until after 1935 did public opinion begin to see Japan as a threat to
Indo–China[4]), together with that malaise of the spirit and body politic which

[1] Cecil, 351. The muddle and impracticability of this new concept of semi-
obligatory sanctions is apparent.
[2] Script of B.B.C. talk by Murray, 26 July 1955, Murray Papers; Madariaga,
'Gilbert Murray and the League' in Murray, *Unfinished Autobiography*.
[3] S. de Madariaga, *Victors, Beware* (London 1946), 129–33. On Madariaga's
1936 proposal for a 'World Fellowship of guiding spirits endowed with vision . . .
to spread throughout the world . . . the principle of world unity', see the relevant
documents in the Murray Papers. For the change of approach on the part of
Arnold Toynbee between 1931 and 1948, when (admittedly in the context of
nuclear weapons) he advocated a division of the world into spheres of interest
between the United States and Soviet Union ('there might be consultations in
which they would say to each other: "You take Manchuria and we will take the
rest of China", and so forth round the globe'), see Morgenthau, *In Defense of the
National Interest*, 155–6.
[4] Renouvin, *La Question d'Extrême-Orient*, 399–401.

burst into prominence in February 1934.[1] Disillusionment with the League—insofar as there can be said to have been illusions about it in the first place—was nevertheless one feature of the French scene, while in a more vicarious form the same was true in the United States. There, the League's failure over Manchuria provided fresh ammunition for those who had long decried it as a body that was futile but dangerous;[2] more soberly, American diplomats and others were in many cases prompted to make revised and less hopeful estimates of the potentiality of an international organisation of this kind. The very term, collective security, was bandied about in a debate that now became more passionate and more confused than ever. Again, the question of power and of force in international relations lay close to the heart of the matter as Dorothy Detzer and others, like Kingsley Martin in Britain, wrestled with the problem of resisting aggression while avoiding the evil of war in any form.[3] The organised peace movement, in the shape of the new, co-ordinating National Peace Conference, soon proved to be irreparably split between what can crudely be designated its isolationist and interventionist wings, with the neutrality legislation of the mid-'30s and the renewed fighting in China in 1937 providing major occasions for displays of disunity.[4] The investigations of the Nye Committee into the munitions industry, continuing social and economic difficulties, and the heightened dangers of the European scene were all among considerations which prompted large numbers of Americans and their Congressional representatives to demand more vehemently than ever that the country be kept out of all foreign entanglements.

A sense of threat from Japan was not lacking after 1933: under Roosevelt the U.S. Navy's building programme was stepped up in order to remedy serious weaknesses vis-à-vis that country which had greatly disturbed the new President, and despite a growing trade balance in America's favour, outcries against unfair Japanese commercial competition were increasingly to be heard. Surveys revealed, however, that few of the public anticipated a conflict between the two countries, while in answer to a question on whether Japan's economic interests in Manchuria had justified her policy there, 'a strong minority of businessmen, lawyers and university people indicated a new trend of opinion by voting in the affirmative'.[5] Moreover as before there is little evidence to show that the mass of the American people, however generally sympathetic they might be at times, saw Chinese affairs as

[1] See Warner; R. Griffiths, *Marshal Pétain* (London, 1970).

[2] See, e.g., *Congressional Record, 72nd Congress*, vol. 77, 1517.

[3] See, e.g., Detzer addresses of 1933 and 1939, Detzer Papers, box 1; Balch memorandum, 1939, 'A Foreign Policy for W.I.L.P.F.', Balch Papers, box 4.

[4] See Borg, *The United States and the Far Eastern Crisis*, 340 ff., and the relevant essays in De Conde, *Isolation and Security*. Cf. Adler; Almond, *The American People*; Divine, *The Illusion of Neutrality*; Osgood, *Ideals and Self-Interest*; A. Offner, *American Appeasement: United States Foreign Policy and Germany, 1933–1938* (Cambridge, Mass., 1969); M. Jonas, *Isolationism In America, 1935–1941* (Ithaca, New York, 1966); W. Cole, *America First: The Battle Against Intervention, 1940–1941* (Madison, 1953); Isaacs, *Scratches on our Minds*; Iriye, *Across the Pacific*; Tupper and McReynolds; Neumann, *America Encounters Japan.*

[5] Tupper and McReynolds, 364.

being of major significance—even as compared to those of Europe, let alone to those within their own country.[1] Occasions like the Amau statement on Japan's Asiatic policy might briefly revive attention, but did not lead to any substantial pressure for action to defend United States interests in the area.[2] Memories persisted of China's own fragile resistance to the invader—in 1944, as noted earlier, Walter Lippmann was still adducing this as a major reason for the world's failure to halt Japan[3]—while by contrast enthusiasm for the defiant gesture of non-recognition perceptibly declined. As early as 1934, for example, Lippmann again, who had contributed something to the formulation of Stimson's first pronouncement on the subject, was suggesting a possible basis for an agreement with Japan that by implication would put an end to it. If Japan would accept that continued naval limitation was desirable, he wrote, and that she did not possess a 'free hand' in the Far East, might not the United States 'recognise that the revival of Russia as a great power in the Far East, the continuing weakness of China, *the separation of Manchuria*, and our withdrawal from the Philippines are new elements in the situation'?[4]

With the renewal of fighting in 1937—together with the shock of the Japanese sinking of the American gunboat *Panay*—anti-Japanese opinion again became more pronounced, and from private life Stimson joined the ranks of those who called for the imposition of economic sanctions (but not military involvement). It has been suggested, indeed, that the Administration may have paid a disproportionate amount of attention to those on the other side who continued to argue in isolationist terms,[5] and certainly there is some evidence to indicate that in the ensuing 1939–41 period opinion in the country as a whole was shifting away from a determined isolationist stance more rapidly than was Congress, despite the appeals of Hoover among others for a retreat into the American stronghold.[6] Even so, actual military engagement remained a formidable prospect, and in this respect the 'appeasement' or limited-liability policies of the Administration towards Europe and Asia alike appear to have commanded the support of the majority up to the moment of Pearl Harbour.[7]

Two further developments within American opinion in this post-Manchurian period deserve notice. One is the gradual reaction in intellectual circles against those idealistic interpretations and panaceas for international politics which had been a feature of the post-1918 period. This new trend of thought was to emerge most clearly after the war, in the writings of Morgenthau, Osgood and others, and bore down upon isolationists and Wilsonians alike. The second development linked this revived respectability of the concept of the national interest to the belief in some quarters that

[1] See, e.g., Cohen, 150, and Borg, *The United States and the Far Eastern Crisis*, 256 ff.

[2] Borg, ibid, 89–90.   [3] See above, 9, n.

[4] Lippmann, *Interpretations, 1933–1935* (New York, 1935), 339, emphasis added.

[5] Borg, ibid, 353–4.

[6] See, e.g., Adler, 256–7. On 21 November 1941, Hoover was writing to Dawes of the 'futility and evils embodied in the Atlantic Declaration'. Dawes Papers, personal files, Hoover.

[7] See, e.g., Offner, passim; Neumann, in De Conde, 51.

America was, indeed, vitally concerned with what occurred in East Asia. As China's sufferings under the Japanese attack increased, the growing connection between Germany and Japan helped foster an identification of China with the Western democracies, and thus a renewal of the Stimsonian vision of a protégé destined to grow in one's own likeness.[1] At the same time some observers now began to shift their emphasis and to decide that the Japanese challenge in the Far East did, after all, touch directly upon American security.[2] As Lippmann was to put it later, retracting one of the arguments he had adduced in 1931–3 against any move that might involve the possibility of war, 'our unawareness of our vital interest caused us to avoid, neglect and refuse the measures which, if taken earlier, would have involved a smaller risk and much less cost of treasure and life.'[3]

A new orthodoxy was thus in the making concerning the Japanese threat, the inevitability of a Japanese–American conflict, and the lost opportunity of earlier years. A special twist was imparted to these notions by the China lobby in the United States during and after the Pacific war, particularly after the shock of Chiang Kai-shek's expulsion from the mainland. Several of those involved—Patrick Hurley, for example—had been strongly opposed to intervention on behalf of China in 1931–3; now they interpreted recent history as revealing America's neglect and betrayal of her Kuomintang allies.[4] Relief was thus found from the dissonance between one's image of the essential China and the undeniable fact of Communist power there by the familiar means of a conspiracy theory—in this case conspiracy on the part of the fellow-travellers or worse in the State Department and elsewhere. Such a process of reasoning was not unknown on the other side of the Atlantic, and there, too, it was now being employed in connection with Far Eastern matters, this time in the form of the charge of wanton betrayal on the part of the National Government which had 'caused' the failure of 1931. Those men in post-war Britain who now clung to this explanation of how the League had come to grief were also often to be found strongly attacking the activities of the China lobby and American cold-war policy in Asia and elsewhere. In at least the processes of discontent, however, the two groups shared a certain bizarre kinship.

The shaping of policy: London and Washington

Like the British and American governments, the French and the Dutch had every reason to look with concern at the Far Eastern scene after 1933. In Paris, however, European affairs continued to eclipse all others, while in The Hague one could only assure Japan of one's desire for friendship (although raising a quota system against her goods in the East Indies[5]) and await the development of policy in London and Washington. It was in those two capitals that the Western response continued to be shaped.

[1] See Iriye, *Across the Pacific*, 205.
[2] Borg, *Historians and American Far Eastern Policy*; Iriye, *Across the Pacific*, 205.
[3] Lippmann, *U.S. War Aims*, 30.
[4] See, e.g., Tang Tsou, *America's Failure in China, 1941–50* (Chicago, 1963); Lohbeck, *Patrick Hurley*.
[5] Clyde, 640–1.

As noted in the previous chapter, one of the conclusions drawn in London from the crisis that had just passed was that the coercive functions of the League must continue to be played down. The Abyssinian affair was to provide a final, major test of this belief, but what needs to be emphasised here is the growing extent to which it was sustained by strategic considerations as the Admiralty contemplated the possibility of a Japanese attack timed to coincide with trouble in Europe. (Here lay the key to the Navy's thinking during the Abyssinian crisis itself: not that they would be unable to defeat the Italians, but that in doing so they might sustain damage that could prove critical in terms of global contingencies.) 'This miserable business of collective security,' wrote the First Sea Lord, 'has run away with all our traditional interests and policies.'[1] For the time being, however, the Covenant in its entirety remained in theory Britain's prime international commitment, and in the spring of 1933 there were those who hoped that the new Administration in Washington would lend a significant amount of weight in the same direction. Roosevelt's propensity for being all things to all men was partly responsible for this, as were well-meant but ill-founded effusions on the part of Norman Davis, of the kind which has already been recorded in connection with Cecil. 'Norman Davis assures me,' wrote Raymond Fosdick to Arthur Sweetser, 'that the President and Cordell Hull are going to establish a degree of cooperation with other nations that will surprise the American people . . . and (cooperation with Geneva) will be the best since the League began.'[2] Observers could also note Roosevelt's request to Congress for powers to suspend arms supplies 'to such countries as the President may designate' in cases where they would be conducive to an increased use of force.[3] Above all, they heard Davis declare to the Disarmament Conference in May 1933 that the United States was prepared to consult with other governments in the event of future threats to peace, and that she would not undermine any collective action taken against a violator of international obligations.[4]

Nevertheless the resulting hopes were swiftly disappointed. Davis's offer at Geneva was conditional upon 'a substantive reduction of armaments', and was thus never operative; in any event it had also contained the proviso that the United States must first 'concur in the judgement rendered as to the responsible and guilty party', and as Hugh Wilson pointed out to a critical Lippmann, 'did not provide for any positive action on our part beyond that of consultation'.[5] Meanwhile the Senate Foreign Relations Committee had objected to Roosevelt's proposed arms-embargo legislation on various grounds of self-interest—and because it might encourage the League to invite Washington to join in such an embargo against Japan. Despite being assured by Cordell Hull, the new Secretary of State, that if such requests

[1] Chatfield to Dreyer, 16 September 1935, Chatfield Papers.
[2] Fosdick to Sweetser, 22 March 1933, Sweetser Papers, box 31.
[3] See Hull to McReynolds and Pittman, 5 April 1933, DS 811.113/280A/B.
[4] Toynbee, Survey, 1933, 275.
[5] Wilson to Lippmann, 13 June 1933, Davis Papers, box 35. Cf. Lippmann to Davis, 29 December 1933, ibid, in which the writer urged that 'the Administration is under a mandate to prepare itself for a neutral position in the event of war . . . and I believe that preparations must be made without loss of time'.

were received 'we would not be disposed to give them favourable consideration', the Senators continued to put up a number of amendments that would emasculate the proposal. To Hull's dismay—he found out through a third party—Roosevelt decided to give way to the isolationists. In the State Department, confusion and ignorance now prevailed as the President dictated policy from the White House; 'everything that is going on here,' observed Moffat, 'political or otherwise, seems to be diverging more and more from the Secretary's hopes'.[1] Those hopes had themselves been modest enough. At the outset of the new régime Moffat had noted: 'Europe is so convinced that the Roosevelt Administration plans to bring us towards the League of Nations that the knowledge, when it comes, that our policy will probably be more cautious than under Mr. Stimson will come as a great shock.' In Hull's mind, the need was to be helpful where possible 'but not to go forward with any plan for leadership', while William Phillips his Under Secretary, MacDonald-like, privately blamed German and Italian belligerence on French thoughts 'that she can dominate Europe through the League'. 'Certainly,' he concluded, 'the United States must keep free from European political struggles.'[2]

The new men in Washington were likewise determined to keep out of trouble in the Far East—as suggested by a minor action of Phillips', for example, when he warned Stimson not to irritate Japan unnecessarily in lectures that the latter was due to give at Princeton.[3] Within the State Department there was widespread acceptance of the view that Hugh Wilson was also privately expressing, that beyond Europe 'positive action of any nature or even its contemplation constitutes a danger to us', and it was partly on these grounds that Hornbeck advocated the passive policy which was followed during the final bout of Sino–Japanese fighting in the spring of 1933.[4] Nor did suggestions for action accompany the warnings that were received from Grew that Japan might be preparing to foster a separatist movement in North China, from Johnson that she was likely to 'advance southward' if and when the United States left the Philippines, and from Johnson again that she was almost certainly fortifying the mandated islands in the Pacific. The latter was unhappy as to the future prospects for American commerce, but as before wrote off Manchuria and thought that little of immediate importance was at stake for the United States in North China; Grew, like Hornbeck, advised that the country should 'speak softly but carry a big stick', although he also saw signs of improvement in American–Japanese relations and remained doggedly hopeful for the future.[5] So far as

[1] Pittman to Hull, 10 May; Hull to Pittman, 15 May; Hull to Roosevelt, 27 May 1933, DS 811.113/297, 308; Moffat Diary, 11 March, 17 April, 10–11 June 1933.

[2] Moffat Diary, 17 March 1933; William Phillips Diary, 7 December 1933.

[3] Phillips Diary, 3 November 1933. Cf. Moffat Diary, 16 May 1933.

[4] Wilson to Lippmann, 13 June 1933, Davis Papers, box 35; Moffat Diary, 23 April 1933; DS 711.94/804; FRUS, 1933, III, 327–9. Cf. Borg, The United States and the Far Eastern Crisis, 22 ff. In all following comments on American policy I am much indebted to Dr. Borg's work. For this reason I have further compressed this aspect of the chapter, as compared to that concerning British policy after 1933, where no comparable study yet exists.

[5] E.g., FRUS, 1933, III, 285; Johnson to Hull, 12 June 1933, Johnson Papers, box 19; Grew, 88, 139; Borg, ibid, 33 ff., 115 ff., 237 ff.

China was concerned, the continuing lack of unity and effective leadership was watched with anxiety and no little gloom. Organisational shortcomings in the State Department helped prevent a full appreciation in Washington of the development of the Communist movement, however, while the possible role of the Soviet Union in the area (for example in the event of a Japanese–American conflict) also received inadequate attention.[1]

The 'big stick' advice of Grew and others coincided, naturally, with that of the Navy, for whom the 1934–5 discussions on a possible extension of international limitation-agreements were as crucial as the reports, exaggerated it seems, concerning the mandated islands.[2] Talks with Japan on limitations in fact came to nothing, and increased appropriations for new vessels were forthcoming; but despite this and the ending of the Washington treaty 'freeze' on fortifications at the end of 1936, the gap between commitments and resources in the Western Pacific was not bridged, either in terms of the size of the fleet and its auxiliaries or of protected bases.[3] To the accompaniment of further splits between the Army and Navy planners, the basic unreality of War Plan 'Orange' became even more marked, despite appeals from the commanders on the spot and frequent tinkerings in Washington.[4] Nevertheless, as the crisis with Japan approached its climax in 1940–1 there were those officials who were able to resolve the problem in their own minds by the significant belief that the Japanese would not dare to offer a military challenge to economic sanctions or some other form of coercion and disapproval that was backed by the might of the United States.

It is not surprising to find among these men two who at times between 1931 and 1933 had looked to the weapon of economic sanctions as a swift and cheap means of bringing Japan to heel on that occasion: Stimson and Hornbeck. On his return to office as Secretary of War in 1940, Stimson took up once more his campaign against any retreat from the Western Pacific, and at the same time proclaimed his confidence in the efficacy of an embargo against the potential enemy:

> Japan has historically shown that when the United States indicates by clear language and bold actions that she intends to carry out a clear and affirmative policy in the Far East, Japan will yield to that policy, even though it conflicts with her own Asiatic policy and conceived interests.

Military Intelligence was another quarter where it was believed that Japan would 'fall apart' under a serious embargo. Hornbeck for his part, having like Stimson advocated sanctions in the firm belief that Japan would not take retaliatory action against Western possessions, unfortunately chose 27 November 1941 to emphasise his confidence that no Japanese attack on the United States was forthcoming. 'Stated briefly,' he concluded, 'the undersigned does not believe that this country is now on the immediate verge of "war" in the Pacific.'[5]

[1] Borg, 51–5; 196 ff., 222–7.
[2] For an early study of the limitations question, see Hepburn memorandum, 14 March, 1933, Davis Papers, box 20; cf. Burns, 'Inspection of Mandates', loc. cit.; Tuleja, 84 ff.; Rappaport, *Navy League*, 154 ff.; Borg, 100 ff.
[3] See above, 72–4, and, e.g., Borg, 250–1.
[4] See Morton, 'War Plan Orange', loc. cit., and *Strategy and Command*.
[5] See Tuleja, 220; Current, *Secretary Stimson*, 146–7; a host of confident

Here again one observes two features which had been prominent in 1931–3:[1] a tendency in conditions of uncertainty to predict that desired events or developments (in the earlier period, for example, a change of Japanese mood under economic difficulties) will actually occur; and secondly the transference to another actor on the international scene, as in the same foregoing example, of the mental processes, reactions and values which, if often missing in practice, might be expected of an idealised, rational political man in one's own environment. There was also a third feature that had existed from the beginning of the century onwards: the continued failure to reach a clear and agreed definition of the American national interest in the Far East and an understanding of what policies were being pursued towards that end. As the Joint Army–Navy Planning Committee plaintively observed in 1939: '(We have) frequently had to work in the dark with respect to what national policy is with respect to a specific problem, or what it may be expected to be.' In Washington in 1940–1, confusion surrounded, not so much what the Japanese might be seeking or might do, but the same questions when applied to the United States herself.[2]

Even before this final phase, there had been major differences of opinion in official circles over the country's approach to Far Eastern problems. As in London, the Treasury was closely concerned, and the exchanges between its Secretary, Morgenthau, and Cordell Hull were lengthy and at times heated.[3] Until the end of the period, however, it was the latter's less assertive inclinations which predominated. Supported both by his senior diplomats in the area and by the President, believing profoundly, in Dr. Borg's words, 'that most of the basic problems of international relations could be solved by moral education',[4] Hull supervised an American policy which even after 1937 is remarkable in retrospect for its passivity above all else.[5] A bigger stick was gradually being developed in the Navy yards, but it was the soft speaking that stood out. Above all—and even where naval bases in the Western Pacific were concerned—Japan was to be irritated as little as possible in order that any deeper involvement in the area should be avoided. Obviously, such a policy provided certain contrasts with the one pursued on the surface between 1931 and 1933. Thoughts of the kind that Stimson had had on a virtually inevitable conflict with Japan were not in evidence, for example, and his public note-writing was speedily and deliberately abandoned. On the other hand enough has been said of the underlying passivity of American policy in that earlier period, and of Stimson's own caution towards Japan during the last six months of his tenure of office, to suggest that there was a strong element of continuity, as well as certain changes,

memoranda by Hornbeck in 1937, 1940 and 1941 are gathered together in the Hornbeck Papers, boxes 83, 145, 155, 253, 254, 309, 318.

[1] Cf. Wohlstetter, 353–4, 397; Iriye, *Across the Pacific*, 217.

[2] Wohlstetter, 73; F. Green, 'The Military View of American National Policy, 1904–1941', *American Historical Review*, vol. LXVI, No. 2, 1961. Cf. Tang Tsou's comments on the confusion surrounding the U.S. interest in China after 1941, and on those aspects of the American political tradition that accentuated 'the natural tendency to view alien things in terms of the image of one's self'. *America's Failure*, e.g. 219 ff., 360 ff.

[3] See, e.g., Borg, 127 ff.   [4] Ibid, 95–6.   [5] See ibid, 522 ff.

between the two Administrations. Above all, in neither period could the other two parties most immediately involved, China and Britain, expect to receive substantial or decisive practical assistance from Washington.

The memory of 1931–3 cast its shadow over policy-making in London as it did in Washington in the following period, and again a substantial degree of overlap can be observed between the official debates that were taking place within the two capitals. Over the final outbreak of fighting before the Tangku truce their policies shared an essential passivity, even fatalism, and although in London there remained alarm over British interests in North China, there was also a transient sense of relief that soon one's problems in the area might disappear. Already the swift Jehol campaign had led Neville Chamberlain to hope that 'our troubles may soon be over in that quarter',[1] while MacDonald was minuting in May: 'We ought to be thinking of the end of this (crisis), which is apparently Japanese victory, both military and political, for only upon that assumption shall we be safe.'[2] Simon explained to the Cabinet—not inaccurately—that the difficulty was that the Japanese, pulled on by Chinese counter-attacks, 'did not know how to stop'; as before, however, it was agreed in the Foreign Office that mediation was practicable only if unequivocally sought by both sides. In the meantime, there was little to do but wait.[3]

Immediate helplessness did not preclude, however, the beginnings of a renewed debate on likely developments in the Far East, and despite—or in an important sense, because of—the growing danger in Europe, it was soon being acknowledged that Britain's problems in the Pacific were far from over.[4] In the Foreign Office much attention continued to be paid to China: to her commercial potential and the possible effects of Japanese invasion on the fortunes of Chinese Communism; to racial conflict as a source of continuing friction and the future role in China of the Soviet Union. At the same time there also remained an instinctive tendency to measure the Chinese people by Western, or more particularly British standards. This was more pronounced in Cadogan, the new Minister there, than it had been in Lampson. Not surprisingly the former found the Nanking Government 'a rather inchoate body of possibly well-meaning and quite intelligent individuals without any authority and directive force', but he also declared that 'what was wrong with China was that there was something wrong with the Chinese—something at least that did not conform to western standards and made them unable properly to adjust to western standards.'[5]

[1] Neville to Hilda Chamberlain, 4 March 1933, Neville Chamberlain Papers.
[2] DBFP, XI, No. 559, note.
[3] Cabinet of 26 April 1933, CAB 23/76; DBFP, XI, Nos. 486, note, 528, 529, 559.
[4] The debate within the Foreign Office is illustrated in Louis, *British Strategy*; cf. N. R. Clifford, *Retreat From China: British Policy in the Far East, 1937–1941* (New York, 1967); I. S. Friedman, *British Relations With China, 1931–1939* (New York, 1939); Gull, *British Economic Interests*.
[5] Cadogan to Vansittart, 29 April 1934 (cf. ibid, 3 June 1934), FO 800/293; Louis, 233–4. The new C. in C. China, Admiral Sir Frederick Dreyer, preferred Cadogan to Lampson, because in his view the latter 'always gave way to China'. Dreyer to Chatfield, 22 October 1934, Chatfield Papers.

In the Cabinet, however, Japan commanded far more attention than China, and here the advice the Government received contained two emphases that were in strong contrast to each other, even though they were not entirely inconsistent. On the one hand there was hope. The Japanese were stiff-necked and exasperating,[1] but given time they would come to their senses and behave in a more acceptable fashion;[2] their ambitions were powerful, but were directed above all towards finding economic outlets, especially in China;[3] they were becoming fierce commercial competitors, but were still anxious to retain close friendship with Britain.[4] Yet on the other hand there remained the new sense of danger which had so transformed Cabinet and Foreign Office thinking about Japan between the autumn of 1931 and the summer of 1932. Lampson, for one, was by now greatly disturbed over the future. 'More and more,' he told Nelson Johnson, 'it was being borne in upon him that the Japanese seemed to have in mind far-reaching plans for establishing their control in Asia and it was difficult to foresee how far these plans might carry (them).'[5] In addition, hopeful generalities about coming to a political and commercial understanding with Tokyo were severely dealt with by the experienced Commercial Counsellor of the Embassy there, who saw no existing basis for a bargain that would be acceptable to the 'aggressive, intractable' officials with whom business now had to be done.[6]

What would happen, moreover, if the Japanese were thwarted in China or exasperated by continued Western disapproval? 'If there was any weakening on the part of the National Government,' warned Hankey, 'as to their intention to assert our sea-power in the Pacific in a war emergency, I am convinced . . . that the effect would be absolutely shattering.'[7] Early in 1935 he was also informing MacDonald and Baldwin that over one million copies had been sold of a book written by a retired Japanese naval officer and entitled *The Certainty of an Anglo–Japanese War*,[8] while in one of his rambling letters to Whitehall the new Commander in Chief, China, also declared: 'The Japanese may do anything.'[9] Even before the end of 1933, Simon had presented the C.I.D. with a more frightening prospect still. Japan was now 'behaving extremely correctly', he reported, but he believed that she had fixed objectives involving the need for raw materials and territory; at the same time the C.I.G.S. had declared that Germany would be ready for

[1] See, e.g., DBFP, XI, No. 560, note.
[2] See, e.g., Louis, 246 ff.
[3] See, e.g., CP 145 (33), CAB 24/241; Cabinet of 31 May 1933, CAB 23/76; Louis, 234–6.
[4] See, e.g., Ronald to Wigram, 21 February 1934, RA G.V, M2333/13, referring to FO 371, F 591/591/23; Simon memorandum, 21 January 1935, MacDonald Papers, RM 1/27.
[5] Johnson note, 17 May 1933, Johnson Papers, box 36.
[6] Sansom memorandum, 12 October 1934, CAB 27/596 and MacDonald Papers, RM 1/27.
[7] Hankey to Baldwin, 23 August 1934, Baldwin Papers, vol. 1.
[8] Hankey to Baldwin and MacDonald, 9 February 1935, MacDonald Papers, RM 1/27.
[9] Dreyer to Chatfield, 5 March 1935, Chatfield Papers.

war in five years time (Simon himself, spurred on by Vansittart, had warned that the Nazi régime was deliberately fostering an attitude of mind 'which could end in only one way'). Might not Germany look round for an ally when the time came, and find one—as the Quai d'Orsay had already begun to fear—in Japan? Bruce of Australia agreed with the Foreign Secretary, and added his own warning to the Committee, that 'we were powerless in the Far East'. MacDonald could only acknowledge that the outlook was a grim one.[1]

The gap between commitments and capabilities appeared if anything to be widening, and as in 1932 discussion returned time and again to the partially-measurable matter of the state of military preparedness. This is not the place to follow the ramifications of the debate within the Cabinet, as the last hopes of achieving some new international agreement on arms limitation went drifting away and a slow start was made (reflected, for example, in the 1935 Defence White Paper) on repairing some of the major defects in the country's defences. Likewise the technical details of the subject—fuel supplies, seaward defences, ship-borne aircraft, and so forth—must be passed over as they pre-occupied the individual Services, the C.I.D. and finally the Defence Requirements Sub-Committee of the C.I.D. in the remainder of 1933 and 1934. As before, Singapore filled the centre of the picture, and a decision to bring forward the completion of its main defences to mid-1936 was widely felt to have at least set a limit to the period of acute danger. With that as a basis one might proceed towards what the Defence Requirements Sub-Committee described as 'an ultimate policy of accommodation and friendship with Japan', by way of 'an immediate and provisional policy of "showing a tooth" for the purpose of recovering the standing which we have sacrificed of recent years'.[2]

Yet even so, 'tooth', and not 'teeth', remained the appropriate term to employ. As Germany's naval strength increased, and particularly when her fast pocket-battleships were about to be supplemented by heavier units, the confident intention of despatching a major force of capital ships to the Far East—an intention repeated at the Imperial Conference of 1937 in response to the anxious enquiries of Australia and New Zealand[3]—began to take on an aura of unreality not unlike the one surrounding Washington's War Plan 'Orange'. As early as 1933 it had been decided not to send the battle-cruisers out to the Far East, even when Singapore was ready to receive them,[4]

---

[1] C.I.D., 9 November, 1933, CAB 2/6; Simon memorandum, CP 129(33), discussed in Cabinet of 17 May 1933, CAB 23/76; Vansittart minutes of 6 May, 4 September 1933, Vansittart Papers; cf. FO 371, C 3990/319/18.

[2] See, e.g., Eyres-Monsell contribution in Cabinet Disarmament Committee, 20 January 1934, CAB 27/505; Chiefs of Staff report and C.I.D. minutes, 6 April 1933, CP 95(33), CAB 24/239, and CAB 2/5; Chief of Air Staff memorandum, 10 April 1933, CP 102(33), CAB 24/240; First Sea Lord memorandum, n.d., CP 163(33), CAB 24/242; Cabinet of 12 April 1933, CAB 23/75; Chiefs of Staff Annual Review, 1933, CP 264(33), CAB 24/244; minutes and report of Defence Requirements Sub-Committee, C.I.D., CAB 16/109; Chatfield to Hankey, n.d., 1933, CAB 21/369; Chatfield to Dreyer, 1 June 1933, 2 February, 7 August 1934; Chatfield to Beatty, 10 October 1934; Dreyer to Chatfield, 19 August, 2 December 1933, Chatfield Papers. Cf. R. Grenfell, *Main Fleet to Singapore* (London, 1951).

[3] C.I.D. 450C, CAB 2/6.   [4] Chatfield to Fisher, 11 May 1934, Chatfield Papers.

and by the time *Scharnhorst, Bismarck* and their respective sister-ships were nearing completion the position vis-à-vis the powerful Japanese fleet was looking a poor one indeed.[1] Singapore was eventually believed to be ready for a major conflict in 1938, but the estimated time that would elapse before its relief by the arrival of the fleet had by then reached 70 days (in 1932, it will be recalled, it had been 38). In July 1939 this in turn became 90 days, and in September of that year, 180; in 1941 the Japanese allowed themselves 100 days to capture the base, and took 70.[2] The eventual and fatal despatch of the *Prince of Wales* and *Repulse* in 1941 was no more than a bluff, aimed, in Churchill's words, at 'steadying the Japanese political situation' and pushed through by him against Admiralty opposition, in the belief that 'Japan will not run into war with [the United States, Britain, China and the Netherlands] unless or until Russia is decisively broken'.[3] This miscalculation—by no means Churchill's only one where Japan was concerned—was based on somewhat different grounds from those which were buoying up confidence in Washington at the time; yet even if the Prime Minister's forecasting had been less inaccurate, how much more could have been done? The risk of sending a few additional capital ships might have been taken; equally, those vessels might well have joined the *Prince of Wales* and *Repulse* as sunken testimony to the diminishing command such units could exercise in an age of air power.

Whatever the type of ship, however, only money could enable them to appear,[4] and in all the defence debates of the post-Manchurian period the Treasury played a major role. Armed with its 'doctrine of normal trade' and still led by Chamberlain and Fisher, that department helped to see to it that whatever the acknowledged seriousness of the situation no major acceleration of defence spending occurred until 1938.[5] In 1934, for example, Chamberlain cut a proposed five-year expenditure of £76 million to £50 million, but the underlying problem of limited resources was also carrying him into the very centre of the discussions on the country's entire international strategy, where his contributions now became far more frequent and weighty than they had been during the 1931–3 crisis. In European terms, he began to expound the idea of a 'limited liability international force'.[6] In a world context (and having begun by demanding from Hankey an explanation of why

---

[1] From the summer of 1937 to the spring of 1938 it was the intention to keep only *Hood* and *Repulse* in European waters in the event of major trouble in the Far East. From the summer of 1939 to the spring of 1940 this had grown to *Hood, Repulse, Renown* and two *Nelson*-class battleships. Note the continued emphasis on the battleship, rather than the aircraft-carrier yardstick.

[2] Kirby, *The War Against Japan*, I, 17–19, 28, cap. XXVII.

[3] Kirby, cap. XXVII; W. S. Churchill, *The Second World War*, III (London, 1950), 523–5, 768–74.

[4] On 19 September 1933, Chatfield wrote to Admiral Sir William Fisher: 'We literally have not got the income to keep up a first-class Navy.' Chatfield Papers.

[5] See Hancock and Gowing, 68–71. As noted earlier, Fisher's awareness of the need for improved defences has often been underestimated. Hankey, however, thought him unsound where the Navy and Pacific requirements were concerned. Hankey to Baldwin, 23 August 1934, Baldwin Papers, vol. 1.

[6] E.g., Neville Chamberlain Diary, 26 April, 3, 9 May 1934.

the Anglo–Japanese alliance had ever been terminated[1]) he developed his arguments from the premise 'that we cannot provide simultaneously for hostilities with Japan and Germany and that the latter is the problem to which we must address ourselves, adapting our policy to some pacific arrangement with Japan'.[2] His ideas took firmer shape in the autumn of 1934 when the vital Far Eastern discussions on naval limitations were approaching, and were eventually put before the Cabinet in a memorandum in his name and Simon's. With the Foreign Secretary now regarded as a broken reed, however,[3] it was Chamberlain's sponsorship that carried the more weight, and in his diary he summarised what he was seeking to do at this time:

> I returned to my former proposal for a Pact of non-aggression (with Japan) . . . and expressed the view that we were not justified in neglecting the opportunity of exploring the situation and finding out how far Japan was prepared to go. I did not suggest that we should guarantee her a free hand in the Far East; on the contrary I recognised that if we were to consider entering into such a Pact we should have to obtain certain assurances respecting the territorial integrity of China and perhaps our own trading position there. But I believe the Japanese would welcome a Pact with us, and would be willing to pay a price for it. The result would be an instantaneous easing of the Australasian position, a new security in the East and possibly a better atmosphere in economic relations with the Japs.[4]

While the Chancellor of the Exchequer developed these eminently reasonable (though not necessarily practicable) ideas, his Permanent Under Secretary was already helping to push the Defence Requirements Sub-Committee in a similar direction, keeping pressure on his colleagues outside the formal meetings of that body. In return, Fisher received the support of the C.I.G.S., now General Sir Archibald Montgomery-Massingberd (not the most distinguished of military minds), who in 1933 had described the ending of the Anglo–Japanese alliance at the Washington Conference as 'insensate folly'. Chatfield, somewhat more cautiously, was also ready to deplore the breach with Japan, while Hankey, too, termed the ending of the alliance 'a great misfortune which was forced upon us by the circumstances of the day and which was greatly regretted by all concerned'.[5] From the China Station,

[1] Hankey to Chamberlain, 30 October 1933, CAB 21/369.

[2] Neville Chamberlain Diary, 6 June 1934.

[3] See above, 95. On 18 November 1933, Chamberlain wrote to his sister Hilda: 'We have had a terrible time with Simon this week, and I feel that somehow or other there will have to be a change at the F.O. before long.' Neville Chamberlain Papers.

[4] Neville Chamberlain Diary, 9 October 1934; Chamberlain–Simon memorandum, CP 223(34), CAB 27/596. Cf. Middlemas and Barnes, 776 ff., and essay No. 4 in Watt, *Personalities and Policies*. It is difficult to judge whether public opinion would have acquiesced in some marked and open form of Anglo–Japanese reconciliation in the period immediately following the Manchurian crisis; coupled with the Genevan factor, it might well have helped the 'America-first' faction in Whitehall to reject such a proposal.

[5] Massingberd to Hankey and Chatfield, 13 September 1933; Chatfield to Massingberd, 15 September 1933; Hankey to Massingberd, 22 September 1933, CAB 21/369. Hankey's description of universal regret was exaggerated.

the new C. in C., Dreyer, also chimed in with sixteen extraordinary pages of 'personal reflections', complete with Biblical texts, written following a visit he had paid to Japan with some of his ships.[1]

Despite the strong sympathy it aroused, however, the Chamberlain–Fisher thesis could not avoid becoming entangled in two other considerations. The first of these, which was argued out in the Defence Requirements Sub-Committee, was whether the greater danger to the Empire was posed by Japan (as Chatfield maintained) or Germany (as Vansittart claimed,[2] although he admitted that apart from Wellesley 'the great majority of the departmental opinion in the Foreign Office' put Japan first). Hankey, who was in the chair, bracketed the two, the Committee's final report naming Japan as the greater immediate threat and Germany as 'the ultimate potential enemy'. There remained the second question, however: how far should one risk offending American susceptibilities when pursuing friendship with Japan? (Here again, in other words, was the old dilemma stretching back into the pre-1914 period.)[3] In this case it was Fisher of the Defence Requirements Sub-Committee who was all for paying less heed to the United States, pointing to the barren experience of the recent crisis as one piece of supporting evidence, while Vansittart hoped 'that the betterment (of Anglo–American relations) would not all be thrown away in order to run after the Japanese'.

Behind Vansittart in this matter there still stood Simon and MacDonald, as Fisher tartly observed to Chamberlain in a note on the naval conversations that were taking place with the Americans at the end of 1934:

> It is desirable to lead gently and by degrees those of your colleagues, to wit the Prime Minister and the Foreign Secretary, who seem so surprisingly shy of the actualities. That the whole trouble is due to the baseless American demands [i.e. over cruiser limitation especially] and the equally baseless terror entertained by those two Ministers of the Americans is as definitely Admiral Chatfield's view as it is my own.[4]

In fact, Chatfield was somewhat less one-sided on the subject than Fisher chose to suggest, although he accepted the need to develop a new line of policy. His private response to the latter's crusading appeals has already been mentioned in passing, as reflecting the essentially defensive British posture in this period; but in the context of the crucial dilemma of 1934—foreshadowed as it had been in 1932—the letter in question deserves quoting at greater length:

> The answer . . . seems to me to move slowly and carefully, but nevertheless to move. We are in the remarkable position of not wanting to quarrel with anybody because we have got most of the world already, or the best parts of it, and we

[1] Dreyer narrative, 3 November 1933, ADM 125/72. 'Now is the "Golden Moment",' he wrote, 'for the people of the British Empire to make friends with those other seafaring people, the Japanese . . . We should realise that they are Orientals and know how to deal with the Chinese far better than we do . . .'
[2] Cf. Vansittart, memorandum, 'The Foreign Policy of the United Kingdom', 19 May 1933, Vansittart Papers.
[3] See Nish II, passim.
[4] Fisher to Chamberlain, 12 November 1934, Chatfield Papers.

only want to keep what we have got and prevent others taking it away from us . . . The last thing I want to do is to threaten Japan. The most we can hope for in the East is to have a sufficient Navy that it can go there in an emergency . . . to prevent her threatening us, and Australia and India. I do not see how we can ever prevent Japan, ourselves, from dominating China so long as the Chinese are so feeble as to let them do it . . . and it is much better to settle our differences over China by diplomatic means, there being plenty of room for both of us in that country . . . I agree with Van(sittart) to the extent that we do not want to propitiate Japan at the expense of a hostile and jealous United States. At the same time I am entirely with you that we do not want to tie ourselves as we have done in the past to the United States, because she is unreliable and does not know her own mind and her statesmen do not know the mind of their own country. Nothing that is said by the President or any of their statesmen can ever be accepted at more than its face value, as we all know.[1]

Although Fisher was to continue his anti-American outbursts into 1937,[2] the desire to settle the question of cruiser numbers had earlier entailed the need to reach some understanding with Washington.[3] Japan's own refusal to accommodate herself to Western desiderata over naval matters in 1934–5 also helped to weaken the more extreme pro-Japanese arguments, while as Hankey discovered during his ostensibly private tour in 1934, there was much anxiety among Commonwealth officials for firm ties to be built up with America. 'I have the strong impression,' he wrote to MacDonald, 'that all the Dominions I visited would attach great importance to the closest possible relations that the peculiar constitution of the United States permits.' In Canada, he had found this sentiment to be especially marked in Army circles; in Australia, where there was much disquiet at what had recently occurred in the Far East, he had been assured that Washington 'could not afford to see Australia and New Zealand overwhelmed by Japan'.[4] Already, in other words, the post-war ANZUS pact was being foreshadowed.

Faced with these conflicting considerations and with the mixture of alarm and hope where Japanese behaviour was concerned, the Defence Requirements Sub-Committee delivered its advice in a form which leant towards Japan, rather than towards the United States, and which, for all its warnings, comfortingly suggested that the former country entertained no aggressive designs upon British possessions in the East:

[1] Chatfield to Fisher, 4 June 1934, ibid.

[2] On 18 December 1937, when, on British initiative, the question of sanctions against Japan was being discussed with the U.S.A., Fisher minuted to Simon (now Chancellor of the Exchequer): 'Over and above the imbecility of economic sanctions, we shd find ourselves left in the lurch sooner or later by the U.S.A. (who incidentally have no special stakes in Asia) and Japan wd scoop Hongkong. Shd we then add to the fatal folly of going to war with Japan and so committing suicide in Europe?' Notes on Possible Sanctions and Economic Reprisals Against Japan, Conversations with U.S.A., November–December 1937, T 160/693, F 15255/01.

[3] This, despite the fact that Chatfield himself preferred an end to all limitations, substituting 'political understandings (and) leaving each Nation free to build what she wants'. Chatfield to Fisher, 4 June 1934, Chatfield Papers.

[4] Hankey to MacDonald, 2 January 1935, MacDonald Papers, RM 1/18; cf. Hankey to Baldwin, 23 August 1934, Baldwin Papers, vol. 1; Mansergh, 154–5.

We cannot overstate the importance we attach to getting back, not to an alliance (since that would not be practical politics), but at least to our old terms of cordiality and mutual respect with Japan. There should be no insuperable difficulty in such a task, for which conditions are now favourable, though there is already some speculation as to the future extent of Japan's relations with Germany. Success on our part would not only bring us increased security, but might enable us to correct or obviate any unhealthy tendency . . . in Japan. Japan is more likely, however, to respect and listen to a Power that can defend its interests than one that is defenceless.

There is much to be said for the view that our subservience to the United States of America in past years has been one of the principal factors in the deterioration of our former good relations with Japan, and that, before the Naval Disarmament Conference in 1935 we ought thoroughly to reconsider our general attitude. At the present moment, however, we cannot overlook the danger created by our total inability to defend our interests in the Far East . . . We do not consider that there is any immediate danger or any present aggressive design. There remains the risk . . . that some unexpected emergency may arise, as in the autumn of 1931, or that Japan might yield to the sudden temptation of a favourable opportunity arising from complications elsewhere. And elsewhere means Europe, and danger to us in Europe will only come from Germany.

Even now the Japanese–American dilemma did not disappear, however, and was to return in acute form after 1937 when the renewed Sino–Japanese conflict forced a consideration of how far it was advisable for Britain to 'co-operate' with Japan in the Far East.[1] There also remained the major complication of trade relations and the perception of a Japanese threat in that respect, as already noted in relation to the closing stages of the 1931–3 crisis.[2] Here, too, the arguments of the Defence Requirements Sub-Committee were relevant, for Fisher had urged in its meetings that in order to recover Japanese friendship one must first win her respect, and that this in turn required a tough line to be taken over matters of trade—especially those involving India. As with military strategy, the details surrounding this subject—including the F.B.I. and Leith–Ross missions to the Far East— must be left aside. It is important, however, to observe that there was considerable confusion in the arguments that were to be heard in Whitehall. For example, was a political agreement with Japan to provide the basis for a commercial one, or vice versa?[3] Nevertheless the Cabinet swept on, with the President of the Board of Trade, the Secretary of State for India and the Chancellor of the Exchequer in the van. At the end of 1933 they decided that the Government of India should be encouraged to place further restrictions on the import of Japanese cotton goods, Britain promising to compensate India for any losses she might incur should the Japanese retaliate, as they threatened, by not buying Indian raw cotton. The need to win back protected markets for Lancashire overshadowed all other considerations during these discussions in London, and even the Viceroy of India was moved to remonstrate that it was short-sighted folly to suppose that Britain's manufacturers would benefit more by risking a breakdown in Indian–Japanese negotiations than by 'the increased prosperity of the agricultural classes which must result from the purchase of 1½ million bales of cotton by Japan'.

[1] See Louis, 238 ff.   [2] See above, 366–7; Gull, passim; Louis, 214 ff.
[3] See, e.g., Simon memorandum, 21 January 1935, MacDonald Papers, RM 1/27.

Once embarked on this course, moreover, little mention was made of Britain's contemporary politico-strategic goals in the Far East, beyond the suggestion in 1934 that when the Japanese Ambassador was informed that his hosts were resuming their freedom of action over various duties and textile quotas in the colonies, it should be done 'with all possible courtesy' and without appearing 'brusque'. The widely-accepted thesis of Wellesley and others, that the problems being created by Japan sprang ultimately from her socio-economic difficulties, faded away before the double-think of officials like Sir Horace Wilson. Chamberlain, too, was ready to admit that Japan 'held most of the good cards'; yet somehow he and others assumed that she would appreciate and accept Britain's case and love her the more dearly for it.[1] Here again, as with Stimson and Hornbeck to name only two, one encounters the deep-seated belief that for all their power the Japanese were often bluffing (in the report on his Far Eastern economic mission, Sir Frederick Leith-Ross described them as 'experts in (this) art'[2]), and that they could be kept in their suitably subordinate place by a token display of Anglo–Saxon might, or even a mere stiffening of the British jaw. Chamberlain, for example—the leader of the campaign within the Cabinet for a renewed understanding with Tokyo—reflected this approach when congratulating himself in his diary on the success of his threat to back India financially in her trade negotiations with Japan:

We felt that really more was at stake than the bleached cotton market in India since this was really the first round in a fight against Japanese competition in many other articles and in many other markets. Moreover the acceptance of Japan's terms would certainly raise very bitter feelings in Lancashire . . . In these circumstances, believing that there was at least a good deal of bluff behind the Jap proposals, I determined on a bold stroke . . . The effect was magical.[3]

In a number of ways the Far Eastern crisis of 1931–3 had greatly disturbed the men who were directly responsible for the making of both British and American foreign policies. Ironically, indeed, one of its effects was to increase the determination of each Western power to be ready to act in defence of its own 'life-line' and surrounding area, as the Japanese had acted according to their lights to preserve theirs. In Washington, for example, there was growing concern to guard against a sudden Japanese strike against the Panama Canal;[4] in London, following similar discussions regarding possible Japanese action to block the fleet's route to the Far East, it was agreed by the C.I.D. to recommend 'that his Majesty's Government should

[1] See Cabinets of 29 March, 24 May 1933; 18 April 1934, CAB 23/75, 76, 79 respectively; Hoare memorandum, 20 July 1933, CP 192(33), CAB 24/242; Cabinet Committee on Indian Cotton, December 1933, CAB 27/556; Cabinet Committee on Japanese Trade Competition, March–June 1934, CAB 27/568.

[2] Leith-Ross report, T 160/620, F 14233/03, 04.

[3] Neville Chamberlain Diary, January 1934; cf. ibid, 6 February 1934; Neville to Ida Chamberlain, 17 December 1933, Neville Chamberlain Papers.

[4] See, e.g., Borg, 494–5, 505, and the Joint Army–Navy Board papers for this period.

be prepared to assume control of the Suez Canal at any time at which the situation appeared to warrant such action'.[1]

Whatever the similarities to be observed between British and American reflexes, however, or between various analyses of the situation that were being offered in their official circles, one major factor among others that continued to make for contrast between the two of them was the differing size of their respective national interests in the Far East as measured in immediate, material terms. It has been suggested earlier[2] that in a way this difference had helped set common limits to their policies during the crisis that had just passed. Once it was accepted in London, however, that developments remained so menacing that they must be steered in a new direction, then the contrast in interests spread back to one that involved responses as well. After 1933, whatever Stimson's vision of the future (and it, like him, was temporarily in eclipse), American interests in the area appeared to be 'vital' only in terms of rubber supplies from South-East Asia—and then only to a few officials in Washington who were specially concerned with that subject.[3] On the other hand, whatever the optimism of a Chamberlain or a Lindley, British money, possessions and Dominions remained at risk to an extent that threatened to involve her very existence as a world power. In the former case passivity, however odd it might seem to some observers in the light of later events, could appear not only attractive but logical; in the latter, despite the difficulties of doing so, one had, in Chatfield's words, to move.

It is not surprising, therefore, to find that while recriminations concerning 1931–3 continued,[4] Anglo–American co-operation over the Far East now reached only a very low level, and that despite London's timidity and uncertainty it was from that side that there came most initiatives, to be met usually by refusals or evasions in Washington. When the Amau statement was issued in 1934, for example, it was Simon who raised the possibility of Anglo–American co-operation over a forthright response, and although no firm British proposals were eventually forthcoming, the American reaction had been negative from the outset.[5] As the 1935 Naval Conference approached, and despite the Treasury's pro-Japanese machinations, it was Baldwin, Simon and MacDonald who sounded out the Americans on a possible Far Eastern alliance, and who received an immediate refusal.[6] At the same time it was Britain which displayed the greater urgency in seeking to find a basis for practical assistance to China where her severe financial and economic difficulties were concerned,[7] and Britain which reacted more swiftly to indications in 1935–6 that the Japanese were increasing their pressure on North China.[8] In 1937 it was Chamberlain who proposed some form of Anglo–American–Japanese agreement to hold the Far Eastern

---

[1] Chatfield to Fisher, 24 January 1935 (cf. ibid, 22 May 1935), Chatfield Papers.
[2] See above, 200–1.   [3] See above, 58.
[4] In addition to the angry exchanges cited, see Cecil to Sweetser, 14 November 1938, Sweetser Papers, box 30, and Simon's appeal to Cordell Hull to help him get kinder treatment from the American press (no doubt to help prop up his position with MacDonald especially): Simon to Hull, 23 November 1934, Davis Papers, box 12.
[5] Borg, *The United States*, 78–87.   [6] Ibid. 103–9.
[7] Ibid, 121 ff.; Louis, 227 ff.   [8] Borg, 147 ff., 189.

situation—a reasonable idea to explore, since the United States had rejected a bilateral arrangement—and who again got no for an answer.[1]

With the renewal of Sino–Japanese fighting in 1937, there remained much caution in London where the League and new commitments were concerned, but at least the idea of local mediation was pursued, as it had been in 1932, some form of swift response also being suggested over the Japanese attacks on the *Panay* and H.M.S. *Ladybird*.[2] For all its underlying reservations, it was again the British Government that worked to bring about the Brussels Nine Power Treaty Conference, proposed that the question of economic sanctions should receive close Anglo–American scrutiny, and undertook to engage in any course of action that the United States might think fit to adopt in the Far East.[3] In turn Washington kept aloof from mediation, took its time over the *Panay* issue, and—despite Norman Davis—would not look at sanctions. Roosevelt's 'quarantine' speech of October 1937, which attracted so much attention and hope in Europe, was never intended as a prelude to action either there or in the Far East, but was rather, in Dr. Borg's words, 'a confused and unsuccessful attempt to solve the dilemma of how to restrict aggression without resorting to threatening measures'.[4] Nor was the mission to London at the end of that year of Captain Ingersoll of the U.S. Navy 'designed to effect any major preparations for the application of forceful pressure against Japan'. (It was also viewed sceptically, needless to say, by Chamberlain and others on the British side.)[5]

In short, when the Imperial Conference of 1937 was told that 'nothing specific can be relied on from the U.S.A.', it was an accurate summary of the situation, and it continued to hold good as Britain faced a direct challenge from the Japanese two years later when the latter blockaded Tientsin.[6] Yet if Japan *were* set upon driving south against the French, British and Dutch—and we have seen that such an intention was then at least in the making—the only hope of successful resistance lay, as Vansittart had pointed out in 1932, in an end to American passivity. Such a happy eventuality still seemed a long way off in 1939—indeed, until Britain's growing peril in her war with Germany helped swing Washington towards a hard line over Japan's threat to the raw materials of South East Asia, it looked almost as if the United States was in the process of giving up all claim to be a major power in Asia and the Western Pacific. For the moment, and as one last attempt was made to avoid war in Europe, Britain's future in the Far East seemed more desperate than at any time since her arrival there as a major power in the nineteenth century. The forebodings of those who had witnessed the departure of her China-Station battleships in 1905, the warnings of Beatty in 1924 and others after him, the predictions of the Chiefs of Staff in 1932: all now appeared likely to be borne out before long. 'I have no doubt,' wrote Chatfield in 1938 as he surveyed Japan's attack on China, 'that sooner or

[1] Ibid, 270 ff.

[2] Ibid, 287 ff., 486 ff.; L. Pratt, 'The Anglo–American Naval Conversations of January 1938', *International Affairs*, October 1971.

[3] Borg, 359 ff., 399 ff.; Louis, 243 ff.

[4] Borg, 382–3.

[5] Ibid, 497; Pratt, 'Naval Conversations', loc. cit.

[6] See, e.g., Louis, 256 ff.

later it will be our turn to face the music'.[1] 'The more one reflects on the situation,' admitted a Foreign Office official in the summer of 1939, 'the more one is obliged to conclude that no satisfactory solution can be found that does not recognise some "new order" in Eastern Asia in which Japan plays a dominant part'.[2] With Matsuoka, as he faced the censure of the League Assembly in 1933, it might have been said: 'We look into the gloom of the future, and can see no certain gleam of light before us.'

[1] Chatfield to Dreyer, 20 January 1938, Chatfield Papers.
[2] DBFP, 3rd series, IX, appendix 1.

CHAPTER TWELVE

CONCLUSIONS

AT THE beginning of this study, a brief outline was given of the main arguments among participants and historians that arose from the crisis of 1931 to 1933.[1] On occasions this debate, if such it can be called, has been of a somewhat ferocious nature, and one reason no doubt lies in the character of events on either side of what occurred in Manchuria itself: in the futile horrors of 1914–18 which helped give the League idea in Britain its creed-like features, and in the unparalleled 'material ruin and moral havoc' of 1939–45 which Churchill and others assured the world could 'easily have been prevented'.[2] For a time after this second conflict, the temptation to explain all by discovering a group of 'guilty men', by lighting upon a 'turning point' at which peace was wantonly betrayed, proved almost irresistible; and while this eventually gave way in a European context to a wider and more critical questioning, the greater general ignorance of Far Eastern affairs may be one reason why even now it remains common for simplistic answers to be accepted where this other sphere is concerned. Meanwhile the new-found comradeship in adversity of the United States and Britain helped to obscure the years of distrust and hostility that had gone before, and to encourage a 'hands-across-the-sea' approach to the history of Anglo-American relations which in turn highlighted such episodes as Stimson's apparent readiness for joint action to stamp out aggression and nascent anarchy in 1932. Secure in the knowledge of the disasters that had followed, it was easy, as we have seen, for a Cecil or a Stimson to overlook his own perplexity and caution of the time and to find in the timidity and short-sightedness of others the reason for the downfall of the League, the triumph of Japan and the perils that awaited the democracies.

Forty years after the event, the notion of Sumner Welles and others[3] that the Manchurian episode was 'the chief cause' of the subsequent acts of aggression in the 1930s has a threadbare look to it. Where war in Europe was concerned, for example, even a preliminary survey can produce so many other factors which have to be considered as possible contributory causes, whether the German problem as it existed from, say, 1871 onwards, or the inherent instability of the 1919 settlement; whether the ancient question of minorities as exacerbated by that settlement and the growing

[1] See above, 7ff.

[2] W. S. Churchill, *The Second World War*, vol. 1 (London, 1950), 16.

[3] See above, 8. Cf. Bell, *Conventions of Crisis*, 20, where the 'crisis slide' of the '30s is dated only from 1936 onwards.

nationalism of the time, or the element of continuity in German war aims between 1914 and 1939; whether the contribution of an individual like Hitler, or the roots of fascism, Nazism and the apotheosis of 'the SS state' in pre-1914 racialism, irrationalism and social-Darwinism, in the strands of German intellectual development in the nineteenth century, or even perhaps, as some would have it, in 'a lashing out of the choked psyche' or 'the ambiguous after-life of religious feeling in Western culture'.[1]

That the Far Eastern crisis preceded, had links with, but did not 'cause' the events which followed in Europe is equally apparent when one examines the individual episodes involved. Over Abyssinia, for example, although Mussolini only finally resolved upon action when Manchuria had probably helped to increase his existing scorn for the League, his reasons for embarking upon a war are to be found elsewhere—in his alarm at German and Austrian developments in 1934, for example; in 'the nature of Italian Fascism . . . and the (domestic) needs of his dictatorship', and even in the degree of encouragement he had been receiving as early as 1931 from the French.[2] In Germany's case, there can be no doubt that Manchuria provided an easy target for the derision of extreme nationalists, nor that it played some part in helping to bring about the eventual alignment of Tokyo and Berlin; on the other hand it did nothing to mould the specific aims of the Nazis—in terms, say, of the absorption of Austria—any more than it contributed to the fact that 'conquest', in Nolte's words, 'bluntly and without reservation, was the focal idea in Hitler's policy'.[3] It was long before the events of 1931–1933, in the heyday of Geneva, in fact, when the future Chancellor was talking confidently and sincerely of 'destroying these ideas such as the belief in reconciliation, understanding, world peace, the League of Nations, and international solidarity'.[4]

But might the Nazis never have come to power in the first place had it not been for Japan's successful defiance in the immediately preceding period? A direct causal relationship between the two events is beyond almost anyone's contriving, but an indirect one is still treasured in some quarters. In this version, the outcome of the Far Eastern crisis ensured the failure of the Disarmament Conference, and this failure in turn paved the way for

---

[1] Briefly, the questions raised above may be followed up in the following works among many others: Robertson (ed.); *The Origins of the Second World War*; E. M. Robertson, *Hitler's Pre-War Policy and Military Plans* (London, 1963); A. J. P. Taylor, *The Origins of the Second World War* (London, 1963); A. Bullock, *Hitler: A Study In Tyranny* (London, 1962); E. H. Carr, *The Twenty Years' Crisis* (London, 1958); Hinsley, *Power and the Pursuit of Peace*; Thorne, *The Approach of War*; F. Fischer, *Germany's Aims in the First World War* (London, 1967); S. J. Woolf (ed.), *European Fascism* (London, 1968); G. L. Mosse, *The Crisis of German Ideology* (London, 1966); E. Nolte, *Three Faces of Fascism* (London, 1965); H. Krausnick et al., *Anatomy of the SS State* (London, 1968); C. A. Macartney, *National States and National Minorities* (London, 1934); E. Wiskemann, *Czechs and Germans* (London, 1967); G. Steiner, *In Bluebeard's Castle* (London, 1971).

[2] See Baer, *The Coming of the Italian-Ethiopian War*, 29 ff. I have also benefited from reading and discussing with E. M. Robertson early drafts of his forthcoming book on Italian foreign policy in this period.

[3] Nolte, 325. Cf. Robertson, *Hitler's Pre-War Policy*, passim.

[4] Bullock, 128–9.

Hitler's accession to power. Quite apart from any chronological straining involved, the argument is open to serious doubt in several respects. Working backwards, so to speak, and while granting that it was not until the fall of Brüning in May 1932 that 'a real turning point (was reached)in the collapse of German democracy',[1] it can be asserted that the malaise that was killing the Weimar Republic was not then to be cured even by striking concessions over reparations and disarmament on the part of the victors of 1918. Whether one looks at the process of disintegration and fear that was taking place at a local level[2] or turns to the findings of a recent and detailed examination of these events nationally,[3] there is little reason to believe that disarmament alone held the key to Germany's political future between February 1932 and January 1933. As for connections between the Conference at Geneva and the conflict in the Far East, that they existed has been demonstrated at some length earlier in the book; but this does not invalidate the conclusion that the immediate crux of the matter so far as disarmament was concerned lay between France and Germany, regardless of what occurred on the Western shores of the Pacific, and that to ascribe failure on this occasion to the Far Eastern factor is merely to add yet another superficial and inadequate explanation to that list of 'if onlys' which, as Strachey has admirably demonstrated,[4] has all too often clogged the study of arms control in general.

Indeed, the entire thesis that success could readily have been achieved by the Western powers in 1931–33, and that in turn this would have either forestalled altogether or brought similar triumphs over later acts of aggression, rests on a series of hypotheses that are no less questionable for being usually implied rather than recognised. Where the Manchurian episode itself is concerned the obstacles to success in both East and West have been explored at length,[5] and it is enough to recall that submission by Japan would have required that one or more of a series of connected eventualities should have come about. At the lowest level, swift and strong condemnation by the West would have had to lead to Shidehara and Wakatsuki's extracting compliance from the Kwantung Army—possibly in the face of that Army's initial and open defiance, and certainly within the context of a highly volatile and fragmented domestic political situation. Failing this, the League and United States would presumably have had to seek the same result by means of diplomatic sanctions such as a withdrawal of ambassadors; failing that again, by economic coercion. Assuming for the moment—highly improbable though it is—that such economic measures had won the active support of Hoover, Congress and a sufficient body of the American people to make them politically practicable in a pre-election period of domestic crisis, then at this stage one of two consequences would have had to ensue. Either the very threat would have had to be sufficient to make the Kwantung Army and their political supporters in Japan willing to admit defeat—something that no Western observer on the spot believed

---

[1] A. J. Nicholls, *Weimar and the Rise of Hitler* (London, 1968), 160.
[2] See W. S. Allen, *The Nazi Seizure of Power* (London, 1966).
[3] Nicholls, 144 ff.
[4] J. Strachey, *On the Prevention of War* (London, 1967), cap. 10.
[5] See, for example, 124–7 above.

likely, even those who were emissaries of the League like Walters, Lytton
and McCoy; or the sanctions themselves would have had to be mounted
with sufficient speed and effectiveness to produce whatever degree of deprivation was required to bring the Kwantung Army and the Japanese
public (men, alas, who were neither imbued with the spirit of John Stuart
Mill nor too proud to fight) to reason (as understood in the West) or to
their knees—and this, moreover, at a cost and in a space of time that could
be accepted and sustained within the domestic political environments of the
sanctioning governments. Even this is based on the additional assumption
that Japan would not, in response, either have blockaded China or struck
against the possessions of those who were seeking to coerce her. At the time,
as we have seen, the Japanese did not have plans prepared for such a contingency; it is equally evident, however, that the military balance in the area
was such that, had the will to act been there, they would have had ample time
and resources to extemporise.

At this point one arrives at the final, hypothetical situation which
Mr. Noel-Baker, for example, would ultimately be prepared to contemplate
in retrospect:[1] a war between the League powers—and, let us again say for
the sake of argument, the United States—on the one hand and Japan on the
other, fought in order to preserve the post-war structure of international
obligations as enshrined in the Covenant. Accepting that such a conflict
would have occurred, as Mr. Noel-Baker argues, in circumstances far more
favourable than those Britain was to face in 1939, the extensive nature of the
costs likely to have been involved can be inferred from our earlier analysis
of the military balance.[2] Above all—and while those responsible for policy
in 1931 did not know, of course, what inferior conditions awaited them eight
years later, they would eventually have had to convince their electorates that
the certain alternative in some form or other was to pay greater costs still
in the long run—the sacrifices involved would again have had to be support-
able in terms of domestic politics in the West. Finally, let it be assumed that,
at whatever cost, success had been achieved in the shape of a Manchuria
restored to China. It does not necessarily follow—indeed, several considerations to the contrary have been suggested above—that potential aggressors in
Europe would thereupon have been warned off altogether. Nor does it
necessarily follow that the governments and publics of the democracies
would thereafter have been ready for their part to plunge again into the
possible costs of halting aggression through the application of sanctions on
a League basis. They might, of course, have acted in the most enlightened,
far-seeing and unselfish fashion; it is by no means impossible, however,
that, having once found the process a painful one, they would have drawn
back from repeating it in a fresh context.

At all stages of the argument there arise questions concerning not only the
likely reactions of individual Western governments, but also the nature
and capabilities of the League itself. In this connection it needs to be
emphasised at the outset that whatever else the Manchurian episode was not,
it did constitute a major blow to the prestige of that organisation, and to that
of Britain especially among its members. Even Mussolini's defiance over

---

[1] See above, 383, note 3.   [2] See above, 63ff.

Corfu had been sufficiently blurred by the way in which the crisis was handled by France and Britain, and by the final Italian departure from the island itself, to allow the hopes of the faithful to remain intact. Now, however, the aggressor had operated on a far larger scale, had defiantly retained his prize, and had departed from Geneva with little more than verbal censure as the price of his deed. In the smaller League states, even in France and Germany as well as Britain and the United States, there was disillusionment and dismay. Whatever the historian may observe at a distance, there is no doubt that in many minds at the time the episode did appear as a turning point; in official circles, it also provided fresh evidence which could be cited, like Corfu before it, as 'proof' that the Covenant of the League was a seriously flawed document.[1]

As the preliminary analysis offered in chapter four of the present work has already suggested, however, the failure of 1931–33 did not 'cause' the downfall of the League, any more than it did the aggression of Nazi Germany; it was, rather, the occasion for showing up some of its main inherent weaknesses.[2] Some of these weaknesses were of the kind likely to arise in any attempt to create a system of genuine collective security, wherein a formidable number of preconditions will need to be fulfilled if success is to be achieved. Practically, for example, there is the requirement that every state in the system shall be vulnerable to whatever kind of sanctions are envisaged; psychologically, as Cecil came to realise, there has to be a readiness on everyone's part to accept suffering in defence of another's security as he would in the case of his own (in other words, so long as a substantial number of people share the view of Professor Dennett, for example,[3] who 'didn't raise his boys to be soldiers to displace Japan', then the system will be seriously jeopardised). In compiling the full list of these preconditions, one encounters problems both of circularity—'collective security cannot work unless states disarm, but states will not disarm until collective security has clearly shown that it merits confidence'[4]—and of self-contradiction—states being seen as 'both irresponsible enough to create the urgent problem of war and responsible enough to solve the problem' through collective security.[5] This is to suppose in the first place, moreover, that aggression can swiftly be defined to the common satisfaction, and that the essential, committed nature of the ensuing response is going to be desirable in every instance.

The likelihood is that there will be much ambivalence among and within states towards such a system, towards its potential costs and what were earlier explored as 'the rules of the game'. The doubtful nature of its effectiveness becomes all the more apparent when one examines further the central, deterrent function that is involved.[6] For example, in order to possess a high capability in this respect an international organisation, like an indi-

---

[1] For later use of the 1931-3 episode in this way in London, see, e.g., Louis, cap. VIII.   [2] For a more extensive analysis, see Claude, cap. 12.

[3] See above, 7,n.   [4] Claude, 237.

[5] Ibid, 258–9. It needs to be said, perhaps, that the Korean episode of 1950-3 was not one in which collective security functioned as such a system required.

[6] The following section owes much to Schelling's *Arms and Influence*, a book which, suitably, first saw light as the Henry L. Stimson memorial lectures at Yale, and in which a far more thorough analysis of deterrence will be found.

vidual state or a regional alliance, may well need to be seen in advance to possess not many options but few of them, so that to the would-be aggressor there will appear all the more likelihood of an immediate and massive response to the action he contemplates. In addition, the organisation may well need to have demonstrated beforehand in some way that it will not itself be deterred by the obvious 'nuisance value'[1] of whatever economic or military action it threatens to take against an aggressor—in other words that it will readily accept the disruptive effects that such action is likely to have on the law-enforcer as well as the law-breaker. Or again—and this is clearly a major requirement where the sanction of so-called 'world opinion' is concerned—there will exist the need adequately to communicate the organisation's deterrent threat, in a world of differing societies with their differing values and political cultures.

Considerations such as these (and they are only a few of those that could be produced) begin to look formidable when placed alongside an organisation that is composed of states which retain their full sovereignty and the governments of which, as the Wilsonian vision required, are democratically responsive to their own electorates. Where deterrence is concerned, they serve to reinforce the observation made in 1919 in the British Government's White Paper on the Covenant of the League, that 'if the nations of the future are in the main selfish, grasping and warlike, no instrument or machinery will restrain them'. Moreover it is evident that problems of a new order will arise if and when the mere existence of such a collective-security system has indeed failed to deter someone from aggression, as was the case with the League in September 1931. The organisation is then required to pass on from deterrence to what has been termed 'compellance', and in this changed situation the threats and responses which are involved are likely to take on certain new characteristics. Not the least difference will be the far more obvious nature of any act of compliance by the transgressor (that is, as compared to merely desisting from aggression in the first place under deterrence), and hence the much greater degree of 'face' involved.

Whether the stage is one of deterring or compelling, moreover, there has yet to appear a state, however powerful, whose government, under certain circumstances, did not have to weigh the costs which might be involved. As Schelling has put it, 'a nation has limited resources in the things that it can get exceptionally concerned about', in the areas of the world with which it can closely identify.[2] An effective deterrent will require the clear prospect of a rising scale of retaliation; yet it is most likely (if not certain) that there will come a moment under some conditions when the risks and costs involved will appear too high a price to pay in order to maintain the transgressor's expectations about one's behaviour. In short—and whether on their own or within a collective-security context—governments will ask the kind of questions that Baldwin was posing on 27 February 1932:

> The very people like Bob Cecil who have made us disarm, and quite right too, are now urging us forward to take action. But where will action lead us to? If we withdraw Ambassadors, that is the first step. What is the next? and the next?[3]

[1] See Q. Wright, *A Study of War* (Chicago, 1942), 319–20.
[2] Schelling, 51, 56.　　　　　　　　　　　[3] Jones, *Diary*, 30.

Granted that one possible reply is that, unless one acts immediately, a step of far greater magnitude and cost will eventually have to be taken (and the dangers of rigidly applying such a notion as a panacea for all international ills have been suggested earlier[1]), the considerations outlined above will not thereby be removed. Given the finest of normative rules for the game, pragmatic ones will continue to make their appearance.[2]

In addition to such problems involved in any attempt to construct a system of collective security—in the background, of course, lying formidable questions concerning the very causes and necessity of war itself[3]—the League faced particular difficulties of its own, as we have seen. Despite the favourable, diffused nature of the international power structure at the time of its creation,[4] there remained the crippling absence of the United States and Soviet Union, the inherent conservatism in a world of rapid change, the essentially Western assumptions, values and preoccupations at a time of declining Western supremacy. Had the United States joined from the outset as envisaged, then no doubt the deterrent capability of the organisation would have been greatly enhanced, and it could be argued that in that event the 1931 challenge might not have arisen in the first place. It is equally valid, however, to speculate that at some time or other a major power that perceived a vital interest to be at stake would have challenged the League system, and that in such an eventuality, as Hugh Wilson acknowledged, the United States would have been found no more prepared to run great risks within the organisation than proved to be the case in her isolation.[5] As it was, the peculiar difficulties of time and place involved in the Manchurian episode were less significant than the challenge it offered to the basic assumptions of those who had drawn up the Covenant, with American collaboration, at the end of the Great War.

Needless to say, successful coercion was not beyond the League in all circumstances. The Greco-Bulgarian dispute had demonstrated as much, while on a larger scale the practical possibilities of bringing down Italy over Abyssinia were to be far greater than they had been where Japan and Manchuria were concerned. Nor should one overlook the achievements of the League in areas other than those of disarmament, security and peace-keeping, or the significance of this 'great experiment', as Cecil rightly called it, in terms of aspirations embracing international relations as a whole. Nevertheless, 'international politics (remain) power politics,'[6] their fluid nature ill-suited to any rigid and all-encompassing structure or formula, however laudable the intentions involved. In the sense of endlessly observing existing and likely future conditions and adjusting one's policies accordingly, a continual balancing of power is inescapable, and where the League failed it did so, not because it was betrayed over Manchuria in 1931, but because, in Hinsley's words, 'its basic conception is impracticable at any time'.[7]

·   ·   ·

[1] See above, 62.   [2] See above, 126.
[3] See, e.g., K. N. Waltz, *Man, The State and War* (New York, 1959); Claude, 197 ff.; Aron, 339 ff.; Wright, passim.
[4] See Claude, 234.
[5] See, e.g., Waltz, *Foreign Policy and Democratic Politics*, 100.
[6] Aron, 703.   [7] Hinsley, 321.

Not all the limitations pressing in upon the League were immutable. And when examining the limits within which the policies of individual Western states were formulated in 1931–33, it is likewise important to recall the distinctions made earlier,[1] between the setting as seen later by the 'omniscient observer' and as perceived at the time by those involved; between limits that were within one's own control and those beyond all manipulation; between what might change or be changed with some speed—public opinion, perhaps—and a factor such as the number of available battleships that had to be accepted for several years ahead. Distinctions of this kind arise, for example, when one compares the effects on policy during the crisis of domestic factors in Britain and the United States. In Britain's case, the magnitude of her economic and financial crisis was considerably less than the one facing Hoover's Government; yet British perceptions of the situation were such as to create an important similarity in this respect, and one that was accompanied by others involving insecure leadership, a strong inward-looking tendency, and deep divisions of public opinion over the Far Eastern issue itself. Here again, however, the distinction has to be made between what can now be observed as a 'fact'—that there *were* these divisions of opinion, even within a body like the L.N.U., or that in the legislatures of the two countries, as in that of France, the debates on the question were relatively brief and cautious—and the images of public opinion that were formed by contemporaries in Whitehall and Washington. In this general area, contrasts as well as similarities begin to emerge, for example between the far wider and stronger organisation of the L.N.U. in Britain than of any American peace society; between the weakness of such attitude groups in the United States in terms of swift and direct influence on their country's policy, and the direct pressure which an interest group like the arms manufacturers or the Firestone Company could on occasions exert on the Administration or through Congressional committees; between the greater pervasiveness of images of domestic opinion in the deliberations of American, as opposed to British, policy-makers, however much the general mood and outer limits of policy were being affected in both instances.

In some cases a man's interpretation of public opinion could change, in emphasis at least, and seemingly in keeping with circumstances as much as in response to alterations in that opinion itself. A similar process of re-valuation has also been evident even in relation to the more measurable factor of what was at stake in material terms in the area of Sino-Japanese conflict, the need to preserve the 'open door' in Manchuria, for example, moving several places down the scale in both London and Washington between September 1931 and February 1933. Meanwhile, and despite the contrasts that existed between Western states in this sphere of material interests, the addition of two other factors—a common inadequacy of resources to defend them, and a common acceptance that Japan might resist an attempt to coerce her by means other than disapproval—brought about an underlying similarity of policies. Whether, like Hoover, one saw too little as being at stake, or, like Baldwin, too much, the risks were seen to be too great to proceed with, say, economic sanctions. It has also been

[1] See above, 12.

suggested that, paradoxically, it was partly this very similarity in fearing to arouse Japan that prevented the development of full trust and cooperation between Britain, the United States and France, a situation which was exacerbated by other issues such as debts and disarmament, and which was essentially a continuation of the largely uncoordinated and mutually suspicious manoeuvrings of the powers in the Far East in the years following the Washington Conference.

Relations between the United States and Britain in particular had deteriorated by the end of the crisis. This can also be attributed in part to their need in the post-Versailles era to idealise their own policies for the benefit of domestic opinion and, for Britain especially, with an eye to opinion at Geneva. Here, too, was one factor which, together with their interests and aspirations in China and elsewhere, ensured that however much each set of Western policy-makers might have liked to allow the crisis to spend itself without their becoming entangled in it, they could not escape involvement in some degree. One outcome was a heightened level of confusion over the nature and rules of the international game itself.[1] In the Western democracies there was no likelihood that this uncertainty would be dissipated with one, abrupt stroke of the kind that the Kwantung Army had now supplied in Japan or that Hitler was about to provide for Germany.

This underlying confusion also contributed to some of those common features which have been encountered in the actual policy-making processes of the three main Western powers, and of Britain and the United States in particular. For example, not only did the wider preferences of individual diplomats frequently reflect their immediate, local circumstances, as one might have expected, but with men like Johnson, Hornbeck and Pratt one also comes across pronounced and sometimes rapid variations in emphasis between the requirements of national self-preservation and the longer-term dictates of international morality and stability. Even so, however, one can observe also a dominant image of the situation being rapidly built up within each foreign-policy organisation (a process sometimes assisted by the grasping of analogies), an image which served in turn as a screen for further incoming messages and hence was all the more difficult to change as time went on. In terms of Japan these dominant images did at times come close to the actual situation obtaining in political and military circles in that country; in general, however, there was a failure to appreciate the full nature and extent of the changes that had been taking place even before the Mukden incident, a failure to establish an adequate perspective and context in terms of Japan's political culture. For the longer term, there was too often a surrender to vague optimism and an implicit projection of one's own, idealised pattern of reactions and rationality on to the other party.

Obviously this general criticism must be modified where certain individuals are concerned. Similarly, there were those within the Foreign Office, State Department and Quai d'Orsay who attempted to produce a thorough analysis of the situation and on that basis to make projections for several years ahead. Nevertheless in both London and Washington (records do not exist for an adequate evaluation in the case of Paris; in The Hague it

---

[1] See above, 126.

appears that there was well-nigh total quiescence) there was a striking lack of any such thorough analysis at government level during the crisis itself. Both in the essentially two-man, President-and-Secretary of State setting for American decisions and the more diffused system of Cabinet responsibility in Britain, it was usually a hand-to-mouth process that prevailed. If Stimson's concern for the future in Asia and for the post-war structure of international agreements helped to leave London supreme in this respect, then it was in Washington that the failure to define the national interests in the Far East was far more blatant. On the part of both governments, moreover, there was a failure to remove—or even to discern in some instances—the marked degree of incoherence which existed, for example, between political and commercial, and political and strategic aspects of their policies. As in Japan, there were those groups within the structures of official organisation who had their own and often narrow goals and criteria—the India Office over Tibet and the Board of Trade over Lancashire markets; the U.S. Navy and its search for a major role in the Pacific; the Treasuries of both countries. During the crisis, however, these other official bodies did not impinge upon Far Eastern policy to any great extent. On this occasion there was nothing approaching the kind of inter-departmental manoeuvring that Huntington, for example, has described in post-war Washington,[1] and matters rested essentially with foreign offices and senior Ministers. In neither the British nor the American case can the outcome be described as a synthesis.[2]

The State Department, Quai d'Orsay and Foreign Office thus exercised a considerable degree of influence on the policy of their respective countries as it emerged on a day-to-day basis. It was in Paris that this characteristic was most apparent and sustained; in London, the Cabinet endorsed and later insisted on maintaining the limits already formulated by Simon's officials, and became deeply involved for a brief period when a crisis of major dimensions arose at Shanghai; in Washington, Hoover's vetoes constituted the most obvious instances of powerful intervention by an Administration. Meanwhile the crisis was serving to bring out some of those separate characteristics of each foreign-policy machine that were noted at the outset.[3] Within the Quai d'Orsay the professionalism of the fonctionnaires was doubtless an asset as governments came and went with some rapidity, but the price may well have been the further development of an unduly centralised and autonomous bureaucracy.[4] Within the State Department and the ranks of American diplomats, on the other hand, confusion and amateurishness had continued to be apparent, notwithstanding the presence of a core of extremely competent professionals, several of whom (Castle; Wilson; Grew; Moffat), while often cool towards Britain herself, had tended to react to the crisis in ways which were closer to those of their British colleagues than to those of their own Secretary of State. In London itself, the efforts of Pratt and Wellesley among others to probe beneath and beyond the immediate

---

[1] Huntington, *The Common Defense*, passim.

[2] This is not to suggest that a country's foreign policy can ever be expected to contain no mutually-conflicting elements; a certain minimum level of harmony can and should be aspired to, however. [3] See above, 78, 87, 96.

[4] The firmness of such a conclusion must depend in part on the answer to the question posed above, 326, note 1.

situation suggest that the familiar criticism of short-sightedness should be
modified, whatever the limitations of the consequent analyses and the underlying structural defects noted earlier. At the same time the degree of general
efficiency, the extent and clarity of internal debate, and the exchange of
information between the centre and missions in the field were all well in
advance of Washington's, while despite serious shortcomings (where
Commonwealth defence planning was involved, for example) the Committee
of Imperial Defence had provided a better setting within which to consider,
say, the situation in March 1932 than anything the Americans had at their
disposal.

The most obvious and commonly cited contrast, however, is that between
the cautious pragmatism of London and the pre-occupation with legal and
moral principles which helped bring Stimson to furnish further support for
Conrad's observation, that 'the air of the New World seems favourable to
the art of declamation'.[1] The background to these diverging responses
having been explored earlier, it is sufficient here to ask what was achieved by
each of them on this occasion. Where the fate of Manchuria was concerned,
neither proclamations nor private and sympathetic pressure affected the
outcome between 1931 and 1933; given the situation within Japanese
military and political circles, specific instances which could be picked out, of
opinion in Japan being inflamed on this date or of Shidehara not being
pressed hard enough on that, are not of great significance. Even Stimson's
own early caution and opposition to a commission of enquiry, while dis-
heartening at Geneva, was probably not of major consequence for the
successes of the Kwantung Army. As for the long-term reactions of the
Japanese, there was again little positive achievement to show for either
private pressure or public condemnation. Britain's restraint could be said to
have helped 'keep Tokyo in play', as the favourite phrase had it, but there
was little likelihood that this would drastically alter for example Japan's
stand over naval limitations when the time came for their renewal.

The most celebrated product of the period (though it was not new) was
the doctrine of non-recognition, which was hailed not only by commentators
like Lippmann but also by an international lawyer like Quincy Wright. 'No
diplomatic note of recent or even more distant years,' wrote the latter of
Stimson's pronouncement of January 1932, 'is likely to go down in history
as of greater significance in the development of international law',[2] while the
application of non-recognition by the League against Japan was seen by the
Secretary of State in later years as 'perhaps the greatest constructive achievement of his public life'.[3] Yet as Wright himself observed at the time, when
arguing that with the Pact of Paris 'the legal case against war and armed

---

[1] Joseph Conrad, *Nostromo* (Harmondsworth, 1963), 80.

[2] Q. Wright, 'The Stimson Note of January 7th, 1932', in *American Journal of
International Law*, vol. 26 (1932), 342–8. The writer emphasised the note's importance concerning the following principles: '(1) De facto occupation of territory
gives no title, (2) treaties contrary to the rights of third states are void, (3) treaties
in making of which non-pacific means have been employed are void. . . . If these
three principles were really made effective, international law would be revolution-
ised.' (One wonders also what the implications of (3) might have been for, say,
the Versailles settlement.)   [3] Stimson and Bundy, 262.

violence in international affairs is complete', 'the problem of organising the peace . . . remained'.[1] Stimson's notes may have served, in his own words, 'to reassert the American conviction that no good could come from the breach of treaties';[2] they did little, however, to hinder Japan or to aid China on that occasion. Moreover, in general terms, such pronouncements (like the subsequent and lengthy American refusal to recognise Communist China) not only come close to what has been described as 'cant in foreign policy',[3] but can in time entail greater discomfort for the issuing state than for the recipient. Where the immediate dangers at Shanghai were concerned, Lampson's endeavours on the spot offered more hope of improving matters than did the Secretary's letter to Senator Borah. In the long run, might Stimson's hard-line approach to the worsening relations between Washington and Tokyo in 1940–41 have reflected in part a need to vindicate in theory and improve upon in practice the utterances for which he had become celebrated?[4] Meanwhile if the United States had to become deeply involved in the destinies of the Far East, as he desired, these pronouncements in 1932 had done nothing to bring home to his own public the difficulties and costs likely to be entailed; if anything they had encouraged the expectation that one could exert influence without accepting responsibility. Stimson's failure in this respect can be bracketed with that of British leaders like MacDonald and Baldwin, who had become alarmed during the period of the crisis at the dangers to which the country might soon become exposed, but who were not inclined to risk their political lives in order to alert their public to the situation, even when hopes of a happier outcome through the Disarmament Conference had become minimal.

One further consequence of Stimson's desire to pronounce 'on the morality of this great situation' was a diminution of that trust and cooperation between Britain and the United States which it was his own wish to bring about. Even so, as Hoffmann has pointed out in another context,[5] the simple dichotomy of 'idealism' versus 'realism' is a false one where international politics are concerned, and the present study has attempted to demonstrate that during the Far Eastern crisis there were present both a cautious pursuit of immediate self-interest in Washington and an awareness of wider issues of principle in London and Paris. A clearer and in many ways more significant contrast was the one which has been stressed throughout, between, on the one hand, the broad consensus over Far Eastern policy which existed in Whitehall in 1931–33, such disagreements as there were being concerned largely with means rather than ends and the dominant goal being that of self-preservation (even the fierce debates of 1934–35 concerning Japan and the United States still revolved around how best this could be achieved); and on the other hand the growing and profound disagreement between

---

[1] Q. Wright, 'The Meaning of the Pact of Paris', in *American Journal of International Law*, vol. 27 (1933), 39–61.

[2] Stimson and Bundy, 234.   [3] Hugo, *Appearance and Reality*, cap. 1.

[4] A similar question arises when one considers Eden's belligerence in 1956, the ineffectual nature of his performance as Foreign Secretary in the 1930s, and the false popular reputation he had nevertheless gained from those earlier years. See Christopher Thorne, 'Nationalism and Public Opinion in Britain', *Orbis*, vol. X, No. 4, 1967, 1128.   [5] Hoffmann, *Gulliver's Troubles*, 125.

Hoover and Stimson in Washington, a conflict which involved others around them, which derived in part from differing views of the nature of the international system, and which embraced not only the means but ultimately the very ends of United States policy.[1] Where Stimson and the U.S. Navy were concerned, goals of self-extension and not merely of self-preservation had continued to be present, and while the two of them were not always at one—over Great Britain, for example, or international peace-keeping—their inclinations still tended in the same direction, towards what Liska has chosen to call 'the international politics of primacy' as the framework for the policies of 'imperial America'.[2]

Both the tension between Hoover and Stimson and the confusion within Stimson's own mind make it difficult to talk accurately of an 'American policy' during the crisis, and the style of execution often matched that of the conception. Even so, these and other shortcomings that have been suggested should not obscure the conclusion that has been argued at various stages of the narrative, that without accepting a high risk of extensive costs there was little that the United States, Britain and France, singly or even together, could do to make the Japanese surrender over Manchuria. At the same time there were those powerful considerations on the other side that made it impossible to accept what was being done with total indifference. In short, while the way in which Simon dithered, prevaricated, and eventually executed British policy was often open to serious criticism, that policy itself in its broadest terms was the best that could be maintained in the circumstances.

Nor should Western shortcomings obscure the major failures which existed on the Japanese side—sometimes in similar areas of policy-making—such as their lack of coherence and coordination, their reluctance to follow through the likely consequences of what was taking place, or their failure to take adequate account of the aspirations and political culture of another society, in this case that of China above all.[3] As for the place of the crisis in Japan's own history, the criticisms made earlier of Western perceptions have already implied that these events constituted a significant episode in the country's progress into what came to be called 'the dark valley' of violence at home and overseas. This broad assertion needs to be followed by two qualifications, however. The first is that in this respect it would again be wrong to conclude that the Manchurian crisis was a sudden 'turning point'. As Scalapino has observed, 'the history of Japan after 1931 represented the logical culmination of previous trends—an era in which ultranationalism and militarism took a dominant position, easily breaking through such negligible obstacles as were placed in their path . . . It did not require a fundamental revolution to push the democratic movement aside in Japan, and, indeed, no such event occurred'. As it was, even then 'the demise of

[1] For some general reflections on this aspect of American leadership from the 1890s onwards, see J. P. Lovell, *Foreign Policy in Perspective* (New York, 1970), 192.

[2] G. Liska, *Imperial America: The International Politics of Primacy* (Baltimore, 1967).

[3] See, e.g., Morley, *Dilemmas of Growth*.

civilian government was not immediate, nor was military control ever complete or wholly unified'.[1]

The second qualification may also be stated briefly, since it has been introduced in the preceding chapter. It is that it would be rash to leap from an awareness of the depth and strength of Japan's defiant nationalism in 1931 to the conclusion which Stimson, the International Tribunal and others were happy to accept in later years,[2] that a direct road of carefully planned guilt on Japan's part led from there to a great-power war in 1941, or that such a war was 'inevitable'. That there was an underlying drift in the direction of solving Japan's problems by violence is clear; but for all their rejection of the existing order of things and their 'quest for autonomy', her military and civilian leaders alike remained greatly influenced by developments in Europe and the Soviet Union. Had events elsewhere taken a different direction, it is doubtful whether the Pacific war would have occurred at the time and in the form it did; nor can it be laid down with certainty that by 1933 its very occurrence had become inevitable, however high the probability may seem. Moreover if one has to find 'roads', then it would be in many ways more sound to start one, not in 1931, but in the period immediately following the Washington Conference, when all the major powers in the Far East failed to cooperate in establishing a clear framework for international relations in the area. Alternatively, one might choose to start with Perry or Theodore Roosevelt and proceed, via Stimson's thoughts on America's national destiny and international role in the Far East, to that country's defeat in Vietnam.

In this connection there also arises the question posed at the beginning of the book,[3] concerning the contribution of the Western powers themselves to the deeper causes of the Pacific war. For the manifest act of aggression that took place in 1941 and the barbarities of the Japanese 'new order' that followed cannot serve to divorce Japan's policies up to that point from the attitudes, assumptions and actions of those states that had dominated the area from the middle of the nineteenth century. Even a look at a few aspects and episodes of the final period before Pearl Harbour is sufficient reminder of the need to avoid a preconceived and all-embracing explanation of the conspiracy variety. During the secret negotiations of 1941, for example, might it not be suggested that the Roosevelt Administration, like the Japanese, were in several respects inflexible and unwilling to see the other's point of view, rejecting more imaginative and constructive courses such as those proposed by Harry Dexter White? (A similar question must hang over the reception in Washington of indications that Japanese leaders were seeking to end the war in the summer of 1945.)[4] If Japanese

---

[1] Scalapino, *Democracy and the Party Movement*, 346, 243. Cf. Hayashi in Morley, *Dilemmas of Growth*; Butow, *Japan's Decision to Surrender*, passim, and Scalapino's introduction to 'The Road to the Pacific War', vol. IV, part 2.

[2] See above, 5, 8.   [3] See above, 6.

[4] Butow, *Japan's Decision to Surrender*, 103 ff. It should be noted that Stimson, who had so often misjudged the Japanese, did (vainly) suggest that the Potsdam declaration should contain a statement to the effect that the Allies did not exclude the possibility of a constitutional monarchy for Japan under the existing dynasty, thus making it easier for Tokyo to accept the terms of surrender. Ibid, 140.

admirals had already adopted a dangerous circularity of thought over the need to drive southwards (such a move to obtain raw materials would make a major war inevitable; a major war was inevitable and therefore these resources must be seized), had not their opposite numbers in Washington, partly in order to justify their own existence, long since argued in similar fashion (war with Japan was highly likely, partly as a result of America's retention of the Philippines; the Philippines must be retained as a vital base for use in the coming war with Japan)? And whilst there was this fatalistic belief in the inevitability of war on each side,[1] was it not a basic political requirement of the American admirals that Japan should 'adopt a government similar to ours and (become) actuated by ideals in harmony with ours'? 'Securus judicat orbis terrarum,' wrote Augustine; for Stimson and Mahan's disciples in Washington it was the judgement and standards of America that were unshakable, and such a conclusion, while of the kind fit to carry John Henry Newman towards the Church of Rome,[2] is not the basis for finding a modus vivendi between nations.

A simple assertion of Japanese guilt and sole responsibility becomes all the more difficult when one examines the setting from the nineteenth century onwards. The Western powers had then arrived at Japan's door and at gunpoint had invited her at best to enter into a game of international politics that was of their designing and on the basis of which they were completing the acquisition of the major share of trade and resources of the East ('we have got most of the world already,' in Chatfield's words, 'or the best parts of it . . .') Although one can quarrel with certain details, there was substance, in other words, in Mr. Justice Pal's observation at the Tokyo trial that

> when Japan came on the field there had already been the Anglo-American economic world order leaving no space for expansion to any new power. From its very nature this did not admit of any sharing with others . . . Even peaceful pursuit on the part of a new aspirant would thus involve some apprehension from these privileged participants, especially when 'their whole conception of the evolution of human affairs from a distant past towards a distant future was that the future belonged to them only', and that others had 'fulfilled their destined function in history by ministering to the divinely appointed advancement of them'.[3]

For all her late start, however, and despite having been tricked out of part of her booty in China in the 1890s, Japan had succeeded by 1918 in playing the West's game to considerable effect. At this point the West then declared that the nature of that game was to be changed, a transformation which as we have seen was accepted only with reluctance in Tokyo, even by an honorary Westerner like Shidehara.[4] Nor could it escape Japan's attention that by this change of rules the major Western powers did not divest themselves of their own empires—indeed, it could be thought that they were seeking to preserve them by new means—or renounce the fruits of past aggression. As Pal was to observe,

[1] See Heinrichs, 'The Role of the U.S. Navy', Hakone Conference paper.
[2] J. H. Newman, *Apologia pro Vita Sua* (London, 1912), 120–1.
[3] IMTFE, *Judgement*, vols. 157–8, 732–4.
[4] See above, 22.

The iniquity, of course, was that of their fathers who had had recourse to the sword for this purpose. But perhaps it is right to say that 'the man of violence cannot both genuinely repent of his violence and permanently profit by it'.[1]

Nor were overt and implicit assumptions of racial superiority abandoned within this new and Western order of international brotherhood, while the major Western powers showed little willingness to desist from interfering in what they saw as their own areas of 'vital interest', any more than they were to do (in Central America and the Middle East, for example) after condemning Japan over Manchuria. Moreover when Japan again became all too successful, this time in that open-door type of commercial competition that was envisaged when the old order in the Far East was buried at the Washington Conference, then, piecemeal, the game was further modified and doors under the control of others were rapidly shut in her face.

This is not to argue for an inverted and equally absurd 'conspiracy' explanation whereby the Western powers become solely responsible for the belligerent nationalism that developed in Japan or for that country's act of aggression in 1941. It does mean, however, that by their selfishness, short-sightedness and hypocrisy, and not least by their often-unconscious racial arrogance, those Western powers had lent strength to the argument of extremists that Japan, too, faced as she was by apparently immense demographic and socio-economic problems, must carve out her own share of the resources of an unsympathetic world. In Professor Iriye's words, 'What united the military, the nationalist groups, and the bulk of the intellectuals [in the 1930s] was the shared perception of the 1920s as a decade of futile attempts at peaceful expansion through international cooperation.'[2] It means also that this reaction of Japan's was in part only one aspect of a widespread Asian revolt, both spiritual and material, against an Occidental world order, political, economic and cultural.[3]

Nowhere had Western superiority and assumptions of superiority appeared more manifest than in China; yet there, too, despite the dreams of a Stimson or the dogmatism of Shanghai expatriates, the movement of self-confidence and self-assertion was gathering momentum. The outburst of 4 May 1919 had been of far greater significance than the haggling over Shantung that had gone on in Paris; for all the hopes reposed by Western governments in Chiang Kai-shek and other nationalist leaders, the ideological inspiration of Western, liberal democracy was already a spent force where the Chinese revolution was concerned.[4] By their victory over Russia in 1904–5 the Japanese had earlier hastened the decline in the prestige of non-Asians; now, in 1931, with the European imperial powers hopelessly over-stretched, Japan had again appeared to demonstrate what the West itself had taught in the previous century, that in the last resort power grew out of the barrel of a gun, and that the rest was so much gloss.[5] In the

[1] IMTFE, *Judgment*, vols. 157–8, 279.
[2] Morley, *Dilemmas of Growth*, 107.
[3] See above, 28–9, and on India, for example, Pandey, 21 ff.
[4] See, e.g., Fitzgerald, 58.
[5] Other factors, not least self-confidence, had of course greatly assisted Britain to hold India, for example.

process, she also helped to harden the nature of that Chinese revolution that in the end was to reject her as successfully as it rejected the West: the sole declaration of war during the Manchurian crisis was the one pronounced against the Japanese by Mao Tse-tung and Chu Teh in April 1932 in the name of the Kiangsi Soviet, and in retrospect it was as significant as the failure of others to follow suit.

For the United States, pursuing at last Stimson's vision of a Pax Americana in the area, the crisis of these years was eventually followed by an entirely new scale of involvement in the Far East for a while. Nevertheless, the defiant action of the Japanese, if not a 'turning point', constituted a major landmark in the decline of the West in Asia. For the seekers of roads or discrete periods of history, in fact, there would be some validity in one which commenced with this overt challenge to the Western order of things in 1931, and ended only eighteen years later with the arrival in power of a new and assertive government in Peking, the British already gone from India and the Dutch and French entering upon the death throes of their empires in the East. As with the Suez operation in another sphere of Western decline, there was the Korean intervention and also the flailing conservatism of Vietnam to come.[1] In terms of four hundred years of Western dominance, however, they were little more than a postscript.

For the European imperial powers in the post-war years, a solution to the growing dilemma of how to bridge the gap between resources and commitments had in part been forced and hastened by the defeat handed out to them by Japan during the early stages of the Pacific war. For the United States there had been a shock of a different kind, in what seemed the rejection of her by the Chinese protégé on whose side—not, as was sometimes believed, on whose behalf—she had fought that same war. (There were, of course, some notable opponents of this ignorant reaction, especially within the State Department and in academic circles concerned with the Far East.) Thereafter, the Japanese themselves appeared to offer consolation to some crusaders—new protégés who General MacArthur had no doubt were 'thirsty for guidance and inspiration', eager for the 'democracy and Christianity' that he had come in triumph to bring them in 1945.[2] Yet time was to reveal that these people, too, might not be nascent Americans after all, and long before defeat had been tacitly accepted in Vietnam, disillusion had begun to cloud over what remained of Stimson's bright vision for the East as a whole. Meanwhile, although the extreme isolationism of the inter-war years was now more impracticable than ever, the spirit of Hoover, even more than that of his Secretary of State, perhaps, continued to find expression in what has been described as the desire to make the world fit for America to leave it.

Following the Pacific war, the 'lesson' of 1931 and subsequent episodes had also brought the United States into the new world organisation that was founded on the ruins of the League. Here again, however, there was a large measure of disillusionment to come, and while the United Nations Charter showed many advances over the Covenant of 1919, it, too, was soon meeting

[1] There were obviously a considerable variety of conscious Western motives in each case.

[2] Kennan, *Memoirs, 1925–1950*, 384.

the strain of having been designed to prevent a repetition of the war that had brought the organisation into existence in the first place. Within ten years, there was talk of a 'new United Nations' evolving piecemeal.[1] The flood of new members after 1955; the 1960 Declaration on the Granting of Independence to Colonial Countries;[2] the triumphant entry of Communist China in 1971: all were far removed from the hopes and assumptions of the Secretary of State who not long before had found only one Filipino politician with a sufficiently Anglo-Saxon mind to be capable of self-rule, and who had looked to his own country, together with Britain and France perhaps, to police the world.

In Geneva, where the old League headquarters still stands in faded gentility by the lake, the new organisation, faced with major issues that in many cases had scarcely begun to be perceived in the 1930s,[3] labours on in the Palais des Nations on the hill above. In the sphere of international power politics and peace-keeping, heavy demands continue to be made on the faith of those who looked to the United Nations to triumph where its predecessor had failed, and many of the expectations that were present in 1945, as in 1919, can easily be shown in retrospect to have been far removed from reality. It remains to be seen whether shocks like the one delivered by the Japanese in 1931 can help produce a more modest and well-founded conception of the role of such organisations, without at the same time the complete loss of that vision which had led Gilbert Murray, Raymond Fosdick and others to join Leonard Woolf after 1914–18 in refusing to yield, 'even to the logic of events'; to pursue, with him, 'the shadow of a shadow of a dream'.[4]

[1] See, e.g., S. Hoffmann, 'The Role of International Organisation', in *International Organisation*, 1956, III.

[2] See, e.g., R. Emerson, 'Colonialism and the U.N.', in *International Organisation*, 1965.

[3] See, e.g., *Le Monde*, 16, 17 October, 1971.

[4] L. Woolf, *The Journey Not The Arrival Matters* (London, 1969), 168–72.

BIBLIOGRAPHIES

HISTORICAL SOURCES

A. *Unpublished Material*

1. Official documents.
   (a) International.
      International Military Tribunal for the Far East, Proceedings, Exhibits and Judgement. (Imperial War Museum, London.)
      League of Nations Archives, files P33–4, R 1862–76; 3309–10, 3606, 3609–12, 3624–6, 3631, 5680–5, 5706–7, 5713–17, 6228; S 29–50. (Palais des Nations, Geneva.)
      League of Nations: Directors' Meetings: Papers and Confidential Circulars (U.N. Library, Geneva.)
   (b) France.
      Ministry of Foreign Affairs Archives. (Quai d'Orsay, Paris.)*
   (c) Germany.
      Foreign Ministry photostat records:
      Büro des Reichsministers, Serial 3088H.
      Büro Staatssekretar von Bulöw, Serial 4619.
      Büro des Staatssekretars, Serial K4620.
      Handakten Ministerial—Direktor Trautmann, Serial 5551H.
      Abteilung IV China, Serials K2049, K2088, K2264, L 1780.
      Büro Reichsministers Völkerbund, Serial 3147.
      (Foreign Office Library, London.)
   (d) Great Britain.
      Prime Minister's Office files, PM 1.
      Committee of Imperial Defence, minutes, CAB 2.
      C.I.D. sub-committees, CAB 16.
      Disarmament Committee and Defence Review, CAB 21.
      Cabinet Conclusions, CAB 23.
      Cabinet documents, CAB 24.
      Cabinet Committees on Far East, Reparations and Debts, Disarmament, War Debts, Arms Industry, India, Indian Cotton, Japanese Trade, CAB 27.
      Imperial Conference, 1930, CAB 32, with Singapore Base Committee in CAB 27.
      Admiralty, General Correspondence, Far East, ADM 125.
      Board of Admiralty, Minutes and Memoranda, ADM 167.

* See relevant note in the Preface

Foreign Office files, FO 371 series.
Dominions Office files, DO 3, DO 35.
Treasury files, T 160. (All Public Record Office, London.)
(e) Netherlands.
Archives of the Ministry of Foreign Affairs, Colonial Ministry and Council of Ministers (The Hague.)*
(d) United States.
Department of State: decimal files 500 A15A4; 793.94; 793.94 Commission; 793.94 P.C.; 811.113; 841.00; 851.00. Various documents from 033.5111; 500 A4; 500C; 693.001; 711.94; 851.20; 893.113; 894.00. (National Archives, Washington, D.C.).
United States Navy Department: General Records, Office of the Secretary, General Correspondence. (National Archives).
United States Navy General Board: War Plans, Hearings, Studies, Arms Limitation. (U.S. Navy Operational Archives, Washington Dockyard).
Joint Army-Navy Board, Record Group 225 (National Archives).

2. Private papers (names as in 1931–33).
(a) Great Britain.
Stanley Baldwin (Cambridge University Library).
Alexander Cadogan (FO 800/293, Public Record Office).
Viscount Cecil (Cecil of Chelwood Papers, British Museum).
Sir Austen Chamberlain (Birmingham University).
Neville Chamberlain (Mrs. Dorothy Lloyd).
Admiral Sir Ernle Chatfield (Southampton University).
China Association (China Association, London).
King George V (Royal Archives, Windsor Castle).
Sir Maurice Hankey (Churchill College, Cambridge).
Arthur Henderson (FO 800/283–4, Public Record Office).
Sir Samuel Hoare (Templewood Papers, Cambridge University Library).
Admiral Sir Howard Kelly (National Maritime Museum, Greenwich).
Ramsay MacDonald (David Marquand, M.P., and Public Record Office).
Kingsley Martin (University of Sussex).
Gilbert Murray (Bodleian Library, Oxford).
Lord Reading (FO 800/226, Public Record Office).
Sir John Simon (FO 800/285–88, Public Record Office).
Sir John Simon (private collection, Institute of Historical Research, University of London).
Sir Robert Vansittart (Churchill College, Cambridge).
Lord Weir (Churchill College, Cambridge).
(b) United States.
Jane Addams (Swarthmore College, Peace Collection).

* See relevant note in the Preface

Newton D. Baker (Library of Congress).
Emily Greene Balch (Swarthmore College, Peace Collection).
William E. Borah (Library of Congress).
William R. Castle (Hoover Library, West Branch, Iowa.)*
Norman H. Davis (Library of Congress).
Charles G. Dawes (Northwestern University, Evanston).
Dorothy Detzer (Swarthmore College Peace Collection).
W. Cameron Forbes (Library of Congress).
Joseph C. Grew (Houghton Library, Harvard University).
Herbert Hoover (Hoover Library, West Branch, Iowa).
Stanley K. Hornbeck (Hoover Institute, Stanford University).
Cordell Hull (Library of Congress).
Nelson T. Johnson (Library of Congress).
General Frank R. McCoy (Library of Congress).
Ogden Mills (Library of Congress).
J. Pierrepont Moffat (Houghton Library, Harvard University).
William Phillips (Houghton Library).
Admiral William V. Pratt (U.S. Navy Operational Archives,
     Washington).
Elihu Root (Library of Congress).
Henry L. Stimson (Stirling Memorial Library, Yale University).
Arthur Sweetser (Library of Congress).
Admiral Montgomery M. Taylor (Library of Congress).
Ray Lyman Wilbur (Hoover Memorial Library, West Branch).
Hugh R. Wilson (Hoover Memorial Library, West Branch).
Women's International League for Peace and Freedom, U.S.
     Section. (Swarthmore College Peace Collection).

B. *Published Official Documents.*

  1. League of Nations.
       Official Journal, 1931–1933 (Geneva, 1931–1933).
       Official Journal, Special Supplements, Nos. 93, 101, 102, 104, 111,
          112, 115 (Geneva, 1931–1933).
       Disarmament: Preparation For the General Conference (Geneva,
          1931).
  2. France.
       Documents Diplomatiques Français, 1ʳᵉ Série:
       Tome I (Paris, 1964).
       Tome II (Paris, 1966).
       Tome III (Paris, 1967).
  3. Germany.
       Documents on German Foreign Policy, 1918–1945, series C, vol. I
          (London, 1957).

* Since his death, Castle's diary has been closed until 1980. I have therefore had to cite passages referred to by those few historians who had already been permitted to see it. The West Branch collection consists of correspondence only.

4. Great Britain.
> *Documents on British Foreign Policy, 1919–1939, second series:*
>> *vol. I*   (London, 1946).
>> *vol. II*   (London, 1947).
>> *vol. III* (London, 1948).
>> *vol. IV* (London, 1950).
>> *vol. V*   (London, 1956).
>> *vol. VII* (London, 1958).
>> *vol. VIII* (London, 1960).
>> *vol. IX* (London, 1965).
>> *vol. X*   (London, 1969).
>> *vol. XI* (London, 1970).

5. United States.
> *Foreign Relations of the United States:*
>> *1931, vols. I, II, III* (Washington, 1946–).
>> *1932, vols. I, III, IV, V* (Washington, 1948–).
>> *1933, vols. I, III* (Washington, 1950–).
>> *Japan, 1931–1941, I* (Washington, 1946).
> *Annual Report of the Secretary of the Navy:*
>> *1930–1933* (Washington, 1931–33).
> *Annual Report of the Secretary of the Treasury:*
>> *1930–1933* (Washington, 1931–34).

C. *Parliamentary Debates.*

> *Annales de la Chambre des Députés. Débats, novembre, 1931–avril, 1933* (7 vols. Paris, 1933–34).
> *Congressional Record, 72nd Congress, vols. 75–77* (Washington, 1932–1933).
> *Hansard, House of Commons, vols. 256–278* (London, 1932–33).
> *Hansard, House of Lords, vols. 85–87* (London, 1932–33).
> *Rijksbegrooting voor het Dienstjaar 1932, III* (The Hague, 1933).

D. *Press.*

> Royal Institute of International Affairs, London: Press-cuttings Library, 12 boxes.
> *North China Herald*, July 1931–June 1933 (Cambridge University Library).
> *New York Times, Washington Post, San Francisco Examiner, Chicago Daily Tribune* (Library of Congress, Press Library microfilms).

E. *Other Primary Sources.*

> *China Year Book, 1931–1932* (Shanghai, 1932).
> Gallup Poll Archives, London (for the poll on Tientsin and Japan, 1939, by kind permission of Dr. Henry Durant).
> League of Nations, *Armaments Year Book, 1930–1931* (Geneva, 1931); *1932–1933* (Geneva, 1933).

F. *Memoirs, Collected Letters, Published Diaries, etc.*

Amery, L. S., *My Political Life, vol. III* (London, 1955).
Angell, N., *After All* (London, 1951).
Cecil, Viscount, *A Great Experiment* (London, 1941).
Chatfield, Lord, *It Might Happen Again* (London, 1947).
Dawes, C. G., *Journal As Ambassador to Great Britain* (New York, 1939).
Detzer, D., *Appointment on the Hill* (New York, 1948).
Feis, H., *Seen From the E.A.* (New York, 1966).
    1933: Characters in Crisis (Boston, 1966).
Fosdick, R. B., *Letters on the League of Nations* (Princeton, 1966).
Grew, J. C., *Ten Years in Japan* (London, 1944).
Herriot, E., *Jadis, vol. 2* (Paris, 1952).
Hoover, H., *Memoirs, 1920–1933* (*London*, 1952).
Hull, C., *Memoirs, vol. 1* (London, 1948).
James, R. R. (ed.), *Memoirs of a Conservative* (London, 1969).
Jones, T., *A Diary With Letters* (London, 1954).
Liddell Hart, B., *Memoirs, vol. I* (London, 1965).
Lippmann, W., *Interpretations, 1931–1933* (London, 1934).
    Interpretations, 1933–1935 (New York, 1935).
Martin, K., *Father Figures* (Harmondsworth, 1969).
    Editor (Harmondsworth, 1969).
Murray, G., *An Unfinished Autobiography* (London, 1960).
Myers, W. S., *The State Papers and Other Public Writings of Herbert Hoover* (2 vols., New York, 1934).
Nixon, E. (ed.), *Franklin D. Roosevelt and Foreign Affairs, vol. I* (Cambridge, Mass., 1969).
Paul-Boncour, J., *Entre Deux Guerres, vol. 2* (Paris, 1945).
Selby, W., *Diplomatic Twilight* (London, 1953).
Shigemitsu, M., *Japan and Her Destiny* (London, 1958).
Shotwell, J. T., *On the Rim of the Abyss* (New York, 1937).
Stimson, H. L., *The Far Eastern Crisis* (New York, 1936).
Stimson, H. L. and Bundy, M., *On Active Service in Peace and War* (New York, 1948).
Temperley, A. C., *The Whispering Gallery of Europe* (London, 1939).
Vansittart, Lord, *The Mist Procession* (London, 1958).
Welles, S., *Time for Decision* (London, 1944).
Wellesley, V., *Diplomacy in Fetters* (London, 1944).
Wilbur, R. L., *Memoirs* (Stanford, 1960).
Wilson, H., *Diplomat Between Wars* (New York, 1941).

G. *Secondary Works*

Adler, S., *The Isolationist Impulse* (New York, 1960).
Allen, G. C., *A Short Economic History of Japan* (London, 1962).
Allen, G. C. and Donnithorne, A. G., *Western Enterprise in Far Eastern Economic Development* (London, 1962).
Almond, G. A., *The American People and Foreign Policy* (New York, 1960).

Azcarté, P. de (ed.), *William Martin: Un Grand Journaliste de Genève* (Geneva, 1970).

Baer, G. W., *The Coming of the Italian–Ethiopian War* (Cambridge, Mass., 1967).

Barros, J., *The Corfu Incident* (Princeton, 1965).
    Betrayal from Within (New Haven, 1969).
    The League of Nations and the Great Powers (Oxford, 1970).

Bassett, R., *Democracy and Foreign Policy* (London, 1952).

Beloff, M., *Imperial Sunset, vol. I* (London, 1969).

Bergamini, D., *Japan's Imperial Conspiracy* (London, 1971).

Bishop, D. G., *The Administration of British Foreign Relations* (Syracuse, 1961).

Bloch, K., *Germany's Interests and Policies in the Far East* (New York, 1940).

Borg, D., *American Policy and the Chinese Revolution, 1925–1928* (New York, 1947).
    The United States and the Far Eastern Crisis of 1933–1938 (Cambridge, Mass., 1964).
  (ed.) *Historians and American Far Eastern Policy* (New York, 1966).

Braisted, W. R., *The United States Navy in the Pacific, 1909–1922* (Austin, Texas, 1971).

Butow, R. J., *Japan's Decision to Surrender* (Stanford, 1954).
    Tojo and the Coming of War (Princeton, 1961).

Byas, H., *Government by Assassination* (London, 1943).

Carlton, D., *MacDonald Versus Henderson* (London, 1970).

Carr, E. H., *The 20 Years' Crisis* (London, 1962).

Clyde, R. H., *The Far East* (Englewood Cliffs, N.J., 1958).

Cohen, W. I., *America's Response to China* (New York, 1971).

Colton, J., *Léon Blum* (New York, 1966).

Craig, G., and Gilbert, F. (eds.), *The Diplomats* (Princeton, 1953).

Crowley, J., *Japan's Quest for Autonomy* (Princeton, 1966).

Current, R. N., *Secretary Stimson: A Study in Statecraft* (New Brunswick, 1954).

De Conde, A. (ed.), *Isolation and Security* (Durham, N. Carolina, 1957).

Divine, R., *The Illusion of Neutrality* (Chicago, 1962).

Drechsler, K., *Deutschland–China–Japan, 1933–1939* (Berlin, 1964).

Duroselle, J-B., *La Politique Extérieure de la France, de 1914 à 1945* (Paris. 1965).

Eayres, L., *In Defence of Canada, vol. I* (Toronto, 1964).

Edwardes, M., *Asia in the European Age* (London, 1961).

Ellis, H. S., *French and German Investments in China* (Honolulu, 1929).

Erickson, J., *The Soviet High Command* (London, 1962).

Farley, M., *America's Stake in the Far East* (New York, 1936).

Ferrell, R. H., *Peace In Their Time* (New Haven, 1952).
    American Diplomacy In the Great Depression (New Haven, 1957).
    The American Secretaries of State and their Diplomacy, XI (New York, 1963).

Fishel, W. R., *The End of Extraterritoriality in China* (Berkeley, 1952).

Fitzgerald, C. P., *The Birth of Communist China* (Harmondsworth, 1964).

        The Chinese View of Their Place in the World (London, 1964).

Fleming, D. F., *The United States and World Organization, 1920–1933* (New York, 1938).

Geneva Special Studies, vol. II Nos. 10–12; vol. III, No. 1 (Geneva, 1931–32).

Ghébali, V-Y., *Les délégations permanentes auprès de la Société des Nations* (Geneva, 1969).

Griswold, A. W., *The Far Eastern Policy of the United States* (New York, 1937).

Gull, E. M., *British Economic Interests in the Far East* (London, 1943).

Hall, D. G., *A. History of South East Asia* (London, 1968).

Hancock, W. K., and Gowing, M., *British War Economy* (London, 1949).

Heinrichs, W. H., *American Ambassador* (Boston, 1965).

Hinsley, F. H., *Power and the Pursuit of Peace* (Cambridge, 1967).

Hofstadter, R., *The American Political Tradition* (London, 1962).

Hornbeck, S. K., *The United States In The Far East* (Boston, 1942).

Hudson, G., *The Far East In World Politics* (London, 1939).

Hulen, B. D., *Inside The State Department* (New York, 1939).

Huntington, S. P., *The Soldier and the State* (New York, 1957).

Ike, N., *Japan's Decision For War* (Stanford, 1967).

Iriye, A., *After Imperialism* (Cambridge, Mass., 1965).

        Across The Pacific (New York, 1967).

Isaacs, H., *Scratches On Our Minds* (New York, 1963).

Jones, F. C., *Manchuria Since 1931* (London, 1949).

Kennedy, M. D., *The Estrangement of Great Britain and Japan, 1917–1935* (Manchester, 1969).

Kennan, G., *American Diplomacy, 1900–1950* (New York, 1951).

Kirby, S. W., *The War Against Japan, vol. I* (London, 1957).

Kuehl, W. F., *Seeking World Order* (Nashville, Tenn., 1969).

Lattimore, O., *Manchuria, Cradle of Conflict* (New York, 1932).

League Year Book, 1933 (London, 1933).

Levy, R., *French Interests and Possessions in the Far East* (New York, 1941).

Lippmann, W., *United States War Aims* (London, 1944).

Lohbeck, D., *Patrick J. Hurley* (Chicago, 1956).

Lowe, P., *Great Britain and Japan, 1911–1915* (London, 1969).

Louis, W. R., *British Strategy In the Far East, 1919–1939* (Oxford, 1971).

Lyons, E., *Herbert Hoover: A Biography* (New York, 1964).

Madariaga, S. de, *Victors, Beware* (London, 1946).

Mansergh, N., *Survey of British Commonwealth Affairs: Problems of External Policy, 1931–1939* (London, 1952).

Martin, L. W., *Peace Without Victory* (New Haven, 1958).

Middlemas, K., and Barnes, J., *Baldwin* (London, 1969).
Mitsubishi Economic Research Bureau, *Japan's Trade and Industry* (London, 1936).
Morgenthau, H., *In Defense of the National Interest* (New York, 1951).
Morison, E. E., *Turmoil and Tradition* (Boston, 1960).
Morley, J. W. (ed.), *Dilemmas of Growth in Pre-War Japan* (Princeton, 1972).
Morton, L., *Strategy and Command: The First Two Years* (Washington D.C., 1962).
Mowat, C. L., *Britain Between The Wars* (London, 1956).
Myers, W. S., and Newton, W. H., *The Hoover Administration* (New York, 1936).
Needham, J., *Within The Four Seas* (London, 1969).
Neumann, W. L., *America Encounters Japan* (Baltimore, 1963).
Nicholls, A. J., *Weimar and the Rise of Hitler* (London, 1968).
Nish, I., *The Anglo-Japanese Alliance* (London, 1966).
　　　Alliance in Decline: A Study In Anglo-Japanese Relations, 1908–1923 (London, 1972).
O'Connor, R. G., *Perilous Equilibrium* (Lawrence, Kansas, 1962).
Ogata, S. N., *Defiance In Manchuria* (Berkeley, 1964).
Osgood, R., *Ideals And Self-Interest In America's Foreign Policy* (Chicago, 1953).
Paige, G. D., *The Korean Decision* (New York, 1968).
Panikkar, K. M., *Asia and Western Dominance* (London, 1953).
Pearson, D. and Brown, C., *The Diplomatic Game* (New York, 1935).
Potter, D. M., *The People of Plenty* (Chicago, 1954).
Pratt, J., *War And Peace in China* (London, 1943).
Pratt, J. W., *The American Secretaries of State And Their Diplomacy, XII.* (New York, 1964).
Presseisen, E. L., *Germany and Japan: A Study In Totalitarian Diplomacy, 1933–1941* (The Hague, 1958).
The Problems of Peace, Third to Eighth Series (London, 1929–1934).
Rappaport, A., *The Navy League of the United States* (Detroit, 1962).
　　　Henry L. Stimson and Japan, 1931–1933 (Chicago, 1963).
Remer, C. F., *American Investments In China* (Honolulu, 1929).
　　　Foreign Investments In China (New York, 1933).
Renouvin, P., *La Question d'Extrême Orient* (Paris, 1953).
Robertson, E. M., *Hitler's Pre-War Policy and Military Plans* (London, 1963).
　　　(ed.), *The Origins of the Second World War* (London, 1971).
Romasco, U. A., *The Poverty of Abundance* (London, 1968).
Roseveare, H., *The Treasury* (London, 1969).
Roskill, S. W., *Naval Policy Between The Wars, vol. I* (London, 1968).
　　　Hankey: Man of Secrets, vol. II (London, 1972).
Rovine, A. W., *The First Fifty Years: The Secretary-General In World Politics* (Leyden, 1970).

Royal Institute of International Affairs, *The Future of the League of Nations* (New York, 1936).

International Sanctions (London, 1938).

Nationalism (London, 1939).

Scalapino, R. A., *Democracy and the Party Movement In Pre-War Japan* (Berkeley, 1962).

Schlote, W., *British Overseas Trade From 1700 to the 1930s* (Oxford, 1952).

Schram, S., *Mao Tse-tung* (Harmondsworth, 1966).

Smith, S. R., *The Manchurian Crisis, 1931–1932* (New York, 1948).

Soulié, M., *La Vie Politique d'Edouard Herriot* (Paris, 1962).

Sprout, H. and M., *Toward A New Order of Sea Power* (London, 1943).

Steiner, Z., *The Foreign Office and Foreign Policy, 1898–1914* (Cambridge, 1969).

Storry, R., *The Double Patriots* (London, 1957).

Suarez, G., *Briand, vol. VI* (Paris, 1952).

Taiheiyo senso e no michi: kaisen gaiko-shi (Tokyo, 1962–63).

Takeuchi, T., *War And Diplomacy In the Japanese Empire* (London, 1936).

Tang, P. S., *Russian and Soviet Policy in Manchuria and Outer Mongolia, 1911–1931* (Durham, N.C., 1959).

Tang Tsou, *America's Failure in China, 1941–50* (Chicago, 1962).

Taylor, A. J. P., *English History, 1941–1945* (Oxford, 1965).

Teichman, E., *Affairs of China* (London, 1938).

Toynbee, A. J., *Survey of International Affairs, 1931; 1932; 1933* (London, 1932, '33, '34).

Tuleja, T. V., *Statesmen and Admirals* (New York, 1963).

Tupper, E., and, McReynolds G., *Japan in American Public Opinion* (New York, 1937).

Varg, P., *Missionaries, Chinese, and Diplomats* (Princeton, 1958).

The Making of A Myth: The United States and China, 1897–1912 (East Lansing, Michigan, 1968).

Walters, F. P., *A History of the League of Nations* (London, 1967).

Warner, G., *Pierre Laval and the Eclipse of France* (London, 1968).

Watt, D. C., *Personalities and Policies* (London, 1965).

Wheeler, G. E., *Prelude to Pearl Harbor* (Columbia, Missouri, 1963).

Wilbur, R. L., and Hyde, A. M., *The Hoover Policies* (New York, 1937).

Willoughby, W. W., *The Sino-Japanese Controversy and the League of Nations* (Baltimore, 1935).

Wilson, A., *World Security: An Essay on Sanctions* (London, 1931).

Winkler, H. R., *The League of Nations Movement In Great Britain, 1914–1919* (Metuchen, N.J., 1967).

Wint, G., *The British In Asia* (New York, 1954).

Wohlstetter, R., *Pearl Harbor: Warning and Decision* (Stanford, 1962).

Wright, R. G., *The American Tariff and Oriental Trade* (Chicago, 1931).

Yoshihashi, T., *Conspiracy at Mukden* (New Haven, 1963).

Zimmern, A., *The League of Nations and the Rule of Law* (London, 1939).

H. *Articles.*

Akagi, R., 'Japan's Economic Relations With China', *Pacific Affairs*, June 1931.

Asada, S., 'Japan's "Special Interests" and the Washington Conference, 1921–2', *American Historical Review*, LXVII, October 1961.

Bailey, T. A., 'The Root-Takahira Agreement of 1908', *Pacific Historical Review*, IX, 1940.

Benes, E., 'The League of Nations: Successes and Failures', *Foreign Affairs*, October 1932.

Burns, R. D., 'Inspection of Mandates, 1919–1941', *Pacific Historical Review*, XXXVII, 1968.

Chay, J., 'The Taft-Katsura Memorandum of 1905', *Pacific Historical Review*, XXXVII, 1968.

Current, R. N., 'The Stimson Doctrine and the Hoover Doctrine', *American Historical Review*, LIX, 1953–54.

Edwards, P. G., 'The Foreign Office and Fascism', *Journal of Contemporary History*, vol. 5, No. 2, 1970.

Green, F., 'The Military View of American National Policy, 1904–1940', *American Historical Review*, LXVI, No. 2, 1961.

Hecht, R. A., 'Great Britain and the Stimson Note of January 7th, 1932', *Pacific Historical Review*, May 1969.

Levy, R., 'Indo-China in 1931–1932', *Pacific Affairs*, March 1932.

Marder, A., 'The Royal Navy and the Ethiopian Crisis of 1935–36', *American Historical Review*, LXXV, No. 5, 1970.

Morton, L., 'War Plan Orange: Evolution of A Strategy', *World Politics*, January 1959.

Pratt, L., 'The Anglo-American Naval Conversations of January, 1938', *International Affairs*, vol. 47, No. 4, 1971.

Pratt, W. V., 'Our Naval Policy', *U.S. Naval Institute Proceedings*, vol. 58, 1932.

Radek, K., 'The War In The Far East: A Soviet View', *Foreign Affairs*, July 1932.

Sauvy, A., 'The Economic Crisis of the 1930s in France', *Journal of Contemporary History*, vol. 4, No. 4, 1969.

Richardson, H. W., 'The Economic Significance of the Great Depression In Britain', *Journal of Contemporary History*, vol. 4, No. 4, 1969.

Thorne, C. G., 'The Shanghai Crisis of 1932: The Basis of British Policy', *American Historical Review*, LXXV, No. 6, 1970.
　　　　'The Quest for Arms Embargoes: Failure in 1933', *Journal of Contemporary History*, vol. 5, No. 4, 1970.
　　　　'Viscount Cecil, The Government and the Far Eastern Crisis of 1931', *Historical Journal*, vol. 14, No. 4, 1971.

Treat, P. J., 'Shanghai, January 28th, 1932', *Pacific Historical Review*, September 1940.

Vandenbosch, A., 'Nationalism In Netherlands East India', *Pacific Affairs*, December 1931.

'Economic and Administrative Policy in the Dutch East Indies', *Pacific Affairs*, October 1932.

Vinson, J. C., 'The Imperial Conference of 1921 and the Anglo-Japanese Alliance', *Pacific Historical Review*, XXXI, 1962.

Wheeler, G. E., 'Republican Philippines Policy, 1921–1933', *Pacific Historical Review*, XXVIII, 1959.

'Isolated Japan', *Pacific Historical Review*, XXX, 1961.

Wright, Q., 'The Stimson Note of January 7th, 1932', and 'When Does War Exist?', *American Journal of International Law*, vol. 26, 1932.

'The Meaning of the Pact of Paris', and 'Some Legal Aspects of the Far Eastern Situation', *American Journal of International Law*, vol. 27, 1933.

I. *Unpublished Papers, etc.*

Aghnides, Th., Oral Testimony (Carnegie Foundation for International Peace, European Centre, Geneva).

Northedge, F. S., 'British Opinion, the League, and the United Nations' (paper prepared for a Chatham House study group, 1953).

Papers prepared for the conference of American and Japanese historians at Hakone, Japan, 1969 (Columbia, East Asia Institute).

Papers prepared for the conference of American Far Eastern historians at Cuernavaca, Mexico, 1970 (Columbia, East Asia Institute).

'The Road to the Pacific War', incomplete translation (Columbia, East Asia Institute).

INTERNATIONAL POLITICS AND FOREIGN POLICY ANALYSIS: SELECT BIBLIOGRAPHY.

Aron, R., *Peace and War: A Theory of International Relations* (London, 1966).

Bailey, F. G., *Stratagems and Spoils* (Oxford, 1969).

Bell, C., *The Conventions of Crisis* (London, 1971).

Boulding, K. E., *The Image* (Ann Arbor, 1956).

Braybrook, D. and Lindblom, C. E., *A Strategy of Decision* (New York, 1963).

Butterfield, H., and Wight, M., (eds.), *Diplomatic Investigations* (London, 1966).

Castles, F. G., *Pressure Groups and Political Culture* (London, 1967).

Charlesworth, J. C. (ed.), *Contemporary Political Analysis* (New York, 1967).

Claude, I., *Swords into Ploughshares* (London, 1964).

Cohen, B. C., *The Press and Foreign Policy* (Princeton, 1963).

De Rivera, J., *The Psychological Dimension of Foreign Policy* (Colombus, Ohio, 1968).

Deutsch, K., *The Nerves of Government* (New York, 1967).

Farrell, J. C. and Smith, A. P., (eds.), *Image and Reality in World Politics* (New York, 1968).

Farrell, R. B. (ed.), *Approaches to Comparative and International Politics* (Chicago, 1966).

Festinger, L., *A Theory of Cognitive Dissonance* (Stanford, 1962).

Frankel, J., *The Making of Foreign Policy* (London, 1963).
            National Interest (London, 1970).

Gore, W. J. and Dyson, J. W., (eds.), *The Making of Decisions* (New York, 1964).

Hugo, G., *Britain in Tomorrow's World* (London, 1969).
          Appearance and Reality in International Relations (London, 1970).

Kelman, H. C., *International Behavior* (New York, 1966).

Knorr, K., and Verba, S., *The International System* (Princeton, 1963).

Lasswell, H. D., and Kaplan, A., *Power and Society* (New Haven, 1950).

Rosenau, J. N., *Public Opinion and Foreign Policy* (New York, 1961).
                (ed.), *International Politics and Foreign Policy* (New York, 1961).
                (ed.), *Domestic Sources of Foreign Policy* (New York, 1967).
                (ed.), *Linkage Politics* (New York, 1969).

Sapin, B. M., *The Making of United States Foreign Policy* (New York, 1966).

Schelling, T. C., *Arms and Influence* (New Haven, 1966).

Snyder, R. C., et al., *Foreign Policy Decision-Making* (New York, 1962).

Sprout, H. and M., *The Ecological Perspective in Human Affairs* (Princeton, 1965).

Vickers, G., *Value Systems and Social Process* (Harmondsworth, 1970).*

Vital, D., *The Making of British Foreign Policy* (London, 1968).

Wiseman, H. V., *Political Systems: Some Sociological Approaches* (London, 1967).

Wolfers, A., *Discord and Collaboration* (Baltimore, 1965).

Wright, Q., *A Study of War* (Chicago, 1942).

* Acknowledgement is gratefully made to Tavistock Publications Ltd, and Sir Geoffrey Vickers for permission to quote from this work.

INDEX*

Abyssinia, 366, 377–8, 382–3, 388, 405, 410
Adachi Kenzo, 132
Adams, Charles Francis, 72, 83, 156–7, 268
Adams, Vyvyan, 342
Aga Khan, 42, 213, 232, 294
Aghnides, Thanassis, 112n.
Aldrovandi, Count Luigi, 278, 282
Aloisi, Baron Pompeo, 332
'Amau Doctrine' (1934), 375, 401
American Boycott Association, 222, 285
Amery, L. S., 108, 140, 342–3
Amoy, 202, 275
Angelino, de Kat, 279, 359
Angell, Norman, 106
Anglo-Japanese Alliance (1902–21), 21–2, 25–7, 123, 396
Anti-Comintern Pact (1936), 374
Antung, 3, 153
Araki Sadao, General, 171, 203, 204, 275, 330–1
Arms trade and embargoes, 215, 244, 337–340, 345, 364–6, 388–9
Astor, William, 279, 280
Atherton, Ray, 87, 122, 256, 258, 261–2, 298, 320, 346
Attlee, Clement, 342, 383
Augustine, Saint, 418
Australia, 17, 24, 28, 42–3, 59, 67, 217, 265, 298, 374, 394, 398
Avenol, Joseph, 112, 183, 377

Baker, Newton D., 222–4, 344
Balch, Emily, 222
Baldwin, Stanley, character and position of, 47, 54, 89–93, 108, 310
  and defence and disarmament, 13, 314–316, 319–20, 324, 409, 415
  and debts, 316
  and Far Eastern crisis, 211, 241, 247, 249–51, 264–5, 295, 337, 364–6, 401, 411
Balfour, Earl, 44, 109
Barthou, Louis, 104
Bassett, R., 89n.
Beatty, Admiral of the Fleet, Lord, 402
Belgium, 174n., 231, 334
Benes, Édouard, 332–3, 337
Berthelot, Admiral, 297
Berthelot, Philippe, 78, 192, 297
Betterton, Sir Henry, 365
Beveridge, Albert J., 20n.
Biddle, Lt. William, 279

* Names, titles, etc. as in 1931–33.

Bingham, Hiram, 346
Birdwood, Field Marshal Sir William, 177
Blakeslee, George, 225n., 279–80, 282n.
Blockland, Beerlaerts van, 213
Blum, Léon, 78, 343
Boal, Pierre, 268
Bolivia, 109, 213, 378
Bonin islands, 21, 28
Borah, William E., 54, 87, 114–15, 121, 139, 140, 158, 211, 224, 226, 263, 298, 299, 307, 308, 317, 319, 343, 345
Borchard, Edwin, 345
Bowyer, Sir George, 45n.
Braadland, Burger, 213
Brenan, J. F., 228–9, 235, 253
Briand, Aristide, position and beliefs of, 41, 78, 112, 213, 231, 319
  and Far Eastern crisis, 136, 146–7 151n., 155, 171, 173–4, 182, 192
Bridgeman, Lord, 358
Bruce, S. M., 333, 394
Brüning, Heinrich, 309, 406
Bryan, William Jennings, 197, 211
Bülow, Bernhard von, 182, 280
Burma, 17, 58, 374
Butler, Nicholas Murray, 114n., 285

Cadogan, Alexander, 99, 151–2, 182, 188, 257, 360, 362, 363, 392
Cahan, C. H., 333, 358
Canada (see also 'Cahan'), 28, 69n., 110, 233, 298–9, 346, 398
Canton, 49, 51, 169, 202, 275, 329, 371–2
Capper, Arthur, 222
Caroline islands, 22, 28
Carr, E. H., 361n., 382, 384
Carter, J. F., 56n.
Castle, William R., position and general Far Eastern views of, 53, 86, 88, 118
  and Far Eastern crisis, 155, 157–60, 186, 194–7, 236ff., 277, 298–301, 346, 349
Castlereagh, Viscount, 243
Cecil, Viscount, character and political beliefs of, 98, 102–3, 106–7, 116, 381, 384, 410
  at League Council and Assembly, 1931–2, 4, 135, 145–6, 151, 174–5, 293
  and problems of Far Eastern policy, 139, 141, 178–82, 217–21, 230–1, 286–7, 339–41
  and disarmament, 119, 219, 287, 304–5, 322, 409
  and crisis in retrospect, 7–8, 134, 206, 380, 404